# SHIELD OF REPUBLIC/
# SWORD OF EMPIRE

# SHIELD OF REPUBLIC/ SWORD OF EMPIRE

*A Bibliography of United States Military Affairs, 1783-1846*

*Compiled by*
JOHN C. FREDRIKSEN

Bibliographies and Indexes in American History, Number 15

GREENWOOD PRESS
New York • Westport, Connecticut • London

**Library of Congress Cataloging-in-Publication Data**

Fredriksen, John C.
    Shield of republic/sword of empire : a bibliography of United
States military affairs, 1783-1846 / compiled by John C. Fredriksen.
        p.   cm.—(Bibliographies and indexes in American history,
    ISSN 0742-6828 ; no. 15)
        ISBN 0-313-25384-6 (lib. bdg. : alk. paper)
        1. United States—Armed Forces—History—19th century—
    Bibliography.   2. United States—Armed Forces—History—18th
    century—Bibliography.   3. United States—History, Military—To
    1900—Bibliography.   I. Title.   II. Series.
    Z1249.M5F73   1990
    [UA23]
    016.355 '00973 '09034—dc20          89-25620

British Library Cataloguing in Publication Data is available.

Library of Congress Catalog Card Number: 89-25620
ISBN: 0-313-25384-6
ISSN: 0742-6828

First published in 1990

Greenwood Press, Inc.
88 Post Road West, Westport, Connecticut 06881

Printed in the United States of America

The paper used in this book complies with the
Permanent Paper Standard issued by the National
Information Standards Organization (Z39.48-1984).

10 9 8 7 6 5 4 3 2 1

To Marika R., my favorite fortune teller.

# CONTENTS

# PREFACE

In many respects, this book is an outgrowth of my previous effort, Free Trade and Sailors' Rights, and at first glance shares some commonalities with it. However, Shield of Republic/Sword of Empire, while containing supplementary information, was conceived more as a companion volume than an identical sequel. There are many inherent differences.

In historical terms, the parameters of this book are large and encompass sixty years of American military affairs. This breaks down roughly into the three decades preceding and following the War of 1812. I initially toyed with the idea of a new bibliography based entirely upon the previous format, but as the vast geographical and chronological expanse revealed itself, this approach became unfeasible. Because flexibility is a function of utility, I settled upon a scheme of only five chapters. Each has its own distinct format, but all are inter-linked through extensive cross-references. Chapter One is a general overview of the entire period and strictly chronological in order. The wars and events are listed separately, with requisite subheadings for politics/diplomacy, prisoners, and contemporary accounts. The next two chapters deal with corporate entities, the U.S. Army and U.S. Navy. Because materials here do not lend themselves to chronological presentation, a topical arrangement was adopted. Starting with nebulous concepts such as history, policy, and administration, these chapters progress towards more tangible subjects such as personnel, materiel, and theaters of deployment. Notable physical entities associated with either service, forts and ships, are listed at the end of each. Where possible I made allowances for chronological subdivions such as 'Early History' or 'Early Policy', but the bulk of this literature is overwhelmingly thematic. Chapter Four, a miscellaneous one, contains everything which would not fit logically elsewhere. When appropriate, the broad categories of militia, Canada and Indians are further delineated by relevant subtopics. Note that in all the aforementioned chapters, the main entries are underlined for ease of identification. A concluding chapter on biographies is arrayed alphabetically, and both name and subject indexes have been appended to enhance user access.

The organization of this book is more complicated than Free Trade and Sailors' Rights owing to the tremendous variety of locations, scope of subjects, and other considerations absent in the previous work. This intrinsic diversity, in turn, required a careful approach toward syndetical devices employed. Because of a strict hierarchical relationship of the chapters to each other, and the internal arrangements of each, cross references always direct reader attention to the rear of the book. This unidirectional placement  obviates the need to flip to and fro about the text in search of related citations. Without exception, cross references are to the rear of where they are found, never forward.

As previously mentioned, this bibliography contains supplementary information which updates <u>Free Trade and Sailors' Rights</u>, especially for biographies of men who served in several wars. Where identical subject headings exist in the earlier volume, in this book they are marked with an asterisk(*). For the full range of writings on these topics, readers are strongly advised to consult both bibliographies. Together, the two represent an aggregate of over 12,000 items which span the historiographical gulf between the Revolutionary and Mexican Wars. From the standpoint of historical research, they should answer most questions regarding sources for the period 1783 to 1846.

This bibliography is the product of five years of intensive research. Many institutions and individuals contributed greatly to it, but are far too numerous to mention. However, I am especially indebted to Dr. Murray Bradley of the U.S. Naval War College Library, Newport, Rhode Island, for repeated access to that splendid facility. The author also gratefully acknowledges receipt of a research grant from the David Library of the American Revolution, Washington Crossing, Pennsylvania, which was instrumental in preparing this volume. I thank you all.

# INTRODUCTION

The six decades spanning 1783 and 1846 were formative ones for the
United States military establishment, and helped define its role in the
national agenda. During this period the young republic evolved rapidly
from a weak confederation of Atlantic states to a burgeoning hemispheric
power on the verge of 'manifest destiny'. But America treaded the uncharted
waters of independence warily, and for many years groped for coherent
military policies. Almost from its inception, American military philosophy
was an uneasy alliance between democratic ideology and legitimate defense
needs. Traditional Whig distrust of standing professional forces was a
centerpiece of the political culture and precluded adoption of European-
style solutions to the problems of national defense. The sometimes furious
debate over the exact nature of the United States military was unprecedented
for its time and the Americans further broke from established tradition
by entrusting national security to a small army, a small navy, and very
large militia forces. This unique system, the product of political
expediency and compromise, was not without merit, nor battle field succe-
sses, but by 1815 its sometimes glaring deficiencies prompted the quest
for new policies and approaches. Thereafter, American armed forces continued
to be numerically small, but enjoyed a quantum jump in efficiency owing to
the growth of professionalism. But equally important, was the fact that the centers of professionalism, West Point and
Annapolis, were firmly wedded to the ideals of republicanism. Both schools
were charged with the task of properly imbuing the officer class, and all
facets of military leadership, with democratic sensibilities. This entire
period  was a careful balancing act between national defense and preservation of personal liberty. Its success is one of the most enduring legacies
of the American Revolution and transcends purely military considerations.

As the maturing United States lost its fear of military oppression,
both branches of service were actively and continuously employed as agents
of national growth. The tasks presented them were numerous and far-ranging,
but not exclusively military in nature. For the army this entailed road
construction, harbor clearing, frontier exploration and Indian removal.
Concurrently, the navy engaged in diplomacy, suppression of piracy and the
slave trade, and global circumnavigation. Both services also pioneered
first applications of steam technology, whose subsequent adoption by
civilians in the guise of railroads and steamships ushered in a transportation revolution. Thus the military establishment, despised and almost
non-existent in 1783, had by 1846 won for itself a trusted and conspicuous
niche among American institutions. As a conduit of expansion, it functioned

brilliantly in the Mexican War. Its triumph, however, was a direct result
of the leaders, events, and judicious readjustments of the previous half-
century.

As this book's title suggests, there was a pronounced dichotomy in
the application of American military force from 1783 to 1846. The United
States was strongly positioned to fend off encroachment by the Old World
while simultaneously consolidating its own in the New. As the roles of
external security and internal expansion became closely intertwined,
American military affairs were never more diverse, sustained, or far-flung
than during this germinal period. Only the Second World War rivals it in
scope.

The problems confronting the young republic were diverse, and required
differing solutions. At the onset, both Confederation and Constitutional
governments were beset by destabilizing insurrections in Massachusetts
and Pennsylvania. No sooner were these resolved than foreign entanglements
culminated in an undeclared war with France, a protracted naval campaign
in North Africa, and a brief but internecine second war with England.
Native Americans also strove to protect and preserve their birthright and
engaged the United States five times in a losing struggle to stop white
expansion. But in every contest save 1812, the nascent American military
surmounted these challenges to the national interest, and secured for
itself a long-standing tradition of victory.

But throughout this tumultuous period, even the peace could be fraught
with peril. Historians seldom appreciate that most defense expenditures
after 1815 were predicated upon the eventuality of a third war with England.
Despite major accords like the Rush-Bagot Agreement of 1817, border tension
with Canada remained high and a detriment to true rapproachement. For
thirty years after the peace of Ghent, a series of incidents ranging from
the Patriot Rebellion to the Oregon Question produced several near-colli-
sions before equitable solutions were reached. The wars and border crises
were small by the then-contemporary standards, but their geographical
span stretching from North Africa to the Pacific Northwest, would have
taxed most European powers. That the United States emerged relatively
unscathed is more a tribute to combat leadership, fighting skill, and
astute diplomacy, than sheer military might. Perhaps her unique approach
to war, spawned of democratic idealism and North American conditions, was
more adept at addressing national interests than traditional scholarship
has implied.

Every age produces memorable figures, and this period hosted several
who left indelible impressions upon American military history and tradition. Revolutionary veterans John Barry, Edward Preble, Henry Knox, and
Anthony Wayne soldiered on and garnered additional luster to already
sterling reputations. They were succeeded by a generation of War of 1812
leaders such as William Bainbridge, David Porter, Winfield Scott, and
Zachary Taylor, all of whom greatly influenced post-war affairs. Junior
officers like Jefferson Davis, Robert E. Lee, William S. Harney and
David G. Farragut also served, and primed themselves for distinction in
a future conflict. The seeds of Civil War leadership were firmly sown at
this time. But the talent pool available to the military was seldom so
large and accomplished, and contributions were made in a great many areas.
Noted explorers like Meriwether Lewis, William Clark, Zeubulon M. Pike,
and John C. Fremont rendered valuable service while capturing public
imagination. Less celebrated engineers like John Ericsson and John A.
Dahlgren blazed similar trails on the frontiers of metallurgy. Medical
knowledge and administration greatly benefitted at the hands of capable
doctors like William Beaumont and James Tilton. Naval scientists like

William Chauvenet and Matthew F. Maury found counterparts in army techno-
crats like Alfred Mordecai and Decius Wadsworth. In the public arena noted
generals George Washington and Andrew Jackson assumed the mantle of
commanders-in-chief while a non-soldier, Thomas Jefferson, sought to
define the military in the context of American democracy. Professional
politicians like Lewis Cass and John C. Calhoun used their appointment
as Secretary of War to enhance presidential aspirations of their own.
Even popular culture was affected. Literary sages like James Fenimore
Cooper, Herman Melville and Edgar Allen Poe were all associated with
military service at this time in their careers. In similar fashion, Native
Americans brought forth accomplished figures like Little Turtle, Tecumseh,
Black Hawk and Osceola.John G. Simcoe and William Lyon Mackenzie were also
present in Canada. This, then, was a dynamic, decisive period in the
history of North America, replete with great lives, ideas and events.
But like many important historical periods, it suffered from a surprising
lack of bibliographic tools to assist scholar and layman in their studies.
This book is an attempt to address that lacunae, and presents researchers
with a wide variety of carefully assembled scholarship on all facets of
the American military equation, from 1783 to 1846.

# I
# WAR, INTERVENTION, BORDER CRISES

## SHAYS' REBELLION

1 Allen, Terry. "Shays' Rebellion and an Unsettling View of History," New England Social Studies Bulletin 44 (1987): 14-18.

2 Baylies, Francis. "Some Remarks on the Life and Character of General David Cobb," New England Historical and Genealogical Register 18 (1864): 5-17.

3 Barry, John S. The History of Massachusetts. 3 Vols. Boston: Henry Barry, 1857. Vol. 3.

4 "Character of the Hon. George Richards Minot," Massachusetts Historical Society Collections 8 (1802): 86-109.

5 Chase, Charles A. "Proceedings," American Antiquarian Society Proceedings 15 (1902): 112-20.

6 Chipman, Daniel. The Life of the Hon. Nathaniel Chipman. Boston: Little, Brown, 1846, 66-69.

7 Crane, Ellery B. "Shays' Rebellion," Worcester Historical Society Collections 5 (1881): 61-111.

8 Culver, David M. "Shays' Rebellion and the Issue of Liberty and Power in a Free Society," New England Social Studies Bulletin 44 (1987): 8-13.

9 Cutler, H.G. "The Nation's First Rebellion," Magazine of American History 12 (1884): 332-47.

10 Damon, Samuel C. History of Holden, 1667-1841. Worcester, MA: Wallace, Ripley, 1841, 84-91.

11 Davis, Andrew M. "The Shays' Rebellion: A Political Aftermath," American Antiquarian Society Proceedings 21 (1911): 57-79.

12 Donovan, Bernard F. "The Massachusetts Insurrection of 1786." Ph. d. dissertation, Boston College, 1938.

13 Dye, Walter A. "Embattled Farmers," New England Quarterly 4 (1931): 460-81.

14  East, R.A. "Massachusetts Conservatives in the Critical Period."
    In: Richard B. Morris, ed. Era of the American Revolution: Studies
    Inscribed to Evarts Bourtell Greene. New York: Columbia University
    Press, 1939, 349-91.

15  Egleston, Thomas. The Life of John Paterson, Major General in the
    Revolutionary Army. New York: G.P. Putnam's Sons, 1898.

16  Farnsworth, Albert. "Shays' Rebellion in Worcester, Massachusetts."
    Ph. D. dissertation, Clarke College, 1927.

17  _____. "Shays' Rebellion," Massachusetts Law Quarterly 12 (1927):
    29-42.

18  Feer, Robert A. "Shays' Rebellion." Ph. D. dissertation, Harvard
    University, 1958.

19  _____. "George Richards Minot's History of the Insurrection: History,
    Propaganda, and Autobiography," New England Quarterly 25 (1962):
    203-28.

20  _____. "Shays' Rebellion and the Constitution: A study in Causation,"
    Ibid 42 (1969): 388-410.

21  Fiske, John . "The Paper Money Craze of 1786 and the Shays' Rebellion,"
    Atlantic Monthly 58 (1886): 376-85.

22  Green, Samuel A. "Groton during Shays' Rebellion," Massachusetts
    Historical Society Proceedings 1 (1884/1885): 298-312.

23  Grinnell, F.W. "The Constitutional History of the Supreme Judicial
    Court of Massachusetts from the Revolution to 1813," Massachusetts
    Law Quarterly 2 (1917): 359-552.

24  Hall, Hilland. "Vermont as a Sovereign and Independent State, 1783-
    1791," Vermont Historical Society Collections 2 (1871): 443-49.

25  Hall,Van Beck. Politics without Parties: Massachusetts, 1780-1791.
    Pittsburgh: University of Pittsburgh Press, 1972.

26  Hansen, Millard W. "The Significance of Shays' Rebellion," South
    Atlantic Quarterly 39 (1940): 305-17.

27  Harding, Samuel B. The Contest over the Ratification of the Federal
    Constitution in the State of Massachusetts. New York: Longmans,
    Green, 1896.

28  Herscopf, Richard. "The New England Farmer and Politics, 1785-1787."
    Master's Thesis, University of Wisconsin, 1947.

29  Holland, Josiah G. History of Western Massachusetts. 2 Vols.
    Springfield, MA: Samuel Bowles, 1855. Vol. 1.

30  Hudson, Alfred S. History of Sudbury, Massachusetts, 1638-1889.
    Boston: R.H. Blodgett, 1889, 426-31.

31  Humphreys, Francis L. The Life and Times of David Humphreys, Soldier-
    Statesman-Poet. 2 Vols. New York: G.P. Putnam's Sons, 1917.

32 Jensen, Merrill. The New Nation: A History of the United States During the Confederation, 1781-1789. New York: Alfred A. Knopf, 1950.

33 Kaplan, Sidney. "Honestus' and the Annihilation of Lawyers," South Atlantic Quarterly 48 (1949): 401-20.

34      . "Shays' Rebellion and the English Press," Boston Public Library Quarterly 8 (1956): 165-67.

35 Karsky, Barbara. "Agrarian Radicalism in the Late Revolutionary Period, 1780-1795." In: Erich Angermann, ed. New Wine in Old Skins: A Comparative View of Socio-Political Structures and Values affecting The American Revolution. Stuttgart, GER: Klett, 1976, 87-114.

36 Kaufman, Martin. Shays' Rebellion: Selected Essays. Westfield, MA: Institute for Massachusetts Studies, 1987.

37 Lincoln, William. History of Worcester, Massachusetts. Worcester: M.D. Phillips, 1837.

38 Lockwood, John H. Westfield and its Historic Influence, 1669-1919. Westfield, MA: The Author, 1922. Vol. 2, 45-157.

39 Lossing, Benson J. "Shays' Rebellion," Harper's Monthly Magazine 24 (1862): 656-62.

40 McGinty, Brian. "Shays' Rebellion," American History Illustrated 21 (1987): 10-13, 46-47.

41 Martyn, Charles. The Life of Artemus Ward, the First Commander-in-Chief of the American Revolution. New York: A. Ward, 1921.

42 Massachusetts General Court. An Address from the General Court to the People of the Commonwealth of Massachusetts. Boston: Adams, Nourse, 1786.

43 Meader, John R. "The Little Wars of the Republic," Americana 5 (1910): 661-70.

44 Middleton, Larmar. Revolt, U.S.A. New York: Stackpole, 1938, 155-82.

45 Moody, Robert E. "Samuel Ely: Forerunner of Shays," New England Quarterly 5 (1932): 105-34.

46 Morris, Richard B. "Insurrection in Massachusetts." In: Daniel Aaron, ed. America in Crisis: Fourteen Crucial Episodes in American History. New York: Knopf, 1952, 21-49.

47 Munroe, James P. "The Shays' Rebellion." In: The New England Conscience with Typical Examples. Boston: R.G. Badger, 1915, 89-116.

48 Nicholls, C.L. Life of Samuel Salisbury, A Boston Merchant in the Revolution. Worcester: American Antiquarian Society, 1926.

49 Noble, John. "A few Notes on the Shays' Rebellion," American Antiquarian Society Proceedings 15 (1902): 200-32.

50  Nobles, Gregory H. "The Politics of Patriarchy in Shays' Rebellion: The Case of Henry McCulloch," Dublin Seminar for New England Life (1985): 37-47.

51  Oliver, Fitch E. Diary of William Pynchon of Salem, Massachusetts. Boston: Houghton, Mifflin, 1980.

52  O'Reilly, Kevin. "Was Shays' Rebellion an Important Cause of the Constitution? Evaluating Cause and Effect Reasoning," New England Social Studies Bulletin 44 (1987): 43-48.

53  Parmenter, C.O. History of Pelham, Massachusetts, 1738-1898. Amherst, MA: Carpenter, Morehouse, 1898, 366-90.

54  Pole, J.R. "Shays' Rebellion: A Political Interpretation." In: Jack P. Greene, ed. The Reinterpretation of the American Revolution, 1763-1789. New York: Harper, Row, 1968, 416-34.

55  Pressman, R.S. "Class Positioning and Shays' Rebellion: Resolving the Contradiction of the Contrast," Early American Literature 21 (1986): 87-102.

56  Ravitz, Abe C. "The Anarchiad and the Massachusetts Centinel, 1786-1787," Boston Public Library Quarterly 4 (1952): 97-101.

57  Reynolds, Grindall, ed. "Concord during the Shays' Rebellion." In his: A Collection of Historical and Other Papers. Concord, MA: The Editor, 1895, 195-244.

58  Sargent, Lucius. Dealings with the Dead. By a Sexton of the Old School. 2 Vols. Boston: Dutton, Wentworth, 1856. No. 29.

59  Sawtelle, Ithamar B. History of the Town of Townsend, Massachusetts, 1676-1878. Fitchburg, MA: The Author, 1878, 213-22.

60  Sawyer, Henry A. "Shays' Rebellion, its Inception and Results," Lynn Historical Society Register 25 (1931): 56-76.

61  Shattuck, Lemuel. Memorials of the Descendants of William Shattuck. Boston: Dutton, Wentworth, 1855.

62  Shriner, Charles A. "Shays' Rebellion," Americana 20 (1926): 236-52.

63  Smith, Johnathan. "Features of Shays' Rebellion," Clinton Historical Society Papers 1 (1912): 9-20.

64  ____. Some Features of Shays' Rebellion. Clinton, MA: W.J. Coulter, 1905.

65  ____. "The Depression of 1785 and Shays' Rebellion," William and Mary Quarterly 5 (1948): 77-94.

66  Smith, Joseph E. The History of Pittsfield, Massachusetts, from the Year 1734 to the Year 1800. 2 Vols. Boston: Lee, Shepard, 1869.

67  Smith, William L. "Springfield in the Insurrection of 1786," Connecticut Valley Historical Society Proceedings 1 (1876/1881); 72-90.

68   Starkey, Marion L. A Little Rebellion. New York: Knopf, 1955.

69   Stearns, Monroe. Shays' Rebellion, 1786-7. New York: Franklin
     Watts, 1968.

70   Swarty, L.E. "American Freedom's First Test," Americana 4 (1909):
     677-90.

71   Szatmary, David P. "New England Crowd Activity, 1783-1788: The
     Story of Shays' Rebellion." Ph. D. dissertation, Rutgers University
     1979.

71A  _____. Shays' Rebellion: The making of an Agrarian Insurrection.
     Amherst: University of Massachusetts, 1980.

72   Taylor, Robert J. Western Massachusetts in the Revolution. Providence:
     Brown University Press, 1954.

73   Vaughn, Alden T. "The Horrid and Unnatural Rebellion of Daniel Shays,"
     American Heritage 17 (1966): 50-53, 77-81.

74   Victor, Orville J. History of American Conspiracies. New York:
     James D. Torrey, 1863.

75   Warren, Joseph P. "The Shays' Rebellion." Ph. D. dissertation,
     Harvard University, 1902.

76   _____. "The Confederation and the Shays' Rebellion," American
     Historical Review 11 (1905): 42-67.

77   Wehtje, Myron F. "Boston's Response to Disorder in the Commonwealth,
     1783-1787," Historical Journal of Massachusetts 12 (1984): 19-27.

78   Wilcox, D.M. "An Episode of Shays' Rebellion," Magazine of History
     22 (1916): 100-07.

79   Winthrop, Robert C. The Life and Services of James Bowdoin.
     Boston: The Author, 1876.

80   Wood, F.J. "Paper Money and Shays' Rebellion," Stone and Webster
     Journal 26 (1920): 333-45, 422-34.

81   _____. "Unrest in the Early Days of the Republic," DAR Magazine
     54 (1920): 391-97.

     SEE ALSO: 2233, 4548, Samuel Adams, Benjamin Lincoln, Daniel Shays

CONTEMPORARY ACCOUNTS

82   "The Belknap Papers," Massachusetts Historical Society Collections
     3 (1877): 1-371.

82A  "The Bowdoin and Belknap Papers," Ibid 9 (1897): 3-488.

83   Brown, E. Francis, ed. "Letter From Joseph Hawley to Ephraim Wright,"
     American Historical Review 36 (1931): 776-78.

84   Brown, Richard D., ed. "Shays' Rebellion and its Aftermath: A View
     From Springfield," William and Mary Quarterly 40 (1983): 598-615.

84A Cumming, James D. "Incidents of Olden Time," American Pioneer 2 (1843): 372-74.

85  Dexter, Franklin B., ed. "Selections from Letters Received by David Daggett, 1786-1802," American Antiquarian Society Proceedings 4 (1885-1887): 367-78.

86  Edwards, William. Memoirs of Colonel William Edwards. Washington, DC: W.F. Roberts, 1897, 19-38.

87  Hale, Edward E., ed. "Letter From J. Wilder on Shays' Rebellion," Massachusetts Historical Society Proceedings 15 (1901-1902): 371-73.

88  Hall, John W. "Reminiscences of Shays' Insurrection," Old Colony Historical Society Collections No. 4 (1889): 79-87.

89  Hibbard, Billy. Memoirs of the Life and Travels of Billy Hibbard. New York: The Author, 1825.

90  Holland, Park. "Reminiscences of Shays' Rebellion," New England Magazine 29 (1901): 538-42.

91  Kaplan, Sidney, ed. "A Negro Veteran in Shays' Rebellion," Journal Of Negro History 33 (1948): 123-29.

92  "Letter of Oliver Prescott Relating to Shays' Rebellion," Massachusetts Historical Society Proceedings 4 (1887-1889): 158-59.

93  "Letter Of Rufus Putnam to Gov. Bowdoin, January 8, 1787," Maine Historical Society Collections 2 (1847): 250-55.

94  Minot, George R. The History of the Insurrections in Massachusetts in the year MDCCLXXXVI, and the Rebellion Consequent Thereon. Worcester: Isaiah Thomas, 1788.

95  Mitchell, H.G., ed. "Reminiscences of Shays' Rebellion," New England Magazine 23 (1901): 538-42.

96  "Observations on the Late Insurrection in Massachusetts," American Museum 2 (1787): 315-20.

97  "Rebellion in 1786," Month at Goodspeed's 23 (1952): 118-23.

98  Riley, Stephen T. "Dr. William Whiting and Shays' Rebellion," American Antiquarian Society Proceedings 66 (1957): 119-66.

99  "Rough Times in Berkshire Hills: Sketch of Rev. Billy Hibbard and his Account of Shays' Rebellion," Berkshire Hills 3 (1902-1903): 23-24.

100 Stebbins, Daniel. "Reminiscences of Olden Time," American Pioneer 1 (1842): 383-88.

101 Thatcher, George. "The Thatcher papers," Historical Magazine 6 (1869): 257-71.

102 Warren, Joseph P., ed. "Documents Relating to Shays' Rebellion," American Historical Review 2 (1896-1897): 693-98.

## OLD NORTHWEST INDIAN WAR

103 Adams, Randolph G. and Howard H. Peckham. Lexington to Fallen Timbers, 1775-1796. Ann Arbor, MI: University of Michigan Press, 1942.

104 Albach, James R. Annals of the West. Pittsburgh: W.S. Haven, 1858, 522-714.

105 Atwater, Caleb. A History of the State of Ohio, Natural and Civil. Cincinnati: Gelezen, Shepard, 1838, 132-49.

106 Barce, Elmore. The Land of the Miamis: An Account of the Struggle To Secure Possession of the Northwest from the End of the Revolution Until 1812. Fowler, IN: Benton Review Bookshop, 1922.

107 Beggs, Stephen R. Pages From the Early History of the West and Northwest. Cincinnati: Methodist Book Concern, 1868.

108 Bird, Harrison. War for the West, 1790-1813. New York: Oxford University Press, 1971.

109 Blanchard, Rufus. Discovery and Conquest of the Northwest with the History of Chicago. 2 Vols. Chicago: R. Blanchard, 1898-1900.

110 Bodley, Temple. History of Kentucky. 4 Vols. Chicago: S.J. Clarke, 1928. Vol. 1, 451-538.

111 Buell, John H. "Fighting Indians in the Northwest," American History Illustrated 3 (1969): 23-26, 35.

112 _____. "Peace in the Northwest," Ibid 3 (1969): 33-35.

113 Burnet, Jacob. Notes on the Early Settlement of the Northwest Territory. Cincinnati: Derby, Bradley, 1847.

114 Burton, Clarence M. History of Wayne County, Michigan. 5 Vols. Chicago: S.J. Clarke, 1930. Vol. 1, 223-37.

115 Butler, Mann. A History of the Commonwealth of Kentucky. Cincinnati: J.A. James, 1836.

116 Byrd, Pratt. "The Kentucky Frontier in 1792," Filson Club Quarterly 25 (1951): 181-203, 286-94.

117 Caruso, John. "Indian War." In his: The Great Lakes Frontier. Indianapolis: Bobbs-Merrill, 1961, 147-81.

118 Centennial History of Butler County, Ohio. N.p., B. F. Bowen, 1905, 59-95.

119 Chase, Lew A. "The Upper Mississippi a Century Ago, " Magazine of History 12 (1910): 135-46.

120 Cist, Charles. Cincinnati Miscellany. 2 Vols. Cincinnati: Caleb Clark, 1845.

121 Compton, Harvey W. "The Americans Win the Northwest," Northwest Ohio Quarterly 4 (1932): 1-13.

122  Craig, Oscar J. Ouiatanon; A Study in Indiana History.
Indianapolis: Bowen-Merrill, 1893, 317-48.

123  Cutler, William P. "Services of the Ohio Company in Defending the
United States Frontier from Invasion," Ohio Archaeological and
Historical Society Quarterly 1 (1888): 283-87.

124  Danford, Herry E. Ohio Valley Pioneers. Chicago: Rand, McNally,
1931, 172-91.

125  Darling, Arthur B. Our Rising Empire, 1763-1803. New York: Yale
University Press, 1940.

126  Dodge, Jacob. Red Men of the Ohio Valley. Springfield, OH: Ruralist
Publishing Co., 1860.

127  Downes, Randolph C. Frontier Ohio, 1788-1803. Columbus: Ohio
Historical Society, 1935.

128  _____. Council Fires on the Upper Ohio: A Narrative of Indian Affairs
in the Upper Ohio Valley Until 1795. Pittsburgh: University of
Pittsburgh, 1940.

129  Downey, Fairfax. Indian Wars of the U.S. Army, 1776-1865.
Garden City, NY: Doubleday, 1963.

130  Ellis, Edward S. The Indian Wars of the United States, from the First
Settlement at Jamestown in 1607 to the Close of the Great Uprising
of 1890-91. New York: Cassell, 1892.

131  Esarey, Logan. A History of Indiana. 2 Vols. Indianapolis: W.K.
Stewart, 1915. Vol. 1, 92-125.

132  Farrand, Max. "The Indian Line Boundary Line," American Historical
Review 10 (1905): 782-91.

133  Flint, Timothy. Indian Wars of the West. Cincinnati: E.H. Flint, 1833.

134  Foik, Paul K. "Among the Indian Chiefs at the Great Miami,"
Illinois Catholic Historical Review 8 (1926): 215-32.

135  Frost, John. Border Wars of the West. Auburn, NY: Derby, Miller, 1853.

136  Galbreath, Charles B. History of Ohio. 5 Vols. Chicago: American
Historical Society, 1925. Vol. 1, 193-269.

137  Gifford, Jack J. "The Northwest Indian War, 1784-1795." Ph. D.
dissertation, University of Southern California, 1964.

138  _____. "One Nation...Making it Work: The Army and the Constitutional
Government," Military Review 67 (1987): 14-23.

139  Harpster, John W., ed. Pen Pictures of early Western Pennsylvania.
Pittsburgh: University of Pittsburgh, 1938, 151-75.

140  Hildreth, Samuel P. Pioneer History; Being an Account of the First
Examinations of the Ohio Valley. Cincinnati: W.H. Derby, 1848.

141  _____. Contributions to the Early History of the Northwest.
Cincinnati: Poe, Hitchcock, 1864.

142  Hinsdale, Burke A. The Old Northwest. New York: Townsend, MacCoun, 1888.

143  Horsman, Reginald. The Frontier in the Formative Years, 1783-1815. New York: Rinehart, Winston, 1970.

144  Howe, Henry. Historical Collections of Ohio. 2 Vols. Cincinnati: Robert Clarke, 1888.

145  Indian Narratives: Containing a Correct and Interesting History of The Indian Wars. Claremont, NH: Tracy & Bros., 1854, 89-128.

146  Jahns, Patricia. The Violent Years: Simon Kenton and the Ohio-Kentucky Frontier. New York: Hastings House, 1962.

147  James, James A. "Some Phases of the History of the Northwest," Proceedings of the Mississippi Valley Historical Association 7 (1913-1914): 168-95.

148  Knapp, Horace S. History of the Maumee Valley. Toldeo: Blade Mammoth Printing, 1877, 62-94.

149  Lanfried, Helen M. "The Indian Campaigns in the Ohio Country, 1787-1795." Master's Thesis, University of Cincinnati, 1944.

150  McKnight, Charles. Our Western Border, its Life, Combats, Adventures. Philadelphia: J. C. McCurdy, 1875.

151  Macleod, William C. The American Indian Frontier. New York: Alfred A. Knopf, 1928.

152  McClung, John A. Sketches of Western Adventure. Covington, KY: Richard H. Collins, 1872.

153  Marshall, Humphrey. The History of Kentucky. 2 Vols. Frankfort: G.S. Robinson, 1824.

154  Martzolff, Clement L. "Big Bottom and its History," Ohio Archaeological and Historical Society Quarterly 15 (1906): 1-30.

155  Mason, Augustus L. Indian Wars and Famous Frontiersmen: the Thrilling Story of Pioneer Life in America. N.p., 1904.

156  Mathews, Alfred. "The Indian War," Magazine of Western History 1 (1884-1885): 193-206, 312-20.

157  Meader, John R. "The Little Wars of the Republic," Americana 5 (1910): 782-90.

158  Moore, Charles. The Northwest Under Three Flags, 1635-1796. New York: Harper Brothers, 1900.

159  Pennock, Ames C. The Centennial Northwest. Madison, WS: Interstate Book Co., 1876.

160  Patterson, A.W. History of the Backwoods; or, the Region of Ohio. Pittsburgh: The Author, 1843.

161  Peters, Joseph G. Indian Battles and Skirmishes on the American Frontier, 1790-1898. New York: Argonaut Press, 1966.

162   Pritts, Joseph. <u>Incidents of Border Life</u>. Chambersburg, PA: J.
      Pritts, 1839, 437-54.

163   Randall, Emilus O. and Daniel J. Ryan. <u>History of Ohio</u>. 5 Vols.
      New York: Century History Co., 1912. Vol. 2, 505-58.

164   Riccards, Michael P. "The Tribes and the Long Knives." In his:
      <u>A Republic if You can keep it: The Foundation of the American</u>
      <u>Presidency, 1700-1800</u>. Westport: Greenwood Press, 1987, 114-27.

165   Rust, Orton G. <u>History of West Central Ohio</u>. 3 Vols. Indianapolis:
      Historical Publishing Co., 1934. Vol. 1, 301-38.

166   Shipman, Fred W. "The Indian Council of 1793: A Clash of Policies."
      Master's Thesis: Clark University, 1933.

167   Sipe, Helen C. <u>The Indian Wars of Pennsylvania</u>. Harrisburg, PA:
      Telegraph Press, 1931, 685-719.

168   Slocum, Charles E. <u>The Ohio Country Between the Years 1783 and 1815</u>.
      New York: G.P. Putnam's Sons, 1910.

169   _____. <u>History of the Maumee River Basin</u>. 3 Vols. Indianapolis:
      Bowen & Slocum, 1905. Vol. 1, 152-234.

170   Smith, Dwight L. "The Contest with the Indians for Ohio Lands,"
      <u>American Heritage</u> 4 (1953): 32-37, 69-70.

171   _____. "Conquest of the Old Northwest: Second Phase, 1783-1795,"
      <u>Old Fort News</u> 21 (1958): 13-26.

172   Smith, William R. <u>The History of Wisconsin</u>. 3 Vols. Madison, WS:
      Beriah Brown, 1852. Vol. 1, 113-232.

173   Smucker, Isaac. <u>Ohio Pioneer History: The Military Expeditions of</u>
      <u>the Northwest Territory</u>. N.p., N.d.

174   Sons of the American Revolution. District of Columbia Society.
      <u>The Battlefields of the Maumee Valley: A Collection of Historical</u>
      <u>Addresses Delivered Before the Sons of the American Revolution</u>.
      Washington, DC: W.F. Roberts, 1896.

175   Stone, William L. <u>Life of Joseph Brant-Thayendanega-including the</u>
      <u>Border wars of the American Revolution and Sketches of the Indian</u>
      <u>Campaigns of Generals Harmar, St. Clair, and Wayne</u>. 2 Vols.
      New York: A.V. Blake, 1838.

176   Sword, Wiley. <u>President Washington's Indian War: The Struggle for</u>
      <u>the Old Northwest, 1790-1795</u>. Norman: University of Oklahoma Press,
      1985.

177   Tanner, Helen. <u>Atlas of Great Lakes Indian History</u>. Norman: University
      of Oklahoma Press, 1987.

178   Tebbel, John and Keith Jennison. <u>The American Indian Wars</u>. New York:
      Harper & Brothers, 1960, 131-46.

179   Trumbull, Henry. <u>History of the Indian Wars</u>. Boston: Phillips,
      Sampson, 1846.

180  Tuttle, Charles R. History of the Border Wars of Two Centuries;
     embracing a Narrative of the Wars with the Indians from 1750 to 1876.
     Madison, WS: A.C. Pennock, 1876.

181  Valley of the Upper Maumee River. 2 Vols. Madison, WS: Brant, Fuller,
     1889. Vol. 1, 81-109.

182  Van Every, Dale. Men of the Western Waters. Boston: Houghton, Mifflin,
     1956.

183  _____. "President Washington's Calculated Risk," American Heritage
     9 (1958): 56-61, 109-11.

184  _____. The Ark of Empire, 1784-1803. New York: William Morrow, 1963.

185  Van Tassel, Charles V. Story of the Maumee Valley, Toledo and the
     Sandusky Region. 2 Vols. Chicago: S.J. Clarke, 1929. Vol. 1, 308-69.

186  Weiss, Harry B. and Grace M. Ziegler. Colonel Erkuries Beatty, 1759-
     1823. Trenton, NJ: Past Times Press, 1958.

187  Wellman, Paul I. The Indian Wars of the West. Garden City, NY:
     Doubleday, 1954.

188  Williamson, G.W. History of Western Ohio and Auglaize County.
     Columbus: W.M. Linn, 1905.

189  Wilson, Frazer E. Advancing the Ohio Frontier, a Saga of the Old
     Northwest. Blanchester, OH: Brown Publishing Co., 1937.

190  _____. "The Northwest Prior to 1795," Ohio Magazine 1 (1906): 337-49.

191  Winter, Nevin O. A History of Northwest Ohio. New York: Lewis
     Publishing Co., 1917, 54-94.

192  Withers, Alexander S. Chronicles of Border Warfare. Cincinnati:
     Robert Clarke, 1895.

     SEE ALSO: 2016, 2817, 2898, 4588, 4589, 4591, 4593, 4594, 4595,
     4599, 4600, 4603, 4605, 4715, 4723, 4724, 4726, 4728, 4737, 4738,
     4744, 4770, 4771, 4772, 4775, 4776, 4777, 4790, 4793, 4811, Fort
     Campus Martius, British-Indian Relations, John Adair, Simon Girty,
     Henry Knox, Benjamin Lincoln, Timothy Pickering, Arthur St. Clair,
     George Washington.

## CONTEMPORARY ACCOUNTS

193  Beatty, Joseph M., ed. "Letters of the Four Beatty Brothers,"
     Pennsylvania Magazine of History and Biography 44 (1920): 193-263.

194  Bliss, Eugene S. Diary of David Zeisberger: A Moravian Missionary
     Among the Indians 2 Vols. Cincinnati: Robert Clarke, 1885.

195  Carmony, Donald F., ed. "Message of Pennsylvania and New Jersey
     Quakers to Indians of the Old Northwest," Indiana Magazine of
     History 59 (1963): 51-58.

196  Bond, Beverly W., ed. "Dr. Daniel Drake's Memoirs of the Miami
     Country, 1779-1794," Ohio Historical and  Philosophical Society
     Publications 18 (1923): 39-89.

197   "Contemporary Description of Ohio in 1788," Ohio Archaeological and
      Historical Society Publications 3 (1900): 82-108.

198   Craig, Neville, ed. "General Butler's Journal, 1785-1786," Olden
      Time 2 (1848): 433-64, 481-531.

199   Edes, Richard S. and W.M. Darlington, eds. The Journal and Letters
      of Colonel John May of Boston relative to Two Journeys to the Ohio
      Country in 1788 and 89. Cincinnati: Robert Clarke, 1873.

200   Faries, Elizabeth. "The Miami Country, 1750-1815," Ohio Archaeological
      and Historical Society Quarterly 57 (1948): 48-65.

201   Harmon, George D. Sixty Years of Indian Affairs, political, economic,
      and Diplomatic, 1789-1850. Chapel Hill: University of North Carolina
      Press, 1941.

202   Helderman, Leonard C. "Danger on the Wabash," Indiana Magazine of
      History 34 (1938): 455-67.

203   Jordan, John W., ed. "Narrtive of John Heckewelder's Journey to the
      Wabash in 1792," Pennsylvania Magazine of History and Biography 9
      (1887): 466-75; 10 (1888): 34-54, 165-84.

204   Knopf, Richard C., ed. The Diary of John Hutchinson Buell.
      Columbus: Anthony Wayne Parkway Board, 1957.

205   Lindley, Jacob, ed. "Account of a Journey to Attend the Indian
      Treaty Prepared at Sandusky in 1793," Friends Miscellany 2 (1832):
      49-156.

206   May, John. "Journal of Colonel John May of Boston Relative to a
      Journey to the Ohio Country, 1789," Pennsylvania Magazine of
      History and Biography 45 (1921): 138-51.

207   Proctor, Thomas. "Narrative of the Journal of Col. Thomas Proctor,
      and the Indians of the Northwest, 1791," Pennsylvania Archives
      2nd Series 4 (1876): 551-662.

208   Quaife, Milo M. "Journal from Detroit to the Miami River," Illinois
      Historical Society Publications 7 (1923): 293-361.

209   Smith, Dwight L. "Notes on the Wabash River in 1795," Indiana
      Magazine of History 50 (1954): 277-90.

210   Smith, E.H. "The Northwest Country in 1797," Magazine of American
      History 19 (1888): 74-77.

211   Stocker, Harry E. "A History of the Moravian Mission Among the
      Indians on the White River in Indiana," Moravian Historical Society
      Transactions 10 (1917): 230-57.

212   Wilson, Paul C. A Forgotten Mission to the Indians: William Smalley's
      Adventures Among the Delaware Indians in 1792. Galveston, TX: N.p.,
      1965.

      SEE ALSO: 2765, 2766

## HARMAR'S CAMPAIGN

213  Adams, Randolph G. "The Harmar Expedition of 1790," Ohio Archaeo-
     logical and Historical Society Quarterly 50 (1941): 60-62.

214  Barry, James P. "The Defeats of Harmar and St. Clair," American
     History Illustrated 3 (1968): 10-19.

215  Brown, Alan S. "The Role of the Army in the Western Settlement:
     Josiah Harmar's Command, 1785-1790," Pennsylvania Magazine of
     History and Biography 93 (1969): 161-78.

216  Dawson, John W. Address of John W. Dawson, delivered Before a Meeting
     of Old Settlers of Allen County. Fort Wayne: R.D. Dunn, 1871.

217  Fort Wayne and Allen County Public Library. General Harmar's Campaign.
     Fort Wayne: The Library, 1954.

218  Griswold, Bert J. The Pictorial History of Fort Wayne. Chicago:
     Robert O. Law, 1917, 102-13.

219  "Harmar's Expedition," Western Review and Miscellaneous Magazine
     2 (1820): 179-82.

220  "History of Ohio," Western Monthly Magazine 1 (1833): 391-403.

221  Huber, John P. "General Josiah Harmar's Command: Military Policy
     and the Old Northwest, 1784-1791." Ph. D. dissertation, University
     of Michigan, 1968.

222  Katzenberger, George A. "Major David Ziegler," Ohio Archaeological
     and Historical Society Quarterly 21 (1912): 127-76.

223  _____. "Major George Adams," Ibid 22 (1913): 522-42.

224  Meek, Basil. "General Harmar's Expedition," Ibid 20 (1911): 74-108.

225  Morris, David H. "General Harmar's Campaign Against the Northern
     Indians in 1790," New Jersey Historical Society Proceedings 60
     (1942): 238-46.

226  Peckham, Howard H. "Josiah Harmar and His Indian Expedition,"
     Ohio Archaeological and Historical Society Quarterly 55 (1946): 227-41.

227  Steele, Mary D. "Military Career of an Officer in Harmar's Regiment,
     1775-1792," Magazine of Western History 10 (1889): 247-55, 377-82.

228   Symmes, John C. "The Trenton Circular, 'To the Respectable Public,'
     of November 26, 1787," Historical and Philosophical Society of Ohio
     Publications 5 (1910): 77-101.

229  Warner, Michael S. "General Josiah Harmar's Campaign Reconsidered:
     How the Americans lost the battle of Kekionga," Indiana Magazine
     of History 83 (1987): 43-64.

230  Winger, Otho. "The Indians Who Opposed Harmar," Ohio Archaeological
     and Historical Society Quarterly 50 (1941): 55-59.

SEE ALSO: 1717 , 1800 , 2860 , Fort Harmar, Ebenezer Denny, Josiah
Harmar, Little Turtle

## CONTEMPORARY ACCOUNTS

231   Butterfield, Consul W., ed. Journal of Captain Johnathan Heart.
      Albany: J. Munsell's Sons, 1885.

232   Cist, Charles. "Recollections of Harmar's Campaign," Cincinnati
      Miscellany 2 (1845): 105-06.

233   Irvin, Thomas. "Harmar's Campaign," Ohio Archaeological and Historical
      Society Quarterly 19 (1910): 393-96.

234   Morris, David H. "General Harmar's Campaign Against the Northern
      Indians in 1790," New Jersey Historical Society Proceedings 60
      (1942): 238-46.

235   Peckham, Howard H. "Captain Thomas Morris on the Maumee," Ohio
      Archaeological and Historical Society Quarterly 50 (1941): 49-54.

      SEE ALSO: 260, 270, 347, 461

## ST. CLAIR'S CAMPAIGN

236   "Biographical Sketch of General William Darke of Virginia,"
      Military and Naval Magazine 6 (1835): 1-10.

237   Booraem, Hendrik V. "William Henry Harrison comes to Cincinnati,"
      Queen City Heritage 45 (1987): 2-22.

238   Brady, Cyrus. "St. Clair's Defeat." In: American Fights and Fighters.
      New York: McClure, Phillips, 1900, 163-78.

239   Dawson, Henry B. Battle of the United States. 2 Vols. New York:
      Johnson, Fry, 1858. Vol. 2, 7-15.

240   Gilman, Chandler R. "Defeat of General St. Clair in 1791,"
      New York Historical Society Proceedings (1847): 34-52.

241   "History of Ohio," Western Monthly Magazine 1 (1833): 489-99.

242   Hunt, Samuel F. "St. Clair's Defeat," Ohio Archaeological and
      Historical Society Quarterly 8 (1900): 373-96.

243   ____. "The Defeat of Major General Arthur St. Clair." In: Orations
      and Historical Addresses. Cincinnati: Robert Clarke, 1908, 254-82.

244   Incidents and Sketches Connected with the Early History and
      Settlement of the West. Cincinnati: J.A. & V.P. James, 1848.

245   Lane, Amos. Speech of Mr. Lane of Indiana, in the House of Repre-
      sentatives of the United States, January 23 and 24. Washington, DC:
      F.P. Blair, 1834.

246   "Major Johnathan Heart," American Historical Record   3 (1874): 318-20.

247   "Major William Ferguson," Ibid 2 (1873): 217-20.

248   Munroe, John A. "Robert Kirkwood," Picket Post No. 23 (1948): 6-8, 11.

249   O'Callaghan, E.B. "The Author of the Ballad Entitled 'St. Clair's
      Defeat'," Historical Magazine 4 (1868): 261-63.

250  Raymond, Richmond. "St. Clair's Defeat: Rout on the Wabash," Army
     33 (1983): 62-65.

251  Roosevelt, Theodore. "St. Clair's Defeat," Harper's Monthly Magazine
     92 (1895): 387-403.

252  "St. Clair's Campaign," Western Review and Miscellaneous Magazine
     3 (1821): 58-61.

253  Schlesinger, Arthur M, Jr. and Roger Burns, eds. Congress Investigates:
     A Documented History, 1792-1794. 5 Vols. New York: Chelsea House
     Publications, 1975.

254  "Sergeant Andrew Wallace, A Scotch Catholic Soldier of the Revolution
     and of the Indian Wars," American Catholic Historical Researches 4
     (1908): 313-17.

255  United States. 2d Congress. House. In the House of Representatives
     of the United States, Tuesday, the 8th of May, 1792. Mr. Fitzsimmons
     From the Committee Appointed to Inquire into the Causes of the Failure
     of the Late Expedition under Major General St. Clair. Philadelphia:
     N.p., 1792.

256  Walsh, William P. "The Defeat of Major General Arthur St. Clair,
     November 4, 1791: A Study in the Nation's Response, 1791-1793."
     Ph. D. dissertation, Loyola University, 1977.

257  Williams, John H. "Defeated Army in Shame," Military History 5 (1988):
     18-25.

258  Wilson, Frazer E. "St. Clair's Defeat," Ohio Archaeological and
     Historical Society Quarterly 11 (1903): 30-43.

259  _____. The Peace of Mad Anthony: An Account of the Subjugation of
     the Northwest Indian Tribes and the Treaty of Greenville by which
     the Territory Beyond the Ohio was opened for Anglo-Saxon Settlement.
     Greenville, OH: C.R. Kemble, 1909.

     SEE ALSO:1717, 1800, 2860, 2877, 2881, 3041, Fort Hamilton, Fort
     Jefferson, Fort St. Clair, Fort Washington, Ebenezer Denny, Little
     Turtle, John Hardin, Arthur St. Clair, Winthrop Sargent, Charles Scott

## CONTEMPORARY ACCOUNTS

260  Bond, Beverly W., ed. "Memoirs of Benjamin Van Cleve," Historical
     and Philosophical Society of Ohio Publications 17 (1922): 3-71.

261  Branshaw, Robert. "Robert Branshaw's Narrative." In: Door County
     Advocate (Sturckon Bay, WS) October 31, 1878.

262  Bunn, Matthew. A Journal of the Adventures of Matthew Bunn.
     Littleton, CT: Thomas Collier, 1796.

263  Campbell, P. Travels in the Interiors Inhabited Parts of North
     America, 1791-2. Edinburgh: Guthrie, 1793.

264  Coates, G.H., ed. "A Narrative of an Embassy to the Western Indians,"
     Memoirs of the Historical Society of Pennsylvania 2 (1827): 61-131.

265   The Columbian Tragedy; containing A Particular and Official Account
      of the Brave and Unfortunate Officers Who Were Slain and Wounded in
      the Ever-Memorable and Bloody Indian Battle. Boston: E. Russell, 1791.

266   "Extract From a Manuscript Journal of A Gentleman Belonging to the
      Army While Under the Command of Major General St. Clair," Massachusetts
      Historical Society Collections 3 (1794): 21-26.

267   Fort Wayne and Allen County Public Library. St. Clair's Defeat, 1791.
      Fort Wayne: The Library, 1954.

268   Harbison, Massy W. A Narrative of the Sufferings of Massy Harbison.
      Pittsburgh: S. Engles, 1825.

269   Irwin, Thomas. "St. Clair's Defeat, as told by an Eyewitness," Ohio
      Archaeological and Historical Society Quarterly 10 (1902): 378-80.

270   Johonnet, Jackson. The Remarkable Adventures of Jackson Johonnet of
      Massachusetts, who served as a Soldier in the Western Army in the
      Expeditions of General Harmar and the Unfortunate General St. Clair.
      Windsor, VT: Alden Spooner, 1793.

271   Loudon, Archibald. A Selection of Some of the Most Interesting
      Narratives of Outrages Committed by the Indians in Their Wars with
      The White People. 2 Vols. Carlisle, PA: Loudon, 1808-1811.

272   McDonough, Michael. "Christmas, 1791," Historical and Philosophical
      Society of Ohio Bulletin 12 (1954): 66-8.

273   "A Memory of St. Clair's Defeat: Original Papers," Magazine of History
      5 (1907): 344-56.

274   Minutes of Debates in Council, on the Banks of the Ottawa River,
      November, 1791. Said to be Held There by the Chiefs of Several
      Indian Nations who Defeated the Army of the United States on the
      4th of that Month. Baltimore: Warner, Hanna, 1800.

275   Poffenbarger, Livia N. Ann Bailey; Thrilling Adventures of the Heroine
      of the  Kanawha Valley. Point Pleasant, W. VA: N.p., 1907.

276   Quaife, Milo M., ed. "A Picture of the First United States Army: The
      Journal of Captain Samuel Newman," Wisconsin Magazine of History 2
      (1918): 40-73.

277   Shepard, Lee. "William Walker on Joseph Brandt: Historical Indian
      Letter," Historical and Philosophical Society of Ohio Bulletin 12
      (1954): 234-9.

278   Symmes, John C. "John Cleves Symmes to Elias Boudinot," Ibid 5 (1910):
      93-101.

279   Van Cleve, Benjamin. "Extracts from Benjamin Van Cleve's Memoranda,"
      Michigan Pioneer 34 (1904): 741-46.

280   _____. "Diary of St. Clair's Disastrous Campaign," American Pioneer
      2 (1843): 135-38, 150-53.

      SEE ALSO: 347, 349 , 354, 461

WAYNE'S CAMPAIGN

281  Barr, Lockwood. Biography of Dr. Joseph Strong. Philadelphia:
     The Author, 1940.

282  Bonney, Catharina V. A Legacy of Historical Gleanings. 2 Vols.
     Albany: J. Munsell, 1875. Vol. 1, 89-108.

283  Boyd, Thomas. "Mad Anthony Wayne: the Fight in the Northwest,"
     Atlantic Monthly 143 (1929): 61-77.

284  Burton, Clarence M. "Anthony Wayne and the Battle of Fallen Timbers,"
     Michigan Pioneer 31 (1901): 472-89.

285  Carswell, Stuart R. "Extracts From General Anthony Wayne's Orderbooks,"
     Infantry Journal 32 (1928): 509-14.

286  Case, Thomas R. "The Battle of Fallen Timbers," Northwest Ohio
     Quarterly 35 (1963): 54-69.

287  Cleves, Freeman. Old Tippecanoe: William Henry Harrison and His Times.
     New York: Charles Scribner's Sons, 1939, 9-21.

288  Compton, H.W. "The Battle of Fallen Timbers," Maumee Valley Pioneer
     Association 3 (1899): 9-21.

289  Davis, W.B. "Casualties of the Battle of Fallen Timbers," Ohio
     Archaeological and Historical Society Quarterly 41 (1932): 527-30.

290  Dawson, Henry B. Battle of the United States. 2 Vols. New York:
     Johnson, Fry, 1888. Vol. 2, 19-26.

291  Edwards, William W. "General Wayne's Campaign Against the Indians of
     the Northwest," Journal of the Military Service Institute 50 (1912):
     414-26.

292  Fort Wayne and Allen County Public Library. General Anthony Wayne's
     Expedition into the Indian Country. Fort Wayne: The Library, 1952.

293  "General Wayne's Campaign of 1794 and the Battle of Fallen Timbers,"
     Northwest Ohio Quarterly Bulletin 1 (1929): 9-16.

294  Helwig, Richard M. Great Winds in the Valley. Defiance, OH: Defiance
     County Historical Society, 1969.

295  Hoberg, Walter R. "A Tory in the Northwest," Pennsylvania Magazine
     of History and Biography 59 (1935): 32-41.

296  Hood, Ronald C. "The Battle of Fallen Timbers," American History
     Illustrated 3 (1969): 4-11, 45-47.

297  Hunt, Samuel F. "General Anthony Wayne and the Battle of Fallen Timbers,"
     Ohio Archaeological and Historical Society Quarterly 9 (1901): 214-37.

298  ____. Orations and Historical Addresses. Cincinnati: Robert Clarke,
     1908, 388-416.

299  "The Illinois Indians to Captain Abner Prior," American Historical
     Review 4 (1898-1899): 107-11.

300   Kimball, Jeffrey P. "The Battle of Fallen Timbers." In: John Loos, ed. Great Events From History, American Series. Englewood Cliffs, NJ: Salem Press, 1973. Vol. 1, 383-88.

301   Larwill, J. Richard. "The Anthony Wayne Parkway," Historical and Philosophical Society of Ohio Bulletin 9 (1951): 40-45.

302   Lynd, William F. "Fallen Timbers: the Effect of a Single Battle on the Course of American History." Master's Thesis, University of California, 1951.

303   McCord, Shirley S., comp. Travel Accounts of Indiana. Indianapolis: Indiana Historical Bureau, 1970, 38-41.

304   Mason, Augustus L. The Story of the Pioneers. Cincinnati: National Book Co., N.d., 937-79.

305   Miles, Richard D. The Stars and Stripes Come to Detroit. Detroit: Wayne University Press, 1951.

306   Nelson, Paul D. "Anthony Wayne's Indian War in the Old Northwest, 1792-1795," Northwest Ohio Quarterly 56 (1984): 115-40.

307   Norris, Caleb H. "Tarhee, the Crane, Chief of the Wyandots," Northwest Ohio Quarterly 7 (1935): 1-13.

308   Ohio State Archaeological and Historical Society. The Anthony Wayne Memorial Parkway Project in Ohio. Columbus: The Society, 1944.

309   Priddy, O.W. "Wayne's Strategic Advance from Fort Greenville to Grand Glaize," Ohio Archaeological and Historical Society Quarterly 39 (1930): 42-76.

310   Reade, Philip. "Wayne's Campaign, 1793-1794." Typescript at the Filson Club Library, Louisville.

311   Robb, H.L. "Mad Anthony Wayne's Campaign Against the Indians in Ohio, 1792-1794," Military Engineer 13 (1921): 474-77.

312   Rogers, Truett. Bibles and Battle Drums. Valley Forge, PA: Judson Press, 1976.

313   Roosevelt, Theodore. "Mad Anthony Wayne's Victory," Harper's Monthly Magazine 92 (1896): 702-16.

314   _____. Anthony Wayne's Expedition into the Northwest. Fort Wayne: Fort Wayne and Allen County Public Library, 1957.

315   Scott, Thomas. "An Incident of Wayne's Campaign," West Virginia Review 20 (1943): 31-33.

316   Shepard, Lee. "A War Casualty of Long Ago," Historical and Philosophical Society of Ohio Bulletin 10 (1952): 48-60.

317   Tebbel, John W. The Battle of Fallen Timbers, August 20, 1794. New York: Franklin Watts, 1972.

318   Van Every, Dale. "President Washington's Calculated Risk," American Heritage 9 (1958): 56-61, 109-11.

319  Will, George. "Wayne's Indian War," American Pioneer 1 (1842): 293-94.

SEE ALSO: 1800 , 2121 , 2143 , 2808 , 2860 , 2867 , 2874 , 2878 , 2879 , 2898 ,
3041 , 3050 , 4831 , Fort Defiance, Fort Miami, Fort Recovery, Fort Wayne,
Blue Jacket, William Clark, John F. Hamtramck, Little Turtle, Winthrop
Sargent, Charles Scott, Anthony Wayne, William Wells, James Wilkinson

CONTEMPORARY ACCOUNTS

320  "Account of Wayne's Campaign," Western Review and Miscellaneous
Magazine 2 (1840): 229-31.

321  "Anecdotes of Wayne's Campaign," Ibid 3 (1821): 112-16.

322  Armstrong, John. "John Armstrong's Journal." In: James McBride.
Pioneer Biography. 2 Vols. Cincinnati: Robert Clarke, 1869. Vol. 1,
118-22.

323  Barr, Lockwood, ed. "Letters from Dr. Joseph Strong to Captain John
Pratt," Ohio Archaeological and Historical Society Quarterly 51
(1942): 236-42.

324  Boyer, John. "Daily Journal of Wayne's Campaign," American Pioneer
1 (1842): 315-22, 351-57.

325  _____. A Journal of Wayne's Campaign. Cincinnati: J.F. Uhlhorn, 1866.

326  "John Bricknell's Narrative," American Pioneer 1 (1842): 50-53.

327  Buell, John H. "A Fragment from the Diary of Major John Hutchinson
Buell, U.S.A., " Journal of the Military Service Institute of the
United States 40 (1907): 102-13, 260-68.

328  _____. "After the Battle of Fallen Timbers: Peace in the Northwest,"
American History Illustrated 4 (1969): 32-35.

329  "By Gones of the Backwoods," Chamber's Journal 9 (1848): 387-91.

330  Carter, Clarence E., ed. Territorial Papers of the United States.
Vol. 2: The Territory Northwest of the River Ohio, 1787-1803.
Washington, DC: Government Printing Office, 1934.

331  Cooke, John . Diary of Captain John Cooke, 1794. Fort Wayne:
Fort Wayne and Allen County Public Library, 1953.

331A  _____. "General Wayne's Campaign in 1794 and 1795: Captain John
Cooke's Journal," American Historical Record 2 (1873): 311-16, 339-45.

332  Chew, John. "The Diary of an Officer in the Indian Country in 1794,"
American Historical Magazine 3 (1908): 639-43; 4 (1909): 69-71.

333  Cruikshank, Ernest A. "The Diary of an Officer in the Indian Country
in 1794," Magazine of Western History 11 (1889-1890): 383-88.

334  Griswold, Alexander V. A Short Sketch of the Life of Mr. Lent Munson.
Littlefield, CT: T. Collier, 1797.

335  Howard, Dresden W., ed. "The Battle of Fallen Timbers as Told by Chief
Kin-jo-i-no," Northwest Ohio Quarterly 20 (1948): 37-49.

336  Jacob, John J. A Biographical Sketch of the Life of the Late Captain Michael Cresap. Cincinnati: J.F. Ulhorn, 1866.

337  Jones, Horatio G., ed. "Extracts from the Original Manuscript Journal of the Rev. David Jones, A.M., Chaplain of the United States Legion under Major General Anthony Wayne, during the Indian Wars of 1794-5-6," Michigan Pioneer 8 (1907): 392-95.

338  Knopf, Richard C. Miscellaneous Notes from the Draper Collection. Columbus: Anthony Wayne Parkway Board, 1952.

339  ____., ed. "Two Journals of the Kentucky Volunteers in 1793 and 1794," Filson Club Quarterly 27 (1953): 247-81.

340  ____, ed. "A Precise Journal of General Wayne's Last Campaign," American Antiquarian Society Proceedings 64 (1954): 273-302.

341  ____, ed. "Wayne's Western Campaign: The Wayne-Knox Correspondence, 1793-1794," Pennsylvania Magazine of History and Biography 78 (1954): 298-341, 424-55.

342  ____, ed. The West Point Orderly Books for the United States Legion May 24, 1792-September 28, 1794. Columbus: Anthony Wayne Parkway Board, 1954.

343  ____, ed. Campaign into the Wilderness: the Wayne-Knox-Pickering-McHenry Correspondence. 5 Vols. Columbus: Anthony Wayne Parkway Board, 1955.

344  ____, ed. The Journal of Joseph Gardner Andrews. Columbus: Ohio Historical Society, 1958.

345  Linn, John B. "General Wayne's Campaign in 1794 and 1795; Captain Cooke's Journal," American Historical Record 2 (1873): 311-16, 339-45.

346  Lytle, William. "Personal narrative of William Lytle," Historical and Philosophical Society of Ohio Quarterly 1 (1906): 3-30.

347  Metcalfe, Samuel. A Collection of Some of the Most Interesting Narratives of Indian Warfare in the West. Lexington, KY: William G. Hart, 1821.

348  "Papers Relating to the Defense of the Frontiers," Pennsylvania Archives 2nd Series 4 (1876):623-776.

349  Scott, John M. "Journal of John M. Scott." In: Horace A. Knapp. History of the Maumee Valley. Toledo: Blade-Mammoth Printing, 1872, 83-85.

350  Shepard, Lee, ed. Journal of Thomas Taylor Underwood, March 26, 1792 to March 18, 1800: An Old Soldier in Wayne's Army. Cincinnati: Society of Colonial Wars in the State of Ohio, 1945.

351  Smith, Dwight L. "From Greenville to Fallen Timbers: A Journal of the Wayne Campaign, July 28-September 14, 1794," Indiana Historical Society Publications 16 (1952): 239-333.

352  ____. With Captain Edward Miller in the Wayne Campaign of 1794. Ann Arbor, MI: William L. Clements Library, 1965.

353  Sudduth, William. "A Sketch of the Early Adventures of William Sudduth in Kentucky," Filson Club Quarterly 2 (1928): 43-70.

354  Wilson, Frazer E. Journal of Captain Daniel Bradley: an Epic of the Ohio Frontier. Greenville, OH: F.H. Jobes & Son, 1935.

     SEE ALSO: 463, 3128

                         POLITICS AND DIPLOMACY

355  Bald, Frederick C. How Michigan Men Helped Make the Treaty of Greenville. Ypsilanti: University Lithoprinters, 1945.

356  Brunson, Charles M. "Along the Greenville Treaty Line," Northwest Ohio Historical Society Quarterly 7 (1935): 1-5.

357  "Centennial Anniversary of General Wayne's Treaty of Greenville, August 3, 1895," Ohio Archaeological and Historical Society Quarterly 7 (1899): 205-58.

358  Cook, Kermit A. "Military Defense of the Frontier in the Northwest Territory, Part II: The Treaty of Greenville," West Virginia History 10 (1949): 93-113.

359  Greenville Treaty Memorial Association. More Than a Scrap of Paper: The National Significance of the Treaty of Greenville. Greenville, OH: Greenville Treaty Memorial Association, 1935.

360  Hanna, W.S. "Indian Boundary Line, Greenville Treaty Line, or Wayne's Treaty Line," Ohio Archaeological and Historical Society Quarterly 14 (1905): 158-63.

361  Harris, Thaddeus M. Journal of a Tour into the Territory Northwest of the Allegheny Mountains. Boston: Manning, Loring, 1805, 241-50.

362  Hunt, Samuel F. "The Treaty of Greenville," Ohio Archaeological and Historical Society Quarterly 7 (1899): 218-40.

363  Kent, Charles A. "Story of a Great Treaty, Whereby the Site of Chicago was Secured From the Indians," Illinois State Historical Society Journal 9 (1917): 568-84.

364  _____. "The Treaty of Greenville, August 3, 1795," Ibid 10 (1918): 567-84.

365  Lanman, James H. History of Michigan from its Earliest Colonization to the Present Time. New York: Harper Bros., 1841, 258-67.

366  Larson, Robert H. "Treaty of Greenville Celebration," Michigan Historical Magazine 30 (1946): 126-30.

367  Libby, Dorothy R. An Anthropological Report on the Piankanshaw Indians. New York: Garland Publishing Co., 1974.

368  "Manuscripts Relating to the Early History of Michigan and the Old Northwest, 1795-1801," Burton Historical Collection 1 (1917): 33-46.

369  Ohio State Archaeological and Historical Society. Guide to the Painting, "The Signing of the Treaty of Greenville." Greenville, OH: Treaty of Greenville Sesquicentennial Commission, 1945.

370  Priestly, L.J. "Sequicentennial Celebration of the Treaty of Green-
     ville," West Virginia History 7 (1946): 101-08.

371  Randall, Emilius O. "The Treaty of Greenville," Ohio Archaeological
     and Historical Society Quarterly 12 (1903): 128-59.

372  Rhees, Morgan J. The Altar of Peace. Philadelphia: Ephraim Conrad,
     1798.

373  Slosson, Preston W. "The Significance of the Treaty of Greenville,"
     Ohio Archaeological and Historical Society Quarterly 55 (1946): 1-11.

374  Smith, Dwight L. "Wayne's Peace Treaty with the Indians of the Old
     Northwest," Ibid 59 (1950): 239-55.

375  _____. "Wayne and the Treaty of Greenville," Ibid 63 (1954): 1-7.

376  Stout, David B. The Piankashaw and Kaskaskia and the Treaty of
     Greenville. New York: Garland Publishing Co., 1974.

377  "Unveiling Greenwood Tablet," Ohio Archaeological and Historical
     Society Quarterly 15 (1906): 499-503.

378  Walker, Richard.  Where is the Legendary Silverheels? Carlville, IL:
     R. Walker, 1980.

379  Wessen, Ernest J. Rufus Putnam Papers. Survey of the Greenville
     Treaty Line. Mansfield, OH: Midland Rare Book Co., N.d.

380  Wilson, Frazer E. The Treaty of Greenville; being an Official Account
     of the Same, together with the Expeditions of General Arthur St. Clair
     and General Anthony Wayne Against the Northwestern Indian Tribes.
     Piqua, OH: Correspondent Press, 1894.

381  _____. "The Treaty of Greenville," Ohio Archaeological and Historical
     Society Quarterly 12 (1903): 128-59.

382  _____. Around the Council Fire; Proceedings at Fort Greenville in
     1795, culminating in the Signing of the Treaty of Greenville by
     General Anthony Wayne and the Indian Chiefs of the Old Northwest.
     Greenville, OH: F.E. Wilson, 1945.

     SEE ALSO: Fort Greenville, Little Turtle, Anthony Wayne

## WHISKEY REBELLION

383  Agrew, Daniel. Major Richard Howell of New Jersey, 1776; a Centennial
     Sketch, 1876. N.p., 1876.

384  Albach, James R. Annals of the West. Pittsburgh: W.S. Haven, 1858,
     685-708.

385  Albert, George D. History of the County of Westmoreland, Pennsylvania.
     Philadelphia: L.H. Everts, 1882, 196-207.

386  Baldwin, Leland D. Whiskey Rebels: The Story of a Frontier Uprising.
     Pittsburgh: University of Pittsburgh, 1939.

387  Barber, William P. "Among the Most Techy Articles of Civil Policy':
     Federal Taxation and the Adoption of the Whiskey Excise," William
     and Mary Quarterly 25 (1968): 58-84.

388  Binkley, Wilfred E. "Anti-Federalists." In: American Political Parties, Their Natural History. New York: A.A. Knopf, 1945, 52-71.

389  Bond, Beverly W. "The Whiskey Insurrection in Pennsylvania," John P. Branch Historical Papers 1 (1902): 68-87.

390  Boyd, Stephen R. The Whiskey Rebellion: Past and Present Interpretations. Westport, CT: Greenwood Press, 1985

391  Brackenridge, Henry M. History of the Insurrection in Western Pennsylvania, Commonly called the Whiskey Insurrection. Pittsburgh: W.S. Haven, 1859.

392  Bright, Royal. "The Whiskey Rebellion." Master's Thesis, Temple University, 1939.

393  Carnahan, James. "The Pennsylvania Insurrection of 1794," New Jersey Historical Society Proceedings 6 (1853): 115-52.

394  Carson, Gerald. "A Tax on Whiskey? Never!" American Heritage 14 (1963): 62-64, 101-5.

395  Claussen, W. Edmunds. "Soldier of the Whiskey Rebellion," Bulletin of the Historical Society of Montgomery County 19 (1974): 288-92.

396  Coakley, Robert W. "Federal Use of Militia and the National Guard in Civil Disturbances: The Whiskey Rebellion to Little Rock." In: Robin Higham, ed. Bayonets in the Streets: The Use of Troops in Civil Disturbances. Lawrence, KS: University Press of Kansas, 1969, 17-34.

397  Cooke, Jacob E. "The Whiskey Insurrection: A Re-Evaluation," Pennsylvania History 30 (1963): 316-46.

398  Corson, O.T. "History  Repeats Itself," Ohio Educational Monthly 70 (1921): 39-43.

399  Craig, Neville B. Sketch of the Life and Services of Isaac Craig. Pittsburgh: J.S. Davison, 1854.

400  ____. "Exposure of the Many Misstatements in H.M. Brackenridge's History of the Whiskey Insurrection." In: History of Pittsburgh. Pittsburgh: J.M. Mellor, 1917, 228-73.

401  Creigh, Alfred. History of Washington County, from its First Settlement to the Present Time. Harrisburg, PA: B. Singerly, 1876, 59-121.

402  Crow, Jeffery T. "The Whiskey Rebellion in North Carolina," North Carolina Historical Review 66 (1989): 1-28.

403  Crumrine, Boyd. History of Washington County, Pennsylvania. Philadelphia: L.H. Everts, 1882, 262-306.

404  Don Passos, John R. "Modern Chivalry." In: Ground We Stand On: Some Examples From the History of a Political Creed. New York: Harcourt, 1941, 381-401.

405  Egle, William H. An Illustrated History of the Commonwealth of Pennsylvania. Harrisburg, PA: DeWitt C. Goodrich, 1876, 223-31.

406  Ellis, Franklin, ed. History of Fayette County, Pennsylvania.
     Philadelphia: L.H. Everts, 1882, 157-80.

407  Ewing, Charles M. Causes of That So-Called Whiskey Insurrection of
     1794. Washington, PA: N.p., 1930.
     At Washington and Jefferson College Library.

408  Felton, Margaret M. "General John Neville." Master's Thesis,
     University of Pittsburgh, 1932.

409  Fennell, Dorothy E. "Western Insurrection: The Popular Classes,
     Culture, and Ideology of Western Pennsylvania, 1700-1800."
     Ph. D. dissertation, University of Pittsburgh, 1981.

410  Ferguson, Russell J. Early Western Pennsylvania Politics.
     Pittsburgh: University of Pittsburgh Press, 1938.

411  Findley, William. History of the Insurrection in the Four Western
     Counties of Pennsylvania in the Year 1794. Philadelphia: Samuel
     H. Smith, 1796.

412  Harper, R. Eugene. "The Class Structure of Western Pennsylvania,
     1783-1796." Ph. D. dissertation, University of Pittsburgh, 1969.

413  Hogg, J. Bernard. "Presley Neville." Master's Thesis, University
     of Pittsburgh, 1935.

414  Humrich, C.P. "The Relations Which the People of Cumberland and
     Franklin Counties Bore to the Whiskey Insurrection of 1794,"
     Kittochtinny Historical Society Papers 3 (1904): 221-47.

415  Jack, William I. "The Federalist Administration and the Whiskey
     Rebellion." Master's Thesis, William and Mary College, 1958.

416  James, Alfred P. "A Political Interpretation of the Whiskey Insur-
     rection," Western Pennsylvania Historical Magazine 33 (1950): 90-101.

417  Jenkins, Howard, ed. Pennsylvania: A History, 1608-1907. 3 Vols.
     Philadelphia: Pennsylvania Historical Publishing Association, 1907.
     Vol. 2, 269-83.

418  Johnson, Allen, ed. Readings in American Constitutional History,
     1776-1876. Boston: Houghton, Mifflin, 1912, 188-96.

419  Jones, Mark H. "Herman Husband: Millenarian Carolina Regulator and
     Whiskey Rebel." Ph. D. dissertation, University of Northern Illinois,
     1983.

420  Kiehl, G.W. "Literature of the Whiskey Insurrection." Master's
     Thesis, Washington and Jefferson College, 1930.

421  Knopf, Richard C., ed. "Personal Notes on the Whiskey Rebels,"
     Historical and Philosophical Society of Ohio Bulletin 12 (1954):
     308-23.

422  Kohn, Richard H. "The Washington Administration's Decision to Crush
     the Whiskey Rebellion," Journal of American History 59 (1972): 567-84.

423  Long, Ronald W. "The Presbyterians and the Whiskey Rebellion,"
     Journal of Presbyterian History 43 (1965): 28-36.

424  Lossing, Benson J. "The Whiskey Rebellion," Harper's Monthly Magazine 24 (1862): 370-76.

425  McGinty, Brain. "Rebel Spirits," American History Illustrated 11 (1976): 4-9.

426  Marder, Daniel. "The Whiskey Rebels and the Elusive Dream," Southern Quarterly 14 (1976): 373-81.

427  Meader, John R. "The Little Wars of the Republic," Americana 5 (1910): 893-903.

428  Middleton, Larmar. Revolt, U.S.A. New York: Stackpole, 1938, 183-214.

429  Miller, William. "The Democratic Societies and the Whiskey Insurrection," Pennsylvania Magazine of History and Biography 62 (1938): 324-49.

430  Millis, Wade F. "First Trial of the Constitution," Journal of Criminal Law 16 (1926): 573-88.

431  Milton [Pseud.] "Whiskey Insurrection," Literary Casket 3 (1842): 162-64.

432  Nevin, Robert P. "Tom the Tinker," Lippincott's Magazine 2 (1868): 374-89.

433  _____. Les Trois Rois. Pittsburgh: J. Eichbaum, 1888, 105-55.

434  "New Light on the Whiskey Rebellion," Magazine of Western History 6 (1887): 514-16; 7 )1887): 104-06.

435  Nolan, J. Bennett. "Reading in the Whiskey Rebellion of 1794," Berkshire County Historical Review 1 (1936): 42-44.

436  Parker, Iola B. "Whiskey Creek keeps Running, but Only with Water," Smithsonian 5 (1974): 82-86.

437  Raphalides, Samuel J. "The President's Use of Troops in Civil Disorder," Presidential Studies Quarterly 8 (1978): 180-87.

438  Riccards, Michael P. "The Whiskey Rebellion." In: A Republic if You Can Keep It: The Foundation of the American Presidency, 1700-1800. Westport, CT: Greenwood Press, 1987, 161-66.

439  Rossman, Kenneth R. Thomas Mifflin and the Politics of the American Revolution. Chapel Hill: University of North Carolina Press, 1952.

440  Rupp, I. Daniel. Early History of Western Pennsylvania and of the West. Pittsburgh: Daniel W. Kaufman, 1846, 271-81.

441  Shriner, Charles A. "The Whiskey Insurrection," Americana 18 (1924): 228-51.

442  Slaughter, Thomas P. The Whiskey Rebellion: Frontier Epilogue to the American Revolution. New York: Oxford University Press, 1981.

443  Tachau, Mary K. "The Whiskey Rebellion in Kentucky: A Forgotten Episode of Civil Disobedience," Journal of the Early Republic 2 (1982): 239-59.

444   Theiss, Lewis. "General John Borrows," Northumberland County
      Historical Society Proceedings 12 (1942): 59-76.

445   Victor, Orville J. History of American Conspiracies. New York: James
      D. Torrey, 1863.

446   Wagner, Pearl E. "Economic Conditions in Western Pennsylvania During
      the Whiskey Rebellion." Master's Thesis, University of Pennsylvania,
      1926.

447   _____. "Economic Conditions in Western Pennsylvania During the
      Whiskey Rebellion," Western Pennsylvania Historical Magazine 10
      (1927): 193-209.

448   Warner, A. History of the Allegheny County, Pennsylvania. Chicago:
      A. Warner, 1889, 149-73.

449   Weyl, Nathaniel. "Whiskey Insurrection." In: Treason: The Story of
      Disloyalty and Betrayal in American History. Washington, DC: Public
      Affairs Press, 1950, 60-86.

450   White, J.W. and A.A. Lambing. Allegheny County: Its Early History
      and Subsequent Development. Pittsburgh: Snowden, Peterson, 1888.

451   Whitten, David O. "An Economic Inquiry into the Whiskey Rebellion of
      1794," Agricultural History 49 (1975): 491-504.

452   Wiley, Richard T. The Whiskey Insurrection: A General View.
      Elizabeth, PA: Herald Printing House, 1912.

453   Wilkinson, Samuel. "The Whiskey Insurrection," Buffalo Historical
      Society Publications 5 (1902): 163-76.

454   Wilson, Frederick T. "The Whiskey Insurrection, 1794." In: Federal
      Aid in Domestic Disturbances, 1783-1903. Washington, DC: Government
      Printing Office, 1903, 33-42.

      SEE ALSO: Albert Gallatin, Alexander Hamilton, Daniel Morgan, George
      Washington

CONTEMPORARY ACCOUNTS

455   Baldwin, Leland D. "Orders Issued by General Henry Lee During the
      Campaign Against the Whiskey Insurrectionists," Western Pennsylvania
      Historical Magazine 19 (1936): 79-111.

456   Brackenridge, Hugh H. Incidents of the Insurrection in the Western
      Parts of Pennsylvania in the Year 1794. Philadelphia: John McCulloch,
      1795.

457   Clunn, John H. "March on Pittsburgh, 1794," Pennsylvania Magazine of
      History and Biography 71 (1947): 44-67.

458   Chambers, D. "Reminiscences of Olden Times," Hesperian 1 (1838):
      29-32, 258-59.

459   Dallas, George M. The Life and Writings of Alexander J. Dallas.
      Philadelphia: J.B. Lippincott, 1871, 29-48, 149-59.

460 No entry

461 "Early Recollections of the West," American Pioneer 2 (1843): 203-17.

462 Egle, William H. "Notes and Queries Relating to the Whiskey Rebellion," Notes and Queries 4 (1896): 93-103.

463 Elliot, James. Poetical and Miscellaneous Works of James Elliot. Greenfield, MA: Thomas Pickman, 1798.

464 "A Few Documents from the Isaac Craig Collection," Carnegie Library Bulletin 16 (1911): 192-97.

465 Finley, William. "William Finley of Westmoreland, Pennsylvania," Pennsylvania Magazine of History and Biography 5 (1881): 440-50.

466 Ford, David. "Journal of Captain David Ford, during the Expedition into Pennsylvania in 1794," New Jersey Historical Society Proceedings 8 (1856-1859): 75-88.

467 Gibson, John B. "Observations on the Statement of Facts Prefixed, in Wharton's State Trials, for Treason in the Western Insurrection," Pennsylvania Historical Society Collections 1 (1853): 349-51.

468 Gould, William. "Journal of Major William Gould of the New Jersey Infantry, during an Expedition into Pennsylvania in 1794," New Jersey Historical Society Proceedings 3 (1848-1849): 173-91.

469 Graydon, Alexander. Memoirs of a Life Passed Chiefly in Pennsylvania within the Last Sixty Years. Harrisburg: John Wyeth, 1811.

470 Hanna, John S. A History of the Life and Services of Samuel Dewees, A Native of Pennsylvania, and Soldier of the Revolution and Last Wars in all of Which he was Patriotically Engaged. Baltimore: R. Neilson, 1844.

471 Linn, John B. and William H. Egle. "Whiskey Rebellion Papers," Pennsylvania Archives 2d Series (1896) Vol. 4, 1-462.

472 McKean, Thomas. "Letter from Thomas McKean, Chief Justice of Pennsylvania, to the Attorney General on the Western Riots," New York Public Library Bulletin 3 (1899): 500-01.

473 Michael, William. "A Journal of the Whiskey Insurrection," Historical Register 1 (1883): 64-74, 134-47.

474 Michael, William. "Autobiography of William Michael," Lancaster County Historical Society Papers 25 (1921): 62-64, 69-77.

475 Report of the Commissioners Appointed by the President of the United States of America to Confer with the  Insurgents in the Western Counties of Pennsylvania. Philadelphia: Childs, Swaine, 1794.

476 Ward, Townsend. "Insurrection in Pennsylvania in 1794," Pennsylvania Historical Society Memoirs 6 (1858): 117-203.

477 Wellford, Robert. "A Diary Kept by Robert Wellford of Fredericksburg, during the March of Virginian Troops to Fort Pitt to Supress the Whiskey Rebellion," William and Mary Quarterly 11 (1902-1903): 1-19.

478 "The Western Insurrection," Olden Time 2 (1848): 547-72.

479  White, Kenneth A., ed. "'Such Disorders Can Only Be Cured by Copious Bleedings': The Correspondence of Isaac Craig During the Whiskey Rebellion," Western Pennsylvania Historical Magazine 67 (1984): 213-42.

## QUASI-WAR WITH FRANCE

480  Abbot, Willis J. Blue Jackets of 1812: A History of the Naval battles of the Second War with Great Britain. To Which is Prefixed an Account of the French War of 1798. New York, Dodd, Mead, 1887.

481  Allen, Gardner W. Our Naval War with France. Boston: Houghton, Mifflin, 1919.

482  Brady, Cyrus T. American Fights and Fighters: Stories of the First Five Wars of the United States, from the Revolution to the War of 1812. New York: McLure, Phillips, 1900.

483  Cox, Henry B. "A Nineteenth Century Archival Search: The History of the French Spoilation Claims papers," American Archivist 33 (1971): 384-401.

484  Dupuy, R. Ernest and William H. Baumer. The Little Wars of the United States: A Compact History from 1798-1920. New York: Hawthorne, 1969.

485  Greer, James A. "Our Minor Naval Wars," American Monthly Magazine 16 (1900): 273-88.

486  Jackson, Melvin H. "The French Privateers in American Waters, 1793-1798: The Failure of a Mission." Ph. D. dissertation, Harvard University, 1957.

487  _____. "The Consular Privateers: an Account of French Privateering in American Waters, April to August, 1793," American Neptune 22 (1962): 91-98.

488  _____. Privateers in Charleston, 1793-1796. Washington: Smithsonian Institute, 1969.

489  Jenkins, Lawrence W. "The Ship 'Mount Vernon' of Salem," Old Time New England 11 (1920): 9-11.

490  Johnston, Charles H. Famous Privateersmen and Adventurers of the Sea. Boston: L.C. Page, 1911.

491  Knight, David C. The Naval War with France, 1798-1800. New York: Franklin J. Watts, 1970.

492  McGee, G.W. "Early Cold Wars: Between 1776 and Pronouncement of the Monroe Doctrine in 1823," Current History 18 (1950): 346-53.

493  Maclay, Edgar S. "Early Victories of the American Navy," Century Magazine 41 (1890): 79-86.

494  Morgan, Mike. "The Remarkable Frigate L'Insurgent," Nautical Research Journal 20 (1974): 134-37.

495  Nash, Howard P. The Forgotten Wars: The Role of the U.S. Navy in the Quasi-War with France and the Barbary Wars, 1798-1805. New York: A.S. Barnes, 1968.

496  Norman, Charles B. The Corsairs of France. London: S. Low, Marston,
     Searle, Rivington, 1887.

497  Palmer, Michael A. Stoddert's War: Naval Operations During the Quasi-
     War with France, 1798-1800. Columbia: University of South Carolina
     Press, 1987.

498  Phillips, James D. "Salem's Part in the Naval War with France,"
     New England Quarterly 16 (1943): 543-66.

499  ____. Salem and the Indies: The Story of the Great Commercial Era
     of the City. Boston: Houghton, Mifflin, 1947.

500 Postgate, Raymond. The Story of a Year: 1798. New York: Harcourt, 1971.

501  "Private Armed ships Belonging to Salem, 1797," Essex Instutute
     Collections 71 (1935): 120-27.

502 Sargent, Nathan. "The Quasi-War with France," United Service 9 (1883):
     1-27.

503  Stull, Henry N. "Our 'partial war' with France," Harper's Magazine
     132 (1915): 36-42.

504  Talbot, Melvin P. "A Review of the Maritime History of the United
     States, from the Treaty of Paris (1783) through the Tripolitan War."
     Typescript at the U.S. Naval War College, Newport.

     SEE ALSO: 597, 1715, 1716, 1725, 2111, 2162, 3555, 3559, 3669, 3670,
     3734 , 3746 , 3761 , 3791 , 4131 , 4278 , USS Boston, USS Constellation,
     USS John Adams, Samuel Barron, John Barry, Moses Brown, Richard Dale,
     Alexander Hamilton, Isaac Hull, James McHenry, Alexander Murray,
     Isaac Phillips, Benjamin Stoddert, Silas Talbot, Thomas Truxton

## POLITICS AND DIPLOMACY

505  Adams, Brooks. "The Convention of 1800 with France," Massachusetts
     Historical Society Proceedings 44 (1911): 377-428.

506  Allen, John. Speech of John Allen, Esq., in the House of Represent-
     atives , the 20th day of April, 1798, relating to Employing the Armed
     Vessels as Convoys. Philadelphia: W. Cobbett, 1798.

507  Archambault, P.J. "From Grand Alliance to Great Schism: France in
     America, 1763-1815," Papers on Language and Literature 12 (1976):
     339-65.

508  Bemis, Samuel F. "The United States and the Abortive Armed Neutrality
     of 1794," American Historical Review 24 (1918): 26-47.

509  Bowman, Albert H. The Struggle for Neutrality: Franco-American
     Diplomacy During the Federalist Era. Knoxville: University of
     Tennessee Press, 1974.

510  Bradley, J.E. "Reprieve of a Loyalist: Count Rumford's Invitation
     Home," New England Quarterly 47 (1974): 368-85.

511  Childs, Frances S. "French Opinion of Anglo-American Relations, 1795-
     1805," French American Review 1 (1948): 21-35.

512  Carnegie Endowment for International Peace. The Controversy over Neutral Rights between the United States and France, 1797-1800: A Collection of American State Papers and Judicial Decisions. New York: Oxford University Press, 1917.

513  DeConde, Alexander. The Quasi-War: The Politics and Diplomacy of the Undeclared War with France, 1797-1801. New York: Scribner's, 1966.

514  _____. "The Quasi-War," American History Illustrated 12 (1977): 4-9, 44-48.

515  _____. "Foreclosure of a Peacemaker's Career: A Criticism of Thomas Jefferson's Isolation," Huntington Library Quarterly 15 (1952): 297-304.

516  _____. "William Vans Murray and the Diplomacy of Peace, 1797-1800," Maryland Historical Magazine 48 (1953): 1-26.

517  Ford, Worthington, ed. "Letters of William Vans Murray to John Quincy Adams, 1797-1813," American Historical Association Annual Report (1912): 341-708.

518  Gebhardt, Adam G. State Papers Relating to the Diplomatic Transactions Between the American and French Governments. 3 Vols. London: J.B.G. Vogel, 1816.

519  Goldsmith, Lewis. An Exposition of the Conduct of France Towards America: Illustrated by Cases Decided in the Council of Prizes in Paris. London: J.M. Richardson, 1810.

520  Grob, Fritz. The Relativity of War and Peace: A Study in Law, History, and Politics. New Haven: Yale University Press, 1949.

521  Harper, Robert G. Observations on the Dispute Between the United States and France. Philadelphia: N.p., 1798.

522  Hill, Peter B. William Vans Murray, Federalist Diplomat: The Shaping of Peace With France, 1797-1801. Syracuse: Syracuse University, 1971.

523  Hill, Peter B. "Prologue to the Quasi-War: Stresses in Franco-American Relations, 1793-1796," Journal of Modern History 49 (1977): 1053-95.

524  James, James A. "French Opinion as a Factor Preventing war between France and the United States, 1795-1800," American Historical Review 30 (1924): 44-55.

525  Kramer, Eugene F. "Some New Light on the XYZ Affair: Elbridge Gerry's Reasons for Opposing War with France," New England Quarterly 29 (1956): 509-13.

526  Kurtz, George W. "Guns for Charleston: A Case of Lend-lease in 1798-1799, with the text of Liston's, Grenville's, and Pickering's Letters," Journal of Southern History 14 (1948): 401-08.

527  Kurtz, Stephen G. "The French Mission of 1799-1800: Concluding Chapters in the Statecraft of John Adams," Political Science Quarterly 30 (1965): 543-57.

528  Lang, Daniel G. Foreign Policy in the Early Republic: The Laws of Nations and the Balance of Power. Baton Rouge: Louisiana State University, 1985.

529  Lyon, E. Wilson. "The Directory and the United States," American Historical Review 43 (1938): 514-32.

530  ____. "The Franco-American Convention of 1800," Journal of Modern History 12 (1940): 305-33.

531  McLemore, Richard A. Franco-American Diplomatic Relations, 1816-1836. Baton Rouge: Louisiana State University, 1941.

532  Morison, Samuel E. "Dupont, Tallyrand, and French Spoilations," Massachusetts Historical Society Proceedings 49 (1915-1916): 63-79.

533  Reindehl, J.H. "The Influence of the French Revolution and Napoleon Upon the United States as Revealed by the Fortunes of the Crowning-shield Family of Salem." Ph. D. dissertation, University of Michigan, 1953.

534  Richmond, Arthur A. "The United States and the Armed Neutrality of 1800." Ph. D. dissertation, Yale University, 1951.

535  ____. "Napoleon and the Armed Neutrality of 1800," Journal of the Royal United Service Institute 104 (1959): 1-9.

536  Scott, James B., ed. The Controversy over Neutral Rights between the United States and France, 1797-1800: A Collection of American State Papers and Judicial Decisions. New York: Oxford University Press, 1917.

537  Smith, James M. "Background for Repression: America's Half-War with France and the Internal Security Legislation of 1798," Huntinton Library Quarterly 18 (1954): 37-58.

538  Soler, William G. "A Reattribution: John Dickinson's Authorship of the pamphlet 'A Caution'," Pennsylvania Magazine of History and Biography 77 (1953): 24-31.

539  Sparks, Edwin E. "Formative Incidents in American Diplomacy," Chautauquan 34 (1904): 247-63.

540  Stinchcombe, William C. The XYZ Affair. Westport, CT: Greenwood Press, 1981.

541  ____. "Tallyrand and the American Negotiations of 1797-1798," Journal of American History 62 (1975): 575-90.

542  Strong, M.K. "Foreign Affairs and Congressional Elections: Elections of 1798," Current History 10 (1946): 342-47.

543  Tolles, Frederick B. "Unofficial Ambassador: George Logan's Mission to France, 1798," William and Mary Quarterly 7 (1950): 3-25.

544  Van Alstyne, Richard W. "Naval War with France, 1798-1800." In: American Diplomacy in Action: A Series of Case Studies. Stanford: Stanford University Press, 1944, 420-32.

SEE ALSO: 642, 6644, John Adams

## PRISONERS

545   Kihn, Phyllis. "The French San Domingo Prisoners in Connecticut," Connecticut Historical Society Bulletin 28 (1963): 47-63.

546   Savageau, David L. "The United States Navy and its 'Half War' Prisoners, 1798-1800," American Neptune 31 (1971): 159-76.

## CONTEMPORARY ACCOUNTS

547   Higginson, Thomas W. The Life and Times of Stephen Higginson. Boston: Houghton, Mifflin, 1907.

548   _____., ed. "Letters of Stephen Higginson," American Historical Association Annual Report (1896): 704-841.

549   Knox, Dudley W.. "Documents on the Naval War with France," United States Naval Institute Proceedings 61 (1935): 535-38.

550   _____., ed. Naval Documents Related to the Quasi-War between the United States and France: Naval Operations from February, 1797, to December, 1801. 7 Vols. Washington, DC: Government Printing Office, 1935-1938.

SEE ALSO: 4278

## TRIPOLITAN WAR

551   Abbot, Willis J. Blue Jackets of '76. A History of the Naval Battles of the American Revolution, together with a Narrative of the War with Tripoli. New York: Dodd, Mead, 1888.

552   Abedin, Syed Z. "In Defense of Freedom: America's First Foreign War. A New Look at U.S.-Barbary Relations, 1776-1816." Ph. D. dissertation, University of Pennsylvania, 1974.

553   Adams, Henry. History of the United States of America during the Administration of Thomas Jefferson. 2 Vols. New York: A. and C. Boni, 1930.

554   Albion, Robert G. and Jennie B. Pope. "Pirates." In: Sealanes in Wartime: The American Experience, 1775-1945. New York: W.W. Norton, 1942, 126-47.

555   Allen, Gardner W. Our Navy and the Barbary Corsairs. Boston: Houghton, Mifflin, 1905.

556   Anderson, Roger C. "Tripoli and Tunis: The Americans in the Mediterranean, 1795-1805." In: Naval Wars in the Levant, 1559-1853. Princeton: Princeton University Press, 1953, 393-426.

557   Bell, Frederick J. Room to Swing a Cat: Being Some Tales of the Old Navy. New York: Longmans, Green, 1938, 25-73.

558   Birge, William S. "Before the Walls of Tripoli," Americana 4 (1909): 478-80.

559   Blyth, Stephen C. History of the War Between the United States and Tripoli, and other Barbary Powers. Salem, MA: Gazette, 1806.

560   Bradford, Ernie D. Mediterranean: Portrait of a Sea. New York: Harcourt, Brace, Jovanovich, 1971.

561  Bryson, Thomas A. "The Barbary Pirates and the Founding of the
     United States Navy, 1794-1816." In: Tars, Turks, and Tankers: The
     Role of the United States Navy in the Middle East, 1800-1879.
     Metuchen, NJ: Scarecrow Press, 1980, 1-19.

562  Burchis, Mustapha and Arthur M. Johnson. "Lost but not Forgotten:
     the Final Resting Place for Heroes of the Barbary Wars," United
     States Naval Institute Proceedings 82 (1956): 968-73.

563  Castor, Avery. The Tripolitan War, 1801-1805: America Meets the
     Menace of the Barbary Pirates. New York: Franklin Watts, 1971.

564  Chambliss, William C. "Lend-lease long Ago," United States Naval
     Institute Proceedings 73 (1947): 1324-27.

565  Chidsey, Donald B. The Wars in Barbary: Arab Piracy and the Birth of
     the United States Navy. New York: Crown, 1971.

566  Cooke, Jean Marie. "The American Experience of the Arab, 1800-1860."
     Ph. D. dissertation, St. John's University, 1970.

567  Currey, Edward H. Sea Wolves of the Mediterranean: The Grand Period
     of the Moslem Corsairs. New York: Frederick A. Stokes, 1929.

568  Dawson, Henry B. Battles of the United States. 2 Vols. New York:
     Johnson, Fry, 1858. Vol. 2, 35-63.

569  Dearden, Seton. "Eaton's March on Tripoli," Cornhill Magazine 1078
     (1973-1974): 133-64.

570  DeMorgan, John. Taming the Barbary Pirates. Springfield, MA:
     McLoughlin Bros., 1933.

571  Dix, John A. "War with Tripoli." In: Speeches and Occasional Addresses
     of John Adams Dix. 2 Vols. New York: D, Appleton, 1864. Vol. 2,
     383-409.

572  Earle, Peter. Corsairs of Malta and Barbary. Annapolis: United States
     Naval Institute Press, 1970.

573  Eller, Ernest M. "To the Shores of Tripoli," United States Naval
     Institute Proceedings 59 (1933): 347-36, 411-14, 1192-93.

574  Ent, Uzal W. "On the Shores of Tripoli," American History Illustrated
     20 (1986): 42-49.

575  Field, James A., Jr. America and the Mediterranean World, 1776-1886.
     Princeton: Princeton University Press, 1969.

576  Fisher, Godfrey. Barbary Legend: War, Trade and Piracy in North
     Africa, 1415-1830. New York: Oxford University Press, 1957.

577  Folayan, Kola. "Tripoli and the War with the U.S.A., 1801-1805,"
     Journal of African History 13 (1972): 261-70.

578  _____. "The Tripolitan War: A Reconsideration of the Causes,"
     Africa 27 (1972): 615-26.

579  Forester, Cecil S. The Barbary Pirates. New York: Random House, 1953.

580  Frost, Hollaway W. "We Fight the Mediterranean Pirates, 1801-1805."
     In: We Build a Navy. Annapolis: United States Naval Institute Press,
     1940, 105-202.

581  Furlong, Charles W. Extracts from Blue Book Magazine of Articles
     Written by Charles Wellington Furlong, 1940-1941. N.p., N.d.

582  Gallagher, Charles F. The United States and North Africa: Morocco,
     Algeria, Tunisia. Cambridge: Harvard University Press, 1963.

583  Geer, Andrew. "To the Shores...," Leatherneck 54 (1971): 38-41.

584  Goldsborough, Charles W. The United States Naval Chronicle.
     Washington: J. Wilson, 1824.

585  Greenhow, Robert. History and Present Condition of Tripoli: with
     Some Accounts of other Barbary States. Richmond: T.W. White, 1835.

586  Headley, Joel T. "Eaton's Barbary Expedition," Harper's Monthly
     Magazine 21 (1860): 496-511.

587  Holland, Rupert S. "How the Young Republic Fought the Barbary Pirates."
     In: Historic Adventures. Philadelphia: George W. Jacobs, 1913, 80-112.

588  Howard, L.C. "American Involvement in Africa South of the Sahara,
     1800-1860." Ph. D. dissertation, Harvard University, 1956.

589  Howe, Russell W. Along the Afric Shore: A Historic Review of Two
     Centuries of U.S.-African Relations. New York: Barnes, Noble, 1975.

590  Howland, Felix. "Eaton's Declaration of the Blockade of Tripoli, 1801,"
     United States Naval Institute Proceedings 58 (1932): 1186-90.

591  _____. "The Blockade of Tripoli, 1801-1802," Ibid 63 (1937): 1702-04.

592  _____. "Tripolitan Background of the War of 1801-1805," Marine Corps
     Gazette 22 (1938): 23-24.

593  Hunt, Livingston. "The Trial of Lieut. Ridgely for Murder," United
     States Naval Institute Proceedings 56 (1930): 985-990.

594  Jamieson, Alan. "The Tangier Galleys and the Wars against the
     Mediterranean Corsairs," American Neptune 24 (1964): 61-69.

595  Jenrich, Charles H. "To the Shores of Tripoli," Rudder 74 (1958):
     19-23.

596  King, Cecil. "France and Tripoli." In: Atlantic Charter. New York:
     Studio, 1943, 53-67.

597  LaFargue, Thomas E. "America's African Odyssey," Scientific Monthly
     55 (1942): 369-74.

598  Lane-Poole, Stanley and J.D. Jerrold Kelley. The Story of the Barbary
     Corsairs. New York: G.P. Putnam's Sons, 1890.

599  Lanier, William P. "The Shores of Tripoli," United States Naval
     Institute Proceedings 68 (1942): 72-78.

600   Leeming, Joseph. "The Bombardment of Tripoli." In: The Book of American
      Fighting Ships. New York: Harper & Bros., 1939, 79-86.

601   Lewis, Charles L. "The Old Navy at Constantinople," United States
      Naval Institute Proceedings 59 (1933): 1442-48.

602   McKee, Linda and Christopher McKee, eds. "An Inquiry into the Conduct
      of Joshua Blake," American Neptune 21 (1961): 130-41.

603   Meader, John R. "The Little Wars of the Republic," Americana 5 (1910):
      1017-25.

604   Miller, Arthur P. "Tripoli Graves Discovered," United States Naval
      Institute Proceedings 76 (1950): 372-77.

605   Montorency, J.E. "Piracy and the Barbary Corsairs," Law Quarterly
      Review 35 (1919): 133-42.

606   Moran, Charles. "Commodore Preble's Sicilian Auxilaries," United
      States Naval Institute Proceedings 65 (1939): 80-82.

607   Munger, Martha P. "A Little-Known Debt" the War with Tripoli,"
      Americana 23 (1929): 11-19.

608   Parrott, Marc. "A Captive Marine and his Rescuers." In: Hazard:
      Marines on a Mission. New York: Doubleday, 1962, 21-68.

609   Pratt, Fletcher. Heroic Years: Fourteen Years of the Republic, 1801-
      1815. New York: Smith, 1935.

610   Rentrow, F. "To the Shores of Tripoli," Leatherneck 12 (1929): 10-11.

611   Richardson, Frank. "Bullies on the Barbary Coast," Blackwood's
      Magazine 312 (1972): 27-36.

612   Richardson, Gardner. "The American Invasion of Tripoli; a Forgotten
      Incident of History," Independent 71 (1911): 861-64.

613   Shippen, Edward. "The Barbarous Moors," United Service 2 (1880):
      580-604.

614   "Sketch of the Barbary States," Analectic Magazine 7 (1816): 105-13.

615   Smith, Gaddis. "The United States vs International Terrorists; a
      chapter from Our Past," American Heritage 28 (1977): 37-43.

616   Soley, James R. "Operations of the American Squadron under Commodore
      Edward Preble, 1803-1804," United States Naval Institute Proceedings
      5 (1879): 51-98.

617   _____. Paper on the Operation of the Mediterranean Squadron Under
      Commodore Edward Preble in 1803-1804. Claremont, NH: N.p., 1879.

618   Thorn, Charles E. Heroic Life and Tragic Death of Lieutenant Johnathan
      Thorn, United States Navy. New York: Reporter Press, 1944.

619   Tucker, Glenn. Dawn Like Thunder: The Barbary Wars and the Birth of
      the United States Navy. Indianapolis: Bobbs-Merrill, 1963.

620 ____. "Our Glorious Little Naval War," American History Illustrated 2 (1968): 4-12.

621 Tyrrell, Frank H. "The Barbary Corsairs," Asiatic Quarterly Review 11 (1891): 438-57.

622 "The United States and the Barbary States," Atlantic Monthly 6 (1860): 641-57.

623 Wallace, Robert. "The Barbary Wars waged Over Tribute Demanded by the Arabs," Smithsonian 5 (1975): 82-91.

624 Wolf, John B. The Barbary Coast: Algiers under the Turks, 1500 to 1830. New York: W.W. Norton, 1979.

625 Wright, C.Q. "The Tripoli Monument," United States Naval Institute Proceedings 48 (1922): 1931-41.

626 Zingg, Paul J. "The United States and North Africa: A Historio-graphical Wasteland," African Studies Review 16 (1973): 107-17.

    SEE ALSO: 3541, 3723, 3740, 4711, USS Constitution, USS Enterprose, USS Intrepid, USS Philadelphia, USS Vixen, William Bainbridge, Richard Dale, Stephen Decatur, William Eaton, Thomas Jefferson, James Lawrence, Richard V. Morris, Presley O'Bannon, Edward Preble, John Rodgers, Richard Somers

## POLITICS AND DIPLOMACY

627 Aube, Raymond F. "Worlds Apart: The Roots of America's Diplomatic Failures in other Cultures—The Barbary Coast in the Early Nine-teenth Century." Ph. D. dissertation, New York University, 1986.

628 BenRejeb, B. Lofti. "To the Shores of Tripoli': The Impact of Barbary on Early American Nationalism." Ph. D. dissetation, Indiana University, 1982.

629 Canton, Milton. "Joel Barlow's Mission at Algiers," Historian 25 (1963): 172-94.

630 Carey, Matthew. A Short Account of Algiers, with a Concise View of the Rupture between Algiers and the United States. Philadelphia: M. Carey, 1794.

631 Carson, David A. "Congress in Jefferson's Foreign Policy, 1801-1809." Ph. D. dissertation, Texas Christian University, 1983.

632 ____. "Jefferson, Congress, and the Question of Leadership in the Tripolitan War," Virginia Magazine of History and Biography 94 (1986): 409-29.

633 Charlick, Carl. "Jefferson's NATO," Foreign Service Journal 31 (1954): 18-21, 58.

634 Dispatches from U.S. Consuls in Tripoli, 1796-1885. Washington, DC: National Archives, 1955.

635 Eilts, Hermann F. "Sayyid Muhammed Bin 'Aqil of Dhufar: Malevolent Maligned?" Essex Institute Historical Collections 109 (1973): 179-230.

636  Hall, Luella J. The United States and Morocco, 1776-1956.
     Metuchen, NJ: Scarecrow Press, 1971.

637  Hamet Caramalli. Documents Respecting the Application of Hamet
     Caramelli, Ex-Bashaw of Tripoli. Washington, DC: Duane & Sons, 1806.

638  Irwin, Ray W. The Diplomatic Relations of the United States with the
     Barbary Powers. Chapel Hill: University of North Carolina Press, 1931.

639  _____. "The Mission of Soliman Mellmelni, Tunisian Ambassador to the
     United States, 1805-1807," Americana 26 (1932): 465-71.

640  _____. "Proteges of the United States in Consequence of the War with
     Triploi, 1801-1807," Ibid 29 (1935): 345-63.

641  Ives, Ernest L. "Colonel Tobias Lear," American Foreign Service
     Journal 13 (1936): 185-87.

642  Lint, Gregg L. "Early American Concepts of International Law, and
     their Influence on Foreign Policy, 1776-1803." Ph. D. dissertation,
     Michigan State University, 1975.

643  Nicholas, Roy F. "Diplomacy in Barbary," Pennsylvania Magazine of
     History and Biography 74 (1950): 113-41.

644  Ross, Frank E. "The Mission of John Lamb to Algiers, 1785-1786,"
     Americana 28 (1934): 287-94.

645  _____. "The Mission of Joseph Donaldson, Jr., to Algiers, 1795-1797,"
     Journal of Modern History 7 (1935): 422-33.

646  Savage, Marie M. "American Diplomacy in North Africa, 1776-1817."
     Ph. D. dissertation, Georgetown University, 1949.

647  Schuyler, Eugene. American Diplomacy and the Furtherance of Commerce.
     New York: C. Scribner's Sons, 1886, 193-232.

648  Taylor, John M. "Adams and Jefferson in the Middle East,"
     Mansucripts 33 (1981): 237-40.

649  Van Alstyne, Richard W. "Mediterranean Trade and the Barbary Pirates."
     In: American Diplomacy in Action: A Series of Case Studies. Stanford:
     Stanford University Press, 1944, 432-38.

650  Wright, Louis B. and Julia A. Macleod. "Mellmelli," Virginia Quarterly
     Review 20 (1944): 555-65.

     SEE ALSO: 666, 3796, 3799, 4851, James L. Cathcart, William Eaton

## PRISONERS

651  Barnby, H.G. The Prisoners of Algiers: An Account of the Forgotten
     American-Algerian War, 1785-1797. Totwa, NJ: Rowman, Littlefield, 1966.

652  Bartlett, Harley H. "American Captivities in Barbary," Michigan Alumnus
     Quarterly Review 61 (1955): 238-54.

653  Foik, Paul O. "In the Clutches of the Barbary Corsairs," Illinois
     Catholic Historical Review 9 (1926): 162-76.

654   Ray, William. Horror of Slavery, or, the American Tars in Tripoli; Containing an Account of the Loss and Capture of the United States Frigate Philadelphia. Troy, NY: Oliver Lyon, 1808.

655   Stevens, James. A Historical and Geographical Account of Algiers, Comprehending a Novel and Interesting Detail of Events relative to the American Captives. Philadelphia: Hogan, McElroy, 1797.

656   Wilson, Gary E. "American Prisoners in the Barbary Nations, 1784–1816." Ph. D. dissertation, North Texas State University, 1979.

657   _____. "The First American Hostages in Moslem Nations, 1784–89," American Neptune 41 (1981): 208–23.

658   _____. "American Hostages in Moslem Nations, 1784–1796: the Public Response," Journal of the Early Republic 2 (1982): 123–41.

SEE ALSO: 4394, USS Philadelphia

CONTEMPORARY ACCOUNTS

659   Adams, Robert. The Narrative of Robert Adams, an American Sailor who was Wrecked on the West Coast of Africa in the year 1810. Boston: Wells, Lilly, 1817.

660   Beran, Edith R. "Letters from Nicholas Harwood, M.D., U.S. Navy, Prisoner of War in Tripoli, 1803–05," Maryland Historical Magazine 40 (1945): 66–70.

661   Blaquiere, E. Letters from the Mediterranean; Containing a Civil and Political Account of Sicily, Tripoli, Tunis and Malta. 2 Vols. London: Henry Colburn, 1813.

662   Breen, John J. "A Connecticut Yankee finds the 'pleasing diversity' of a Sailor's life," New England Galaxy 17 (1976): 3–7.

663   Cantor, Milton, ed. "A Connecticut Yankee in a Barbary Coast: Joel Barlow's Algerian Letters to his Wife," William and Mary Quarterly 19 (1962): 172–94.

664   Clark, Edward D. Travels in Various Countries of Europe, Asia and Africa. 3 Vols. London: T. Cadell, W. Davis, 1813. Vol. 3.

665   Cowdery, Jonathan. American Captives in Tripoli; or, Dr. Cowdery's Journal in Miniature. Kept during his late Captivity in Tripoli. Boston: Belcher, Armstrong, 1806.

666   Cutting, Nathaniel. "Journey of an Embassy to Algiers in 1793 under Colonel David Humphries," Historical Magazine 4 (1860): 262–65, 296–98, 359–63.

667   Evans, Gordon H. Sufferings in Africa: Captain Riley's Narrative. New York: Clarkson N. Potter, 1965.

668   Fielding, Xan. Corsair Country: The Diary of a Journey along the Barbary Coast. London: Secks, Warburg, 1958.

669   Foss, John. A Journal of Captivity and Suffering by John Foss; several years a Prisoner in Algiers. Newburyport, MA: A. March, 1798.

670  Gee, Joshua. Narrative of Joshua Gee, of Boston, Massachusetts, while
     he was a Captive in Algeria of the Barbary Pirates. Hartford:
     Wadsworth Athenaeum, 1943.

671  Humphreys, David. The Miscellaneous Works of David Humphreys, Late
     Minister Plenipotentiary...to the Court of Madrid. New York: T & J
     Swords, 1804.

672  Knox, Dudley W., ed. Documents Related to the United States Wars with
     the Barbary Pirates: Naval Operations including Diplomatic Background
     from 1785 through 1807. 6 Vols. Washington, DC: Government Printing
     Office, 1939-1944.

673  Lincoln, Charles H., ed. The Hull-Eaton Correspondence during the
     Expedition Against Tripoli, 1804-1805. Worcester, MA: American
     Antiquarian Society, 1911.

674  Martin, Maria. History of the Captivity and Sufferings of Mrs. M.
     Martin, who was Six Years a Captive in Algiers. Boston: Crory, 1807.

675  Pellow, Thomas. The Adventures of Thomas Pellow, of Penryu, Mariner;
     three and twenty Years in Captivity among the Moors. New York:
     Macmillan, 1890.

676  Rodgers, Robert S. "Closing Events in the War with Tripoli: McMaster's
     Account compared with Official Records and other Reliable Sources,"
     United States Naval Institute Proceedings 34 (1908): 889-916.

677  Spence, Robert T. "A Tripolitan War Record: Letter Dated November 12,
     1804, written by  Midshipman Robert T. Spence, U.S. Navy," Ibid 49
     (1923): 625-30.

678  Tully, Miss. Narrative of Ten Years Residence at Tripoli, in Africa,
     from Original Correspondence. London: Henry Colburne, 1816.

679  Tyler, Royall. The Algerine Captive, or. the Life and Adventures of
     Dr. Updike Underhill [Pseud]; six years a Prisoner among the Algerines.
     Walpole, NH: David Carlisle, 1797.

## *WAR OF 1812

680  Coles, Harry. "The War of 1812 and the Mexican War." In: Russell
     Weigley, ed. New Dimensions in Military History: an Anthology.
     San Rafael, CA: Presidio Press, 1975, 311-26.

681  Horsman, Reginald. "On to Canada: Manifest Destiny and the United
     States Strategy in the War of 1812," Michigan Historical Review
     13 (1987): 1-24.

682  Mahon, John K. "British Command Decisions in the Northern Campaigns
     of the War of 1812," Canadian Historical Review 46 (1965): 219-27.

683  Selement, George. "Impressment and the American Merchant Marine,
     1782-1812: An American View," Mariner's Mirror 59 (1973): 409-18.

684  Strum, Harvey. War Scare of 1807 and the Embargo. Lockport, NY:
     Niagara County Historical Society, 1986.

685  White, Patrick C. "A Mere Matter of Marching: A Military History of
     the War of 1812 in British North America." In: Loyal She Remains: A
     History of Ontario. Toronto: United Empire Loyalists, 1984, 124-68.

SEE ALSO: 1880, 2013, 2122, 2177, 2223, 2229, 2230, 2233, 2252, 2253
2349, 2379, 2775, 2861, 2876, Canada-War of 1812

☆WEST

686  Antal, Sandor. "The Thames Campaign in the War of 1812." Master's
     Thesis, Carleton University, 1984.

687  Biel, John G. "The Savage Preface to 1812," Society of Indiana
     Pioneers Yearbook (1956): 5-11.

688  Brady, Cyrus T. Border Fights and Fighters. New York: McClure,
     Philips, 1902, 269-88.

689  Bolt, Robert. "Vice President Richard M. Johnson of Kentucky: Hero
     of the Thames- or the Great Amalgamator?" Register of the Kentucky
     Historical Society 75 (1977): 191-203.

690  Carter-Edwards, Dennis. "The War of 1812 along the Detroit Frontier:
     A Canadian Perspective," Michigan Historical Review 13 (1987): 25-49.

691  Conlin, Mary Lou. Simon Perkins of the Western Reserve. Cleveland:
     Western Reserve Historical Society, 1968, 74-94.

692  "Death of Peter Navarre, the Famous Scout of the War of 1812,"
     Michigan Pioneer 5 (1884): 188-90.

693  Evelyn, George J. "A Feather in the Cap? The Affair at River Carnard,
     16th July, 1812," Military Historian and Collector 39 (1987): 169-71.

694  Expedition under General McArthur," Michigan Pioneer 8 (1886): 652-54.

695  "Frontier Incident," Army Navy Chronicle 6 (1838): 359.

696  "General Trotter's Tomb," Kentucky Historical and Genealogical
     Magazine 1 (1899): 21-25.

697  Harris, James R. "Kentuckians in the War of 1812: A Note on Numbers,
     Losses, and Sources," Register of the Kentucky Historical Society
     82 (1984): 277-86.

698  Kantor, Alvin R. "Harrison and the Battle of the Thames," Manuscripts
     21 (1969): 282-84.

699  Lippincott, Thomas. "The Wood River Massacre," Western Monthly
     Magazine 1 (1833): 280-84.

700  Patterson, Nicholas and John M. Peck. "The Boon's Lick Country,"
     Missouri Historical Society Bulletin 6 (1950): 442-71.

701  Perrin, J. Nick. "The Wood River Massacre," Illinois State Historical
     Society Journal 3 (1911): 70-73.

702  Pratt, Fletcher. "Richard M. Johnson: Rumpsey Dumpsey." In: Eleven
     Generals: Studies in American Command. New York: William Sloan,
     1949, 81-98.

703  Randall, Emilius O. "The Harrison Table Rock and Ball's Battlefield,'
     Ohio Archaeological and Historical Society Quarterly 19 (1910): 360-69.

704  Richmond, Volney. "The Wood River Massacre," Illinois State
     Historical Society Transactions (1901): 93-95.

705  Strouse, Isaac R. "The Wabash Country Prior to 1800," Magazine of
     American History 17 (1887): 408-13.

706  Sugden, John. Tecumseh's Last Stand. Norman, OK: University of
     Oklahoma Press, 1985.

707  "A Trait of Frontier warfare," Western Monthly Magazine 5 (1836):
     139-50.

     SEE ALSO: 930, 931, 932, 937, 949, 952, 953, 955, 959, 960, 966,
     4671, 4742, 4766, 4769, Fort Dearborn, Fort Madison, Fort Meigs,
     Fort Osage, Fort Wayne, Kentucky militia, British-Indian relations,
     Billy Caldwell, Lewis Cass, Main Poc, Henry Procter, Zachary Taylor,
     Tecumseh

## *NIAGARA FRONTIER-LAKE ONTARIO

708  "The American Invasion, 1812-1813," Canadian Antiquarian and
     Numismatic Journal 7 (1879): 128-36.

709  Boeth, David J. "Battle of Sackett's Harbor," Soldiers 40 (1985):
     44-45.

710  Hein, Edward B. "The Niagara Frontier and the War of 1812."
     Ph. D. dissertation, University of Ottawa, 1949.

711  Heller, Charles F. "Those are Regulars, by God!" Army 37 (1987):
     52-54.

712  Crackel, Theodore J. "The Battle of Queenston heights, 13 October,
     1813." In: Charles E. Heller and William A. Sofft, eds. America's
     First Battles, 1776-1965. Lawrence, KS: University Press of Kansas,
     1986, 33-56.

713  "Battle of Queenston Heights," Ontario Historical Society Papers
     and Records 6 (1905): 76-77.

714  Frazer, John. "The Battle of Queenston Heights," Magazine of
     American History 24 (1890): 203-11.

715  "The Battle of Lundy's Lane," Army and Navy Chronicle 3 (1836):
     296-97.

716  Crosswell, Daniel K. "A Near Run Thing on the Niagara: The Battle of
     Lundy's lane." In: Sharing Past and Future. Toronto: Ontario
     Genealogical Society, 1987, 33-56.

717  Leavitt, Thaddeus W. History of Leeds and Grenville, Ontario, from
     1749 to 1879. Brockville, ON: Recorder Press, 1879, 69-71.

718  "Recollections of Lundy's Lane," Army and Navy Chronicle 3 (1836):
     218-19; 7 (1838): 145-47.

719  Upham, C.W. "The Capture of General Riall," Historical Magazine 1
     (1873): 252-53.

     SEE ALSO: 921, 924, 925, 932, 936, 938, 940, 941, 943, 944, 966, 971,
     2399, Fort Erie, Hugh Brady, Isaac Brock, Jacob Brown, James Fitz-
     gibbon, James Hall, Winfield Scott, Stephen Van Rensselaer

*ST. LAWRENCE-LAKE CHAMPLAIN

720  "The Battle of Plattsburg," Army and Navy Chronicle 1 (1835): 275-76.

721  "The Battle of Plattsburg," Ibid 9 (1839): 129-30.

722  "The Battle of Plattsburg," Army and Navy Chronicle and Scientific Repository 2 (1843): 434-41.

723  Croil, James. Dundas; or, Sketches of Canadian History. Montreal: B. Dawson, 1861, 78-95.

724  Gaines, William H. Thomas Mann Randolph, Jefferson's Son-in-Law. Baton Rouge: Louisiana State University, 1966, 82-100.

725  Galloway, Strome. "Why the Maple Leaf is Our National Emblem," Canadian Geographic 102 (1982): 30-35.

726  McKell, Wayne. "The Battle of Chauteauguay," Chauteauguay Valley Historical Society Annual Report 6 (1973): 81-86.

727  Macomb, Alexander. "The Battle of Plattsburg," Journal of the Military Service Institute 12 (1891): 76-79.

728  "Major General Benjamin Mooers, of Plattsburg, New York," Historical Magazine 11 (1872): 92-94.

729  Nelson, Gladys G. "The Battle of Plattsburg," University of Rochester Library Bulletin 3 (1848): 30-34.

730  Stevenson, James. "Opening Address," Literary and Historical Society of Quebec Transactions (1877-1879): 13-20.

731  Walter, Philip G. and Raymond Walters, Jr. "The American Career of David Parish," Journal of Economic History 4 (1944): 149-66.

732  Weise, A.J. The Swartwout Chronicles, 1338-1899. New York: Trow Directory, printing, and Book Binding Co., 1899.

733  Wood, Col. J.H. "Plattsburg, 1814," Women's Canadian Historical Society Transactions No. 5 (1905): 10-16.

     SEE ALSO: 939, 940, 941, 942, 945, 965, Leonard Covington, Wade Hampton, John E. Wool

*LAKE WAR

734  Allen, E.S. "Sailors on Wheels," Motor Boating 113 (1964): 148-51.

735  Belovarac, Allan. "A Brief Overview of the Battle of Lake Erie and the Perry-Elliott Controversy," Journal of Lake Erie Studies 17 (1988): 3-6.

736  Burchard, Roswell D. "Significance of Raising and Rebuilding of the 'Niagara'," Journal of American History 8 (1914): 50-57.

737  Cain, Emily. "Building Lord Nelson," Inland Seas 41 (1985): 121-29.

737A Clanin, Douglas E., ed. "The Correspondence of William Henry Harrison and Oliver Hazard Perry, July 5, 1813-July 31, 1815," Northwest Ohio Quarterly 60 (1988): 153-80.

738  Clark, Francis. "Monroe County: Action of Lake Ontario at the Mouth of the Genessee River, War of 1812," Yesteryears 17 (1973): 34-38.

739 Cooper, James F. Ned Myers, or, A Life before the Mast.
New York: Putnam, 1899, 46-81.

740 Curry, Frederick C. "Six Little Schooners," Inland Seas 2 (1946):
185-90.

741 Donaldson, Gordon. "When Kingston Built the World's Mightiest Ships,"
Canadian Geographic 103 (1984): 55-61.

742 Drake, Frederick C. "A Loss of Mastery: The British Squadron on Lake
Erie, May-September, 1813," Journal of Erie Studies 17 (1988): 47-75.

743 Gagne, Leonne. "Lake Champlain and its Importance during Wars,"
Vermont History 29 (1961): 87-91.

744 Haller, Willis and C. Gerard Hoard. The Building of Chauncey's Fleet.
N.p., N.d., 1983.

745 Jury, Elsie M. "USS Tigress-HMS Confiance, 1813-1831," Inland Seas
28 (1972): 3-16.

746 Little, C.H. "Naval Activities on the Lakes: Past and Present,"
Canadian Geographic 67 (1963): 202-15.

747 Lord, Barry. "Two Armed Schooners from the War of 1812." In:
David L. Matersen, ed. Naval History: The Sixth Symposium of the
United States Naval Academy. Wilmington, DE: Scholarly Resources,
1987, 354-58.

748 Murphy, Rowley. "Resurrection at Penetanguishene," Inland Seas 10
(1954): 3-8.

749 Nelson, Dan. "Sinking of the Hamilton and Scourge: How Many Men
were Lost?" Freshwater 2 (1987): 4-7.

750 Saunders, Robert. "When Newfoundland Saved Canada," Newfoundland
Quarterly 62 (1963): 15-17, 20-23.

751 See, Scott W. "The War of 1812: Battle of Interpretations." In:
Jennie G. Versteeg, ed. Lake Champlain: Reflection on our Past.
Burlington, VT: University of Vermont, 1987, 163-74.

752 Snodgrass, James M. "A Racing Sailor Looks at the Battle of Lake
Erie," Inland Seas 44 (1988): 132-38.

753 Stevens, John R. "HM Provincial Marine Schooner 'General Hunter',"
Nautical Research Journal 3 (1952): 125-7.

754      . The Story of HM Armed Schooner Tecumseh. Halifax: Maritime
Museum of Canada, 1961.

755 "U.S. Naval Vessels on Lake Ontario during the War of 1812: Vessels
bulit for the Navy," Yesteryears 29 (1986): 4-10.

756 Valle, James E. "The Battle of Lake Erie: A Victory for Commodore
Perry," Pennsylvania Heritage 14 (1988): 30-37.

SEE ALSO: 945, 946, 954, 3706, 3709, 3729, 4836, Fort Ontario,
USS Eagle, USS New Orleans,   Robert H. Barclay, John Cassin, Isaac
Chauncey, Daniel Dobbins, Henry Eckford, Jesse D. Elliot,

Thomas MacDonough, Usher Parsons, Oliver H. Perry, Daniel Turner, Melanchthon T. Woolsey

*ATLANTIC SEABOARD

757 Anderson, Russell. The British Raid on Essex, April 8, 1814. Essex, CT: Essex County Historical Society, 1981.

758 Brown, Donald. "Eastport: A Maritime History," American Neptune 28 (1968): 113-27.

759 Drisko, George W. Narrative of the Town of Machias, the Old and the New. Machias, ME: Press of the Republican, 1904.

760 Grutz, George. This Bold Corner. Old Lyme, CT: Lyme House, 1957.

761 Hincks, William B. Bridgeport and Vicinity in the Revolution and the War of 1812. Bridgeport, CT: Gould, Stiles, 1876.

762 Lynch, Frank C. "The Battle of Stonington in Retrospective: Its Strategy, Politics, and Personalities," Stonington Historical Society Historical Footnotes 1 (1964): 5-14.

763 "Mother Bailey," My Country 7 (1973): 14-17.

764 Murdock, Richard K. "The Battle of Stonington: A New Look," Stonington Historical Society Historic Footnotes 10 (1973): 1-3, 6-9.

765 "New Canaan's Part in the War of 1812," New Canaan Historical Society Annual 3 (1954): 279-81.

766 Peet, Martha D. "My Home in Connecticut Fifty Years Ago," Connecticut Historical Society Bulletin 11 (1946): 9-16.

767 Smith, Marion J. General William King. Camden, ME: Down East Books, 1980.

   SEE ALSO: 823, 963, 967, 4547, 4700. Fort Nathan Hale, Fort Sullivan

*CHESAPEAKE BAY

768 Barton, Wilfred M. The Road to Washington. Boston: R.G. Badger, 1919.

769 "Battle of Baltimore," Army and Navy Chronicle and Scientific Repository 3 (1844): 90-91.

770 "By the Dawn's Early Light," Army Digest 25 (1970): 14-19.

771 Chace, James and Caleb Carr. "The Burning of Washington: Absolute Vunerability." In: The Quest for Absolute Security: From the War of 1812 to Star Wars. New York: Summit Books, 1988, 17-40.

772 Foytik, Rodney C. "Aspects of the Military Life of Troops Stationed around Norfolk Harbor, 1812-1814," Chesopiean 22 (1984): 12-20.

773 Francis, J. Henry. "The Star-Spangled Banner: How and Why it came to be Written," West Virginia History 3 (1942): 305-13.

774 Hallahan, John M. The Battle of Craney Island: A Matter of Credit. Portsmouth, VA: St. Michael's Press, 1986.

775  Hecht, Arthur. "The Post Office Department in St. Mary's County in
     the War of 1812," Maryland Historical Magazine 52 (1957): 142-57.

776  Howard, John T. Our American Music; Three Hundred Years of it.
     New York: Thomas Y. Crowell, 1931.

777  Huntsberry, Thomas V. North Point, War of 1812. Baltimore: J. Mart,
     1985.

778  "General Winder and the Capture of Washington," Historical Magazine
     5 (1861): 227-29.

779  McGarry, John H. "The War of 1812 and its effect on Montgomery
     County," The Montgomery County Story 26 (1983): 43-50.

780  "Minutes of the Committee of Defense of Philadelphia, 1814-1815,"
     Memoirs of the Historical Society of Pennsylvania 8 (1867): 5-420.

781  Mogilka, Gerard H. "The British Campaign in the Chesapeake during
     the latter part of August, 1814." Master's Thesis, DePaul University,
     1975.

782  Sheads, Scott S. The Rocket's Red Glare: The Maritime Defenses of
     Baltimore in 1814. Centerville, MD: Tidewater Press, 1986.

783  Simmons, Edwin S. "The Battle of Craney Island and Hampton,"
     Fortitudine 15 (1985): 3-7.

784  Sioussat, Anne M. Old Baltimore. New York: Macmillan, 1931.

785  Taylor, Blaine. "Battle of North Point," National Guard 40 (1986):

786  _____. "Twilight's Last Gleaming: the Battle of Fort McHenry,"
     Ibid 40 (1986): 16-18.

     SEE ALSO: 929, 968, 4567, 4570, George Cockburn, Francis S. Key

*SOUTH

787  Barber, Douglas. "Council Government and the Genesis of the Creek War,"
     Alabama Review 38 (1985): 163-74.

788  Brannon, Peter A., ed. "Death of Lieutenant Wilcox," Alabama
     Historical Quarterly 19 (1957): 228-31.

789  Cawthen, William L. "Clinton: County Seat on the Georgia Frontier,
     1808-1821." Master's Thesis, University of Georgia, 1984.

790  Chenault, Lynn. "New Orleans, 1815: The End and a New Beginning,"
     American Society of Arms Collecting Bulletin No. 54 (1986): 2-9.

791  Coker, William S. "How General Andrew Jackson learned about British
     plans before the Battle of New Orleans," Gulf Coast Historical Review
     3 (1987): 85-96.

792  DeGrummond, Jane L. "The Fair Honoring the Brave," Louisiana History
     3 (1962): 54-58.

793  Foner, Philip S. Morale Education in the American Army. New York:
     International Publishers, 1944, 25-29.

794   Greene, Jerome A. Jean Lafitte National Historic Park and Preserve. Washington, DC: U.S. Department of the Interior, 1985.

795   "John Bull before New Orleans," American Historical Record 2 (1873): 435-38.

796   Kantor, Alvin R. "John Houstoun McIntosh and the East Florida Question," Manuscripts 38 (1986): 284-91.

797   Kimball, Jeffrey P. "The Battle of New Orleans." In: John Loos, ed. Great Events From History, American Series. Englewood Cliffs, NJ: Salem Press, 1975, 533-38.

798   Kirk, Cooper. William Lauderdale, Andrew Jackson's Warrior. Fort Lauderdale, FL: Manatee Books, 1982.

799   McCracken, Joseph H. "Victory at New Orleans," American Society of Arms Collecting Bulletin No. 41 (1979): 3-7.

800   Mackenzie, George C. The Indian Breastwork in the Battle of Horseshoe Bend; its size, location, and Construction. Washington, DC: U.S Office of Archaeology and Historic Preservation, 1969.

801   McLemore, Richard A. A History of Mississippi. 2 Vols. Hattiesburg, MS: University Press of Mississippi, 1977. Vol. 1, 217-50.

802   Owen, Thomas M. The History of Alabama. 4 Vols. Chicago: S.J. Clarke, 1921.

803   Pakenham, Valerie. "Sir Edward Pakenham and the Battle of New Orleans," Irish Sword 9 (1975): 32-37.

804   Roberts, W. Adolphe. "By the Eternal!" In: Lake Pontchartrain. Indianapolis: Bobbs-Merrill, 1946, 107-25.

805   Smith, Joseph B. The Plot to Steal Florida: James Madison's Phoney War. New York: Arbor House, 1983.

806   Sternberg, Richard R. "Louisiana and West Florida: A few notes," Southwest Social Science Quarterly 18 (1937): 244-54.

807   Wilgus, A. Curtis. "Spanish-American Patriot Activity Along the Gulf Coast of the United States, 1811-1822," Louisiana Historical Quarterly 7 (1925): 193-215.

      SEE ALSO: 928, 929, 934, 942, 947, 948, 951, 956, 957, 972, 1738, 2206, 3742, 4605, Fort Morgan, Fort Mims, Alexander Ccchrane, Benjamin Hawkins, David Holmes, Andrew Jackson

## *SOUTHWEST

808   Almarez, Felix D. Tragic Cavalier: Governor Manuel Salcedo of Texas, 1805-1813. Austin: University of Texas Press, 1971.

809   Bridges, Katherine. "Lieutenant Augustus William Magee," Louisiana Studies 6 (1967): 291-98.

810   Carter, Hodding. Doomed Road of Empire: The Spanish Trail of Conquest. New York: McGraw Hill, 1971.

811   Garrett, Julia K., ed. "Dr. John Sibley and the Louisiana-Texas
      Frontier, 1803-1814," Southwestern Historical Quarterly 49 (1946):
      405-31.

812   Haggard, Juan V. "The Neutral Ground between Louisiana and Texas."
      Ph. D. dissertation, University of Texas, 1943.

813   Jarrett, Rie. Gutierrez de Lara, Mexican Texan; the Story of a
      Creole Hero. Austin: Creole Texana, 1949.

814   Milligan, James C. "Jose Bernardo Gutierrez de Lara, Mexican
      Frontiersman, 1811-1841." Master's Thesis, Texas Technological
      University, 1975.

815   Nasatir, Abraham P. Borderlands in Retreat:From Spanish Louisiana
      to the Far Southwest. Albuquerque: University of New Mexico, 1976.

816   Warren, Harris G. "Jose Alvarez de Toledo's initiation as a Filli-
      buster," American Historical Review 20 (1940): 56-82.

      SEE ALSO: 950

## *NAVAL WAR

817   Furber, Holden, ed. "How William James came to be a Naval Historian,"
      American Historical Review 38 (1932): 74-85.

818   Langley, Harold D. "Respect for Civilian Authority: the Tragic
      Career of Captain Angur," American Neptune 40 (1980): 23-37.

819   Maclay, Edgar S. "Laurels of the American Tar in 1812," Century
      Magazine 41 (1890): 205-20.

820   Morison, Samuel E. "The Roosevelt Collection of Naval Art," United
      States Naval Institute Proceedings 89 (1963): 81-96.

821   Scott, Kenneth. "U.S. Seamen imprisoned in England in 1814,"
      National Genealogical Society Quarterly 71 (1983): 131-34.

822   Valle, James E. "The Navy's battle doctrine in the War of 1812,"
      American Neptune 65 (1984): 171-78.

      SEE ALSO: 935, 963, 3510, 3513, 3710, 3790, 4079, 4113, 4197, 4204,
      4700, USS Chesapeake, USS Constitution, William H. Allen, William
      Bainbridge, William Burrows, Stephen Decatur, John M. Gamble, Isaac
      Hull, Jacob Jones, James Lawrence, Charles Morris, David Porter, John
      T. Shubrick, Charles Stewart, Provo Wallis, Lewis Warrington

## *PRIVATEERS

823   Baker, William A. A Maritime History of Bath, Maine, and the Kennebec
      River Region. Bath, ME: Maine Research Society, 1973. Vol. 1, 186-201.

824   "The Cleopatra Barge," Historical Magazine 3 (1874): 38-40.

825   Cruikshank, Ernest A. "Colonial Privateers in the War of 1812,"
      Canadiana 1 (1889): 129-37.

826   _____. "Cruises of a Nova Scotian Privateer," Ibid 1 (1889): 81-86.

827   Huntberry, Thomas V. Maryland War of 1812 Privateers. Baltimore:
      J. Mart, 1983.

828   Kert, Faye M. "Fortunes of War: Privateering in Atlantic Canada
      in the War of 1812." Master's Thesis, Carleton University, 1986.

829   McNutt, William S.  The Atlantic Provinces: the Emergence of a
      Colonial Society, 1762-1857. Toronto: McClelland, Stewart, 1965.

830   Mason, George S. "The Private armed Brig Yankee," American Historical
      Register 4 (1896): 161-75.

831   Nelson, George A. "The First Cruise of the Privateer 'Harpy',"
      American Neptune 1 (1942): 116-22.

832   Peabody, Robert E. "The Third 'Grand Turk'." In: The Logs of the
      Grand Turks. Boston: Houghton, Mifflin, 1926, 153-215.

833   "A Seafight of 1813," Magazine of History 9 (1909): 7-9.

      SEE ALSO: USS General Armstrong, Samuel C. Reid

## *POLITICS AND DIPLOMACY

834   Allaben, Frank. "Divine Purpose in the War of 1812," Journal of
      American History 8 (1914): 99-102.

835   Clancy, Herbert J. The Democratic Party: Jefferson to Jackson.
      New York: Fordham University Press, 1962, 120-43.

836   Clayton, Bruce L. "Mr. Madison's War and Mr. Wilson's Crusade,"
      Journal of Erie Studies 13 (1984): 48-66.

837   Cooper, Joseph. "Jeffersonian Attitudes toward Executive Leadership
      and Committee Development in the House of Representatives," Western
      Political Quarterly 18 (1965): 45-63.

838   Green, Daniel. Great Cobbett: the Noblest Agitator. Toronto:
      Hodder, Stoughton, 1983.

839  Haynes, Robert V. "The Secretary of War and the War of 1812,"
     Louisiana History 5 (1964): 41-51.

840   Heale, J.M. "Towards Republican Harmony." In: The Making of American
      Politics, 1750-1850. New York: Longman, 1972, 89-102.

841   Hess, John C. "Was it Mr. Madison's War?" Master's Thesis, Texas
      Christian University, 1968.

842   Horsman, Reginald. The Diplomacy of the New Republic, 1776-1815.
      Arlington Heights, IL: Harlan, Davidson, 1985.

843   Ketcham, Ralph L. Presidents above Party: the First American Presi-
      dency, 1789-1829. Chapel Hill: University of North Carolina, 1984.

844   Lucey, William. "The Treaty of Ghent: A Study of Diplomacy in Action,"
      History Bulletin 29 (1950): 28-38.

845  McLaughlin, Patrick L., David R. Nofziger, and Richard C. Ruhrs. "A Computer Program for Gutman Scaling of Roll Calls," Historical Methods 18 (1985): 45-50.

846  Polakoff, Keth I. Political Parties in American History. New York: John Wiley, 1981, 79-91.

847  Rutland, Robert A. The Democrats from Jefferson to Carter. Baton Rouge: Louisiana State University Press, 1979, 29-53.

848  Warwick, Charles. "Our Last War with England," American Historical Register 2 (1895): 1469-73.

849  Watts, Steven. The Republic Reborn: War and the Making of Liberal America, 1790-1820. Baltimore: Johns Hopkins University Press, 1988.

850  Wharton, Anne H. Social Life in the Early Republic. Philadelphia: J.B. Lippincott, 1902.

851  Wise, Floy S. "The Growth of Political Democracy in the States, 1776-1828." Ph. D. dissertation, University of Texas, 1945.

     SEE ALSO: 961, 3781, 4590, 5612, 5619, John Q. Adams, James Madison

                              * WEST

852  Bloom, Jo Tice. "The Territorial Delegates of Indiana," Old Northwest 12 (1986): 7-26.

853  Brown, Stephen G. Voice of the New West: John G. Jackson's Life and Times. Macon, GA: Mercer University Press, 1985.

854  Cayton, Andrew R. The Republic: Ideology and Politics in the Ohio Country, 1780-1825. Kent, OH: Kent State University Press, 1986.

855  Foley, William E. "Territorial Politics in Frontier Missouri, 1804-1820." Ph. D. dissertation, University of Missouri, Columbia, 1967.

856  Weisenberger, Francis P. "A Wartime Congressman." In: The Life of John McLean. Columbus: Ohio State University Press, 1937, 8-21.

     SEE ALSO: 970

                            *NORTHEAST

857  Banner, James M. "A Shadow of Secession? The Hartford Convention, 1814," History Today 38 (1988): 24-30.

858  Baxter, Maurice G. "Anti-War Congressman." In: One and Inseparable: Daniel Webster and the Union. Cambridge, MA: Belknap Press, 1984, 37-51.

859  Ballard, Harlan H. "A Forgotten Fraternity," Berkshire History and Social Sciences Collections 3 (1899): 279-98.

860  Chatfield, John H. "Already We are A Fallen Country': The Politics and Ideology of Connecticut Federalism, 1792-1812." Ph. D. dissertation, Columbia University, 1988.

861   Cress, Lawrence D. "Cool and Serious Reflection: Federalist Attitudes
      towards the War of 1812," Journal of the Early Republic 7 (1987):
      123-45.

862   Eastman, Anthony F. "Federalist Ideology and Secession, 1796-1815."
      Ph. D. dissertation, University of Southern Mississippi, 1972.

863   Kirker, Harold, and James Kirker. Bullfinch's Boston, 1787-1817.
      New York: Oxford University Press, 1964, 233-56.

864   Levine, Robert. "The Separation of the District of Maine from
      Massachusetts, 1785-1820." Ph. D. dissertation, Clark University,
      1933.

865   McBride, Rita M. "Roger Griswold, Connecticut Federalist." Ph. d.
      dissertation, Yale University, 1948.

866   Renzulli, L. Marx. "The Extent of Rhode Island Participation in the
      War of 1812." Master's Thesis, University of Rhode Island, 1958.

867   Robinson, William A. "The Federalist Reaction." In: Jeffersonian
      Democracy in New England. New Haven: Yale University Press, 1916,
      76-94.

868   Ruth, George L. "Verse Satire on Faction, 1790-1815," William and
      Mary Quarterly 17 (1960): 471-85.

869   "The Story of the Rhode Island Pig," History Magazine 9 (1871): 43.

870   Thomas, Edmund B. "Politics in the land of Steady habits: Connecti-
      cut's Political Party System, 1789-1820." Ph. D. dissertation,
      Clarke University, 1972.

871   Varg, Paul A. New England and Foreign Relations, 1789-1850.
      Hanover, NH: University Press of New England, 1983, 52-73.

872   Welling, James C. Connecticut Federalism, or, Aristocratic  Politics
      in a Social Democracy. New York: New York Historical Society, 1890.

      SEE ALSO: 922 , 926 , 927 , 962 , 969 , Timothy Pickering

*MIDDLE ATLANTIC STATES

873   Chazanof, William. "The Political Influence of Joseph Ellicot in
      Western New York." Ph. D. dissertation, University of Syracuse, 1955.

874   Henderson, Elizabeth K. "Some Aspects of Sectionalism in Pennsylvania,
      1790-1812." Ph. D. dissertation, Bryn Mawr College, 1935.

875   Karin, Daniel B. "Towards the Empire State:  New York Politics and
      Economic Growth, 1800-1815." Ph. D. dissertation, State University
      of New York, Buffalo, 1987.

876   Kaufman, Martin. "War Sentiment in Western Pennsylvania, 1812,"
      Pennsylvania History 31 (1964): 436-88.

877   Levine, Peter. "The New Jersey Federalist Party Convention of 1814,"
      Journal of the Rutgers University Library 33 (1969): 1-8.

878   Nadler, Soloman. "Federal Patronage and New York Politics, 1801-1830."
      Ph. D. dissertation, New York University, 1973.

879   Rodgers, Robert M. "Some Phases of New Jersey History in the
      Jeffersonian Period." Master's Thesis, University of Chicago, 1930.

880   Siry, Steven E. "Spokesman for a New Political Economy: A Biography
      of DeWitt Clinton, 1769-1828." Ph. D. dissertation, University of
      Cincinnati, 1986.

881   Strum, Harvey. "New Jersey Politics and the War of 1812," New Jersey
      History 105 (1987): 37-70.

882   Wilson, James G. The Memorial History of the City of New York. 4
      Vols. New York: New York Historical Co., 1893. Vol. 3, 219-94.

CHESAPEAKE*

883   Brooks, Lester. "Sentinels of Federalism: Rhetoric and Ideology of
      the Federalist Party in Maryland, 1800-1815." Ph. D. dissertation,
      University of Michigan, 1986.

884   Fisher, Pauline T. "The Attitude of Virginia to the War of 1812,
      from 1805 to 1815." Master's Thesis, Columbia University, 1928.

885   Gilje, Paul A. "Le Menu Peuple' in America: Identifying the Mob in
      the Baltimore Riots of 1812," Maryland Historical Magazine 81 (1986):
      50-66.

886   Lowery, Charles P. "War's Wild Alarm." In: James Barbour: A Jeffer-
      sonian Republican. University, AL: University of Alabama Press, 1984.

887   Peterson, Norma L. "War and Innovation." In: Littleton Walker
      Tazewell. Charlotteville: University of Virginia, 1983, 72-84.

888   Shulim, Joseph I. "The Old Dominion and Napoleon Bonaparte: A Study
      in American Opinion." Ph. D. dissertation, Columbia University, 1944.

889   Wendelken, David H. "The Rhetoric of John Randolph of Roanoke: A
      New Evaluation." Ph. D. dissertation, Ohio State University, 1984.

      SEE ALSO: 964

SOUTH*

890   Fortune, Porter L. "George M. Troup: Leading States' Rights Advocate."
      Ph. D. dissertation, University of North Carolina, 1949.

891   Haynes, Robert V. "A Political History of the Mississippi Territory."
      Ph. D. dissertation, Rice University, 1959.

892   Hutton, Hamilton M. "Southern Nationalism, 1790-1817." Master's Thesis,
      University of Virginia, 1940.

893   Kaplanoff, M.D. "Making the South Solid: Politics and the Structure
      of Society in South Carolina, 1790-1815." Ph. D. dissertation,
      Cambridge University, 1980.

894   Ogden, Warren C. "Langdon Cheves, 1776-1857." Master's Thesis,
      Duke University, 1930.

895  Russo, David L. "The Southern Republicans and American Political Nationalism, 1815-1825." Ph. D. dissertation, Yale University, 1966.

896  Vipperman, Carl J. William Lowndes and the Transition of Southern Politics, 1782-1822. Chapel Hill: University of North Carolina Press, 1989.

897  Winn, Larry J. "The War Hawks' Call to Arms: Appeals for a Second War with Great Britain," Southern Speech Communication Journal 37 (1972): 402-12.

898  Winters, John D. "William C.C. Claiborne: Profile of a Democrat," Louisiana History 10 (1969): 189-209.

899  Wright, Homer E. "Diplomacy of Trade on the Southern Frontier: A Case Study of the Influence of William Panton and John Forbes, 1784-1817." Ph. D. dissertation, University of Georgia, 1972.

SEE ALSO: 1039

## *NEWSPAPERS

900  Avery, Donald R. "American over European Community: Newspaper Content Changes, 1808-1812," Journalism Quarterly 63 (1986): 311-14.

901  Fisher, Josephine. "Francis James Jackson and Newspaper Propaganda in the United States, 1809-1814," Maryland Historical Magazine 30 (1935): 93-113.

902  Hoffman, Ellen P. "Unnecessary, Unjustified and Ruinous: Anti-war Rhetoric in Massachusetts Federalist Newspapers." Ph. D. dissertation, University of Massachusetts, 1984.

903  Kilpatrick, Delbert H. "Nativism in American Journalism, 1784-1814," South Carolina Historical Society Proceedings (1948): 3-14.

904  Sloan, William D. "The Party Press: The Newspaper Role in National politics, 1789-1816." Ph. D. dissertation, University of Texas, 1981.

## *ECONOMICS

905  Andrews, Archie D. "Agriculture in Virginia, 1789-1820." Master's Thesis, University of Virginia, 1950.

906  Blackwell, Cecil L. "The Port of Norfolk and its Decline as a Result of the Embargo of 1807 and the War of 1812." Master's Thesis: William and Mary College, 1959.

907  Copeland, Charles H. "To the Farthest Port of the Rich East," American Heritage 6 (1955): 10-19, 114-15.

908  Crow, Frank W. "The Age of Promise: Societies for Social and Economic Improvement in the United States, 1783-1815." Ph. D. dissertation, University of Wisconsin, 1952.

909  Dunham, Douglas. "The French Element in the American Fur Trade, 1760-1816." Ph. D. dissertation, University of Michigan, 1950.

910  Fenstermaker, J. Van. "The Statistics of American Commercial Banking, 1782-1818," Journal of Economic History 25 (1965): 400-13.

911  Hartz, Louis. Economic Policy and Democratic Thought: Pennsylvania, 1776-1860. Cambridge, MA: Harvard University Press, 1948.

912  Kagin, Donald H. "Monetary Aspects of the Treasury Notes of the War of 1812," Journal of Economic History 44 (1984): 69-88.

913  Lasky, Herbert. "David Parish: A European in American Finance, 1806-1816." Ph. D. dissertation, New York University, 1972.

914  Lingelbach, W.E. "Historical Investigation  and the Commerical History  of the Napoleonic Era," American Historical Review 19 (1914): 257-81.

915  Muller, H.N. "Smuggling into Canada: How the Champlain Valley Defied Jefferson's Embargo," Vermont History 38 (1970): 5-21.

916  Parkinson, C. Northcote, ed. "The American Trade." In: The Trade Winds: A Study of British Overseas Trade during the French Wars, 1793-1815. London: Allen, Unwin, 1948, 194-226.

917  Schur, Leon M. "The Second Bank of the United States and the Inflation after the War of 1812," Journal of Political Economics 68 (1960): 118-34.

918  Todd, Charles L., and Robert Sonkin. "War Years in New York and Washington." In: Alexander Bryan Johnson: Philosophical Banker. Syracuse: Syracuse University Press, 1977, 57-83.

919  Whitehurst, George W. "The Commerce of Virginia, 1789-1815." Master's Thesis, University of Virginia, 1951.

920  Wright, Peter M. "The Public Debt and the Recharter of the Second Bank of the United States, 1775-1836." Ph. D. dissertation, University of Wyoming, 1978.

CONTEMPORARY ACCOUNTS

921  Attica News, Attica, New York. Reminiscence of the War of 1812. N.p., 1940.

922  Baker, Edward W. "Extracts from the Diary of Benjamin Goddard," Brookline Historical Society Proceedings 18 (1911): 16-48.

923  Barrickman, John. Captain John Barrickman's Diary, Account and General Record Book in the War of 1812. Chicago: Genealogical Services and Publications, 1980.

924  "The Battle of Queenston Heights, by an Officer in the Army," United Service Journal 2 (1851): 161-64.

925  Beardsley, Levi. Reminiscences, Personal and other Incidents. New York: C. Vinten, 1852, 150-51.

926  Bell, Shubael. "An Account of the Town of Boston written in 1817," Bostonian Society Publications 3 (1909): 15-65.

927  Bentley, William. The Diary of William Bentley, D.D. 4 Vols. Salem: Essex Institute, 1905-1914.

928 Brannon, Peter A., ed. "John Coffee in Alabama, 1814: Letters written to his Wife while on Campaign," Arrow Points 14 (1929): 67-72.

929 Brown, David. Diary of a Soldier, 1805-1827. Androsan, ENG: A. Guthrie & Sons, 193-.

930 Campbell, John T. "Some Comments on Tipton's Journal," Indiana Magazine of History 3 (1907): 30-33.

931 Cruikshank, Ernest A., ed. Documents Relating to the Invasion of Canada and the Surrender of Detroit, 1812. Ottawa: Government Printing Bureau, 1912.

932 Douglas, David B. "Reminiscences of the Campaign of 1814 on the Niagara Frontier," Historical Magazine 2 (1873): 1-12, 65-76, 127-42, 216-24.

933 Draper, Lyman C., ed. "Lawe and Grignon Papers, 1794-1821," Wisconsin Historical Society Collections 10 (1888): 90-141.

934 Ellis, William. "Captive's Diary." In: The Aurora (Philadelphia) January 4, 1815.

935 "An Eventful day: A True Story," Military and Navy Magazine 2 (1834): 4-9.

936 Fredriksen, John C., ed. "Memoirs of Captain Ephraim Shaler: A Connecticut Yankee in the War of 1812," New England Quarterly 57 (1984): 411-20.

937 _____., ed. "Kentucky at the Thames: A Rediscovered Narrative by William Greathouse," Register of the Kentucky Historical Society 83 (1985): 93-107.

938 _____., ed. "The Memoirs of Johnathan Kearsley: A Michigan Hero from the War of 1812," Indiana Military History Journal 10 (1985): 4-16.

939 _____., ed. "A New Hampshire Volunteer in the War of 1812: the Experiences of Charles Fairbanks," Historical New Hampshire 40 (1985): 156-78.

940 _____., ed. "A Poor but Honest Sodger": Colonel Cromwell Pearce, the 16th U.S. Infantry, and the War of 1812," Pennsylvania History 52 (1985): 131-61.

941 _____. "Plow-Joggers for Generals': the Experiences of a New York Ensign in the War of 1812," Indiana Military History Journal 11 (1986): 16-27.

942 _____., ed. "A Georgian Officer in the War of 1812: the Letters of Colonel William Clay Cumming," Georgia Historical Quarterly 71 (1987): 668-91.

943 _____., ed. "Lawyer, Soldier, Judge: Incidents in the Life of Joseph Lee Smith of New Britain, Connecticut," Connecticut Historical Society Bulletin 51 (1986): 102-21.

944 _____., ed. "The Pennsylvania Volunteers in the War of 1812: An Anonymous Journal of Service for the Year 1814," Western Pennsylvania Historical Magazine 70 (1987): 123-57.

945    ____., ed. "The War of 1812 in Northern New York: The Observations of Captain Rufus McIntire," New York History 68 (1987): 297-324.

946    ____., ed. "A Grand Moment for our Beloved Commander': Sailing Master William V. Taylor's Account of the Battle of Lake Erie," Journal of Erie Studies 17 (1988): 133-22.

947    Gaines, George S. "Notes on the Early Days of South Alabama," Alabama Historical Quarterly 26 (1964): 133-229.

948    Gattel, Frank O., ed. "Boston Boy in Mr. Madison's War: Letters by John Palfrey and his Sons, Henry and Edward," Louisiana Historical Quarterly 44 (1961): 148-59.

949    Gibson, John. "Some Letters of John Gibson," Indiana Magazine of History 1 (1905): 128-31.

950    Gulick, Charles A. and Katherine Elliots, eds. The Papers of Mirabeau B. Larmar. 6 Vols. Austin, TX: A.C. Baldwin, 1921-28. Vol. 1.

951    Hamilton, Peter J. and Thomas M. Owens, eds. "Topographical Notes and Observations on the Alabama River, August, 1814," Transactions of the Alabama Historical Society 2 (1898): 130-77.

952    Hubbard, Gordon S. "Col. G.S. Hubbard's Narrative." In: Addresses Delivered at the Annual Meeting of the Chicago Historical Society. Chicago: Fergus Printing, 1877, 41-46.

953    "Journal of an Officer, 1814-1815," DeBow's Review 16 (1854): 641-46.

954    "Kennon Letters," Virginia Magazine of History and Biography 37 (1929): 46-51.

955    Knopf, Richard C., ed. Documentary Transcriptions of the War of 1812 in the Northwest. 6 Vols. Columbus: Anthony Wayne Parkway Board, 1959.

956    Latour, Arsene L. Historical Memoir of the War in West Florida and Louisiana in 1814-15, with an Atlas. 2 Vols. Philadelphia: John Conrad, 1816.

957    "Letters of the War of 1812," Magazine of History 17 (1913): 163-73.

958    Levering, N. "War Anecdotes of 1812," Iowa Historical Record 4 (1888): 361-65.

959    McDouall, Robert. "Capture of Fort McKay, Prairie Du Chien in 1814," Report on Canadian Archives (1887): civ-cix.

960    "Miscellaneous Documents Relating to the War of 1812," Michigan Pioneer 8 (1886): 620-59.

961    Morris, Anthony. Castles in Spain: Anthony Morris's Letters to his Children, 1813-1817. Philadelphia: Wyck Association, 1982.

962    Morse, Frances R. Henry and Mary Lee, Letters and Journals. Boston: T. Todd, 1926, 167-228.

963    McLaughlin, Philip K. "Blockading the New England Coast: the Journal of Lieutenant Henry Napier," American Neptune 45 (1985): 5-9.

964  Parr, Marylin K. "Augustus John Foster and the 'Washington Wilder-
     ness': Personal Letters of a British Diplomat." Ph. D. dissertation,
     George Washington University, 1987.

965  Preston, Richard A. "The Journals of Sir. F.P. Robinson, G.C.B.,"
     Canadian Historical Review 37 (1956): 352-55.

966  Quaife, Milo M., ed. The John Askin Papers. 2 Vols. Detroit:
     Detroit Library Commission, 1928-1931. Vol. 2, 711-76.

967  "A Reminiscence of the Last war," Army and Navy Chronicle 11 (1840):
     366-67.

968  Rowley, Peter, ed. "Captain Robert Rowley Helps to Burn Washington,
     D.C.," Maryland Historical Magazine 82 (1987): 240-50; 83 (1988):
     247-53.

969  Scott, David N., ed. "Additions to the Letters of Abijah Bigelow,"
     American Antiquarian Society Proceedings 79 (1969): 245-52.

970  Washburn, E.B., ed. The Edwards Papers. Chicago: Chicago Historical
     Society, 1884.

971  "War Reminiscences," Army and Navy Chronicle 9 (1839): 101-03.

972  Wrottelsey, George, ed. Life and Correspondence of Field Marshal
     John Fox Burgoyne, Bart. 2 Vols. London: Bentley & Sons, 1873.
     Vol. 1, 301-03.

## ALGERIAN WAR

973  Bowen, Abel. The Naval Monument, Containing Official and Other
     Accounts of the Battles Fought Between the Navies of the United
     States and Great Britain during the Late War, and an Account of the
     War with Algiers. Boston: A. Bowen, 1816.

974  Davis, Paris M. An Authentic History of the Late War Between the
     United States and Great Britain...to which will be added the War
     with Algiers and the Treaty of Peace. New York: Davis, 1829.

975  George, Noah J. A Concise and Brief Journal of the Late War with
     Great Britain, to which is Added a Short Account of the War with
     Algiers. Andover, NH: E. Chase, 1819.

976  Kanof, Abram and David Markowitz. "Joseph B. Nones: the Affable
     Midshipman," American Jewish Historical Society Publications 46
     (1956): 1-18.

977  O'Connor, Thomas. An Impartial and Correct History of the War
     Between the United States of America and Great Britain. New York:
     John Low, 1816, 313-28.

978  Spencer, William. Algiers in the Age of Corsairs. Norman:
     University of Oklahoma Press, 1976.

979  Sokol, Anthony E. "The Barbary Corsairs--A Lesson in Appeasement
     and International Cooperation," United States Naval Institute
     Proceedings 75 (1949): 796-803, 542-43.

980  Smith, Johnathan S. The Siege of Algiers. Philadelphia: J. Maxwell,
     1823.

981   Thornbury, George W. Old Stories Retold. London: Chapman, Hall, 1870.

POLITICS AND DIPLOMACY

982   Ives, Ernest L. "An Adventurer turns Diplomat," American Foreign
      Service Journal 13 (1936): 628-33.

983   Lear, Tobias. "Mission to Algiers: An 1815 Post Report," Ibid 28
      (1951): 15-17.

PRISONERS

984   Nicholson, Thomas. An Affecting Narrative of the Captivity and
      Sufferings of Thomas Nicholson, a Native of New Jersey, who has
      Been Six Years a Prisoner among the Algerines, and from whom He
      Fortunately made his escape   a few Months Previous to Commodore
      Decatur's Late Expedition. Boston: N. Coverly, 1818.

985   Noah, Mordecai M. Correspondence and Documents Relative to Attempts
      to Negotiate for the Release of the American captives at Algiers,
      1813-1814. Washington, DC: N.p., 1816.

986   Pananti, Filippo. Narrative of a Residence in Algiers, comprising
      a Geographical and Historical Account of the Regency, Biographical
      Sketches of the Dey, and his Ministers, and Anecdotes of the Late
      War. London: Henry Colburn, 1818.

987   Pitts, Joseph. Narrative of the Captivity of Joseph Pitts Among the
      Algerines. Fredericktown, Hardt, Cross, 1815.

      SEE ALSO: William Bainbridge, Stephen Decatur, James Hall

CONTEMPORARY ACCOUNTS

988   "Account of Operations of the American Squadron under Commodore
      Decatur, against Algiers, Tunis and Tripoli," Analectic Magazine
      7 (1816): 113-26.

989   Holbrook, Samuel F. Threescore Years: An Autobiography; Containing
      Incidents of Voyages and travels, including six years in a Man-of-War.
      Details of the War Between the United States and the Algerian
      Government. Boston: J. French, 1857.

990   "An Incident at Algiers during the Visit of Decatur's Squadron in
      1815," Army and Navy Chronicle 1 (1835): 98-99.

991   Shaw, Elijah. Short Sketch of the Life of Elijah Shaw, who served
      Twenty-one years in the United States Navy, taking Active Part in
      Four Different Wars. Rochester, NY: Strong, Davis, 1843.

ASTORIA

992   Elliot, T.C. "The Surrender of Astoria in 1818," Oregon Historical
      Quarterly 14 (1918): 271-82.

993   _____. "An event of One Hundred Years ago," Ibid 19 (1918): 183-87.

994   Judson, Katherine B. "The British side of the Restoration of Fort
      Astoria," Ibid 20 (1919): 243-60, 305-30.

995   Koch, P. "The Story of Astoria," Magazine of American History 13
      (1885): 269-76.

996   Paullin, Charles O. "The First Naval Voyage to Our West Coast,"
      Americana 4 (1909): 964-70.

      SEE ALSO: USS Ontario, James Biddle

## FIRST SEMINOLE WAR

997   Anderson, Robert L. "The End of an Idyll," Florida Historical
      Quarterly 42 (1963): 35-47.

998   Arbuthnot, Alexander. The Trials of A. Arbuthnot & R.C. Ambrister,
      Charged with Exciting the Seminole Indians to War Against the United
      States. London: James Ridgeway, 1819.

999   Baker, Maury. "The Spanish War Scare of 1816," Mid America 45 (1963):
      67-78.

1000  Becton, Joseph. "Old Hickory and the Negro Fort: Exodus to Freedom,"
      Pensacola History Illustrated 2 (1986): 25-32.

1001  Boyd, Mark F. "Events at Prospect Bluff on the Apalachicola River,
      1808-1818," Florida Historical Quarterly 16 (1937): 55-96.

1002  Brown, William H. The Glory Seekers: the Romance of the would-be
      Founders of Empire in the Early days of the Great Southwest.
      Chicago: McClurg, 1906.

1003  Bruce, H. Addington. The Romance of American Expansion. New York:
      Moffat, Yard, 1909.

1004  Clay, Henry. Speech of the Hon. Henry Clay in the House of Represent-
      atives of the United States on the Seminole War. Washington: N.p.

1005  Coulter, Ellis M. "The Chehaw Affair," Georgia Historical Quarterly
      49 (1965): 369-95.

1006  Cresson, W.P. "The Seminole War and the Florida Treaty." In:
      James Monroe. Chapel Hill: University of North Carolina Press,
      1946, 377-84.

1007  Curry, J.L. "The Acquisition of Florida," Magazine of American
      History 19 (1888): 286-301.

1008  Dewhurst, W.W. "Disputes between the United States and Spain over
      Florida Settled by the Treaty of 1819." In: Proceedings of the
      Fifteenth Annual Session of the Florida State Bar Association.
      (1922): 103-18.

1009  Foster, Lawrence. "Negro-Indian Relations in the Southeast." Ph. D.
      dissertation, University of Pennsylvania, 1931.

1010  Gibbs, C.R. "Negro Fort," CAMP Periodical 5 (1973): 14-16.

1011  Griffin, John W., ed. "Some Comments on the Seminoles in 1818,"
      Florida Anthropologist 10 (1957): 41-49.

1012  "Inquiry into Jackson's Reasons for Attacking the Negro Fort,"
      15th Congress. 2d Session (1818-1819). House Document 119.

1013  "Jackson gives 'em the Old Hickory," Month at Goodspeed's 19 (1948):
      147-49.

1014  Knox, Dudley W. "A Forgotten Fight in Florida," United States Naval
      Institute Proceedings 62 (1936): 507-13.

1015  Mays, Elizabeth. "The March of Andrew Jackson in the First Seminole
      war." Master's Thesis, Emory University, 1923.

1016  Mercer, Charles F. Speech of the Hon. Mr. Mercer in the House of
      Representatives on the Seminole War. N.p., 1819.

1017  Narrative of a Voyage to the Spanish Main in the Ship Two Friends;
      The Occupation of Ameila Island by McGregor &c...with an Appendix
      Containing a Detail of the Seminole War, and the Execution of
      Arbuthnot and Armbrister. London: J. Miller, 1819.

1018  Overton, John. A Vindication of the Measures of the President and
      and His Commanding Generals in the Commencement and Termination of
      the Seminole War. Washington, DC: Gales, Seaton, 1819.

1019  Owsley, Frank L. "Armbrister and Arbuthnot: Adventurers or Martyrs
      for British Honor?" Journal of the Early Republic 5 (1985): 289-308.

1020  _____. "Prophet of War: Josiah Francis and the Creek War," American
      Indian Quarterly 9 (1985): 273-94.

1021  Paine, Charles R. "The Seminole War of 1817-1818." Master's Thesis,
      University of Oklahoma, 1938.

1022  Phinney, A. H. "The Second Spanish-American War," Florida Historical
      Quarterly 5 (1926): 103-11.

1023  Porter, Kenneth W. "Negroes and the Seminole War, 1817-1818,"
      Journal of Negro History 36 (1951): 249-80.

1024  Satz, Ronald N. "Remini's Andrew Jackson: Jackson and the Indians,"
      Tennessee Historical Quarterly 38 (1979): 158-66.

1025  Saurez, Annette M. "The War Path across Georgia made by Tennessee
      Troops in the First Seminole War," Georgia Historical Quarterly 38
      (1954): 29-42.

1026  Schouler, James. "Jackson in Florida." In: History of the United
      States of America under the Constitution. 8 Vols. New York: Dodd,
      Mead, 1894. Vol. 3, 57-93.

1027  _____. "Monroe and the Rhea letter," Magazine of American History
      12 (1884): 308-22.

1028  "The Seminole War," 15th Congress. 2d Session. House Executive
      Document 14, 1818.

1029  Simmons, William H. Notices of East Florida, with an Account of the
      Seminole Nation of Indians. Charleston: A.E. Miller, 1822.

1030   Smyth, Alexander. Speech of the Hon. Alexander Smyth in the House
       of Reprsentatives, on the Seminole War. N.p., 1819.

1031   Soulter, Shelton. "Jackson in Florida." Master's Thesis, Emory
       University, 1924.

1032   Stenberg, Richard R. "Jackson's Rhea Letter Hoax," Journal of
       Southern History 2 (1936): 480-96.

1033   Storrs, Henry R. Speech of the Hon. Mr. Storrs in the House of
       Representatives, on the Seminole War. Washington, DC: N.p., 1818.

1034   Tebbel, John and Keith Jennison. The American Indian Wars. New York:
       Harper & Bros., 1960, 181-90.

1035   U.S. 15th Congress. 2d Session, 181-1819. House. Debate in the House
       of Representatives...on the Seminole War in January and February.
       Washington, DC: National Intelligencer, 1819.

1036   United States. President, 1817-1825. Message from the President of
       the United States transmitting information in relation to the War
       with the Seminoles. Washington, DC: E. DeKrafft, 1818.

1037   White, David H. "The John Forbes Company: Heir to the Florida Indian
       Trade, 1801-1819." Ph. D. dissertation, University of Alabama, 1973.

1038   Williams, John L. The Territory of Florida; or, sketches of the
       Topography, Civil and natural History. New York: A.T. Goodrich, 1837.

       SEE ALSO: 4865 , Andrew Jackson, William McIntosh

CONTEMPORARY ACCOUNTS

1039   Amos, Alcione M. "Captain Hugh Young's Map of Jackson's 1818 Seminole
       Campaign in Florida," Florida Historical Quarterly 55 (1977): 336-46.

1040   Banks, John. A Short Biographical Sketch of the Undersigned by
       Himself, John Banks. N.p., N.d.
       In the Ayers Collection, Newberry Library.

1041   Barber, Eunice. Narrative of the Tragic Death of Mr. Decius Barber
       and his Seven Children, who were inhumanely butchered by the Indians
       in Lauder County, Georgia, January 26, 1818. Boston: Hazen, 1818.

1042   Boyd, Mark F. and Gerald M. Ponton, eds. "A Topographical Memoir of
       West Florida with Itineraries of General Jackson's Army, 1818,"
       Florida Historical Quarterly 13 (1934): 16-50, 82-102, 129-64.

1043   A Concise Narrative of the Seminole Campaign. By an Officer attached
       to the Expedition. Nashville, TN: M'Lean, Tunstall, 1819.

1044   Correspondence between Gen. Andrew Jackson and John C. Calhoun,
       President and Vice-President of the United States...on Occurences
       in the Seminole War. Washington, DC: Green, 1831.

1045   Destler, C.M., ed. "Additional Correspondence of Gov. David Brydie
       Mitchell," Georgia Historical Quarterly 28 (1944): 93-104.

1046   Dibble, Ernest F. "Captain Hugh Young and his 1818 Topographical
       Memoir," Florida Historical Quarterly 55 (1977): 321-35.

1047  "Dunlap-Brady Correspondence," American Historical Magazine 8 (1903): 256-61.

1048  Gadsen, James. "The Defenses of the Floridas: A Report of Captain James Gadsen, Aide de Camp to General Andrew Jackson, August 1, 1818," Florida Historical Quarterly 15 (1937): 242-48.

1049  "Incidents of the Florida War. By a Looker on," Western Literary Emporium 2 (1848): 297-304. At Wisconsin Historical Society.

1050  Patrick, Rembert W., ed. "A New Letter of James Monroe on the cession of Florida," Florida Historical Quarterly 23 (1945): 197-201.

1051  Van Ness, William P. A Concise Narrative of General Jackson's First Invasion of Florida, and of his Immortal Defense of New Orleans. New York: E.M. Murden, A. Ming, 1827.

1052  Walker, Joel P. A Pioneer of Pioneers; Narrative of Adventures thro' Alabama, Florida, New Mexico, Oregon, California, etc. Los Angeles: Glen Dawson, 1953.

1053  Wilkinson, Thomas. Memorial of Thomas Williamson and other Officers Engaged in the Expedition Against the Seminole Indians in 1818. U.S. 18th Cong. 1st Session. House Document 42.

1054  Woodward, Thomas S. Woodward's Reminiscences of the Creek and Muscogee Indians. Montgomery , AL: Barrett, Wimbish, 1859.

1055  Wright, J. Leitch, ed. "A Note on the First Seminole War as Seen by the Indians, Negroes, and their British advisors," Journal of Southern History 34 (1968): 565-75.

ARIKARA WAR

1056  Berry, Don. A Majority of Scoundrels: An Informal History of the Rocky Mountain Fur Company. New York: Harper, 1961, 33-47.

1057  Camp, Charles L., ed. James Clyman, American Frontiersman. San Francisco: California Historical Society, 1928, 12-22.

1058  Eller, W.H. "The Arickari Conquest of 1823," Nebraska State Historical Society Transactions 5 (1893): 35-43.

1059  Hafen, LeRoy R. and William H. Ghent. Broken Hand; the Life Story of Thomas Fitzpatrick, Chief of the Mountain Men. Denver, CO: Old West Publishing Co., 1931, 18-30.

1060  Morgan, Dale L. Jedediah Smith and the Opening of the West. Indianapolis: Bobbs-Merrill, 1953, 59-77.

1061  Nasatir, Abraham P. "The International Significance of the Jones and Immell Massacre and the Aricara Outbreak in 1823," Pacific Northwest Quarterly 30 (1939): 77-108.

1062  Nichols, Roger L. "The Arikara Indians and the Missouri River Trade: A Quest for Survival," Great Plains Quarterly 2 (1982): 77-93.

1063  _____. "Backdrop for Disaster: Causes of the Arikara War of 1823," South Dakota History 14 (1984): 93-113.

1064   Rawling, Gerald. The Pathfinders: The History of America's First
       Westerners. New York: Macmillan, 1964, 123-40.

1065   Sunder, John E. Bill Sublette, Mountain Man. Norman: University of
       Oklahoma Press, 1959, 34-45.

1066   _____ . Joshua Pilcher, Fur Trader and Indian Agent. Norman:
       University of Oklahoma Press, 1968.

                          CONTEMPORARY ACCOUNTS

1067   Paul Wilhelm, Duke of Wuerttemberg. "General Leavenworth's Expedition
       against the Aricaras," South Dakota Historical Collections 19 (1938):
       404-06.

1068   Robinson, Doane, ed. "Official Correspondence Pertaining to the
       Leavenworth Expedition of 1823 into South Dakota for the Conquest
       of the Ree Indians," Ibid 1 (1902): 181-256.

1069   U.S. War Department. Correspondence Relative to Hostilities of the
       Arickaree Indians. Washington: Gales, Seaton, 1823.

       SEE ALSO: William H. Ashley, Henry Leavenworth

                             BLACK HAWK WAR

1070   Armstrong, Perry A. The Sauks and the Black Hawk War, with
       Biographical Sketches, etc. Springfield, IL: H.W. Rokker, 1887.

1071   Atwood, John A. The Story of the Battle of Stillman's Run, fought at
       Stillman Valley, Illinois, May 14, 1832. Stillman Valley: J.A. Atwood,
       1904.

1072   Backus, Electus. "The War with the Sac and Fox Indians under Black
       Hawk in Illinois in 1832," Historical Magazine 2 (1873): 353-60.

1073   Baldwin, Elmer. History of LaSalle County, Illinois. Chicago:
       Rand, McNally, 1877, 95-104.

1074   Barton, Albert O. "Echoes of the Black Hawk War," Wisconsin Magazine
       of History 16 (1932-1933): 404-11.

1075   Beckwith, Hiram W. "The Illinois and Indiana Indians," Fergus
       Historical Series No. 27 (1884): 99-183.

1076   Beggs, Stephen R. Pages from the Early History of the West and
       Northwest. Cincinnati: Methodist Book Concern, 1868, 213-20.

1077   Biddle, James W. "Account of the Battle of Pekatonica," Wisconsin
       Historical Society Collections 4 (1859): 85-87.

1078   "Black Hawk War," Chronicles of the North American Savages 1 (1835):
       28-32, 49-61.

1079   "The Black Hawk War," Wisconsin Historical Society Collections 5
       (1867): 285-320.

1080   "Black Hawk's Fate. The Battle of Bad Axe." In: The Chicago Times,
       June 20, 1885.

1081   Boss, Henry R. Sketches of the History of Ogle County, Illinois.
       Polo, IL: H.R. Boss, 1859, 36-49.

1082   Bracken, Charles and Peter Parkinson. "Pekatonica Battle Controversy,"
       Wisconsin Historical Society Collections 2 (1855): 365-92.

1083   Brown, Orlando, ed. "Causes of the Black Hawk War," Ibid 10 (1888):
       223-26.

1084   Brunson, Alfred. "Sketch of Hole-in-the-Day," Ibid 5 (1868): 387-99.

1085   Buckner, E. "A Brief History of the War with the Sac and Fox Indians
       in Illinois and Michigan in 1832," Michigan Pioneer 12 (1887): 424-36.

1086   Buley, Carlyle. The Old Northwest. 2 Vols. Bloomington: Indiana
       University Press, 1951.

1087   Channing, Edward. The Story of the Great Lakes. New York: Macmillan,
       1909, 201-14.

1088   "Chapters in Fox River Valley History," Wisconsin Historical Society
       Proceedings (1912): 146-220.

1089   Clemens, Orion. City of Keokuk in 1856... also a Sketch of the Black
       Hawk War. Keokuk, IA: O. Clemens, 1856.

1090   Coe, Edwin P. The Black Hawk Tragedy. N.p., 1896.

1091   Cole, Cyrenus. A History of the People of Iowa. Cedar Rapids, IA:
       Torch Press, 1921, 81-113.

1092   _____. Iowa Through the Years. Iowa City, IA: State Historical Society
       of Iowa, 1940, 63-98.

1093   Currey, Josiah S. Chicago: its History and its Builders, a Century
       of Marvelous Growth. 5 Vols. Chicago: S.J. Clarke, 1912. Vol. 1,
       185-200.

1094   Dawson, Henry B. Battle of the United States. 2 Vols. New York:
       Johnson, Fry, 1858. Vol. 2, 426-39.

1095   Duis, Etzard. The Good old Times in McLean County, Illinois.
       Bloomington, IL: Leader Publishing & Print House, 1874, 97-124.

1096   Dunn, Julia M. Sau-ke-nuk, the Story of Black Hawk's Tower.
       Moline, IL: DeSaulniers, 1905.

1097   Eby, Cecil. 'That Disgraceful Affair': The Black Hawk War. New York:
       W.W. Norton, 1973.

1098   Eckert, Allan W. Twilight of Empire. Boston: Little, Brown, 1988.

1099   Efflandt, Lloyd H. The Black Hawk War, Why? Rock Island, IL:
       Rock Island Arsenal Historical Society, 1986.

1100   Elliott, E.S. Black Hawk's Last Victory. Stillman Valley: N.p., 1900.

1101   Fisher, Kathy. "The Forgotten Dodge," Annals of Iowa 40 (1970):
       296-305.

1102 Fitch, Matthew G. "The Battle of Peckatonica," Wisconsin Historical Society Collections 10 (1883-1885): 178-83.

1103 Ford, Thomas. A History of Illinois, from its Commencement as a States in 1818 to 1847. New York: Ivison, Pinney, 1854, 109-65.

1104 Fulton, Alexander R. The Red Men of Iowa. Des Moines, IA: Mills & Co., 1882, 186-230.

1105 Gurko, Miriam. Indian America, the Black Hawk War. New York: Crowell, 1970.

1106 Hagan, William T. "The Black Hawk War." Ph. D. dissertation, University of Wisconsin, 1950.

1107 _____. The Sac and Fox Indians. Norman: University of Oklahoma Press, 1958.

1108 Hamilton, Henry R. The Epic of Chicago. Chicago: Willett, Clark, 1932, 183-210.

1109 Hauberg, John H. The Black Hawk Watch Tower in the County of Rock Island, State of Illinois. Rock Island, IL: Duffill, 1925.

1110 _____. "The Black Hawk War, 1831-1832," Illinois State Historical Society Transactions (1932): 91-134.

1111 Haydon, James R. Chicago's True Founder: Thomas J.V. Owen. Lombard: Privately Printed, 1934, 78-118.

1112 Homan, Harriet L. From Revolution to Massacre, with a Description in Word and Artistic Portrayal of the Indian Creek Massacre, May 20, 1832, An Incident in the Black Hawk War. Waterman, IL: Waterman Press, 1976.

1113 Jackson, Donald and William J. Petersen. "The Black Hawk War," Palimpsest 43 (1962): 65-113.

1114 Jones, George W. "Robert S. Black and the Black Hawk War," Wisconsin Historical Society Collections 10 (1888): 229-31.

1115 Kellogg, Louise P. "Wisconsin Heights Battlefield," Wisconsin Magazine of History 1 (1923): 20-12, 28-31.

1116 Lambert, Joseph I. "The Black Hawk War: A Military Analysis," Illinois States Historical Society Journal 32 (1939): 442-73.

1117 Lebron, Jeanne. "Colonel James W. Stephenson; Galena Pioneer," Ibid 35 (1942): 347-67.

1118 Little, Henry. "A History of the Black Hawk War," Michigan Pioneer 5 (1882): 152-78.

1119 Lonn, Ella. "Ripples of the Black Hawk War in Northern Indiana," Indiana Magazine of History 20 (1924): 288-307.

1120 Lurie, Nancy O. "In Search of Chaetar: New Findings on Black Hawk's Surrender," Wisconsin Magazine of History 71 (1988): 163-83.

1121  McGrain, Gertrude C. "Michigan's Role in the Black Hawk War."
      Master's Thesis, University of Detroit, 1937.

1122  McHarry, Jessie. "John Reynolds," Illinois States Historical Society
      Journal 6 (1913-1914): 5-51.

1123  Martin, Deborah B. History of Brown County, Wisconsin, Past and
      Present. 2 Vols. Chicago: S.J. Clarke, 1913.

1124  Meese, William A. Early Rock Island. Moline, IL: Desaulniers, 1905.

1125  Miller, Stanley. "Massacre at Bad Axe," American History Illustrated
      19 (1984): 30-35, 48.

1126  Newlands, R.W. "The Black Hawk War, an Account of the Discovery of
      the Graves of Men who Fell in the Battle of Stillman's Run," Illinois
      State Historical Library Publications No. 6 (1901): 117-20.

1127  Nichols, Roger L. "The Black Hawk War: Another View," Annals of Iowa
      36 (1963): 523-33.

1128  _____. "The Black Hawk War in Retrospect," Wisconsin Magazine of
      History 65 (1982): 239-46.

1129  O'Byrne, Michael C. History of LaSalle County, Illinois. 3 Vols.
      Chicago: Lewis Publishing Co., 1924. Vol. 1, 71-84.

1130  Pease, Theodore C. The Frontier State, 1818-1870. Springfield, IL:
      Illinois Centennial Commission, 1918.

1131  Petersen, William J. "The Terms of Peace," Palimpsest 12 (1932):
      74-89; 43 (1962): 95-111.

1132  _____. The Story of Iowa. 4 Vols. New York: Lewis Historical Co.,
      1952. Vol. 1, 117-35.

1133  Porter, C.V. "The Black Hawk War. Second Battle of Bad Axe." In:
      DeSoto (Wisconsin) Chronicle, January 15-February 2, 1887.

1134  Prince, Erza M. "McLean County in the Black Hawk War, 1832,"
      McLean County Historical Society Transactions 1 (1899): 12-18.

1135  Rayman, Ronald. "The Black Hawk Purchase: Stimulus to the Settlement
      of Iowa, 1832-1851," Western Illinois Regional Studies 3 (1980): 141-53.

1136  Richman, Irving B. John Brown among the Quakers and other Sketches.
      Des Moines, IA: Iowa History Department, 1904, 79-119.

1137  Roach, J.V. "The Story of Black Hawk and his Wars," Americana 5
      (1910): 46-62.

1138  Rooney, Elizabeth B. "The Story of the Black Hawk War," Wisconsin
      Magazine of History 40 (1956-1957): 274-83.

1139  Ross, Harvey L. The Early Pioneers and Pioneer Events of the State
      of Illinois. Chicago: Eastman Brothers, 1849.

1140  Roulston, Jessie A. "The Effect of the Black Hawk War on Development
      of the Northwest." Ph. D. dissertation, University of Chicago, 1910.

1141   Salisbury, Albert. "Green County Pioneers," Wisconsin Historical Society Collections 6 (1872): 401-15.

1142   Scanlan, Charles M. Indian Creek Massacre and Captivity of the Hall Girls. Milwaukee, WS: Reic Publishing Co., 1915.

1143   Smith, William P. The History of Wisconsin. 3 Vols. Madison, WS: Beriah Brown, 1854. Vol. 1, 258-85.

1144   Snyder, John F. Adam W. Snyder and his Period in Illinois History, 1817-1842. Springfield, IL: H.W. Rokker, 1903.

1145   Spencer, John W. The Early Day of Rock Island and Davenport. Davenport, IA: Griggs, Watson, Day, 1872.

1146   Stark, William F. Along the Black Hawk Trail. Sheboygan, WS: Zimmerman Press, 1984.

1147   Stevens, Frank E. The Black Hawk War, including a Review of Black Hawk's Life. Chicago: F.E. Stevens, 1903.

1148   _____. "Stillman's Defeat," Illinois States Historical Society Transactions 7 (1902): 170-79.

1149   _____. "A Forgotten Hero: General James Dougherty Henry," Ibid (1934): 77-120.

1150   Stout, Steve. "Indian Creek: A Battle of the Black Hawk War," Illinois Magazine 22 (1983): 30-34.

1151   Strong, Moses M. "The Indian Wars of Wisconsin," Wisconsin Historical Society Collections 8 (1877-1879): 241-86.

1152   Tebbel, John and Keith Jennison. The American Indian Wars. New York: Harper & Bros., 1960, 191-208.

1153   Thwaites, Reuben G. "The Black Hawk War," Magazine of Western History 5 (1886): 32-45, 181-96.

1154   _____. "The Story of the Black Hawk War," Wisconsin Historical Society Collections 12 (1892): 217-65.

1155   Titus, William A. "Historic Spots in Wisconsin: The Battle of Wisconsin Heights," Wisconsin Magazine of History 3 (1920-1921): 55-60.

1156   _____. "Historic Spots in Wisconsin: The Battle of Bad Axe," Ibid 3 (1920-1921): 196-99.

1157   Tuttle, Charles R. History of the Border wars of Two Centuries, Embracing a Narrative of the Wars with the Indians from 1750 to 1874. Chicago: C.A. Wall, 1874, 292-329.

1158   Vander Zee, Jacob. "The Black Hawk War and the Treaty of 1832," Iowa Journal of History and Politics 13 (1915): 416-28.

1159   _____. The Black Hawk War. Iowa City, IA: State Historical Society of Iowa, 1918.

1160   Wakefield, John A. History of the War Between the United States and
       the Sac and Fox Nations of Indians. Jacksonville, IL: Calvin Goudy,
       1834.

1161   Wallace, Anthony F. Prelude to Disaster: The Course of Indian-White
       Relations which led to the Black Hawk War of 1832. Springfield, IL:
       Illinois States Historical Library, 1970.

1162   Warren, William. The Battle of St. Croix Falls. St. Paul: Minnesota
       Historical Society Press, 1984.

1163   Whitney, Ruth M., comp. The Black Hawk War, 1831-1832. Springfield,IL:
       Illinois State Historical Library, 1978.

1164   Williams, J.R. "Sketch of the Life of General John R. Williams,"
       Michigan Pioneer 29 (1899-1900): 491-96.

1165   Zackem, Mathilde Z. "Michigan's Aid in the Black Hawk War." Master's
       Thesis, Wayne State University, 1943.

       SEE ALSO: 1891, 2782 , 2798 , 2826 , 6516, Fort Winnebago, Illinois
       Militia, Henry Atkinson, Black Hawk, Jefferson Davis, Henry Dodge,
       Charles Gratiot, Albert S. Johnston, Keokuk, Abraham Lincoln, George
       A. McCall, Winfield Scott, Shabbona

                          CONTEMPORARY ACCOUNTS

1166   Allaman, John L. "Incidents in the Life of an Old Pioneer: The
       Memoirs of Field Jarvis," Western Illinois Regional Studies 9 (1986):
       5-18.

1167   An Account of the Indian Chief Black Hawk and his Tribes, the Sac
       and Fox Indians, with affecting narrative of a Lady who was taken
       Prisoner by the Indians. Philadelphia: N.p., 1834.

1168   Anderson, Robert. "Reminiscences of the Black Hawk War," Wisconsin
       Historical Society Collections 10 (1888): 167-76.

1169   _____. "Robert Anderson and the Black Hawk War," Chicago History
       3 (1952): 151-59.

1170   _____. "Letter to E.B. Washburne, dated Tours, France, May 10, 1870,"
       Illinois State Historical Society Journal 10 (1917): 422-28.

1171   Armstrong, James. Life of a Woman Pioneer, as Illustrated in the
       Life of Elsie Strawn Armstrong, 1789-1871. Chicago: J.F. Higgins,
       1931, 80-110.

1172   Bracken, Charles. "Further Strictures on Gov. Ford's History of the
       Black Hawk War," Wisconsin Historical Society Collections 2 (1856):
       402-14.

1173   Breese, Sidney S., ed. "Reminiscences of the Black Hawk War" An
       Interesting letter from General Robert Anderson to E.B. Washburn,"
       Illinois State Historical Society Journal 10 (1917-1918): 421-28.

1174   Brown, Ebenezer. "Autobiographical Notes," Michigan Pioneer 30
       (1906): 424-94.

1175  Brunson, Alfred. "Memoir of T.P. Burnett," Wisconsin Historical Society Collections 2 (1856): 233-325.

1176  _____. "A Methodist Circuit Rider's Horseback Tour from Pennsylvania to Wisconsin, 1835," Ibid 15 (1900): 264-91.

1177  Brush, Daniel H. Growing Up in Southern Illinois, 1820 to 1861. Chicago: Lakeside Press, 1944.

1178  Bryan, William S. and Robert Rose. A History of the Pioneer Families of Missouri with Numerous Sketches, Anecdotes, Adventures, etc., Relating to Early days in Missouri. St. Louis: Bryan, Brand, 1876, 455-97.

1179  Burton, Charles M. "The Black Hawk War papers of General John R. Williams," Michigan Pioneer 31 (1902): 313-471.

1180  Camp, Charles L., ed. James Clyman, American Frontiersman, 1792-1881. San Francisco: California Historical Society, 1928.

1181  Carter, Clarence E., ed. Territorial papers on the United States. Vol. 12: The Territory of Michigan, 1829-1837. Washington: Government Printing Office, 1945.

1182  Chetlain, Augustus L. Recollections of Seventy Years. Galena, IL: Galena Publishing Co., 1899, 17-23.

1183  Childs, Ebenezer. "Recollections of Wisconsin since 1820," Wisconsin Historical Society Collections 4 (1859): 153-95.

1184  "Edward D. Beochard's Vindication," Ibid 7 (1876): 289-96.

1185  Elliott, Richard S. Notes Taken in Sixty Years. St. Louis: R.P. Studley, 1883.

1186  Ellsworth, Spencer. Records of the Olden Time, or Fifty Years on the Prairies. Lacon, IL: Home Journal Steam Printing, 1880, 98-112.

1187  Fox, J. Sharpless, ed. "Territorial papers, 1831-1836," Michigan Pioneer 37 (1909-1910): 207-420.

1188  Greene, Evarts B. and Clarence W. Alvord, eds. The Governor's Letter-books, 1818-1834. Springfield, IL: Illinois State Historical Society, 1909.

1189  Grignon, Augustin. "Seventy-Two years Recollection of Wisconsin," Wisconsin Historical Society Collections 3 (1857): 197-296.

1190  Hobart, Chauncey. Recollections of my Life: Fifty Years of Itinerary in the Northwest. Red Wing, MN: Red Wing Print Co., 1885

1191  Hollman, Frederick G. The Autobiography of Frederick G. Hollman. Platteville, WS: R.I. Dugdale, n.d. At Wisconsin Historical Society.

1192  Iles, Elijah. Sketches of Early Life and Times in Kentucky, Missouri, and Illinois. Springfield, IL: Springfield Print Co., 1883.

1193  "Indian Campaign of 1832," Military and Naval Magazine 1 (1833): 321-33.

1194  Jerome, Edwin. "Incidents in the Black Hawk War," Michigan Pioneer 1 (1877): 48-51.

1195  Kingston, John T. "Early Western Days," Wisconsin Historical Society Proceedings 7 (1876): 297-344.

1196  Kinzie, Juliette A. Wau-bun, the 'Early Day' in the Northwest. New York: Jackson, Derby, 1856.

1197  Lewis, Hannah. Narrative of the Captivity and Providential Escape of Mrs. Jane Lewis. New York: N.p., 1833.

1198  Lockwood, James H. "Early Times and Events in Wisconsin," Wisconsin Historical Society Collections 2 (1856): 98-196.

1199  Marsh, Cutting. "Extracts from Marsh's Journal, during the Black Hawk War," Ibid 15 (1900): 60-65.

1200  McPheeters, Addison. "Illinois Commentary: the Reminiscences of Addison McPheeters," Illinois State Historical Society Journal 67 (1974): 212-26.

1201  "Narrative of Alexis Clermont," Wisconsin Historical Society Collections 15 (1900): 452-57.

1202  "Narrative of Spoon Decorah," Ibid 13 (1895): 448-62.

1203  Narrative of the Capture and Providential Escape of Misses Frances and Almira Hall, two Respectable young Women of the ages of 16 and 18, who were taken Prisoners by the Savages at a Frontier Settlement, near Indian Creek, in May, 1832. New York: N.p., 1835.

1204  "Notes and Reminiscences of an Officer of the Army," Army and Navy Chronicle 11 (1840): 282-84.

1205  Orr, William. "The Indian War," Illinois State Historical Society Journal 5 (1912): 66-79.

1206  Parkinson, Daniel M. "Pioneer Life in Wisconsin," Wisconsin Historical Society Collections 2 (1856): 326-64.

1207  Parkinson, Peter. "Strictures upon Gov. Ford's History of the Black Hawk War," Ibid 2 (1856): 393-401.

1208  _____. "Notes on the Black Hawk War," Ibid 10 (1888): 184-212.

1209  Patton, James W., ed. "Letters From North Carolina; Emigrants from the Old Northwest, 1830-1834," Mississippi Valley Historical Review 47 (1960): 263-77.

1210  Quaife, Milo M., ed. "A Journal of Events and Proceedings with the Rock River Band of Winnebago Indians," Ibid 12 (1925): 396-407.

1211  _____. The Early Days of Rock Island and Davenport; the Narratives of J.W. Spencer and J.M.D. Burrows. Chicago: Lakeside Press, 1942.

1212   Recollections of the Pioneers of Lee County. Dixon, IL: Inez A.
       Kennedy, 1893, 239-51.

1213   "Reminiscences of Black Hawk and the Black Hawk War," Wisconsin
       Historical Society Collections 5 (1867-1869): 287-90.

1214   "Reminiscences of Wisconsin in 1833," Ibid 10 (1888): 231-34.

1215   Reynolds, John. My Own Times, Embracing also the History of My Life.
       Belleville, IL: H.L. Davison, 1855, 349-416.

1216   Satterlee, John L. The Black Hawk War and the Sangamo Journal, 1832.
       Springfield, IL: Satterlee, 1982.

1217   Smith, Henry. "Indian Campaign of 1832," Wisconsin Historical Society
       Collections 10 (1888): 150-66.

1218   Spencer, John W. Reminiscences of Pioneer Life in the Mississippi
       Valley. Davenport, IA: Watson, Day, 1872.

1219   Thayer, Crawford B. Hunting a Shadow: the Search for Black Hawk;
       An Eyewitness Account of the Black Hawk War of 1832. Fort Atkinson, WS:
       C.B. Thayer, 1981.

1220   _____. The Battle of Wisconsin Heights: An Eyewitness Account of the
       Black Hawk War of 1832. Fort Atkinson, WS: Thayer, 1983.

1221   _____. Massacre at Bad Axe: An Eyewitness Account of the Black Hawk
       War of 1832. Fort Atkinson, WS: C.B. Thayer, 1984.

1222   Thornburn, Grant. Life and Writings of Grant Thorburn; prepared by
       Himself. New York: Edward Walker, 1852, 277-308.

1223   "A Voyage on the Upper Mississippi," Military and Naval Magazine
       3 (1834): 245-52, 349-57.

1224   St. Vrain, Felix. "A Diary of the Black Hawk War," Iowa Journal of
       History and Politics 8 (1910): 265-69.

1225   Washburn, Elihu B. "Letter to John Dixon, Dated Paris, December 15,
       1874," Illinois State Historical Society Journal 6 (1913): 214-31.

1226   Whittlesey, Charles. "Recollections of a Tour through Wisconsin in
       1832," Wisconsin Historical Society Collections 1 (1855): 64-85.

1227   "A Woman Pioneer's Story. Selena Truett, Daughter of General Dodge,
       Territorial Governor of Wisconsin, Relates her Experiences in the
       Black Hawk War." In: Evening Wisconsin, February 20, 1897.
       At Wisconsin Historical Society.

1228   Woodruff, George H. Fifty Years Ago, or, Gleanings Respecting the
       History of Northern Illinois a few years previous to, and during,
       the Black Hawk War. Joliet, IL: Joliet Republic, 1883, 21-62.

       SEE ALSO: 2782 , 3478 , 4779, 4786, 4787

QUALLAH BATTOO

1229   "A Battle at Quallah Battoo," Salem Gazette, July 19, 1831.

1230   Campbell, John F. "Pepper, Pirates and Grapeshot," American Neptune
       21 (1961): 292-302.

1231   Daley, R.F. "The Attack on Quallah Battoo," United States Naval
       Institute Proceedings 79 (1953): 761-71.

1232   Endicott, Charles M. "Narrative of Piracy and Plunder of the Ship
       'Friendship'," Essex Institute Historical Collections 1 (1859): 15-32.

1233   Gould, James W. "American Interests in Sumatra, 1784-1873." Ph. D.
       dissertation, Fletcher School of Diplomacy, 1955.

1234   Long, David F. "Martial Thunder': The First Official American Armed
       Intervention in Asia," Pacific Historical Review 42 (1973): 143-62.

1235   Maclay, Edgar S. "Chastisement of the Quallah Battooans," Harper's
       Monthly Magazine 88 (1894): 858-70.

1236   Nalty, Bernard C. "Pirates and Pepper," Leatherneck 41 (1960): 50-53.

1237   Phillips, James D. Pepper and Pirates: Adventures in the Sumatra
       Pepper Trade of Salem. Boston: Houghton, Mifflin, 1949.

1238   Powell, Edward A. The Road to Glory. New York: Charles Scribner's
       Sons, 1915.

1239   Putnam, George G. Salem Vessels and their Voyages: A History of the
       Pepper Trade with the Island of Sumatra. Salem, MA: Essex Institute,
       1922.

1240   Wright, James N. "Quallah Battoo," Leatherneck 24 (1941): 14-16.

       SEE ALSO: 3897, 3900, 5583, USS John Adams, USS Potomac, John Downes

## SECOND SEMINOLE WAR

1241   Adams, George R. "Caloosahatchee Massacre: Its Significance in the
       Second Seminole War," Florida Historical Quarterly 48 (1970): 368-80.

1242   Allen, Desmond W. "Dade's Massacre in the Second Seminole War,"
       Order of the Indian Wars Journal 2 (1981): 18-32.

1243   Alvord, Benjamin. Address Before the Dialectic Society of the Corps
       of Cadets. New York: Wiley, Putnam, 1839.

1244   Azoy, Anastasio C. "Dade and His Command," Esquire Magazine 21 (1944):
       60-61.

1245   Bellamy, Jeanne, ed. "The Perrines at Indian Key, Florida, 1838-
       1840," Tequesta 7 (1947): 69-78.

1246   Bittle, George C. "The First Campaign of the Second Seminole War,"
       Florida Historical Quarterly 46 (1967): 39-45.

1247   Bockelman, Charles W. Six Columns and Fort New Smyrna. Deleon Springs:
       E.O. Painter, 1985.

1248   Boyd, Mark F. "Florida Aflame: Background and Onset of the Second
       Seminole War, 1835," Florida Historical Quarterly 30 (1951): 1-115.

1249    ____. "Horatio S. Dexter and Events leading to the Treaty of Moultrie Creek with the Seminole Indians," Florida Anthropologist 11 (1958): 65-95.

1250    Brady, Cyrus T. Border Fights and Fighters. New York: McClure, Phillips, 1902, 191-202.

1251    Brawley, Benjamin. A Social History of the American Negro. New York: Macmillan, 1921, 91-115.

1252    Brinton, Daniel G. Notes on the Floridian Penninsula, Its Literary History, Indian Tribes, and Antiquities. Philadelphia: J. Sabin, 1859.

1253    Brown, George M. Ponce de Leon Land and Florida War Record. St. Augustine: Brown, 1902.

1254    Buckmaster, Henrietta. The Seminole Wars. New York: Collier Books, 1966.

1255    Coe, Charles H. Red Patriots: The Story of the Seminoles. Cincinnati: Editor Publishing Co., 1898.

1256    Cooke, David C. Indians on the Warpath. New York: Dodd, Mead, 1957.

1257    Covington, James W. "The Armed Occupation Act of 1842," Florida Historical Quarterly 40 (1961): 41-52.

1258    ____. "Cuban Bloodhounds and the Seminoles," Ibid 33 (1954): 111-19.

1259    ____. "Exploring the Ten Thousand Islands in 1838, Tequesta 18 (1958): 7-13.

1260    Cubberly, Frederick. The Dade Massacre. Washington: Government Printing Office, 1921.

1261    Davis, T. Frederick. "Pioneer Florida: Indian Key and Wrecking in 1833," Florida Historical Quarterly 22 (1943): 57-61.

1262    Dawson, Henry B. Battles of the United States. 2 Vols. New York: Johnson, Fry, 1858. Vol. 2, 439-44.

1263    Douglas, Marjory S. The Everglades: River of Glass. New York: Rinehart, 1947.

1264    Drake, Samuel G. Biography and History of the Indians of North America. Boston: J. Drake, 1834, 414, 461-99.

1265    Dye, Dewey A. "The Indian Key Massacre," United States Naval Institute Proceedings 100 (1974): 74-78.

1266    Ervin, William R. The Seminole War: Prelude to Victory, 1823-1838. Holly Hill, FL: W. & S. Ervin, 1983.

1267    Fairbanks, George R. History of Florida from its Discovery by Ponce de Leon in 1512, to the Close of the Florida War in 1842. Philadelphia: J.B. Lippincott, 1871.

1268    Fishburne, Charles C. Of Chiefs and Generals: A History of Cedar Keys to the End of the Second Seminole War. Cedar Keys, FL: Sea Hawk, 1982.

1269    Halbe, James M. Tales of the Seminole War. Okeechobe, FL: Okeechobe News, 1950.

1270  Hanna, Alfred J. and Kathyrn A. Lake Okeechobee. New York: Bobbs-
      Merrill, 1948.

1271  Haydon, Frederick S. "First Attempts at Military Aviation in the
      United States," Military Affairs 2 (1938): 131-38.

1272  Howard, Cecil H. Life and Public Services of General John Wolcott
      Phelps. Brattleboro, VT: F.E. Housh, 1887.

1273  Huse, Harriet P. "An Untold Story of the Florida War," Harper's
      Monthly Magazine 83 (1891): 591-94.

1274  ____. "Some Old Florida Traditions-Social and Others," United
      Service 7 (1892): 267-74.

1275  "Indian Murders," Florida Historical Quarterly 8 (1930): 200-03.

1276  "Jacksonville and the Seminole War, 1835-36," Ibid 3 (1925): 10-14,
      15-21; 4 (1925): 22-30.

1277  Jelks, Edward. "Dr. Henry Perrine," Jacksonville Historical Society
      Annual (1933-1934): 69-75.

1278  Jones, Charles C. Antiquities of Florida Indians. New York: D.
      Appleton, 1873.

1279  Kimball, Allen C. "The Seminole Negro Indian Scouts," Order  of the
      Indian Wars Journal 2 (1981): 28-31.

1280  Knotts, Tom. "History of the Blockhouse on the Withlacoochee,"
      Florida Historical Quarterly 49 (1971): 245-54.

1281  Laumer, Frank. Massacre!  Gainesville, FL: University of Florida
      Press, 1968.

1282  ____. "Encounter by the River," Florida Historical Quarterly 46
      (1968): 322-39.

1283  Lawton, Edward P. "William Elon Bassinger: A Georgian who died for
      Florida," Georgia Historical Quarterly 45 (1961): 105-19.

1284  McReynolds, Edwin C. The Seminoles. Norman: University of Oklahoma
      Press, 1957.

1285  Mahon, John K. History of the Second Seminole War, 1835-1842.
      Gainesville, FL: University of Florida Press, 1967.

1286  ____. "The Second Seminole War, 1835-1842," U.S. Army Military
      History Research Collections 4 (1976): 106-22.

1287  Martin, Sidney. Florida During Territorial Days. Athens, GA:
      University of Georgia Press, 1944.

1288  Mellen, T.A. "Captain Charles Mellon," Florida Historical Quarterly
      15 (1937): 281-83.

1289  Mauncey, Albert C. "Some Military Affairs in Territorial Florida,"
      Ibid 25 (1946): 202-11.

1290  Meltzer, Milton. Hunted like a Wolf. New York: Farrar, Strauss, 1972.

1291  Monk, J. Floyd. "Christmas Day in Florida," _Tequesta_ 38 (1978): 5-38.

1292  Montross, Lynn. "War with the Seminoles," _Leatherneck_ 54 (1971): 42-45.

1293  Moulton, Gary E. "Cherokees and the Second Seminole War," _Florida Historical Quarterly_ 53 (1975): 296-305.

1294  "Negroes &¢. Captured from Indians in Florida, &c. " 25th Cong. 3d Session. _House Document_ 225 (1839): 1-126.

1295  Parker, H.H. "The Battle of Okeechobee," _American Philatelist_ 61 (1948): 808-10.

1296  Parrish, John O. _Battling the Seminoles, Featuring John Atkins, Scout._ Lakeland, FL: Southern Printing Co., 1930.

1297  Pasco, Samuel. "Jefferson County, Florida, 1827-1910," _Florida Historical Quarterly_ 7 (1929): 234-57.

1298  Peters, Virginia B. _The Second Seminole War, 1835-1842._ Hamden, CT: Shoestring Press, 1979.

1299  Pierce, Philip N. and Frank O. Hough. "The Seven Years War," _Marine Corps Gazette_ 32 (1948): 32-38.

1300  Porter, Kenneth W. "Abraham," _Phylon_ 2 (1941): 107-16.

1301  _____. "John Caesar: A Forgotten Hero of the Seminole War," _Journal of Negro History_ 28 (1943): 53-65.

1302  _____. "Louis Pacheco: The Man and the Myth," _Ibid_ 28 (1943): 65-72.

1303  _____. "Three Fighters for Freedom: Maroons in Massachusetts; John Caesar, a Forgotten Hero of the Seminole War, Louis Pacheco," _Ibid_ 28 (1945): 53-72.

1304  _____. "John Caesar, Seminole Negro Partisan," _Ibid_ 31 (1946): 190-207.

1305  _____. "The Negro Abraham," _Florida Historical Quarterly_ 25 (1946): 1-43.

1306  _____. "The Founder of the 'Seminole Nation', Secoffee or Cowkeeper," _Ibid_ 37 (1949): 362-84.

1307  _____. "Negro Guides and Interpreters in the Early Stages of the Seminole War, December 25, 1835-March 6, 1837," _Journal of Negro History_ 35 (1950): 174-82.

1308  _____. The Cowkeeper Dynasty of the Seminole Nation," _Florida Historical Quarterly_ 30 (1952): 174-82.

1309  _____. "Florida Slaves and the Free Negroes in the Seminole War, 1835-1842," _Journal of Negro History_ 28 (1964): 427-50.

1310  _____. "Negroes and the Seminole War, 1835-1842," _Journal of Southern History_ 30 (1964): 427-50.

1311  Roberts, Albert H. "The Dade Massacre," _Florida Historical Quarterly_ 5 (1927): 123-38.

1312   Richards, Zack. "Seminole Warriors," Soldiers 32 (1977): 45-6.

1313   Roberts, Albert H. "The Dade Massacre," Florida Historical Quarterly
       5 (1927): 123-38.

1314   Sarkesian, Sam C. America's Forgotten Wars. Westport, CT: Greenwood
       Press, 1984, 155-65.

1315   Schloenback, Helen H. "The Seminole War, 1835-1842." Master's Thesis,
       University of Georgia, 1940.

1316   "The Seminole Indians-War in Florida," Army and Navy Chronicle 2
       (1836): 42-43.

1317   "The Seminole War," Family Magazine 3 (1835-1836): 439-40.

1318   Sherburne, John H. "Proposal for Ending the Second Seminole War,"
       American Indian Journal 2 (1976): 12-14.

1319   Sprague, John T. The Origins, Progress, and Conclusion of the Florida
       Gainesville, FL: University of Florida Press, 1964.

1320   Sprague, Oren D. "Second Seminole War, 1835-1842," Military Review
       68 (1988): 52-59.

1321   Steele, W.S. "Last Command: The Dade Massacre," Tequesta 46 (1986):
       5-19.

1322   Summerall, Charles P. "Soldiers Connected with Florida History since
       1812," Florida Historical Quarterly 9 (1931): 242-58.

1323   Tanner, Earl C. "The Early career of Edwin T. Jenks," Ibid 30 (1952):
       261-75.

1324   Tebeau, Charlton W. A History of Florida. Miami: University of
       Miami Press, 1972.

1325   Tebbel, John and Keith Jennison. American Indian Wars. New York:
       Harper & Bros., 1960, 209-19.

1326   Tierney, John. "America's Forgotten Wars: Guerilla Campaigns in U.S.
       History," Conflict 2 (1980): 223-49.

1327   Trussell, John B. "Seminoles in the Everglades: A Case Study in
       Guerilla Warfare," Army 12 (1961): 41-45.

1328   Tyler, Martha. "Reminiscences of the Indian Uprising near Fort Gatlin,
       Florida," Florida Historical Quarterly 3 (1924): 37-41.

1329   U.S. Quartermaster's Department. Records of Officers and Soldiers
       Killed in Battle and Died in Service during the Florida War.
       Washington, DC: Government Printing Office, 1842.

1330   Valliere, Kenneth L. "The Creek War of 1836, a Military History,"
       Chronicles of Oklahoma 57 (1979): 463-85.

1331   Van Ness, W.P. "An Incident of the Seminole War," Journal of the
       Military Service Institute 50 (1912): 267-71.

1332   Walker, Hester P. "Massacre at Indian Key, August 7, 1840,"
       Florida Historical Quarterly 5 (1926): 18-42.

1333   Walton, George. Fearless and Free: The Seminole Indian War, 1835-
       1842. Indianapolis: Bobbs-Merrill, 1977.

1334   Watts, Jill M. "We do Not Live for Ourselves Only: Seminole Black
       Perceptions and the Second Seminole War," UCLA History Journal 7
       (1986): 5-28.

1335   Weidenbach, Nell F. "Lieutenant John T. McLaughlin: Guilty or
       Innocent?" Florida Historical Quarterly 46 (1967): 46-52.

1336   Welsh, Michael E. "Legislating a Homestead Bill: Thomas Hart Benton
       and the Second Seminole War," Ibid 57 (1978): 157-72.

1337   White Nathan W. Private Joseph Sprague of Vermont, the Last Soldier-
       Survivor of Dade's Massacre in Florida, 28 December, 1835.
       Fort Lauderdale: N.H. White, 1981.

1338   Whiting, Henry. "The Florida War," North American Review 54 (1842):
       1-34.

1339   Williams, John T. The Territory of Florida; or, Sketches of the
       Topography, Civil, and Natural History. New York: Goodrich, 1837.

1340   Williams, Ernest L. "Negro Slavery in Florida," Florida Historical
       Quarterly 28 (1949): 93-110.

1341   Woodward, A.L. "Massacre in Gadsen County," Ibid 1 (1908): 17-25.

1342   Woodward, Sara. "The Second Seminole War with Especial Reference
       to Congress." Master's Thesis, Columbia University, 1933.

       SEE ALSO: 1735, 2265, 3035, 3037, 3047, 3502, 3503, 3504, 3505, 3512,
       3722, 3751, 4154, 4529, 4561, 4718, 4722, 4731, 4736, 4762, 4773,
       4781, 4783, 4798, 4820, Second Dragoons, Fort Brooke, Fort Dade,
       Fort Foster, Fort King, Fort McNeil, Fort Maitland, Fort Marion,
       Fort Mellon, Fort Meyers, Fort Taylor, Florida Militia, Missouri
       Militia, Billy Bowlegs, Richard K. Call, Thomas Childs, Duncan L.
       Clinch, Coacoochee, Edmund P. Gaines, William S. Harney, Archibald
       Henderson, Ethan A. Hitchcock, Andrew H. Humphreys, Thomas S. Jesup,
       George A. McCall, Stephen R. Mallory, David Moniac, Osceola, Benjamin
       K. Pierce, Winfield Scott, Zachary Taylor, Tiger Tail

CONTEMPORARY ACCOUNTS

1343   "The Army-Battle of Kissimmee," Army and Navy Chronicle 6 (1838): 141.

1344   An Authentic Narrative of the Seminole War and the Miraculous Escape
       of Mrs. Mary Godfrey. Providence: D.F. Blanchard, 1836.

1345   Backus, Electus. "Diary of a Campaign in Florida in 1837-1838,"
       Historical Magazine 10 (1866): 279-85.

1346   Barr, James. Correct and Authentic Narrative of the Indian War, with
       a Description of Maj. Dade's Massacre. New York: J. Narine, 1836.

1347   "Battle of Withlacoochee, 31st December, 1835," Army and Navy
       Chronicle 3 (1836): 323-24.

1348  Blanchard, Daniel F. An Authentic Narrative of the Seminole War, its
      Cause, Rise, and Purpose. Providence: D.F. Blanchard, 1836.

1349  "The Blood Hounds," Army and Navy Chronicle 10 (1840): 114-18.

1350  Carter, Clarence E., ed. Territorial Papers of the United States:
      Florida Territory, 1834-1835. Washington: Government Printing Office,
      1960-1962. Vols. 15, 16, 22-26.

1351  Chandler, William. "Original narratives of Indian Attacks in Florida:
      A Tallahassee Alarm of 1836," Florida Historical Quarterly 8 (1930):
      197-99.

1352  Clark, Ransom. The Surprising Adventures of Ransom Clark. Binghamton,
      NY: J.R. Orton, 1839.

1353  Cohen, Myer M. Notices of Florida and the Campaigns. Charleston:
      Burges, Honour, 1836.

1354  Davis, Doris S., comp. Register of the Levi-Twiggs Papers, 1834-1850.
      Quantico, VA: USMC Museum, 1970.

1355  Day, Hannibal. "Scrap Book of Newspaper Clippings Relating to the
      Second Seminole War and the Army of the United States."
      At the United States Military Academy Library, West Point.

1356  Dodd, Dorothy. "Letters from East Florida," Florida Historical
      Quarterly 15 (1936): 51-64.

1357  Drimmer, Frederick, ed. Scalps and Tomahawks: Narratives of Indian
      Captivity. New York: Coward, McCann, 1961, 268-71.

1358  Elderkin, James D. Biographical Sketches and Anecdotes of a Soldier
      of Three Wars. Detroit: Privately Printed, 1899, 16-38.

1359  "Florida Campaign-1837," Army and Navy Chronicle 8 (1839): 94, 154-55.

1360  "The Florida War," North American Review 54 (1842): 1-34.

1361  "Florida War, No. 4," Army and Navy Chronicle 8 (1839): 219-20.

1362  Gadsden, James. "Letter of Colonel James Gadsen on the Seminole Council,"
      Florida Historical Quarterly 7 (1929): 350-56.

1363  Horn, Stanley F., ed. "Tennessee Volunteers in the Seminole Campaign
      of 1836: The Diary of Henry Hollingsowrth," Tennessee Historical
      Quarterly 1 (1942): 269-74, 344-66; 2 (1943): 61-73, 163-78, 236-56.

1364  Howe, Charles. "A Letter From Indian Key, 1840," Florida Historical
      Quarterly 20 (1941): 197-202.

1365  Hoyt, William D. "A Soldier's View of the Second Seminole War, 1838-
      39: Three Letters of James B. Dallam," Ibid 25 (1947): 356-62.

1366  Judson, E.Z. "Sketches of the Florida War," Western Literary Journal
      and Monthly Review 1 (1845): 97-100, 168-71, 213-16, 218-82, 333-35.

1367  Laumer, Frank. "The Incredible Adventures of Ransom Clark," Tampa Bay
      History 3 (1981): 5-18.

1368   McGaughy, Felix P. "The Squaw-Kissing War: Bartholomew M. Lynch's
       Journal of the Second Seminole War, 1836–1839." Master's Thesis,
       Florida States University, 1965.

1369   Mahon, John K., ed. "The Journal of A.B. Meek and the Second Seminole
       War, 1836," Florida Historical Quarterly 38 (1960): 302–18.

1370   _____., ed. "Letters from the Second Seminole War," Ibid 36 (1958):
       331–52.

1371   Moore, John H. "A South Carolina Lawyer Visits St. Augustine, 1837,"
       Ibid 43 (1965): 361–78.

1372   Munroe, Kirk. Through Swamps and Glade. New York: Charles Scribner's
       Sons, 1896.

1373   A Narrative of the Life and Sufferings of Mrs. Jane Johns, who was
       Barbarously wounded and Scalped by Seminole Indians in East Florida.
       Baltimore: J. Lucas, E.K. Dearer, 1837.

1374   "The Narrative of Ransom Clark," Army and Navy Chronicle 4 (1837):
       369–70.

1375   "Notes on the Passage Across the Everglades," Tequesta 20 (1960):
       57–65.

1376   "Original Narratives of Indian Attacks in Florida: Indian Murders,"
       Florida Historical Quarterly 8 (1930): 200–03.

1377   The Pathetic and Lamentable Narrative of Miss Perine, on the Massacre
       and Destruction of Indian Key Village in April, 1840. Philadelphia:
       E.C. Gill, 1840.

1378   Peek, Peter V. Inklings of Adventure in the Campaigns of the Florida
       Indian War; and a Sketch of the Life of the Author. Schenectady, NY:
       I. Riggs, 1846.

1379   Phelps, John W. "Letters of Lieutenant John W. Phelps, U.S.A., 1837–
       1838," Florida Historical Quarterly 6 (1927): 67–84.

1380   Pond, Frederick E. Life and Adventures of 'Ned Buntline'. New York:
       Cadmus Book Shop, 1919.

1381   Potter, Woodbourne. The War in Florida: Being an Exposition of its
       Causes and an Accurate History of the Campaigns of Generals Clinch,
       Gaines, and Scott. Baltimore: Lewis, Coleman, 1836.

1382   Preble, George H. "Diary of a Canoe Expedition in the Everglades and
       Interior of Southern Florida in 1842," United Service 8 (1905): 26–46.

1383   "Recollections of a Campaign in Florida," Yale Literary Magazine 11
       (1846): 72–80, 130–37.

1384   Rowles, W.P. "Incidents and Observation in Florida in 1836,"
       The Southran 1 (1841): 54–55, 116–18, 157–61, 199–204.

1385   Scenes   in the Florida War; by a Carolinian. Charleston: Walker, 1838.

1386   "Seminole War-Treaty of Paine's Landing," Army and Navy Chronicle
       6 (1838): 282–84, 344–45.

1387   Sheldon, Jane M. "Original Narratives of Indian Attacks in Florida:
       Seminole Attacks near New Smyrna," Florida Historical Quarterly 8
       (1930): 188-96.

1388   Simmons, James W. "Recollections of the Late Campaign in East Florida."
       In the Ayers Collection, Newberry Library.

1389   Smith, W.W. Sketch of the Seminole War during a Campaign. By an
       Officer of the Left Wing. Charleston: J.W. Dowling, 1836.

1390   Solano, Matthew. Documents Respecting Capt. Sprague's Book, relating
       to the Seminole War. Washington, DC: N.p., 1848.

1391   Sketches of the Indian War in Florida, embracing a Minute Account of
       the Principal Cruel and horrible Indian Massacres. New York: N.p., 1837.

1392   "Sketches of the Seminole War. By a Lieutenant of the Left Wing,"
       Southern Literary Journal 3 (1836): 76-81.

1393   "A Thrilling Adventure Among the Florida Indians," Army and Navy
       Chronicle and Scientific Repository 2 (1843): 326-28.

1394   "Seminole War," Army and Navy Chronicle 2 (1836): 55-56.

1395   A True and Authentic Account of the Indian War in Florida Giving the
       the Particulars Respecting the Murder of the Widow Robbins, and the
       Provencial Escape of her daughter, Aurelia. New York: Saunders, Van
       Welt, 1836.

1396   U.S. War Department. Letter from the Secretary of War, Transmitting
       Documents in Relation to Hostilities of Creek Indians. 24th Cong.
       1st Session. House Document 276 (1836).

1397   _____. Court of Inquiry-Operations in Florida &c. Letter from the
       Secretary of War, Transmitting Copies of the Proceedings of a Court
       Martial Inquiry, convened at Fredericktown in Relation to the
       Operations against the Seminole and Creek Indians. 25th Cong.
       2d Session House Document 278 (1836).

1398   White, Frank F., ed. "Macomb's Mission to the Seminoles: John T.
       Sprague's Journal kept during April and May, 1839," Florida Historical
       Quarterly 35 (1956): 130-93.

1399   _____., ed. "A Scouting Expedition along Lake Panasofflee," Ibid
       31 (1953): 282-89.

1400   _____., ed. "The Journal of Lieutenant John Pickell, 1836-1837,"
       Ibid 38 (1959): 142-71.

1401   _____., ed. "A Journal of Lieut. Robert C. Buchanan during the
       Seminole War," Ibid 29 (1950): 132-51.

1402   Wik, Reynold M., ed. "Captain Nathaniel Wyche Hunter and the Florida
       Indian Campaigns, 1837-1841," Ibid 39 (1960): 62-75.

       SEE ALSO: 2850 , 2854 , 2855 , 2856 , 2857, 2862, 2863, 2864, 2865, 4042

## MONTEREY

1403   Bancroft, Hubert H. History of California. 4 Vols. San Francisco: Historical Company, 1886. Vol. 4, 298-329.

1404   Bechtell, K.K. Commodore Jones' War, 1842. San Francisco: Grabhorn Press, 1948.

1405   Brooke, George M. "The Vest Pocket War of Commodore Jones," Pacific Historical Review 31 (1962): 217-33.

1406   Feipel, Louis N. "The United States Navy in Mexico, 1821-1914," United States Naval Institute Proceedings 41 (1914): 489-97.

1407   Gapp, Frank W. "The 'Capture' of Monterey in 1842," Ibid 105 (1979): 46-54.

1408   Guinn, James M. "The Capture of Monterey, October 19, 1842," Historical Society of Southern California Publications 4 (1896): 70-73.

1409   Hanks, Robert J. "Commodore Jones and his Private War with Mexico," American West 16 (1979): 30-33, 60-63.

1410   Hathewsay, G.G. "Commodore Jones' War," History Today 16 (1966): 194-201.

1411   High, James. "Jones at Monterey, 1842," Journal of the West 5 (1966): 173-86.

1412   Larkin, Thomas O. The Affair at Monterey, October 20 and 21, 1842. Los Angeles: Zamorano Club, 1964.

1413   Smith, Gene A. "The War that Wasn't: Thomas ap Catsby Jones' Seizure of Monterey," California History 66 (1987): 104-13, 155-57.

1414   Tessendorf, K.C. "Pardon my Conquest," Foreign Service Journal 46 (1969): 39-41.

## CONTEMPORARY ACCOUNTS

1415   Franklin, Samuel R., ed. Memories of a Rear Admiral; who has served For More than Half a Century in the Navy of the United States. New York: Harper & Bros., 1898, 49-51.

1416   Jackson, Alonzo C. The Conquest of California: Alonzo C. Jackson's Letter in Detail of the Seizure of Monterey in 1842. New York: Eberstadt, 1953.

1417   Kemble, John H., ed. Visit to Monterey in 1842. Los Angeles: G. Dawson, 1955.

SEE ALSO: USS Cyane, USS United States, Thomas ap Catsby Jones

## PATRIOT WAR

1418   Alexander, Edward P. "The Hunter's Lodges of 1838," New York History 19 (1938): 64-39.

1419   An Impartial and Authentic Account of the Civil War in the Canadas. London: J. Saunders, Jr., 1838.

1420  Barber, John W. "The Battle of Prescott," Michigan Pioneer 21 (1892): 609-12.

1421  Beauclerk, Charles. Lithographic Views of Military Operations in Canada under his Excellency, Sir John Colbourne, during the late Insurrection. London: A. Flint, 1840.

1422  Bellasis, Margaret. Rise, Canadians! Montreal: Palm Publishers, 1955.

1423  Booth, Philip. "Soldering in Bygone Days in Canada," Dalhousie Review 47 (1967): 355-59.

1424  Canada in the Great World War: An Authentic Account of the Military History of Canada from the Earliest Days to the Close of the War of the Nations. Toronto: Morang, 1918.

1425  Cleary, Francis. "The Battle of Windsor," Essex Historical Society Papers 2 (1914): 5-33.

1426  Colquhoun, A.H., ed. "The Niagara Frontier in 1837-38," Niagara Historical Society Publications No. 29 (1916): 4-40.

1427  Corey, Albert. Canadian-American Relations Along the Detroit River. Detroit: Wayne State University, 1957.

1428  Coventry, George. "A Concise History of the Late Rebellion in Upper Canada to the Evacuation of Navy Island, 1838," Ontario Historical Society Papers and Records 17 (1919): 113-74.

1429  Crampton, Emeline J. "An Incident of the Patriot War," Journal of American History 18 (1924): 345-47.

1430  Cross, D.W. "The Canadian Rebellion of 1837," Magazine of Western History 7 (1887-1888): 359-70, 521-29.

1431  Cruikshank, Ernest A. "The Insurrection in Short Hills in 1838," Ontario Historical Society Papers and Records 8 (1907): 5-23.

1432  _____. "The Invasion of Navy Island in 1837-38," Ibid 32 (1937): 7-84.

1433  _____. "A Twice-Told Tale," Ibid 23 (1926): 180-222.

1434  DeCelles, Alfred D. The 'Patriotes' of 1837. A Chronicle of the Lower Canada Rebellion. Toronto: Glasgow, Brook, 1916.

1435  Dent, John C. The Story of the Upper Canadian Rebellion: Largely Derived from Original Sources and Documents. 2 Vols. Toronto: Robinson, 1885.

1436  G.T.D. "The Burning of the 'Caroline'," Canadian Monthly 3 (1873): 289-92.

1437  Dougall, James. "That Windsor Battle: The Account of it from a Canadian Standpoint," Michigan Pioneer 7 (1884): 82-88.

1438  Douglas, R. Alan. "The Battle of Windsor," Ontario History 61 (1969): 137-52.

1439  Drew, Andrew. A Narrative of the Capture and Destruction of the Steamer 'Caroline'. London: Spottiswood, 1864.

1440   Duffy, John and Nicholas Muller. "The Great Wolf Hunt: The Regular
       Response in Vermont to the Patriote Uprising of 1837," Journal of
       American Studies 8 (1974): 153-69.

1441   Durant, Samuel W. History of St. Lawrence County, New York.
       Philadelphia: L.H. Everts, 1878, 468-75.

1442   Fleming, Roy F. "Steamer 'Caroline' burned at Niagara, 1837,"
       Inland Seas 25 (1969): 21-25.

1443   Fraser, John. Canadian Pen and Ink Sketches. Montreal: Gazette
       Printing  Co., 1890, 71-109.

1444   Fryer, Mary B. Volunteers and Redcoats-Rebels and Raiders: A Military
       History of the Rebellions in Upper Canada. Toronto: Dundurn, 1987.

1445   Gray, John M. "The life and Death of 'General' William Putnam,"
       Ontario History 46 (1954): 3-20.

1446   Green, Ernest. "War Clouds over the Short Hills," Welland County
       Historical Society Papers and Records 5 (1938): 153-62.

1447   Guillet, Edwin C. The Lives and Times of the Patriots: An Account of
       the Rebellion in Upper Canada, 1837-38, and of the Patriot Agitation
       in the United States, 1837-1842. Toronto: University of Toronto Press,
       1938.

1448   _____ . "The Coburg Conspiracy," Canadian Historical Review 18 (1937):
       28-47.

1449   Hamil, Fred C. "American Recruits for the Invasion of Windsor,"
       Detroit Historical Society Bulletin 15 (1959): 7-14.

1450   Hamilton, Alexander. The Niagara Frontier in 1837-38. Niagara, ON:
       Niagara Historical Society, 1916.

1451   Hand, Augustus N. "Local Incidents of the Papineau Rebellion,"
       New York History 15 (1934): 376-81.

1452   Harmon, John H. "Battle of Windsor," Essex Historical Society Papers
       and Addresses 2 (1915): 19-24.

1453   Harrison, William. "The Two Colonels," Canadian Magazine 29 (1907):
       321-25.

1454   Head, Francis B. A Narrative, with Notes by William Lyon Mackenzie.
       Toronto: McClelland, Stewart, 1969.

1455   "History of the Recent Insurrection in the Canadas," United States
       Magazine and Democratic Review 4 (1838): 74-104.

1456   Horsey, Amey. "Battle of the Windmill, 1838," Women's Canadian
       Historical Society Transactions 5 (1912): 37-42.

1457   Hough, Franklin B. History of St. Lawrence and Franklin Counties.
       Albany: J. Munsell, 1860, 656-74.

1458   "The Hunter's Lodges of 1838," New York History 19 (1938): 64-69.

1459   Ireland, John. "Andrew Drew: The Man who Burned the 'Caroline',"
       Ontario History 59 (1967): 137-56.

1460   Jachman, Sydney W. "Galloping Head: the Life of Right and Honorable
       Sir Francis Bond Head, Bart, P.C, etc, 1793-1875, Late Lieutenant
       Governor of Upper Canada." Ph. D. dissertation, Harvard University,
       1953.

1461   Johnson, Walter S.   The Rebellion of 1837. Montreal: McGill
       University, 1925

1462   Jones, Howard. "The Caroline Affair," Historian 38 (1976): 485-502.

1463   Kinchen, Oscar A. The Rise and Fall of the Patriot Hunters. New York:
       Bookman Associates, 1956.

1464   Kurtz, Henry I. "The Undeclared War between Britain and America,"
       1837-1842," History Today 12 (1962): 777-83, 872-80.

1465   Landon, Fred. "London and its Vicinity, 1837-38," Ontario Historical
       Society  Papers and Records 24 (1927): 410-38.

1466   _____. "The Duncombe Uprising of 1837 and some of its Consequences,"
       Royal Society of Canada Transactions 25 (1931): 83-98.

1467   _____. "The Common Man in the Era of the Rebellion in Upper Canada,"
       Canadian Historical Association Annual Report (1937): 76-91.

1468   Leach, Hamish A. "A Politico-Military Study of the Detroit River
       Boundary Defense during the December, 1837-March, 1838 Emergency."
       Ph. D. dissertation, University of Ottawa, 1963.

1469   Lindsey, E.G. A History of Events which Transpired during the Navy
       Island Campaign. Lewiston, NY: J.A. Harrison, 1838.

1470   Link, Eugene P. "Vermont Physicians and the Canadian Rebellion of
       1837," Vermont History 37 (1969): 177-83.

1471   Lizars, Robina. Humours of 1837, Grave, Gay and Grim; Rebellious
       Times in the Canadas. Toronto: W. Briggs, 1897.

1472   McCrae, John. "Battle of Windsor, Canada, December 4th, 1838,"
       Ontario Historical Society Papers and Records 6 (1905): 78-81.

1473   McFarland, Robert. "The Patriot War: The Battle of Fighting Island,"
       Michigan Pioneer 7 (1884): 89-92.

1474   McLeod, Donald. A Brief Review of the Settlement of Upper Canada by
       the U.E. Loyalists and Scotch Highlanders, 1783. Cleveland: F.B.
       Penniman, 1841.

1475   McRae, John. "The Battle of Fighting Island, February, 1838," Essex
       Historical Society Papers 1 (1913): 28-30.

1476   Mann, Michael. A Particular Duty: The Canadian Rebellions, 1837-1839.
       Salisbury, ENG: Russell, 1986.

1477   Manning, Helen T. The Revolt in French Canada, 1800-1835: A Chapter
       in the History of the British Commonwealth. New York: St. Martin's
       Press, 1962.

1478   Martyn, John P. "Upper Canada and Border Incidents, 1837-18: A Study
       of the Troubles on the American Frontier following the Rebellion of
       1837." Master's Thesis, University of Toronto, 1962.

1479   _____. "The Patriot Invasion of Pelee Island," Ontario History 56
       (1964): 153-65.

1480   Meader, John R. "Little Wars of the Republic: The Patriot War,"
       Americana 6 (1911): 867-74.

1481   Middleton, Jesse E. and Fred Landon. The Province of Ontario:
       A History. 5 Vols. Toronto: Dominion Publishing Co., 1927-1928.

1482   Monet, Jacques. The Last Cannon Shot: A Study of French-Canadian
       Nationalism, 1837-1850. Toronto: University of Toronto Press, 1969.

1483   Morrison, Neil F. "The Battle of Fighting Island and Pelee Island,"
       Michigan History 48 (1964): 227-32.

1484   Morton, Desmond. Rebellions in Canada. Toronto: Grolier, 1979.

1485   Muggeridge, John. "John Rolph-A reluctant Rebel," Ontario History
       51 (1959): 217-29.

1486   Muller, H.N. "Trouble on the Border, 1838: A Neglected Incident from
       Vermont's Neglected History," Vermont History 44 (1976): 97-102.

1487   Natress, Thomas. "Fort Malden and Old Fort Days," Essex Historical
       Society Papers 1 (1913): 69-84.

1488   Needler, George H. Colonel Anthony Von Egmond, from Napoleon to
       Mackenzie and Rebellion. Toronto: Burns, MacEachern, 1956.

1489   Nelson, Peter. "The Battle of Diamond Island," New York State
       Historical Association Proceedings 3 (1922): 35-51.

1490   New, Chester. "The Rebellion of 1837 in its Larger Setting," Canadian
       Historical Association Annual Report (1937): 5-17.

1491   Overman, William D., ed. "A Sidelight on the Hunter's Lodges of 1838,"
       Canadian Historical Review 19 (1938): 165-72.

1492   Palfrey, J.G. "Affair of the'Caroline'," North American Review 53
       (1841): 412-31.

1493   Palmer, Friend. "The Battle of Windsor," Essex Historical Society
       Papers 2 (1915): 30-33.

1494   Partridge, G.F. "A Yankee on the New York Frontier, 1833-1851,"
       New England Quarterly 10 (1937): 752-72.

1495   Pearce, Bruce M. The First Grand Master: A Biography of William Mercer
       Wilson. Simcoe, ON: Pearce Publishing Co., 1932.

1496   Read, Colin F. "The Rising in Western Upper Canada, 1837-1838: The
       Duncombe Revolt and After." Ph. D. dissertation, University of
       Toronto, 1974.

1497   _____. "The Shorthills raid of June, 1838, and its Aftermath,"
       Ontario History 68 (1976): 93-115.

1498  Read, David B. The Canadian Rebellion of 1837. Toronto: C.B. Robinson, 1896.

1499  Riddell, William R. "A Contemporary Account of the Navy Island Episode," Royal Society of Canada Transactions 13 (1914): 57-76.

1500  _____. "The 'Patriot' Generals." In: Old Province Tales, Upper Canada. Toronto: Glasgow, Brook, 1920, 192-216.

1501  _____. "A Patriot General," Canadian Magazine 44 (1914): 32-36.

1502  _____. "Another Patriot General," Ibid (47 (1916): 218-22.

1503  Rosentreter, Roger L. "'To Free Upper Canada': Michigan and the Patriot War, 1837-1838." Ph. D. dissertation, University of Michigan, 1983.

1504  _____. "Liberating Canada: Michigan and the Patriot War," Michigan History 67 (1983): 32-34.

1505  Ross, Robert B. "The Patriot War," Michigan Pioneer 21 (1894): 509-608.

1506  Schull, Joseph. Rebellion; the Rising in French Canada, 1837. Toronto: Macmillan of Canada, 1971.

1507  Scott, Keith F. Prescott's Famous Battle of the Windmill, November 13-18, 1838. Prescott, ON: St. Lawrence Printing, 1970.

1508  Senior, Elinor K. Redcoats and Patriotes: the Rebellion in Lower Canada, 1837-1838. Stittsville, ON: Canada's Wings, 1985.

1509  _____. "Supressing Rebellion in Lower Canada: British Military Policy and Practice, 1837-38," Canadian Defense Quarterly 17 (1988): 50-55.

1510  _____. "Rebellion along the Chauteauguay, 1838," Chauteuaguay Valley Historical Society Journal 21 (1988): 7-14.

1511  Severence. Frank H. "Contributions Towards a Bibliography of the Niagara Region: The Upper Canada Rebellion, 1837-38," Buffalo Historical Society Publications 5 (1902): 427-96.

1512  _____. "Illustrative Documents Bearing on the Canadian Rebellion," Ibid 8 (1905): 119-29.

1513  Smith, George C. The Life of John Colborne, Field Marshal Lord Seaton. London: J. Murray, 1903.

1514  Stagg, Ronald J. "The Younge Street Rebellion of 1837: An Examination of the Social Background and a Re-assessment of the Events. Ph. D. dissertation, University of Toronto, 1976.

1515  Stanley, George F. "Invasion 1838-the Battle of the Windmill," Ontario History 54 (1962): 237-52.

1516  Stevens, Alfred J. "Some Historical Notes Concerning Fighting Island in Detroit River," Essex Historical Society Papers 3 (1921): 50-58.

1517  Stevens, Kenneth R. "The 'Caroline' Affair: Anglo-American Relations and Domestic Politics, 1837-1842." Ph. D. dissertation, Indiana University, 1982.

1518  Stone, L. "St. Eustache, some Incidents of its defense and its defenders in 1837," Canadian Magazine 51 (1918): 353-61.

1519  Sullivan, John D. "The Canadian Rebellion of 1837-38," Essex Historical Society Papers 2 (1915): 6-18.

1520  Sumner, Elsie G. "Activities of Canadian Patriots in the Rochester District," Ontario Historical Society Papers and Records 36 (1944): 28-32.

1521  Theller, Edward A. Canada in 1837-38: Showing by Historical Facts the Cause of the Late Attempted Revolution and its Failure. Philadelphia: Henry F. Anners, 1841.

1522  Tiffany, Orrin L. "The Relations of the United States to the Canadian Rebellion of 1837-38," Buffalo Historical Society Publications 8 (1905): 1-147.

1523  ____. "The Relations of the United States to the Canadian Rebellion of 1837-1838." Ph. D. dissertation, University of Michigan, 1905.

1524  Wallace, Stewart W. A Chronicle of the Rebellion in Upper Canada. Toronto: Glasgow, Brook, 1920.

1525  Wallace, William C. The Family Compact; a Chronicle of the Rebellion in Upper Canada. Toronto: Glasgow, Brook, 1915.

1526  Waterson, Elizabeth. "Gilbert Parker and the Rebellion of 1837," Journal of Canadian Studies 20 (1985): 80-89.

1527  Wells, George C. "The Battle of Windmill Point," Canadian Magazine 47 (1916): 149-52.

        SEE ALSO: 4455, 4619, 4620, 4630, 4639, 4644, Hugh Brady, William L. Mackenzie, Alexander McLeod, Winfield Scott

POLITICS AND DIPLOMACY

1528  Brown, George W. "The Durham Report and the Upper Canadian Scene," Canadian Historical Review 20 (1939): 136-60.

1529  Burroughs, Peter. British Attitudes towards Canada, 1822-1844. Scarborough, ON: Prentice-Hall of Canada, 1971.

1530  ____. The Canadian Crisis and British Colonial Policy, 1828-1841. Toronto: Macmillan of Canada, 1972.

1531  Carter, George E. "Daniel Webster and the Canadian Rebellions, 1837-1838," Canadian Historical Association Annual Report (1970): 120-31.

1532  Clark, S.D. Movements of Political Protest in Canada, 1640-1840. Toronto: University of Toronto Press, 1959.

1533  Corey, Albert B. The Crisis of 1830-1842 in Canadian-American Relations. New Haven, CT: Carnegie Endowment for International Peace, 1941.

1534  Craig, Gerald M. "The American Impact on the Upper Canada Reform Movement before 1837," Canadian Historical Review 29 (1948): 333-52.

1535  Creighton, D.G. "The Economic Background of the Rebellions of 1837," Canadian Journal of Economics and Political Science 3 (1937): 322-34.

1536  DeCelles, Alfred D. Papineau Cartier. Toronto: Morang, 1904.

1537  Derbishine, Stewart. "Stewart Derbishine's Report to Lord Durham on Canada," Canadian Historical Review 18 (1937): 48-62.

1538  Dunham, Aiken. Political Unrest in Upper Canada, 1815-1836. New York: Longmans, Green, 1927.

1539  Durham, John G. Lord Durham's Report on the Affairs of British North America. Oxford: Claredon Press, 1912.

1540  Eady, Ronald J. "Anti-American Sentiment in Essex County in the Wake of the Rebellions of 1837," Ontario History 61 (1969): 1-8.

1541  Elliot, Thomas F. The Canadian Controversy; its origin, nature and merits. London: Longman, Orme, Brown, Green, 1838.

1542  Fairchild, George M. Lower Canada Affairs in 1836. Quebec: Telegraph Printing Co., 1910.

1543  Frank, Douglas. "The Canadian Rebellion and the American Public," Niagara Frontier 16 (1969): 96-104.

1544  Garland, M.A. "Some Frontier and American Influences in Upper Canada prior to 1837," London and Middlesex Historical Society Transactions 13 (1929): 5-33.

1545  Hamil, Fred C. "The Reform Movement in Upper  Canada." In: Profiles of a Province: Studies in the History of Ontario. Toronto: Ontario Historical Society, 1967, 9-19.

1546  Longley, R.S. "Emigration and the Crises of 1837 in Upper Canada," Canadian Historical Review 17 (1936): 29-40.

1547  Martin, Chester. "Lord Durham's Report and its Consequences," Canadian Historical Review 20 (1939): 178-94.

1548  Martin, Ged. "Self-Defense: Francis Bond Head and Canada, 1841-1870," Ontario History 73 (1981): 3-18.

1549  Moore, David R. Canada and the United States, 1815-1830. Chicago: Jennings, Graham, 1910.

1550  Morey, William C. Diplomatic Episodes: a Review of Certain Historical incidents Bearing upon International relations and Diplomacy. New York: Longmans, 1926.

1551  Morrell, William P. British Colonial Policy in the Age of Peel and Russell. Oxford: Claredon Press, 1930.

1552  Ryerson, Stanley B. 1837: the Birth of Canadian Democracy. Toronto: Francis White, 1937.

1553  Saint-Pierre, Telesphore, comp. The Americans and Canada in 1837-38: Authentic Documents. Montreal: A.P. Pigeon, 1897.

1554  Saunders, Robert F. "What was the Family Compact?" Ontario History 49 (1957): 165-78.

1555  Shortridge, Wilson P. "The Canadian-American Frontier during the Rebellion of 1837-1838," Canadian Historical Review 7 (1926): 13-26.

1556   Smith, Elizabeth. "Historic Attempts to Annex Canada to the United States," Journal of American History 5 (1911): 215-30.

1557   Stavrianos, L.S. "Is the Frontier Theory Applicable to the Canadian Rebellion of 1837-38?" Michigan History Magazine 22 (1938): 326-37.

1558   Stevens, Kenneth R. "James Grogan and the Crisis in Canadian-American relations, 1837-1842," Vermont History 50 (1982): 219-26.

1559   Wise, Sydney F. and Robert C. Brown. Canada Views the United States: Nineteenth Century Political Attitudes. Seattle: University of Washington Press, 1962.

1560   _____. "The Family Compact: A Negative Oligarchy." In: David L. Earl, ed. The Family Compact: Aristocracy or Oligarchy? Toronto: Coppclark Publishing Co., 1967, 142-45.

1561   Wittke, Carl. "Ohioans and the Canadian-American Crises of 1837-1838," Ohio Archeological and Historical Society Quarterly 58 (1949): 21-34.

PRISONERS

1562   Barnett, J. Davis. "The Books of the Political Prisoners and Exiles of 1838," Ontario Historical Society Papers and Records 16 (1918): 10-18.

1563   Borthwick, John D. History of the Montreal Prison from A.D. 1784 to A.D. 1886; containing a Complete Record of the Troubles of 1837-1838. Montreal: A. Periard, 1886.

1564   Hemmeon, Douglas. "The Canadian Exiles of 1838," Dalhousie Review 7 (1927): 13-16.

1565   Landon, Fred. "Trial and Punishment of the Patriots captured at Windsor, December, 1838," Michigan History Magazine 18 (1934): 25-32.

1566   Riddell, William R. "A Trial for High Treason in 1838," Ontario Historical Society Papers and Records 18 (1920): 50-58.

1567   Scott, Ernest. "The Canadian and United States Transported Prisoners of 1839," Journal and Proceedings of the Royal Australian Historical Society 21 (1935): 1-18.

1568   Scott, Stuart C. "The Patriot game: New Yorkers and the Patriot Rebellion of 1837-1838," New York History 68 (1987): 281-96.

1569   Struthers, Irving E. "The Curious Case of Benjamin Mott," Canadian Magazine 45 (1915): 497-501.

1570   Watt, R.C. "The Political Prisoners in Upper Canada," English Historical Review 41 (1926): 526-55.

      SEE ALSO: 1580, 1581, 1582, 1584, 1590, 1591, 1593, 1595, 1599, 1600, 1616, 1618, 4709

CONTEMPORARY ACCOUNTS

1571   "An American Account of the Prescott Raid of 1838," Canadian Defense Quarterly 9 (1926-1927): 393-98.

1572  Bellingham, Sydney. Some Personal Recollections of the Rebellion of 1837 in Canada. Dublin: Browne, Nolan, 1902.

1573  Bishop, Levi. "Recollections of the Patriot War of 1838-39 on this Frontier," Michigan Pioneer 12 (1887): 414-24.

1574  Brown, Thomas S. 1837-My Connection with it. Quebec: R. Renault, 1898.

1575  Compton-Smith, C., comp. The Upper Canadian Rebellion: A Collection of Documents and Records, together with Factual Reports, dealing with the Events of the Day. Toronto: McGraw-Hill of Canada, 1968.

1576  Davenport, E.M. The Life and Recollections of E.M. Davenport, Major, H.M. 16th Regiment. London: Hatchards, 1869.

1577  Durand, Charles. Reminiscences of Charles Durand. Totonto: Hunter, Rose, 1898.

1578  Elgin Histoical and Scientific Institute. Reminiscences of Early Settlers and other Records. St. Thomas, ON: The Institute, 1911.

1579  De la Fosse, F.M., ed. "Diary of Lieutenant-Colonel Robert D. Rogers," Ontario Historical Society Papers and Records 13 (1932): 429-30.

1580  Gates, Lillian F. "A Canadian Rebel's Appeal to George Bancroft," New England Quarterly 41 (1968): 96-104.

1581  Gates, William. Recollection of Life in Van Dieman's Land. Lockport, NY: C.S. Grandal, 1850.

1582  Greenwood, F. Murray. Land of a Thousand Sorrows: Australian Prison Journal, 1840-1842, of the Exiled Canadien Patriote Francois-Maurice Lepailleur. Vancouver, BC: University of British Columbia, 1980.

1583  Henry, Walter. Trifles from my Portfolio, or, Recollections of Scenes and Small Adventures during Twenty-Nine Years Military Service. 2 Vols. Quebec: W. Neilson, 1839.

1584  Heustis, Daniel D. A Narrative of the Adventures and Sufferings of Captain D. Heustis and his Companions in Canada and Van Dieman's Land during a long Captivity. Boston: S.W. Wilder, 1847.

1585  A History of Events which Transpired during the Navy Island Campaign; to which is Added the Correspondence of Different Public Officials. Lewiston, NY: E.G. Lindsay, 1838.

1586  Hunt, Jedediah. An Adventure on a Frozen Lake: A Tale of the Canadian Rebellion of 1837-8. Cincinnati: Ben Franklin Book and Job, 1859.

1587  King, John. The Other side of the 'Story'; being some Reviews of Mr. J.C. Dent's First Volume of the Story of the Upper Canada Rebellion. Toronto: J. Murray, 1886.

1588  Knaplund, Paul, ed. Letters From Lord Sydenham, Governor-General of Canada, 1839-1841, to Lord John Russell. London: Allen, Unwin, 1931.

1589  Land, John H. "The Recollections of Lieut. John Land, a Militiaman in the Rebellion of 1837," Wentworth Historical Society Papers 8 (1919): 20-24.

1590   Landon, Fred. "The Exiles of 1838 from Canada to Van Dieman's Land,"
       London and Middlesex Historical Society Transactions (1927): 5-20.

1591   Lyon, Caleb. Narrative of Recollections of Van Dieman's Land, during
       a three year's captivity of Stephen S. Wright. New York: Winchester,
       1844.

1592   Lysons, Daniel. Early Reminiscences, by General Sir David Lysons.
       London: J. Murray, 1896.

1593   Marsh, Robert. Seven Years of my Life, of, Narrative of a Patriot
       Exile. Buffalo: Foxon, Stevens, 1848.

1594   Miller, H. Orlo, ed. "The Letters of Rebels and Loyalists," Canadian
       Science Digest 1 (1938): 70-78.

1595   Miller, Linus W. Notes of an Exile to Van Dieman's Land; Comprising
       Incidents of the Canadian Rebellion in 1838. Fredonia, NY:
       W. McKinstry, 1846.

1596   Norton, Lewis A. Life and Adventure of Col. L.A. Norton, Written by
       Himself. Oakland, CA: Pacific Press Publishing House, 1887.

1597   Ormsby, William, ed. Crisis in the Canadas, 1838-1839; The Grey
       Journals and Letters. Toronto: Macmillan of Canada, 1964.

1598   Pipping, Ella. Soldier of Fortune: The Story of a Nineteenth Century
       Adventurer. Boston: Gambit, 1971.

1599   Poutre, Felix. Escaped from the Gallows: Souveniers of a Canadian
       State  Prisoner in 1838. Montreal: DeMontigny, 1862.

1600   Prieur, Francois X. Notes of a Convict of 1838. Sydney, AUS: D.S.
       Ford, 1949.

1601   Read, Colin and Ronald J. Stagg, eds. The Rebellion of 1837 in Upper
       Canada: A Collection of Documents. Toronto: Champlain Society and
       Carleton University Press, 1985.

1602   Riddell, William R., ed. "A Contemporary Account of the Rebellion in
       Upper Canada, 1837," Ontario Historical Society Papers and Records
       17 (1919): 113-74.

1603   Sanderson, Charles R., ed. The Arthur Papers. 2 Vols. Toronto:
       University of Toronto Press, 1957.

1604   Scadding, Henry. Extracts from the Diary of Rev. Henry Scadding,
       1837-1838. Toronto: Women's Canadian Historical Society, 1906.

1605   Severence, Frank H. "Misadventures of Robert Marsh." In: Old Trails
       on the Niagara Frontier. Buffalo: Matthews-Northup Co., 1899.

1606   Simcoe County Pioneer and Historical Society. Pioneer Papers.
       Barrie, ON: The Society, 1918.

1607   Sissons, C.B. "Dr. John Rolph's Own Account of the Flag of Truce
       Incident in the Rebellion of 1837," Canadian Historical Review 19
       (1938): 56-59.

1608   Snow, Samuel. The Exile's Return; or, Narrative of Samuel Snow, who
       was Banished to Van Dieman's Land. Cleveland: Smend, Lowles, 1846.

1609  Spragge, George W., ed. "A Diary of 1837 by John Sandfield MacDonald," Ontario History 47 (1955): 1-11.

1610  Stacey, Charles P., ed. "The Crisis of 1837 in a Back Township of Upper Canada, being the Diary of Joseph Richard Thompson," Canadian Historical Review 11 (1930): 223-31.

1611  _____. "An American account of the Prescott Raid of 1838," Canadian Defense Quarterly 9 (1932): 393-98.

1612  Sutherland, Thomas J. A Letter to her Majesty, the British Queen, with Letters to Lord Durham, Lord Gleneig, and Sir George Arthur. Albany: C. Van Benthuysen, 1841.

1613  Szulc, Michael C. "Letter to J.R. Palmer dated Fort Henry, Ontario, 1 December, 1838," Polish-American Studies 9 (1952): 90-92.

1614  Tomlin, Roswell. "Roswell Tomlin's Reminiscences of the Rebellion of 1837," Elgin Historical and Scientific Institute Publications 4 (1911): 29-44.

1615  Wait, Benjamin. The Wait Letters. Erin, ON: Press Porcepic, 1976.

1616  Welch, Samuel M. Home History. Recollections of Buffalo during the Decade from 1830 to 1840, or Fifty Years since. Buffalo: P. Paul, 1891, 274-92.

1617  Williams, Samuel. "Reminiscences of Samuel Williams: The Rebellion of '37'," Elgin Historical and Scientific Institute Publications 4 (1911): 64-69.

1618  Wright, Stephen S. Narrative and Recollections of Van Dieman's Land during a Three Year's Captivity of Stephen S. Wright. New York: J. Winchester, 1844.

## OREGON QUESTION

1619  Ambler, Charles H. "The Oregon Country, 1810-1830: A Chapter in Territorial Expansion," Mississippi Valley Historical Review 30 (1943): 3-24.

1620  Blue, George V. "The Oregon Question, 1818-1828: A Study of Dr. John Floyd's Efforts in Congress to Secure the Oregon Country," Oregon Historical Quarterly 23 (1922): 193-219.

1621  Bourne, Edward G. "Aspects of Oregon History Before 1840," Ibid 6 (1906): 255-75.

1622  Cleland, Robert G. "Asiatic Trade and the American Occupation of the Pacific Coast," American Historical Association Annual Report for the Year 1914 (1916): 283-89.

1623  Coughlin, Magalen. "California Ports: A Key to Diplomacy for the West Coast, 1820-1845," Journal of the West 5 (1966): 153-72.

1624  DeVoto, Bernard. The Course of Empire. Boston: Houghton, Mifflin, 1952.

1625  Franklin, John H. "The Southern Expansionists of 1846," Journal of Southern History 25 (1959): 323-38.

1626  Graebner, Norman A. "Polk, Politics and Oregon," East Tennessee
      Historical Society Publications No. 24 (1952): 11-25.

1627  ____. "Maritime Factors in the Oregon Compromise," Pacific Historical
      Review 20 (1951): 331-45.

1628  ____. "Politics and the Oregon Compromise," Pacific Northwest
      Quarterly 52 (1961): 7-14.

1629  Gluek, Alvin C. "The Struggle for the British Northwest: A Study in
      Canadian-American Relations." Ph. D. dissertations, University of
      Minnesota, 1953.

1630  Hansen, William A. "Thomas Hart Benton and the Oregon Question,"
      Missouri Historical Review 63 (1969): 489-97.

1631  Haste, Richard A. "Fifty-Four, Forty or Fight: A National Bluff
      that was Called," Canadian Magazine 62 (1924): 311-14.

1632  Howe, Daniel W. "The Mississippi Valley in the Movement for Fifty-
      Four-Forty or Fight," Mississippi Valley Historical Association
      Proceedings (1912): 99-116.

1633  Husband, Michael B. "Senator Lewis F. Linn and the Oregon Question,"
      Missouri Historical Review 66 (1971): 1-19.

1634  Johansen, Dorothy O. "Oregon's Role in American History: An Old
      Theme Recast," Pacific Northwest Quarterly 40 (1949): 84-92.

1635  Ledbetter, William H. "Military History of the Oregon Country, 1804-
      1859." Master's Thesis, University of Oregon, 1935.

1636  McCabe, James O. "Arbitration and the Oregon Question," Canadian
      Historical Review 41 (1961): 308-27.

1637  Merk, Frederick. The Oregon Question: Essays in Anglo-American
      Diplomacy and Politics. Cambridge: Harvard University Press, 1967.

1638  Miles, Edwin A. "Fifty-Four-Forty or Fight-an American Political
      Legend," Mississippi Valley Historical Review 44 (1957): 291-309.

1639  "Oregon and the Oregon Question," Southern Quarterly Review 8 (1845):
      191-243.

1640  Pratt, Julius W. "James Knox Polk and John Bull," Canadian
      Historical Review 24 (1943): 341-49.

1641  Schafer, Joseph. "Oregon Pioneers and American Diplomacy." In:
      Guy S. Ford, ed. Essays in American History Dedicated to Frederick
      Jackson Turner. New York: Holt, 1910, 35-55.

1642  Soward, F.H. "President Polk and the Canadian Frontier," Canadian
      Historical Association Annual Report (1930): 71-80.

1643  Shippee, Lester B. "The Federal Relations of Oregon," Oregon
      Historical Quarterly 19 (1918): 89-133, 186-230, 283-331.

1644  Van Alstyne, Richard W. "International Rivalries in the Pacific
      Northwest," Oregon Historical Quarterly 46 (1945): 185-218.

1645   Young, F.G. "The Oregon Trail," Oregon Historical Quarterly 1
       (1900): 339-70.

       SEE ALSO: 4574 , 4587 , 4601 , 4702 , Lewis and Clark Expedition

                          AROOSTOOK WAR

1646   Bradley, Caleb. "Rev. Caleb Bradley on the Madawaska War," Maine
       Historical Society Collections 9 (1898): 418-25.

1647   Burrage, Henry S. Maine in the Northeastern Boundary Controversy.
       Portland, ME: Marks, 1919.

1648   ____. "The American Attitude of Maine in the Northeastern Boundary
       Controversy," Maine Historical Society Collections 1 (1904): 353-68.

1649   Ferris, I.F. "Our Last War with England, the so-called 'Aroostook
       War'," Munsey's Magazine 65 (1918): 172-74.

1650   Ganong, William F. "A Monograph on the Evolution of the Boundries of
       the Province of New Brunswick," Royal Society of Canada Transactions
       6 (1901): 241-361.

1651   Gill, George J. "Edward Everett and the Northeastern Boundary,"
       New England Quarterly 42 (1969): 201-13.

1652   Hasse, A.R. "The Northeastern Boundary," New York Public Library
       Bulletin 4 (1900): 391-411.

1653   Irish, Maria M. "The Northeastern Boundary of Maine," Journal of
       American History 16 (1922): 311-22.

1654   Jones, Howard. "The Attempt to Impeach Daniel Webster," Capitol
       Studies 3 (1975): 31-44.

1655   ____. "Anglophobia and the Aroostook  War," New England Quarterly
       48 (1975): 519-39.

1656   Jones, Wilbur D. "Lord Ashburton and the Maine Boundary Negotiations,"
       Mississippi Valley Historical Review 40 (1953): 177-90.

1657   LeDuc, Thomas. "The Maine Frontier and the Northeastern Boundary
       Controversy," American Historical Review 53 (1947): 30-41.

1658   Lowenthal, David. "The Maine Press and the Aroostook  War,"
       Canadian Historical Review 32 (1951): 315-36.

1659   Lucey, W.L. "Some Correspondence of the Maine Commissioners Regarding
       the Webster-Ashburton Treaty," New England Quarterly 15 (1942): 332-48.

1660   Maine, Council. Aroostook  War. Historical Sketch and Roster of
       Commissioned Officers and Enlisted Men called into Service for the
       Protection of the Northeastern Frontier of Maine. Augusta, ME:
       Kennebec Journal Print Co., 1904.

1661   Nicholson, M.R. "The Relations of New Brunswick with the State of
       Maine and the United States, 1837-1849." Master's Thesis, University
       of New Brunswick, 1952.

1662   "The Northeastern Boundary Question," United States Magazine and
       Democratic Review 3 (1838): 29-49.

1663   Rowell, George S. "John Baker, a Hero of Madawaska."
       Clippings at Maine Historical Society.

1664   Sprague, John F. "The Northeastern Boundary Controversy and the
       Aroostook  War." In: Historical Collections of Piscataquis County,
       Maine. Dover, ME: Observer Press, 1910, 216–81.

1665   Washburne, Israel. "The Northeastern Boundary," Maine Historical
       Society Collections 3 (1881): 1–106.

1666   White, James. "Boundary Disputes and Treaties." In: Adam Shortt, ed.
       Canada and its Provinces. 23 Vols. Toronto: Edinburgh University
       Press, 1914–1916. Vol. 8, 749–958.

1667   Winsor, Justin. "The Settlement of the Northeastern Boundary,"
       Massachusetts Historcal Society Proceedings 3 (1887): 349–69.

## POLITICS AND DIPLOMACY

1668   Adams, Ephraim D. "Lord Ashburton and the Treaty of Washington,"
       American Historical Review 17 (1912): 764–82.

1669   Baldwin, J.R. "The Ashburton-Webster Boundary Settlement," Canadian
       Historical Association Annual Report (1938): 121–33.

1670   Biggar, Hazel. "The Ashburton Treaty," Women's Canadian Historical
       Society Transactions 6 (1915): 85–91.

1671   Current, Richard N. "Webster's Propaganda and the Ashburton Treaty,"
       Mississippi Valley Historical Review 34 (1947): 187–200.

1672   Gordon, Hugh T. The Treaty of Washington, Concluded August 9, 1842,
       by Daniel Webster and Lord Ashburton. Berkeley: University of
       California Press, 1908.

1673   Jones, Wilbur D. "Lord Ashburton and the Maine Boundary Negotiations,"
       Mississippi Valley Historical Review 40 (1953): 477–90.

1674   LeDuc, Thomas. "The Webster-Ashburton Treaty and the Minnesota Iron
       Ranges," Journal of American History 51 (1964): 476–81.

1675   Merk, Frederick. "The Oregon Question in the Webster-Ashburton
       Negotiations," Mississippi Valley Historical Review 43 (1956): 379–
       404.

1676   Mills, Dudley. "British Diplomacy and Canada: The Ashburton Treaty,"
       United Empire 2 (1911): 683–712.

1677   Sage, Walter N. "The Oregon Treaty of 1846," Canadian Historical
       Review 27 (1946): 349–67.

1678   Schuyler, Robert L. "Polk and the Oregon Compromise of 1846,"
       Political Science Quarterly 26 (1911): 443–61.

1679   Scott, Leslie M. "Influence of American Settlement Upon the Oregon
       Boundary Treaty of 1846," Oregon Historical Quarterly 29 (1928): 1–19.

1680   Tait, W.M. "Fixing the Borderline," Canadian Magazine 45 (1915):
       209–16.

1681   Weatherbe, J. "The Canadian Boundary Dispute and the Ashburton
       Treaty," Nova Scotia Historical Society Collections 6 (1887-1888):
       17-52.

1682   Whiteley, Emily S. "Small Talk of a Great Affair," Virginia
       Quarterly Review 6 (1930): 21-36.

# II
# UNITED STATES
# ARMY

PUBLIC DOCUMENTATION

1683  Annals of the Congress of the United States, 1789-1824. 42 Vols.
      Washington, DC: Gales, Seaton, 1834-1856.

1684  Congressional Globe, Containing the Debates and Proceedings, 1833-
      1873. 111 Vols. Washington, DC: F.&J. Rives, George Bailey, 1834-
      1873.

1685  Ford, Worthington C. and Gail G. Hunt, eds. Journals of the Contin-
      ental Congress, 1774-1789. 34 Vols. Washington, DC: Manuscript
      Division of the Library of Congress, 1904-1937.

1686  Peters, Richard, et al. The Public Statutes at Large of the United
      States of America, 1789-1873. 27 Vols. Boston: C.C. Little, J.
      Brown, 1848-1873.

1687  Register of Debates in Congress, 1825-1837. Washington, DC: Gales,
      Seaton, 1825-1837.

1688  Richardson, James D., ed. The Messages and Papers of the Presidents,
      1789-1897. 10 Vols. Washington, DC: Government Printing Office,
      1907.

                              *HISTORY

1689  Albion, Robert G. Introduction to Military History. New York:
      Century Co., 1929.

1690  Bond, P.S. and Enoch B. Garey. Wars of the American Nation.
      Annapolis: New Military Library, 1923.

1691  Cloke, H.E. Condensed Military History of the United States; a
      Condensed Discussion of the Most Important Military Campaigns of
      the United States. Cambridge, MA: Technology Press, 1928.

1692  Decker, Leslie E. America's Major Wars: Crusaders, Critics and
      Scholars, 1775-1972. 2 Vols. Reading, MA: Addison, Wesley, 1973.

1693  Dupuy, Richard E. and William H. Baumer. The Little Wars of the
      United States: A Compact History from 1798 to 1920. New York:
      Hawthorne, 1968.

1694  Frost, John. The Book of the Army. New York: D. Appleton, 1845.

1695  Ganoe, William A. The History of the United States Army.
      New York: D. Appleton, 1924.

1696  Hero Tales of the American Soldier and Sailor as Told by the Heroes
      Themselves and Their Comrades. New York: W.W. Wilson, 1899.

1697  Laurent, Francis W. Organization for Military Defense of the United
      States, 1789-1959. Madison: University of Wisconsin Press, 1960.

1698  Merrill, James M., ed. Uncommon Valor: The Exciting Story of the
      Army. Chicago: Rand, McNally, 1964.

1699  Millis, Walter. Arms and Men: A Study of American Military History.
      New York: Putnam's Sons, 1958.

1700  Palmer, Dave R. Early American Wars and Military Institutions.
      Wayne, NJ: Avery Publishing Group, 1986.

1701  Palmer, John M. America in Arms: The Experiences of the United States
      with Military Organization. New Haven: Yale University Press, 1946.

1702  Phisterer, Frederick. Statistical Record of the Armies of the United
      States. New York: Scribner's, 1884.

1703  Ryan, Garry D. and Timothy K. Nenninger. Soldiers and Civilians:
      The U.S. Army and the American People. Washington, DC: National
      Archives & Records Administration, 1987.

1704  Weigley, Russell F. History of the United States Army. New York:
      Macmillan, 1967.

1705  Wood, Leonard. Our Military History: Its Facts and Fallacies.
      Chicago: Reilly, Britton, 1916.

EARLY HISTORY

1706  Bonner, James C. "The Historical Basis of the Southern Military
      Tradition," Georgia Review 9 (1955): 74-85.

1707  Childress, David T. "The Army in Transition: The United States Army,
      1815-1846." Ph. D. dissertation, Mississippi State University, 1974.

1708  Coffman, Edward M. The Old Army: A Portrait of the American Army in
      Peacetime, 1784-1898. New York: Oxford University Press, 1986.

1709  Coles, Harry J. "From Peaceable Coercion to Balenced Forces, 1807-
      1815." In: Kenneth J. Hagan and William R. Roberts, eds. Against
      All Enemies: Interpretations of American Military History from
      Colonial Times to Present. Westport, CT: Greenwood, 1986, 71-90.

1710  Crackel, Theodore J. Mr. Jefferson's Army: Political and Social
      Reform of the Military Establishment, 1801-1809. New York: New
      York University Press, 1987.

1711  ____. "Jefferson, Politics, and the Army: An Examination of the
      Military Peace Establishment Act of 1802," Journal of the Early
      Republic 2 (1982): 21-38.

1712  Cress, Lawrence D. "Reassessing American Military Requirements, 1783-
      1807." In: Kenneth J. Hagan and William R. Roberts, eds. Against
      All Enemies: Interpretations of American Military History from
      Colonial Times to Present. Westport, CT: Greenwood, 1986, 49-69.

1713  Cunliffe, Marcus. Soldiers and Civilians: The Martial Spirit in America, 1775-1865. New York: Free Press, 1973.

1714  ____. "The American Military Tradition." In: Harry C. Allen and C.P. Hill, eds. British Essays in American History. New York: E. Arnold, 1957, 207-24.

1715  Gaines, William H. "The Forgotten Army: Recruiting for a National Emergency," Virginia Magazine of History and Biography 56 (1948): 269-79.

1716  Godfey, Carlos E. "Organization of the Provisional Army of the United States in the Anticipated War with France, 1798-1800," Pennsylvania Magazine of History and Biography 38 (1914): 129-82.

1717  Guthman, William.H. March to Massacre: A History of the First Seven Years of the United States Army, 1784-1781. New York: McGraw Hill,

1718  Higginbotham, Don. The War of American Independence: Military Attitudes, Policies, and Practices, 1763-1789. New York: Macmillan, 1973.

1719  Jacobs, James R. The Beginnings of the U.S. Army, 1783-1812. Princeton: Princeton University Press, 1947.

1720  Kohn, Richard. Eagle and Sword: The Federalists and the Creation of the Military Establishment in America, 1783-1802. New York: Free Press, 1975.

1721  ____. "The Creation of the American Military Establishment, 1783-1802." In: Peter Karsten, ed. The Military in America: From Colonial Era to the Present. New York: Free Press, 1980, 73-84.

1722  Mahon, John K. "Pennsylvania and the Beginnings of the Regular Army," Pennsylvania History 21 (1954): 33-44.

1723  ____. "Military Relations Between Georgia and the United States, 1789-1794," Georgia Historical Quarterly 43 (1959): 138-55.

1724  Martin, James K. and Mark E. Lender. A Respectable Army: The Military Origins of the Republic, 1763-1789. Arlington Heights, IL: Harlan Davidson, 1982.

1725  "Orderly Book-1800," Union County Historical Society Proceedings 2 (1934): 42-92.

1726  Pogue, Forrest C. "Economy before Preparedness," Defense Management Journal 12 (1976): 14-18.

1727  Prucha, Francis P. The Sword of the Republic: The United States Army on the Frontier, 1783-1846. New York: Macmillan, 1969.

1728  Reamer, Ida S. "The Army of the United States from the Revolution to 1821," Coastal Artillery Journal 64 (1926): 139-54.

1729  Schenck, A.D. "The U.S. Army in the Year 1801," Journal of the Military Service Institute 32 (1903): 443-44.

1730  Skelton, William B. "The United States Army, 1821-1837: An Institutional History." Ph. D. dissertation, Northwestern University, 1968.

1731      _____. "The Army in the Age of the Common Man, 1815-1845." In:
          Kenneth J. Hagan and William R. Roberts, eds. Against all Enemies:
          Interpretations of American Military History from Colonial Times to
          the Present. Westport, CT: Greenwood Press, 1986, 91-112.

1732      Spaulding, Oliver L. "The Thirty Year's Peace: An Interlude in the
          History of the United States Army," Army Ordnance 17 (1937): 218-21.

1733      Stessel, Harold E. "Pen and Swords: The Image of the Soldier in
          Early Nineteenth Century American Literature." Ph. D. dissertation,
          University of Pennsylvania, 1980.

1734      Thomson, Earl W. "The Army of the United States from 1830 to 1840,"
          Coastal Artillery Journal 79 (1936): 440-43.

1735      Walker, S.H. Florida and the Seminole Wars: Brief Observations on
          the Conduct of the Officers and the Discipline of the Army of the
          United States. Washington, DC: N.p., 1840.

1736      Weigley, Russell F. "The Anglo-American Armies and Peace, 1783-1868."
          In: Joan R. Challinor and Robert L. Beisner, eds. Arms at Rest: Peace-
          Making and Peace-keeping in American History. Westport, CT: Greenwood
          Press, 1987, 133-60.

1737      Williams, T. Harry. "From the Revolution to 1860." In: Americans at
          War: The Development  of the American Military System. Baton Rouge:
          Louisiana State University Press, 1960, 1-45.

1738      Young, Tommy R. "The United States Army in the South, 1789-1835."
          Ph. D. dissertation, Louisiana State University, 1973.

1739      _____. "The United States Army and the Institution of Slavery in
          Louisiana, 1803-1815," Louisiana Studies 13 (1974): 201-22.

## MILITARY POLICY

1740      Bacon, Eugene H. and C. Joseph Bernardo. American Military Policy.
          Harrisburg, PA: Military Service Publications, 1955.

1741      Campbell, John W. "Evolution of a Doctrine: The Principles of War,"
          Marine Corps Gazette 54 (1970): 39-42.

1742      Carter, William H. "Interdependence of Political and Military
          Policies," North American Review 194 (1911): 837-47.

1743      _____. "Prophets of Preparedness," Journal of the Military Service
          Institute 60 (1917): 329-44.

1744      Dutcher, George M. "National Safety of the United States, past and
          future," South Atlantic Quarterly 15 (1916): 183-88.

1745      Follansbee, G.G. "National Defense-1775-1929; 154 Years of American
          Military Policy," Infantry Journal 34 (1929): 488-95.

1746      Kennon, L.W. "Standing Armies," Journal of the Military Service
          Institute 50 (1912): 305-17.

1747      McCarthy, Charles H. "National Preparedness as Illustrated by American
          History," Catholic World 102 (1916): 787-95.

1748  MacIsaac, David and Samuel F. Wells. "The American Military: A 'Minuteman' Tradition," Wilson Quarterly 3 (1979): 109-24.

1749  O'Connor, Raymond. American Defense Policy in Perspective: From Colonial Time to the Present. New York: Wiley, 1965.

1750  Palmer, Williston B. The Evolution of Military Policy in the United States. Carlisle Barracks, PA: Army Information School, 1946.

1751  Pettit, James S. "How Far Does Democracy Affect the Organization and Discipline of Our Armies," Journal of the Military Service Institute 38 (1906): 1-38.

1752  Phayre, Ignatius. "The Defense Policy of the United States," Royal United Service Institute Journal 79 (1934): 317-30.

1753  Weigley, Russell F. Towards an American Army: Military Thought from Washington to Marshall. New York: Columbia University Press, 1962.

1754  _____. The American Way of War: A History of the United States Military Strategy and Policy. New York: Macmillan, 1973.

EARLY POLICY

1755  Bartky, Elliot M. "War and the American Founding: Volunteerism and the Origins of American Military Policy." Ph. D. dissertation, Rutgers University, 1983.

1756  Carp, E. Wayne. "The Problem of National Defense and Public Order in the Early American Republic." In: Jack P. Greene, ed. The American Revolution: Its Character and Limits. New York: New York University Press, 1987, 14-50.

1757  Clarfield, Gerald H. "Protecting the Frontier: Defense Policy and the Tariff Question in the First Washington Administration," William and Mary Quarterly 32 (1975): 443-64.

1758  Crane, Charles J. "Our Military Policy from the End of the War of 1812-1815 to the Begining of the Civil War.," Journal of the United States Infantry Association 4 (1907-1908): 562-88, 677-709.

1759  Cress, Lawrence D. "Republican Liberty and National Security: American Military Policy as an Ideological Problem, 1783-1789," William and Mary Quarterly 38 (1981): 73-96.

1760  Fraser, Richard H. "The Foundation of American Military Policy, 1783-1800." Ph. D. dissertation, University of Oklahoma, 1959.

1761  Hedberg, Lloyd F. "A Critical Consideration of the History and Development of the Basic Organizational Policy of the Army of the United States, up to the Passage of the National Defense Act of 1920, in Relation to the Theory of a Citizen Army." Master's Thesis, Georgetown University, 1945.

1762  Heffron, Paul A. "The Anti-Military Tradition of the Founding Fathers and its Continuation in the Writings of Carl Schurtz, Charles A. Beard, and Walter Millis." Ph. D. dissertation, University of Minnesota, 1974.

1763  Hickey, Donald R. "Federalist Defense Policy in the Age of Jefferson, 1801-1812," Military Affairs 45 (1981): 63-70.

1764  Higginbotham, Don. "The Debate over National Military Institutions:
      An Issue Slowly Resolved." In: William M. Fowler and Wallace Coyle,
      eds. The American Revolution: Changing Perspectives. Boston:
      Northeastern University Press, 1979, 153-68.

1765  _____. "The Early American Way of War: Reconnaissance and Appraisal,"
      William and Mary Quarterly 44 (1987): 230-73.

1766  Holt, William S. "The United States and the Defense of the Western
      Hemisphere, 1815-1840," Pacific Historical Review 10 (1941): 29-38.

1767  Morton, Louis. "The Origins of American Military Policy," Military
      Affairs 22 (1958): 75-82.

1768  Smith, Carlton B. "Congressional Attitudes Towards Military Prepar-
      edness during the Monroe Administration," Military Affairs 40
      (1976): 22-25.

1769  _____. "The American Search for a 'Harmless' Army," Essays in
      History 10 (1964-1965): 29-43.

1770  Stuart, Reginald C. War and American Thought: From the Revolution
      to the Monroe Doctrine. Kent, OH: Kent State University Press, 1982.

1771  _____. "Engines of Tyranny': Recent Historiography on Standing Armies
      during the Era of the American Revolution," Canadian Journal of
      History 19 (1984): 183-99.

1772  Watson, Richard R. "Congressional Attitudes Towards Military Prepar-
      edness, 1829-1835," Mississippi Valley Historical Review 34 (1948):

1773  Wesley, Edgar B. "The Military Policy of the Critical Period,"
      Coastal Artillery Journal 68 (1930): 281-90.

      SEE ALSO: 2167, 2200, Frontier Policy, Alexander Hamilton

CIVILIAN CONTROL

1774  Ekirch, Arthur. The Civilian and the Military. New York: Oxford
      University Press, 1956.

1775  Huntington, Samuel P. The Soldier and the State: The Theory and
      Policy of Civil-Military Relations. Cambridge:  Harvard University
      Press, 1957

1776  _____. "Civilian Control of the Military: A Theoretical Statement."
      In: Heinz Eulau, Samuel J. Eldersveld and Morris Janowitz, eds.
      Political Behavior: A Reader in Theory and Method. Glencoe, NY:
      Free Press, 1956, 379-85.

1777  _____. "Civilian Control and the Constitution," American Political
      Science Review 50 (1956): 676-99.

1778  Lieber, G. Norman. "The Use of the Army in Aid of Civil Power." In:
      Charles McClure, ed. A Digest of Opinions of the Judge-Advocates
      General of the Army. Washington, DC: Government Printing Office,
      1901, 759-92.

1779  Linethal, Edward T. "From Hero to Antihero: The Transformation of
      the Warrior in Modern America," Soundings 63 (1980): 79-93.

1780  Merriam, Charles E. "Security without Militarism: Preserving Civilian
      Control in American Political Institutions." In: Jerome Kerwin, ed.
      Civil-Military Relationships in American Life. Chicago: University
      of Chicago Press, 1948, 156-72.

1781  Miles, Jack L. "The Fusion of Military and Political Considerations:
      Threat or Challenge to the Military," Marine Corps Gazette 52 (1968):
      22-29, 44-52.

1782  Morton, Louis. "Civilian or Soldiers," Ibid 47 (1963): 24-29.

1783  Smith, Louis. American Democracy and Military Power: A Study of Civil
      Control of Military Power in the United States. Chicago: University
      of Chicago Press, 1951.

      SEE ALSO: 2107, 6620

## WAR POWERS

1784  Burnham, James. "And the Sword," Marine Corps Gazette 44 (1960): 10-14.

1785  Lofgren, Charles A. "War-making under the Constitution: The Original
      Understanding," Yale Law Journal 81 (1972): 672-702.

1786  _____. "War Powers, Treaties, and the Constitution." In: Leonard W.
      Levy and Dennis J. Mahoney, eds. The Framing of the Constitution.
      New York: Macmillan, 1987, 242-58.

1787  May, Ernest R. "The President Shall be Commander-in-Chief." In:
      The Ultimate Decision: The President as Commander-in-Chief. New York:
      G. Braziller, 1960, 3-20.

1788  Reveley, W. Taylor. "War Powers of the President and Congress: Who
      Decides whether America Fights?" This Constitution (1985): 19-24.

1789  Shewmaker, Kenneth F. "Congress only Can Declare War' and 'The
      President is Commander-in-Chief': Daniel Webster and the War Power,"
      Diplomatic History 12 (1988): 383-409.

1790  Sofaer, Abraham. War, Foreign Affairs, and Constitutional Power:
      The Origins. Cambridge, MA: Ballinger, 1976.

1791  Stuart, Reginald C. "War Powers of the Constitution in Historical
      Perspective," Parameters 10 (1980): 65-71.

1792  White Howard. Executive Influence in Determining Military Policy in
      the United States. Urbana, IL: University of Illinois, 1925.

1793  Wormuth, Francis D. and Edwin B. Firmage. To Chain the Dog of War:
      The War Power of Congress in History and in Law. Dallas: Southern
      Methodist University Press, 1986.

## ADMINISTRATION

1794  Hamersly, Thomas H. Complete Regular Army Register of the United
      States...Also, a Military History of the Department of War and of
      Each Staff Department of the Army. Washington, DC: Hamersly, 1880.

1795  Histories of Administrative Bureaux of the War Department.
      Washington, DC: Government Printing Office, 1901.

1796  Ingersoll, Lurton D. A History of the War Department of the United
      States, with Biographical Sketches of the Secretaries. Washington:
      F.B. Mohun, 1879.

1797  O'Connell, Charles F. "The United States Army and the Origins of
      Modern Management, 1818-1860." Ph. D. dissertation, Ohio State
      University, 1982.

1798  Smith, Carlton B. "The United States War Department, 1815-1842."
      Ph. D. dissertation, University of Virginia, 1967.

1799  Stafford, G.M., ed. "The Autobiography of George Mason Graham,"
      Louisiana Historical Quarterly 20 (1937): 43-57.

1800  Ward, Harry M. The Department of War, 1781-1795. Pittsburgh:
      University of Pittsburgh, 1962.

1801  White, Leonard D. The Federalists: A Study in Administrative History,
      1789-1802. New York: Macmillan, 1948.

1802  _____. The Jeffersonians: A Study in Administrative History, 1801-
      1829. New York: Macmillan, 1951.

1803  _____. The Jacksonians: A Study in Administrative History, 1801-1829.
      New York: Macmillan, 1961.

      SEE ALSO: John Bell, John C. Calhoun, Lewis Cass, William H. Crawford,
      James McHenry, William L. Marcy, Benjamin Stoddert

                              GENERAL STAFF

1804  Carter, William G. Creation of the American General Staff; Personal
      Narrative of the General Staff System of the American Army.
      Washington, DC: Government Printing Office, 1924.

1805  DeWitt, John L. "Brief Historical Description of the Organization
      of the War Department General Staff," Quartermaster Review 12 (1932):
      29-32.

1806  Eliot, George F. "The Hilt of the Sword," Marine Corps Gazette 53
      (1969): 20-27.

1807  Hargreaves, Reginald. "The Brass," United States Naval Institute
      Proceedings 100 (1974): 63-70.

1808  Hittle, James D. The Military Staff: Its History and Development.
      Harrisburg, PA: Military Service Publishing Co., 1949.

1809  A Memoir on the Principles and the Means of Organizing the General
      Staff of the United States Military Power. N.p., 1812.

1810  Murphy, James. "Evolution of the General Staff Concept," Defense
      Management Journal 12 (1976): 34-39.

1811  Semonie, Frank L. Structure and Policy: The Evolution of the Military
      Staff. New York: New York University Press, 1975.

1812  Tarr, Curtis W. "Unification of America's Armed Forces: A Century
      and a Half of Conflict." Ph. D. dissertation, Stanford University,
      1962.

1813  Thian, Raphael P. Legislative History of the General Staff of the Army of the United States...from 1775 to 1901. Washington, DC: Government Printing Office, 1901.

1814  Vaulx 8 [Pseud] "The Evolution of a General Staff," Journal of the Military Service Institute 33 (1903): 200-06.

SEE ALSO: 2974

### ADJUTANT GENERAL'S DEPARTMENT

1815  Fry, James B. A Sketch of the Adjutant General's Department, U.S. Army, from 1775 to 1875. New York: N.p., 1875.

1816  Hughes, Patrick J. "The Adjutant General's Office, 1821-1861: A Study in Administrative History." Ph. D. dissertation, Ohio State University, 1977.

### INSPECTOR GENERAL'S DEPARTMENT

1817  Clary, David A. and Joseph W. Whithorne. The Inspector Generals of The United States Army, 1777-1903. Washington, DC: Office of the Inspector General, 1987.

1818  Marcy, Randolph B. Historical Sketch of the Inspector General's Department. Washington, DC: N.p., 1876.

1819  Sanger, J.P. "The Inspector General's Department." In: Theophilus Rodenbough and William L. Haskin, eds. The Army of the United States. New York: Maynard, Merrill, 1896, 12-32.

1820       . "The Inspector General's Department," Journal of the Military Service Institute 16 (1895): 417-37.

SEE ALSO: 2783, Sylvester Churchill

### JUDGE ADVOCATE GENERAL'S DEPARTMENT

1821  The Army Lawyer: A History of the Judge Advocate General's Corps, 1775-1975. Washington, DC: Government Printing Office, 1975.

1822  Clous, J.W. "The Judge Advocate General's Department." In: Theophilus Rodenbough and William L. Haskin, eds. The Army of the United States. New York: Maynard, Merrill, 1896, 33-37.

1823  Fratcher, William F. "Notes on the History of the Judge Advocate General's Department, 1775-1941," Judge Advocate Journal 1 (1944): 5-15.

1824       . "History of the Judge Advocate General's Corps, United States Army," Military Law Review 4 (1959): 89-122.

1825       . and Thomas M. Green. "History of the Judge Advocate General's Department," Army Lawyer 30 (1975): 13-16.

1826  Generous, William T. "Swords and Scales: The Development of the Uniform Code of Military Justice." Ph. D. dissertation, Stanford University, 1971.

1827  Stansfield, George J. "A History of the Judge Advocate General's Department, United States Army," Military Affairs 9 (1945): 219-37.

1828  Winthrop, William W. Military Law and Precedents. 2 Vols.
      Boston: Little, Brown, 1896.

1829  Wurfel, Seymour W. "Military Habeas Corpus," Michigan Law Review
      49 (1951): 493-528.

*QUARTERMASTER'S DEPARTMENT

1830  Cooke, Jacob E. Tench Coxe and the Early Republic. Chapel Hill:
      University of North Carolina Press, 1978.

1831  Fitzgerald, F.V. "Footprints in History and Steps in its Development,"
      Quartermaster Review 10 (1931): 11-19.

1832  Hagen, Fred E. "The Story of the Quartermaster Corps, 1775-1927,"
      Ibid 7 (1927): 33-37.

1833  _____. "Early Military Records and Memoranda," Ibid 15 (1935): 30-40.

1834  Kieffer, C.L. "Quartermaster Generals of the Past," Ibid 32 (1953):
      18-21, 124-28.

1835  Long, Oscar F. "The Quartermaster General's Department." In: Theoph-
      philus Rodenbaugh and William Haskin.  The Army of the United States.
      New York: Maynard, Merrill, 1896, 38-66.

1836  Risch, Erna. "Quartermasters General of the Past," Quartermaster
      Review 32 (1953): 31-34, 159-62.

1837  Rowan, John V. "Origin and Function of the Quartermaster Corps,"
      Ibid 16 (1936): 29-34, 74.

1838  System of Accountability for Clothing and Camp Equipage Issued to
      the Army of the United States. Washington, DC: James C. Dunn, 1827.

1839  U.S. Quartermaster Department. Regulations of the Quartermaster
      Department. Washington, DC: J. & G.S. Gideon, 1841.

      SEE ALSO: Food and Supplies, Thomas S. Jesup

*MEDICAL DEPARTMENT

1840  Ashburn, Percy M. A History of the Medical Department of the United
      States Army. Boston: Houghton, Mifflin, 1929.

1841  _____. "Gleanings from Medical Department History," Military Surgeon
      64 (1929): 442-50.

1842  Duncan, Louis C. "How the Medical Department Secured Rank in the Army,"
      Military Surgeon 45 (1929): 870-72.

1843  Gillett, Mary C. The Army Medical Department, 1818-1865. Washington:
      Center of Military History, 1987.

1844  Morgan, William G. "Contributions of the Medical Department of the
      United States Army to the Advancement of Knowledge," Military Surgeon
      66 (1930): 779-90.

1845  Owen, William O. A Chronicle of Congressional Legislation Relating
      to the Medical Corps of the United States Army from 1785 to 1917.
      Chicago: American Medical Association, 1918.

1846  Pilcher, James E. The Surgeon Generals of the Army of the United
States of America. Carlisle, PA: Association of Military Surgeons,
1905.

1847  Regulations for the Medical Department of the Army. Washington, DC:
Charles H. Barron, 1832.

1848  Scheirer, George A. Notes on the Army Surgeon General's Office in
Washington, 1818-1948. Washington, DC: N.p., 1948.

1849  Smart, Charles. "The Medical Department." In: Theophilus Rodenbough
and William L. Haskin, eds. The Army of the United States. New York:
Maynard, Merrill, 1896, 83-99.

SEE ALSO: Military Medicine, James Tilton

SUBSISTENCE DEPARTMENT

1850  Barriger, John W. Legislative History of the Subsistence Department,
U.S. Army, 1775-1876. Washington: Government Printing Office, 1876.

1851  ____. "The Subsistence Department." In: Theophilus Rodenbough and
William L. Haskin, eds. The Army of the United States. New York:
Maynard, Merrill, 1896, 67-82.

1852  Regulations for the Subsistence Department of the Army. Washington:
Blair, Rivers, 1835.

ORDNANCE DEPARTMENT

1853  DeCaindry, William A. A Compilation of the Laws of the United States
Relating to and Affecting the Ordnance Department. Washington, DC:
Government Printing Office, 1872.

1854  Dutton, C.E. "The Ordnance Department." In: Theophilus Rodenbough
and William L. Haskin, eds. The Army of the United States. New York:
Maynard, Merrill, 1896, 126-35.

1855  U.S. Ordnance Department. Ordnance Manual for the Use of Officers
of the United States Army. Washington, DC: J. & G.S. Gideon, 1841.

1856  ____. Regulations for the Government of the Ordnance Department.
Washington, DC: Francis P. Blair, 1834.

SEE ALSO: Alfred Mordecai, Decius Wadsworth

PAY DEPARTMENT

1857  Carey, Asa B. Sketch of the Organization of the Pay Department of
the U.S. Army from 1775 to 1876. Washington, DC: Government Printing
Office, 1876.

1858  ____. "The Pay Department." In: Theophilus Rodenbough and William
L. Haskin, eds. The Army of the United States. New York: Maynard,
Merrill, 1896, 100-10.

1859  Exley, Thomas M. A Compendium of the Pay of the Army from 1785 to
1888. Washington, DC: Government Printing Office, 1888.

PRINTED REGULATIONS

1860  American State Papers: Military Affairs. 7 Vols. Washington, DC:
      Gales, Seaton, 1832-1861.

1861  Callan, John F. Military Laws of the United States. Baltimore:
      John Murphy, 1858.

1862  Cooling, Benjamin F. The New American States Papers: Military Affairs.
      19 Vols. Wilmington, DE: Scholarly Resources, 1979.

1863  Cross, Trueman. Military Laws of the United States to which is
      Prefixed the Constitution of the United States. Washington, DC:
      E. DeKrafft, 1825.

1864  Hetzel, Abner R., comp. Military Laws of the United States; including
      those Relating to the Army, Marine Corps, Volunteers, Militia, and
      to Bounty Lands and Pensions. Washington, DC: George Templeman, 1846.

1865  Laws of the United States of America, from March 1789 to March
      Washington, DC: John Biven, W. John Duane, 1815.

1866  Macomb, Alexander. Memoir of the Organization of the Army of the
      United States, with a View to its Giving effect to the Militia,
      when called into Actual Service. Georgetown, DC: James C. Dunn,
      1826.

1867  Mordecai, Alfred. A Digest of the Laws Relating to the Military
      Establishment of the United States. Washington, DC: Thompson,
      Homans, 1833.

1868  War Department. General Regulations for the Army; of Military
      Institutes. Philadelphia: M. Carey & Sons, 1821.

1869  _____. Regulations Established for the Organization and Government
      of the Military Academy at West Point, New York. New York: Wiley,
      Putnam, 1839.

1870  _____. General Regulations for the Army of the United States, 1841.
      Washington, DC: J. & G.S. Gideon, 1841.

CONTEMPORARY ACCOUNTS

1871  "Army Attack and National Defense," American Whig Review 4 (1846):
      146-60.

1872  "Army of the United States," American Quarterly Review 13 (1833):
      298-313.

1873  Alexander, James E. "Notes on the Army of the United States,"
      Military and Naval Magazine 1 (1833): 97-108.

1874  "The Army and Navy of the United States in 1840," Museum of Foreign
      Literature 41 (1841): 599-603.

1875  "Army of the United States," Military and Naval Magazine 2 (1833):
      21-36.

1876  "Army of the United States," North American Review 23 (1826): 245-74.

1877   "Army Organization," United States Magazine and Democratic Review 16 (1845): 121-36.

1878   Butler, Benjamin F. The Military Profession in the United States, and the means of Promoting its usefulness and Honor. New York: Samuel Colman, 1839.

1879   "Foreign Miscellany," Army and Navy Chronicle 8 (1839): 369-76.

1880   A Memoir on the Present Military Posture of the Affairs of the United States, and on the Means by which the Measures of the Government may be Rendered More Efficient than they have been Since the Declaration of War. N.p., 1812.

1881   "Military Affairs of the Nation," North American Review 61 (1845): 320-49.

1882   The Military Monitor, or, Advice to the Officers and Soldiers of the American Army. Baltimore: J.C. O'Reilly, 1813.

1883   "National Defense," North American Review 52 (1841): 1-30.

1884   "Notes on Our Army," Southern Literary Messenger 10 (1844): 86-88, 155-57, 246-51, 283-87, 372-77, 750-53.

1885   "Notes on the Army of the United States of America," Military and Naval Magazine 1 (1833): 98-108.

1886   "On Popular Prejudices Against Military Establishments," Military and Naval Magazine 1 (1833): 292-303.

1887   Perry, Milton F., ed. "The American Military of 1825 through Foreign Eyes," Military Collector and Historian 8 (1956): 95-97.

1888   Poinsett, Joel R. "Army Organization," United States Magazine and Democratic Review 16 (1845): 121-36.

1889   Prucha, Francis P. "The United States Army as Viewed by British Travellers, 1825-1860," Military Affairs 17 (1953): 113-24.

1890   "Some Account of the American Army," Port Folio 4 (1817): 9-36.

*INFANTRY

1891   Balough, George W. "The Regular Army in the Black Hawk War," Order of the Indian Wars Journal 1 (1980): 18-27.

1892   Coakley, Robert L. Evolution of the Enlisted Grade Structure of the U.S. Army, 1775-1959. Washington, DC: Office, Chief of Military History, 1966.

1893   Mahon, John K. Infantry, Part I: Regular Army. Washington, DC: Office, Chief of Military History, 1972.

1894   "Outline Histories of Infantry Regiments," Infantry Journal 19 (1921): 659-70.

1895   Urwin, Gregory J. and Darby Erd. The United States Infantry: An Illustrated History, 1775-1918. Dorset, ENG: Blanford Press, 1988.

RIFLE REGIMENT

1896    Austerman, Wayne R. "This Excellent and Gallant Rifle Corps,"
        Man at Arms 3 (1981): 18-24, 44.

1897    Lewis, Berkeley. "Early U.S. Riflemen: Their Arms and Training,"
        American Riflemen 106 (1958): 30-33.

        SEE ALSO: 2300 , 2308 , 2376 , Yellowstone Expedition

FIRST INFANTRY

1898    Buchwald, Donald M. "History of the First United States Infantry
        Regiment, 1741-1860." Master's Thesis, Fairleigh Dickinson University,
        1966.

1899    "The First Regiment of Infantry," Journal of the Military Service
        Institute 16 (1895): 197-209.

SECOND INFANTRY

1900    Shaw, Frederick B. One Hundred and Forty Years of Service in Peace
        and War; History of the Second Infantry. Detroit: Strathmore Press,
        1930.

1901    Wright, W.M. "The Second Regiment of Infantry," Journal of the
        Military Service Institute 16 (1895): 438-55.

THIRD INFANTRY

1902    McRae, J.H. "The Third Regiment of Infantry," Journal of the Military
        Service Institute 16 (1895): 674-93.

FOURTH INFANTRY

1903    "History of the Old Fourth Infantry," House Reports  322. 27th Cong.
        2d Session. (1841-1843), I.

1904    Hodges, C.B. "An Old Regiment of Regulars," Ohio Illustrated Magazine
        3 (1907): 211-18.

1905    Leyden, James A. A Historical Sketch of the Fourth Infantry from
        1796 to 1891. Fort Sherman, ID: Regimental Press, 1891.

1906    _____. "Fourth Regiment of Infantry," Journal of the Military Service
        Institute 15 (1894): 219-32.

1907    Powell, William H. A History of the Organization and Movement of the
        Fourth Regiment of Infantry, U.S. Army, from May 30, 1796 to December
        31, 1870. Washington, DC: M'Gill, Witherow, 1871.

FIFTH INFANTRY

1908    "The Fifth Regiment of Infantry," Journal of the Military Service
        Institute 15 (1894): 1093-1106.

SIXTH INFANTRY

1909    Babcock, Elkanah. A War History of the Sixth U.S. Infantry from
        1798 to 1903. Kansas City, MO: Hudson Kimberly, 1903.

1910   Byrne, Charles. "The Sixth Regiment of Infantry," Journal of the
       Military Service Institute 15 (1894): 642-59.

1911   Ryther, Dwight W. "The One Hundredth Anniversary of the Organization
       of the Sixth U.S. Infantry," Journal of the Military Service Institute
       43 (1908): 277-80.

                          SEVENTH INFANTRY

1912   Johnson, Alfred B. "The Seventh Regiment of Infantry," Journal of
       the Military Service Institute 15 (1894): 896-908.

                          EIGHTH INFANTRY

1913   Wilhelm, Thomas. History of the Eighth U.S. Infantry, from its
       Organization in 1838. 2 Vols. New York: Eighth Infantry, 1873.

1914   Wilson, Richard H. "The Eighth Regiment of Infantry," Journal of
       the Military Service Institute 15 (1894): 660-74.

                          *CAVALRY

1915   Barton, Henry W. "The United States Cavalry and the Texas Rangers,"
       Southwest Historical Quarterly 63 (1960): 495-510.

1916   Brackett, Albert G. History of the United States Cavalry, from the
       Foundation of the Federal Government to the 1st of June, 1861.
       New York: Harper & Bros, 1865.

1917   Butterworth, William E. Soldiers on Horseback: The Story of the
       United States Cavalry. New York: W.W. Norton, 1968.

1918   Carter, William H. "Early History of the American Cavalry," Cavalry
       Journal 34 (1925): 7-18.

1919   Essin, Emmett M. "The Cavalry and the Horse." Ph. D. dissertation,
       Texas Christian University, 1968.

1920   Herr, John K. and Edward S. Wallace. The Story of the U.S. Cavalry,
       1775-1942. Boston: Little, Brown, 1953.

1921   Hickok, H.R. "Our Cavalry Organization as Viewed in the Light of its
       History and Legislation," Journal of the U.S. Cavalry Association
       22 (1911-1912): 995-1009.

1922   Langellier, John P. "Sabers, Saddles and Shakos: The Formative
       Years of the Regiment of Dragoons, 1833-1846," Gateway Heritage
       4 (1983): 38-48.

1923   Merrill, James M. Spurs to Glory: The Story of the U.S. Cavalry.
       New York: Rand-McNally, 1966, 15-50.

1924   Sawicki, James A. Cavalry Regiments of the U.S. Army. Dumfries, VA:
       Wyvern Press, 1987.

1925   Urwin, Gregory J. The United States Cavalry: An Illustrated History.
       Dorset, ENG: Blandford Press, 1983.

1926   Wormser, Richard. The Yellowlegs: The Story of the United States
       Cavalry. Garden City, NY: Doubleday, 1966, 41-78.

1927  Young, Otis E. "The Rise of Cavalry in the Old West," Westerners
      Brand Book 14 (1957): 49-51, 55-56.

      SEE ALSO: Cavalry Expeditions, Military Escorts, 2251, 2256, 2259,
      2345, 2354, 2357, 2363, 2369, 2372, 2384, 2385, 2395, 2755, 2758,
      2768, 2799, 2859

MOUNTED RANGER BATTALION

1928  Foreman, Grant. Pioneer Days in the Early Southwest. Cleveland:
      Arthur H. Clark, 1926, 85-108.

1929  Irving, Washington. The Crayon Miscellany. Philadelphia: Carey,
      Lea, Blanchard, 1835, 47-181.

1930  Latrobe, Charles J. The Rambler in North America. 2 Vols. London:
      R.B. Seeley, W. Burnside, 1835. Vol. 1, 179-248.

1931  U.S. War Department. Rules and Regulations for Government of the
      Mounted Rangers. Washington, DC: F.P. BLair, 1832.

1932  Young, Otis E. "The United States Mounted Ranger Battalion, 1832-
      1833," Mississippi Valley Historical Review 41 (1954): 453-70.

      SEE ALSO: Henry Dodge

FIRST DRAGOONS

1933  "The First Regiment of Cavalry, United States Army," Cavalry Journal
      30 (1921): 343-53.

1934  Hughes, Willis B. "The First Dragoons on the Western Frontier, 1834-
      1846," Arizona and the West 12 (1970): 115-38.

1935  Parrot, James C. "The First United States Dragoons," Iowa Historical
      Record 6 (1890): 523-26.

1936  "United States Dragoons," Military and Naval Magazine 3 (1834):
      427-34.

1937  "United States Dragoons," Ibid 1 (1833): 118-22.

1938  Wainwright, R.P. "The First Regiment of Cavalry," Journal of the
      Military Service Institute 16 (1895): 177-96.

1939  ____. History of the First U.S. Cavalry, 1833-1906. Fort Clark:
      Regimental Press, 1906.

1940  ____. "The First Regiment of Cavalry," By Valor and Arms 1 (1975):
      32-47.

      SEE ALSO: Philip St. G. Cooke, Henry Dodge, Henry Leavenworth,
      Richard B. Mason

SECOND DRAGOONS

1941  Bates, Alfred E. "The Second Regiment of Cavalry," Journal of the
      Military Service Institute 13 (1892): 623-42.

1942  Brackett, Albert G. "The Story of A Regiment," American Historical
      Record 1 (1872): 488-94.

1943  Fleming, David. "The Second Dragoons," Journal of the Military Service
      Institute 49 (1911): 193-208.

1944  Hostetter, John D. "The Second Dragoons and American Expansion."
      Master's Thesis, Florida States University, 1964.

1945  Lambert, Joseph I. One Hundred Years with the Second Cavalry.
      Fort Riley: Capper Printing Co., 1939.

1946  "Remounting the Second Dragoons." 28th Cong. 1st Session. House
      Report 77 (Serial 445) 1844.

1947  Rodenbough, Theophilus F. From Everglade to Canon with the Second
      Dragoons. New York: Van Nostrand, 1875.

1948  Ruggles, W.B. "The Story of a Regiment: The Second Dragoons,"
      Magazine of History 14 (1911): 31-42.

1949  "Sketch of the Second Cavalry," Midwestern 2 (1908): 39-66.

1950  Thompson, Christopher P. and Kenneth E. Morrison. "Second Dragoons
      Mark their 150th Anniversary of Continuous Service," Armor 95 (1986):
      22-29.

      SEE ALSO: William S. Harney

## *ARTILLERY

1951  "The Ancient and Honorable Artillery Company of Massachusetts, 1638-
      1884," United Service 12 (1885): 156-68.

1952  Azoy, A.C. "Great Guns: A History of the Coast Artillery Corps,"
      Coastal Artillery Journal 84 (1941): 426-34.

1953  Babcock, D.S. "The History of Battery 'D', 1st Field Artillery,
      1792-1934," Field Artillery Journal 24 (1934): 483-504.

1954  Bazelon, Bruce S. and William F. McGuinn. A Directory of Military
      Dealers and Makers, 1785-1885. Harrisburg, PA: Privately Printed,
      1987.

1955  Birnie, Rogers. "Origins of our Modern Guns, the Transition from
      Iron to Steel," Army Ordnance 16 (1934): 147-57.

1956  Bush, George F. "Early American Rockets," Aerospace Historian 16
      (1969): 22-25.

1957  Caruana, Adrian B. "Iron Mortars in 1812," Arms Collecting 25 (1987):
      125-30.

1958  Casey, Powell A. "Early History of the Washington Artillery of New
      Orleans," Louisiana Historical Quarterly 23 (1940): 471-84.

1959  Downey, Fairfax. Sound of the Guns: The Story of American Artillery
      from the Ancient and Honorable Company to the Atom Cannon and Guided
      Missles. New York: McKay, 1956.

1960  "Early Artillery Organization," Coastal Artillery Journal 69 (1928):
      418-25.

1961 Falk, Stanley. "Artillery for the Land Service: The Development of a System," Military Affairs 28 (1964): 94-122.

1962 Ezell, Edward C. "The Development of Artillery for the United States Land Service before 1861: with Special Emphasis on the Rodman Gun." Master's Thesis, University of Delaware, 1963.

1963 Haskin, William L. "The Organization and Material of the Artillery before the Civil War," Journal of the Military Service Institute 3 (1882): 403-09.

1964 Hatch, H.J. "A History of the Coast Artillery Board and its Work," Coastal Artillery Journal 60 (1924): 453-69.

1965 "Horse Artillery," Army and Navy Chronicle 10 (1840): 227-28.

1966 Hunt, Henry J. "Our Experience in Artillery Administration," Journal of the Military Service Institute 12 (1891): 197-224.

1967 Kahler, Herbert E. "Hot Shot Furnaces," Regional Review 2 (1939): 11-13.

1968 Larter, Harry C. "Material of the First American Light Artillery," Military Collector and Historian 4 (1952): 53-63.

1969 Manucy, Albert. Artillery Through the Ages. Washington, DC: Government Printing Office, 1949.

1970 Olejar, Paul D. "Rockets in Early American Wars," Military Affairs 10 (1946): 16-34.

1971 Paulding, J.N. The Cannon and Projectiles invented by Robert Parker Parrott. New York; N.p., 1879.

1972 Peterson, Harold L. Roundshot and Rammers. Harrisburg, PA: Stackpole Books, 1969.

1973 Poore, Benjamin P. "The Ancient and Honorable Artillery Company of Massachusetts, 1638-1884," United Service 12 (1885): 156-68.

1974 Raoul, Margaret L. "Gouverneur Kemble and the West Point Foundary," Americana 30 (1936): 461-73.

1975 Schenck, A.D. "Evolution of the Organization of Field Artillery," United Service 2 (1902): 565-626.

1976 Trussell, John B. "The Spirit of the Corps-A Guide for the Future," Anti-Aircraft Journal 96 (1953): 11-14.

1977 Tschappat, William H. "Early History of American Ordnance: A Chronology of Munitions in the United States," Army Ordnance 13 (1933): 333-38; 14 (1934): 14-18, 76-82.

1978 Wade, William. "Early Systems of Artillery," Ordnance Notes No. 25 (1874): 79-87.

1979 Wynne, James. Memoir of Major Samuel Ringgold, United States Army. Baltimore: J. Murphy, 1847.

SEE ALSO: 2095, 2272, 2982, 3011, Henry Burbeck, Alfred Mordecai Louis de Tousard, Decius Wadsworth

FIRST ARTILLERY

1980   Haskin, William L. The History of the First Artillery, from its
       Organization in 1821 to January 1, 1876. Portland, ME: B. Thurston,
       1879.

SECOND ARTILLERY

1981   Simpson, W.A. "The Second Regiment of Artillery." In: Theophilus
       Rodenbough and William L. Haskin, eds. The Army of the United States.
       New York: Maynard, Merrill, 1896, 312-27.

THIRD ARTILLERY

1982   Birkhimer, William E. "The Third Regiment of Artillery." In: Theophilus
       Rodenbough and William L. Haskin, eds. The Army of the United States.
       New York: Maynard, Merrill, 1896, 328-50.

FOURTH ARTILLERY

1983   Dyer, Alexander B. "The Fourth Regiment of Artillery." In: Theophilus
       Rodenbough and William L. Haskin, eds. The Army of the United States.
       New York: Maynard, Merrill, 1896, 351-75.

*ENGINEERS

1984   Abbot, Henry L. "The Corps of Engineers." In: Theophilus Rodenbough
       and William L. Haskin, eds. The Army of the United States. New York:
       Maynard, Merrill, 1896, 111-25.

1985   Allin, Lawrence C. "Four Engineers on the Missouri: Long, Fremont,
       Humphreys, and Warren," Nebraska History 65 (1984): 58-83.

1986   Beers, Henry P. "A History of the Topographical Engineers, 1813-
       1863," Military Engineer  34 (1942): 384-52.

1987   Burr, Edward. Historical Sketch of the Corps of Engineers, U.S. Army.
       Washington, DC: Government Printing Office, 1939.

1988   Calhoun, Daniel H. "The American Civil Engineer, 1792-1843." Ph. D.
       dissertation, Johns Hopkins University, 1956.

1989   Casey, Thomas L. Letter from the Chief of Engineers to the Secretary
       of War, Containing a Historical Sketch of the Corps of Engineers.
       Washington, DC: Government Printing Office, 1876.

1990   Crump, Irving. Our Army Engineers. New York: Dodd, Mead, 1954.

1991   Cullum, George W. Biographical Sketch of Captain William H. Swift of
       the Topographical Engineers, United States Army, 1832-1849. New York:
       A.G. Sherwood, 1880.

1992   _____. In Memory of Col. James Monroe. New York: N.p., 1870.

1993   Drakes-Wilkes, L.P.  "United States Army: History and Traditions
       of the Corps of Engineers," Canadian Army Journal 6 (1953): 57-73.

1994   Forman, Sidney. "The United States Military Philosophical Society,
       1802-1813," William and Mary Quarterly 2 (1945): 273-85.

1995 Hill, Forest G. "The Role of the Army Engineers in the Planning and Encouragement of Internal Improvement." Ph. D. dissertation, Columbia University, 1950.

1996 Holden, Edward S, ed. "Biographical memoirs of William H.C. Bartlett, 1804-1893," National Academy of Sciences. Biographical Memoirs (1911): Vol. 7, 171-93.

1997 Holt, W. Stull. The Office of the Chief of Engineers of the Army: Its Non-Military History, Activities and Organization. Baltimore: Johns Hopkins University Press, 1923.

1998 Jewett, Henry C. "History of the Corps of Engineers to 1915," Military Engineer 14 (1922): 304-6, 385-88.

1999 Johnson, Leland R. "A History of the Operations of the Corps of Engineers, U.S. Army in the Cumberland and Tennessee River Valleys." Ph. D. dissertation, Vanderbilt University, 1972.

2000 _____. "Army Engineers on the Cumberland and Tennessee, 1824-1954," Tennessee Historical Quarterly 31 (1972): 149-69.

2001 _____. "Nineteenth Century Military Engineering: The Contest of 1824," Military Engineer 65 (1973): 166-71.

2002 _____. "Sword, Shovel, and Compass," Ibid 68 (1976): 159-65.

2003 Kanarek, Harold. "The U.S. Army Corps of Engineers and Early Internal Improvements in Maryland," Maryland Historical Magazine 72 (1977): 99-109.

2004 Lenny, John J. Caste System in the American Army: A Study of the Corps of Engineers and the West Point System. New York: Ib Greenberg, 1949.

2005 O'Connell, Charles F. "The Corps of Engineers and the Rise of Modern Management." In: Military Enterprise and Technological Change: Perspectives on the American Experience. Cambridge, MA: MIT Press, 1985, 87-116.

2006 Ryan, Garry D. "War Department Topographical Bureau, 1831-1863: An Administrative History." Ph. D. dissertation, American University, 1968.

2007 Schubert, Frank N., ed. The Nation Builders: A Sesquicentennial History of the Corps of Topographical Engineers, 1838-1863. Washington, DC: Government Printing Office, 1988.

2008 Shallat, Todd A. "Structures in the Stream: A History of Water, Science, and Civil Activities of the U.S. Army Corps of Engineers, 1700-1861." Ph. D. dissertation, Carnegie-Mellon University, 1986.

2009 Stoddard, Francis R. "Amiel Weeks Whipple, 1817-1863," Chronicles of Oklahoma 28 (1950): 226-34.

2010 Thian, Raphael. Notes Illustrating the Military Geography of the United States, 1813-1880. Washington, DC: Government Printing Office, 1881.

2011 United States. Engineering School Museum. Genesis of the Corps of Engineers, including Portraits and Profiles of its Forty Chiefs. Fort Belvoir, VA: N.p., 1953.

2012   U.S. Army. Office of the Chief of Engineers. Laws of the United States Relating to the Improvement of Rivers and Harbors, from August 11, 1790 to January 2, 1939. 3 Vols. Washington, DC: Government Printing Office, 1913, 1940.

2013   Walker, Charles E. "Engineers in the War of 1812." Typescript at the Historical Division, U.S. Army Corps of Engineers, Fort Belvoir, Virginia.

2014   Youngberg, Gilbert A. History of the Engineer Troops in the United States Army, 1775-1901. Washington, DC: Engineer School Press, 1910.

        SEE ALSO: 2143, 2374, 2712, 2718, 2727, 2730, 2897, 2899, 2935, 2945, 2982, Simon Bernard, Rene DeRussy, Charles Gratiot, Andrew Humphreys, Robert E. Lee, Ormsby M. Mitchel, Joseph G. Swift, George W. Whistler

## U.S. MILITARY ACADEMY

2015   Ambrose, Stephen. Duty, Honor, Country: A history of West Point. Baltimore: Johns Hopkins Press, 1966.

2016   Bell, William G. "A Test of the Academy's Independence," Military Review 44 (1964): 57-62.

2017   Boynton, Edward C. History of West Point, and its Military Importance during the Revolution, and the Origin and Progress of the U.S. Military Academy. New York: D. Van Nostrand, 1863.

2018   Carter, William H. "West Point in Literature," Journal of the Military Service Institute 43 (1908): 378-83.

2019   Crackel, Theodore J. "The Founding of West Point: Jefferson and the Politics of Security," Armed Forces and Society 7 (1981): 529-43.

2020   Cullum, George W. "The Early Years of the United States Military Academy." In: Biographical Register of the Officers and Graduates of the United States Military Academy at West Point, New York, from its Establishment in 1802 to 1890. 3 Vols. New York: Houghton, Mifflin, 1891. Vol. 3, 467-672.

2021   Denton, Edgar. "The Formative Years of the United States Military Academy." Ph. D. dissertation, Syracuse University, 1964.

2022   Dupuy, R. Ernest. Where They Have Trod: The West Point Tradition In American Life. New York: Frederick A. Stokes, 1940.

2023   Ellis, Joseph and Robert Moore. School for Soldiers: West Point and the Profession of Arms. New York: Oxford University Press, 1974.

2024   Farley, J.P. "West Point-Past and Present," United Service 7 (1905): 174-89.

2025   Fleming, Thomas J. West Point: the Men and the Times of the United States Military Academy. New York: William Morrow, 1969.

2026   Forman, Sidney. West Point: A History of the United States Military Academy. New York: Johns Hopkins Press, 1950.

2027   _____. "Why the U.S. Military Academy was Established in 1802," Military Affairs 29 (1965): 16-25.

2028  Hicks, F.H. "The Story of West Point," Mentor 12 (1924): 6-17.

2029  Holden, Edward S. "Origins of the United States Military Academy,
      1777-1802." In: Centennial of the United States Military Academy at
      West Point, New York, 1802-1902. 2 Vols. Washington: Government
      Printing Office, 1904. Vol. 1, 201-22.

2030  Knowlton, Miner. Lands Belonging to the United States at West Point.
      Washington, DC: N.p., 1839.

2031  McMaster, Richard K. West Point's Contribution to Education, 1802-1952.
      El Paso, TX: McMath Printing Co., 1951.

2032  "The Military Academy at West Point," American Journal of Education
      13 (1863): 17-48.

2033  Morrison, James L. The Best School in the World: West Point, the
      Pre-Civil War Years, 1833-1866. Kent, OH: Kent State Press, 1986.

2034  Park, Roswell. A Sketch of the History and Topography of West Point
      and the U.S. Military Academy. Philadelphia: Henry Perkins, 1840.

2035  Preston, Richard A. "Perspectives in the History of Military Education
      and Professionalism," Harmon Memorial Lectures in Military History
      22 (1980): 1-37.

2036  Rodenbough, Theophilus F. "Early West Point," Journal of the Military
      Service Institute 117 (1910): 431-35.

2037  Segwick, Theodore. "West Point in 1824," Nation 90 (1910): 455-56.

2038  Tillman, S.F. "A Review of West Point's Military History," Journal
      of the Military Service Institute 58 (1916): 184-96.

2039  U.S. Military Academy. Regulations for the U.S. Military Academy at
      West Point, New York. 20 Vols. Washington, DC: Government Printing
      Office, 1820-1932.

2040  Waugh, E.D. West Point. New York: Macmillan, 1944.

      SEE ALSO: 2110, 2375, Henry Burbeck, Jefferson Davis, Robert E. Lee,
      Denis H. Mahan, Jared Mansfield, David Moniac, Alfred Mordecai, Alden
      Partridge, Edgar A. Poe, Sylvanus Thayer, Louis DeTousard, Johnathan
      Williams

                          MILITARY EDUCATION

2041  Ambrose, Stephen E. "This Monotonous Life," American History
      Illustrated 6 (1971): 27-32.

2042  Budka, Metchie J. "Minerva versus Archimedes," Smithsonian Journal
      of History 1 (1966): 61-64.

2043  Chaput, Donald. "The Early Missouri Graduates of West Point, Officers
      or Merchants?" Missouri Historical Review 72 (1978): 262-70.

2044  Couper, William. Cladius Crozet: Soldier, Scholar, Educator, Engineer,
      1789-1864. Charlottesville, VA: Historical Publishing Co., 1936.

2045  Dudley, Edgar S. "Was 'Secession' Taught at West Point?" Century
      Magazine 78 (1909): 632-35.

2046  Dupuy, Richard E. Men of West Point: The First 150 Years of the United States Military Academy. New York: Sloane, 1951.

2047  Fowler, Frank. "The Sully Portraits at the U.S. Military Academy," Scribner's Magazine 43 (1908): 125-28.

2048  A Guidebook to West Point and Vicinity. New York: J.H. Colton, 1844.

2049  Hall, Robert H. "Early Discipline at the United States Military Academy," Journal of the Military Service Institute 2 (1882): 448-74.

2050  Hamilton, Doris H. "Early Days at West Point," Hobbies 63 (1958): 110-11.

2051  Hruby, Dale E. "The Civilian Careers of West Point Graduates, Classes of 1802 through 1833." Master's Essay, Columbia, 1965.

2052  Kombs, John. "The Height and Weight of West Point Cadets: Dietary Change in Antebellum America," Journal of Economic History 47 (1987): 897-927.

2053  McIver, George W. "North Carolinians at West Point Before the Civil War," North Carolina Historical Review 7 (1930): 15-45.

2054  Maddox, Robert. "The Grog Mutiny: One Merry Christmas at West Point," American History Illustrated 16 (1981): 32-37.

2055  Molloy, Peter M. "Technical Education and the Young Republic: West Point as America's Ecole Polytechnique, 1802-1833." Ph. D. dissertation, Brown University, 1975.

2056  Morrison, James L. "The Struggle Between Sectionalism and Nationalism at Antebellum West Point, 1830-1861," Civil War History 19 (1973): 138-48.

2057  Ness, George T. "Missouri at West Point: Her Graduates through the Civil War Years," Missouri Historical Review 38 (1944): 162-69.

2058  Parmly, Eleazar. "West Point Folklore," New York History 33 (1952): 294-302.

2059  Rosenwaite, Ira. "Simon M. Levy: West Point Graduate," American Jewish Historical Quarterly 61 (1971): 69-73.

2060  Shaughnessy, Thomas E. "Beginnings of National Professional Military Education in America, 1775-1825." Ph. D. dissertation, Johns Hopkins University, 1957.

2061  Tilman, Samuel. "The Academic History of the Military Academy, 1802-1902." In: Centennial of the United States Military Academy at West Point, New York, 1802-1902. 2 Vols. Washington, DC: Government Printing Office, 1904. Vol. 1, 223-438.

2062  United Confederate Veterans. "A View of the Constitution," Confederate Veteran 22 (1914): 353-56.

2063  Welch, M.L. "Early West Point French Teachers and Influences," Journal of the American Society of the French Foreign Legion 26 (1955): 27-43.

2064  Winton, George P. "Antebellum Military Instruction of West Point Officers and its Influence upon Confederate Military Organization and Operations." Ph. D. dissertation, University of South Carolina, 1972.

CONTEMPORARY ACCOUNTS

2065   "Academy at West Point," American Quarterly Review 16 (1834): 358-75.

2066   Bernard, Augusta B. Reminiscences of West Point in the Olden Time. East Saginaw, MI: Evening News Printing and Binding House, 1886.

2067   Church, Albert. Personal Reminiscences of the United States Military Academy, from 1824 to 1831. West Point: U.S. Military Press, 1879.

2068   Conover, Cheryl, ed. "To Please Papa: The Letters of John Walker Barry, West Point Cadet, 1826-1830," Register of the Kentucky Historical Society 80 (1982): 182-212.

2069   Forman, Sidney, ed. Cadet Life Before the Mexican War. Episodes in Cadet Life Drawn from the Manuscript Collections in the Library of the United States Military Academy. West Point: USMA Printing Office, 1945.

2070   James, Joseph B. "Life at West Point One Hundred Years Ago," Mississippi Valley Historical Review 31 (1944): 21-40.

2071   Johnson, Richard M. "Military Academy," Military and Naval Magazine 4 (1834): 136-51.

2072   Latrobe, John H. Reminiscences of West Point from September, 1818, to March, 1882. East Saginaw, MI: Evening Printing News, 1887.

2073   _____. A Journal of March, performed by the Corps of Cadets of the United States Military Academy, in the year Eighteen Hundred and Twenty One. Newburgh: W.M. Gazlay, 1822.

2074   [Temple, Lieut.] "Military Academy," North American Review 34 (1832): 246-62.

2075   "The Military Academy," Ibid 57 (1843): 269-92.

2076   "Military Academy at West Point," Analectic Magazine 2 (1820): 171-76.

2077   "Military Academy at West Point," American Quarterly Review 22 (1837): 77-131.

2078   Morrison, James L., ed. "Getting through West Point: The Cadet Memoirs of John C. Tidball, Class of 1848," Civil War History 26 (1980): 304-25.

2079   Quiff [Pseud]. "A Plebe's Account of Himself: My Reception," Military and Naval Magazine 2 (1833): 83-87.

2080   Ramsay, George D. "Recollections of the Cadet Life of George D. Ramsay." In: George W. Cullum. Biographical Register of the Officers and Graduates of the United States Military Academy at West Point, from its Establishment in 1802 to 1890. 3 Vols. New York: Houghton, Mifflin, 1891. Vol. 3, 612-32.

2081   Rees, James. "West Point," United States Military Magazine 2 (1840): 53-55.

2082   "Report of the Board of Visitors of the United States Military Academy," Quarterly Christian Spectator 6 (1834): 345-71.

2083   Scott, Franklin D., ed. "A Swedish View of West Point in 1820,"
       New York History 33 (1952): 313–21.

2084   Sizer, Theodore. "Memoirs of West Point during the Two Decades
       Preceding the Civil War," New York Historical Society Quarterly
       41 (1957): 109–41.

2085   Smith, Francis H. "United States Military Academy," Southern Literary
       Messenger 9 (1843): 665–70.

2086   _____. West Point Fifty Years Ago. New York: D. Van Nostrand, 1879.

2087   Turner, Charles W., ed. "The Education of Col. David Bullock Harris,
       C.S.A., using his West Point Letters, 1829–1835," West Virginia
       History 46 (1985–1986): 45–57.

2088   "U.S. Military Academy," Army and Navy Chronicle and Scientific
       Repository 1 (1843): 346–50.

2089   "The United States Military Academy at West Point," American Journal
       of Education 6 (1828): 328–38.

2090   "West Point," American Journal of Scientific and Useful Knowledge
       1 (1835): 41–45.

2091   "West Point," Family Magazine or Monthly Abstract of General
       Knowledge 2 (1836): 423–27.

2092   "West Point Academy," American Quarterly Review 11 (1832): 495–503.

2093   "West Point and the United States Military Academy," New England
       Magazine 3 (1832): 265–78.

2094   "West Point Military Academy," North American Review 52 (1841): 23–30.

## MILITARY SCHOOLS

2095   Arthur, Robert. The Coastal Artillery School, 1824–1927. Fort Monroe,
       VA: Coastal Artillery School, 1928.

2096   Barnard, Henry. "Military Schools and Education," American Journal
       of Education 12 (1862): 3–400.

2097   Bond, O.J. The Story of the Citadel. Richmond: Garnett, Massie, 1936.

2098   Kraus, John D. "The Civilian Military College," Military Review 56
       (1976): 77–87.

2099   Webb, Lester A. "The Origin of Military Schools in the United States,
       Founded in the Nineteenth Century." Ph. D. dissertation, University
       of North Carolina, 1958.

2100   Wise, Jennings C. Sunrise of the Virginia Military Institute as a
       School of Arms; Spawn of the Cincinnati. Lexington, VA: N.p., 1958.

2101   _____. The Military History of the Virginia Military Institute from
       1839 to 1865. Lynchburg, VA: J.P. Bell, 1915.

## PERSONNEL

2102   Benton, William. "Pennsylvania Revolutionary Officers and the Federal
       Constitution," Pennsylvania History 31 (1964): 419–35.

2103  Brown, Russell K. "Fallen Stars," Military Affairs 45 (1981): 9-12.

2104  _____. Fallen in Battle: American General Officer Combat Fatalities
      From 1775. Westport, CT: Greenwood Press, 1988.

2105  Caldwell, Norman W. "The Frontier Army Officer, 1790-1814," Mid America
      37 (1955): 101-28.

2106  Coffman, Edward M. "The Young Officer in the Old Army," Harmon Memorial
      Lectures in Military History 18 (1976): 1-17.

2107  _____. "The Army Officer and the Constitution," Parameters 17
      (1987): 2-12.

2108  Floyd, Dale E. "U.S. Army Officers in Europe, 1815-1861." In: David
      H. White and John W. Gordon, eds. Proceedings of the Citadel Conference
      on War and Diplomacy. Charleston, SC: The Citadel, 1977, 26-30.

2109  Fredriksen, John C. Officers of the War of 1812 with Portraits and
      Anecdotes. Lewiston, NY: Edwin Mellen Press, 1989.

2110  Gordon, William A. A Compilation of Registers of the Army of the United
      States from 1815 to 1837. Washington, DC: James C. Dunn, 1937.

2111  Gough, Robert. "Officering the American Army, 1798," William and Mary
      Quarterly 43 (1986): 460-71.

2112  Hamersly, Thomas H. Complete Regular Army Register of the United States
      for One Hundred Years, 1779-1879. Washington, DC: Government Printing
      Office, 1880.

2113  Heitman, Francis B. Historical Register and Dictionary of the United
      States Army. 2 Vols. Washington, DC: Government Printing Office, 1903.

2114  Kaplan, Sidney. "Veteran Officers and Politics in Massachusetts, 1783-
      1787," William and Mary Quarterly 9 (1952): 29-57.

2115  Kemble, Charles R. "The Image of the Army Officer: The Nineteenth
      Century." Ph. D. dissertation, George Washington University, 1969.

2116  Kindred, Marilyn A. "The Army Officer Corps and the Arts: Artistic
      Patronage and Practice in America, 1820-1885." Ph. D. dissertation,
      University of Kansas, 1981.

2117  McGregor, Marylee G. "Your Friend, James Monroe," Manuscripts 39
      (1987): 219-25.

2118  Middleton, William H. The History of My Friend; shewing how He was
      Deprived of his Military Commission and left (a Cripple) to starve
      in Time of Peace. New York: N.p., 1816.

2119  Morrison, James L. "Educating the Civil War Generals: West Point, 1833-
      1861." Military Affairs 38 (1974): 108-11.

2120  Powell, William H. List of Officers of the Army of the United States
      from 1779 to 1900. New York: L.R. Hamersly, 1900.

2121  "Roster of the Officers of 'The Legion of the United States', commanded
      by Major General Anthony Wayne," Pennsylvania Magazine of History and
      Biography 16 (1892): 423-29.

2122   Senter, Nathaniel G. A Vindication of the Character of Nathaniel G.
       Senter. Hallowell, ME: E. Goodale, 1815.

2123   Skelton, William B. "The Commanding General and the Problem of Command
       in the United States Army, 1821-1841." Military Affairs 34 (1970):
       117-22.

2124   _____. "Professionalization in the U.S. Army Officer Corps during the
       Age of Jackson," Armed Forces and Society 1 (1975): 443-71.

2125   _____. "Officers and Politicians: The Origins of Army Politics in the
       United States Before the Civil War," Ibid 6 (1979): 22-48.

2126   Spiller, Roger J., ed. Dictionary of American Military Biography.
       Westport, CT: Greenwood Press, 1984.

2127   Trussell, John B. "The Role of the Professional Military Officer in
       the Preservation of the Republic," Western Pennsylvania Historical
       Magazine 60 (1977): 1-21.

2128   Wade, Arthur P. "Roads to the Top: An Analysis of General Officer
       Selection in the United States Army, 1789-1898," Military Affairs
       40 (1976): 157-63.

2129   Wright, Robert K. Soldier Statesmen of the Constitution. Washington
       Center of Military History, 1987.

       SEE ALSO: 2728 , 4810 , Edward R.S. Canby, Henry W. Halleck, William J.
       Hardee, Theophilus H. Holmes, David Hunter, Philip Kearny, Gustavus
       Loomis, Nathaniel Lyon, John B. Magruder, Montgomery C. Meigs, Martin
       Scott, Isaac Ingalls, Alexander P. Stewart, Edwin V. Sumner, David E.
       Twiggs, William Whistler

## SOCIETY OF THE CINCINNATI

2130   Adams, Samuel. "Letter of Samuel Adams to Elbridge Gerry, 1785,"
       Collector 23 (1909): 15-16.

2131   Alderman, Mrs. L. The Indentification of the Society of the Cincinnati
       with the First Authorized Settlement of the Northwest Territory at
       Marietta, Ohio, April 7, 1788. Marietta, OH: E.R. Alderman, 1888.

2132   Alexander, Charles B. "The Society of the Cincinnati and its Future,"
       Grafton Magazine 1 (1908): 1-9.

2133   Cochrane, John. "The Centennial of the Cincinnati," Magazine of
       American History 10 (1883): 171-93.

2134   Davies, Wallace E. "The Society of the Cincinnati in New England,
       1783-1800," William and Mary Quarterly 5 (1948): 3-25.

2135   Davis, Charles L. "The Society of the Cincinnati in the Southern
       States," Southern Historical Association Publications (1898): 29-33.

2136   Davis, Curtis C. Revolution's Godchild: The Birth, Death, and
       Resurrection of the Society of the Cincinnati in North Carolina.
       Chapel Hill: University of North Carolina Press, 1976.

2137   Feller, John Q. The Society of the Cincinnati, 1783-1983. Salem, MA:
       Peabody Museum, 1983.

2138  Hansen, Millard W. "The Society of the Cincinnati: Its political
      Influence in the Years 1783-1787," South Atlantic Quarterly 44
      (1945): 185-94.

2139  Hoey, Edwin A. "A 'New, Strange Order of Man'," American Heritage
      19 (1968): 44-49, 72-75.

2140  Hume, Edgar E. LaFayette and the Society of the Cincinnati.
      Baltimore: Johns Hopkins University Press, 1934.

2141  ____. "The Role of the Society of the Cincinnati in the Birth of
      the Constitution of the United States," Pennsylvania History 5
      (1938): 101-07.

2142  ____. "The Attempt to Establish a State Society of the Cincinnati
      in Kentucky," Register of the Kentucky Historical Society 32 (1934):
      199-223.

2143  ____. "The Society of the Cincinnati and the Corps of Engineers,"
      Military Engineer 25 (1933): 468-73.

2144  ____. "Early Opposition to the Cincinnati," Americana 30 (1936):
      597-638.

2145  ____. "The Naming of the City of Cincinnati," Ohio Archaeological
      and Historical Society Quarterly 44 (1935): 81-91.

2146  ____. "Steuben and the Society of the Cincinnati," American-German
      Review 1 (1935): 17-19, 54.

2147  Johnston, Alexander. "Some Account of the Society of the Cincinnati,"
      Historical Society of Pennsylvania Memoirs 6 (1858): 15-55.

2148  Kilbourne, John D. "The Society of the Cincinnati of Maryland: Its
      First One Hundred Years, 1783-1883," Maryland Historical Magazine
      78 (1983): 169-85.

2149  Lamb, John K. "The Society of the Cincinnati," Queen City Heritage
      41 (1983): 7-9.

2150  Lewis, Alonzo N. Historical Sketches of the Venerable and Illustrious
      Order of the Cincinnati. Montpelier: Argus Patriot Press, 1907.

2151  Myers, Minor. Liberty without Anarchy: A History of the Society of
      the Cincinnati. Charlottesville: University of Virginia Press, 1982.

2152  Pennington, William S. "The Beginnings of the Society of the Cincin-
      nati." In: Historical Papers Read Before the Society of the Cincin-
      nati in the State of New Jersey. New York: Collins, Day, 1897.

2153  Raiford, William R. West Point and the Society of the Cincinnati.
      Washington, DC: N.p., 1967.

2154  Roe, William J. "America's Order of Nobility," Americana 5 (1910):
      169-76.

2155  Saunders, Richard F. "The Origin and Early History of the Society of
      the Cincinnati, the Oldest Hereditary and Patriotic Organization in
      the United States." Ph. D. dissertation, University of Georgia, 1970.

2156  Sibley, Frederick T. "A Sketch of the Origin of the Society of the
      Cincinnati." In: War Papers Read Before the Commander of the State
      of Michigan Military Order of the United States. Detroit, Winn, 1893.

2157   Society of the Cincinnati. Sword and Firearm Collection of the
       Society of the Cincinnati in the Anderson House, Washington, D.C.
       Washington, DC: N.p., 1965.

2158   Stimpson, Mary S. "The Society of the Cincinnati," New England
       Magazine 44 (1911): 70-76.

2159   Thomas, William S. The Society of the Cincinnati, 1783-1935.
       New York: G.P. Putnam's Sons, 1935.

2160   Van Domelen, John E. "Hugh Henry Brackenridge and the Order of the
       Cincinnati," Western Pennsylvania Historical Magazine 47 (1964):
       47-53.

2161   Warren, Winslow. The Society of the Cincinnati, a History of the
       General Society of the Cincinnati. Boston: Massachusetts Society
       of the Cincinnati, 1929.

       SEE ALSO: 6631, 6632, Henry Knox, Winthrop Sargent

                              ENLISTED MEN

2162   Boyd, J.P. "An Eighteenth Century Recruiting Poster," Pennsylvania
       Magazine of History and Biography 60 (1936): 186-88.

2163   Carleton, William G. "Raising Armies Before the Civil War," Current
       History 54 (1968): 327-32, 363-64.

2164   Donohue, Bernardo and Marshal Smelser. "The Congressional Power to
       Raise Armies: The Constitutional and Ratifying Conventions, 1787-88,"
       Review of Politics 33 (1971): 202-12.

2165   Hargreaves, Reginald." What Sort of Recruit," Military Review 52
       (1972): 58-67.

2166   Hershey, Lewis B. "Procurement of Manpower in American Wars," Annals
       of the American Academy of Political and Social Science 241 (1945):
       15-25.

2167   Jackson, Donald. "Jefferson, Meriwether Lewis, and the Reduction of
       the United States Army," Proceedings of the American Philosophical
       Society 124 (1980): 91-96.

2168   Janowitz, Morris. "Military Insitutions and Citizenship in Western
       Societies," Armed Forces and Society 2 (1976): 185-204.

2169   Kreidberg, Marvin A. and Henry G. Merton. History of Military
       Mobilization in the United States Army, 1775-1915. Washington, DC:
       Government Printing Office, 1955.

2170   Lerwill, Leonard D. The Personnel Replacement System in the United
       States Army. Washington, DC: Department of the Army, 1954.

2171   Levine, Herbert M. "Armies of Democracy: A Problem of Historiography,"
       Studies in History and Society 6 (1975): 1-30.

2172   Logan, John A. The Volunteer Soldier of America. New York: Peale, 1887.

2173   Olsson, Nils W. "Swedish Enlistments in the U.S. Army before 1851,"
       Swedish Pioneer Historical Quarterly 1 (1951): 3-13, 17-38.

2174   "Reducing the Army A Century Ago," Cavalry Journal 32 (1923): 53-55.

2175  Regulations for the Recruiting Service of the Army of the United
      States. Washington: Francis P. Blair, 1834.

2176  Sparrow, John C. History of Personnel Demobilization in the United
      States Army. Washington: Chief of Military History, 1951.

2177  Stagg, J.C.A. "Enlisted Men in the United States Army, 1812-1815:
      A Preliminary Survey," William and Mary Quarterly 43 (1986): 615-45.

2178  Tanham, George K. "The Soldier and the Citizen," Marine Corps
      Gazette 48 (1964): 20-25.

2179  Tompkins, Avery. "Demobilization, past and Present," Infantry
      Journal 16 (1919): 93-100.

2180  War Department. Strength of the Army at Stated Periods from the
      Beginning of the Government to Date. 45th Cong. 3d Session House
      Executive Document No. 23 (1879).

2181  Williams, Wesley R. "Call to Arms: Notes from the Pages of Army
      Recruiting History," Army Digest 25 (1970): 41-44.

2182  U.S. Army. War College. History Section. A Study of Volunteer Enlist-
      ments, Army of the United States, 1775-1945. N.p., 1945.
      At U.S. Army Historical Research Center, Carlisle Barracks.

## CONSCRIPTION

2183  Armstrong, Paul G. "Selective Service: Its History and its Functions,"
      State Government 23 (1950): 267-70.

2184  Axtell, George C. and Robert S. Stubbs. "UMT: A Study," George
      Washington Law Review 20 (1952): 450-88.

2185  Barker, J. Ellis. "How America Became a Nation in Arms," Nineteenth
      Century 78 (1915): 507-40.

2186  Chambers, John W. Draftees or Volunteers: A Documentary History of
      the Debate over Military Conscription in the United States, 1787-
      1973. New York: Garland Publications, 1975.

2187  _____. "Soldiers When they Chose to Be." In: To Raise an Army: The
      Draft Comes to Modern America. New York: Free Press, 1987, 13-39.

2188  Cutler, Frederick M. "The History of Military Conscription, with
      Especial Reference to the United States." Ph. D. dissertation, Clark
      University, 1922.

2189  Davis, Henry C. "The System of Military Conscription Proposed by
      George Washington and General Henry Knox," Journal of the Military
      Service Institute 58 (1916): 1-13.

2190  Duggan, Joseph C. The Legislative and Statutory Development of the
      Federal Concept for Military Service. Washington, DC: Catholic
      University Press, 1946.

2191  Griffith, Robert K. "Conscription and the All-Volunteer Army in
      Historical Perspective," Parameters 10 (1980): 61-69.

2192  Holley, I.B. "To Defend the Nation: Conscription and the All-Volunteer
      Army in Historical Perspective," Public Historian 6 (1984): 65-71.

2193  Knight, Bruce W. "How to Round up Cannon Fodder," American Mercury 34 (1935): 31-39.

2194  Leach, Jack F. "The Law, Theory and Politics of National Conscription in the United States to the End of the Civil War." Ph. D. dissertation, University of California, Berkeley, 1943.

2195  ____. Conscription in the United States: Historical Background. Rutland, VT: C.E. Tuttle, 1952.

2196  Lewis, George G. and John Mewha. History of Prisoner of War Utilization by the United States Army, 1776-1945. Washington, DC: Department of the Army, 1955.

2197  Lofgren, Charles A. "Compulsary Military Service under the Constitution," William and Mary Quarterly 33 (1976): 61-88.

2198  Philipps, Denis S. "The American People and Compulsary Military Service." Ph. D. dissertation, New York University, 1956.

2199  Rankin, Robert H. "A History of the Selective Service," United States Naval Institute Proceedings 77 (1951): 1072-81.

2200  Renner, Richard W. "Conscientious Objection and the Federal Government," Military Affairs 78 (1974): 142-45.

2201  Rilling, Alexander W. "The Question of Universal Military Training," United States Naval Institute Proceedings 93 (1967): 65-75.

2202  Russell, R.R. "Development of Conscientious Objector Recognition in the United States," George Washington Law Review 20 (1952): 409-48.

2203  Schlissel, Lillian, ed. Conscience in America: A Documentary History of Conscientious Objection in America, 1757-1967. New York: E.P. Dutton, 1968.

2204  Tansill, Charles C. "Historical Background of Compulsary Military Service," Thought 15 (1940): 623-40.

BLACKS IN THE ARMY

2205  Arnold, Paul T. "Negro Soldiers in the United States Army," Magazine of History 10 (1909): 185-93.

2206  Ballard, Mary R. Black Liberation in Cumberland Island in 1815. DeLeon Springs, FL: E.O. Painter, 1983.

2207  Clark, Walter. "Negro Soldiers," North Carolina Booklet 18 (1918): 57-62.

2208  Davis, Paul C. "The Negro in the Armed Services," Virginia Quarterly Review 24 (1948): 499-520.

2209  Fabel, R. "King Dick-Captive Black Leader," Negro History Bulletin 36 (1973): 58-61.

2210  McGlone, John. "Monuments and Memorial to Black Military History, 1775 to 1891." Ph. D. dissertation, Middle Tennessee State University, 1985.

2211  Reddick, L.D. "The Negro Policy of the United States Army, 1775-1945,"
      Journal of Negro History 34 (1949): 9-29.

2212  Wilkes, Laura E. Missing Pages in American History, Revealing the
      Services of Negroes in the Early wars of the United States of America,
      1641-1815. Washington, DC: Press of R. L. Pendleton, 1919.

      SEE ALSO: 5594 , 5598

                              WOMEN

2213  Coffman, Edward M. "Women and Children in the Army, 1784-1812,"
      CAMP Periodical 46 (1982): 31-39.

2214  Stimson, Julia C. "The Forerunners of the American Army Nurse,"
      Military Surgeon 58 (1926): 133-41.

2215  Stewart, Miller J. "Army Laundresses: Ladies of the 'Soap Suds Row',"
      Nebraska History 61 (1980): 421-36.

      SEE ALSO: 3239 , 3403

                          VETERANS AFFAIRS

2216  Bodenger, Robert G. "Soldiers' Bonuses: A History of Veterans Benefits
      in the United States, 1776-1967." Ph. D. dissertation, Pennsylvania
      State University, 1971.

2217  Cetina, Judith G. "A History of Veterans' Homes in the United States,
      1811-1930." Ph. D. dissertation, Case Western University, 1977.

2218  Crowell, Chester T. "The Old Army game," American Mercury 35 (1935):
      458-63.

2219  Davies, Wallace E. Patriotism on Parade: The Story of Veterans' and
      Hereditary Organizations in America, 1783-1900. Cambridge: Harvard
      University Press, 1955.

2220  Freund, Rudolph. "Military Bounty Lands and the Origins of the Public
      Domain," Agricultural History 20 (1946): 8-18.

2221  Glasson, William H. "History of Military Pension Legislation in the
      United States." Ph. D. dissertation, Columbia University, 1900.

2222  _____. Federal Military Pensions in the United States. New York:
      Oxford University Press, 1918.

2223  Hay, Peter. Proceedings of the National Convention of the Soldiers
      of the War of 1812. Philadelphia: Brown's Steam Power Book, Card,
      and Job Printing Office, 1854.

2224  Howard, Oliver O. "Military and Naval Pensions of the United States,"
      Journal of the Military Service Institute 11 (1890): 1-15.

2225  Ijams, George E. and Philip B. Matz. "History of the Medical and
      Domicilary Care of Veterans," Military Surgeon 76 (1935): 113-33.

2226  Lawton, Eba. History of the Soldiers Home, Washington, D.C.
      New York: G.P. Putnam's Sons, 1914.

2227   Oberly, James M. "Acres and Old Men: Military Land warrants, 1847-1860."
       Ph. D. dissertation, University of Rochester, 1982.

2228   _____. "Gray-Haired Lobbyists: War of 1812 Veterans and the Politics
       of Bounty Land Grants," Journal of the Early Republic 5 (1985): 35-58.

2229   _____. "Westward Who? Estimates of a Native White Interstate Migration
       after the War of 1812," Journal of Economic History 46 (1986): 431-40.

2230   O'Callaghan, Jerry A. "The War Veteran and the Public Lands,"
       Agricultural History 28 (1954): 163-68.

2231   Park, Siyoung. "Land Speculation in Western Illinois: Pike County,
       1821-1835," Illinois State Historical Society Journal 77 (1984): 115-28.

2232   Rezab, Gordana. "Land Speculation in Fulton County, 1817-1832,"
       Western Illinois Regional Studies 3 (1980): 22-35.

2233   Severo, Richard and Lewis Milford. The Wages of War: When America's
       Soldiers Came Home-From Valley Forge to Vietnam. New York:
       Simon, Schuster, 1989.

2234   Vivian, Jean H. "Military Land Bonuses During the Revolutionary and
       Confederation Periods," Maryland Historical Magazine 61 (1966): 231-56.

## MILITARY DISCIPLINE

2235   Carswell, Stuart R. "Old Military Records," Infantry Journal 26 (1925):
       28-33; 27 (1925): 293-98.

2236   "Colonel Thomas Butler and General Wilkinson's 'Roundhead Order',"
       Pennsylvania Magazine of History and Biography 17 (1893): 501-12.

2237   Foreman, Carolyn T. "Military Discipline in Early Oklahoma,"
       Chronicles of Oklahoma 6 (1928): 140-44.

2238   Gates, William. Proceedings of a General Court-Martial for the Trial
       of Major William Gates, of the Second Regiment of Artillery. New York:
       J. Narine, 1837.

2239   Harwood, W.S. "Soldiers of 1794: Baron Von Steuben's Ideas on the
       Order and Discipline of the Troops of the United States," Harper's
       Weekly Magazine 41 (1897): 659-62.

2240   Hickey, Donald R. "The United States Army vs Long Hair: The Trials
       of Colonel Thomas Butler, 1801-1805," Pennsylvania Magazine of History
       and Biography 101 (1977): 462-74.

2241   _____. "Andrew Jackson and the Haircut: Individual Rights vs Military
       Discipline," Tennessee Historical Quarterly 35 (1976): 365-78.

2242   Kenny, Alice P. "The Bathtub Courtmartial, " New York Historical
       Society Quarterly 50 (1966): 281-97.

2243   Knopf, Richard C. "Crime and Punishment in the American Legion,"
       Historical and Philosophical Society of Ohio Bulletin 14 (1956): 232-38.

2244   McAnaney, William P. "Desertion in the United States Army," Journal
       of the Military Service Institute 10 (1889): 450-65.

2245  Macomb, Alexander. A Treatise on Martial Law and Courts-Martial as
      Practiced in the United States of America. Charleston, SC: Hoff, 1809.

2246  Miles, Thomas W. "Hair!" DAR Magazine 105 (1971): 4-8, 72, 90.

2247  Pasley, Robert S. "The Federal Courts look at the Court Martial,"
      University of Pittsburgh Law Review 12 (1950): 7-34.

2248  Philips, Verne D. "The American Military Court of Inquiry," Military
      History of Texas and the Southwest 14 (1978): 45-52.

2249  Ulmer, J.R. "Military Punishments in the Old Days," Infantry Journal
      43 (1936): 57-59.

## DRILL AND TACTICS

2250  Carswell, Stuart R. "Infantry School of 1826," Infantry Journal 24
      (1924): 263-67.

2251  Godfrey, E.S. "Cavalry Fire Discipline," By Valor and Arms 2 (1976):
      30-36.

2252  Graves, Donald E. "'Dry Books of Tactics': U.S. Infantry Manuals of
      the War of 1812 and After," Military Collector and Historian 38 (1986):
      50-61, 173-77.

2253  _____. and John C. Fredriksen. "Dry Books of Tactics, Revisited,"
      Ibid 39 (1987): 65-66.

2254  Green, Fred M. "The Evolution of Infantry Drill," Infantry Drill 40
      (1933): 109-16.

2255  Hindman [Pseud] "The New Infantry tactics," Army and Navy Chronicle
      1 (1835): 332-33.

2256  Kearny, Stephen W. Carbine Manual, or Notes for the Exercise and
      Maneuveres for the U.S. Dragoons. Washington, DC: U.S. War Department,
      1837.

2257  Ney, Virgil. The Evolution of the U.S. Army Field Manual: Valley Forge
      to Vietnam. Fort Belvoir, VA: Combat Operations Research Group, 1966.

2258  Osterhoudt, Henry J. "The Evolution of U.S. Army Assault Tactics, 1778-
      1919: The Search for Sound Doctrine." Ph. D. dissertation, Duke
      dissertation, 1986.

2259  Peladeau, Marius B. "The U.S. Dragoon Manual of 1837," Arms Collecting
      25 (1987): 43-51.

2260  "Scott's Military Tactics," New York Review 8 (1840): 358-75.

2261  Toomey, Thomas M. The History of the Infantry Drill Regulation of the
      United States Army. St. Louis: N.p., 1917.

2262  Vigman, Fred K. "William Duane's American Military Library," Military
      Affairs 8 (1944): 321-25.

## MATERIEL

2263  Abbott, Jacob. "The Armory at Springfield," Harper's Monthly Magazine
      5 (1852): 145-61.

2264 Bricker, E.D. "Watervliet Arsenal: Its History and Place in Our Plan of National Defense," Army Ordnance 8 (1927): 133-40.

2265 Brown, M.L. "Notes on U.S. Arsenals, Depots, and Martial Firearms of the Second Seminole War," Florida Historical Quarterly 61 (1983): 445-58.

2266 Dobbs, Judy. A History of the Watertown Arsenal, Watertown. Watertown, MA: Army Materials and Mechanics Research Center, 1977.

2267 Haight, Floyd L. "History of the Detroit Arsenal in Dearborn," Michigan History 42 (1958): 88-96.

2268 Horney, Oduc C. "The Frankfort Arsenal, 1816-1926," Army Ordnance 6 (1926): 233-36.

2269 Miller, Clifford A. "Springfield Arms: milestones of a Great National Armory," Ibid 20 (1939): 12-21.

2270 Nothstein, Ira O. "Rock Island and the Rock Island Arsenal," Illinois State Historical Society Journal 33 (1940): 304-40.

2271 O'Brien, William J. "The Washington Arsenal, Historic Landmark of the Nation's Capital," Ibid 16 (1935): 32-37.

2272 Smith, Hugh. "Manufacture of Cannon at Watervliet Arsenal," Ibid 8 (1927): 149-55.

2273 Smith, Merritt R. "Military Arsenals and Industry Before World War I." In: B. Franklin Cooling, ed. War, Business, and American Society: Historical Perspectives on the Military Industrial Complex. Port Washington, NY: Kennikat Press, 1977, 24-42.

2274 _____. "The Harper's Ferry Arsenal and the 'New Technology' in America, 1794-1854." Ph. D. dissertation, Pennsylvania State University, 1971.

2275 Swantek, John E. "Watervliet: America's Oldest and Newest Arsenal," Ordnance 3 (1985): 18-21.

2276 Uselding, Paul J. "Technical Progress at the Springfield Armory, 1820-1850," Explorations in Economic History 9 (1972): 291-316.

2277 Wade, Arthur P. "Mount Dearborn: The National Armory at Rocky Mount, South Carolina, 1802-1829," South Carolina Historical Magazine 81 (1980): 207-31.

2278 Whittlesey, Derwent S. "The Springfield Armory: A Study of Institutional Development." Ph. D. dissertation, University of Chicago, 1920.

GUN MAKING

2279 Birnie, Rogers. "Gun Making in the United States," Journal of the Military Service Institute 12 (1891): 385-526.

2280 Carey, Arthur M. American Firearms Makers: When, Where, and What they Made from the Colonial Period to the End of the Nineteenth Century. New York: Thomas Y. Crowell, 1953.

2281 Cesari, Gene S. "American Arms-Making Machine Tool Development, 1798-1855." Ph. D. dissertation, University of Pennsylvania, 1970.

2282 Deyrup, Felicia J. Arms-makers of the Connecticut Valley: A Regional
     Study of the Economic Development of the Small Arms Industry, 1798–
     1870. Northampton, MA: Smith College, 1938.

2283 Fries, Russell I. "A Comparative Study of British and American Arms
     Industries, 1790–1890." Ph. D. dissertation, Johns Hopkins
     University, 1972.

2284 Green, Constance M. Eli Whitney and the Birth of American Technology.
     Boston: Little, Brown, 1956.

2285 Kissling, Herbert H. "United States Musket Factory, 1796–1835."
     Typescript at Harper's Ferry National Historic Park.

2286 Satterlee, Leroy D. and Arcadi Gluckman. American Gun Makers.
     Harrisburg, PA: Stackpole Co., 1953.

2287 Smith, Merrit R. "Army Ordnance and the American System of Manufact-
     uring, 1815–1861." In: Military Enterprise and Technological Change:
     Perspectives on the American Experience. Cambridge: MIT, 1985, 39–86.

2288 _____. "From Craftsman to Mechanic: The Harper's Ferry Experience,
     1798–1854." In: I.M. Quimby and P.A. Earl, eds. Technological Inno-
     vation and the Decorative Arts. Charlottesville: University of
     Virginia Press, 1974, 103–39.

2289 Woodbury, Robert S. "The Legend of Eli Whitney and Interchangeable
     Parts," Technology and Culture 1 (1960): 235–53.

2290 Wooward, William. "Fire Arms: Their Evolution and Worcester's Part
     in Them," Worcester Historical Society Publications 1 (1933): 264–78.

### *FIREARMS

2291 Brown, Stuart E. The Guns of Harper's Ferry. Berryville, VA:
     Virginia Book Co., 1968.

2292 Butler, David F. United States Firearms: The First Century, 1776–
     1875. New York: Winchester Press, 1971.

2293 Correll, John T. "Brown Bess had her Limits," Airman 17 (1973): 42–
     47.

2294 Davis, Carl L. "Army Ordnance and Interia Towards Change in Samll
     Arms through the Civil War." Master's Thesis, Oklahoma State
     University, 1959.

2295 Demeritt, Dwight B. "John Hall and the Origin of the Breechloader,"
     American Society of Arms Collectors Bulletin No. 42 (1980): 24–29.

2296 Fairbairn, Charlotte J. and C. Meade Patterson. "Captain Hall,
     Inventor," The Gun Report 5 (1959): 6–10, 15–22, 25–26.

2297 Fuller, Claude E. Springfield Muzzle-Loading Shoulder Arms.
     New York: Bannerman & Sons, 1930.

2298 _____. The Breechloader in the Service, 1816–1917. New Milford, CT:
     N. Flayderman, 1965.

2299 Garavaglia, Louis A. and Charles G. Worman. Firearms of the American
     West, 1803–1865. Albuerquerque: University of New Mexico Press, 1984.

2300  Gerber, William E. "Harper's Ferry Rifles: Comparing the Models 1803 and 1814," American Society of Arms Collectors No. 38 (1978): 17-21.

2301  Gluckman, Arcadi. United States Muskets, Rifles, and Carbines. Buffalo, NY: Otto Ulbruch, 1948.

2302  Grider, Rufus A. "Powder Horns, their History and Use," New York Historical Society Bulletin 15 (1931): 3-24.

2303  Guthman, William H. U.S. Army Weapons, 1784-1791. Cleveland: American Society of Arms Collectors, 1875.

2304  Hargreaves, Reginald. "The Dominant Weapon," American Rifleman 100 (1952): 13-16.

2305  _____. "Soldiers' Weapon," Marine Corps Gazette 43 (1959): 44-53.

2306  Hicks, James E. Notes on United States Ordnance, 1776-1940. 2 Vols. Mt. Vernon, NY: James E. Hicks, 1940.

2307  Holt, Thomas E. "Pennsylvania 1798 Contract Muskets," American Society of Arms Collectors Bulletin No. 2 (1956): 19-24.

2308  Holt, Richard A. "Pre-1814 U.S. Contract Rifles," Ibid No. 47 (1982): 7-19.

2309  _____. "U.S. 1798 Contract Muskets," Ibid No. 21 (1970): 8-14.

2310  Hughes, Nicky. "The Role of Kentucky in America's Military Heritage," Ibid No. 48 (1983): 3-5.

2311  Huntington, Roy T. "Hall Breech-loading Arms," Gun Report 2 (1958): 6-8, 12-14.

2312  _____. Hall's Breechloaders: John H. Hall's Invention of a Breechloading Rifle with Precision-made Interchangable Parts and its Introduction into the United States Service. York, PA: G. Shumway, 1972.

2313  _____. "Hall Rifles at Harper's Ferry," Gun Magazine 7 (1961): 30-31, 45-47.

2314  Kennedy, R.N. "Notes on the Model 1816 U.S. Flintlock Musket," American Society of Arms Collectors Bulletin No. 31 (1975): 41-49.

2315  King, James C. "The Frontier Gunsmith and Indian Relations," Western Pennsylvania Historical Magazine 50 (1967): 23-32.

2316  Kley, Ron. "Rifles to the Missouri: The Fate of Hall's Hundred," Man at Arms 7 (1985): 22-28.

2317  Lewis, Berkeley R. Small Arms and Ammunition in the United States Service, 1776-1865. Washington, DC: Smithsonian Institute, 1956.

2318  _____. "The First U.S. Repeaters," American Rifleman 97 (1949): 38-42.

2319  McMurray, John C. "U.S. Martial Flintlock Rifles," American Society of Arms Collectors Bulletin No. 17 (1968): 8-14.

2320  Nehrbass, Arthur F. "The Failure of the 1812 Musket Pattern," Man at Arms 4 (1982): 42-45.

2321    ____. "Contract Production of the 'Model 1812' Musket," Man at Arms
        8 (1986): 35-37.

2322    Patterson, C. Meade. "Harper's Ferry and its Firearms," American
        Society of Arms Collectors Bulletin No. 11 (1965): 21-30.

2323    Reichmann, Felix. "The Pennsylvania Rifle: A Social Interpretation
        of Changing Military Techniques," Pennsylvania Magazine of History
        and Biography 69 (1945): 3-14.

2324    Reilly, Robert M. United States Military Small Arms, 1816-1865.
        Baton Rouge, LA: Eagle Press, 1970.

2325    ____. United States Martial Flintlocks. Lincoln, RI: Andrew Mowbray,
        1987.

2326    ____. "Harper's Ferry and John Hall," American Society of Arms
        Collectors Bulletin No. 26 (1972): 16-29.

2327    Rosebush, Waldo E. American Firearms and the Changing Frontier.
        Spokane, WA: Eastern Washington State Historical Society, 1962.

2328    Russell, Carl P. Guns on the Early Frontiers. Berkeley: University
        of California Press, 1957.

2329    Sawyer, Charles W. Fire Arms in American History. 3 Vols. Boston:
        The Author, 1910-1920.

2330    Schmidt, Peter A. "The Model 1833 North/Hall Carbine, Type III,"
        American Society of Arms Collecting Bulletin No. 54 (1986): 25-31.

2331    Sharpe, Philip B. The Rifle in America. New York: Morrow, 1938.

2332    Sheehan, Michael S. "A Manual for the Identification of Small Arms
        Ordnance Material," Bulletin and Journal of Archaeology for New York
        State No. 93 (1986): 27-50.

2333    Sprague, Richard K. "U.S. Flintlock Musket Model 1835," Man at Arms
        6 (1984): 37-39.

2334    Steuart, Richard D. "Historical Military Firearms as Preserved in the
        Bowie Collection at Fort McHenry," Army Ordnance 19 (1938): 93-98.

2335    Wasson, Robert G. The Hall Carbine Affair, a Study in Contemporary
        Folklore. New York: Pandick Press, 1948.

2336    Weller, Jac. "Flintlock to Percussion Rifle: Fifteen Critical Years
        in Infantry Weapons Development," Ordnance 37 (1952): 446-49.

        SEE ALSO: 2545, 2549, Naval Firearms

                              PISTOLS

2337    Gluckman, Arcadi. United States Martial Pistols and Revolvers.
        Buffalo: Otto Ulbrich, 1944.

2338    Kalman, James M. A Pictorial History of U.S. Single Shot Martial
        Pistols. New York: Charles Scribner's Sons, 1957.

2339  North, S.D. and Ralph H. North. Simeon North, First Official Pistol
      Maker of the United States. Concord, NH: Rumford Press, 1913.

2340  Sawyer, Charles W. United States Single Shot Martial Pistols.
      Boston: The Arms Company, 1913.

2341  Severen, James E. Colt Firearms from 1836. Santa Ana, CA:
      Foundation Press, 1954.

2342  Smith, Samuel E. and Edwin W. Bitter. Historical Pistols: The American
      Martial Flintlock, 1760-1845. New York: Scalamandre, 1985.

2343  Taylerson, Anthony W. The Revolver, 1818-1865. New York: Crown
      Publishers, 1968.

## SWORDS AND SABERS

2344  Altmayer, Jay P. American Presentation Swords: A Study of the Design
      and Development of Presentation Swords in the U.S. from the Post-
      Revolutionary Times Until after the Close of the Spanish-American
      War. Mobile, AL: Rankin Press, 1958.

2345  Armstrong, Don. "U.S. Dragoons and their Sabers," American Society
      of Arms Collecting Bulletin No. 56 (1987): 2-8.

2346  Belote, Theodore T. American and European Swords in the Historical
      Collections of the United States National Museum. Washington, DC:
      Smithsonian Institute, 1932.

2347  Coffin, Patricia. "First President's Variety of Swords," Smithsonian
      5 (1975): 114-18.

2348  Hamilton, John D. The Ames Sword Company, 1829-1935. Providence:
      Andrew Mowbray, 1983.

2349  ____. "A Roland for an Oliver: Swords Awarded by the State of New
      York during the War of 1812," American Society of Arms Collecting
      Bulletin No. 57 (1987): 2-11.

2350  ____. "A Swan Among the Ugly Ducklings: Daniel Pettibone's 1812
      U.S. Sword Contract," Man at Arms 7 (1985): 20-23.

2351  ____ " Ugly Ducklings: Iron-Hilted Swords of the Federal Republic,
      1795-1815," Ibid 5 (1983): 32-54.

2352  ____. "The Ames Century, 1829-1929," Ibid 2 (1980): 22-30.

2353  Hicks, James E. Nathan Starr, the First Official Swordmaker.
      Mt. Vernon, NY: J.E. Hicks, 1940.

2354  Hopkins, Alfred F. "The Long Horseman's Sword," Society of American
      Sword Collectors Bulletin 3 (1950): 2-7.

2355  "The Sword of Captain Nathan Heald," Ibid 2 (1948): 5-8.

2356  ____. "Some American Military Swords," Regional Review 4 (1910): 11-16.

2357  Johnson, Richard. "U.S. Cavalry Sabers," American Society of Arms
      Collectors Bulletin No. 46 (1982): 7-17.

2358  Mowbray, E. Andrew. The American Eagle Pommel Sword: The Early Years,
      1793-1830. Lincoln, RI: Andrew Mowbray, 1988.

2359  Nehrbass, Arthur F. "Rose 1812 Non-Commissioned Officer Sword,"
      Man at Arms 7 (1985): 59-61.

2360  Peterson, Harold L. The American Sword, 1775-1945. Philadelphia:
      Ray Riling Books, 1965.

2361  Sawyer, Charles W. United States Single Shot Martial Pistols.
      Boston: The Arms Company, 1913.

2362  Stryker, Russell F. "The Last Resort of the Foot Soldier," American
      Sword Collector's Bulletin 3 (1950): 10-14.

2363  _____. "The American Trooper's Sabre," Society of American Sword
      Collectors' Bulletin 3 (1949): 6-13.

                          BAYONETS

2364  Hardin, Albert N. The American Bayonet, 1776-1964. Philadelphia:
      Riling, Lentz, 1964.

2365  Reilly, Robert M. "The Evolution of the Socket Bayonet in America,"
      Man at Arms 7 (1985): 17-23.

2366  Webster, Donald B. American Socket Bayonets, 1717-1873. Ottawa:
      Museum Restoration Service, 1964.

                          POLE ARMS

2367  "American Pole Arms or Shafted Weapons, with Examples from the Fort
      Ticonderoga Collection," Fort Ticonderoga Museum Bulletin 5 (1939):
      66-103.

2368  Dean, Bashford. "On American Pole Arms, especially those in the
      Metropolitan Museum of Art," American Military Historical Foundation
      Journal 1 (1937): 108-21, 177-85.

2369  Thiele, Thomas. "Some Notes on the Lance and Lancers in the United
      States Cavalry," Military Collector and Historian 7 (1955): 31-37.

      SEE ALSO: Naval Polearms

                          *UNIFORMS

2370  Albert, Alphaeus H. Record of American Uniform and Historical Buttons.
      Boyertown, PA: Boyertown Publishing Co., 1973.

2371  "Army Uniform," Army and Navy Chronicle 10 (1840): 73-74.

2372  Bird, Harrison K. "Early American Cavalry Helmets," Fort Ticonderoga
      Museum Bulletin 5 (1940): 142-51.

2373  _____. "The Uniform Collection," Ibid 4 (1937): 109-19.

2374  Buzzaird, Raleigh B. "Insignia of the Corps of Engineers," Military
      Engineers 50 (1958): 25-29.

2375  "Cadets: Why They wear Gray," Americana 7 (1912): 1083-84.

2376  Campbell, J. Duncan. "Notes on the Insignia of the Riflemen, U.S.
      Army," Military Collector and Historian 1 (1949): 6-8.

2377  _____. "The Eagle Militant," Early American Life 9 (1978): 32-35.

2378 ____. and Edgar M. Howell. American Military Insignia, 1800-1851. Washington, DC: Smithsonian Institute, 1963.

2379 Chartrand, Rene. "The United States Forces of 1812-1816, as Drawn by Charles Hamilton Smith, Officer and Spy," Military Collector and Historian 35 (1983): 142-50.

2380 Curtis, Lawrence A. "Uniform of the Army," Infantry Journal 20 (1922): 414-20.

2381 Emerson, William K. "Cockcades and Eagles," Military Collector and Historian 35 (1983): 104-12.

2382 Gardiner, Asa B. "The Uniform of the American Army," Magazine of American History 1 (1877): 461-92.

2383 Holabird, S.B. "Army Clothing," Journal of the Military Service Institute 2 (1882): 356-87.

2384 Huntington, Roy T. Accoutrements of the United States Infantry, Riflemen and Dragoons, 1834-1839. Alexandria Bay, NY: Museum Restoration Service, 1987.

2385 ____. "Dragoon Accoutrements and Equipments, 1834-1849: An Identification Guide," Plains Anthropologist 12 (1967): 345-55.

2386 Jacobsen, Jacques N. Accoutrements of the Army of the United States as Described in the Ordnance Manuals of 1839, 1841, 1850 & 1861. Staten island, NY: Manor, 1968.

2387 Johnson, Richard. "U.S. Army Accoutrements, 1840-1860," American Society of Arms Collectors Bulletin No. 45 (1981): 17-23.

2388 Johnson, David F. Uniform Buttons: American Armed Forces, 1784-1948. 2 Vols. Watkins Glen, NY: Century House, 1948.

2388A Katcher, Philip. U.S. Infantry Equipments, 1775-1910. London: Osprey Publishing, 1989.

2389 Kerksis, Sydney C. Plates and Buckles of the American Military, 1795-1874. Kennesaw, GA: Gigal Press, 1974.

2390 Kloster, Donald E. "Uniforms of the Army Prior and Subsequent to 1872," Military Collector and Historian 14 (1962): 103-12.

2391 ____. and Edgar M. Howell. United States Army Headgear to 1854. Washington, DC: Smithsonian Institute, 1969.

2392 Long, Oscar F. Changes in the Uniforms of the Army, 1774-1895. Washington, DC: N.p., 1896.

2393 Ludington, Marshal T. Uniform of the Army of the United States from 1774 to 1889. New York: American Lithographic Co., 1890.

2394 Lewis, Waverly P. U.S. Military Headgear, 1770-1880. Devon, CT: N.p., 1960.

2395 Olsen, Stanley J. "The Development of the U.S. Army Saddle," Military Collector and Historian 7 (1955): 1-7.

2396  Peterson, Mendel. "American Military Epaulettes, 1775-1820,"
      Military Collector and Historian 2 (1950): 17-21.

2397  _____. "American Military Epaulettes, 1814-1872," Ibid 3 (1951):
      1-14.

2398  Repman, Harry J. "U.S. Buckles and Plates, 1830-1860," American
      Society of Arms Collecting Bulletin No. 33 (1976): 81-88.

2399  Schneider, David H. "Gray Uniforms of the Niagara," Military Coll-
      ector and Historian 33 (1981): 170-72,

2400  "Uniforms Presented by Mrs. Blake Lawrence," Fort Ticonderoga Museum
      Bulletin 9 (1956): 268-75.

2401  U.S. Quartermaster Department. Uniforms of the Army of the United
      States, from 1774-1889, 1898-1907. 2 Vols. New York: American
      Lithographic Co., 1909.

2402  Wycoff, Martin A. United States Military Buttons of the Land Services;
      1787-1902. Bloomington, IN: McLean County Historical Society, 1984.

      SEE ALSO: 3377, 3397

### FLAGS

2403  Davis, Gherardi. The Colors of the United States Army, 1789-1912.
      New York: Gilliss, 1912.

2404  Finke, Detmar H. "United States Army Colors and Standards, 1784-
      1808," Military Collector and Historian 15 (1963): 69-72.

2405  "History of the Flags," Journal of the Military Service Institute
      57 (1915): 440-46.

2406  Kuhn, Edward C. "U.S. Army Colors and Standards of 1808," Military
      Affairs 5 (1941): 263-67.

      SEE ALSO: 3714

### MUSIC

2407  Bowman, Kent A. Voices of Combat: A Century of Liberty and War Songs.
      Westport, CT: Greenwood Press, 1987.

2408  Camus, Raoul F. "The Military Band in the United States Army to
      1834." Ph. D. dissertation, New York University, 1969.

2409  Ferguson, Allan J. "Trumpets, Bugles and Horns in North America,
      1750-1815," Military Collector and Historian 36 (1984): 2-7.

2410  Hernandez, R.J. "Pride of the Capital: The United States Army Band,"
      Quartermaster Review 12 (1933): 35-40.

2411  McCormick, David C. "A History of the United States Army Band to
      1846." Ph. D. dissertation, Northwestern University, 1970.

2412  Mattson, Donald E. and Louis D. Walz. Old Fort Snelling Instruction
      Book for Fife with Music of Early America. St. Paul: Minnesota
      Historical Society, 1974.

2413  Nelson, Larry L. "Two Military bands of Music on the Northwestern
      Frontier during the War of 1812," Military Collector and Historian
      36 (1984): 67-69.

2414   Simmons, David. "The Band of Music in the American Army of 1797,"
       Ibid 37 (1985): 135-37.

2415   White, William C. The History of Military Music in America. New York:
       Exposition Press, 1944.

       SEE ALSO: 3361, 3715

                          FRONTIER EXPLORATION

2416   Alford, Terry L. "The West as A Desert in American Thought Prior to
       Long's 1819-1820 Expedition," Journal of the West  8 (1969): 515-25.

2417   _____. "Western Desert Images in American Thought, 1800-1860."
       Ph. D. dissertation, Mississippi State University, 1970.

2418   Allen, Milford F. "United States Government Exploring Expeditions
       and Natural History, 1800-1840." Ph. D. dissertation, University
       of Texas, 1958.

2419   Bartlett, Richard A. Great Surveys of the West. Norman: University
       Oklahoma, 1962.

2420   Blackburn, Bob L. "First Lieutenant James B. Wilkinson." In: Joseph
       A. Stout, ed. Frontier Adventurers: American Explorers in Oklahoma.
       Oklahoma City: Oklahoma Historical Society, 1976, 6-18.

2421   Blackburn, Forrest R. "The Army in Western Exploration," Military
       Review 51 (1971): 75-90.

2422   Cox, Isaac J. "The Exploration of the Louisiana Frontier, 1803-1806,"
       American Historical Association Annual Report (1904): 151-74.

2423   Flores, Dan L., ed. Jefferson and Southwestern Exploration: The
       Freeman and Custis Accounts of the Red River Expedition of 1806.
       Norman: University of Oklahoma Press, 1986.

2424   Goetzmann, William H. Army Explorations in the American West, 1803-
       1863. New Haven: Yale University Press, 1959.

2425   _____. "The West and the American Age of Exploration," Arizona and
       the West 2 (1960): 265-78.

2426   Gilbert, Edmund W. The Explorations of Western America, 1800-1850;
       A Historical Geography. New York: Cooper Square, 1966.

2427   _____. Exploration and Empire: The Explorer and the Scientist in
       the Winning of the West. New York: Alfred A. Knopf, 1966.

2428   Goodwin, Cardinal L. "Early Explorations and Settlements of Missouri
       and Arkansas, 1803-1822," Missouri Historical Review 14 (1920): 385-424.

2429   Hawgood, John A. American Western Frontiers: The Story of Explorers
       and Settlers who opened the Trans-Mississippi West. New York: Alfred
       A. Knopf, 1967.

2430   Jackman, Sydney W. and John F. Freeman, eds. American Voyageur: The
       Journal of David Bates Douglass. Marquette: Northern Michigan
       University Press, 1969.

2431  Lewis, G. Malcom. "Early American Exploration and Cis-Rocky Mountain
      Desert, 1803-1823," Great Plains Journal 5 (1965): 1-11.

2432  Rawlings, Gerald. The Pathfinders, the History of America's First
      Westerners. New York: Macmillan, 1964.

2433  Symons, Thomas W. "The Army and the Exploration of the West," Journal
      of the Military Service Institute 4 (1883): 205-49.

2434  Thomas, Philip D. "The United States Army as the Early Patron of
      Naturalists in the Trans-Mississippi West, 1803-1820," Chronicles
      of Oklahoma 56 (1978): 171-93.

2435  Wheat, Carl J. Mapping the Trans-Mississippi West, 1540-1861. 3 Vols.
      San Francisco: Institute of Historical Cartography, 1957-1958.

2436  Van Orman, Richard A. The Explorers: Nineteenth Century Expeditions
      in Africa and the American West. Albuquerque: University of New Mexico
      Press, 1984.

2437  Wells, Harry L. "Who was the Pathfinder," Overland 16 (1890): 242-50.

      SEE ALSO: 3569, 3570, Benjamin Bonneville, Lewis Cass, Stephen W.
      Kearny, Randolph B. Marcy

## LEWIS AND CLARK EXPEDITION

2438  Abrams, Rochonne. "A Song of the Promise of the Land: The Style of
      the Lewis and Clark Journals," Missouri Historical Society Bulletin
      32 (1976): 141-57.

2439  Adam, Graeme M. The Lewis and Clark Expedition, 1804-1806. New York:
      University Society, 1904.

2440  Allaben, Frank A. "Lewis and Clark's Expedition over the Rocky
      Mountains, 1804-1806," Journal of American History 18 (1924): 253-64.

2441  Allen, John L. Passage Through the Gardens: Lewis and Clark and the
      Image of the American Northwest. Urbana, IL: University of Illinois
      Press, 1975.

2442  _____. "An Analysis of the Exploratory Process: The Lewis and Clark
      Expedition of 1804-1806," Geographical Review 62 (1972): 13-39.

2443  _____. "Lewis and Clark on the Upper Missouri: Decision at the Marias,"
      Montana 21 (1971): 2-17.

2444  Allen, Paul. Lewis and Clark; Pioneers of the Great American Northwest
      New York: D.M. MacLellan Book Co., 1910.

2445  Andrist, Ralph K. To the Pacific with Lewis and Clark. New York:
      American Heritage Press, 1967.

2446  Appelman, Roy E. Lewis and Clark: Historic Places Associated with
      Their Transcontinental Exploration. Washington, DC: National Park
      Service, 1975.

2447  _____. "The Lost Site of Camp Wood," Journal of the West 7 (1968):
      270-74.

2448 _____. "Joseph and Rubin Field, Kentucky Frontiersmen of the Lewis and Clark Expedition, and their Father Abraham," Filson Club Quarterly 49 (1975): 5-36.

2449 Bailey, Robert G. River of No Return (The Great Salmon River of Idaho) A Century of Central Idaho and Eastern Washington History. Lewiston: Bailey-Blake Print Co., 1935.

2450 Bakeless, John E. Lewis and Clark: Pioneers in Discovery. New York: William Morrow, 1947.

2451 _____. The Adventures of Lewis and Clark. Boston: Houghton, Mifflin, 1962.

2452 Bancroft, Hubert H. History of the Northwest Coast. 2 Vols. San Francisco: History Company, 1890. Vol. 2, 1-87.

2453 Bashford, Herbert. Stories of Western Pioneers. San Francisco: Harr Wanger, 1928.

2454 Berthold, Mary P. Including Two Captains: A Later Look Westward. Detroit: Harlo, 1975.

2455 No entry

2456 Bordwell, Constance. March of the Volunteers; Soldiering with Lewis and Clark. Portland, OR: Beaver Books, 1960.

2457 Brebner, John B. The Explorers of North America, 1492-1806. New York: New York: Macmillan Co., 1933.

2458 Brooks, Noah. First Across the Continent: The Story of the Exploring Expedition of Lewis and Clark in 1803-4-5. New York: C. Scribner's Sons, 1901.

2459 Brown, D. Alexander. "The Lewis and Clark Adventure," American History Illustrated 4 (1969): 4-9, 41-47.

2460 Burk, Redmond and Robert Kelly. "The Lewis and Clark Expedition Papers: The Genesis of a Case," DePaul Law Review 7 (1952): 162-71.

2461 Burroughs, Raymond D. Exploration Unlimited: The Story of the Lewis and Clark Expedition. Detroit: Wayne State University Press, 1953.

2462 Caywood, Louis R. "The Exploratory Excavation of Fort Clatsop," Oregon Historical Quarterly 49 (1948): 205-10.

2463 Chidsey, Donald B. Lewis and Clark, the Great Adventure. New York: Crown Publishers, 1970.

2464 Coues, Elliott, ed. History of the Expedition under the Command of Lewis and Clark. 4 Vols. New York: Francis P. Harper, 1893.

2465 Crawford, Anthony R. "Exploring the Wilderness: The Lewis and Clark Expedition," Gateway Heritage 2 (1981): 8-21.

2466 Cutright, Paul R. "Lewis and Clark Begin a Journey," Missouri Historical Society Bulletin 24 (1967): 20-35.

2467 Daugherty, James H. Of Courage Undaunted: Across the Continent with Lewis and Clark. New York: Viking Press, 1951.

2468 Davis, Julia. No Other White Men. New York: E.P. Dutton, 1937.

2469 DeVoto, Bernard. "An Inference Regarding the Expedition of Lewis and Clark," American Philosophical Society Proceedings 99 (1955): 185-94.

2470 Duncan, Dayton. Out West, and American Journal. New York: Viking Press, 1987.

2471 Eide, Ingvard H. American Odyssey: The Journey of Lewis and Clark. Chicago: Rand McNally, 1969.

2472 Elson, Henry W. Sidelights on American History. New York: Macmillan, 1912.

2473 Ericksen, Vernon. "Lewis and Clark on the Upper Missouri," North Dakota History 40 (1973): 34-37.

2474 Fields, Wayne D. "The Meaning of Lewis and Clark," Gateway Heritage 2 (1981): 2-7.

2475 Goetzman, William H. "A National Epic: The Journals of Lewis and Clark, A Review Essay," New Mexico Historical Review 63 (1988): 273-79.

2476 Gray, Charles D. "Lewis and Clark at the Mouth of Wood River," Illinois States Historical Society Journal 13 (1921): 180-91.

2477 Greely, Adolphus W. Explorers and Travelers. New York: Scribner's Sons, 1895, 105-62.

2478 Guinness, Ralph B. "The Purpose of the Lewis and Clark Expedition," Mississippi Valley Historical Review 20 (1933): 90-100.

2479 Harris, Burton. John Colter: His Years in the Rockies. New York: Scribner, 1952.

2480 Hawke, David F. Those Tremendous Mountains: The Story of the Lewis and Clark Expedition. New York: W.W. Norton, 1980.

2481 Henriksen, Stephen E. "This Place of Encampment: Fort Clatsop," American History Illustrated 20 (1985): 22-33.

2482 Hitchcock, Ripley. The Lewis and Clark Expedition. Boston: Ginn & Co., 1905.

2483 Holloway, David. Lewis and Clark and the Crossing of North America. New York: Saturday Review Press, 1974.

2484 Hosmer, James K. History of the Expedition of Lewis and Clark. 2 Vols. Chicago: McClurg, 1902.

2485 Hulbert, Archer B. Pilots of the Republic: The Romance of the Pioneer Promoter in the Middle West. Chicago: McClurg, 1906.

2486 Jackson, Donald. Among the Sleeping Giants: Occasional Pieces on Lewis and Clark. Urbana: University of Illinois, 1988.

2487 _____. "A Footnote to the Lewis and Clark Expedition," Manuscripts 24 (1972): 3-21.

2488 _____. "A New Lewis and Clark Map," Missouri Historical Society Bulletin 17 (1961): 117-32.

2489 Johnston, Charles H. Famous Scouts, Pioneers, and Soldiers of the Frontier. Boston: L.C. Page, 1910, 123-39.

2490 Karsten, M.O. Hunter and Interpreter for Lewis and Clark; George Drouillard. Glendale, CA: Arthur H. Clark, 1968.

2491 Kasson, John A. "The Expansion of the Republic West of the Mississippi," Annals of Iowa 5 (1901): 177-98.

2492 Keller, Linda Q. "Jefferson's Western Diplomacy: The Lewis and Clark Expedition." Master's Thesis, University of Virginia, 1971.

2493 Koch, Elers. "Lewis and Clark Route Retraced Across the Bitter Roots," Oregon Historical Quarterly 41 (1940): 160-74.

2494 Lankiewicz, Donald P. "The Camp on Wood River: A Winter of Preparation for the Lewis and Clark Expedition," Illinois State Historical Society Journal 75 (1982): 115-20.

2495 Laut, Agnes C. Pathfinders of the West. New York: Macmillan, 1902.

2496 Lavender, David. The Way to the Western Sea: Lewis and Clark Across the Continent. New York: Harper, Row, 1988.

2497 "Lewis and Clark's Expedition over the Rocky Mountains, 1804-06," Journal of American History 18 (1924): 253-64.

2498 "Lewis and Clark's Travels," Analectic Magazine 5 (1815): 127-49, 210-34.

2499 Lighton, William R. Lewis and Clark: Meriwether Lewis and William Clark. Boston: Houghton, Mifflin, 1901.

2500 Link, Louis W. Lewis and Clark Expedition, 1804-1806; from St. Louis, Missouri, to Pacific Ocean and Return, with Particular Reference to the Upper Missouri and Yellowstone Rivers. Cardwell, MT: N.p., 1962.

2501 Loughborough, J. "Lewis and Clark's Expedition to and From the Pacific," Western Journal and Civilian 3 (1849): 363-79; 4 (1850): 6-14.

2502 Lyman, Horace S. "The Lewis and Clark Expedition," American Historical Magazine 1 (1906): 329-66, 439-56.

2503 Mahan, Bruce E. "Explorations of Iowa," Palimpsest 5 (1924): 363-69.

2504 Majors, Harry M. "Lewis and Clark in the Bitteroot Valley," Northwest Discovery 7 (1987): 244-378.

2505 _____. "Lewis and Clark Enter the Rocky Mountains: North Fork Salmon River, August 30--September 3, 1805," Ibid 7 (1987): 4-120.

2506 Mirsky, Jeannette. The Westward Crossings: Balboa, Mackenzie, Lewis and Clark. New York: Alfred A. Knopf, 1946.

2507 Mott, David C. "The Lewis and Clark Expedition in its Relation to Iowa History and Geography," Annals of Iowa 13 (1921): 99-125, 163-92.

2508 Murphy, Dan and David Muench. Lewis and Clark: Voyage of Discovery. Las Vegas: KC Publications, 1977.

2509  Nichols, William. "Lewis and Clark Probe the Heart of Darkness,"
      American Scholar 49 (1979–1980): 94–101.

2510  Olmstead, Gerald W. Fielding's Lewis and Clark Trail. New York:
      Fielding Travel Books, 1986.

2511  Osgood, Ernest S. "Clark on the Yellowstone, 1806," Montana 18 (1968):
      8–29.

2512  Overland, Helen H. "Fabled Friendship: Lewis and Clark," Ibid 5 (1955):
      2–19.

2513  Peebles, John J. Lewis and Clark in Idaho. Boise: Idaho Historical
      Society, 1966.

2514  _____. "Rugged Water Trails and Campsites of Lewis and Clark in the
      Salmon River Country," Idaho Yesterdays 8 (1964): 2–17.

2515  _____. "On the Lolo Trail: Route Campsites of Lewis and Clark,"
      Ibid 9 (1965): 2–15; 10 (1966): 16–27.

2516  _____. "The Return of Lewis and Clark," Ibid 10 (1966): 16–27.

2517  Perrine, Fred S. "Early Days on the Willamette," Oregon Historical
      Quarterly 25 (1924): 295–312.

2518  Petersen, William J. The Story of Iowa. 4 Vols. New York: Lewis
      Historical Co., 1952. Vol. 1, 220–29.

2519  Rawling, G.S. "The Lewis and Clark Expedition," History Today 10
      (1960): 760–69.

2520  Riegel, Robert E. America Moves West. New York: Henry Holt, 1930.

2521  Robinson, Doane. "Our First Family," South Dakota Historical
      Collections 13 (1926): 46–68.

2522  Rogers, Julia. Lewis and Clark in Missouri. St. Louis: Meredco, 1981.

2523  Salisbury, Albert P. Two Captains West: A Historical Tour of the
      Lewis and Clark Trail. Seattle, WA: Superior Publishing Co., 1950.

2524  Salter, William. "The Western Border of Iowa in 1804 and 1806,"
      Iowa Historical Record 10 (1894): 71–78.

2525  Satterfield, Archie. The Lewis and Clark Trail. Harrisburg, PA:
      Stackpole Press, 1978.

2526  Skarsten, M.O. Drouillard: Hunter and Interpreter for Lewis and Clark,
      and Fur Trader, 1807–1810. Glendale, CA: Arthur H. Clark, 1964.

2527  Skinner, Constance L. Adventurers of Oregon: A Chronicle of the Fur
      Trade. New Haven: Yale University Press, 1920.

2528  Smyth, Clifford. Lewis and Clark, Pioneers in America's Westward
      Expansion. New York: Funk, Wagnalls, 1931.

2529  Snyder, Gerald S. In the Footsteps of Lewis and Clark. Washington, DC:
      National Geographic Society, 1970.

2530  Space, Ralph S. The Lolo Trail. Lewiston, ID: Printcraft, 1970.

2531  Stevens, Phillip H. Search Out the Land: A History of America's
      Military Scouts. Chicago: Rand McNally, 1969.

2532  "To Meriwether Lewis and William Clark, Pioneer Explorers of the
      American West," Washington Academy of Science Journal 44 (1954): 333-73.

2533  Tomkins, Calvin. The Lewis and Clark Trail. New York: Harper, 1965.

2534  Vincent, William D. The Lewis and Clark Expedition. Pullman, WA:
      State College of Washington, 1929.

2535  Vinton, Stallo. John Colter, Discoverer of Yellowstone Park. New York:
      E. Eberstadt, 1926.

2536  Wheeler, Olin D. The Trail of Lewis and Clark, 1804-1904: A Story of
      the Great Exploration Across the Continent. 2 Vols. New York: G.P.
      Putnam's Sons, 1904.

2537  Young, F.G. "The Higher Significance of the Lewis and Clark Expedition,"
      Oregon Historical Quarterly 6 (1905): 1-25.

      SEE ALSO: 2800, 2804, 2810, 2819, 2822, 2834, 2838, 2839, 2843, 2847,
      William Clark, Charles Floyd, Patrick Gass, Thomas Jefferson,
      Meriwether Lewis, Nathaniel Pryor, Sacajawea

## MISCELLANEOUS ASPECTS

2538  Adelman, Seymour. "Equipping the Lewis and Clark Expedition,"
      American Philosophical Society Library Bulletin, 1945 (1946): 39-44.

2539  Bakeless, John E. "Lewis and Clark's Background for Exploration,"
      Washington Academy of Science Journal 44 (1954): 334-38.

2540  Bedini, Silvio A. "The Scientific Instruments of the Lewis and Clark
      Expedition," Great Plains Quarterly 4 (1984): 54-69.

2541  Clarke, Charles G. The Men of the Lewis and Clark Expedition: A
      Biographical Roster of the Fifty-Two Members. Glendale: Clark, 1970.

2542  Criswell, Elijah H. Lewis and Clark: Linguistic Pioneers. Columbia:
      University of Missouri Press, 1940.

2543  Cutright, Paul R. Lewis and Clark: Pioneering Naturalists. Urbana:
      University of Illinois Press, 1969.

2544  Garver, F.H. "Tents for Lewis and Clark," Palimpsest 25 (1944): 90-96.

2545  Hunt, Ruby E. Guns of the Lewis and Clark Expedition. Seattle, WA:
      Washington State Historical Society, 1960.

2546  Jackson, Donald. "The Public Image of Lewis and Clark," Pacific
      Northwest Quarterly 57 (1966): 1-7.

2547  _____. "Some Books Carried by Lewis and Clark," Missouri Historical
      Society Bulletin 16 (1959): 3-13.

2548  Lewis, Grace. "Financial Records, "Exploration to the Pacific Ocean',"
      Missouri Historical Society Bulletin 10 (1954): 465-89.

2549  Russell, Carl P. "The Guns of the Lewis and Clark Expedition,"
      North Dakota History 27 (1960): 25-34.

2550  Willingham, William F. Enlightenment Science in the Pacific Northwest:
      The Lewis and Clark Expedition. Portland, OR: Dynagraphics, 1984.

      SEE ALSO: 4716, 4721, 4730, 4743, 4749, 4760, 4761, 4763

                          CONTEMPORARY ACCOUNTS

2551  Allen, Paul, ed. History of the Expedition Under the Command of
      Captains Lewis and Clark to the Sources of the Missouri. 2 Vols.
      Philadelphia: Bradford, Inskeep, 1817.

2552  Cappan, Lester J. "Who is the Author of 'History of the Expedition
      under the Command of captains Lewis and Clark'?" William and Mary
      Quarterly 19 (1962): 257-68.

2553  Cutright, Paul R. "The Journal of Private Joseph Whitehouse, a Soldier
      with Lewis and Clark," Missouri Historical Society Bulletin 28 (1971-
      1972): 143-61.

2554  _____. A History of the Lewis and Clark Journals. Norman: University
      of Oklahoma Press, 1976.

2555  Bakeless, John E. The Journals of Lewis and Clark: A New Selection
      with an Introduction. New York: New American Library, 1964.

2556  DeVoto, Bernard, ed. The Journals of Lewis and Clark. 2 Vols. Boston:
      Houghton, Mifflin, 1953.

2557  Eide, Ingvard. American Odyssey: The Journals of Lewis and Clark.
      New York: Rand, McNally, 1955.

2558  Finley, Helen D. "The Lewis and Clark Expedition," Missouri Historical
      Historical Review 42 (1948): 249-70, 343-66; 43 (1949): 48-70, 145-59.

2559  Jackson, Donald. "The Race to Publish Lewis and Clark," Pennsylvania
      Magazine of History and Biography 85 (1961): 163-77.

2560  _____., ed. Letters of the Lewis and Clark Expedition: with Related
      Documents, 1783-1854. Urbana: University of Illinois Press, 1962.

2561  _____. "Some Advice to the Next Editor of Lewis and Clark," Missouri
      Historical Society Bulletin 24 (1967): 52-62.

2562  "Lewis and Clark in North Dakota," North Dakota History 14 (1947):
      5-45, 173-241, 281-391; 15 (1948): 15-74.

2563  Moulton, Gary E. "The Specialized Journals of Lewis and Clark,"
      American Philosophical Society Proceedings 127 (1983): 194-201.

2564  _____. Atlas of the Lewis and Clark Expedition. Lincoln: University
      of Nebraska Press, 1983.

2565  _____., ed. Journals of the Lewis and Clark Expedition. 4 Vols.
      Lincoln: University of Nebraska Press, 1986-1987.

2566  Ordway, John. "Letters of John Ordway of the Lewis and Clark Expedition
      to His Parents," Oregon Historical Quarterly 22 (1922): 268-69.

2567   Quaife, Milo M., ed. "New-found Records of Lewis and Clark,"
       Mississippi Valley Historical Review 2 (1915-1916): 106-17.

2568   _____. "Journals of Captain Meriwether Lewis and Sgt. John Ordway,
       kept on the Expedition of Western Exploration, 1803-1806," Wisconsin
       Historical Society Collections 22 (1916): 13-405.

2569   Teggart, Frederick J. "Notes Supplementary to any Edition of Lewis
       and Clark," American Historical Association Annual Report (1908):
       183-95.

2570   Thwaites, Reuben G. "Newly Discovered Personal Records of Lewis and
       Clark," Scribner's Magazine 35 (1904): 685-700.

2571   _____., ed. Original Journals of the Lewis and Clark Expedition.
       New York: Dodd, Mead, 1904-1905.

2572   _____. "The Story of the Lewis and Clark Journals," Oregon Historical
       Quarterly 6 (1905): 26-53.

## PIKE EXPEDITION

2573   Adams, Alva. The Louisiana Purchase and its First Explorer, Zeubulon
       Montgomery Pike. Pueblo, CO: N.p., 1894.

2574   Carter, Carol J. Pike in Colorado. Fort Collins, CO: Old Army Press,
       1978.

2575   Carter, Harvey L. "A Soldier with Pike Tried for Murder," Colorado
       Magazine 33 (1956): 218-34.

2576   _____. Zeubulon Montgomery Pike, Pathfinder and Patriot. Colorado:
       Dentan Print Co., 1956.

2577   Dellenbaugh, Frederick S. "Pike Up the Mississippi and Across the
       Plains." In: Breaking the Wilderness. New York: Putnam's Sons, 1905,
       178-92.

2578   Duffus, Robert L. "El Viagero Piake." In: Santa Fe Trail. New York:
       Tudor Publishing Co., 1930, 32-54.

2579   Dunbar, John B. The White Man's Foot in Kansas. Topeka: Kansas State
       Historical Society, 1908.

2580   Folwell, William W. A History of Minnesota 4 Vols. St. Paul: Minnesota
       Historical Society, 1921-1950. Vol. 1, 91-97.

2581   Glazier, Willard. Headwaters of the Mississippi, Comprising
       Biographical Sketches of Early and Recent Explorers of the Great
       River. Chicago: Rand, McNally, 1895, 163-93.

2582   Greely, Adolphus W. Explorers and Travelers. New York: Scribner's
       Sons, 1895, 163-93.

2583   Grinnell, George B. "Zeubulon M. Pike." In: Trails of the Pathfinders.
       New York: Charles Scribner's Sons, 1911, 207-52.

2584   Harvey, Charles M. "The Pike Exploration Centennial," Review of Reviews
       34 (1906): 333-37.

2585 Hitchcock, Ripley. "Pike's Expedition." In: The Louisiana Purchase. Boston: Ginn & Co., 1904, 199-207.

2586 Hoffman, M.M. "Yankee Captain and Spanish Priests," Catholic World 136 (1933): 672-79.

2587 Hollon, W. Eugene. "Zeubulon Montgomery Pike's Mississippi Voyage, 1805-1806," Wisconsin Magazine of History 32 (1949): 445-55.

2588 Jackson, Donald. "Zeubulon M. Pike 'tours' America," American West 3 (1966): 67-71, 89-93.

2589 _____. "Zeubulon Pike and Nebraska," Nebraska History 47 (1966): 355-69.

2590 _____. "How Lost Was Pike," American Heritage 16 (1985): 10-15, 75-80.

2591 Mahan, Bruce E. "Pike's Hill," Palimpsest 2 (1921): 282-89.

2592 Martin, Ethyl E. "The Expedition of Zeubulon M. Pike to the Sources of the Mississippi," Iowa Journal of History and Politics 9 (1911): 335-58.

2593 Martin, George W. "The Flag in Kansas," Magazine of History 4 (1906): 106-12.

2594 Meigs, Cornelia. As the Crow Flies. New York: Macmillan, 1927.

2595 Petersen, William J. "The Zeubulon M. Pike Expedition," Palimpsest 36 (1955): 165-204.

2596 _____. The Story of Iowa. 4 Vols. New York: Lewis Historical Co., 1952. Vol. 1, 229-36.

2597 Quaife, Milo M., ed. The Southwestern Expedition of Zeubulon M. Pike. Chicago: R.R. Donnelly, 1925.

2598 Sabin, Edwin L. Lost with Lieutenant Pike. Philadelphia: Lippincott, 1919.

2599 Salter, William. "The Eastern Border of Iowa in 1805-6," Iowa Historical Record 10 (1894): 107-21.

2600 Scheffer, Theodore H. "Following Pike's Expedition from the Smoky Hill to the Soloman," Kansas Historical Quarterly 15 (1947): 240-47.

2601 Snell, Jessie K. "Captain Pike and his Journeying." In: Lore of the Great Plains. Colby, KS: Colby Community College, 1970, 61-74.

2602 Stockwell, Wilhelmina G. "Pike on the Upper Mississippi, 1806-1806." In: New Spain and the Anglo-American; Historical Contributions Presented to Herbert Eugene Bolton. 2 Vols. Los Angeles: Privately Printed, 1932. Vol. 2, 1-20.

2603 Twitchell, Ralph E. "The Expedition under Zeubulon M. Pike." In: The Leading Facts of New Mexico History 5 Vols. Cedar City, IA: Torch Press, 1911-1917. Vol. 1, 461-69.

2604 "Z.M. Pike's Exploration in Minnesota, 1805-1806," Minnesota Historical Society Collections 1 (1872): 368-416.

SEE ALSO: 4713, 4720, 4750, 4753, 4764, Zeubulon M. Pike

## LONG'S EXPEDITION

2605  Benson, Maxine F. "Edwin James: Scientist, Linguist, Humanitarian."
      Ph. D. dissertation, University of Colorado, 1968.

2606  Christianson, Theodore. "The Long and Beltrami Explorations in
      Minnesota One Hundred Years Ago," Minnesota Historical Bulletin
      5 (1923): 249-64.

2607  Connelley, William E. Standard History of Kansas and Kansans. 5 Vols.
      Chicago: Lewis Publishing Co., 1918. Vol. 1, 79-84.

2608  Everett, Edward. "Long's Expedition," North American Review 16 (1823):
      242-69.

2609  "Explanation of the Map," Kansas Historical Collections 9 (1905-1906):
      565-78.

2610  Hill, Alfred J. "Constantine Belltrami," Minnesota Historical Society
      Collections 2 (1889): 183-96.

2611  McDermott, John F. "Early Sketches of T.R. Peale," Nebraska History
      33 (1952): 186-89.

2612  _____. "Samuel Seymour: Pioneer Artist of the Plains and the Rockies,"
      Smithsonian Institute Annual Report (1950): 497-509.

2613  Miceli, Augusto P. The Man with the Red Umbrella: Giacomo Constantino
      Beltrami in America. Baton Rouge: Claitor's Publishing Division, 1974.

2614  Miles, Wyndham P. "A Versatile Explorer: A Sketch of William H.
      Keating," Minnesota History 36 (1959): 294-99.

2615  Pammel, L.H. "Dr. Edwin James," Annals of Iowa 8 (1907): 161-85, 277-95.

2616  Phillips, Maurice E. "Long's Expedition," Frontiers 20 (1956): 79-81,
      95-97.

2617  Sparks, Jared. "Review of Keating's Account of Long's Expedition,"
      North American Review 21 (1825): 178-88.

2618  Starr, John T. "Long's Expedition to the West," Military Review 53
      (1961): 116-18.

2619  Thomas, Alfred B. "The Yellowstone River, Stephen H. Long, and Spanish
      Reaction to American Intrusion into Spanish Dominions, 1818-1819,"
      New Mexico Historical Review 4 (1929): 164-77.

2620  Tucker, John M. "Major Long's Route from the Arkansas to the Canadian
      River, 1820," Ibid 38 (1963): 185-219.

2621  Wood, Richard G. "Dr. Edwin James: A Disappointed Explorer,"
      Minnesota History 34 (1955): 284-86.

      SEE ALSO: Stephen H. Long

## CONTEMPORARY ACCOUNTS

2622  Benson, Maxie, ed. From Pittsburgh to the Rocky Mountains: Major
      Stephen Long's Expedition, 1819-1820. Golden, CO: Fulcrum, 1988.

2623  Fuller, Harlin M. and LeRoy R. Hafen, eds. The Journal of Captain John
      R. Bell, Official Journalist of the Stephen H. Long Expedition to the
      Rocky Mountains. Glendale, CA: Arthur H. Clarke, 1957.

2624  James, Edwin. Account of an Expedition from Pittsburgh to the Rocky
      Mountains, performed in the years 1819 and '20, by order of the Hon.
      J.C. Calhoun, Secretary of War, under the Command of Major Stephen H.
      Long. 2 Vols. Philadelphia: H.C. Carey, I. Lea, 1823.

2625  Keating, William H. Narratives of an Expedition to the Source of St.
      Peter's River, Lake Winnepeck, Lake of the Woods, &c. &c. 2 Vols.
      Philadelphia: H.C. Carey, I. Lea, 1823.

2626  Thwaites, Reuben G., ed. Early Western Travels, 1748-1846. Cleveland:
      Arthur H. Clarke, 1905. Vols. 14-17.

## YELLOWSTONE EXPEDITIONS

2627  Babbitt, Charles H. Early Days at Council Bluffs. Washington, DC:
      Byron S. Adams, 1916.

2628  Goodwin, Cardinal L. "A Larger View of the Yellowstone Expedition,
      1819-1820," Mississippi Valley Historical Review 4 (1917): 299-313.

2629  Nichols, Roger L. "Martin Cantonment and American Expansion in the
      Missouri valley," Missouri Historical Review 64 (1969): 1-17.

2630  Remsburg, George. "Isle au Vache," Kansas Historical Collections 8
      (1903): 436-41.

2631  Watkins, Albert. Notes of the Early History of the Nebraska Country.
      Lincoln: Nebraska State Historical Society, 1922.

2632  Wesley, Edgar B. "A Still Larger View of the so-called Yellowstone
      Expedition," North Dakota Historical Quarterly 5 (1931): 219-38.

2633  "Yellowstone Expedition," Nebraska Historical Society Publications
      20 (1922): 23-30.

      SEE ALSO: 2942, Fort Atkinson, Neb., Henry Atkinson

## CONTEMPORARY ACCOUNTS

2634  Nichols, Roger L., ed. The Missouri Expedition, 1818-1820: The Journal
      of Surgeon John Gale with Related Documents. Norman: University of
      Oklahoma Press, 1969.

2635  "Notes on the Missouri River, and Some of the Native Tribes in its
      Neighborhood, by a Military Gentleman attached to the Yellowstone
      Expedition in 1819," Analectic Magazine 1 (1820): 293-313, 342-75.

2636  Padgett, James A., ed. "The Life and Letters of James Johnson of
      Kentucky," Register of the Kentucky Historical Society 35 (1937):
      301-38.

2637  Reid, Russell and Clell G. Gannon, eds. "Journal of the Atkinson-
      O'Fallon Expedition, 1825," North Dakota Historical Quarterly 4 (1929):
      4-56.

      SEE ALSO: 2932, Henry Atkinson

FREMONT EXPEDITIONS

2638   Barnes, Gertrude. "Following Fremont's Trail Through Northern Colorado,"
       Colorado Magazine 19 (1942): 185-89.

2639   Byington, Lewis F. "The Historic Expedition of Col. John  C. Fremont
       and Kit Carson to California, 1843-44," Society of California Pioneers
       8 (1931): 184-91.

2640   Farquhar, Francis P. "Fremont in the Sierra Nevada," Sierra Club
       Bulletin 15 (1930): 74-95.

2641   Fletcher, Fred N. Early Nevada: the Period of Exploration. Reno:
       A. Carlisle, 1929.

2642   Fremont, Jessie B. "Origin of the Fremont Explorations," Century
       Magazine 41 (1891): 766-71.

2643   _____. "Resume of Fremont's Expeditions," Ibid 19 (1890): 759-71.

2644   "Fremont's Explorations," United States Magazine and Democratic Review
       17 (1845): 68-77.

2645   French, Joseph L. The Pioneer West: Narratives of the Westward March
       of Empire. Boston: Little, Brown, 1923.

2646   Greely, Adolphus W. Explorers and Travelers. New York: Scribner's
       Sons, 1895, 212-39.

2647   Horton, Lilburn H. Fremont's Explorations Through Kansas, 1842-1854.
       Hays, KS: Fort Hays Kansas State College, 1962.

2648   Johnson, Henry W. "Where Did Fremont Cross the Tehachopi Mountains in
       1844?" Historical Society of California Publications 13 (1927): 365-73.

2649   Monaghan, James. "John Fremont." In: The Overland Trail. Indianapolis:
       Bobbs-Merrill, 1947, 218-37.

2650   "Nicollet and Fremont," South Dakota Historical Collections 10 (1920):
       69-129.

2651   Rochlin, Phillip. "Fremont on the Rocky Mountains," Historical Society
       of Southern California Quarterly 35 (1953): 325-34.

2652   Sabin, Edwin L. With Carson and Fremont, Being the Adventures in the
       the Years 1842-43-44. Philadelphia: Lippincott, 1912.

2653   Smith, Herbert G. Historic Deeds of Danger and Daring. New York:
       Christian Herald, 1906.

2654   Smith, James U. "John C. Fremont's Expedition in Nevada, 1843-1844,"
       Nevada Historical Society Report 2 (1911): 106-52.

       SEE ALSO: John C. Fremont

CONTEMPORARY ACCOUNTS

2655   Carey, Charles H., ed. The Journals of Theodore Talbot, 1843 and 1849-52;
       with the Fremont Expedition of 1843, and with the First Military Company
       in Oregon Territory, 1849-1852. Portland, OR: Metropolitan Press, 1931.

2656  Des Montaignes, Francois. The Plains; being No Less than a Collection
      of Veracious Memoranda Taken During the Expedition of Exploration in
      The Year 1845. Norman: University of Oklahoma Press, 1972.

2657  Gudde, Erwin G. and Elizabeth K. Exploring with Fremont: The Private
      Diaries of Charles Preuss, Cartographer for John C. Fremont on his
      First, Second and Fourth Expeditions to the Far West. Norman:
      University of Oklahoma Press, 1958.

2658  Hive, Robert V. and Savoie Lottinville, eds. Soldier in the West:
      Letters of Theordore Talbot during his Services in California, Mexico
      and Oregon, 1845-1853. Norman: University of Oklahoma Press, 1972.

## CAVALRY EXPEDITIONS

2659  Abert, James W. Guadal P'a: The Journal of Lieutenant J.W. Abert from
      Bent's Fort to St. Louis in 1845. Canyon, TX: Panhandle-Plains
      Historical Society, 1941.

2660  Agnew, Brad. "The Dodge-Leavenworth Expedition of 1834," Chronicles
      of Oklahoma 53 (1975): 376-96.

2661  _____. "Brigadier General Henry Leavenworth and Colonel Henry Dodge."
      In: Joseph A. Stout, ed. Frontier Adventures: American Explorers in
      Oklahoma. Oklahoma City: Oklahoma Historical Society, 1976, 91-100.

2662  Allen, James and Henry B. Schoolcraft. Expedition to the Northwestern
      Indians,1832. 23rd Cong. 1st Session House Document 323 (1834).

2663  Bray, Edmund C. and Martha C. Joseph Nicollet on the Plains and
      Prairies: Expeditions of 1838-39, with Journals, letters, and Notes
      on the Indians. St. Paul: Minnesota Historical Society, 1976.

2664  Briggs, John E., ed. "The Expedition of 1835," Palimpsest 16 (1935):
      105-36.

2665  _____. "When Iowa was Young," Ibid 6 (1925): 117-27.

2666  _____. "With  Captain Allen in 1844," Ibid 25 (1944): 193-209.

2667  Connelley, William E., ed. The Expedition of Major Clifton Wharton
      in 1844," Kansas Historical Collections 16 (1923-1925): 272-305.

2668  "Dragoon Expedition," Army and Navy Chronicle 9 (1839): 285-86.

2669  "The Dragoon Expedition from the Journal of an Officer," Military
      and Naval Magazine 5 (1835): 49-50.

2670  "Dragoon Expedition-Indian Talk," Ibid 6 (1835): 178-87, 237-48, 317-
      29, 412-23.

2671  "Dragoon Expedition, Fort Leavenworth, Oct. 3, 1839," Army and Navy
      Chronicle 9 (1839): 285-6.

2672  [Ford, Lemuel] "A Summer upon the Prairie," Ibid 2 (1836): 277-78,
      292-93, 311-12, 321-22, 337-38, 369-70, 385-86; 3 (1836): 1-2, 17-18,
      33-34.

2673  Foreman, Grant. Pioneer Days in the Early Southwest. Cleveland:
      Arthur H. Clark, 1926, 123-39.

2674  "A Fragment of History," Chronicles of Oklahoma 13 (1935): 481-84.

2675  Gardner, Hamilton. "The March of the First Dragoons from Jefferson
      Barracks to Fort Gibson in 1833-1834," Ibid 31 (1953): 22-36.

2676  Hildreth, James. Dragoon Campaigns to the Rocky Mountains; Being a
      History of the Enlistment, Organization, and First Campaigns of the
      Regiment of United States Dragoons. New York: Wiley, Long, 1836.

2677  Hulbert, Archer B., ed. "A Summer Upon the Prairie." In: The Call of
      the Columbia: Iron Men and Saints Take the Oregon Trail. Denver, CO:
      Denver Public Library, 1934, 228-305.

2678  Kingsbury, Gaines P. "Journal of the March of a Detachment of Dragoons
      under the Command of Colonel Dodge During the Summer of 1835,"
      American State Papers: Military Affairs 6: 130-44.

2679  Lucas, J.G. "March of the Dragoons: Colonel Kearny's Expedition
      Impressed the Indians," Annals of Iowa 27 (1945): 85-96.

2680  Lupton, David W. and Dorothy R., eds. "A Dragoon in Arkansas Territory
      in 1833," Arkansas Historical Quarterly 45 (1986): 217-27.

2681  McDermott, John F., ed. Indian Sketches Taken During an Expedition to
      the Pawnee Tribes, 1833. Norman: University of Oklahoma Press, 1955.

2682  Morrison, James D. "Travis G. Wright and the Leavenworth Expedition
      in Oklahoma," Chronicles of Oklahoma 25 (1947): 7-14.

2683  Mumey, Nolie, ed. March of the First Dragoons to the Rocky Mountains
      in 1835: The Diaries and Maps of Lemuel Ford. Denver, CO: Eames Bros.,
      1957.

2684  Pelzer, Louis. Marches of the Dragoons in the Mississippi Valley.
      Iowa City: State Historical Society of Iowa, 1917.

2685  _____., ed. "A Journal of Marches by the First United States Dragoons,
      1834-1835," Iowa Journal of History and Politics 7 (1909): 331-78.

2686  _____., ed. "Captain Lemuel Ford's Journal of an Expedition to the
      Rocky Mountains, 29 May to 16 September, 1835," Mississippi Valley
      Historical Review 12 (1926): 550-79.

2687  Perrine, Fred S., ed. "Hugh Evans Journal of Colonel Henry Dodge's
      Expedition to the Rocky Mountains in 1835," Ibid 14 (1927): 192-214.

2688  _____. and Grant Foreman, eds. "The Journal of Hugh Evans, Covering
      the First and Second Campaigns of the United States Dragoon Regiment
      in 1834 and 1835," Chronicles of Oklahoma 3 (1925): 175-215.

2689  Petersen, William J. "Across the Prairies of Iowa," Palimpsest 12
      (1931): 326-34.

2690  _____. "Jean Marie Cardinal," Ibid 12 (1931): 414-20.

2691  _____. "Trailmaking on the Frontier," Ibid 12 (1931): 298-314.

2692  _____. The Story of Iowa. 4 Vols. New York: Lewis Historical Co.,
      1952. Vol. 1, 261-72.

2693 _____. "Up the Missouri with Atkinson," Palimpsest 12 (1931): 315-25.

2694 "Reminiscences of Some Incidents in the Career of A United States Dragoon between the Years 1839 and 1844," Texas Quarterly 1 (1966): 6-20.

2695 Rutland, Robert A. "A Journal of the First Dragoons in the Iowa Territory, 1844," Iowa Journal of History and Politics 51 (1953): 57-78.

2696 _____. "The Dragoons in the Iowa Territory, 1845," Ibid 51 (1953): 156-82.

2697 Schoolcraft, Henry R. Narrative of an Expedition through Upper Missouri to Itasca Lake. New York: Harper, 1834, 163-241.

2698 Schubert, Frank N. , ed. March to South Pass: Lt. William B. Franklin's Journal of the Kearny Expedition of 1845. Washington, DC: Office of the Chief of Engineers, 1979.

2699 Shirk, George H. "Peace on the Plains," Chronicles of Oklahoma 28 (1950): 2-41.

2700 Stevenson, C. Stanley, ed. "Expeditions into Dakota," South Dakota Historical Collections 9 (1918): 347-68.

2701 Thoburn, Joseph B. and Muriel H. Wright. Oklahoma: A History of the States and its People. 3 Vols. New York: Lewis Historical Publishing Co., 1929. Vol. 1, 179-86.

2702 Thoburn, Joseph B. "The Dragoon Campaigns to the Rocky Mountains," Chronicles of Oklahoma 8 (1930): 35-41.

2703 Van der Zee, Jacob, ed. "Captain James Allen's Dragoon Expedition From Fort Des Moines, Territory of Iowa, in 1844," Iowa Journal of History and Politics 11 (1913): 68-108.

2704 _____., ed. "Captain Edwin V. Sumner's Dragoon Expedition in the Iowa Territory, 1845," Ibid 11 (1913): 259-66.

2705 Wheelock, Thompson B. "Colonel Henry Dodge and his Regiment of Dragoons on the Plains in 1834," Annals of Iowa 17 (1930): 173-97.

2706 Wheelock, Thompson B. "Journal of Colonel Dodge's Expedition from Fort Gibson to the Pawnee Pict Village," American State Papers, Military Affairs 5: 373-82.

2707 Whitcomb, Mary R. "Reminiscences of Gen. James C. Parrott," Annals of Iowa 3 (1898): 369-83.

2708 Williams, Stanley T. and Barbara D. Simison, eds. Washington Irving on the Prairie; or, A Narrative of the Southwest in the Year 1832. New York: American Book Co., 1937.

2709 Williams, Maj. William. "Historical Sketches-Northwestern Iowa," Annals of Iowa 1 (1893): 132-36.

2710 Woolworth, Nancy. "Captain Edwin V. Sumner's Expedition to Devil Lake in the Summer of 1845," North Dakota History 28 (1961): 79-98.

SEE ALSO: 2859, 4719, Nathan Boone, James H. Carleton, Philip St. G. Cooke, Henry Dodge, Stephen W. Kearny, Albert M. Lea, Henry Leavenworth

FRONTIER DEVELOPMENT

2711 Barry, Louise. The Beginning of the West: Annals of the Kansas Gateway to the American West, 1540-1854. Topeka: Kansas State Historical Society, 1972.

2712 Borger, Henry C. "The Role of the Army Engineers in the Westward Movement in the Lake Huron-Michigan Basin Before the Civil War." Ph. D. dissertation, Columbia University, 1954.

2713 Brown, Everett S. "Jefferson's Plans for a Military Colony in Orleans Territory," Mississippi Valley Historical Review 8 (1921): 373-76.

2314 Clous, John W. "The Army as a Pioneer of Civilization, and as a Constructive Agency under our Government," Journal of the Military Service Institute 49 (1911): 45-56.

2315 Colgrove, Kenneth W. "The Attitude of Congress Towards the Pioneers of the West, 1789-1820," Iowa Journal of History and Politics 8 (1910): 3-129.

2716 Crimmins, M.L. "Texas in the 'Army and Navy Chronicle', 1836," Southwestern Historical Quarterly 49 (1945): 390-98.

2717 Garver, John B. "The Role of the United States Army in the Colonization of the Trans-Missouri West: Kansas, 1804-1861." Ph. D. Dissertation, Syracuse University, 1981.

2718 Goetzmann, William A. "The Corps of Topographical Engineers in the Exploration and Development of the Trans-Mississippi West." Ph. D. dissertation, Yale University, 1957.

2719 McFarling, Lloyd, ed. Exploring the Northern Plains, 1800-1876. Caldwell, ID: Caxton Printers, 1955.

2720 Nichols, Roger L. "The Army and Early Perceptions of the Plains," Nebraska History 56 (1975): 121-35.

2721 Oliva, Leo E. "The Army and Continental Expansion." In: Robin Higham and Carol Brandt, eds. The United States Army in Peacetime. Manhattan, KS: Military Affairs Publications, 1975, 21-39.

2722 _____. "The Army and the Fur Trade," Journal of the West 26 (1987): 21-26.

2723 Prucha, Francis P. "The Settler and the Army in Frontier Minnesota," Minnesota History 29 (1948): 231-46.

2724 _____. "The Scythe of Civilization: A Study of the United States Army as a Civilizing Force on the Northwest Frontier." Ph. D. dissertation, Harvard University, 1950.

2725 _____. Broadax and Bayonet: The Role of the United States Army in the Development of the Northwest, 1815-1860. Madison: State Historical Society of Wisconsin, 1953.

2726 Robinson, W. Stitt. "The Role of the Military in Territorial Kansas." In: Territorial Kansas: Studies Commemorating the Centennial. Lawrence: University of Kansas Publications, 1954, 70-102.

2727  Schubert, Frank N. Vanguard of Expansion: Army Engineers in the Trans-
      Mississippi West, 1819–1879. Washington, DC: Office of the Chief of
      Engineers, 1980.

2728  Skaggs, David C. "Military Contributions to the Development of
      Territorial Kansas." Master's Thesis, University of Kansas, 1960.

2729  Storrow, Samuel A. "The Northwest in 1817: A Contemporary Letter,"
      Wisconsin Historical Society Collections 6 (1872): 154–87.

2730  Stunkel, Kenneth P. "Military Scientists of the American West,"
      Army 13 (1963): 50–59.

2731  Tate, Michael L. "The Multi-Purpose Army on the Frontier: A Call for
      Further Research." In: Ronald Lora, ed. The American West: Essays in
      Honor of W. Eugene Hollon. Toldeo: University of Toledo, 1980, 171–208.

2732  Thomas, David Y. A History of Military Government in Newly Acquired
      Territory of the United States. New York: Columbia University Press,
      1904.

2733  Utley, Robert M. "The Contribution of the Frontier to the American
      Military Tradition." In: James P. Tate, ed. The American Military
      on the Frontier. Washington, DC: Office of Air Force History, 1978,
      3–13.

2734  _____. "The Frontier and the American Military Tradition." In:
      Paul A. Hutton, ed. Soldiers West: Biographies From the Military
      Frontier. Lincoln: University of Nebraska Press, 1986, 1–10.

2735  Vestal, S.C. "The Role of the Army in the Winning of the West,"
      Infantry Journal 37 (1930): 59–64.

2736  Wallace, Edward S. The Great Reconnaissance: Soldiers, Artists, and
      Scientists on the Frontier. Boston: Little, Brown, 1955.

2737  Wesley, Edgar B. "The Army and the Westward Movement," Minnesota
      History 15 (1934): 375–81.

## FRONTIER POLICY

2738  Adams, Mary P. "Jefferson's Military Policy with Special Reference
      to the Frontier, 1805–1809." Ph. D. dissertation, University of
      Virginia, 1958.

2739  Beers, Henry P. The Western Military Frontier, 1815–1846. Philadelphia:
      Henry P. Beers, 1935.

2740  Crowe, Fletcher S. "National Policy of Frontier Defense, 1815–1825."
      Master's Thesis, Washington University, St. Louis, 1922.

2741  "Defense of the Western Frontier," Army Navy Chronicle 6 (1838): 231–2.

2742  Gallagher, Ruth. "The Military-Indian Frontier, 1830–1835," Iowa
      Journal of History and Politics 15 (1917): 393–428.

2743  Holmes, Virginia. "With Broad Ax and Bayonet: The American Military
      and the Early Frontier, 1810–1840," Order of the Indian Wars Journal
      2 (1981): 1–6.

2744   Mattison, Ray H. "The Military Frontier on the Upper Mississippi,"
       Nebraska History 37 (1956): 159-82.

2745   _____. "The Indian Frontier on the Upper Missouri, to 1865," Ibid
       39 (1958): 241-66.

2746   Neal, Annie. "Policing the Frontier, 1816-1827." Master's Thesis,
       University of Wisconsin, 1923.

2747   Prucha, Francis P. "Distribution of Regular Troops before the Civil
       War," Military Affairs 16 (1952): 169-73.

2748   Robbins, Roy M. "The Defense of the Western Frontier, 1825-1840."
       Master's Thesis, University of Wisconsin, 1926.

2749   Wesley, Edgar B. Guarding the Frontier: A Study of Frontier Defense
       from 1815 to 1825. Minneapolis: University of Minnesota Press, 1935.

2750   Wooster, Robert A. "Military Strategy in the American West, 1815-
       1860." Master's Thesis, Larmar University, 1979.

       SEE ALSO: Henry Atkinson, Edmund P. Gaines, Henry Leavenworth

## MILITARY LIFE

2751   Bicker, Ralph P., ed. Frontier Life in the Army, 1845-1861.
       Glendale, CA: Arthur H. Clarke, 1932.

2752   Caldwell, Norman W. "The Enlisted Soldier at the Frontier Military
       Post, 1790-1814," Mid America 37 (1955): 195-204.

2753   _____. "Civilian Personnel at the Frontier Military Post, 1790-1814,"
       Ibid 38 (1956): 101-19.

2754   Coffman, Edward M. "Army Life on the Frontier," Military Affairs
       20 (1956): 193-201.

2755   Davis, Carl L. and Leroy H. Fischer. "Dragoon Life in Indian
       Territory, 1833-1846," Chronicles of Oklahoma 48 (1970): 2-24.

2756   Gamble, Richard D. "Garrison Life at Frontier Military Posts, 1830-
       1860." Ph. D. dissertation, University of Oklahoma, 1956.

2757   Graham, Stanley S. "Life of the Enlisted Soldier on the Western
       Frontier, 1815-1845." Ph. D. dissertation, North Texas State, 1972.

2758   _____. "Routine at Western Cavalry Posts, 1833-1861," Journal of
       the West 15 (1976): 49-59.

2759   King, James T. "The Sword and the Pen: The Poetry of the Military
       Frontier," Nebraska History 47 (1966): 229-45.

2760   Kohn, Richard H. "The Social History of the American Soldier: A
       Review and Prospectus for Future Research," American Historical
       Review 86 (1981): 553-67.

2761   Kurtz, Henry I. "Soldier's Life," American History Illustrated 7
       (1972): 24-35.

2762   Stewart, Miller J. "A Touch of Civilization: Culture and Education
       in the Frontier Army," Nebraska History 65 (1984): 257-82.

SEE ALSO: 2991, 3075, 3083, 3091, 3096, 3097, 3165, 3187, 3476, 4821

CONTEMPORARY ACCOUNTS

2763  "An Adventure on the Prairie," Army and Navy Chronicle 10 (1840): 123.

2764  Bearden, Jacqueline K. "I Wish to Come Home Once More: The Letters of
Nathaniel Sherburne," Escribano 15 (1978): 37-48.

2765  Beatty, Erkuries. "Diary of Major Erkuries Beatty, Paymaster of the
Western Army, May 15, 1786 to June 5, 1787," Magazine of American
History 1 (1877): 175-79, 235-43, 309-15, 380-84, 432-38.

2766  Brevoort, Henry B. "The Sufferings of Soldiers in Early Days,"
Michigan Pioneer 8 (1886): 447-49.

2767  Butler, Mann. "Details of Frontier Life," Register of the Kentucky
Historical Society 62 (1964): 206-29.

2768  "Domestic Intelligence," Army and Navy Chronicle 4 (1837): 378-81.

2769  Drumm, Stella M., ed. "Letters of William Carr Lane, 1819-1831,"
Glimpses of the Past 7 (1940): 47-114.

2770  Fry, James B. Army Sacrifices, or, Briefs from Official Pigeon Holes.
Sketches Based on Official Reports Grouped Together for the Purpose
of Illustrating the Services and Experiences of the Regular Army of
the United States on the Indian Frontier. New York: D. Van Nostrand,
1879.

2771  Gray, Charles M. The Old Soldier's Story: Autobiography of Charles
Martin Gray, Co. A, 7th Regiment, U.S.I., Embracing Interesting and
Exciting Incidents of Army Life on the Frontier, in the Early Part
of the Present Century. Edgefield, SC: Edgefield Advertiser Print,
1868.

2772  Haynes, Harvey. "A Trip from Rome to Mackinaw in Territorial Days,
with Powder and Clothing for Soldiers at the Fort," Michigan Pioneer
13 (1889): 520-25.

2773  [Hill, Daniel H.] "The Army in Texas," Southwestern Historical
Quarterly 9 (1846): 434-57.

2774  Keyes, Eramus D. Fifty Year's Observation of Men and Events. New York:
Charles Scribner's Sons, 1885.

2775  Levin, Alexandra L. "An Army Wife's Letters from Pittsburgh during
the War of 1812," Western Pennsylvania Historical Magazine 61 (1978):
351-57.

2776  "Military Journal of Captain Isaac Guidon, 1797-1799." In: Seventh
Annual Report of the Director of the Department of Archives and
History of Mississippi. Nashville: Brandon, 1909, 27-113.

2777  Mitchell, Donald G. Daniel Tyler: A Memorial Volume. New Haven:
Privately Printed, 1883.

2778  "Notes and Reminiscences of an Officer of the Army," Army and Navy
Chronicle 10 (1840): 386-87; 11 (1840): 10-11, 60-62, 67-68, 91-93,
122-24, 169-71, 187-88, 200-02, 216-19.

2779  Payne, Darwin. "Camp Life in the Army of Occupation, Corpus Christi, July 1845, to March, 1846," Southwestern Historical Quarterly 73 (1969-1970): 326-42.

2780  Prucha, Francis P., ed. Army Life on the Western Frontier: Selections from the Official Reports Made Between 1826 and 1845 by Colonel George Croghan. Norman: University of Oklahoma Press, 1958.

2781  Recollections of the United States Army. A Series of Thrilling Tales and Sketches by an American Soldier, written during a Period in "the Service". since 1830. Boston: James Monroe, 1845.

2782  "Scenes and Adventures in the Army: Sketches of Indians and Life Beyond the Border," Southern Literary Messenger 8 (1842): 405-14, 453-68, 573-90, 655-64, 701-4; 9 (1843): 109-24.

2783  Shippee, Lester P., ed. "Report of Inspection of the Ninth Military Department, 1819," Mississippi Valley Historical Review 7 (1920): 261-74.

2784  "A Stampedo," Military and Naval Magazine 4 (1834): 296-98.

2785  Storrow, Samuel A. "Narrative of a Tour in the Summer of 1817 on the Shores of Lake Superior and Other Northern lakes of the United States," Wisconsin Historical Society Collections 6 (1872): 154-87.

2786  Welter, Everhard. Forty-Two Years of Eventful Life in Two Wars, in the Great Wild West, and in Washington, D.C. Washington: N.p., 1888.

2787  Wesley, Edgar B., ed. "Diary of James Kennerly, 1823-1826," Missouri Historical Society Collection 6 (1928): 41-97.

2788  White, Helen M. "Frontier Feud, 1819-1820: How Two Officers Quarreled all the Way to the Site of Fort Snelling," Minnesota History 42 (1970): 99-114.

SEE ALSO: Military Medicine, Contemporary Accounts, 2908, 2909, 2920, 2988, 2991, 3005, 3128, 3147, 3178, 3185, 3199, 3211, 3340, 3372, 3373, 3399, 3411, 3444, 3451, 3482, 4817, 5523, 6236

## MILITARY MEDICINE

2789  Archer, G.W. "George Edward Mitchell, Physician and Soldier," Military Surgeon 88 (1941): 670-73.

2790  Alvord, Benjamin. "Mortality in Each Year Among the Officers of the Army for Fifty Years, from 1824 to 1873, as derived from the Army Registers," Proceedings of the American Association for the Advancement of Science 23 (1874): 57-59.

2791  Ashburn, Percy M. "One Century Ago," Military Surgeon 59 (1926): 33-43.

2792  Ayars, Charles W. "Some Notes on the Medical Service of the Army, 1812-1839," Ibid 50 (1922): 505-24.

2793  Barboriak, Peter N. "Reporting to the Surgeon General: The Peacetime Practice of Military Surgeons in Antebellum America, 1818-1861. Ph. D. dissertation, Duke University, 1987.

2794  Barr, R.N. "Army Diseases," Ohio Medical and Surgical Journal 14 (1826): 95-116.

2795  Bayne-Jones, Stanhope. The Evolution of Preventative Medicine in the
      United States Army, 1607-1931. Washington, DC: Office of the Surgeon
      General, 1968.

2796  Black, Wilfred W. "The Army Doctor in the Trans-Mississippi West,
      1775-1860," Southwestern Social Science Quarterly 24 (1943): 118-28.

2797  Breeden, James O. "Health of Early Texas: The Military Frontier,"
      Ibid 80 (1977): 357-98.

2798  Chambers, John S. The Conquest of Cholera, America's Greatest
      Scourge. New York: Macmillan, 1938.

2799  Chitty, W.D. "Historical Sketch of the Veterinary Service of the
      United States Army," Journal of the United States Cavalry Assoc-
      iation 20 (1909-1910): 45-60.

2800  Chuinard, Eldon G. Only One Man Died: The Medical Aspects of the
      Lewis and Clark Expedition. Glendale, CA: Arthur H. Clark, 1979.

2801  Cooney, James P. "Some Notes on the Historical Development of the
      Medical Service Corps," U.S. Armed Forces Medical Journal 8 (1957):
      254-63.

2802  Duncan, Louis C. "Sketches of the Medical Service in the War of
      1812," Military Surgeon 72 (1933): 144-50, 241-46, 324-29.

2803  Erwin, Marie H. "Statistical Reports on the Sickness and Mortality
      of the Army of the United States, 1819-1860," Annals of Wyoming 15
      (1943): 451-73.

2804  Fent, Cindy. "Some Medical Aspects of the Lewis and Clark Expedi-
      tion," North Dakota History 53 (1986): 24-28.

2805  Foote, C.J. "Benjamin Church, First Surgeon General," Connecticut
      Medical Journal 13 (1949): 211-14.

2806  Forry, Samuel. The Climate of the United States and its Endemic
      Influences. Based Chiefly on the Records of the Medical Department
      and Adjutant General, United States Army. New York: Langley, 1842.

2807  Garrison, Fielding H. "Notes on the History of the Medical Service,"
      Military Surgeon 50 (1922): 578-602.

2808  Hall, Virginius C. "Richard Allison, Surgeon of the Legion," Hist-
      orical and Philosophical Society of Ohio Bulletin 9 (1951): 283-98.

2809  Hall, C.R. "The Beginnings of American Military Medicine," Annals
      of Medical History 4 (1942): 122-31.

2810  Hammarsten, Charles F. "Physicians and the Lewis and Clark Exped-
      ition," Transactions of the American Clinical and Climatological
      Association 91 (1979): 115-27.

2811  Henderson, Thomas. Hints on the Medical Examination of Recruits for
      the Army; and on the Discharge of Soldiers from the Service on
      Surgeon's Certificate. Philadelphia: Haswell, Barrington, 1840.

2812  Heustis, Jabez W. Physical Observations on Medical Tracts and
      Researches on Topography and Diseases of Louisiana. New York:
      Swords, 1817.

2813   _____ . "Observations on the Disease which Prevailed in the Army at
Camp Terreaux-Boefs in June, July and August of the Year 1808,"
Medical Repository 3 (1817): 33-41.

2814   Hume, Edgar E. "The Foundation of Medical Meterology by the United
States Army Medical Department," Military Surgeon 87 (1940): 89-116.

2815   _____ . Victories of Army Medicine: Scientific Accomplishments of the
Medical Department of the United States Army. Philadelphia: J.B.
Lippincott, 1943.

2816   Knopf, Richard C.  Physicians of the Indian Wars. Columbus: Ohio
Medical Association, 1953.

2817   _____ . Notes on Surgeons of the Indian Wars and War of 1812. Columbus:
Anthony Wayne Parkway Board, 1957.

2818   Koehler, Herman J. "Historical Resume of Physical Training of Cadets
at the United States Military Academy," United States Infantry
Association Journal 4 (1908): 841-47.

2819   Larsell, Olof. "Medical Aspects of the Lewis and Clark Expedition,"
Oregon Historical Quarterly 56 (1955): 211-25.

2820   Lull, George F. "Army Medical Personnel Early in the 19th Century,"
Military Surgeon 77 (1935): 223-25.

2821   Marsh, Edwin S. "The United States Army and its Health, 1819-1821,"
Ibid 108 (1951): 501-13.

2822   Meany, Edward S. "Doctor Saugrain helped Lewis and Clark," Washington
Historical Quarterly 22 (1931): 295-311.

2823   "Medical Staff of the United States Army," Boston Medical and Surgical
Journal 19 (1838): 78-80.

2824   Merritte, Weber I. "The Medical Corps of the Army and Scientific
Medicine," U.S. Armed Forces Medical Journal 5 (1954): 1785-1801.

2825   Orr, H.W. "Biographic Notes Regarding Some American Military Surgeons,"
Quarterly Bulletin, Northwestern University Medical School 20 (1946):
11-27.

2826   Phalen, James M. "The Cholera Epidemic During the Black Hawk War,"
Military Surgeon 83 (1938): 452-56.

2827   _____ . The Chiefs of the Medical Department, United States Army.
Army Medical Bulletin No. 52 (1940): 1-158.

2828   _____ . "Richard Allison-Surgeon to the Legion," Military Surgeon
86 (1940): 377-79.

2829   _____ . Sinnissippi, A Valley under a Spell. Washington, DC: Association of Military Surgeons, 1942.

2830   _____ . "Charles Stuart Tripler, 1806-1866," Army Medical Bulletin
No. 61 (1942): 176-81.

2831   Reasoner, Matthew A. "The Development of the Medical Supply Service,"
Military Surgeon 63 (1928): 1-21.

2832  Reedy, Michael J. "Army Doctors—Long Years Attaining Military Rank
      and Command," Military Medicine 130 (1965): 813-20.

2833  _____. "Army Doctors: Four Short Term Medical Chiefs," Ibid 132
      (1967): 188-94.

2834  Robinson, Doane. "The Medical Adventures of Lewis and Clark,"
      South Dakota Historical Collections 12 (1924): 53-84.

2835  "Sickness in the Army at New Orleans in 1809," Medical Repository
      14 (1811): 85-87.

2836  Simmons, James S. "Military Preventative Medicine: A Keystone of
      Military Strength," Phi Chi Quarterly 49 (1952): 118-28.

2837  Skinner, George A. "Influence of Epidemic Diseases on Military
      Operations in the History of the Western Hemisphere," Military
      Surgeon 69 (1931): 579-94.

2838  Snoddy, Donald D. "Medical Aspects of the Lewis and Clark Exped-
      ition," Nebraska History 51 (1970): 114-51.

2839  Stanley, L.L "Medicine and Surgery of the Lewis and Clark Exped-
      ition," Medical Journal and Record 127 (1928): 275-78, 306-7, 364-66,
      536-40, 598-99, 655-58.

2840  Stevenson, Isobel. "Beginnings of American Military Medicine,"
      Ciba Symposium 1 (1940): 344-59.

2841  Stewart, M.J. Moving the Wounded: Litters, Cacolets and Ambulence
      Wagons. Fort Collins, CO: Old Army Press, 1979.

2842  Trent, Josiah C. "Benjamin Waterhouse (1754-1846)," Journal of the
      History of Medicine 1 (1946): 357-64.

2843  War Department. Surgeon General's Office. Statistical Report on the
      Sickness and Mortality in the Army of the United States from January
      1819 to January 1839. Washington, DC: Jacob Gideon, 1840.

2844  _____. Statistical Report on the Sickness and Mortality in the Army
      of the United States from January 1839 to January 1855. Washington,
      DC: A.O.P. Nicholson, 1856.

2845  Wier, James A. "Nineteenth Century Army Doctors on the Frontier and
      in Nebraska," Nebraska 61 (1980): 192-214.

2846  Will, Drake W. "The Medical and Surgical Practices of the Lewis and
      Clark Expedition," Journal of the History of Medicine 14 (1959):
      273-97.

2847  _____. "Lewis and Clark: Westering Physicians," Montana 21 (1971):
      2-17.

2848  Wolfe, Edwin P. "The Genesis of the Medical Department of the United
      States Army," New York Academy of Medicine Bulletin 5 (1929): 829-31.

      SEE ALSO: Naval Medicine, 3064, 3085, 3093, 3094, 3150, 3359, 3367,
      3384, 3405, 3406, 3480, 5893, William Beaumont, James Tilton

## CONTEMPORARY ACCOUNTS

2849  Beard, J. Howard. "The Medical Observations and Practices of Lewis
      and Clark," Science Monthly 20 (1925): 506-20.

2850  Bemrose, John. Reminiscences of the Second Seminole War. Gainesville:
University of Florida Press, 1966.

2851  Cutright, Paul R. "I Gave Him Barks and Saltpeter," American Heritage
15 (1963): 59-61, 94-101.

2852  Eaton, K.K. "Military Medicine on the Louisiana Frontier: Letters of
Melines Conklin Leavenworth to Dr. Eli Todd," Bulletin of the History
of Medicine 24 (1950): 247-53.

2853  Forry, Samuel. "On Scorbutus which Prevailed in the United States Army
at Council Bluffs and St. Peter's," American Journal of Medical
Studies 3 (1842): 307-24.

2854  _____. "Letters of Samuel Forry, Surgeon, U.S. Army, 1837-1838,"
Florida Historical Quarterly 6 (1928): 133-48, 206-19; 7 (1928): 88-105.

2855  Hammond, E.A., ed. "Dr. Strobel Reports on South East Florida, 1836,"
Tequesta 21 (1961): 65-75.

2856  _____. "Bemrose's Medical Case Notes from the Second Seminole War,"
Florida Historical Quarterly 47 (1969): 401-13.

2857  Jarvis, Nathan S. "An Army Surgeon's Notes of Frontier Service, 1833-
1848," Journal of the Military Service Institute 39 (1906): 275-86,
451-60; 40 (1907): 269-77, 435-521.

2858  Jones, Harold W., ed. "A Hospital Inspector's Diary, being an Account
of the Journey of Tobias Watkins, Assistant Surgeon General, U.S. Army,
in the year 1818," Bulletin of the History of Medicine 7 (1939): 210-35.

2859  Jones, Harold W., ed. "The Diary of Assistant Surgeon Leonard McPhail
on his Journey to the Southwest in 1835," Chronicles of Oklahoma 18
(1940): 281-92.

2860  Juettner, Otto. "The Medical Records of the Indian Campaigns of
Generals Harmar, St. Clair, and Wayne," New York Medical Journal
101 (1915): 732-35.

2861  "Letters of Dr. Benjamin Waterhouse to General Varnum," Military
Surgeon 63 (1928): 68-76.

2862  Mahon, John K. "Postscript to John Bemrose's Reminiscences," Florida
Historical Quarterly 47 (1968): 59-62.

2863  Mott, Jacob R. Journey into Wilderness: An Army Surgeon's Account of
Life in Camp and Field during the Creek and Seminole Wars, 1836-1838.
Gainesville: University of Florida, 1953.

2864  Stafford, Robert C. "The Bemrose Manuscript on the Seminole War,"
Florida Historical Quarterly 18 (1940): 285-92.

2865  Sunderman, James F., ed. "Army Surgeon Reports on the Lower East
Coast," Tequesta 10 (1950): 25-33.

SEE ALSO: 3128

RELIGION

2866  Axton, John T. Brief History of Chaplains in the Army. Fort
Leavenworth: General Service Schools, 1925.

2867  Davidson, James A. "Reverend David Jones, M.A.," The Chronicle 4
      (1941): 126-40, 151-67.

2868  Gamble, Richard D. "Army Chaplains at Frontier Posts, 1830-1860,"
      Historical Magazine of the Protestant Episcopal Church 27 (1958):
      286-306.

2869  Honneywell, Roy J. Chaplains of the United States Army. Washington:
      Office of the Chief of Chaplains, 1958.

2870  Hughes, William J. "The Methodist Ministry to American Military
      Personnel to 1900." Master's Thesis, New Mexico State University,
      1974.

2871  Norton, Herman A. The United States Chaplaincy: Struggling for
      Recognition, 1791-1865. Washington, DC: Office of the Chief of
      Chaplains, 1977.

      SEE ALSO: 3368, 3695

                        FOOD AND SUPPLIES

2872  Atherton, Lewis E. "The Merchant Sutler in the Pre-Civil War Period,"
      Southwestern Social Science Quarterly 19 (1938): 140-51.

2873  _____. "Western Foodstuffs in the Army Provisions Trade," Agricultural
      History 14 (1940): 161-69.

2874  Brettschneider, Carl A. "Some of the Personalities and Problems of
      Supply Affecting the Indian Campaign of 1792-1794," Historical and
      Philosophical Society of Ohio Bulletin 9 (1951): 299-318.

2875  Brown, W.C. "The Army Ration, Old and New," Quartermaster Review 1
      ((1921): 12-16.

2876  Chartrand, Rene. "The U.S. Army's 'Supply Crisis' during the War of
      1812," Military Collector and Historian 40 (1988): 63-65.

2877  Furlong, Patrick J. "Problems of Frontier Logistics in St. Clair's
      1791 Campaign." In: Robert J. Holden, ed. Selected Papers from the
      1983 and 1984 George Rogers Clark Trans-Appalachian Frontier History
      Conference. Vincennes, IN: Eastern National Park and Monument
      Association, 1985, 101-16.

2878  Knopf, Richard C., ed. A Letterbook of James O'Hara, Quartermaster
      General to the Legion of the United States, 1792-1794. Columbus:
      Anthony Wayne Parkway Board, 1954.

2879  "Letters from General Wayne and General Wilkinson to the Quartermaster
      General," Michigan Pioneer 25 (1907): 617-37.

2880  Merlin, John R. "Critique of the Army ration, Past and Present,"
      Military Surgeon 50 (1922): 38-60, 163-87.

2881  Peifer, William H. "St. Clair's Quartermaster," Quartermaster Review
      31 (1951): 108-14.

2882  Prucha, Francis P. "Army Sutlers and the American Fur Company,"
      Minnesota History 40 (1966): 22-31.

2883   Tapson, Alfred J. "The Sutler and the Soldier," <u>Military Affairs</u> 21
       (1957): 175-81.

2884   Welty, Raymond L. "Supplying the Frontier Military Posts," <u>Kansas
       Historical Society Quarterly</u> 7 (1938): 154-69.

       SEE ALSO: Rivers

## AGRICULTURE

2885   Hall, Edith T. "The Army Took to Farming," <u>Tradition</u> 5 (1962): 19-23.

2886   Nichols, Roger L. "Soldiers as Farmers: Army Agriculture in the
       Missouri Valley, 1818-1827," <u>Nebraska History</u> 52 (1971): 239-54.

2887   Stewart, Miller J. "To Plow, To Sow, To Reap, To Mow: The U.S. Army
       Agriculture Program," <u>Ibid</u> 63 (1982): 194-215.

## ROADS

2888   Agnew, Brad. "Military Roads in Indian Territory," <u>Red River Valley
       Historical Review</u> 6 (1981): 31-47.

2889   Casey, Powell A. "Military Roads in the Florida Parishes of Louisiana,"
       <u>Louisiana History</u> 15 (1974): 229-42.

2890   Catlin, George B. "Michigan's Early Military Roads," <u>Michigan
       Historical Magazine</u> 13 (1929): 196-207.

2891   Cole, Harry E. "The Old Military Road," <u>Wisconsin Magazine of History</u>
       9 (1925): 47-62.

2892   Corbett, William P. "Rifles and Ruts: Army Road Builders in Indian
       Territory," <u>Chronicles of Oklahoma</u> 60 (1982): 294-309.

2893   Culberson, James. "The Fort Towson Road; a Historic Trail," <u>Ibid</u>
       5 (1927): 414-21.

2894   Durbin, Richard D. and Elizabeth. "Wisconsin's Old Military Road:
       Its Genesis and Construction," <u>Wisconsin Magazine of History</u> 68
       (1984): 3-42.

2895   Garner, Mrs. Bert. "A Notable United States Military Road," <u>Michigan
       Historical Magazine</u> 20 (1936): 177-84.

2896   Goodrich, Carter. "National Planning for Internal Improvements,"
       <u>Political Science Quarterly</u> 63 (1948): 16-44.

2897   Hill, Forest G. <u>Roads, Rails, and Waterways: The Army Engineers and
       Early Transportation</u>. Norman: University of Oklahoma, 1957.

2898   Hulbert, Archer B. <u>Military Roads of the Mississippi Basin: The
       Conquest of the Old Northwest</u>. Cleveland: Arthur H. Clark, 1904.

2899   Jackson, W. Turrentine. "The Army Engineers as Road Builders in
       Iowa," <u>Iowa Journal of History and Politics</u> 47 (1949): 15-33.

2900   Love, William A. "General Jackson's Military Road," <u>Mississippi
       Historical Society Publications</u> 11 (1911): 403-17.

2901  Nelson, Harold L. "Military Roads for Peace and War, 1791-1836,"
      Military Affairs 19 (1955): 1-14.

2902  McClosky, Joseph F. "History of Military Road Construction,"
      Military Engineer 41 (1949): 353-56.

2903  "The Old Military Road," Palimpsest 51 (1970): 249-80.

2904  Pray, Carl F. "A Historic Michigan Road," Michigan Historical
      Magazine 11 (1927): 325-41.

2905  Quinn, Yancey M. "Jackson's Military Road," Journal of Mississippi
      History 41 (1979): 335-50.

2906  Robbins, Eloise F. "The Orginal Military Post Road between Fort
      Leavenworth and Fort Scott," Kansas History 1 (1978): 90-100.

2907  Smith, Duane A. "The Army and Western Transportation." In: 1959
      Brand Book of the Denver Posse of the Westerners (1960): 279-308.

                    CONTEMPORARY ACCOUNTS

2908  Foreman, Carolyn T., ed. "Report of Captain John Stuart on the
      Construction of the Road from Fort Smith to Horse Prairie on the
      Red River," Chronicles of Oklahoma 5 (1927): 333-47.

2909  Nicholas, Roger L., ed. "The Camp Missouri-Chariton Road, 1819: The
      Journal of Lt. Gabriel Field," Missouri Historical Society Bulletin
      24 (1967-1968): 139-52.

2910  U.S. War Department. Report of the Reconnaissance and Survey of a
      Route for a National Road. 24th Cong. 1st Sess. House Document 169
      (1836).

      SEE ALSO: 3336

                      MILITARY ESCORTS

2911  Beers, Henry P. "The Army and the Oregon Trail to 1846," Pacific
      Northwest Quarterly 28 (1937): 339-62.

2912  _____. "Military Protection of the Santa Fe Trail to 1843," New
      Mexico Historical Review 12 (1937): 113-33.

2913  Goldman, Henry H. "A Survey of Federal Escorts of the Santa Fe Trail,
      1829-1843," Journal of the West 5 (1966): 504-16.

2914  Oliva, Leo E. Soldiers on the Santa Fe Trail. Norman: University of
      Oklahoma Press, 1967.

2915  Perrine, Fred S. "Military Escorts on the Santa Fe Trail," New Mexico
      Historical Review 2 (1927): 175-93, 269-304; 3 (1928): 265-300.

2916  Wyman, Walker D. "The Military Phase of Santa Fe Freighting," Kansas
      Historical Quarterly 1 (1933): 415-28.

2917  Young, Otis E. "Military Protection of the Santa Fe Trail and Trade,"
      Missouri Historical Review 49 (1954): 19-32.

2918  _____. "Dragoons on the Santa Fe Trail in the Autumn of 1843,"
      Chronicles of Oklahoma 32 (1954): 42-51.

CONTEMPORARY ACCOUNTS

2919 Journal of Lieutenant J.W. Abert from Bent's Fort to St. Louis, in 1845. 29th Cong. 1st Session Senate Document 438, Serial 477 (1845).

2920 "Major Alfonso Wetmore's Diary of a Journey to Santa Fe, 1828," Missouri Historical Review 8 (1914): 177-97.

2921 Young, Otis E. The First Military Escort on the Santa Fe Trail, 1829; from the Journal and Reports of Major Bennett Riley and Lieutenant Phillip St. George Cooke. Glendale, CA: Arthur H. Clark, 1952.

SEE ALSO: 4645, 4805, Phillip St. G. Cooke, Bennett Riley

RAILROADS

2922 Campbell, Edward G. "Railroads in National Defense, 1829-1848," Mississippi Valley Historical Review 27 (1940): 361-78.

2923 Taylor, George R. The Transportation Revolution, 1815-1860. New York: Harper, Row, 1968.

SEE ALSO: Edmund P. Gaines

RIVERS

2924 Chittenden, Hiram M. History of Early Steamboat Navigation on the Missouri River. Glendale, CA: Arthur H. Clark, 1903.

2925 Firth, Winchester. "American Pioneers of Steam Naviagtion," Magazine of History 4 (1906): 326-43.

2926 Foreman, Grant. "River Navigation in the Early Southwest," Mississippi Valley Historical Review 15 (1928): 34-55.

2927 Havinghurst, Walter. "Steamboat to the Rockies," American West 7 (1970): 4-11, 61-62.

2928 Hughes, Thomas. "History of Steamboating on the Minnesota River," Minnesota Historical Society Collections 10 (1905): 131-63.

2929 Hunt, John C. "Steamboats on the Plains," American History Illustrated 1 (1966): 51-57.

2930 Hunter, Louis. Steamboats on the Western Waters: An Economic and Technological History. Cambridge, MA: Harvard University Press, 1949.

2931 _____. "The Invention of the Western Steamboat," Journal of Economic History 3 (1943): 201-20.

2932 McLarty, Vivian K., ed. "The First Steamboats on the Missouri: Reminiscences of Captain W.D. Hubbell," Missouri Historical Review 51 (1957): 373-81.

2933 Merrick, George B. and William R. Tibbals. "Genesis of Steam Naviagtion on Western Waters," Wisconsin Historical Society Proceedings (1912): 97-148.

2934 Murray, Robert A. "Water-Walking War Waggons: Steamboats in the Western Indian Campaigns," By Valor and Arms 3 (1977): 48-56.

2935  Nichols, Roger L. "Army Contributions to River Transportation, 1818-
      1825," Military Affairs 33 (1969): 242-49.

2936  Petersen, William J. "Troops and Military Supplies on the Upper
      Mississippi River Steamboats," Iowa Journal of History and Politics
      33 (1935): 260-86.

2937  _____. Steamboating on the Upper Mississippi: The Waterway to Iowa.
      Iowa City: State Historical Society of Iowa, 1917.

2938  _____. "The 'Virginia", the 'Claremont' of the Upper Mississippi,"
      Minnesota History 9 (1928): 347-62.

2939  Pope, James S. "A History of Steamboating on the Lower Missouri,
      1838-1849, St. Louis to Council Bluffs, Iowa Territory." Ph. D.
      dissertation, St. Louis University, 1984.

2940  Renwick, James. "Reminiscences of the First Introduction of Steam
      Navigation," Historical Magazine 2 (1858): 225-30.

2941  "The Steamboat," Hesperian 1 (1838): 457-65.

2942  Watkins, Albert. "First Steamboat Trip up the Missouri," Nebraska
      Historical Society Collections 17 (1913): 162-205.

2943  Williams, Roy D. "Steamboats on the Missouri," Missouri Historical
      Review 22 (1928): 125-35.

2944  Wood, Richard G. "Exploration by Steamboat," Journal of Transport-
      ation History 2 (1955): 121-23.

      SEE ALSO: 4755, 5875

                              FORTIFICATIONS

2945  Allen, Richard S. "19th Century American Fortifications: Training
      Ground for Engineers," Consulting Engineer 19 (1962): 114-19.

2946  "Fortifications and Sieges," American Quarterly Review 13 (1833):
      337-75.

2947  Grant, Bruce. American Forts, Yesterday and Today. New York:
      E.P. Dutton, 1965.

2948  Haas, Irvin. Citadels, Ramparts, and Stockades: America's Historic
      Forts. New York: Everest House Publishers, 1979.

2949  Hammond, John M. Quaint and Historic Forts of North America.
      Philadelphia: J.B. Lippincott, 1915.

2950  Hinds, James R. and Edmund Fitzgerald. "An Introduction to Fortif-
      ication in the Musket Era," CAMP Periodical 8 (1976): 24-28.

2951  Peterson, Harold L. Forts in America. New York: Charles Scribner's
      Sons, 1964.

2952  Prucha, Francis P. Guide to the Military Posts of the United States,
      1789-1895. Madison: State Historical Society of Wisconsin, 1964.

2953  Roberts, Robert B. Encyclopedia of Historic Forts. New York:
      Macmillan, 1987.

2954   Robinson, Willard B. American Forts: Architectural Form and Function. Urbana: University of Illinois Press, 1977.

SEE ALSO: 4607, 4631, 4649

COASTAL FORTS

2955   Allen, Richard S. "American Coastal Forts: The Golden Years," CAMP Periodical 5 (1973): 2-7.

2956   "The Ancient Defenses of Portland," Journal of the United States Artillery 7 (1896): 193-206.

2957   Arthur, Robert. "Early Coastal Fortification," Coastal Artillery Journal 7 (1929): 134-44.

2958   _____. "Early Coastal Fortification," Military Engineer 13 (1961): 279-81.

2959   Bright, Samuel R. "Coast Defense and the Southern Coasts before Fort Sumter." Master's Thesis, Duke University, 1958.

2960   Browning, Robert S. "Providing for the Common Defense: Military Attitudes Towards U.S. Fortifications, 1794-1812." In: Charles J. Bates, ed. Coloquium on Military History Proceedings. Chicago: N.p., 1979, 85-98.

2961   _____. "Shielding the Republic: American Coastal Defense Policy in the Nineteenth Century." Ph. D. dissertation, University of Wisconsin, 1981.

2962   _____. Two if By Sea: The Development of American Coastal Defense Policy. Westport, CT: Greenwood Press, 1983.

2963   Coleman, James C. and Irene C. Pensacola Fortifications, 1698-1980: Guardians of the Gulf. Pensacola: Pensacola Historical Society, 1982.

2964   Cullum, George W. "Defenses of Narraganset Bay, Rhode Island: Historical Sketch," Magazine of American History 9 (1884): 465-96.

2965   _____. "History of the Sea Coast Fortifications of the United States, III: Narraganset Bay," Journal of the United States Artillery 8 (1897): 51-62, 187-204.

2966   "Early Coast Fortification," Coastal Artillery Journal 70 (1929): 134-44.

2967   Hastings, Hugh. "Early Fortifications around New York City." In: The Public Papers of Daniel D. Tompkins, Governor of New York, 1807-1817: Military. 3 Vols. Albany: J.B. Lyon, 1898-1902. Vol. 1, 55-78.

2968   _____. "History of the Sea Coast Fortifications of the United States, VI: Early Fortifications around New York," Journal of the United States Artillery 9 (1898): 194-210.

2969   Hawthorne, Harry L. "History of the Sea Coast Fortifications of the United States,II: Boston Harbor," Ibid 6 (1898): 359-75.

2970   Hinds, James R. "Potomac River Defenses, the First Twenty Years," CAMP Periodical 5 (1973): 1-17.

2971   Kirchner, David P. "American Harbor Defense Forts," United States Naval Institute Proceedings 84 (1958): 92-101.

2972   Leary, Peter. "History of the Sea Coast Fortifications of the United
       States, I: Portland, Maine," Journal of the United States Artillery
       6 (1896): 193-206.

2973   Lewis, Emanuel R. Seacoast Fortifications of the United States.
       Washington, DC: Smithsonian Institute Press, 1970.

2974   Moore, Jamie W. The Fortification Board, 1816-1828, and the Definition
       of National Security. Charleston, SC: The Citadel, 1981.

2975   _____. "The Bernard Board and Coastal Defense Evolution," CAMP
       Periodical 14 (1986): 3-13.

2976   "On Fortifications," Army and Navy Chronicle 6 (1838): 188-89.

2977   Peterson, Lois P., ed. The Defenses of Norfolk in 1807. Chesapeake
       Norfolk County Historical Society, 1970.

2978   Robinson, Willard B. "North American Martello Towers," Journal of
       the Society of Architectural Historians  33 (1974): 158-64.

2979   Sutcliffe, Sheila. Martello Towers. Rutherford, NJ: Farleigh Dickinson
       University Press, 1972.

2980   Thompson, Kenneth E. "Federal Fort Construction in Essex County,
       1794-1809," Essex Institute Historical Collections 121 (1985): 245-56.

2981   Tompkins, Daniel D. "History of the Sea Coast Fortifications of the
       United States, V: Early Fortifications Around New York City,"
       Journal of the United States Artillery 9 (1898): 194-210.

2982   Wade, Arthur P. "Artillerists and Engineers: The Beginnings of
       American Seacoast Fortifications, 1794-1815." Ph. D. dissertation,
       Kansas State University, 1977.

2983   Wesley, Edgar B. "The Beginnings of Coast Fortifications," Coastal
       Artillery Journal 67 (1927): 281-90.

2984   Williams, Ames W. "The Old Fortifications of New York Harbor,"
       Military Collector and Historian 22 (1970): 37-45.

       SEE ALSO: 4140, Simon Bernard

### FORT ADAMS, RI

2985   Ingersoll, Ernest. "At Fort Adams," Harper's Weekly Magazine 39
       (1895): 496.

2986   Robinson, Willard B. "Fort Adams: American Example of French Military
       Architecture," Rhode Island History 34 (1975): 77-96.

2987   _____. "The Rock on Which the Storm shall Beat!" CAMP Periodical
       9 (1977): 3-16.

### FORT BROOKE

2988   Brooke, George M. "Early Days at Fort Brooke," Sunland Tribune 1
       (1974): 1-18.

2989  Chamberlin, Donald L. "Fort Brooke: A History." Master's Thesis,
      Florida State University, 1968.

2990  ____. "Fort Brooke, Frontier Outpost, 1824-1842," Tampa Bay History
      7 (1985): 5-59.

2991  Covington, James B. "The Establishment of Fort Brooke: Four Letters
      from Colonel George M. Brooke," Florida Historical Quarterly 31
      (1953): 273-78.

2992  ____. "Life at Fort Brooke, 1824-1836," Ibid 36 (1958): 319-30.

2993  Grismer, Karl H. Tampa, A History of the City of Tampa and the Tampa
      Bay Region. St. Petersburg, FL: St. Petersburg Press, 1950.

                          FORT CONSTITUTION

2994  Frost, Thomas B. History of Fort Constitution and 'Walbach Tower',
      Portsmouth Harbor, New Hampshire. Portsmouth: C.W. Brewster, 1865.

2995  Lacy, Harriet S. "Fort William and Mary Becomes Fort Constitution,"
      Historical New Hampshire 39 (1974): 281-93.

2996  ____. Fort Constitution. Concord, NH: New Hampshire Department of
      Resources and Economic Development, 1975.

2997  Sherwin, Harry E. "Fort Constitution," New Hampshire Profiles 1
      (1951): 32-34.

2998  Wade, Arthur P. "The Defenses of Portsmouth Harbor, 1794-1821: The
      First and Second Systems of Sea Coast Fortification," Historical
      New Hampshire 33 (1978): 25-51.

                            FORT DALLAS

2999  Shappee, Nathan D. "Fort Dallas and the Naval Depot on Key Biscayne,"
      Tequesta 21 (1961): 13-40.

                          *FORT MCHENRY

3000  Rivardi, J.J. "Plan of Fort McHenry," Maryland Historical Magazine
      8 (1913): 286-90.

                            FORT MONROE

3001  Arthur, Robert. History of Fort Monroe. Fort Monroe, VA: Coast
      Artillery School, 1930.

3002  ____. "Fort Monroe," Quartermaster Review 14 (1934): 33-45.

3003  Dalby, J. Arnold. A History of Old Point Comfort and Fortress Monroe,
      from 1608 to January 1, 1881. Norfolk, VA: Landmark Steam Book and
      Job Presses, 1881.

3004  Dowdy, Clifford S. "Historic Fort Monroe," Virginia Record 80 (1958):
      5-7, 57-61; 88 (1966): 17-19, 39-43.

3005  Eby, Cecil D., ed. "Recollections of Fort Monroe, 1826-1828: From the
      Autobiography of Lieutenant Alfred Beckley," Virginia Magazine of
      History and Biography 72 (1964): 478-89.

3006   Fulgham, Matthew J. "Historic Fort Monroe," Ironworker 16 (1952): 1-12.

3007   Honts, Emily G. "Fort Monroe: The Gibraltar of the Chesapeake Bay," DAR Magazine 105 (1971): 512-14, 559.

3008   Rachal, William M. "Walled Fortress and Resort Hotels," Virginia Cavalcade 2 (1952): 20-27.

3009   Tales of Old Fort Monroe. Newport News, VA: Committee for the Fort Monroe Casemate Museum, 1953-1957.

3010   Wamsley, James S. "Taps for Fort Monroe?" Commonwealth 46 (1979): 12-15, 16-20.

3011   Weinert, Richard P. The Guns of Fort Monroe. Fort Monroe, VA: Fort Monroe Casemate Museum, 1974.

3012   ____. and Robert Arthur. Defender of the Chesapeake: The Story of Fort Monroe. Annapolis, MD: Leeward Publications, 1978.

SEE ALSO: Robert E. Lee

FORT MORGAN

3013   Chandler, Hatchett. The Cradle of American History: Fort Morgan, Alabama. Gulf Shores, AL: N.p., 1958.

3014   ____. Little Gems from Fort Morgan, the Cradle of American History. Boston: Christopher Publishing House, 1964.

3015   Cullen, E.J. "Under Five Flags: The History of the Fortification at Mobile Bay," Coastal Artillery Journal 59 (1923): 223-32.

3016   Jenkins, William H. "Alabama Forts, 1700-1838," Alabama Review 12 (1959): 163-79.

3017   Robinson, Willard B. "Military Architecture at Mobile Bay," Journal of the Society of Architectural Historians 30 (1971): 119-37.

3018   Stapleton, Earl W. "A History of Fort Morgan, Alabama, from 1813-1864." Master's Thesis, University of Alabama, 1951.

3019   Toulmin, Harry. "Toulmin Letter," Register of the Kentucky Historical Society 48 (1950): 86-86.

FORT MOULTRIE

3020   Bearess, Edwin C. The First Two Fort Moultries: A Structural History. Washington: U.S. Office of Archaeology and Historic Preservation, 1968.

3021   Church, Henry F. "The Harbor Defense of Charleston," Military Engineer 23 (1931): 11-14.

3022   Riley, Edward M. "Historic Fort Moultrie in Charleston Harbor," South Carolina Historical and Genealogical Magazine 51 (1950): 63-74.

3023   Thomas, Ebenezer S. Reminiscences of the Last Sixty-Five Years. 2 Vols. Hartford, CT: Case, Tiffany, Burnham, 1840. Vol. 2, 61-64.

FORT NATHAN HALE

3024  Adams, Leonard E. Fort Nathan Hale, Hew Haven Harbor: The War of 1812.
New Haven, CT: Fort Nathan Hale Restoration Project, 1981.

3025  Greene, Maria L. "New Haven Defenses in the Revolution and the War
of 1812," Connecticut Quarterly 4 (1898): 272-90.

3026  Gumprecht, Edward C. "Fort Nathan Hale and Black Rock Fort on New
Haven's Historic East Shore," Connecticut Antiquarian 35 (1983): 20-23.

FORT SULLIVAN

3027  Depaoli, Neill. Beneath the Barracks: Archaeology at Fort Sullivan.
Eastport, ME: Border Historical Society, 1986.

3028  Dunnack, Henry E. Maine Forts. Augusta, ME: Charles E. Nash, 1924.

3029  Williams, Ames W. "Fort at Moose Island," CAMP Periodical 5 (1973): 8-9.

3030  Zimmerman, David. Coastal Fort: A History of Fort Sullivan, Eastport,
Maine. Eastport: Border Historical Society, 1984.

FORT WOOL

3031  Beard, William E. "The Castle of Rip Raps," Coastal Artillery Journal
78 (1935): 44-46.

3032  Weinert, Richard P. "Saga of Old Fort Wool," CAMP Periodical 8 (1976-
1977): 3-14.

FRONTIER FORTS

3033  Athearn, Robert G. Forts of the Upper Mississippi. Englewood Cliffs,
NJ: Prentice Hall, 1967.

3034  Briggs, John E. Iowa Old and New. Lincoln: University of Nebraska Press,
1939, 85-114.

3035  Brown, Tom O. "Locating Seminole Indian War Forts," Florida Historical
Quarterly 40 (1962): 310-13.

3036  Casey, Powell A. Encyclopedia of Forts, Posts, Named Camps and other
Military Installations in Louisiana, 1700-1981. Baton Rouge: Claitor's
Publication Division, 1983.

3037  Chaffer, H.J. "Florida Forts Established prior to 1860."
Typescript in the P.K. Younge Library, University of Florida.

3038  "Early Military Posts, Missions, and Camps," Kansas State Historical
Society Transactions 1-2 (1888): 263-70.

3039  Frazer, Robert W. Forts of the West: Military Forts and Presidios and
Posts Commonly Called Forts West of the Mississippi. Norman: University
of Oklahoma, 1965.

3040  Graham, Albert A. "The Military Posts, Forts, and Battlefields within
the State of Ohio," Ohio Archaeological and Historical Society
Publications 3 (1891): 298-310.

3041  Green, James A. "A Visit in 1929 to the Sites of Forts in Western Ohio
      built by Generals Arthur St. Clair, Anthony Wayne, and William Henry
      Harrison," Ohio Archaeological and Historical Society Quarterly 38
      (1929): 601-12.

3042  Harden, J. Fair. "Fort Jesup, Fort Seldon, Camp Sabine, Camp Salubrity:
      Four Forgotten Frontier Army Posts of Western Louisiana," Louisiana
      Historical Quarterly 16 (1933): 5-26, 278-92, 441-53, 670-80; 17
      (1933): 139-68.

3043  Harris, Mac R. "Early Military Forts, Posts and Camps in Oklahoma."
      In: Odie Faulk and others, ed. Early Military Forts and Posts of
      Oklahoma. Oklahoma City: Oklahoma Historical Society, 1978, 122-27.

3044  Hart, Herbert M. Tour Guide to Old Western Forts. Fort Collins, CO:
      Old Army Press, 1980.

3045  Kalisch, Philip A. and Beatrice J. "Indian Territory Forts: Charnel
      Houses of the Frontier, 1839-1865," Chronicles of Oklahoma 50 (1971):
      65-81.

3046  Lackey, Vinson. The Forts of Oklahoma. Tulsa: N.p., 1963.

3047  Olsen, S.J. "Seminole War Fort Site in Northern Florida," American
      Antiquity 30 (1965): 491-94.

3048  Pagano, Mary C. "Early Military Forts in Colorado." Master's Thesis,
      University of Denver, 1943.

3049  Ruth, Kent. Great Day in the West: Forts, Posts, and Rendezvous Beyond
      the Mississippi. Norman: University of Oklahoma Press, 1963.

3050  Simmons, David. The Forts of Anthony Wayne. Fort Wayne, IN: Historic
      Fort Wayne, 1977.

3051  _____. "Military Architecture on the American Frontier." In: Robert
      J. Holden, ed. Selected papers from the 1983 and 1984 George Rogers
      Clark Trans-Appalachian Frontier History Conference. Vincennes:
      Eastern National Park and Monument Association, 1985, 81-100.

3052  Swett, Morris. "The Forerunners of Sill," Field Artillery Journal
      28 (1938): 453-63.

3053  U.S. National Park Service. Founders and Frontiersmen: Historic Places
      Commemorating Early Nationhood and the Westward Movement, 1783-1828.
      Washington, DC: Government Printing Office, 1967.

3054  Van Zandt, Howard F. "The History of Camp Holmes and Chouteau's
      Trading Post," Chronicles of Oklahoma 13 (1935): 316-37.

3055  Vander Zee, Jacob. "Forts in the Iowa Country," Iowa Journal
      of History and Politics 12 (1914): 163-204.

3056  Webster, Noah. "Letters from Noah Webster to Erza Stiles Respecting
      the Fortifications in the Western Country," Carey's American Museum
      6 (1789): 27-30, 136-41; 7 (1790): 323-28.

      SEE ALSO: 5862

FORT ADAMS, Tn.

3057  Roper, James E. "Fort Adams and Fort Pickering," Western Tennessee
Historical Society Papers 24 (1970): 5-29.

*FORT AMANDA

3058  June, O. Wickersham. "Fort Amanda," The Reporter 16 (1960): 1-7.

FORT ARBUCKLE

3059  Gardner, James H. "One Hundred Years Ago in the Region of Tulsa,"
Chronicles of Oklahoma 11 (1933): 765-85.

3060  Morrison, William B. "Fort Arbuckle," Ibid 6 (1928): 26-34.

3061  _____ . "Fort Arbuckle." In: Military Camps and Posts in Oklahoma.
Oklahoma City: Harlow Publishing Corporation, 1936, 93-103.

3062  Shirk, George H. "The Site of Old Camp Arbuckle," Chronicles of
Oklahoma 27 (1949): 313-15.

FORT ARMSTRONG

3063  Babson, Jane F. "The Architecture of Early Illinois Forts," Illinois
State  Historical Society Journal 61 (1968): 9-40.

3064  Hauberg, John A. "U.S. Army Surgeons at Fort Armstrong," Ibid 24
(1931-1932): 609-29.

3065  Johnston, Oda B. "History of Fort Armstrong, 1816-1836." Master's
Thesis, University of Iowa, 1940.

3066  Meese, William A. Early Rock Island. Moline, IL: DeSaulniers, 1905.

3067  Miller, Gerard H. "Wooden walls on the Mississippi: Fort Armstrong,"
Military Collector and Historian  24 (1972): 1-10.

3068  Peck, Maria. "Fort Armstrong," Annals of Iowa 1 (1895): 602-13.

3069  Rock Island County Historical Society. Official Book of the Fort
Armstrong centennial Celebration, June 18-24, 1916. Rock Island,IL:
E.O. Vaile, 1916.

FORT ATKINSON, Ia.

3070  Carter, William H. "Fort Atkinson, Iowa," Annals of Iowa 4 (1899-1901):
448-53.

3071  Mahan, Bruce E. "Old Fort Atkinson," Palimpsest 2 (1921): 333-50.

3072  McKusick, Marshall B. and David Archie. "A Tale of Two Forts,"
Iowan Magazine 15 (1966): 50-51.

3073  _____ . "Fort Atkinson Artifacts," Palimpsest 56 (1975): 15-21.

3074  Nichols, Roger L. "The Founding of Fort Atkinson," Annals of Iowa
37 (1965): 589-97.

3075  Williams, Bradley B. "A Soldier's Life at Fort Atkinson," Palimpsest
63 (1982): 162-73.

FORT ATKINSON, Neb.

3076   Babbitt, Charles H. Early Days at Council Bluffs. Washington, DC:
       B.S. Adams, 1916.

3077   Carlson, Gayle F. Archaeological Investigations at Fort Atkinson,
       Washington County, Nebraska. Lincoln: Nebraska State Historical
       Society, 1979.

3078   Eller, W.H. "Old Fort Atkinson," Nebraska State Historical Society
       Transactions 4 (1982): 18-28.

3079   _____. "Camp on the Missouri: Old Fort Atkinson," National Magazine
       18 (1893): 29-36.

3080   Johnson, Sally A. "Cantonment Missouri, 1819-1820," Nebraska History
       37 (1956): 121-33.

3081   _____. "Fort Atkinson at Council Bluffs," Ibid 38 (1957): 229-36.

3082   _____. "The Sixth's Elysian Fields: Fort Atkinson on the Council Bluffs,"
       Ibid 40 (1959): 1-38.

3083   _____. "Military Life at Fort Atkinson, 1819-1827." Master's Thesis,
       University of Nebraska, 1957.

3084   Kivett, Marvin F. "Excavations at Fort Atkinson, Nebraska: A
       Preliminary Report," Nebraska History 40 (1959): 39-66.

3085   Levine, Victor E. "Scurvy in Nebraska," American Journal of Digestive
       Diseases 22 (1955): 9-17, 294-95.

3086   Murphy, William D. "A History of State  Parks and Recreation Areas
       in Nebraska." Ph. D. dissertation, Indiana University, 1975.

3087   Nelson, Ray E. "Old Fort Atkinson, 1819-1827." Master's Thesis,
       University of Chicago, 1940.

3088   Ney, Virgil. "Abandoning Fort Atkinson," CAMP Periodical 6 (1974): 9-20.

3089   _____. "Fort Atkinson, 1819-1827: A Historical Evaluation," Ibid 7
       (1975): 22-26.

3090   _____. "Prairie Generals and Colonels at Cantonment Missouri and Fort
       Atkinson," Nebraska History 56 (1975): 51-76.

3091   _____. "Daily Life at Fort Atkinson on the Missouri, 1820-1827,"
       Military Review 59 (1977): 36-48, 50-66.

3092   _____. Fort on the Prairie: Fort Atkinson on the Council Bluffs.
       Washington, DC: Command Publications, 1978.

3093   Nichols, Roger L. "Scurvy at Cantonment Missouri, 1819-1820," Nebraska
       History 49 (1968): 333-47.

3094   Reals, William J. "Scurvy at Fort Atkinson, 1819-1820," Bulletin of
       the History of Medicine 23 (1949): 137-54.

3095   Watkins, Albert. "Why Fort Atkinson was Established," Nebraska History
       2 (1919): 4-5.

3096    Wesley, Edgar B. "Life at a Frontier Western Post: Fort Atkinson, 1823–1826," Journal of the American Military Institute 3 (1939): 203–9.

3097    _____. "Life at Fort Atkinson," Nebraska History 30 (1949): 348–58.

FORT ATKINSON, Ws.

3098    McMillen, Florence C. "Settlement and Development of Fort Atkinson, Wisconsin, 1832–1860." Bachelor's Thesis, University of Wisconsin, 1914.

3099    Mayne, Dexter D. "The Old Fort at Fort Atkinson," Wisconsin Historical Society Proceedings (1899): 197–201.

3100    Rankin, Aaron. "My First Trip West. Fort Atkinson, as I saw it." Typescript at Wisconsin Historical Society.

3101    Schreiner, Lillian S. "An Important Historical memorial," Americana 5 (1910): 134–36.

FORT BELLE FONTAINE

3102    Gregg, Kate L. "Building of the First American Fort West of the Mississippi," Missouri Historical Review 30 (1936): 345–64.

3103    Magnaghi, Russell M. "The Belle Fountaine Indian Factory, 1805–1808," Ibid 75 (1981): 396–416.

3104    Norton, W.T. "Old Fort Belle Fontaine," Illinois State Historical Society Journal 4 (1911): 334–39.

FORT CAMPUS MARTIUS

3105    Hawes, E.M. "Ohio's Campus Martius," Art and Archaeology 33 (1932): 309–15.

3106    Hildreth, Samuel P. "A Description of Campus Martius," American Pioneer 1 (1842): 83–89.

3107    "Plan of an Ancient Fortification at Marietta, Ohio, 1787," American Academy of Arts and Sciences Memoirs 5 (1850): 25–28.

3108    Schneider, Norris F. Campus Martius State Memorial Museum. Marietta: MacDonald Print Co., 1932.

FORT COFFEE

3109    Littlefield, Daniel E. and Lonnie E. Underhill. "Fort Coffee and Frontier Affairs, 1834–1838," Chronicles of Oklahoma 54 (1976): 314–38.

3110    Morrison, William B. "Forts Coffee and Wayne." In: Military Posts and Camps in Oklahoma. Oklahoma City: Harlow Publishing Corporation, 1936, 59–70.

FORT CRAWFORD

3111    Atwater, Caleb. Remarks Made on a Tour to Prairie du Chein, Thence to Washington City, in 1829. Colombus: Jenkins, Grover, 1831.

3112    Davis, Susan B. Old Forts and Real Folks. Madison, WS: Bayliss, 1939.

3113  Durries, Daniel S. The Early Outposts of Wisconsin. Madison, WS:
      State Historical Society of Wisconsin, 1872.

3114  Fonda, John H. "Early Wisconsin," Wisconsin Historical Society
      Collections 5 (1868): 242-45.

3115  Mahan, Bruce E. Old Fort Crawford and the Frontier. Iowa City: State
      Historical Society of Iowa, 1926.

3116  _____. "Old Fort Crawford," Palimpsest 42 (1961): 449-512.

3117  Snelling, William J. "Early Days at Prairie du Chien and the
      Winnebago Outbreak of 1827," Wisconsin Historical Society Collect-
      ions 5 (1868): 123-53.

                          FORT DADE

3118  Laumer, Frank. "The Fort Dade Site," Florida Anthropologist 16
      (1963): 33-42.

3119  _____. "This Was Fort Dade," Florida Historical Quarterly 45 (1966):
      1-11.

                        *FORT DEARBORN

3119A Currey, Josiah S. "Disputed Points in the Story of Old Fort
      Dearborn," Dial 53 (1912): 186-87.

3120  _____. "More about the Story of Old Fort Dearborn," Ibid 53 (1912):
      282-83.

3121  _____. The Story of Old Fort Dearborn. Chicago: McClurg, 1912.

3122  Cass, Lewis. "Letter," Chicago History 4 (1955): 134-46.

3123  "Fort Dearborn, 1803-1812," Ibid 2 (1949): 97-102.

3124  "Memories of the Fort Dearborn Massacre: Who Was David Kennison,"
      Illinois Catholic Historical Review 2 (1919): 50-60.

3125  Van Natter, F.M. "The Story of Fort Dearborn," National Republic
      21 (1933): 1-3.

3126  Wilson, James G. "Sketch of Fort Dearborn," United States Service
      Magazine 4 (1865): 320-23.

                        FORT DEFIANCE

3127  Carter, William, comp. Fort Defiance Centennial, August 7, 8, and 9,
      1894. Defiance, OH: Cresent Print, 1894.

3128  Knopf, Richard C., ed. "A Surgeon's Mate at Fort Defiance: The
      Journal of Joseph Gardner Andrews for the Year 1795," Ohio Historical
      Quarterly 66 (1957): 57-86. 159-85, 238-68.

3129  Some Interesting facts about Fort Defiance, issued in Commemoration
      of the 150th Anniversary of the Arrival of General 'Mad' Anthony
      Wayne. Defiance, OH: City Park Commission, 1944.

                        FORT DES MOINES

3130  "Fort Des Moines, No. 1," Annals of Iowa 3 (1898): 351-63.

3131   "Fort Des Moines, No. 2," Annals of Iowa 4 (1899): 161-78.

3132   Briggs, John E. "The Second Fort Des Moines," Palimpsest 24 (1943): 161-72.

3133   Gallaher, Ruth A. Fort Des Moines in Iowa History. Iowa City: State Historical Society of Iowa, 1919.

3134   McKusick, Marshall B. "Fort Des Moines (1834-1837): An Archaeological Test," Annals of Iowa 42 (1975): 513-22.

3135   McLaughlin, W.M. "Old Fort Des Moines," Ibid 25 (1943): 31-37.

3136   Petersen, William J. The Story of Iowa. 4 Vols. New York: Lewis Historical Company, 1952. Vol. 1, 252-60.

3137   Polk, Harry H. "Old Fort Des Moines," Annals of Iowa 36 (1962): 425-36.

3138   Sawhill, W.R. "Captain James Allen and Fort Des Moines," Ibid 20 (1937): 547-48.

3139   Seeburger, Vernon R. "Fort Des Moines and Des Moines," Ibid 25 (1943): 20-31.

3140   Williams, Ora. "Des Moines First Hundred Years," Ibid 25 (1943): 7-20.

FORT DUNLAP

3141   Cone, Stephen D. "Indian Attack on Fort Dunlap," Ohio Archaeological and Historical Society Quarterly 17 (1908): 64-72.

*FORT ERIE

3142   Owen, David A. Fort Erie (1764-1823): A Historical Guide. Niagara, ON: Niagara Parks Commission, 1986.

   SEE ALSO: William G. Belknap, Thomas Childs

FORT FAYETTE

3143   Davis, Mrs. Elvert M. "Fort Fayette," Western Pennsylvania Historical Magazine 10 (1927): 65-84.

FORT FOSTER

3144   Schene, Michael G. History of Fort Foster. Tallahassee, FL: Florida Division of Archives, History and Management, 1974.

3145   _____. "Fort Foster: A Second Seminole War Fort," Florida Historical Quarterly 54 (1976): 319-39.

FORT GIBSON

3146   Agnew, Brad. Fort Gibson: Terminal on the Trail of Tears. Norman: University of Oklahoma, 1980.

3147   Boydstun, Q.B. "Fort Gibson Barracks, Powder Magazine and Bake Oven," Chronicles of Oklahoma 50 (1972): 289-96.

3148   _____. "The Restoration of Old Fort Gibson," Ibid 58 (1980): 176-91.

3149   Bristow, Joseph Q. Tales of Old Fort Gibson: Memories Along the Trail
       to Yesterday of the Oklahoma Indian Territory and the Old South.
       New York: Exposition Press, 1961.

3150   Coolidge, Richard H. "On the Medical Topography and Diseases of
       Fort Gibson, Arkansas," Southern Medical Reports 2 (1850): 440-52.

3151   Foote, Rensselaer W. "Letters Postmarked Cantonment Gibson, 1842,"
       Chronicles of Oklahoma 36 (1958): 88-89.

3152   Foreman, Carol T. "Reports from Fort Gibson, 1835 to 1839,"
       Ibid 31 (1953): 207-11.

3153   Foreman, Grant. Fort Gibson: A Brief History. Norman: University of
       Press, 1936.

3154   _____. "The Centennial of Fort Gibson," Chronicles of Oklahoma 2
       (1924): 119-28.

3155   Gardner, James H. "The Lost Captain: J.L. Dawson of Old Fort Gibson,"
       Ibid 21 (1943): 217-49.

3156   Historic Fort Gibson. Fort Gibson, OK: Fort Gibson Historic
       Preservation and Landmark Commission. N.d.
       At Oklahoma Historical Society.

3157   Keller, Lee H. "From New York to Fort Gibson," Sturm's Oklahoma
       Magazine 9 (1909): 66-71.

3158   Morrison, William B. "Fort Gibson." In: Military Posts and Camps in
       Oklahoma. Oklahoma City: Harlow Publishing Corporation, 1936, 28-47.

3159   "Old Fort Gibson," Sturm's Statehood Magazine 1 (1905): 89-92.

3160   Rohrs, Richard C. "Fort Gibson." In: Odie Faulk and Others, eds.
       Early Military Forts and Posts of Oklahoma. Oklahoma City: Oklahoma
       Historical Society, 1978, 26-38.

3161   Shockley, P.M. "The Charnel House of the Frontier," Quartermaster
       Review 12 (1933): 31-36.

3162   Thoburn, Joseph B. "Fort Gibson's Historic Relation to Oklahoma,"
       Sturm's Oklahoma Magazine 9 (1909): 71-76.

3163   West, C.W. Fort Gibson: Gateway to the West. Muskogee, OK: Muscogee
       Publishing Co., 1974.

       SEE ALSO: Pierce M. Butler, Gustavus Loomis, James B. Many

FORT GRATIOT

3164   Bancroft, William L. "History of the Military Reservation at Fort
       Gratiot," Michigan Pioneer 11 (1888): 249-61.

3165   Hawkins, Bruce. Sentries in the Wilderness: Life at Fort Gratiot,
       Michigan Territory, 1814-1821. Port Huron, MI: Museum of Arts, 1986.

3166   "History of Fort Gratiot," Michigan Pioneer 18 (1892): 667-76.
       SEE ALSO: Charles Gratiot

## FORT GREENVILLE

3167   Arnold, James O. "Fort Greenville Traditions," Ohio Archaeological
       and Historical Society Publications 17 (1908): 60-63.

3168   Perry, Robert E. Treaty City, A Story of Old Fort Greenville.
       Bradford, OH: R.E. Perry, 1945.

## FORT HAMILTON

3169   Cone, Stephen D. Biographical and Historical Sketches. A Narrative
       of Hamilton and its Residents from 1791 to 1896. 2 Vols.
       Hamilton, OH: Republican Publishing Co., 1896.

3170   McClung, D.W. Anniversary of the City of Hamilton, Ohio, September
       17-19, 1891. Hamilton, OH: Laramie Print Co., 1892.

3171   Miller, William C. "History of Fort Hamilton," Ohio Archaeological
       and Historical Society Publications 13 (1904): 97-111.

3172   _____. "Powder Magazine at Fort Hamilton," Ibid 14 (1905): 404-7.

3173   Proceedings of the Buckeye Celebration in Commemoration of the Day
       on Which General St. Clair named 'Fort Hamilton' at Hamilton, Ohio.
       Hamilton, OH: N.p., 1835.

       SEE ALSO: 3444

## FORT HARMAR

3174   "A Description of Fort Harmar," Magazine of Western History 1 (1884-
       1885): 26-31.

3175   "Fort Harmar, the First Permanent Settlement in Ohio," American
       Pioneer 1 (1842): 25-30.

3176   History of the Upper Ohio Valley, with Family History and Biographical
       Sketches. 2 Vols. Madison, WS: Brant, Fuller, 1891. Vol. 1, 326-31.

3177   Reiter, Edith S. Marietta and the Northwest Territory, 1788.
       Marietta, OH: Seevers Printing, 1960.

## *FORT HOLMES

3178   Anderson, Charles A., ed. "Frontier Mackinac Island, 1823-1834:
       Letters of William Montague and Amanda White Ferry," Journal of
       The Presbyterian Historical Society 26 (1948): 182-91.

3179   Clark, E.M. "Restoration of Old Fort Holmes on Mackinac island,"
       Michigan Historical Magazine 20 (1936): 295-300.

3180   Dunnigan, Brian L. "The Post of Mackinac, 1779-1812." Master's Thesis,
       Coopertown New York, 1976.

3181   _____. Fort Holmes. Lansing, MI: Mackinac  States Park Commission,
       1985.

3182   Jenks, William L. "Patrick Sinclair, Builder of Fort Mackinac,"
       Michigan Pioneer 39 (1915): 61-85.

3183  "Mackinac," Army and Navy Chronicle 13 (1841): 115-19.

3184  Spooner, Harry L. "At Fort Mackinac a Century Ago," Michigan History 12 (1928): 505-12.

3185  "A Trip to Mackinac," Military and Naval Magazine 6 (1835): 20-28.

3186  White, Peter. "Old Fort Holmes," Michigan Pioneer 38 (1912): 85-89.

3187  Widder, Keith B. Reveille till Taps: Soldier Life at Fort Mackinac, 1780-1895. Lansing, MI: Mackinac Island State Park Commission, 1986.

       SEE ALSO: 4973, William Beaumont

## FORT HOWARD

3188  "Arrival of American Troops at Green Bay in 1816," Wisconsin Historical Society Collections 13 (1895): 441-47.

3189  Biddle, James W. "Recollections of Green Bay in 1816-1817," Ibid 1 (1855): 49-63.

3190  Evans, William L. "The Military History of Green Bay," State Historical Society of Wisconsin Proceedings (1899): 128-46.

3191  "Fort Howard," Green Bay Historical Bulletin 4 (1928): 2-29.

3192  Haeger, John D. "A Time of Change, 1815-1824," Wisconsin Magazine of History 54 (1971): 285-98.

3193  Kellogg, Louis P. "Old Fort Howard," Ibid 18 (1934): 125-40.

3194  Kemper, Jackson. "Journal of an Episcopalian Missionary's Tour to Green Bay, 1834," Wisconsin Historical Society Collections 14 (1898): 394-449.

3195  Lockwood, James H. "Early Times and Events in Wisconsin," Ibid 2 (1856): 103-04.

3196  McMurray, Donald L., ed. "The Military Occupation of Green Bay," Mississippi Valley Historical Review 13 (1927): 549-53.

3197  Martin, Deborah B. Historic Green Bay, 1634-1840. Green Bay: The Author, 1893.

3198  Martin, Elizabeth. "A Visit to Fort Howard in 1836," State Historical Society of Wisconsin Proceedings (1911): 181-87.

3199  "Trip from Mackinac to Green Bay," Military and Naval Magazine 6 (1835): 248-56.

## FORT INDUSTRY

3200  Knabenshue, Samuel S. "Old Fort Industry," Ohio Archaeological and Historical Society Publications 12 (1903): 126-27.

3201  Sherman, Walter J. Fort Industry: A Historical Mystery. Columbus: F.J. Herr, 1929.

3202   Sherman, Walter J. "Old Fort Industry and the Conflicting Historical Accounts," Northwest Ohio Quarterly 2 (1930): 1-13.

SEE ALSO: 3291

FORT JACKSON

3203   Parker, James W. "Fort Jackson after the War of 1812," Alabama Review 38 (1985): 119-30.

FORT JEFFERSON, Fla.

3204   Kinney, Sheldon H. "Dry Tortugas," United States Naval Institute Proceedings 76 (1950): 424-29.

3205   Roth, Clayton D. "The Military Utilization of Key West and the Dry Tortugas from 1822 to 1900." Master's Thesis, University of Miami, 1970.

FORT JEFFERSON, Oh.

3206   "Monument at Fort Jefferson," Ohio Archaeological and Historical Society Publications 17 (1908): 112-31.

3207   Wilson, Frazer E. Fort Jefferson: The Frontier Post of the Upper Miami Valley. Lancaster, PA: Intelligencer Print Co., 1950.

FORT KING

3208   Cubberly, Frederick. "Fort King," Florida Historical Quarterly 5 (1927): 139-52.

3209   Ott, Eloise R. "Fort King: A Brief History," Ibid 46 (1967): 29-38.

FORT KNOX

3210   Black, Glenn A.   The Location of Fort Knox, Knox County, Indiana. Bloomington, IN: N.p., 1959.
       At Indiana Historical Society.

3211   Quaife, Milo M., ed. "Fort Knox Orderly Book, 1793-97," Indiana Magazine of History 32 (1936): 137-69.

3212   Watts, Florence G. "Fort Knox: Outpost on the Wabash, 1787-1816," Ibid 62 (1966): 51-78.

FORT LARAMIE

3213   Anthony, Ross O. "A History of Fort Laramie." Master's Thesis, University of Southern California, 1930.

3214   Boyack, Hazel N. "History of Fort Laramie, the Hub of Early Western History, 1834-1849," Annals of Wyoming 21 (1949): 170-80.

3215   Chappell, Gordon. "The Fortifications of Old Fort Laramie," Ibid 34 (1962): 145-62.

3216   Edwards, William W. "Old Fort Laramie," Journal of the Military Service Institute 52 (1913): 121-36.

3217   Flannery, A.L. "Little-known Facts about Fort Laramie," Annals of Wyoming 32 (1960): 104-08.

3218   Greenburg, Dan W. "How Fort William, Now Fort Laramie, was Named,"
       Annals of Wyoming 12 (1940): 56-62.

3219   Hafen, LeRoy R. and Francis M. Young. Fort Laramie and the Pageant
       of the West, 1834-1890. Glendale, CA: Arthur H. Clarke, 1938.

3220   Hanson, Charles E. "Fur Trade Activities in the Fort Laramie Region,
       1834-1849," Journal of the West 26 (1987): 8-13.

3221   Hieb, David L. Fort Laramie National Monument, Wyoming. Washington, DC:
       Government Printing Office, 1954.

3222   Johnson, Sally A. "A New Look at Fort Laramie," Museum News 40 (1962):
       11-15.

3223   Lombard, Jess H. "Old Bedlam," Annals of Wyoming 13 (1941): 87-91.

3224   Mattes, Merrill J. "Fort Laramie: Guardian of the Oregon Trail,"
       Ibid 17 (1945): 3-22.

3225   _____. Fort Laramie Park History, 1834-1977. Denver, CO: U.S. National
       Park Service, 1980.

3226   Munkres, Robert L. "Fort Laramie: Symbol  of the Frontier," Overland
       Journal 4 (1986): 53-69.

3227   Murray, Robert A. Fort Laramie: Visions of a Grand Old Post. Fort
       Collins, CO: Old Army Press, 1974.

3228   Nadeau, Remi. Fort Laramie and the Sioux. Lincoln: University of
       Nebraska Press, 1967.

3229   Nelson, Robert. "Inside Fort Laramie, Once a Major Fur Trading Post,"
       Wyoming Wild Life 34 (1970): 14-21.

3230   "Old Fort Laramie," Journal of the Military Service Institute 32
       (1903): 439-41.

3231   Pomplun, Ray. "Fort Laramie-Old Bedlam to the Tourist Trade,"
       CAMP Periodical 10 (1978): 36-42.

## FORT LEAVENWORTH

3232   Blackburn, Forrest R. "Cantonment Leavenworth, 1827-1832," Military
       Review 51 (1971): 57-66.

3233   _____. "Fort Leavenworth" Logistical Base for the West," Ibid 53
       (1973): 3-12.

3234   "Building Fort Leavenworth 102 Years Ago under Col. Henry Leavenworth."
       Clippings at Kansas States Historical Society.

3235   DeZurko, Edward R. "A Report and Remarks on Cantonment Leavenworth,"
       Kansas Historical Quarterly 15 (1947): 353-59.

3236   Evans, Wilma M. "Fort Leavenworth, a Frontier Outpost." Master's Thesis,
       University of Iowa, 1940.

3237   Gardner, Hamilton. "Romance of Old Cantonment Leavenworth," Kansas
       Historical Quarterly 22 (1956): 97-113.

3238  Hall, Jesse A. and Larry T. Hand. "Fort Leavenworth." In: History of
      Leavenworth County, Kansas. Topeka: Historical Publishing Co., 1921,
      171-80.

3239  Holt, Daniel D. and Marilyn I. "The Pleasures of Female Society at
      Cantonment Leavenworth," Kansas History 8 (1985): 21-35.

3240  Hunt, Elvid and Lorence Walter. History of Fort Leavenworth, 1827-1937.
      Fort Leavenworth: Command and General Staff School Press, 1937.

3241  Johnston, J.H. "Fort Leavenworth." In: Looking Back. Leavenworth, KS:
      J.H. Johnston, 1982, 164-81.

3242  _____. "Fort Leavenworth, Kansas," Winners of the West 3 (1925): 6-7.

3243  Kanaga, Clinton W. "Early-Day Fort Leavenworth, Missouri," Trail Guide
      1 (1956): 7-20.

3244  Langellier, John. "Gateway to the West: Fort Leavenworth and the
      Frontier Advance," Order of the Indian Wars Journal 2 (1981): 7-11.

3245  McGregor, Edward W. "The Leavenworth," Military Review 36 (1956): 62-76.

3246  Reinhardt, George C. "Fort Leavenworth is Born," Ibid 33 (1953): 3-8.

3247  _____. "Fort Leavenworth Grows Up," Ibid 33 (1954): 16-33.

3248  Shindler, Henry. "History of Fort Leavenworth."
      Typescript at Kansas State Historical Society.

3249  Stanley, Arthur J. "Fort Leavenworth: Dowager Queen of Frontier Posts,"
      Kansas Historical Quarterly 42 (1976): 1-23.

3250  Walton, George. Sentinel of the Plains: Fort Leavenworth and the
      American West. Englewood Cliffs, NJ: Prentice Hall, 1973.

      SEE ALSO: William G. Belknap, Henry Leavenworth

                          FORT MCINTOSH

3251  Graham, Louis E. "Fort McIntosh," Western Pennsylvania Historical
      Magazine 15 (1932): 93-119.

                           FORT MCNEIL

3252  Gentry, Daniel E. "Orange County's Forgotten Fort: Fort McNeil,"
      Orange County Historical Quarterly 2 (1969): 1-3.

                           FORT MACOMB

3253  Milner, P.M. "Fort Macomb," Louisiana Historical Society Publications
      7 (1913-1914): 143-52.

                          *FORT MADISON

3254  "Fort Madison, an  Article Prepared at the War Department, Washington,"
      Annals of Iowa 3 (1897-1899): 97-110.

3255  Jackson, Donald, ed. "A Critic Views Iowa's First Military Post,"
      Iowa Journal of History and Politics 58 (1960): 31-36.

3256  Knapp, Horace E. "J.H. Knapp, First Permanent Settler,"
      Annals of Iowa 10 (1911): 161-65.

3257  McKusick, Marshall B. and David Archie. "A Tale of Two Forts,"
      Iowan Magazine 15 (1966): 10-15.

3258  "A Personal Narrative," Michigan Pioneer 8 (1885): 662-69.

## FORT MAITLAND

3259  Hanna, Alfred J. Fort Maitland: Its Origins and History. Maitland,
      FL: Fort Maitland Committee, 1936.

## FORT MARION

3260  Eby, Cecil D., ed. "Memoir of a West Pointer in St. Augustine, 1824-
      1826," Florida Historical Quarterly 41 (1962): 154-64; 43 (1964):
      307-20.

3261  "Fort Marion, St. Augustine, East Florida," Military and Naval
      Magazine 5 (1835): 97-100.

3262  Singleton, Esther, ed. Historic Buildings of America as Seen and
      Described by Famous Writers. New York: Dodd, 1906.

3263  Young, Rogers W. "Fort Marion during the Seminole War, 1835-1842,"
      Florida Historical Quarterly 13 (1935): 193-223.

      SEE ALSO: 4756

## FORT MASSAC

3264  Armstrong, Fern. A Short History of Fort Massac. Metropolis, IL:
      Herald Printing Co., 1905.

3265  Baily, Francis. Journal of a Tour in Unsettled Parts of North America
      in 1796 and 1797. London: Baily Brothers, 1856.

3266  Caldwell, Norman W. "Fort Massac: The American Frontier Post, 1778-
      1805," Illinois State Historical Society Journal 43 (1950): 265-81.

3267  _____. "Fort Massac: Since 1805," Ibid 44 (1951): 47-60.

3268  Farrar, William G. Historic Profiles of Fort Massac. Carbondale, IL:
      Southern Illinois University Press, 1970.

3269  Hammond, John M. "Fort Massac near Metropolis, Illinois." In: Quaint
      and Historic Forts of North America. Philadelphia: J.B. Lippincott,
      1913, 141-46.

3270  Hogg, Victor. Historic Fort Massac: The Development of the American
      Fort. Carbondale, IL: Southern Illinois University Press, 1970.

3271  Johnson, Leland R. "The Doyle Mission to Massac, 1794," Illinois
      States Historical Society Journal 73 (1980): 2-16.

3272  Smith, George W. Old Forts of Southern Illinois. Tamaroa, IL: Elbert
      Waller, N.d.
      At Illinois State Library.

3273  Scott, Julia G. "Old Fort Massac," Illinois State Historical Society Journal 8 (1904): 38-64.

3274  ____. "Old Fort Massac, Illinois," Magazine of History 10 (1909): 287-92.

*FORT MEIGS

3275  Boehm, Robert B. and Randall L. Buchman, eds. Journal of the Northwestern Campaign of 1812-1813 under Major General William Henry Harrison, by Bvt. Lieut. Col. Eleazar Derby Wood, Captain, Corps of Engineers. Defiance, OH: Defiance College Press, 1975.

3276  Nelson, Larry. Men of Patriotism, Courage and Enterprise: Fort Meigs in the War of 1812. Canton, OH: Darling Books, 1985.

3277  ____. "The Mapping of Fort Meigs," Northwest Ohio Quarterly 58 (1986): 123-42.

3278  Spencer, Rex L. "The Gibraltar of the Maumee: Fort Meigs in the War of 1812." Ph. D. dissertation, Ball State University, 1988.

FORT MELLON

3279  Francke, Arthur E. Fort Mellon, 1837-1842: Microcosom of the Second Seminole War. Miami: Banyan Books, 1977.

FORT MIAMI

3280  Bald, Clever F. "Fort Miami," Northwest Ohio Quarterly 15 (1943): 127-37.

3281  ____. "Fort Miami, Outpost of Empire," Ibid 16 (1944): 75-115.

3282  Canada. Public Archives. Transactions of Manuscripts from the Canadian Archives Pertaining to the Indian Wars and the Building of Fort Miami. Columbus: Anthony Wayne Parkway Board, N.d. At Ohio Historical Society Library.

3283  "The Fight to Save Fort Miami," Northwest Ohio Quarterly 16 (1944): 119-24.

3284  "Fort Miami, built by the British in 1794 at the Foot of the Rapids on the Maumee River," Ibid 16 (1944): 73-116.

3285  Johnston, James A. "The War did not End at Yorktown," Virginia Magazine of History and Biography 60 (1952): 444-57.

3286  Knopf, Richard C. "Fort Miamis: The International Background," Ohio Archaeological and Historical Society Quarterly 61 (1952): 142-66.

3287  Norris, C.H. "Address delivered Before the Pioneers at their Reunion at Fort Meigs, August 12, 1896," Maumee Valley Pioneer Association Addresses (1897): 7-23.

3288  Peckham, Howard H. "Fort Miami and the Maumee Communication," Northwest Ohio Quarterly 14 (1942): 30-41.

3289  Rainey, L. Thomas. Cincinnati's Great Part in the Northwest Territory. Cincinnati: Cincinnati Gas & Electric, 1950.

3290  Sherman, W.J. "Fort Miami at the Foot of the Rapids of the Miami of the Lake," Northwest Ohio Quarterly 9 (1937): 1-7.

3291   Slocum, Charles E. "Fort Miami and Fort Industry," Ohio Archaeological
       and Historical Society Quarterly 12 (1903): 120-25.

3292   Spitzer, Carl B. "Construction and Physical Appearance of Fort Miami,"
       Northwest Ohio Quarterly 16 (1944): 112-16.

       SEE ALSO: Anthony Wayne

                              FORT MIFFLIN

3293   Jackson, John W. Fort Mifflin: Valiant Defender of the Delaware.
       Philadelphia: Old Fort Mifflin Historical Society, 1986.

3294   Shelton, Frederick L. "Old Fort Mifflin," Philadelphia Numismatic and
       Antiquarian Society 29 (1922): 105-38.

3295   Thibault, Jacqueline. "Deceiphering Fort Mifflin," Military Collector
       and Historian 27 (1975): 100-12.

                              *FORT MIMS

3296   Marks, Laurence H. "Fort Mims: A Challenge," Alabama Review 18 (1965):
       275-80.

                           FORT MITCHELL, Ala.

3297   Chase, David W. Fort Mitchell: An Archaeological Exploration in Russell
       County, Alabama. Moundville, AL: Alabama Archaeological Society, 1974.

                           FORT MITCHELL, Neb.

3298   Mattes, Merrill J. "A History of Old Fort Mitchell," Nebraska History
       24 (1943): 71-82.

3299   _____. "Fort Mitchell, Scott's Bluff, Nebraska Territory," Ibid 33
       (1952): 1-34.

                              FORT MYERS

3300   Godown, Marian and Alberta Rawchuck.  Yesterday's Fort Myers.
       Miami: E.A. Seeman Publishing, 1975.

3301   Gonzalez, Thomas A. The Caloosahatchee, Miscellaneous Writings
       Concerning the History of the Caloosahatchee River and the City of
       Fort Myers, Florida. Estero, FL: Koreshan Unity Press, 1932.

3302   Grismer, Karl H. The Story of Fort Myers. The History of the land of
       the Caloosahatchee and Southwest Florida. St. Petersburg: St. Peter-
       sburg Print Co., 1949.

3303   Willson, Minnie M. History of Osceola County; Florida Frontier Life.
       Orlando, FL: Indland Press, 1935.

                              *FORT NIAGARA

3304   Brown, Ernest C. "Niagara-Master Key that Unlocked America to the
       English Race," Journal of American History 2 (1908): 383-400.

3305   Bull, Canon. "Fort Niagara, N.Y., 1783-1796," Niagara Historical Society
       Transactions No. 2 (1897): 3-7.

3306   Carnochan, Janet. "Fort Niagara," Niagara Historical Society
       Publications No. 23 (1912): 1-15.

3307   Dunnigan, Brian L. A History and Guide to Old Fort Niagara. Youngstown,
       NY: Old Fort Niagara Association, 1985.

3308   Hultzen, Claud H. Old Fort Niagara; the Story of an Ancient Gateway
       to the West. Buffalo: Baker, Jones, Hausauer, 1933.

3309   Loker, Donald E. "The 1812 Military Cemetery at Old Fort Niagara,"
       Yesteryears 9 (1965): 61-70.

3310   McClellan, S. Grove. "Old Fort Niagara," American Heritage 4 (1953):
       32-41.

3311   Porter, Peter A. "Old Fort Niagara," New York States Historical
       Association Journal 6 (1925): 121-30.

3312   Robinson, Jane H. "Fort Niagara," DAR Magazine 11 (1897): 23-34.

*FORT ONTARIO

3313   Bertsch, W.H. "The Defenses of Oswego," New York State Historical
       Society Proceedings 13 (1914): 108-27.

3314   Dunn, James T., ed. "The Surrender of Fort Ontario, 1796," New York
       History 31 (1950): 100-04.

FORT OSAGE

3315   Anderson, James. "Fort Osage: An Incident of Territorial Missouri,"
       Missouri Historical Society Bulletin 4 (1948): 174-76.

3316   Gregg, Kate L. "The History of Fort Osage," Missouri Historical Review
       34 (1940): 439-88.

3317   Grove, Nettie T. "Fort Osage: First Settlement in Jackson County,"
       Annals of Kansas City, Missouri 1 (1922): 56-70.

3318   Mathews, John J. "Fort Osage and the War of 1812." In: The Osages:
       Children of the Middle Waters. Norman: University of Oklahoma Press,
       1961, 393-419.

3319   Meriwether, David. My Life in the Mountains and the Plains. Norman:
       University of Oklahoma Press, 1965, 103-13.

3320   White, Emma. "Life at the Fort in Early days," Annals of Kansas City,
       Missouri 1 (1922): 74-83.

3321   Woolridge, Rhoda. Fort Osage: Opening of the American West.
       Independence, MO: Independence Press, 1983.

       SEE ALSO: William Clark

FORT PIERCE

3322   Clausen, Carl J. The Fort Pierce Collection. Tallahassee: Florida
       Department of State, 1970.

3323  Clausen, Carl J. "The Fort Pierce American Goldfind," _Florida Quarterly_ 47 (1968): 51-58.

FORT PLATTE

3324  Lupton, David W. "Fort Platte, Wyoming, 1841-1845: Rival of Fort Laramie," _Annals of Wyoming_ 49 (1977): 83-108.

FORT RECOVERY

3325  Frazier, Ida H. _Fort Recovery: A Historical Sketch Depicting its Role in the History of the Old Northwest._ Columbus: Ohio State Archaeological and Historical Society, 1941.

3326  Knopf, Richard C. "Fort Recovery," _Museum Echoes_ 29 (1956): 91-94.

3327  Rohr, Martha E. _Historical Sketch of Fort Recovery._ Fort Recovery, OH: Journal Publishing Co., 1932.

3328  "Unveiling of Fort Recovery Monument," _Ohio Archaeological and Historical Society_ Quarterly 22 (1913): 419-54.

FORT SAGINAW

3329  Emery, Benjamin F.  _Fort Saginaw, 1822-1823: The Story of a Forgotten Frontier Post._ Detroit: N.p., 1932.

3330  _____. "Fort Saginaw," _Michigan Historical Magazine_ 30 (1946): 476-503.

FORT ST. CLAIR

3331  Brooke, Mary G. _Historic Eaton and Fort St. Clair._ Eaton, OH: Register-Herald, 1930.

3332  Dawson, Henry B. _Battles of the United States._ 2 Vols. New York: Johnson, Fry, 1858. Vol. 2, 16-19.

3333  Preble County Historical Society. "Fort St. Clair, Celebration of St. Clair Day," _Ohio Archaeological and Historical Society Quarterly_ 32 (1923): 506-29.

3334  Randall, E.O. "Fort St. Clair," _Ibid_ 11 (1902): 161-63.

FORT SANFORD

3335  Carter, William H. "Fort Sanford, Iowa," _Annals of Iowa_ 4 (1899-1901): 284-93.

FORT SCOTT

3336  Barry, Louise. "The Fort Leavenworth-Fort Gibson Military Road and the Founding of Fort Scott," _Kansas Historical Quarterly_ 11 (1942): 115-29.

3337  Calhoun, William G. "The Fort of Fort Scott." in: _Fort Scott, A Pictorial History._ N.p., 1978, 3-12.

3338  Cornish, Dudley T. "The Historical Significance of Fort Scott, Kansas," _Fort Scott Tribune_ 30 November, 1963.

3339  Isley, Bliss. "Soldering in Kansas in 1842," _Progress in Kansas_ 8 (1941-1942): 119-22.

3340  Myers, Harry C., ed. "From 'The Crack Post of the Frontier': Letters of Thomas and Charlotte Swords," Kansas History 5 (1982): 184-213.

3341  Oliva, Leo E. Fort Scott on the Indian Frontier. Topeka: Kansas Historical Society, 1984.

3342  Richards, Ralph. The Forts of Fort Scott and the Fateful Borderland. Kansas City, MO: Lowell Press, 1976.

3343  Robley, Thomas F. History of Bourbon County, Kansas. Fort Scott: Monitor Book and Print Co., 1894, 9-17.

3344  Shoemaker, Earl A. The Permanent Indian Frontier: The Reason for the Construction and Abandonment of Fort Scott, Kansas, during the Dragoon Era; a Special Historical Study. Washington, DC: National Park Service, 1986.

3345  Thompson, Erwin N. Fort Scott, Kansas: Historic Structures Report. Washington, DC: National Park Service, 1968.

FORT SMITH

3346  Baird, W. David. "Fort Smith and The Red Man," Arkansas Historical Quarterly 30 (1971): 337-48.

3347  Bearess, Edwin C. and Arrell M. Gibson. Fort Smith, Little Gibraltar on the Arkansas. Norman: University of Oklahoma Press, 1969.

3348  _____. "In Quest of Peace on the Indian Border: The Establishment of Fort Smith," Arkansas Historical Quarterly 23 (1964): 123-53.

3349  Butler, William J. Fort Smith Past and Present: A Historical Summary. Fort Smith, AK: First National Bank, 1972.

3350  Faulk, Odie, and Billy Mac Jones. Fort Smith, and Illustrated History. Fort Smith, AK: Old Fort Museum, 1983.

3351  Foreman, Carolyn T. "William Bradford," Arkansas Historical Quarterly 13 (1954): 341-51.

3352  Haskett, James N. "The Final Chapter in the Story of the First Fort Smith," Ibid 25 (1966): 214-28.

3353  Hicks, Edwin P. The Fort Smith Story: Fort Smith National Historic Site. N.p., N.d.

3354  Mapes, Ruth B. Old Fort Smith: Cultural Center on the Southwestern Frontier. Little Rock: Pioneer Press, 1965.

3355  Morrison, William B. "Fort Smith." In: Military Camps and Posts in Oklahoma. Oklahoma City: Harlow Publishing Corporation, 1936, 15-27.

3356  Ryan, Harold W. "Matthew Arbuckle come to Fort Smith," Arkansas Historical Quarterly 19 (1960): 287-92.

3357  Vaught, Elsa. Captain John Rogers, Founder fo Fort Smith. Van Buren, AK: Press-Argus Print, 1959.

3358  Yadon, Julia E. Reflections of Fort Smith. Fort Smith, AK: Fort Smith Historical Press, 1976.

FORT SNELLING

3359   Armstrong, John M. "Edward Purcell, First Physician of Minnesota,"
       Annals of Medical History 7 (1935): 169-76.

3360   Babcock, Willoughby M. "Historic Fort Snelling," DAR Magazine 91
       (1957): 601-5, 678.

3361   Beck, Roger L. "Military Music at Fort Snelling, Minnesota, from 1819
       to 1858: An Archival Study." Ph. D. dissertation, University of
       Minnesota, 1987.

3362   Bliss, John H. "Reminiscences of Fort Snelling," Minnesota Historical
       Society Collections 6 (1894): 335-53.

3363   Beeson, Lewis, ed. Memoirs of a Boyhood at Fort Snelling. Minneapolis:
       Privately Printed, 1939.

3364   Callender, John M. New Light on Old Fort Snelling: An Archaeological·
       Exploration, 1957-1958. St. Paul: Minnesota Historical Society, 1959.

3365   Doty, James D. "Official Journal, 1820," Wisconsin Historical Society
       Collections 13 (1895): 163-246.

3366   "Early Days at Fort Snelling," Minnesota Historical Society Collections
       1 (1902): 345-59.

3367   Eckman, James. "The First Contribution to A Medical Journal from
       Minnesota: An Epidemic of Scarlet Fever at Fort Snelling, 1847-1848,"
       Minnesota Medicine 34 (1952): 996-1004.

3368   Edsall, Samuel. "Rev. Ezekiel Gilbert Gear, Chaplain at Fort Snelling,
       1838-1858," Minnesota Historical Society Collections 12 (1908): 691-69.

3369   "The Far West," Army and Navy Chronicle 4 (1837): 345-46.

3370   Folwell, William W. A History of Minnesota. 4 Vols. St. Paul: Minnesota
       Historical Society, 1921-1930. Vol. 1, 131-69.

3371   _____. "The Sale of Fort Snelling," Minnesota Historical Society
       Collections 15 (1915): 394-410.

3372   Forsyth, Thomas. "Journal of a Voyage from St. Louis to the Falls of
       St. Anthony in 1819," Wisconsin Historical Society Collections 6
       (1872): 188-215.

3373   _____. "Fort Snelling: Col. Leavenworth's Expedition to Establish it
       in 1819," Minnesota Historical Society Collections 3 (1880): 139-67.

3374   "Fort Snelling," Gopher Historian 21 (1966): 1-19.

3375   Fridley, Russell W. "Fort Snelling, from Military Post to Historic
       Site," Minnesota History 33 (1956): 178-92.

3376   Grant, Joseph H. "Old Fort Snelling," Quartermaster Review 13 (1934):
       21-24, 71-72.

3377   Grossman, John F. Army Uniforms at Fort Snelling, 1821-1832.
       St. Paul: Minnesota Historical Society, 1974.

3378   Hall, Steve. Fort Wilderness: Colossus of the Wilderness.
       St. Paul: Minnesota Historical Society, 1987.

3379   Hansen, Marcus L. Old Fort Snelling, 1819-1858. Iowa City: State
       Historical Society of Iowa, 1918.

3380   Harwood, William S. "Fort Snelling, Old and New," Harper's Weekly
       Magazine 39 (1895): 442-44.

3381   Heilbron, Bertha. "Fort Snelling and Minnesota History," Minnesota
       History 29 (1948): 316-20.

3382   Holcombe, Return I. "Fort Snelling," American Historical Magazine 1
       (1906): 110-33.

3383   Holt, John R. Historic Snelling. St. Paul: Perkins-Tracy Print Co.,
       1938.

3384   Jarvis, Nathan S. "An Army Surgeon's Notes on Frontier Service, 1833-
       1848," Journal of the Military Service Institute 39 (1906): 3-8,
       131-35.

3385   _____. "Letter Dated June 18, 1833," Academy Bookman 2 (1949): 14-15.

3386   Johnson, Loren. "Reconstructing Old Fort Snelling," Minnesota History
       42 (1970): 82-98.

3387   Johnson, Richard W. "Fort Snelling and its History," Western Magazine
       15 (1920): 44-46, 170-73.

3388   _____. "Fort Snelling from its Foundation to the Present Time,"
       Minnesota Historical Society Collection 8 (1898): 427-48.

3389   Jones, Evan. Citadel in the Wilderness: The Story of Fort Snelling
       and the Old Northwest Frontier. New York: Coward-McCann, 1966.

3390   McKasy, Donlin M. "Commandant's House Interpretation Plan."
       Typescript at the Minnesota Historical Society.

3391   McDermott, John F. "A Journalist at Old Fort Snelling," Minnesota
       History 31 (1950): 209-21.

3392   Minnesota Historical Society. "The Key to Historic Fort Snelling,"
       Hennepin County History 28 (1969): 4-18.

3393   Minnesota Outdoor Recreation Resources Commission. Fort Snelling.
       St. Paul: The Commission, 1965.

3394   Neill, Edward D. "Fort Snelling Echoes," Magazine of Western History
       10 (1889): 604-12; 11 (1889-1890): 20-28.

3395   _____. "Fort Snelling, Minnesota, While in Command of Colonel Josiah
       Snelling, Fifth Infantry," Ibid 8 (1888): 171-80, 373-81.

3396   _____. "Occurences in and Around Fort Snelling, from 1819 to 1840,"
       Minnesota Historical Society Collections 2 (1889): 102-42.

3397   Osman, Stephen E. "Army Uniforms at Fort Snelling, 1819-1865,"
       Hennepin County History 38 (1979): 3-11.

3398   Pederson, Kern O. The Story of Fort Snelling. St. Paul: Minnesota
       Historical Society, 1966.

3399  Prucha, Francis P. "An Army Private at Old Fort Snelling in 1849,"
      Minnesota History 36 (1958): 13-17.

3399A Rhoads, James B. "The Fort Snelling Area in 1835: A Contemporary Map,"
      Ibid 35 (1956): 22-29.

3400  Sibley, H.H. "Reminiscences, Historical and Personal," Minnesota
      Historical Society Collections 1 (1872): 457-85.

3401  Snelling, Henry H. Memoirs of a Boyhood at Fort Snelling. Minneapolis:
      N.p., 1939.

3402  Snelling, William J. "Running the Gauntlet: A Thrilling Incident of
      the Early Days at Fort Snelling," Minnesota Historical Society
      Collections 1 (1872): 439-56.

3403  Upham, Warren. "The Women and Children of Fort Saint Anthony, later
      Named Fort Snelling," Magazine of History 21 (1915): 25-39.

3404  Van Cleve, Charlotte O. 'Three Score Years and Ten': Life-long
      Memories of Fort Snelling, Minnesota, and Other Parts of the West.
      Minneapolis: Privately Printed, 1888.

3405  Wiggins, Davis S. "Minnesota's First Hospital: The Practice of
      Medicine at Fort Snelling," Minnesota Medicine 59 (1976): 867-73, 886.

3406  _____. 'Service in 'Siberia': Five Surgeons at Early Fort Snelling.
      St. Paul: Minnesota Historical Society, 1977.

3407  Williams, J. Fletcher, ed. "Early Days at Red River Settlement and
      Fort Snelling: Reminiscences of Mrs. Ann Adams, 1821-1829," Minnesota
      Historical Society Collection 6 (1894): 75-115.

3408  Zeck, Albert F. "Historical Development of Fort Snelling." Master's
      Thesis, University of Southern California, 1939.

3409  Ziebarth, Marilyn and Alan Ominsky. Fort Snelling: Anchor Post of
      the Northwest. St. Paul: Minnesota Historical Society, 1970.

      SEE ALSO: Henry Leavenworth, Josiah Snelling, Zachary Taylor

                          FORT STODDERT

3410  Craighead, Erwin. Mobile; Fact and Tradition, Noteworty People and
      Events. Mobile, AL: Powers Printing Co., 1930.

3411  Holmes, Jack P. "Fort Stoddart [Sic] in 1799: Seven Letters of Captain
      Bartholomew Schaumbaugh," Alabama Historical Quarterly 26 (1964): 231-52.

3412  Short, Peter. "Brief Accounts of Journeys in the Western Country, 1809-
      1812," Historical and Philosophical Society of Ohio Publications 5
      (1910): 5-31.

                          FORT TAYLOR

3413  England, Howard S. Fort Zachary Taylor. Key West, FL: England, 1977.

3414  Jameson, Colin. East Martello Tower. Key West, FL: Key West Art and
      Historical Society, 1980.

3415   William, Ames W. "Stronghold of the Straits: A Short History of Fort
Zachary Taylor," Florida Historical Quarterly 21 (1930): 211-49.

FORT TOWSON

3416   Lewis, Kenneth. 1971 Archaeological Investigations at Fort Towson,
Choctaw County, Oklahoma. Norman, OK: Archaeological Survey, 1972.

3417   McGuigan, Patrick B. "Bulwark of the American Frontier: A History of
Fort Towson." In: Odie Faulk and others, eds. Early Military Forts
and Posts of Oklahoma. Oklahoma City: Oklahoma Historical Society,
1978, 9-25.

3418   Morrison, William B. "Fort Towson," Chronicles of Oklahoma 8 (1930):
226-32.

3419   _____. "Fort Towson." In: Military Posts and Camps in Oklahoma.
Oklahoma City: Harlow Publishing Corporation, 1936, 48-58.

3420   Oglesby, Eliza. Fort Towson. Detroit: Harlo Press, 1965.

3421   Shoemaker, Edward C. "Fort Towson: An Early Communications Route to
Oklahoma," Red River Valley Historical Review 7 (1982): 18-29.

SEE ALSO: Gustavus Loomis, James B. Many

FORT UNION

3422   Culpin, Mary S. and Richard Borjes. "The Architecture of Fort Union:
A Symbol of Dominance," Rendezvous 4 (1981): 135-40.

3423   Dougherty, Dolorita M. "A History of Fort Union (North Dakota), 1829-
1867." Ph. D. dissertation, St. Louis University, 1957.

3424   Garraghan, Gilbert J., ed. "An Early Missouri River Journal by
Nicholas Point," Mid America 2 (1931): 236-54.

3425   Harper, Frank B. Fort Union and its Neighbors on the Upper Missouri:
A Chronological Record of Events. St. Paul: N.p., 1925.

3426   Koenig, Myrna L. "Fort Union as a Missouri River Post." Master's
Thesis, University of Iowa, 1933.

3427   Mattison, Ray H. "Fort Union and its Role in the Upper Missouri Fur
Trade," North Dakota History 29 (1962): 181-210.

3428   Thompson, Erwin N. Fort Union Trading Post: Fur Trade Empire on the
Upper Missouri. Medora, ND: Theodore  Roosevelt Nature and History
Association, 1986.

FORT VASQUEZ

3429   Hafen, LeRoy R. "Fort Vasquez," Colorado Magazine 41 (1964): 198-212.

3430   Judge, W. James. "The Archaeology of Fort Vasquez," Ibid 48 (1971):
181-203.

3431   Peterson, Guy L. "Fort Vasquez: Fact and/or Fantasy?" Master's Thesis,
Colorado State University, 1974.

FORT WASHINGTON, Md.

3432  Clinton, Amy C. "Historic Fort Washington," Maryland Historical
      Magazine 32 (1937): 228-47.

3433  Kendall-Lowther, Minnie. Marshall Hall and Other Potomac Points in
      Story and Picture. Baltimore: Read-Taylor, 1925.

3434  Morgan, James D. "Historic Fort Washington on the Potomac," Columbia
      Historical Society Records 7 (1904): 1-19.

3435  Salay, David L. [V]ery Picturesque, but Regarded as Nearly Useless':
      Fort Washington, Maryland, 1816-1872," Maryland Historical Magazine
      81 (1986): 67-86.

FORT WASHINGTON, Oh.

3436  Baby, Raymond S. "Additional Structural Features of the Fort Washington
      Powder Magazine," Historical and Philosophical Society of Ohio Bulletin
      11 (1953): 320-25.

3437  Havinghurst, Walter. Wilderness for Sale, the Story of the First
      Western Land Rush. New York: Hastings House, 1956.

3438  Jones, Robert R. Fort Washington at Cincinnati, Ohio. Cincinnati:
      Society of Colonial Wars in the State of Ohio, 1902.

3439  King, Arthur G. "The Exact Site of Fort Washington and Daniel Drake's
      Error," Historical and Philosophical Society of Ohio Bulletin 11 (1953):
      128-46.

3440  ____. "Cincinnati's Earliest Hospital," Cincinnati Journal of Medicine
      34 (1958): 350-52.

3441  Knopf, Richard C., Raymond S. Baby and Dwight L. Smith. "The Redis-
      covery of Fort Washington," Historical and Philosophical Society
      of Ohio Bulletin 11 (1953): 2-12.

3442  McCulloch, Delia A. "Forts along the Ohio," Americana 6 (1911): 851-66.

3443  Ohio State  Archaeological and Historical Society. "Monument on the
      Site of Fort Washington: Ceremonies at the Unveiling of Monument,"
      Ohio Archaeological and Historical Society Quarterly 10 (1901): 1-20.

3444  Simmons, David A. "An Orderly Book from Fort Washington and Fort
      Hamilton, 1792-1793," Cincinnati Historical Society Bulletin 36
      (1978): 125-44.

FORT WASHITA

3445  Harbour, Emma E. "A Brief History of the Red River Country Since 1803,"
      Chronicles of Oklahoma 16 (1938): 58-88.

3446  Howard, James A. "Fort Washita." In: Odie Faulk and Others, eds. Early
      Military Forts and Posts of Oklahoma. Oklahoma City: Oklahoma
      Historical Society, 1978, 39-53.

3447  Lewis, Kenneth E., ed. Fort Washita From Past to Present: An Arch-
      aeological Report. Oklahoma City, Oklahoma Historical Society, 1975.

3448   Morrison, William B. "Fort Washita," Chronicles of Oklahoma 5
       (1927): 251-58.

3449   _____. "A Visit to Old Fort Washita," Ibid 7 (1929): 175-79.

3450   _____. "Fort Washita." In: Military Posts and Camps in Oklahoma.
       Oklahoma City: Harlow Publishing Corporation, 1936, 81-92.

3451   Shirk, George H. "Mail Call at Fort Washita," Chronicles of Oklahoma
       33 (1955): 14-35.

                        FORT WAYNE, Ark.

3452   Littlefield, Daniel F. "Fort Wayne and the Arkansas Frontier, 1838-
       1840," Arkansas Historical Quarterly 35 (1976): 334-59.

3453   _____. "Fort Wayne and Border Violence," Ibid 36 (1977): 3-20.

                        *FORT WAYNE, Ind.

3454   Ankenbruck, John. Five Forts. Fort Wayne, IN: News Publishing, 1972.

3455   Banta, Richard E. The Glorious Gate. Fort Wayne, IN: Allen County
       Fort Wayne Historical Society, 1951

3456   Dinnen, Catherine M. "A Study of the Early History of Fort Wayne,
       Indiana." Master's Thesis, University of Southern California, 1950.

3457   Geib, George. "Fort Wayne: Imperial Outpost, 1811-1819," Indiana
       Military History Journal 10 (1985): 16-19.

3458   Horsman, Reginald. "Fort Wayne as a Frontier Outpost, 1802-1815,"
       Old Fort News 27 (1964): 19 pp.

3459   Hosmer, Hezekiah L. Early History of the Maumee Valley. Toldeo:
       Hosmer, Harris, 1858, 9-70.

3460   Poinsatte, Charles R. "A History of Fort Wayne, Indiana, from 1716
       to 1829: A Study of its Early Development as a Frontier Village."
       Master's Thesis, University of Notre Dame, 1951.

3461   Quaife, Milo M., ed. "Fort Wayne in 1790," Indiana Historical Society
       Publications 7 (1923): 293-361.

3462   Roberts, Bessie K. Fort Wayne, the Frontier Post. Fort Wayne, IN:
       Public Library of Fort Wayne and Allen County, 1965.

3463   Woehrmann, Paul J. "Fort Wayne, Indiana Territory, 1794-1819: A Study of
       a Frontier Post." Ph. D. dissertation, Kent State University, 1967.

                        FORT WAYNE, Mich.

3464   Irwin, James R. "Fort Wayne, a Century of Service," Michigan Alumnus
       Quarterly 55 (1948): 68-79.

3465   Jennings, Richard H. "Fort Wayne," Detroit Historical Society Bulletin
       6 (1950): 5-10.

3466   Millis, Wade. "Fort Wayne, Detroit," Michigan Historical Magazine 20
       (1936): 21-29.

3467  Phenix, William P. "Historic Fort Wayne," Michigan History 65
      (1981): 17-31.

3468  Prance, Lois, and James R. Irwin. "History of Fort Wayne," Michigan
      Historical Magazine 30 (1946): 5-40.

3469  Rossetti Associates, Inc. Historic Fort Wayne, Detroit, Michigan:
      An American Revolution Bicentennial Project. Detroit: Detroit
      Historical Commission, 1973.

3470  Slemmons, Harvey F. "A Prolegomenon to the History of Fort Wayne,"
      Military Historian 1 (1961): 1-16.

                            FORT WILKINS
3471  Chase, Lew A. "Fort Wilkins, Copper Harbor, Michigan," Michigan
      Historical Magazine 4 (1920): 608-11.

3472  Emery, Benjamin O. Fort Wilkins, 1844-46, A Frontier Stockaded Post
      Built to Protect Michigan's Copper Mines. Detroit: N.p., 1932.

3473  Fadner, Lawrence T. Fort Wilkins, 1844, and the U.S. Mineral Land
      Agency. New York: Vantage Press, 1966.

3474  Fisher, James. "Fort Wilkins," Michigan Historical Magazine 29
      (1945): 155-65.

3475  Foehler, Charles F. "Fort Wilkins, Symbol of an Era," Michigan
      Conservation 23 (1960): 18-21.

3476  Friggens, Thomas. "Fort Wilkins: Army Life on the Frontier,"
      Michigan History 61 (1977): 220-50.

3477  Swykert, N.L. "Fort Wilkins," Michigan Historical Magazine 13
      (1929): 421-35.

                            FORT WINNEBAGO

3478  Clark, Satterlee. "Early Times at Fort Winnebago and Black Hawk War
      Reminiscences," Wisconsin Historical Society Collections 8 (1879):
      309-21.

3479  Kellogg, Louise. "The Agency House at Fort Winnebago," Wisconsin
      Magazine of History 14 (1931): 437-48.

3480  Tennant, Mrs. Herscehl V. "The Surgeon's Quarters at Portage,"
      Wisconsin," DAR Magazine 87 (1953): 375-76.

3481  Thomas, William. "The Winnebago 'War' of 1827," Illinois State
      Historical Society Transactions 12 (1907): 265-69.

3482  Thwaites, Reuben G. "Fort Winnebago Orderly Book, 1834-36,"
      Wisconsin Historical Society Collections 14 91898): 103-17.

3483  Turner, Andrew J. "History of Fort Winnebago," Ibid 14 (1898): 65-
      102.

                            JEFFERSON BARRACKS

3484  Banta, Byron B. "A History of Jefferson Barracks, 1826-1860."
      Ph. D. dissertation, Louisiana State University, 1981.

3485   Croghan, George. "Jefferson Barracks, 1827," Missouri Historical
       Society Bulletin 9 (1952-1953): 139-40.

3486   DePeyster, F. Watts. "The Beginnings of Jefferson Barracks," Missouri
       Historical Society Collections 3 (1908-1911): 198-99.

3487   Fusco, Tony. A Pictorial History of Jefferson Barracks. St. Louis:
       The Author, 1969.

3488   "Jefferson Barracks Closes," Missouri Historical Society Bulletin 2
       (1946): 55-56.

3489   Layton, Ruth. The Story of Jefferson Barracks. St. Louis: Layton and
       Associates, 1961.

3490   Mitchell, Harry E. "History of Jefferson Barracks."
       Typescript at Missouri Historical Society.

3491   Mueller, Richard E. "Jefferson Barracks: The Early Years, " Missouri
       Historical Review 67 (1972): 7-30.

3492   Webb, Henry W. "The Story of Jefferson Barracks," Mississippi Valley
       Historical Review 21 (1946): 185-208.

SEE ALSO: 4892

# III
# UNITED STATES NAVY

## PUBLIC DOCUMENTATION

3493 American State Papers: Naval Affairs. 4 Vols. Washington, DC: Gales, Seaton, 1832.

3494 Bauer, K. Jack, ed. The New American State Papers, Naval Affairs. Wilmington, DE: Scholarly Resources, 1981.

3495 Callan, John F. and A. W. Russell. Laws of the United States Relating to the Navy and Marine Corps from the Formation of the Government to 1859. Baltimore: John Murphy, 1859.

## *HISTORY

3496 Alden, Carroll S. and Allan Westcott. The United States Navy: A History. Philadelphia: J.B. Lippincott, 1943.

3497 Beach, Edward L. The United States Navy: 200 Years. New York: Henry Holt, 1986.

3498 Belknap, George E. "The Old Navy," Papers of the Military History Society of Massachusetts 12 (1902): 22-59.

3499 Boyeson, Hjalmar H. "Old American Seafights," Cosmopolitan 32 (1901): 189-98.

3500 Brescia, Anthony M., ed. "The American Navy, 1817-1822: Comments of Richard Rush," American Neptune 31 (1971): 217-25.

3501 "The British and American Navies," Edinburgh Review 71 (1840): 120-70.

3502 Buker, George E. "Lieutenant M. Powell, U.S. Navy: Pioneer of River- ine Warfare," Florida Historical Quarterly 47 (1969): 253-75.

3503 _____. Swamp Sailors: Riverine Warfare in the Everglades, 1835-1842. Gainesville: University of Florida Press, 1975.

3504 _____. "The Mosquitio Fleet's Guides and the Second Seminole War," Florida Historical Quarterly 57 (1979): 308-26.

3505 _____. "Lt. John McLaughlin, U.S. Navy, and the Second Seminole War, 1835-1842," Order of the Indian Wars Journal 1 (1980): 12-24.

3506   Brunner, Frank J. "In the Hallowed Area of our Early Sea Struggles,"
       DAR Magazine 57 (1923): 83-87.

3507   Clare, Israel. The Naval History of the United States. New York:
       Union Book Co., 1901.

3508   Clark, George R. The Navy, 1775-1909. Baltimore: Lord Baltimore
       Press, 1910.

3509   Davis, Gherardi. The United States Navy and Merchant Marine.
       New York: Gillis Press, 1923.

3510   Denison, John L. A Pictorial History of the Navy of the United States.
       New York: Henry Bill, 1860.

3511   Evans, Waldo. "The Development and Growth of the American Navy,"
       United States Naval Institute Proceedings 52 (1926): 1897-1915.

3512   Flannery, Edmund P. "Naval Operations during the Second Seminole
       War." Master's Thesis, University of Florida, 1958.

3513   Fowler, William M. Jack Tars and Commodores: The American Navy,
       1783-1815. Boston: Houghton, Mifflin, 1984.

3514   Frost, Holloway H. "The Traditions of the Naval Service," United
       States Naval Institute Proceedings 42 (1916): 1530-36.

3515   Haven, Erastus O. The National Handbook of American Progress. New
       York: E.B. Treat, 1889, 138-66, 453-94.

3516   Knapp, Samuel. Lectures of American Literature, with Remarks on Some
       Passages of American History. New York: E. Bliss, 1829, 266-85.

3517   Krafft, Herman F. "Seapower and American Destiny," United States
       Naval Institute Proceedings 47 (1921): 473-86.

3518   Langley, Harold D. "Robert Y. Hayne and the Navy," South Carolina
       Historical Magazine 82 (1981): 311-30.

3519   McCandless, Bruce and Arthur L. Rogers. "The Navy of 1845," United
       States Naval Institute Proceedings 91 (1965): 166-67.

3520   McKinley, Mike. "Cutlasses and Broadsides," All Hands No. 835 (1986)
       12-16.

3521   "The Navy," North American Review 53 (1841): 360-85.

3522   "The Navy," Ibid 30 (1830): 360-88.

3523   Oskinson, John M. "From John Paul Jones to Dewey: The Typically
       American Development of the Sea-fighting Arm of our Military Service,"
       World's Work 29 (1915): 447-69.

3524   "Our Navy," New York Review 9 (1841): 139-69.

3525   "Our Navy," American Quarterly Review 19 (1836): 467-501.

3526   Potter, E.B., ed. The United States and World Sea Power. Englewood
       Cliffs, NJ: Prentice Hall, 1955.

3527   Pratt, Fletcher. "The Basis of our Naval Tradition," United States
       Naval Institute Proceedings 63 (1937): 1107-14, 1779-80.

3528  Reynolds, Francis J. The United States Navy from the Revolution to
      Date. New York: P.F. Collier, 1917.

3529  Reynolds, G. Clark. "The Sea in the Making of America," United States
      Naval Institute Proceedings 102 (1976): 36-51.

3530  Sprout, Harold and Margaret. The Rise of American Naval Power, 1776-
      1918. Princeton: Princeton University Press, 1939.

3531  Sweetman, Jack. American Naval History: An Illustrated Chronology.
      Annapolis: Naval Institute Press, 1984.

EARLY HISTORY

3532  Adams, Charles F., ed. "The True Origin and Foundation of the
      American Navy." In: The Works of John Adams, Second President of
      the United States. 10 Vols. Boston: Little, Brown, 1850. Vol. 3.

3533  Albion, Robert G. "The First Days of the Navy Department," Military
      Affairs 21 (1948): 1-11.

3534  Barnes, James. "The Beginnings of the American Navy," Harper's
      Monthly Magazine 95 (1897): 547-60.

3535  Bolander, Louis H. "An Incident in the Founding of the American
      Navy," United States Naval Institute Proceedings 55 (1929): 491-94.

3536  Carter, Edward C. "Matthew Carey, Advocate of American Naval Power,
      1785-1814," American Neptune 26 (1966): 177-88.

3537  Chadwick, French E. "The American Navy, 1775-1815," Massachusetts
      Historical Society Proceedings 46 (1913): 191-208.

3538  Cross, F.E. "The Father of the American Navy," United States Naval
      Institute Proceedings 53 (1927): 1296-97.

3539  Farenholt, Ammen. "A Short Account of Legislative Action in Regard
      to the U.S. Navy up to the War of 1812," Ibid 34 (1908): 1279-96.

3540  Frost, Holloway H. "How We got Our Navy," Ibid 59 (1933): 43-48.

3541  Gleeson, Paul F. "Attacks by Algerian Pirates Create Demand for
      American Navy," Rhode Island History 2 (1943): 41-48.

3542  Hattendorf, John B. "The American Navy in the World of Franklin and
      Jefferson, 1755-1826," War and Society 2 (1977): 7-19.

3543  Hislam, Percival A. "The Beginnings of the United States Navy,"
      Army and Navy Life 9 (1906): 623-31.

3544  _____. "The United States Navy" Its First Decline and Resurrection,"
      United Service 34 (1906): 16-21.

3545  Klingelhofer, Herbert F. "Abolish the Navy!" Manuscripts 33 (1981):
      277-84.

3546  Lewis, Winston B. "The Birth of a Navy," United States Naval
      Institute Proceedings 101 (1975): 58-65.

3547  Leyland, John. "The United States Navy in the Making," Nineteenth
      Century 80 (1916): 785-98.

3548  Norris, Walter B. "Who is the Father of the American Navy?" Current
      History 27 (1927): 354-60.

3549  Powers, Stephen E. "The Decline and Extinction of American Naval Power,
      1781-1787." Ph. D. dissertation, University of Notre Dame, 1965.

3550  Paullin, Charles O. "When was our Navy Founded?" United States Naval
      Institute Proceedings 36 (1910): 255-61.

3551  Pratt, Fletcher. "The Sword is Forged." In: The Navy: A History.
      Garden City, NY: Doubleday, 1938, 112-35.

3552  Smelser, Marshall. "Whether to Provide and Maintain a Navy," United
      States Naval Institute Proceedings 83 (1957): 944-53.

3553  ____. "The Passing of the Naval Act of 1794," Military Affairs 22
      (1958): 1-12.

3554  ____. Congress Founds the Navy, 1787-1798. Notre Dame, IN: University
      of Notre Dame Press, 1959.

3555  Spears, John R. "Beginnings of the American Navy," Harper's Monthly
      Magazine 108 (1903): 87-90.

3556  Symonds, Craig L. Navalists and Anti-Navalists: The Naval Policy Debate
      in the United States, 1785-1827. Newark, DE: University of Delaware
      Press, 1978.

3557  ____. "The Anti-Navalists: The Opponents of Naval Expansion in the
      Early National Period," American Neptune 39 (1979): 22-28.

3558  Waite, Henry E. Extracts Relating to the Origin of the American Navy.
      Boston: New England Historical and Genealogical Society, 1890.

3559  Welsh, Donald N. "The Quasi War with France and the Creation of
      the United States Navy." Master's Thesis, University of Akron, 1940.

3560  Werner, H.O. "The Beginnings of the United States Navy." In: Elmer B.
      Potter, ed. Seapower: A Naval History. Englewood Cliff, NJ: Prentice
      Hall, 1960, 187-206.

      SEE ALSO: 4119 , 4120 , 4131 , John Adams, John Barry, Albert Gallatin,
      Alexander Hamilton

## NAVAL POLICY

3561  Albion, Robert G. Makers of Naval Policy, 1798-1947. Annapolis:
      Naval Institute Press, 1980.

3562  Bauer, K. Jack. "The Navy in an Age of Manifest Destiny: Some
      Suggestions for Sources and Research." In: Richard A. Von Doenhoff,
      ed. Versatile Guardian: Research in Naval History. Washington, DC:
      Howard University Press, 1979, 161-75.

3563  Binder, Frederick M. "American Shipbuilding and Russian Naval Power,
      1837-1846," Military Affairs 21 (1957): 79-84.

3564  Henrich, Joseph G. "The Triumph of Ideology: The Jeffersonians and
      the Navy, 1779-1807." Ph. D. dissertation, Duke University, 1971.

3565  Holmes, Wilfred J. "The Foundation of Naval Policy," United States
      Naval Institute Proceedings 60 (1934): 457-69.

3566  Hooper, Edwin B. "Developing Naval Concepts: The Early Years, 1815-
      1842," Defense Management Journal 12 (1976): 19-24.

3567  Leiner, Frederick C. "Saving the Big-Ship Navy," United States Naval
      Institute Proceedings 103 (1977): 76-77.

3568  "The Navy and its Use," Hunt's Merchant Magazine 7 (1842): 148-59.

3569  "The Navy and the West," Southern Literary Messenger 9 (1843): 1-5.

3570  O'Connor, Raymond G. "The Navy on the Frontier." In: James P. Tate, ed.
      The American Military on the Frontier. Washington: Office of Airforce
      History, 1978, 37-49.

3571  Piggott, Francis. The Freedom of the Seas Historically Treated.
      London: Humphrey Milford, 1919.

3572  Predergast, William B. "The Navy and Civil Liberty," United States
      Naval Institute Proceedings 74 (1948): 1263-67.

3573  Roosevelt, Theodore, Jr., ed. American Naval Policy as Outlined in
      Messages of the Presidents of the United States. Washington:
      Government Printing Office, 1924.

3574  Sennott, John P. "Mr. Jefferson's Mothball Fleet," Navy 14 (1971): 22-26.

3575  Sheirrer, G. Terry. "In Search For a Naval Policy, 1783-1812." In:
      Kenneth Hagan, ed. In Peace and War: Interpretations of American Naval
      History, 1775-1984. Westport, CT: Greenwood Press, 1984, 27-45.

      SEE ALSO: 5629, 5635, 5637, 5638

## ADMINISTRATION

3576  Afterguard [Pseud] "Our Navy, Economy, and Good Order," United States
      Nautical Magazine 1 (1845): 307-13.

3577  Albion, Robert G. "The Administration of the Navy, 1798-1945,"
      Public Administration Review 5 (1945): 293-302.

3578  _____. "The Naval Affairs Committees, 1816-1916," United States Naval
      Institute Proceedings 78 (1952): 1227-37.

3579  Bolander, Louis H. "A History of Regulation in the United States Navy,"
      Ibid 73 (1947): 1355-61.

3580  "The Bureau of Supplies and Accounts," Ibid 75 (1979): 343-54.

3581  Calkins, Carlos G. "Tradition and Progress in the Navy: A Review of
      Service Opinions," Ibid 39 (1913): 1184-1216.

3582  "Conditions and Needs of Our Navy, 1815, by the Board of Navy
      Commissioners, David Porter and John Rodgers, U.S.N., " Ibid 53
      (1927): 1309-15.

3583  Furer, Julius A. "The Structure of Naval Appropriation Acts," Ibid
      74 (1948): 1517-27.

3584  Guggenheimer, Jay C. "The Development of the Executive Departments, 1775-1789." In: J. Franklin Jameson, ed. Essays in the Constitutional History of the United States in the Formative Period, 1775-1789. Boston: Houghton, Mifflin, 1889, 116-85.

3585  Haugen, Rolf N. "The Settling of Internal Administrative Communication in the United States Naval Establishment, 1775-1820." Ph. D. dissertation, Harvard University, 1953.

3586  Kennon, B. "B. Kennon to Thomas W. Gilmer, February 22, 1844," William and Mary Quarterly 20 (1911): 19-21.

3587  Long, David F. "The Navy under the Board of Navy Commissioners." In: Kenneth Hagan, ed. In Peace and War: Interpretations of American Naval History, 1775-1984. Westport, CT: Greenwood Press, 1984, 62-78.

3588  McClellan, Edwin N. "Will History Repeat Itself?" United States Naval Institute Proceedings 49 (1923): 249-52.

3589  McIntosh, K.C. "Ships and Shoes and Sealing Wax," Ibid 74 (1949): 135-47.

3590  Neeser, Robert W. "The Department of the Navy," American Political Science Review 9 (1917): 59-75.

3591  Paullin, Charles O. Paullin's History of Naval Administration, 1775-1911. Annapolis: Naval Institute Press, 1968.

3592  _____. "Naval Administration under Secretaries of the Navy Smith, Hamilton and Jones," United States Naval Institute Proceedings 32 (1906): 1289-1328.

3593  _____. "Early Administration under the Constitution," Ibid 32 (1906): 1001-30.

3594  _____. "Naval Administration under the Navy Commissioners, 1815-1842," Ibid 33 (1907): 598-641.

3595  _____. "Naval Administration, 1842-1861," Ibid 33 (1907): 1435-77.

3596  _____. "New England Secretaries of the Navy," New England Magazine 37 (1908): 651-68.

3597  Ray, Thomas W. "The Bureaus Go On Forever," United States Naval Institute Proceedings 94 (1968): 50-63.

3598  Smith, Geoffrey S. "An Uncertain Passage: The Bureaus Run the Navy, 1842-1861." In: Kenneth Hagan, ed. In Peace and War: interpretations of American Naval History, 1775-1984. Westport, CT: Greenwood Press, 1984, 70-106.

3599  Weber, Gustavus A. The Hydrographic Office: Its History, Activities, ans Organization. Baltimore: Johns Hopkins Press, 1926.

3600  _____. The Naval Observatory: Its History, Activities and Organization. Baltimore: Johns Hopkins University Press, 1926.

3601  Welch, P.P. "The High Command," Marine Corps Gazette 19 (1935): 35-37.
      SEE ALSO: George Bancroft, John Branch, Mahlon Dickerson, Thomas W. Gilmer, James McHenry, James K. Paulding, Joel R. Poinsett, Robert Smith, Benjamin Stoddert, Abel P. Upshur

NAVY YARDS

3602  Alden, John . "Portsmouth Naval Shipyard," United States Naval
      Institute Proceedings 90 (1964): 89-105.

3603  Bearess, Edwin V. Charlestown Navy Yard, 1800-1842. 2 Vols.
      Washington, DC: U.S. Department of the Interior, 1984.

3604  Bonaffon, Edward W. "The Old Days of the Washington Navy Yard,"
      Journal of American History 11 (1917): 33-43.

3605  Buell, Thomas B. "Saga of Drydock One," United States Naval Institute
      Proceedings 96 (1970): 60-67.

3606  Cairo, Robert F. "Shipyard and Service Craft: A Portfolio of Plans,"
      Nautical Research Journal 21 (1975): 78-86.

3607  Ferguson, Eugene S. "Mr. Jefferson's Dry Docks," American Neptune
      11 (1951): 108-14.

3608  Foss, William O. The United States Navy in Hampton Roads. Norfolk:
      Donning Co., 1984.

3609  Higginson, Stephen. "The Letters of Stephen Higginson." In: American
      Historical Association Annual Report for the year 1896 (1897): Vol. 1.

3610  Hunnewell, James F. "Aid to Glory," Massachusetts Historical Society
      Proceedings 36 (1902): 182-86.

3611  Johnston, Robert C. "Navy Yards and Drydocks: A Study of the Bureau
      of Yards and Docks, 1842-1871." Master's Thesis, Stanford University,
      1954.

3612  Kauffman, James L. Philadelphia's Navy Yards, 1801-1948. Princeton:
      Princeton University Press, 1948.

3613  Leahy, William D. "Early History of the Washington Navy Yard,"
      United States Naval Institute Proceedings 54 (1928): 869-74.

3614  Lull, Edward P. History of the United States Navy Yard at Gosport,
      Virginia. Washington, DC: Government Printing Office, 1874.

3615  Matthews, Davida. "Shipyards: Midwives of the Early Fleet," All Hands
      No. 713 (1976): 14-17.

3616  Nicilosi, Anthony S. "Foundation of the Naval Presence in Narragansett
      Bay, An Overview," Newport History 52 (1979): 61-82.

3617  Paullin, Charles O. "Washington City and the Old Navy," Columbia
      Historical Society Records 33-34 (1932): 163-77.

3618  Pearce, George F. The U.S. Navy in Pensacola: From Sailing Ships to
      Naval Aviation, 1825-1930. Pensacola: University Presses of Florida,
      1980.

3619  _____. "The United States Navy Comes to Pensacola," Florida Historical
      Quarterly 55 (1976): 37-47.

3620  Peltier, Eugene J. The Bureau of Yards and Docks of the Navy. New York:
      Newcomen Society of America, 1961.

3621 Rachal, William M. "When Virginia Owned a Shipyard: The Story of the Norfolk Navy Shipyard at Portsmouth to the time of its purchase by the United States in 1801," Virginia Cavalcade 2 (1952): 31-35.

3622 Stuart, Charles B. The Naval Dry Docks of the United States. New York: C.B. Norton, 1852.

3623 Valette, Henry M. "History and Reminiscences of the Philadelphia Navy Yard," Potter's American Monthly Magazine 6 (1976): 9-14, 88-91, 177-81, 256-60, 327-33, 407-12.

## U.S. NAVAL ACADEMY

3624 Alden, Carroll S. "Story of the Naval Academy-Annapolis," Mentor 12 (1924): 18-28.

3625 Benjamin, Park. The United States Naval Academy. New York: G.P. Putnam's Sons, 1900.

3626 Brown, F.M. "A Half-Century of Frustration: A Study of the Failure of Naval Academy Legislation between 1800 and 1845," United States Naval Institute Proceedings 80 (1954): 630-35.

3627 Crane, John D. United States Naval Academy: The First Hundred Years. New York: McGraw Hill, 1945.

3628 Description and History of the Naval Academy, from its Origin to the Present Time. N.p., 1869.

3629 Dugan, M.C. Outline History of Annapolis and the Naval Academy. Baltimore: B.G. Eichelberger, 1902.

3630 Duval, Ruby R. "Fort Severn: The Battery at Windmill Point," United States Naval Institute Proceedings 59 (1933): 843-48.

3631 Foster, C.H. "The Requirements for Admission to the Naval Academy- A Historical Review," Ibid 44 (1917): 339-53.

3632 Lull, Edward P. Description and History of the United States Naval Academy, from its Origins to the Present Time. Annapolis: Government Printing Office, 1869.

3633 MaGruder, P.H. "A Walk through Annapolis in Bygone Days," United States Naval Institute Proceedings 55 (1929): 511-17.

3634 Marshal, Edward C. History of the United States Naval Academy with Biographical Sketches and Names of all Superintendents, Professors, and Graduates. New York: D. Van Nostrand, 1862.

3635 "Naval Schools," Southern Literary Messenger 8 (1842): 205-7.

3636 Paullin, Charles O. "The Beginnings of the United States Naval Academy," United States Naval Institute Proceedings 50 (1924): 173-94.

3637 Puleston, W.C. Annapolis: Gangway to the Quarterdeck. New York: Appleton, 1942.

3638 Riley, Elihu S. "Early Days of the Naval Academy," United Service 7 (1905): 209-14,

3639  Soley, James R. Historical Sketch of the United States Naval Academy.
      Washington, DC: Government Printing Office, 1876.

3640  Sturdy, Henry F. "The Establishment of the Naval School at Annapolis,"
      United States Naval Institute Proceedings 71 (1945): 1-17.

3641  _____. "The Founding of the Naval Academy by Bancroft and Buchanan,"
      Ibid 61 (1935): 1367-85.

3642  Sweetman, Jack. The U.S. Naval Academy. Annapolis: Naval Institute
      Press, 1979, 3-18.

3643  Tisdale, Mahlon S. "A Cruise Through the First Academic Journal and
      Some Modern Analogies," United States Naval Institute Proceedings
      50 (1924): 352-72.

3644  Todorich, Charles. The Spirited Years: A History of the Antebellum
      Naval Academy. Annapolis: Naval Institute Press, 1984.

3645  West, Richard S. "The Superintendents of the Naval Academy,"
      United States Naval Institute Proceedings 71 (1945): 801-09.

      SEE ALSO: 6467 , George Bancroft, Franklin Buchanan, William Chauvent

## PERSONNEL

3646  Bolander, Louis H. "The Navy Register: its Evolution," New York Public
      Library Bulletin 58 (1954): 337-43.

3647  Burns, Robert C. "General and Admiral, too," East Tennessee Historical
      Society Publications 48 (1976): 29-33.

3648  Callahan, Edward W. List of Officers of the Navy of the United States,
      and of The Marine Corps from 1775 to 1900. New York: Hamersly, 1901.

3649  Davis, Francklyn W. Robert Mercer, 1759-1828: A Philadelphia Sea
      Captain. Greenwich, NJ: The Author, 1976.

3650  Fasano, Lawrence. Naval Rank: Its Inception and Development. A Short
      History of the Evolution and Genealogy of the Naval Officer. New York:
      Horizon House, 1936.

3651  Ford, Thomas G. "American Navigators of the Colonial Period and the
      Yankee Midshipman," United States Naval Institute Proceedings 32
      (1906): 861-970.

3652  Grant, Richard S. "Captain William Sharp of Norfolk, Virginia,"
      Virginia Magazine of History and Biography 57 (1949): 44-54.

3653  Hamersly, Thomas H. General Register of the United States Navy and
      Marine Corps, 1782-1882. Washington, DC: Thomas Hamersly, 1882.

3654  Holmes, Jack D. "The Naval Career of Lawrence Rousseau," Louisiana
      History 9 (1968): 341-54.

3655  Key, Francis S. Daniel Murray, Late Lieutenant in the American Navy.
      N.p., N.d.

3656  McKee, Christopher. "The Pathology of a Profession: Death in the United
      States Navy Officer Corps, 1797-1815," War and Society 3 (1985): 1-25.

3657  Massey, Robert J. Evolution of Officer Personnel Policy and Practice in the United States Navy, 1821-1861. Washington, DC: American University Press, 1962.

3658  Paullin, Charles O. "Dueling in the Old Navy," United States Naval Institute Proceedings 35 (1909): 1155-1197.

3659  Riley, Elihu S. "American Midshipmen, Past and Present," Army and Navy Life 9 (1906): 33-38.

3660  Rosenwaike, Ira. "Bernard Henry: His Naval and Diplomatic Career," American Jewish History 69 (1980): 488-96.

3661  Shackelford, George G. "George Wythe Randolph, Midshipman," American Neptune 36 (1976): 101-21.

3662  Sprince, Richard H. "From Admirals to Midshipmen," United States Naval Institute Proceedings 82 (1956): 1188-93.

3663  Wegner, Dana M. "Dirty Bill' Porter," Ibid 103 (1977): 40-49.

3664  Wehmann, Howard H. "Noise, Novelties and Nullifiers: A U.S. Navy Officer's Impression of the Nullification Controversy," South Carolina Historical Magazine 76 (1975): 21-24.

3665  Weidenbach, Nell L. "Lieutenant John T. McLaughlin: Guilty or Innocent," Florida Historical Quarterly 46 (1967): 46-52.

SEE ALSO: 3724 , 3725 , 3748 , 3777 , 3779 , 3783 , 3787 , 4230 , George S. Blake, Franklin Buchanan, David Conner, James F. Cooper, Francis G. Dallas, Charles H. Davis, Samuel F. Dupont, David G. Farragut, James M. Gillis, Duncan N. Ingraham, Uriah P. Levy, John Long, Matthew F. Maury, John B. Montgomery, Hiram Paulding, Matthew C. Perry, David D. Porter, John Rodgers, Benjamin F. Sands, Raphael Semmes, John Shaw, William B. Shubrick, John D. Sloat, Charles Stedman, Josiah Tattnall, Henry K. Thatcher, Stephen D. Trenchard

## ENLISTED MEN

3666  Radom, Matthew. "The Americanization of the U.S. Navy," United States Naval Institute Proceedings 63 (1937): 231-34.

3667  Rucker, Bob. "Naval Militia: Forerunner of the Reserves," All Hands No. 760 (1980): 12-17.

3668  McKee, Christopher. "Foreign Seamen in the United States Navy: A Census of 1807," William and Mary Quarterly 42 (1985): 383-93.

3669  Wood, Daniel W. "The All-Volunteer Force in 1798," United States Naval Institute Proceedings 105 (1979): 45-48.

SEE ALSO: 4035

## BLACKS IN THE NAVY

3670  Logan, Rayford W. "The Negro in the Quasi War, 1798-1800," Negro History Bulletin 14 (1951): 128-32.

3671  Nelson, Dennis D. The Integration of the Negro into the United States Navy, 1776-1947. Washington, DC: Government Printing Office, 1948.

3672  Putney, Martha S. Black Sailors: Afro-American Merchant Seamen and Whalemen Prior to the Civil War. New York: Greenwood Press, 1987.

SEE ALSO: 6086

DISCIPLINE

3673  Chapel, Robert B. "The Word Against the Cat: Melville's Influence on Seaman's Rights," American Neptune 42 (1982): 57-65.

3674  Dunn, Herbert O. "Discipline in the Old Navy," United States Naval Institute Proceedings 42 (1916): 1603-05.

3675  Farenholt, Oscar W. "Punishment in the Old Navy," Military Surgeon 76 (1935): 210-13.

3676  Glen, Myra C. "The Naval Reform Campaign Against Flogging: A Case Study in Changing Attitudes Towards Corporal Punishment, 1830-1850," American Quarterly 35 (1983): 408-25.

3677  Horan, Leo T. "Flogging in the U.S. Navy: Unfamiliar Facts Regarding its Origin and Abolition," United States Naval Institute Proceedings 76 (1950): 968-75.

3678  Krafft, Herman F. "The Navy and Flogging," Ibid 55 (1929): 270-73.

3679  Langley, Harold D. "The Humanitarians and the United States Navy, 1789-1862." Ph. D. dissertation, University of Pennsylvania, 1960.

3680  _____. Social Reform in the United States Navy, 1798-1862. Urbana, IL: University of Illinois Press, 1967.

3681  Lockwood, John A. "Flogging in the Navy," United States Magazine and Democratic Review 25 (1849): 97-115, 225-42, 318-37, 417-32.

3682  Low, A.M. "The Lash and the Branding Iron," Harper's Weekly Magazine 45 (1901): 1076-77.

3683  McKee, Christopher. "Fantasies of Mutiny and Murder: A Suggested Psycho-History of Seamen in the U.S. Navy, 1798-1815," Armed Forces and Society 4 (1978): 293-304.

3684  McKinley, Mike. "Shadow of the Cat: A Look back at Bygone Approaches to Navy Discipline," All Hands No. 839 (1987): 18-19.

3685  McNally, William. Evils and Abuses in the Naval and Merchant Service Exposed, with Proposals and Redress. Boston: Cassady, March, 1839.

3686  Observer. An Inquiry into the Necessity and General Principles of Reorganization in the U.S. Navy, with an Examination of the True Sources of Subordination. Baltimore: John Murphy, 1842.

3687  Sargent, Nathan. "The Evolution of Courts-Martial," United States Naval Instutute Proceedings 9 (1883): 693-711.

3688  Snedeker, James. A Brief History of Courts-Martial. Annapolis: Naval Institute Press, 1954.

3689  Stessel, H. Edward. "Melville's White Jacket: A Case Against the Cat," Clio 13 (1983): 37-55.

3690   Valle, James E. Rocks and Shoals: Order and Discipline in the Old Navy, 1800-1861. Annapolis: Naval Institute Press, 1980.

3691   William, Charles R. "On the History of Discipline in the Navy," United States Naval Institute Proceedings 45 (1919): 355-76.

3692   Winston, Alexander. "The Brutal Whip," American History Illustrated 6 (1972): 10-14.

       SEE ALSO: 5907, USS Somers, Abel P. Upshur

RELIGION

3693   Davis, Hugh H. "The American Seaman's Friend Society and the American Sailor, 1828-1838," American Neptune 39 (1979): 45-57.

3694   Drury, Clifford M. The History of the Chaplain Corps, United States Navy. Vol. 1, 1778-1939. Washington, DC: Bureau of Naval Personnel, 1984.

3695   Edel, William H. "The Golden Age of Naval Chaplaincy, 1830-1835," United States Naval Institute Proceedings 50 (1924): 875-85.

3696   Germain, Aidan H. "Catholic Military and Naval Chaplains, 1776-1917." Ph. D. dissertation, Catholic University, 1929.

3697   Meehan, Thomas F. "Catholic Navy Chaplains," U.S. Catholic Historical Researches 32 (1941): 104-14.

3698   "Moral and Religious Improvement in the Navy," Southern Literary Messenger 9 (1843): 73-76.

EDUCATION

3699   Burr, Henry L. "Education in the Early Navy." Ph. D. dissertation, Temple University, 1939.

3700   Crawford, John W. "Get'em Young and Train 'em Right," United States Naval Institute Proceedings 113 (1987): 103-8.

3701   DeChristofaro, S. "The Naval Lyceum," Ibid 77 (1951): 868-73.

3702   Drury, C.M. "Famous Chaplain Teachers of Midshipmen, 1800-1845," Ibid 72 (1946): 681-89.

3703   Heitzmann, W. Ray. "In-Service Naval Officer Education in the 19th Century: Voluntary Committment to Reform," American Neptune 39 (1979): 109-25.

3704   Skinner, John S. Nautical Education...Letter from a Friend to a Young Gentleman on His Entrance into the Navy of the U.S. N.p., 1841.

3705   Stevens, William O. "Two Early Proposals for Naval Education," United States Naval Institute Proceedings 39 (1913): 127-33.

       SEE ALSO: 4370, Arthur Sinclair

## MATERIEL

3706  Skillman, J.H. "The Evolution of the Navy Ration," United States
      Naval Institute Proceedings 60 (1934): 1678-81.

### NAVAL FIREARMS

3707  Martin, Harrison P. "Small Arms and the Navy," United States Naval
      Institute Proceedings 63 (1937): 1753-59.

### NAVAL SWORDS

3708  Clark, Ellery H. "Famous Swords at the U.S. Naval Academy," United
      States Naval Institute Proceedings 66 (1940): 1769-72.

3709  Hamilton, John D. "So Nobly Distinguished': Congressional Swords
      for the Battle of Lake Erie Sailing Masters and Midshipmen," Journal
      of Erie Studies 17 (1988): 76-84.

3710  _____. "So Nobly Distinguished": Congressional Swords for Sailing
      Masters and Midshipmen in the War of 1812," Man at Arms 7 (1985):
      30-37.

3711  Hopkins, Alfred F. "Lions or Eagles," Society of American Sword
      Collectors Bulletin 3 (1950): 5-9.

3712  Keester, George B. "Naval Dirks in the Collection of the U.S. Academy
      Museum," Military Collector and Historian 8 (1956): 31-34.

### NAVAL POLEARMS

3713  Brown, Rodney H. American Polearms, 1526-1865: The Lance, Halberd,
      Spontoon, Pike, and Naval Boarding Weapons. New Milford, CT:
      Norman Flayderman, 1967.

### NAVAL FLAGS

3714  Cluverius, W.T. "Trophies of the Nation," Army and Navy Life 10
      (1907): 388-94.

### MUSIC

3715  Neeser, Robert W. American Naval Songs and Ballads. New Haven:
      Yale University Press, 1938.

      SEE ALSO: 3731

### *NAVAL UNIFORMS

3716  McBarron, H. Charles, Albert W. Haarman, and James C. Tily.
      "Boarding Party, U.S. Navy, 1815: Naval War with Algiers," Military
      Collector and Historian 13 (1961): 114-15.

3717  Smith, Horatio D. "Old Uniforms of the U.S. Service," United Service
      2 (1889): 192-201, 260-71, 375-88.

3718  Tily, James C. "Uniforms of the Navy of the United States, 1797,"
      Military Collector and Historian 15 (1963): 122-23.

3719  Williams, Dion. "War Decorations," United States Naval Institute
      Proceedings 45 (1919): 493-535.

      SEE ALSO: 3726

### *U.S. MARINE CORPS

3720  Altoff, Gerard T. "War of 1812 Leathernecks on Lake Erie,"
      Leatherneck 71 (1988): 36-43.

3721  Bartlett, Tom. "Marines in the Frigate Navy," Leatherneck 66 (1983): 18-21.

3722  Caygill, Harry W. "Flames over the Lighthouse," Ibid 38 (1955): 30-33.

3723  Collum, Richard S. "Our Marines in the Levant," United Service 7 (1882): 358-61.

3724  Donnelly, Ralph W. "Officer Selection in the Old Corps," Marine Corps Gazette 66 (1982): 81-87.

3725  Dunn, Lucius. "The U.S. Navy's First Seagoing Marine Officer," United States Naval Institute Proceedings 25 (1949): 919-24.

3726  "The Early Years of the Marine Corps," Marine Corps Gazette 4 (1919): 259-67.

3727  Evans, Frank E. "The Corps a Hundred Years Ago," Ibid 1 (1916): 43-62.

3728  Heinl, R.D. "A Cat with More than Nine Lives," United States Naval Institute Proceedings 80 (1954): 659-71.

3729  King, Mary E. "More Light on the Ballad of James Bird," New York Folklore 7 (1951): 142-44.

3730  Leonard, John W. and Fred F. Chitty. The Story of the United States Marines: Compiled from Authentic Records, 1740-1919. New York: Marine Corps Publicity Bureau, 1920.

3731  McClellan, Edwin A. "How the Marine Corps Band Started," United States Naval Institute Proceedings 49 (1923): 581-86.

3732  _____. "The First Commandant of the Marine Corps, William Ward Burrows," DAR Magazine 59 (1925): 155-59.

3733  _____. "From 1783-1798," Marine Corps Gazette 7 (1922): 273-86.

3734  _____. "The Naval War with France," Ibid 7 (1922): 339-64.

3735  _____. "Marine Corps History, 1807-1812," Ibid 8 (1923): 24-43.

3736  _____. "Marine Corps History, 1815-1817," Ibid 8 (1923): 269-93.

3737  _____. "Marine Corps History, 1817-1821," Ibid 9 (1924): 69-93.

3738  _____. Uniforms of the American Marines, 1775 to 1932. Washington, DC: N.p., 1932.

3739  Moe, Albert F. "Leatherneck: A Borrowed Name," Names 13 (1965): 225-27.

3740  Parrott, Marc. "A Captive Marine and His Rescuers: Ray, Eaton, and O'Bannon." In" Hazard: Marines on a Mission. Garden City, NJ: Doubleday, 1962, 21-68.

3741  Magruder, John H. "U.S. Marine Corps, 1797-1804," Military Collector and Historian 8 (1956): 15-16.

3742  _____. "U.S. Marine Corps, 1834-1841," Ibid 7 (1955): 77-79.

3743  _____. "United States Marine Corps, 1826," Ibid 9 (1957): 12-14.

3744 Marini, Alfred J. "Political Perceptions of the Marine Forces: Great
     Britain, 1699-1739, and the United States, 1798-1804," Military
     Affairs 44 (1980): 171-75.

3745 Metcalf, C.H. "The Early Years of the Marine Corps," Marine Corps
     Gazette 20 (1936): 28-32, 72-83.

3746 O'Quinlivan, Michael. "The Navy and Marine Corps at Curacao," Navy
     2 (1959): 58-59.

3747 Parker, William D. A Concise History of the United States Marine Corps,
     1775-1969. Washington, DC: Historical Division, Head Quarters, USMC,
     1970.

3748 "Portraits of the Commandants, 1775-1975," Marine Corps Gazette 59
     (1975): 31-46.

3749 Simmons, Edwin H. The United States Marines, 1775-1975. New York:
     Viking Press, 1976.

3750 ____. "The United States Marine Corps," Marine Corps  Gazette 57
     (1973): 23-28, 35-40; 58 (1974): 44-50, 44-46.

3751 ____. "The United States Marines on the Gulf Coast." In: William S.
     Coker, ed. The Military Presence on the Gulf Coast. Pensacola, FL:
     History and Humanities Conference, 1978, 64-81.

3752 ____. "Major Carmick at New Orleans," Fortitudine 14 (1985): 3-8.

3753 Strowbridge, Truman R. and Edwin Turnbladh. "Lieutenant Ichabod Crane,
     United States Marine Corps," New Jersey Historical Society Proceedings
     84 (1966): 170-73.

3754 Thacker, Joel D. "Highlights of United States Marine Corps Activities
     in the District of Columbia," Columbia Historical Society Records
     51-52 (1955): 78-86.

     SEE ALSO: 3843, 4230, 4270, 4279, John M. Gamble, Archibald Henderson,
     Presley O'Bannon

                         U.S. COAST GUARD

3755 Bloomfield, Howard V. The Compact History of the United States Coast
     Guard. New York: Hawthorne, 1966.

3756 A Brief Sketch of the Character of Captain Joshua Sturgis of the
     United States Revenue Service. Boston: White, Lewis, 1844.

3757 Brown, Riley. The Story of the Coast Guard: Men, Wind and Sea.
     Garden City, NY: Blue Ribbon Books, 1943.

3758 Capron, Walter C. The U.S. Coast Guard. New York: Franklin Watts, 1965.

3759 Cayford, John E. "Father of the U.S. Coast Guard: Hopley Yeaton,"
     New England Galaxy 20 (1978): 26-34.

3760 Copeland, Peter F. "The U.S. Revenue Cutter Service," Military
     Collector and Historian 17 (1965): 122-23.

3761 Daly, R.W. "The Revenue Cutters in the Quasi War with France, 1798
     -1800," United States Naval Institute Proceedings 68 (1942): 1713-23.

3762  Evans, Stephen H. The United States Coast Guard, 1790-1915: A
      Definitive History. Annapolis: Naval Institute Press, 1949.

3763  Gray, S.F. "The Story of the Coast Guard," Military Engineer 29
      (1937): 35-41.

3764  Johnson, Harvey E. The United States Coast Guard: Some Adventures.
      Princeton: Princeton University Press, 1941.

3765  Kaplan, Hymen R. "Hamilton's Revenue Fleet," United States Naval
      Institute Press 88 (1962): 160-63.

3766  King, Irving H. George Washington's Coast Guard: Origins of the U.S.
      Revenue Cutter Service, 1789-1801. Annapolis: Naval Institute Press,
      1979.

3767  Parker, John W. "The Revenue Cutter Service," Nautical Research
      Journal 4 (1952): 199-22.

3768  Ross, W.G. "Our Coast Guard: A Brief History of the United States
      Revenue Marine Service," Harper's Monthly Magazine 73 (1886): 909-22.

3769  Smith, Horatio D. Early History of the United States Revenue Marine
      Service, or United States Revenue Cutter Service. Baltimore: R.L.
      Polk Print Co., 1932.

3770  _____. "The United States Revenue Cutter Service," United Service
      2 (1889): 454-66, 579-91; 3 (1890): 38-42, 154-63, 272-81, 380-99.

3771  Wilson Rufus R. "The Police of the Coast." In: The Sea Rovers.
      New York: B.W. Dodge, 1906, 121-48.

## DIPLOMACY AND DEPLOYMENT

3772  Carrison, D.J. "Medal or Court-martial?" United States Naval Institute
      Proceedings 81 (1955): 277-81.

3773  Chester, Colby M. "Diplomacy of the Quarterdeck," American Journal
      of International Law 8 (1914): 443-76.

3774  Dunn, Lucius C. "The United States Navy and 104 Years of the Monroe
      Doctrine," United States Naval Institute Proceedings 54 (1928): 1067-79.

3775  Fenwick, Charles G. American Neutrality: Trial and Failure. New York:
      Oxford University Press, 1940.

3776  Goetzmann, William H. When the Eagle Screamed: The Romantic Horizon
      in American Diplomacy, 1800-1860. New York: John Wiley, 1966.

3777  Knapp, H.S. "The Naval Officer in Diplomacy," United States Naval
      Institute Proceedings 53 (1927): 309-17.

3778  Lang, Daniel G. Foreign Policy in the Early Republic: The Law of
      Nations and the Balance of Power. Baton Rouge: Louisiana State
      University Press, 1985.

3779  Long, David F. Gold Braid and Foreign Relations: Diplomatic Activities
      of U.S. Naval Officers, 1798-1883. Annapolis: Naval Institute Press,
      1988.

3780  Langley, Lester D. "American Foreign Policy in an Age of Nationalism, 1812-1840." In: Gerald K. Haines and J. Samuel Walker, eds. American Foreign Relations: A Historiographical Review. Westport, CT: Greenwood Press, 1981, 33-47.

3781  McColley, Robert, ed. Federalists, Republicans, and Foreign Entanglements, 1789-1815. Englewood Cliffs, NJ: Prentice Hall, 1969.

3782  Moore, Charles G. "International Relations of Our Navy in Peacetime," DAR Magazine 70 (1936): 1105-09.

3783  Paullin, Charles O. Diplomatic Negotiations of American Naval Officers, 1778-1883. Baltimore: Johns Hopkins Press, 1912.

3784  Rochester, H.A. "The Navy's Support of Foreign Policy," United States Naval Institute Proceedings 67 (1931): 1491-1500.

3785  Talbot, Melvin F. "The Inter-relationship of Foreign and Naval Policies in American History," Ibid 76 (1940): 650-60.

3786  Van Alstyne, Richard W. "The American Empire makes it Bow on the World Stage, 1803-1845." In: William A. Williams, ed. From Colony to Empire: Essays in the History of American Foreign Relations. New York: John Wiley & Sons, 1972, 83-113.

3787  Vroom, G.B. "The Place of Naval Officers in International Affairs," United States Naval Institute Proceedings 47 (1921): 685-700.

3788  Woolsey, L.H. "Early Cases on the Doctrine of Continuous Voyage," American Journal of International Law 4 (1910): 823-47.

      SEE ALSO: 3810, 3835, 3844, 3847, 3848, 3849, 3863, 3871, 3883, 3904, 3916, 3925, 3930, 3933, 3935, 3939

COMMERCE

3789  Brauner, Kinley J. "1821-1860: Economics and the Diplomacy of American Expansionism." In: William H. Becker and Samuel F. Wells, eds. Economics and World Power: An Assessment of American Diplomacy Since 1789. New York: Columbia University Press, 1984, 55-118.

3790  Crawford, Michael J. "The Navy's Campaign Against the Licensed Trade in the War of 1812," American Neptune 46 (1986): 165-72.

3791  Hutchins, John G. The American Maritime Industries and Public Policy, 1789-1914. Cambridge: Harvard University Press, 1941.

3792  Langley, Harold D. "Trade as a Precursor of Diplomacy: The Beginnings of American Commercial Relations with the Pacific and Indian Ocean Areas." In: Joan R. Challinor and Robert L. Beisner, eds. Arms at Rest: Peacemaking and Peacekeeping in American History. Westport, CT: Greenwood Press, 1987, 39-74.

3793  Mannix, Richard J. "The Embargo: Its Administration, Impact, and Enforcement." Ph. D. dissertation, New York University, 1975.

3794  Savage, Carleton, ed. The Policy of the United States Toward Maritime Commerce in War. 2 Vols. Washington, DC: Government Printing Office, 1934-1936.

3795   Schroeder, John H. Shaping a Maritime Empire: The Commercial and
       Diplomatic Role of the American Navy, 1829-1861. Westport, CT:
       Greenwood Press, 1985.

3796   Zingg, Paul J. "To the Shores of Barbary: The Ideology and Pursuit
       of American Commercial Expansion, 1816-1906," South Atlantic Quarterly
       79 (1980): 408-24.

       SEE ALSO: 3799, 3930, 3938

                        MEDITERRANEAN

3797   Albion, Robert G. "Distant Stations," United States Naval Institute
       Proceedings 80 (1954): 265-73.

3798   Daniel, Robert L. "American Influences in the Near east before 1861,"
       American Quarterly 16 (1964): 72-84.

3799   Keene, Charles A. "The American Commitment to the Mediterranean
       Marketplace, 1776-1801." Ph. D. dissertation, University of California,
       Santa Barbara, 1979.

                     CONTEMPORARY ACCOUNTS

3800   Schroeder, Francis. Shores of the Mediterranean, with Sketches of
       Travel. New York: Harper & Bros., 1846.

3801   "Scraps from the Journal of a Reefer," Military and Naval Magazine
       2 (1834): 288-94, 338-41.

3802   "Sketches of Naval Life," American Quarterly Review 6 (1829): 216-39.

3803   "Two and a Half Years in the Navy," Ibid 12 (1832): 457-75.

       SEE ALSO: 4086, 4225, 4251, 4276, 4305, 4316, 4357, 4365,4368 ,4478 ,
       4479, 4481

                           AFRICA

3804   Anderson, Robert E. Liberia: America's African Friend. Chapel Hill:
       University of North Carolina Press, 1952.

3805   Ashmun, Jehudi. History of the American Colony in Liberia, from
       December, 1821 to 1823. Washington, DC: Way, Gideon, 1826.

3806   Booth, Alan R. "The United States African Squadron, 1843-1861." In:
       Jeffrey Butler, ed. Boston University Papers in African History.
       Boston: Boston University Press, 1964, 77-117.

3807   Duke, Marvin L. "The Navy Founds a Nation," United States Naval
       Institute Proceedings 96 (1970): 68-70.

3808   Fox, E.L. "The American Colonization Society, 1817-1840." Ph. D.
       dissertation, Johns Hopkins University, 1919.

3809   Griffis, William E. "British and American Co-operation in Africa,"
       Landmark 7 (1925): 613-16.

3810   Harris, Katherine. "The United States, Liberia, and their Foreign
       Relations to 1847." Ph. D. dissertation, Cornell University, 1982.

3811  Harmon, Judd S. "Marriage of Convenience: The United States Navy in Africa, 1820-1843," American Neptune 32 (1972): 264-74.

3812  MacMaster, Richard K. "United State Navy and African Exploration," Mid America 46 (1964): 187-203.

3813  Pfautz, James C. "The African Squadron and the United States Navy, 1843-1861." Master's Thesis, American University, 1968.

3814  Shufeldt, Robert W. The U.S. Navy in Connection with the Foundation, Growth and Prosperity of the Republic of Liberia. Washington, DC: G.L. Ginck, 1877.

      SEE ALSO: Andrew H. Foote, Matthew C. Perry

                        CONTEMPORARY ACCOUNTS

3815  Bridge, Horatio. Journal of an African Cruiser: Comprising Sketches of the Canaries, the Cape de Verde, Liberia, Maderia, Sierra Leone, and Other Places of Interest on the West Coast of Africa. New York: Putnam, 1845.

                            SLAVE TRADE

3816  Brooke, George M. "The Role of the United States Navy in the Supression of the African Slave Trade," American Neptune 21 (1961): 28-41.

3817  Drake, Frederick C. "Secret History of the Slave Trade to Cuba, Written by an American Naval Officer, Robert Wilson Schufelt, 1861," Journal of Negro History 55 (1970): 218-35.

3818  DuBois, W.E.B. The Supression of the African Slave Trade to the United States of America, 1638-1860. New York: Dover, 1970.

3819  Harmon, Judd S. "The United States Navy and the Supression of the Illegal Slave Trade, 1830-1850." In: Craig L. Symonds, ed. New Aspects of Naval History. Annapolis: Naval Institute, 1981, 211-19.

3820  _____. "Supress and Protect: The United States Navy and the African Slave Trade, and Maritime Commerce, 1794-1862." Ph. D. dissertation, William and Mary College, 1977.

3821  Howard, Warren S. American Slavers and the Federal Law, 1837-1862. Berkeley: University of California Press, 1963.

3822  MacMaster, Richard K. "The United States, Great Britain, and the Supression of the Cuban Slave Trade, 1835-1860." Ph. D. dissertation, Georgetown University, 1968.

3823  McNeilly, Earl E. "The U.S. Navy and the Supression of the West African Slave Trade." Ph. D. dissertation, Case Western University, 1973.

3824  "The Navy and the Late Treaty, Hunt's Merchant Magazine 8 (1843): 49-56.

3825  Soulsby, Hugh G. The Right of Search and the Slave Trade in Anglo-American Relations. Baltimore: Johns Hopkins University, 1933.

      SEE ALSO: 4160, 4301, 6473

CARIBBEAN

3826 Allen, Gardner W. Our Navy and the West Indian Pirates. Salem: Essex Institute, 1929.

3827 Baker, Maury D. "The United States and Piracy during the Spanish-American Wars of Independence." Ph. D. dissertation, Duke, 1947.

3828 Barbour, Violet. "Privateers and Pirates of the West Indies," American Historical Review 16 (1911): 529-66.

3829 Barton, William P. Hints for Naval Officers Cruising in the West Indies. Philadelphia: E. Littel, 1830.

3830 Birkner, Michael. "The Foxardo Affair Revisited: Porter, Pirates, and the Problem of Civilian Authority in the Early Republic," American Neptune 42 (1982): 165-78.

3831 Bradlee, Francis B. Piracy in the West Indies and its Supression. Salem: Essex Institute, 1923.

3832 Bunce, K.W. "American Interests in the Caribbean Islands, 1783-1850." Ph. D. dissertation, Ohio State University, 1939.

3833 Butler, Howard R. "Lieutenant William Howard Allen, U.S.N.," United States Naval Institute Proceedings 44 (1918): 49-52.

3834 Calkins, Carlos G. "The Repression of Piracy in the West Indies, 1814-1825," Ibid 37 (1911): 1197-1238.

3835 Colby, Chester. "Diplomacy of the Quarterdeck," American Journal of International Law 8 (1914): 443-76.

3836 Feipel, Louis N. "The United States in Mexico, 1821-1914," United States Naval Institute Proceedings 41 (1915): 33-52, 489-97, 889-903.

3837 Goodrich, Caspar F. "Our Navy and the West Indian Pirates: A Documentary History," Ibid 42 (1916): 1171-92, 1461-83, 1923-39; 43 (1917): 83-98,313-24, 483-96, 683-98, 973-84, 1197-1206, 1449-61, 1727-38, 2023-35.

3838 Green, Samuel A. "Pirates off the Florida Coast," Massachusetts Historical Society Proceedings 44 (1911): 453-59.

3839 A History of the Pirates...to Which is Added a Correct Account of ...the Expedition of Commodore Porter. Haverbill, MA: Carey, 1825.

3840 Jenkins, H.J. "Privateers, Picaroons, Pirates: West Indian Commerce Raiders, 1793-1801," Mariner's Mirror 73 (1987): 181-86.

3841 Kendall, John S. "Piracy in the Gulf of Mexico, 1816-1825," Louisiana Historical Quarterly 7 (1925): 341-68.

3842 Langley, Lester D. The Struggle for the American Mediterranean: United States-European Rivalry in the Gulf-Caribbean, 1776-1904. Athens: University of Georgia Press, 1976.

3843 LeClaire, Charles A. "The Marines Have Landed," Marine Corps Gazette 43 (1959): 24-30.

3844 Logan, Rayford W. The Diplomatic Relations of the United States with Haiti, 1776-1891. Chapel Hill: University of North Carolina, 1941.

3845  Montague, Ludwell L. <u>Haiti and the United States, 1714-1938</u>.
      New York: Russell, Russell, 1966.

3846  Morgan, William A. "Seapower in the Gulf of Mexico and the Caribbean
      during the Mexican and Columbian Wars of Independence, 1815-1830."
      Ph. D. dissertation, University of Southern California, 1969.

3847  Shoemaker, Raymond L. "Diplomacy from the Quarterdeck: The United
      States Navy in the Caribbean, 1815-1830." Ph. D. dissertation,
      Indiana University, 1976.

3848  ____. "Diplomacy from the Quarterdeck: The U.S. Navy in the Caribbean,
      1815-1830." In: Robert W. Love, ed. <u>Changing Interpretations and New</u>
      <u>Sources in Naval History</u>. New York: Garland, 1980, 169-79.

3849  Tansil, Charles C. <u>The United States and Santo Domingo, 1798-1873:</u>
      <u>A Chapter in Caribbean Diplomacy</u>. Baltimore: Johns Hopkins, 1938,

3850  Tays, George. "Commodore Edward B. Kennedy, U.S.N. versus Governor
      Nicholas Gutierrez; an Incident of 1836," <u>California Historical</u>
      <u>Society Quarterly</u> 12 (1933): 137-46.

3851  Warren, Harris G. "The Firebrand Affair: A Forgotten Incident of
      the Mexican Revolution," <u>Louisiana Historical Quarterly</u> 21 (1938):
      203-12.

3852  Whipple, Addison B. "Porter vs the Pirates." In: <u>Pirates</u>. New York:
      Doubleday, 1957, 244-54.

3853  Wheeler, Richard. <u>In Pirate Waters: Captain David Porter, U.S. Navy,</u>
      <u>and America's War on Piracy in the West Indies</u>. New York: Thomas Y.
      Crowell, 1969.

      SEE ALSO: David Porter

CONTEMPORARY ACCOUNTS

3854  Lincoln, Barnabas. <u>Narrative of the Capture, Suffering, and Escape of</u>
      <u>Captain Barnabas Lincoln and his Crew, who were taken by a Piratical</u>
      <u>Schooner, December, 1821, off Key Largo</u>. Boston: Lincoln, 1822.

3855  "Naval Life, No. 2," <u>Military and Naval Magazine</u> 3 (1834): 364-68,
      4 (1834): 5-14.

3856  Newell, Thomas M. "Thomas M. Newell to David Porter on Piracy in the
      West Indies in 1832," <u>New York Public Library Bulletin</u> 9 (1905): 48-49.

3857  "Scraps from my Port Feuille, No. 1," <u>Military and Naval Magazine</u>
      6 (1835): 422-26.

      SEE ALSO: 4087

SOUTH AMERICA

3858  Auchmuty, James J. <u>The United States Government and Latin American</u>
      <u>Independence, 1810-1830</u>. London: P.S. King, 1937.

3859  Bauer, K. Jack. "The Sancala Affair: Captain Philip F. Voorhees seizes
      and Argentine Squadron," <u>American Neptune</u> 29 (1969): 174-86.

3860  Bierck, Harold. "The First Instance of U.S. Foreign Aid: Venezuelan Relief in 1812," Inter-American Economic Affairs 9 (1955): 47-59.

3861  Dickens, P.D. "The Falkland Islands Dispute Between the United States and Argentina," Hispanic American Historical Review 9 (1929): 471-87.

3862  Dyer, George B. and Charlotte L. "The Beginnings of a U.S. Strategic Intelligence System in Latin America, 1809-1826," Military Affairs 14 (1950): 65-83.

3863  Froehlich, Richard C. "The United States Navy and Diplomatic Relations with Brazil, 1822-1871." Ph. D. dissertation, Kent State University, 1971.

3864  Giffin, Donald W. "The American Navy at Work on the Brazilian Station, 1827-1860," American Neptune 19 (1959): 239-56.

3865  Goebel, Julius. Struggle for the Falkland Islands: A Study in Legal and Diplomatic History. New York: Yale University Press, 1927.

3866  Gray, Anthony W. "The Evolution of U.S. Naval Policy in Latin America." Ph. D. dissertation, American University, 1982.

3867  Griffin, Charles C. The United States and the Disruption of the Spanish Empire, 1810-1822. New York: Columbia University Press, 1937.

3868  _____. "Privateers from Baltimore during the Spanish-American Wars of Independence," Maryland Historical Magazine 35 (1940): 1-25.

3869  Hoskins, Halford L. "The Hispanic-American Policy of Henry Clay, 1816-1828," Hispanic-American Historical Review 7 (1927): 460-78.

3870  Klafter, Craig E. "United States Involvement in the Falkland Islands Crisis of 1831-1833," Journal of the Early Republic 4 (1984): 395-420.

3871  Randall, Robert W. "Captains and Diplomats: Americans in the Rio De La Plata, 1843-1846," American Neptune 46 (1986): 230-39.

3872  Solnick, Bruce B. "American Opinion Concerning the Spanish-American Wars of Independence, 1808-1824." Ph. D. dissertation, New York University, 1960.

3873  Thompson, Edgar K. "Yankee Admiral under the Chilean Flag," Mariner's Mirror 64 (1978): 157-62.

3874  Wheelock, Phyllis D. "An American Commodore in the Argentine Navy," American Neptune 6 (1946): 5-18.

3875  Whitaker, Arthur P. The United States and the Independence of Latin America, 1800-1830. Baltimore: Johns Hopkins University Press, 1941.

3876  Wilgus, A. Curtis. "Spanish-American Patriot Activity Along the Gulf Coast of the United States, 1811-1822," Louisiana Historical Quarterly 8 (1925): 193-215.

3877  _____. "Some Notes on Spanish-American Patriot Activity along the Atlantic Seaboard, 1816-1822," North Carolina Historical Review 4 (1927): 172-81.

CONTEMPORARY ACCOUNTS

3878  "Guyaquil in 1833," Naval Magazine 1 (1836): 227-35.

3879  Manning, William R., ed. Diplomatic Correspondence of the United States
      Concerning the Independence of the Latin American Nations. 3 Vols.
      Washington: Carnegie Endowment for International Peace, 1940-1943.

3880  "Rambling Notes on Sea and Shore," Military and Naval Magazine 3
      (1834): 419-27; 4 (1834): 17-25.

3881  "Recollections of a Sailor," Ibid 5 (1835): 340-45; 6 (1835): 43-49.

      SEE ALSO:  3968, 4211, 4219, 4307, 4484, 4486, Western South America,
      Oliver H. Perry

PACIFIC

3882  Battisini, Lawrence. The Rise of American Influence in Asia and the
      Pacific. East Lansing, MI: Michigan State University Press, 1960.

3883  Callahan, James M. American Relations in the Pacific and Far East,
      1784-1900. Baltimore: Johns Hopkins University Press, 1901.

3884  Cummins, Bernard D. "The United States Navy in the Pacific: A History
      of the Pacific Station Before the Mexican War, 1818-1846." Master's
      Thesis, Wichita State University, 1975.

3885  Dennett, Tyler. Americans in Eastern Asia: A Critical Study of the
      United States with Reference to China, Japan and Korea. New York:
      Barnes, Noble, 1931.

3886  Henderson, Daniel M. Yankee Ships in China Seas: Adventures of Pioneer
      Americans in the Troubled Far East. New York: Hastings House, 1946.

3887  Johnson, Robert E. "United States Forces on Pacific Station, 1818-1923."
      Ph. D. dissertation, Claremont Graduate School, 1956.

3888  _____. Thence Round Cape Horn: The Story of United States Naval Forces
      on the Pacific Station, 1818-1823. Annapolis: Naval Institute, 1963.

3889  _____. Far China Station: The U.S. Navy in Asian Waters, 1800-1898.
      Annapolis: Naval Institute Press, 1979.

3890  Lewis, Charles. "Our Navy in the Pacific and the Far East Long Ago,"
      United States Naval Institute Proceedings 69 (1943): 857-64.

3891  Maloney, Linda M. "The U.S. Navy's Pacific Squadron, 1824-1827." In:
      Robert W. Love, ed. Changing Interpretations and New Sources in Naval
      History. New York: Garland, 1980, 180-91.

3892  Merrill, James M. "The Asiatic Squadron, 1835-1907," American Neptune
      29 (1969): 106-17.

3893  Michener, James A. and A. Grove Day. "Rascals in Paradise: The 'Globe'
      Mutineers." In: Rascals in Paradise. New York: Random House, 1957, 7-43.

3894  Morison, Samuel E. "Pacific Strategy," Marine Corps Gazette 46 (1962):
      34-40.

3895 Morison, Samuel E. "Historical Notes on the Gilberts and Marshall Islands," American Neptune 4 (1944): 87-118.

3896 "Navigation of the South China Seas," North American Review 45 (1837): 361-90.

3897 Paullin, Charles O. American Voyages to the Orient, 1690-1865. Annapolis: Naval Institute Press, 1970.

3898 _____. "Early Voyages of American Naval Vessels to the Orient," United States Naval Institute Proceedings 36 (1910): 429-63, 707-34,

3899 Shewmaker, K.E. "Forging the 'Great Chain': Daniel Webster and the Origins of American Foreign Policy Towards East Asia and the Pacific," American Philosophical Society Proceedings 129 (1985): 225-59.

3900 Tate, E. Mowbray. "Navy Justice in the Pacific, 1830-1870: A Pattern of Precedents," American Neptune 35 (1975): 20-31.

3901 Ward, Ralph G. American Activities in the Central Pacific, 1790-1870: A History, Geography and Ethnography Pertaining to American Involvement and Americans in the Pacific. 8 Vols. New York: Gregg, 1966-1972.

SEE ALSO: 4284, 4302, 4304, 4374, 4474

## WESTERN SOUTH AMERICA

3902 Billingsley, Edward B. In Defense of Neutral Rights: The United States Navy and the Wars of Independence in Chile and Peru. Chapel Hill: University of North Carolina Press, 1967.

3903 Neumann, William L. "The Role of the United States in the Chilean Wars of Independence." Ph. D. dissertation, University of Michigan, 1948.

3904 Nolan, L.C. "The Diplomatic and Commercial Relations of the United States and Peru, 1826-1875." Ph. D. dissertation, Duke University, 1935.

3905 O'Neil, Daniel J. "The United States Navy in California, 1840-1850." Ph. D. dissertation, University of Southern California, 1969.

3906 Shurbett, T. Ray. "Chile, Peru, and the Pacific Squadron, 1827-1850." In: Craig L. Symonds, ed. New Aspects of Naval History. Annapolis: Naval Institute Press, 1981, 201-10.

3907 Simmons, Edwin H. "The Secret Mission of Archibald Gillespie," Marine Corps Gazette 52 (1968): 60-67.

3908 Worcester, Donald E. Sea Power and Chilean Independence. Gainesville: University of Florida Press, 1963.

SEE ALSO: 3968, 4213, 4300, 4303, 4304, 4653, 4405, 4410, 4484

## HAWAII

3909 Bradley, Howard W. The American Frontier in Hawaii, 1789-1843: The Pioneers. Stanford: Stanford University Press, 1942.

3910 _____. "Hawaii and the American Penetration of the Northeastern Pacific, 1800-1845," Pacific Historical Review 12 (1943): 277-86.

3911  Brookes, Jean I. International Rivalry in the Pacific Islands, 1800-1875. Berkeley: University of California Press, 1941.

3912  Stevens, Sylvester K. American Expansion in Hawaii, 1842-1898. Harrisburg: Archives Publishing Co., 1945.

3913  Strauss, Wallace P. "Early American Interest and Activity in Polynesia, 1783-1842." Ph. D. dissertation, Columbia University, 1958.

3914  _____. Americans in Polynesia, 1783-1842. East Lansing, MI: Michigan State University Press, 1963.

3915  Taylor, Albert P. "The American Navy in Hawaii," United States Naval Institute Proceedings 53 (1927): 907-24.

      SEE ALSO: Thomas ApC. Jones, John Percival

## JAPAN

3916  Bartlett, Merrill L. "Commodore James Biddle and the First Naval Mission to Japan, 1845-1846," American Neptune 41 (1981): 25-35.

3917  Burton, E.S. "Commodore Biddle's Failure to Enter Japan in 1846," Independent Magazine 59 (1905): 497-501.

3918  Cole, Allan B. "The Dynamics of American Expansion Toward Japan, 1791-1860." Ph. D. dissertation, University of Chicago, 1940.

3919  _____. "Captain David Porter's Proposed Expedition to the Pacific and Japan, 1815," Pacific Historical Review 9 (1940): 61-65.

3920  Dulles, Foster R. Yankees and Samurai: America's Role in the Emergence of Modern Japan, 1791-1900. New York: Harper, Row, 1965.

3921  Larson, Sarah. "East India Squadron Letters: A Passage of Arms," Prologue 13 (1981): 39-48.

3922  Luce, Stephen B. "Commodore Biddle's Visit to Japan in 1846," United States Naval Institute Proceedings 31 (1905): 556-63.

3923  Shunzo, Sakamaki. "Japan and the United States, 1790-1853," Transactions of the Asiatic Society of Japan 18 (1939): 4-11.

3924  Van Doenhoff, Richard A. "Biddle, Perry, and Japan," United States Naval Institute Proceedings 92 (1966): 78-87.

3925  Wada, Teijuhn. American Foreign Policy Towards Japan during the 19th Century. Tokyo: Tokyo Bunko, 1928.

      SEE ALSO: James Biddle

## CHINA

3926  Dulles, Foster R. The Old China Trade. Boston: Hoghton, Mifflin, 1930.

3927  Dunn, Lucius C. "The U.S. Navy and the Open Door Policy," United States Naval Institute Proceedings 75 (1949): 53-65.

3928  Fairbank, John K. Trade and Diplomacy of the China Coast: The Opening of the Treaty Ports. 2 Vols. Cambridge: Harvard University Press, 1953.

3929  Foster, John W. American Diplomacy in the Orient. Boston: Houghton, Mifflin, 1903.

3930  Griffin, Elder. Clippers and Consuls: American Consular and Commercial Relations with Eastern Asia, 1845-1846. Ann Arbor, MI: Edwards, 1938.

3931  Haviland, E.K. "Early Steam Navigation to China," American Neptune 26 (1966): 5-32.

3932  Henson, Curtis T. Commissioners and Commodores: The East India Squadron and American Diplomacy in China. University, AL: University of Alabama Press, 1982.

3933  ____. "The United States Navy and China, 1839-1861." Ph. D. dissertation, Tulane University, 1965.

3934  Kirker, James. Adventures to China: Americans in the Southern Oceans, 1792-1812. New York: Oxford University Press, 1970.

3935  Latourette, Kenneth S. "The History of Early Relations Between the United States and China, 1784-1844." Ph. D. dissertation, Harvard University, 1917.

3936  Snyder, James W. "Bibliography for Early American China Trade, 1784-1815," Americana 34 (1940): 297-345.

3937  Swisher, Earl. "China and the United States, 1841-1861." In: China's Management of the Barbarians: A Study of Sino-American Relations, 1841-1861. New Haven: Yale University Press, 1953, 1-54.

3938  Tate, E. Mowbray. "American Merchant and Naval Contacts with China, 1784-1850," American Neptune 31 (1971): 177-91.

3939  Tong, Te-kong. United States Diplomacy in China, 1840-1860. Seattle: University of Washington, 1964.

3940  Wood, James B. "The American Response to China, 1784-1844: Consensus Policy and the Origin of the East India Squadron." Ph. D. dissertation, Duke University, 1969.

SEE ALSO: Lawrence Kearny

CONTEMPORARY ACCOUNTS

3941  Armstrong, James. "Official Manuscript Log of a Naval Officers who Served under Commodore Isaac Hull on the Pacific Station, 1824-1825," Month at Goodspeeds 27 (1956): 201-03.

3942  "Canton and Macao," Military and Naval Magazine 5 (1835): 116-22.

3943  Fanning, Edmund. Voyages Round the World with Selected Sketches of Voyages to the South China Seas, North and South Pacific Oceans, China, etc. New York: Collins, Hannay, 1833.

3944  "First American Voyage to Canton," Army and Navy Chronicle 4 (1835): 258-60.

3945  Monoghan, Jay, ed. The Private Journal of Louis McLane. Los Angeles: Dawson's Book Store, 1971.

3946 Murrell, Benjamin. Narrative of Four Voyages, to the South Seas, North and South Pacific Ocean, China Sea, Ethiopic and South Atlantic Ocean, Indian and Antarctic Ocean, from the Year 1822 to 1831. New York: J.J. Harper, 1832.

3947 "Nautical Reminiscences," Military and Naval Magazine 1 (1833): 174-83.

3948 "Notes in the Pacific," Army and Navy Chronicle 8 (1839): 218-19.

3949 "Pirate of the South Pacific," Ibid 1 (1835): 313-15.

3950 Ruschenberger, William S. Three Years in the Pacific, Including Notices of Brazil, Chile, Bolivia and Peru. By an Officer of the U.S. Navy. Philadelphia: Carey, Lea, Blanchard, 1834.

3951 ____. A Voyage Around the World, Including an Embassy to Muscat and Siam in 1835-1837. Philadelphia: Carey, Lea, Blanchard, 1838.

3952 "The Sandwich Islands," Military and Naval Magazine 5 (1835): 6-11.

## U.S. EXPLORING EXPEDITION

3953 American Geographical Society of New York. Memorial Volume of the Transcontinental Excursion of 1912. New York: The Society, 1915, 105-13.

3954 Andrist, Ralph K. "Ice Ahead!" American Heritage 17 (1966): 60-63, 92-103.

3955 Barnes, Horace R. "Rear Admiral William Reynolds: A Distinguished Lancastrian, 1815-1879," Lancaster County Historical Society Papers 38 (1924): 61-66.

3956 Bartlett, Harley H. "The Report of the Wilkes Expedition," American Philosophical Society Proceedings 82 (1940): 601-705.

3957 Bertrand, Kenneth J. Americans in Antarctica, 1775-1948. New York: American Geographic Society, 1971.

3958 Bixby, William. The Forgotten Voyage of Charles Wilkes. New York: McKay, 1966.

3959 Borthwick, Doris E. "Outfitting the United States Exploring Expedition: Lieutenant Charles Wilkes' European Assignment, August-November, 1836," American Philosophical Society Proceedings 109 (1965): 159-72.

3960 Bradford, Gershorn. "On a Lee Shore," American Neptune 12 (1952): 282-87.

3961 Brewer, Robert P. and William J. Miller, eds. "To America-with Pride," United States Naval Institute Proceedings 102 (1976): 52-59.

3962 A Brief Account of the Discoveries and Results of the U.S. Exploring Expedition. New Haven: B.L. Hamen, 1843.

3963 Bryan, G.S. "The Wilkes Exploring Expedition," United States Naval Institute Proceedings 65 (1939): 1452-64.

3964 Buck, Peter H. Explorers of the Pacific: European and American Discoveries in Polynesia. Honolulu: Bernice P. Bishop Museum, 1953.

3965  Bryan, George S. "The Purpose, Equipment, and Personnel of the Wilkes Expedition," American Philosophical Society Publications 82 (1940): 551-60.

3966  _____. "The Wilkes Exploring Expedition," United States Naval Institute Proceedings 65 (1939): 1452-64.

3967  Carrell, A.E. "The First American Exploring Expedition," Harper's New Monthly Magazine 44 (1971): 60-64.

3968  Chandler, Charles L. "The Wilkes Exploring Expedition in Brazil, Argentina, Chile, and Peru, 1838-1839," Pan American Magazine 23 (1916): 233-36.

3969  Conklin, Edwin G. "Centenary Celebration of the Wilkes Exploring Expedition of the United States Navy, 1838-1842," American Philosophical Society Proceedings 82 (1940): 519-947.

3970  Cooley, Mary E. "The Exploring Expedition in the Pacific," Ibid 82 (1940): 707-19.

3971  Dodge, Ernest S. Beyond the Capes: Pacific Exploration from Captain Cook to the Challenger. Boston: Little, Brown, 1971.

3972  Dupree, A. Hunter. Science in the Federal Government: A History of Policies and Activities to 1948. Cambridge: Harvard University Press, 1957.

3973  "The Exploring Expedition," North American Review 56 (1843): 257-70.

3974  "The Exploring Expedition," Southern Quarterly Review 8 (1845): 1-6.

3975  "Exploring Expedition of the U.S., " Westminister Review 44 (1845): 241-54.

3976  "Exploring Exedition: Thoughts Suggested by its Approaching Departure," Southern Literary Messenger 4 (1838): 566-69.

3977  "Exploring Expedition to the South Seas," Ibid 3 (1837): 698-700.

3978  Fanning, Edward. Voyages and Discoveries in the South Seas, 1792-1832. Salem: Marine Research Society, 1924.

3979  Farenholt, Ammen. "Vendovi," Military Surgeon 74 (1934): 305-10.

3980  Feipel, Louis N. "The Wilkes Exploring Expedition: Its Progress through Half a Century, 1826-1876," United States Naval Institute Proceedings 40 (1914): 1323-50.

3981  "The First American Exploring Expedition," Harpers Monthly Magazine 44 (1871): 60-64.

3982  Haskell, Daniel C. The United States Exploring Expedition, 1838-1842, and its Publications, 1844-1874. New York: Public Library, 1942.

3983  Hayden, F.V. "United States Government Surveys," American Journal of Science and the Arts 24 (1862): 98-101.

3984  Hurst, Bess S. "One Hundred Years Ago," United States Naval Institute Proceedings 44 (1938): 1624-27.

3985  Jackson, C. Ian. "Exploration as Science: Charles Wilkes and the U.S. Exploring Expedition, 1838-1842," American Scientist 73 (1985): 450-61.

3986  Jackson, Donald D. "Around the World in 1,392 Days with the Navy's Wilkes and His Scientifics," Smithsonian 16 (1985): 48-63.

3987  Jenkins, John S. The Voyage of the U.S. Exploring Expedition, Commanded by Captain Charles Wilkes, U.S.N., in 1838-42. Auburn, NY: J.M. Alden, 1850.

3988  Kazar, John D. "The United States Navy and Scientific Exploration, 1837-1860." Ph. D. dissertation, University of Massachusetts, 1973.

3989  Martin, Lawrence. "Antarctica Discovered by a Connecticut Yankee," Geographical Review 30 (1940): 529-52.

3990  Mawson, Douglas. "Wilkes Antarctic Landfalls," Royal Geographic Society of Australia Proceedings 34 (1934): 70-113.

3991  Mitterling, Philip I. Americans in the Antarctic to 1840. Urbana: University of Illinois Press, 1959.

3992  Morsberger, Robert E. and W. Patrick Strauss. "Lands Below the Horn." In: Clayton R. Barrows, ed. America Spreads Her Sails. Annapolis: Naval Institute Press, 1973, 21-40.

3993  _____. "The Wilkes Expedition, 1838-1842," American History Illustrated 7 (1972): 4-10.

3994  Palmer, James C. Antarctic Mariner's Song. New York: Van Nostrand, 1868.

3995  Pillsbury, John E. "Wilkes and D'urbville's Discoveries in Wilkes Land," United States Naval Institute Proceedings 36 (1910): 465-68.

3996  Poinsett, Joel R. "The Exploring Expedition," North American Review 56 (1843): 259-71.

3997  Ponko, Vincent. Ships, Seas, and Scientists: U.S. Naval Exploration and Discovery in the Nineteenth Century. Annapolis: Naval Institute Press, 1974.

3998  Ramage, Helen. "The Wilkes Exploring Expedition on the Pacific Slope, 1841." Master's Thesis, University of California, 1916.

3999  _____. "Wilkes Exploring Expedition in California, 1841," Overland Monthly 68 (1916): 470-74.

4000  Ramsdell, L.G. "Wilkes Expedition of 1838-1842: Magnificent Voyage," All Hands No. 834 (1986): 6-10.

4001  Rehn, James A. "Connection of the Academy of Natural Sciences in Philadelphia with Our First Nautical Exploring Expedition," American Philosophical Society Proceedings 82 91940): 543-49.

4002  "A Review of 'Narrative of the United States Exploring Expedition'," Littells Living Age 9 (1846): 430-38.

4003  "Review of 'Narrative of the United States Exploring Expedition," Westminister Review 49 (1845): 469- 96.

4004   "Review of 'Narrative of the United States Exploring Expedition During the Years 1838-1842," North American Review 61 (1845): 54-107.

4005   "Review of 'Synopsis of the Cruise of the United States Exploring Expedition'," Ibid 56 (1843): 257-70.

4006   "Review of the 'United States Exploring Expedition', by Charles Wilkes," British Quarterly Review 17 (1853): 327-32.

4007   Reynolds, John N. An Address on the Subject of a Surveying and Exploring Expedition to the Pacific Ocean. New York: Harper, 1836.

4008   _____. The Pacific and Indian Oceans, or, the South Sea Surveying and Exploring Expedition: Its Inception, Progress, and Objects. New York: Harper, 1841.

4009   Ross, Frank E. "The Antarctic Explorations of Lieutenant Charles Wilkes, U.S. Navy," Royal Geographical Society of Australia Proceedings 35 (1935): 70-113, 130-41.

4010   Ross, James C. A Voyage of Discovery and Research in the Southern and Antarctic Regions during the Years, 1839-1843. 2 Vols. London: Murray, 1847.

4011   "Scientific Results of the Exploring Expedition," North American Review 63 (1846): 211-36.

4012   Smith, Geoffrey S. "The Navy before Darwinism: Science, Exploration, and Diplomacy in Antebellum America," American Quarterly 28 (1976): 41-55.

4013   Stanton, William. The Great United States Exploring Expedition of 1838-1842. Berkeley: University of California Press, 1975.

4014   Strauss, Wallace P. "Preparing the Wilkes Expedition: A Study in Disorganization," Pacific Historical Review 28 (1959): 221-32.

4015   Palmer, James C. Thulia, a Tale of the Antarctic. New York: S. Colman, 1843.

4016   Tyler, David B. The Wilkes Expedition: The First U.S. Exploring Expedition. Philadelphia: American Philosophical Society, 1968.

4017   "The United States Exploring Expedition," American Journal of Science and the Arts 44 (1843): 393-408.

4018   "The United States Exploring Expedition," Merchant's Magazine 12 (1845): 444-52.

4019   "The United States Exploring Expedition," North American Review 61 (1845): 54-107.

4020   Viola, Herman and Carolyn Margolis, eds. Magnificent Voyagers: The United States Exploring Expedition, 1838-1842. Washington, DC: Smithsonian Institute, 1986.

4021   Walker, William H. Memorial of Officers of the Exploring Expedition, Praying the Investigation of Certain Statements and Allegations. 29th Cong. Senate Document 494.

4022  Wickman, John E. "Political Aspects of Charles Wilkes' Work and
      Testimony, 1842-1849." Ph. D. dissertation, Indiana University, 1964.

4023  Wright, Helen S. The Seventh Continent: History of the Discovery and
      Exploration of Antarctica.  Boston: Richard C. Badger, 1918.

CONTEMPORARY ACCOUNTS

4024  Cleaver, Ann H. and E. Jeffrey Stanns, eds. Voyage to the Southern
      Ocean: The Letters of Lieutenant William Reynolds from the U.S.
      Exploring Expedition, 1838-1842. Annapolis: Naval Institute, 1988.

4025  Clark, Joseph G. Lights and Shadows of a Sailor's Life: Exemplified
      in Fifteen Years' Service. Boston: B.B. Munsey, 1848.

4026  David, Charles H. "Narrative of the United States Exploring Exped-
      ition," North American Review 61 (1845): 54-107.

4027  Emmons, George F. "Extracts from Emmon's Journal," Oregon Historical
      Quarterly 26 (1925): 263-73.

4028  Erskine, Charles. Twenty Years before the Mast, with the Most
      Thrilling Scenes and Incidents while Circumnavigating the Globe.
      Philadelphia: Jacobs, 1896.

4029  "Narrative of the United States Exploring Expedition during the
      Years 1838-1842," Edinburgh Review 93 (1846): 431-52.

4030  Reynolds, Jeremiah N. Exploring Expedition. Correspondence by
      Jeremiah N. Reynolds and the Hon. Mahlon Dickerson under the
      Respective Signatures of 'Citizen' and 'Friend to the Navy'.
      New York: N.p., 1838.

      SEE ALSO: 4376, 4484, USS Peacock, USS Vincennes, Charles Wilkes

NAVAL LIFE

4031  Allen, Priscilla. "White Jacket: Melville and the Man-of-War
      Microcosom," American Quarterly 25 (1973): 32-47.

4032  Buckingham, John S. "The United States Navy in 1842 as seen by
      a Britisher," United States Naval Institute Proceedings 93 (1967):
      142-44.

4033  Daly, Robert W. "Pay and Prize Money in the Old Navy," Ibid 74
      (1948): 967-71.

4034  Hall, Basil. Travels in North America in the Years 1827-1828.
      2 Vols. Philadelphia: Carey, Lea, Carey, 1829.

4035  Langley, Harold D. "The Grass Roots Harvest of 1828," United States
      Naval Institute Proceedings 90 (1964): 51-59.

4036  Lathrop, Constance. "Grog: Its Origin and Use in the United States
      Navy," Ibid 61 (1935): 377-80.

4037  Leggett, W. Naval Stories. New York: Carrill, 1834.

CONTEMPORARY ACCOUNTS

4038  Adee, David G. "In The United States Navy Fifty Years Ago,"
      United Service 9 (1883): 565-88; 14 (1895): 262-85.

4039  Ames, Nathaniel. Nautical Reminiscences. Providence: W. Marshall, 1832.

4040  Ammen, Daniel. The Old Navy and the New. Philadelphia: Lippincott, 1891.

4041  Burts, Robert. "Naval Fragments," Military and Naval Magazine 4 (1835): 419-21.

4042  Bryan, John R. Diary of John Randolph Bryan, Midshipman, U.S.N., 1823-1829. Richmond: Whittet, Shepperson, 1941.

4043  Cobb, J.A. A Green Hand's First Cruise: Roughed Out from the Logbook of Twenty-Five Years' Standing. 2 Vols. Boston: Otis, Broaders, 1841.

4044  Delta [Pseud]. "Extract from a Log," Military and Naval Magazine 4 (1835): 353-55.

4045  ____. "Life in a Steerage," Ibid 4 (1835): 356-58.

4046  DeMeissner, Sophie R. Old Navy days: Sketches from the Life of Rear Admiral William Radford, U.S.N. New York: Henry Holt, 1920.

4047  De Roos, John F. Personal Narrative of Travels in the United States and Canada in 1826; with Remarks on the Present State of the American Navy. London: W.A. Ainsworth, 1827.

4048  "Extracts from the Journal of an American Naval Officer," Southern Literary Messenger 7 (1841): 479-84, 654-61.

4049  Forbes, Robert B. Personal Reminiscences. Boston: John Wilson, 1876.

4050  Hazen, Jacob A. Five Years Before the Mast, or, Life in the Forecastle aboard a Whaler and Man-of-War. Philadelphia: Willis P. Hazard, 1854.

4051  Hoole, W. Stanley, ed. Florida Territory in 1844: The Diary of Master Edward C. Anderson, United States Navy. University, AL: University of Alabama, 1977.

4052  Hutchins, Elias. The Old Sailor: A Thrilling Narrative of the Life and Adventures of Elias Hutchins, during Forty Years on the Ocean. Biddleford, ME: Eastern Journal Job Office, 1854.

4053  Ingersoll, Royal R. Cruising in the Old Navy. Washington, DC: Naval Historical Foundation, 1974.

4054  Isaacs, Nicholas D. Twenty Years Before the Mast, or, Life in a Forecastle. New York: J.P. Beckwith, 1845.

4055  Langley, Harold D. "A Naval Dependent in Washington, 1837-1842: Letters of Marion Coote Speiden," Columbia Historical Society Records 50 (1980): 105-22.

4056  Lynch, William F. Naval Life, or Observations Afloat and Ashore. New York: Charles Scribner's, 1851.

4057  Marryat, Frederick. A Diary in America, with Remarks on Its Institutions. 2 Vols. Philadelphia: Carey, Hart, 1839.

4058  ____. Second Series of a Diary in America, with Remarks on its Institutions. Philadelphia: T.k. & P.G. Collins, 1840.

4059 Maury, M.F. "Scraps from the Lucky Bag, <u>Southern Literary Messenger</u> 6 (1840): 233-40, 306-20, 786-800.

4060 Melville, Herman. <u>White Jacket, or, the World in a Man of War.</u> Boston: L.C. Page, 1892.

4061 Merrill, Walter M., ed. <u>Belhold Me Once More: The Confessions of James Holley Garrison, Brother of William Lloyd Garrison.</u> Boston: Houghton, Mifflin, 1954.

4062 Monaghan, Jay. <u>The Private Journal of Louis McLane, U.S.N., 1844-1848.</u> Los Angeles: Dawson's Book Shop, 1971.

4063 "Naval Life," <u>Military and Naval Magazine</u> 3 (1835): 364-68; 4 (1835): 5-14.

4064 "Nautical Reminiscences," <u>American Monthly Magazine</u> 5 (1835): 349-53.

4065 Nordhoff, Charles. <u>Man-of-War Life: A Boy's Experience in the United States Navy, during a Voyage Around the World in a Ship of the Line.</u> New York: Dodd, Mead, 1855.

4066 Page, Thomas J. "Autobiographical Sketch of Thomas Jefferson Page," <u>United States Naval Institute Proceedings</u> 49 (1923): 1661-91.

4067 Parker, William H. <u>Recollections of a Naval Officer, 1841-1865.</u> New York: Charles Scribner's, 1883.

4068 Phelps, Thomas S. "Reminiscences of the Old Navy," <u>United Service</u> 6 (1882): 385-88; 7 (1882): 147-54, 480-505, 628-52.

4069 _____. "Reminiscences of the Old Navy," <u>Ibid</u> 41 (1905): 743-71, 795-821.

4070 Phelps, William D. <u>Fore and Aft, or, Leaves From the Life of an Old Sailor.</u> Boston: Nichols, Hall, 1871.

4071 Revere, Joseph W. <u>Keel and Saddle: A Retrospective of Forty Years of Military and Naval Service.</u> Boston: J.R. Osgood, 1872.

4072 Rockwell, Charles. "In the Navy of the United States. <u>In: Sketches of Foreign Travel and Life at Sea.</u> 2 Vols. Boston: Tappan, Dement, 1842. Vol. 2, 383-411.

4073 Shippen, Edward. <u>Thirty Years at Sea: The Story of a Sailor's Life.</u> Philadelphia: Lippincott, 1879.

4074 Stockell, William. <u>The Eventful Narrative of Captain William Stockell, of His Travels, of His Signal Engagements.</u> Cincinnati: S. Ward, 1840.

4075 Warren, H.V. <u>Afloat with Old Glory. By a Blue Jacket of the Old Navy.</u> New York: Abbey Press, 1901.

SEE ALSO: Naval Medicine-Contemporary Accounts, 4202, 4207, 4208, 4210, 4211, 4212, 4213, 4219, 4220, 4225, 4237, 4250, 4251, 4276, 4284, 4289, 4297, 4299, 4300, 4301, 4302, 4303, 4304, 4305, 4306, 4307, 4309, 4316, 4338, 4357, 4362, 4364, 4365, 4368, 4372, 4374, 4401, 4405, 4407, 4409, 4410, 4472, 4473, 4475, 4476, 4478, 4479, 4480, 4481, 4484, 4486, 4488

## * NAVAL MEDICINE

4076  Bradley, George P. "Brief Sketch of the Origin and History of the Medical Corps of the U.S. Navy," Journal of the Association of Military Surgeons of the United States 10 (1902): 487-528.

4077  Bring, Hans. "Navy Medicine Comes Ashore: Establishing the First U.S. Navy Hospital," Journal of the History of Medicine 4 (1986): 257-92.

4078  Campbell, H.J. "The Congressional Debate over the Seaman's Sickness and Disability Act of 1798," Bulletin of the History of Medicine 43 (1974): 423-26.

4079  Cushman, Paul. "Naval Surgery in the War of 1812," New York State Journal of Medicine 72 (1972): 1881-87.

4080  Cutbush, Edward. Observations on the Means of Preserving the Health of Soldiers and Sailors. Philadelphia: Fry, Kammerer, 1808.

4081  Danilson, Harry G. "The First U.S. Naval Medical School," Military Surgeon 80 (1937): 53-60.

4082  Estes, J. Worth. "Naval Medicine in the Age of Sail: The Voyage of the New York, 1802-1803," Bulletin of the History of Medicine 56 (1982): 238-53.

4083  Gibson, J.E. "John Bullus-Reading Physician and Naval Surgeon," Transactions and Studies of the College of Physicians 12 (1944): 108-14.

4084  Gleason, Edmund H. "The Advance of Naval Preventative Medicine," United States Naval Institute Proceedings 84 (1958): 66-71.

4085  Horan, Leo F. "Naval Surgeon Pioneer," Ibid 75 (1949): 919-23.

4086  Horner, Gustavus. Medical Topographical Observations Upon the Mediterranean. Philadelphia: Haswell, Barrington, Haswell, 1839.

4087  _____. Medical Topography of Brazil and Uruguay, with Incidental Remarks. Philadelphia: Lindsay, Blakiston, 1845.

4088  Hyde, James N. Medical Corps of the U.S. Navy, with Some Details Respecting its Past and Present. Carlisle: Association of Military Surgeons, 1905.

4089  Johnson, Lucius W. "Yellow Jack: Master of Strategy," United States Naval Institute Proceedings 76 (1950): 1074-83.

4090  Jordan, Philip D. "A Naval Surgeon in Paris, 1835-1836," Annals of Medical History 2 (1940): 526-35; 3 (1941): 73-81, 148-64.

4091  Kerr, William M. "Peter St. Medard, Surgeon in the Navy of the United States, 1756-1822," U.S. Navy Medical Bulletin 16 (1922): 867-74.

4092  _____. "William Maxwell Wood, the First Surgeon General of the United States Navy," Annals of Medical History 6 (1924): 387-425.

4093  _____. "Benjamin Henry Latrobe, 1764-1820: Designer of the First Naval Hospital," U.S. Navy Medical Bulletin 17 (1922): 615-36.

4094  _____. "Johnathan Cowdery, Surgeon in the United States Navy, 1767-1852," Ibid 17 (1923): 63-87.

4095  Kramer, Howard D. "An Ohio Doctor in the Early Navy," Ohio Archaeo-
      logical and Historical Society Quarterly 60 (1951): 155-74.

4096  Langley, Harold D. "Medical Men of the Old Navy: A Study in the
      Development of a Profession, 1797-1833." In: New Aspects of Naval
      History. Annapolis: Naval Institute Press, 1985, 69-79.

4097  McBarron, H. Charles and James C. Tily. "Medical Officers of the U.S.
      Navy, 1830-1841," Military Collector and Historian 13 (1961): 18-20.

4098  McInnis, Katherine. "When Small Pox Struck," United States Naval
      Institute Proceedings 97 (1971): 78-82.

4099  Pleadwell, Frank L. "Edward Cutbush, M.D., the Nestor of the Medical
      Corps of the Navy," Annals of Medical History 5 (1923): 337-86.

4100       . "Lewis Hearmann, Surgeon in the United States Navy," Ibid
      5 (1923): 113-45.

4101       . "Ninian Pinkney, Surgeon, United States Navy," Ibid 1 (1929):
      666-97.

4102       . "William Paul Crillon Barton, Surgeon, United States Navy:
      A Pioneer in American Naval Medicine," Military Surgeon 46 (1930):
      241-81.

4103  Richman, Allen M. "The Development of Medical Services in the United
      States Navy in the Age of Sail, 1815-1850." Ph. D. dissertation,
      University of Minnesota, 1973.

4104  Roddis, Louis H. A Short History of Naval Medicine. New York: Paul
      B. Hoeber, 1941.

4105       . "The Bureau of Medicine and Surgery: A Brief History," United
      States Naval Institute Proceedings 75 (1949): 457-67.

4106       . "Thomas Harris, M.D., Naval Surgeon and Founder of the First
      School of Naval Medicine in the New World," Journal of the History
      of Medicine 5 (1950): 236-50.

4107       . "Johnathan M. Foltz, Surgeon of the Navy," Military Surgeon
      90 (1942): 445-49.

4108  Schultz, H.S. "First Decade of the Bureau of Medicine and Surgery,"
      Ibid 99 (1946): 136-42.

4109  Stockton, Charles H. Origin, History, Laws and Regulation of the United
      States Naval Asylum, Philadelphia. Washington, DC: Government Printing
      Office, 1886.

4110  Thayer, William R. "The Marine Hospitals of New England in 1817,
      Massachusetts Historical Society Proceedings 50 (1917): 60-72.

4111  Vogel, K. "Two Medical Sailors," Proceedings of the Charaka Club 9
      (1938): 52-72.

4112  Watson, William M. "Thomas Robertson, Naval Surgeon, 1793-1828,"
      Bulletin of the History of Medicine 46 (1972): 131-49.

      SEE ALSO: 4194, 4206, 4256, 4264, 4406, 5641, Usher Parons

CONTEMPORARY ACCOUNTS

4113  Benedict, Theodore W., ed. "An Autobiography of Samuel Russell Trevett, Jr., M.D., Surgeon in the U.S. Navy during the War of 1812," New Canaan Historical Society Annual 3 (1954): 233-46.

4114  Darlington, William. Reliquiae Baldwinianae: Selections from the Correspondence of the Late William Baldwin, M.D., Surgeon in the U.S. Navy, with Occasional Notes and a Short Biography. Philadelphia: Kimber, Sharpless, 1843.

4115  Foltz, Charles S. Surgeon of the Seas: The Adventurous Life of Surgeon General Johnathan M. Foltz, in the Days of Wooden Ships, told from His Notes of the Moment. Indianapolis: Bobbs-Merrill, 1931.

4116  Forbes, Hildegarde B. Correspondence of Dr. Charles H. Wheelwright, Surgeon of the United States Navy. Boston: N.p., 1958.

4117  Pinkney, Ninian. "Report of Some Operations, performed During a Late Cruise in the Pacific," American Journal of Medical Studies 12 (1846): 330-36.

4118  Werner, Charles J. Dr. Isaac Hulse, Surgeon, U.S. Navy, 1797-1856: His Life and Letters. New York: C.J. Werner, 1922.

SHIPS

4119  Baker, Maury. "Cost Overrun; an Early Naval Precedent: Building the First United States Warships, 1794-98," Maryland Historical Magazine 72 (1977): 361-72.

4120  Bauer, K. Jack. "Naval Shipbuilding Programs, 1794-1860," Military Affairs 29 (1965): 29-40.

4121  Benham, Edith W. and Anne M. Hall. Ships of the United States Navy and Their Sponsors, 1797-1913. Norwood, MA: Privately Printed, 1913.

4122  Bolander, Louis H. "The Ships of the Line of the Old Navy," United States Naval Institute Proceedings 64 (1938): 1425-30.

4123  Carson, Hampton L. "Samuel Humphreys: Chief Naval Constructor of the United States," Pennsylvania Magazine of History and Biography 8 (1884): 216-22.

4124  Chapelle, Howard I. The History of the American Sailing Navy. New York: W.W. Norton, 1949.

4125  Edson, Merritt. "Naval Steam Frigates of 1848," Nautical Research Journal 22 (1976): 131-46.

4126  Farenholt, A. "An Enumeration and Short Account of Names of Men-of-War during the Early United States Naval History," United States Naval Institute Proceedings 35 (1908): 889-94.

4127  Fowler, William M. "America's Super Frigates," Mariner's Mirror 59 (1973): 49-56.

4128  Gluntz, Marvin. "Naval Construction on the Great Lakes," United States Naval Institute Proceedings 83 (1957): 133-45.

4129  Henderson, James. The Frigates: An Account of the Lesser Warships of
      the Wars from 1793 to 1815. New York: Dodd, Mead, 1970.

4130  Henrich, Joseph G. "Thomas Paine's Short Career as a Naval Archi-
      tect, August-October, 1807," American Neptune 34 (1974): 123-34.

4131  Leiner, Frederick C. "The Subscription Warships of 1798, Ibid 48
      (1986): 141-58.

4132  Maurer, Maurer. "Copper Bottoms for the United States Navy, 1794-
      1803," United States Naval Institute Proceedings 71 (1945): 693-99.

4133  Murphey, John M. American Ships and Shipbuilders. New York: C.W.
      Baker, 1860.

4134  "Observations on the Construction of Frigates," Naval Chronicle 36
      (1816): 377-83.

4135  Porter, Holbrook F. "The Delameter Ironworks-The Cradle of the
      Modern Navy," Society of Nautical Architects and Marine Engineers
      26 (1918): 1-32.

4136  Preble, George H. "Ships of the 19th Century," United Service 10
      (1884): 130-37.

4137  Roosevelt, Franklin D. "Our First Frigates: Some Unpublished Facts
      about their Construction," Society of Naval Architects and Marine
      Engineers 12 (1914): 139-55.

      SEE ALSO: Henry Eckford, John Ericsson, Josiah Fox, Joshua Humphreys

STEAM POWER

4138  "The American Steam Navy," Journal of the Franklin Institute 48
      (1849): 330-32, 443.

4139  Barnaby, Nathaniel. Naval Development in the Century. Toronto:
      Linscott, 1904.

4140  Barnard, John G. "Harbor Defense by Fortifications and Steam
      Vessels," Southern Literary Messenger 11 (1845): 25-30.

4141  Bartol, Barnabas H. A Treatise on the Marine Boilers of the United
      States. Philadelphia: R.W. Barnard, 1851.

4142  Baxter, James P. "The Iron-clad Warship to 1862." Ph. D. dissert-
      ation, Harvard University, 1926.

4143  Bennett, Frank M. The Steam Navy of the United States: A History of
      the Growth of the Steam Vessel of War in the U.S. Navy, and of the
      Naval Engineer Corps. Pittsburgh: W.T. Nicholson, 1896.

4144  Bowen, Harold G. One Hundred of Steam in the United States.
      Princeton: Princeton University Press, 1937.

4145  Brodie, Bernard. Sea Power in the Machine Age: Major Naval Invent-
      ions and Their Consequences on International Politics, 1814-1940.
      Princeton: Princeton University Press, 1941.

4146  Bynre, Alexander S. Observations on the Best Methods of Propelling
      Ships. New York: C.S. Francis, 1841.

4147  Dyson, George W. "Charles H. Haswell and the Steam Navy," United
      States Naval Institute Proceedings 65 (1939): 225-30.

4148   Geoghegan, William E. "The Auxilary Steam Packet Massachusetts,"
       Nautical Research Journal 16 (1969): 27-35.

4149   _____. "Steamboat Bill of Facts," Ibid 17 (1970): 26-33.

4150   Lyman, John. "Our Early Steam Navy and Merchant Marine," United
       States Naval Institute Proceedings 78 (1952): 1366-67.

4151   Morison, Elting E. "Inventing a Modern Navy," American Heritage 37
       (1986): 81-96.

4152   Morrison, John H. History of American Steam Navigation. New York:
       W.F. Sametz, 1903.

4153   Mueller, Edward R. "East Coast Florida Steam Boating, 1831-1861,"
       Florida Historical Quarterly 40 (1962): 241-60.

4154   _____. "Steamboat activity in Florida during the Second Seminole
       War," Ibid 64 (1986): 407-31.

4155   Mucham, H.A. "Early Great Lakes Steamboats: The Battle of the
       Windmill and Afterwards, 1838-1842," American Neptune 8 (1948): 37-60.

4156   "On Steamers of War," Naval Magazine 1 (1836): 347-55.

4157   Orth, Michael. "The Stevens Battery," United States Naval Institute
       Proceedings 92 (1966): 92-99.

4158   Preble, George H. "Notes for a History of Steam Navigation," United
       Service 6 (1882): 555-60.

4159   _____. A Chronological History of the Origin and Development of
       Steam Navigation, 1543-1882. Philadelphia: Hamersly, 1883.

4160   Rose, J. Holland. "Steam Power and the Supression of the Slave Trade."
       In: Man and the Sea. Boston: Houghton, Mifflin, 1936, 240-63.

4161   Rowland, K.T. Steam at Sea: History of Steam Navigation. New York:
       Praeger, 1970.

4162   Sargent, John O. A Lecture on the Late Improvments in Steam Navi-
       gation and the Art of Naval Warfare, with a brief Notice of Eric-
       ssons's Caloric Engine. New York: Wiley, Putnam, 1844.

4163   Smelser, Marshal. "Clinton Roosevelt's 'Invunerable Steam Battery',
       1835," American Neptune 20 (1960): 167-73.

4164   Stanton, Samuel W. Nineteenth Century United States Steam Vessels.
       Meriden, CT: Gravure, 1964.

4165   The Stevens Iron-Clad Battery. New York: D. Van Nostrand, 1874.

4166   Stuart, Charles B. The Naval and Mail Steamers of the United States.
       New York: C.B. Norton, 1853.

4167   Taggart, Robert. "The Early Developments of the Screw Propeller,"
       American Society of Naval Engineering Journal 71 (1959): 259-76.

SEE ALSO: USS Michigan, John Ericsson, John Stevens

## *ORDNANCE

4168  Adams, William T. "Guns for the Navy," Ordnance 45 (1961): 508-11.

4169  Bathe, Greville. Ship of Destiny: A Record of the Steam Frigate Merrimac, 1855-1862, with an Appendix on the Development of U.S Naval Cannon. St. Augustine, FL: N.p., 1851.

4170  Bolander, Louis H. "The Introduction of Shot and Shell Guns in the United States Navy," Mariner's Mirror 17 (1931): 105-12.

4171  "The Bureau of Ordnance," United States Naval Institute Proceedings 75 (1949): 213-24.

4172  Davis, Morton. "The Old Cannon Foundry Above Georgetown, D.C. and its First Owner, Henry Foxall," Columbia Historical Society Records 9 (1908): 16-70.

4173  Edson, M.A. "Eighteenth Century Gun Carriages and Fittings," Nautical Research Journal 12 (1964): 113-16.

4174  Fisher, Charles. "The Great Guns of the Navy, 1797-1843," American Neptune 36 (1936): 276-95.

4175  Gorr, Louis F. "The Foxall-Columbia Foundry: An Early Defense Contractor in Georgetown," Columbia Historical Society Records (1971-1972): 34-60.

4176  Guiler, R.P. "The Naval Gun Factory," United States Naval Institute Proceedings 50 (1924): 1107-21.

4177  Hornsby, Thomas. "Oregon and Peacemaker: 12 Inch Wrought Iron Guns," American Neptune 6 (1946): 212-22.

4178  Johnson, Roxanne J. "An Analysis of Early Record Keeping in the Dupont Company, 1800-1818." Ph. D. dissertation, Pennsylvania State University, 1987.

4179  Lewis, Emanuel R. "The Ambiguous Columbiads," Military Affairs 18 (1964): 111-22.

4180  Lundeberg, Philip K. Samuel Colt's Submarine Battery. Washington, DC: Smithsonian Institute Press, 1974.

4181  Martin, Tyrone G. "Top Guns in the Early Sailing Navy," Man at Arms 9 (1987): 12-20.

4182  "New Maritime Artillery," American Quarterly Review 4 (1828): 480-506.

4183  Peck, Taylor. Roundshots to Rockets: A History of the Washington Navy Yard and U.S. Naval Gun Factory. Annapolis: Naval Institute Press, 1949.

4184  Perry, Percival. "The Naval-Stores Industry in the Old South," Journal of Southern History 34 (1968): 509-26.

4185  Rowan, S.C. "Notes on Old Sea Cannon," Mariner 6 (1932): 35-47.

4186  Simons, Bentham. "Some Notes on Old Guns," United States Naval Institute Press 63 (1937): 653-58.

4187  Tucker, Gary S. "The Early Columbiads," Military Collector and Historian 10 (1958): 40-42.

4188   Tucker, Spencer C. "The Carronade," United States Naval Institute
       Proceedings 90 (1973): 65-70.

4189   _____. "Arming the Fleet: Early Cannon Founders to the U.S. Navy,"
       American Neptune 45 (1985): 35-41.

4190   _____. "U.S. Navy Gun Carriages from the Revolution through the
       Civil War," Ibid 47 (1987): 108-18.

4191   _____. Arming the Fleet: U.S. Naval Ordnance in the Muzzle-Loading
       Era. Annapolis: Naval Institute Press, 1989.

4192   Washburn, Mabel T. "In Service of the Republic," Journal of American
       History 9 (1915): 593-97.

       SEE ALSO: USS Princeton, John A. Dahlgren

                          *USS JOHN ADAMS

4193   Dunne, W.M. "The South Carolina Frigate: A History of the U.S. Ship
       John Adams," American Neptune 47 (1987): 22-32.

4194   Lockwood, John A. "Medical Notes of a Cruise in the U.S. Ship John
       Adams," American Journal of Medical Sciences 11 (1846): 64-75.

4195   "Washington City," Army and Navy Chronicle 9 (1839): 328-31.

       SEE ALSO: 4210

                          *USS ARGUS

4196   Chapelle, Howard I. "U.S. Brig of War Argus," Mariner 7 (1933): 1-7.

4197   Paltsits, Victor H. "Gift of a Naval Manuscript," New York Library
       Bulletin 22 (1918): 463-64.

                          USS BOSTON

4198   Allen, Gardenr W. "The Boston and the Berceau," Massachusetts
       Historical Society Proceedings 65 (1940): 163-68.

4199   Ames, Ellis. "Battle Between the Boston and the Berceau," Ibid 20
       (1883): 249-69.

4200   "Extracts from the Log of the Frigate Boston," Ibid 16 (1883): 270-75.

4201   Maclay, Edgar S. "Early Victories of the American Navy," Century
       Magazine 19 (1890): 179-86.

4202   Phelps, Thomas S. "Reminiscences of the Old Navy, the Loss of the
       U.S. Sloop-of-War Boston on the Island of Eleuthera, Decmeber 15,"
       1846," United Service 6 (1882): 686-96.

                          USS BRANDYWINE

4203   Thompson, Edgar K. "Lafayette in the Frigate Brandywine," American
       Neptune 26 (1966): 258-61.

       SEE ALSO: 4276
                          *USS CHESAPEAKE

4204   Coutts, H.B. "Shannon vs Chesapeake, June 1, 1813." In: Famous Duels
       of the Fleet and Their Lessons. London: W. Blackwood, 1908, 275-99.

4205  Strum, Harvey. "The Leopard–Chesapeake Incident of 1807: The
      Arrogance of Seapower," Warship 43 (1987): 157-64.

      SEE ALSO: James Lawrence, Provo Wallis

                          USS COLUMBIA

4206  Coale, Dr. Edward. "Notes on the Scurvey, as it Appeared on Board
      the U.S. Frigate Columbia in her Cruise Around the World, 1838-39-
      40," American Journal of the Medical Sciences 3 (1842): 68-77.

4207  Henshaw, Joshua A. Around the World: A Narrative of a Voyage in the
      East Indian Squadron under the Command of George C. Read. 2 Vols.
      New York: C.S. Francis, 1840.

4208  Murrell, William M. Cruise of the Frigate Columbia Around the World;
      under the Command of Commander George C. Read in 1838, 1839 and
      1840. Boston: B. Mussey, 1840.

4209  Neeser, Robert W. "Historic Ships of the Navy," United States Naval
      Institute Proceedings 59 (1933): 1165-68.

4210  Taylor, Fitch W. The Flag Ship, or, A Voyage Round the World in the
      U.S. Frigate Columbia, attended by the Sloop of War John Adams and
      Commanded by Commodore George C. Read. New York: D. Appleton, 1840.

                          USS CONGRESS

4211  Brackenridge, Henry M. Voyage to Buenos Ayres, performed in the Years
      1817 and 1818 by Order of the American Government. 2 Vols.
      Baltimore: J.D. Toy, 1819.

4212  Briggs, Carl. Quarterdeck and Saddlehorn: The Story of Edward F.
      Beale, 1822-1893. Glendale, CA: Arthur H. Clarke, 1983.

4213  Colton, Walter. Deck or Port, or Incidents of a Cruise in the United
      States Frigate Congress to California. New York: A.S. Barnes, 1850.

4214  Galligan, James F. "Fire–Bill of the U.S. Frigate Congress, 1842-
      1846," United States Naval Institute Proceedings 75 (1949): 826-27.

4215  Kennon, Elizabeth B. "A Gala Evening in the U.S.S. Congress, 1812,"
      Ibid 94 (1968): 138-39.

4216  Neeser, Robert W. "Historic Ships of the Navy: Congress," Ibid 62
      (1936): 345-51.

4217  Paltsits, Victor H. "Log Book of the U.S. Frigate Congress, 1845-
      1849," New York Public Library Bulletin 38 (1934): 714-15.

4218  Plumb, Robert J. "The Alcade of Monterey," United States Naval
      Institute Proceedings 95 (1969): 72-83.

4219  Stewart, Charles S. Brazil and La Plata: The Personal Record of a
      Cruise. New York: G.P. Putnam, 1856.

4220  Van Denburgh, Elizabeth D. My Voyage in the Frigate Congress.
      New York: D. Fitzgerald, 1913.

4221   Wainwright, Nicholas B. "Voyage of the Frigate Congress, 1823,"
       Pennsylvania Magazine of History and Biography 75 (1951): 170-88.

                            *USS CONSTELLATION

4222   Brady, Cyrus T. "Constellation in the War with France," McClure's
       Magazine 14 (1900): 272-81.

4223   _____. "Prize Crew on L'Insurgente," Cosmopolitan 31 (1901): 287-89.

4224   Chapelle, Howard I. and Leon D. Pollard. The Constellation Question.
       Washington, DC: Smithsonian Institute Press, 1970.

4225   Colton, Walter. Ship and Shore, or Leaves from the Journal of a
       Cruise to the Levant. New York: Leavitt, Lord, 1835.

4226   "Constellation's 175th Anniversary," Port of Baltimore Bulletin
       (October, 1972): 2-6.

4227   Crosby, Allyn J. "Our Beloved Constellation," Newport Historical
       Society Bulletin No. 98 (1937): 3-13.

4228   Davis, Charles G. Constellation, 36 Gun Frigate, Built in Baltimore,
       1797. Cazenovia, NY: The Author, 1935.

4229   Dawson, Henry B. Battles of the United States. 2 Vols. New York:
       Johnson, Fry, 1858. Vol. 2, 27-35.

4230   Dunn, Lucius C. "The Constellation's First Marine Officer," Maryland
       Historical Magazine 43 (1948): 210-19.

4231   _____. "The Frigate Constellation Puts to Sea," United States Naval
       Institute Proceedings 74 (1948): 1004-7.

4232   _____. "U.S.S. Constellation," Ibid 76 (1950): 679-80.

4233   Dunne, W.M. "The Constellation and the Hermione," Mariner's Mirror
       70 (1984): 82-85.

4234   Duval, Ruby R. "The Frigate Constellation: Oldest Vessel in our Navy,"
       United States Naval Institute Proceedings 61 (1935): 1780-86.

4235   Edward, Brother C. "The U.S.S. Constellation," American History
       Illustrated 9 (1974): 12-25.

4236   Ferguson, Eugene S. "The Launch of the United States Frigate Const-
       ellation," United States Naval Institute Proceedings 74 (1947):
       1090-95.

4237   Hoxe, John. The Yankee Tar. An Authentic Narrative of the Voyages
       and Hardships of John Hoxe and the Cruises of the U.S. Frigate
       Constellation and Her Enagements with the French Frigates La
       Insurgente and La Vengeance. Northampton, MA: J. Metcalfe, 1840.

4238   Jameson, Edwin M. Yankee Racehorse: The U.S. Frigate Constellation.
       Dublin, NH: W.L. Bauhan, 1977.

4239   Leeming, Joseph. "The Constellation's Victories in the War with
       France." In: The Book of American Fighting Ships. New York: Harper
       & Bros., 1939, 57-70.

4240 McIntosh, James Mc. The Memorial of Commander James McIntosh, United States Navy, for Compensation for 'Performing the Duties belonging to those of a Higher Grade'.New York: J.W. Ball, 1843.

4241 Morgan, Michael. Men of the Constellation: A History of the Naval War with France. N.p., 1969.
At the Naval Historical Foundation Library.

4242 Randolph, Evan. "USS Constellation, 1797 to 1979," American Neptune 39 (1979): 235–55.

4243 Roberts, W. Adoplhe. "The Constellation vs the Insurgente." In: The U.S. Navy Fights. Indianapolis: Bobbs-Merrill, 1942, 39–50.

4244 Scarlett, Charles. "The Yankee Race Horse: U.S.S. Constellation," Maryland Historical Magazine 56 (1961): 15–31.

4245 Scott, A.C. "Early Naval Strategy," United States Naval Institute Proceedings 62 (1936): 229–30.

4246 Sternlich, Sanford V. U.S.F. Constellation: 'Yankee Racehorse'. Cockeysville, MD: Liberty Publishing Co., 1981.

4247 Stewart, Donald. "The Yankee Racehorse," DAR Magazine 95 (1961): 532–33.

4248 Todd, Thomas A. "U.S.F. Constellation as She May have Appeared in the Period 1797 to 1800," Nautical Research Journal 31 (1985): 55–67.

4249 Whipple, Addison B. Tall Ships and Great Captains. New York: Harper 7 Bros., 1960, 115–26.

4250 Wight and Bowen. Notes of a Voyage Around the World in the U.S. Ship Constellation. Boston: J.E. Farwell, 1844.
At the Peabody Library, Essex Institute.

4251 Wines, Enoch C. Two and a Half Years in the Navy, or, Journal of a Cruise in the Mediterranean and Levant on Board the U.S. Frigate Constellation in the Years 1829, 1830, and 1831. 2 Vols. Philadelphia: Carey, Lea, 1832.

SEE ALSO: Charles Gordon, Thomas Truxton

*USS CONSTITUTION

4252 Baldridge, Harry A. "Old Ironsides in the Mediterranean off Tripoli," United States Naval Institute Proceedings 53 (1927): 618–22.

4253 Barrows, John S. "The Beginnings and Launching of the U.S. Frigate Constitution," Bostonian Society Proceedings (1925): 23–27.

4254 Bass, William P. and Ethel C. Constitution, Second Phase, 1802–07: Mediterranean, Tripoli, Malta, More. Melbourne, FL: Shipresearch, 1981.

4255 Belohlavek, John M. "Assault on the President: The Jackson-Randolph Affair of 1833," Presidential Studies Quarterly 12 (1981): 361–68.

4256 Bradburn, H.B. "The Medical Log of Old Ironsides," Connecticut Medicine 40 (1976): 859–68.

4257 Brawley, Paul J. "With Sides of Iron," United States Naval Institute Proceedings 111 (1985): 10–13.

4258  Brewington, Marion V. Ship Carvers of North America. Barre, MA: Barre Publishing Co., 1962 , 121-38.

4259  Canfield, Frederick A. "The Figurehead of Jackson," Tennessee Historical Quarterly 8 (1924): 144-45.

4260  "The Chase," Yankee 29 (1965): 98-103, 148-53.

4261  Cooper, James F. "Old Ironsides," Putnam's Monthly 1 (1853): 473-87, 593-607.

4262  Coutts, H.B. "Constitution vs Java, December 29, 1812." In: Famous Duels of the Fleet and Their Lessons. London: W. Blackwood, 1908, 243-73.

4263  Craig, Harden, ed. "The U.S. Frigate Constitution in Borneo, 1845," American Neptune 4 (1944): 217-23.

4264  Cushman, Paul. "Amos Evans, M.D., Surgeon on U.S.S. Constitution in the War of 1812," New York State Journal of Medicine 11 (1980): 1753-56.

4265  Dow, J.E. "Old Ironsides at Malta," United States Military Magazine 2 (1840): 4-5.

4266  Duval, Ruby R. "The Frigate Constitution, Oldest Vessel in Our Navy Today," United States Naval Institute Proceedings 61 (1935): 1780-86.

4267  Emery, William M. Colonel George Claghorn, Builder of the Constitution. New Bedford, MA: Old Dartmouth Historical Society, 1931.

4268  Goldsborough, Netta. "The Story of the Original Masts of the Old Frigate Constitution," American Monthly Magazine 23 (1905): 428-32.

4269  Harris, Charles E. "Figureheads of the Constitution," Antiques 30 (1936): 10-13.

4270  The Historian. "The American Marines of 'Old Ironsides'," Marine Corps Gazette 16 (1931): 26-32.

4271  Hollis, Ira N. "The Constitution at Tripoli." In: Naval Actions and Operations Against Cuba and Porto Rico, 1593-1815. Boston: Military History Society of Massachusetts, 1901, 65-94.

4272  Holmes, Charles N. "The 'Constitution', last of the 'Old Navy'," Magazine of History 20 (1915): 62-67.

4273  Holzer, Harold. "Her Thunder Shook the Mighty Deep," American History Illustrated 22 (1987): 24-31.

4274  Houston, Glenna. "Old Ironsides-the Spirit of the U.S.S. Constitution," All Hands No. 797 (1983): 18-27.

4275  Jarvis, Russell. A Biographical Notice of Commodore Jesse D. Elliott... and a History of the Figure Head of the U.S. Frigate Constitution. Philadelphia: The Author, 1835.

4276  Jones, George. Sketches of Naval Life with Notices of Men, Manners, and Scenery of the Shores of the Mediterranean, in a Series of Letters from the Brandywine and Constitution Frigates. 2 Vols. New Haven: Howe, 1829.

4277  Langley, Harold D. "William Patterson of 'Old Ironsides'," Maryland Historical Magazine 59 (1964): 217-21.

4278  McKee, Christopher, ed. "The Constitution in the Quasi-War with France: The Letters of John Roche, Jr., 1798-1801," American Neptune 27 (1967): 135-49.

4279  Magruder, John H. "A Touch of Tradition: Bush," Marine Corps Gazette 42 (1958): 32-33.

4280  Martin, Tyrone G. "Isaac Hull's Victory Revisited," American Neptune 47 (1987): 14-21.

4281  _____. "The Constitution Connection," Journal of Erie Studies 17 (1988): 39-46.

4282  _____. "Old Ironsides: Relevant Relic," United States Naval Institute Proceedings 102 (1976): 106-9.

4283  Middendorf, J. William. "The U.S.S. Constitution: A Study in Command," Sea History No. 44 (1987): 14-16.

4284  Mercier, Henry J. Life in a Man-of-War, or Scenes in Old Ironsides During Her Cruise in the Pacific, by a Fore-top-man. Philadelphia: L.R. Bailey, 1841.

4285  Mitchell, Helen. Ships that Made U.S. History. New York: Whittlesey House, 1950.

4286  Morgan, James. "Brood of the Constitution," United States Naval Institute Proceedings 42 (1916): 125-38, 925-26, 1259-60.

4287  Morris, Noadish. "The Constitution off Tripoli, 1804: A Letter from N. Morris, September 8, 1804," United States Naval Institute Proceedings 52 (1926): 1271-79.

4288  "Old Ironsides: U.S.S. Constitution, 1794-1931," Marine Corps Gazette 16 (1931): 44-47.

4289  Price, Norma A., ed. Letters from Old Ironsides, 1813-1815: Pardon Mawney Whipple. Tempe, AZ: Beverly-Merriam Press, 1984.

4290  Reilly, John C. The Constitution Gun Deck. Washington, DC: Naval Historical Center, 1983.

4291  Seiken, Jeff. "Not a Look of Fear Was Seen," American History Illustrated 22 (1987): 12-23, 47.

4292  "Ship's Detachment, 1812," Leatherneck 35 (1952): 44-47.

4293  "Sketches from the Log of Old Ironsides," Gentleman's Magazine 5 (1839): 13-17, 101-04, 138-44, 179-81, 272-76, 300-03; 6 (1840): 40-42, 63-64, 118-20, 184.

4294  Smith, Horatio D. "History of the United States Frigate Constitution," United Service 6 (1891): 41-51, 154-80, 258-75, 345-64, 459-78, 577-96; 7 (1892): 15-29.

4295  Smith, Whitney. "Constitution's Not-so-Tattered Ensign," American Neptune 37 (1977): 128-37.

4296  Stanford, Peter. "The U.S.S. Constitution: Reaching Out Over the Horizon," Sea History No. 44 (1987): 11-13.

4297  Stevens, Benjamin F. "A Cruise on the Constitution: Around the World in Old Ironsides, 1844-1847," United Service 5 (1904): 330-49, 414-32, 536-59, 698-705; 6 (1904): 14-20.

4298  Vallette, Henry M. "Old Ironsides on a Lee Shore," Potter's American Monthly 7 91876): 27-31.

4299  Warden, David B. "Journal of a Voyage from Annapolis to Cherbourg on Board the Frigate Constitution, August 1 to September 6, 1811," Maryland Historical Magazine 9 (1916): 127-41, 204-17.

SEE ALSO: Isaac Hull, Joshua Humphreys, John Percival, Charles Stewart

USS CYANE

4300  Kemble, John H., ed. Journal of a Cruise to California and the Sandwich Islands in the U.S. Sloop of War Cyane, 1841-1844. San Francisco: Grabhorn Press, 1955.

4301  Trenchard, Edward. "Extract from the Journal of the U.S.S. Cyane, 1820; an Incident in the Supression of the Slave Trade," Magazine of American History 30 (1893): 92-95.

USS DALE

4302  Craven, Tunis A. "Notes from the Journal of Lieutenant T.A.M. Craven, United States Navy, U.S.S. Dale, Pacific Squadron, 1846-1849," United States Naval Institute Proceedings 14 (1888): 119-48, 301-36.

4303  Meyers, William H. Naval Sketches of the War in California. New York: Random House, 1939.

4304  White, Philo. Narrative of a Cruise in the Pacific to South America and California on the U.S. Sloop of War Dale, 1841-1843. Denver, CO: Old West Publishing Co., 1965.

USS DELAWARE

4305  Israel, John. Journal of a Cruise in the U.S.S. Delaware in the Mediterranean in the Years 1833 and 1834. Port Mahon: Serra, 1835.

4306  "Letter From a Gentleman on Board," United States Navy Register. 2 Vols. (1822). Vol. 2, 84-87.

4307  Peterson, Mendel L., ed. The Journal of Daniel Noble Johnson, 1822-1863; Journal of a Cruise to the Brazils on Board the U.S.S. Delaware, 1841-42, and Notes while on Board the Schooner Enterprise. Washington, DC: Smithsonian Institute, 1959.

4308  Preston, Charles F. "Tamanend vs Tecumseh: Identification of the Figurehead of the U.S. Ship-of-the-Line Delaware," United States Naval Institute Proceedings 40 (1914): 721-25, 1787.

4309  Selfridge, Thomas O. "Extracts from Letters of Lieutenant Thomas O. Selfridge, written in 1833, during a Cruise of the U.S.S. Delaware," Ibid 53 (1927): 184-87.

4310  "The Ship Delaware in 1833," Naval Magazine 1 (1836): 79-93; 2
      (1837): 169-80, 382-90, 484-97.

4311  "Tecumseh: Figurehead of the U.S.S. Delaware," United States Naval
      Institute Proceedings 56 (1930): 674-77.

                        USS DETROIT

4312  Barry, James P. "The Sloop Detroit," Inland Seas 26 (1970): 36-39.

                        USS DOLPHIN

4313  Chapelle, Howard I. "Naval Schooners, 1820: Aliigator, Dolphin,
      Porpoise, Shark," Mariner 7 (1934): 3-10.

4314  Neeser, Robert W. "Historic Ships of the Navy: Dolphin," United
      States Naval Institute Proceedings 61 (1935): 14-15.

      SEE ALSO: Hiram Paulding, John Percival


                        USS EAGLE

4315  Crisman, Kevin J. The Eagle: An American Brig on Lake Champlain
      during the War of 1812. Shelburne, VT: New England Press, 1987.

                        *USS ENTERPRISE

4316  Aegyptus, Tiphys. The Navy's Friend; or, Reminiscences of the Navy,
      Containing Memoirs of a Cruise in the U.S. Schooner Enterprise.
      Baltimore: The Author, 1843.

4317  Johnson, Edwin L. "Between Wind and Water," Nautical Research
      Journal 23 (1977): 81-84.

4318  Koury, Mike, ed. "The Cruise of the Enterprise," By Valor and Arms
      3 (1977): 12-23.

4319  Roberts, W. Adolphe. "The Enterprise at Tripoli." In: The U.S. Navy
      Fights. Indianapolis: Bobbs-Merrill, 1942, 51-64.

                        USS EXPERIMENT

4320  Maloney, Linda M. "A Naval Experiment," American Neptune 34 (1974):
      188-96.


                        *USS ESSEX

4321  Paine, Ralph D. "Building the 'Essex' Ship." In: Ships and Sailors
      of Old Salem. New York: Outing Publishing Co., 1909, 288-309.

4322  _____. "How the Town Built a Fighting Frigate," Outing 52 (1908):
      296-305.

4323  Preble, George H. "The First Cruise of the United States Frigate
      Essex," Essex Institute Historical Collections 10 (1869): 1-108.

4324  Smith, Philip C. Frigate 'Essex' Papers: Building the Salem Frigate,
      1798-1799. Salem, MA: Peabody Museum, 1974.

4325  Toner, Raymond J. "U.S.F. Essex," United States Naval Institute
      Proceedings 82 (1956): 1136-39.

## USS GANGES

4326  Votaw, Homer C. "The Sloop of War Ganges," United States Naval Institute Proceedings 98 (1972): 82–85.

## *USS GENERAL ARMSTRONG

4327  Carney, R.B. "The American Marine Thermopylae," United States Naval Institute Proceedings 63 (1937): 551–54.

4328  "The Figure Head of the General Armstrong, Privateer," Historical Magazine 2 (1867): 288–89.

4329  "Naval and Diplomatic," United Service Journal 1 (1850): 45–46.

SEE ALSO: Samuel C. Reid

## *USS HORNET

4330  Clift, David H. "The Hornet Bible," New York Public Library Bulletin 39 (1935): 441–45.

## *USS INDEPENDENCE

4331  Farenholt, A. "The U.S.S. Independence: An Appreciation," United States Naval Institute Proceedings 40 (1914): 129–34.

4332  Goodwin, J.F. "Ships Orders–1815," Ibid 66 (1940): 78–82.

4333  Hunt, Marguerite. "The Passing of Uncle Sam's Oldest warship," Overland 58 (1911): 257–60.

4334  Musick, Michael P. "Under Skyscraper-Henry Wise aboard the Razee Independence," Prologue 3 (1971): 160–73.

4335  "U.S. Ship Independence in Russia," Naval Magazine 2 (1837): 558–68.

## USS INTREPID

4336  Dixon, Benjamin F. Shores of Tripoli: U.S.S. Intrepid, Tripoli, 1803, First Hospital Ship, American Navy. Washington, DC: N.p., 1944.

4337  "A Naval Reminiscence," Army and Navy Chronicle 3 (1836): 70–71.

SEE ALSO: Richard Somers

## USS MACEDONIAN

4338  DeBlois, C.J., ed. "Private Journal Kept aboard the U.S. Frigate Macedonian," United States Naval Institute Proceedings 36 (1910): 481–500, 707–16.

4339  Johnson, Robert E. "The Cruise of the Macedonian," Ibid 89 (1963): 72–77.

4340  Saegesser, Lee D. "The U.S.S. Macedonian and the Hurricane of 1818," Ibid 96 (1970): 88–90.

## USS MICHIGAN

4341  Braisted, F.A. "The Navy's First Iron Man-of-War," United States Naval Institute Proceedings 79 (1953): 319–20.

4342 Brown, Walter E. "The Daddy of 'em All," United States Naval Institute
     Proceedings 50 (1924): 1687-94.

4343 Chellis, Edgar S. "The First Iron Ship in Our Navy," Seven Seas 2
     (1916): 26-28.

4344 Fowle, Frank F. "100th Anniversary of the First Iron Steamship on
     the Great Lakes," Journal of the Western Society of Engineers 48
     (1943): 174-84.

4345 Hanks, Carlos C. "An Iron Patriarch Passes," United States Naval
     Institute Proceedings 68 (1942): 1103-06.

4346 Howard-Filler, Saralee P. "U.S.S. Michigan," Michigan History 70
     (1986): 44-48.

4347 Metcalf, Clarence S. "First Iron Vessel on the Great Lakes," Inland
     Seas 13 (1957): 24-28.

4348 Musham, H.A. "Early Great Lakes Steam Boats: Warships and Iron Hulls,
     1841-1846," American Neptune 8 (1948): 132-49.

4349 Oliver, Frederick L. "Our First Iron Man-of-War," United States Naval
     Institute Proceedings 75 (1948): 1262-65.

4350 Penton, Henry. "The U.S.S. Michigan, now Called 'Wolverine',"
     Society of Naval Architects and Marine Engineers Proceedings 16
     (1908): 8-12.

4351 Quaife, Milo M. "The Ironship," Burton Historical Collection Leaflet
     7 (1928): 17-32.

4352 Spencer, Herbert R. U.S.S. Michigan-U.S.S. Wolverine. Erie, PA:
     Erie Bookstore, 1966.

4353 Spencer, Herbert R. "The Iron Steamer," American Neptune 4 (1944):
     183-92.

4354 Underwood, E.B. "Wolverine nee Michigan-A bit of the Old Navy,"
     United States Naval Institute Proceedings 50 (1924): 597-602.

USS MISSISSIPPI

4355 Maccoun, R.T. "Reminiscences of the U.S. Ship Mississippi," United
     Service 5 (1881): 552-58.

USS MISSOURI

4356 Adams, Scarrett. "A Warm Evening at the Rock," American Heritage
     19 (1968): 36-39, 104-07.

4357 Bolton, William. A Narrative of the Last Cruise of the U.S. Steam
     Frigate Missouri. Boston: S.N. Dickinson, 1843.

4358 Dysart, Marjorie. "Missouri's Namesakes in the Navy," Missouri
     Historical Review 49 (1956): 225-34.

4359 Farenholt, Ammen. "The Destruction of the U.S. Steam Frigate Missouri at
     Gibraltar, August 26, 1843," United States Naval Institute Proceedings
     38 (1912): 557-62.

## USS NEW ORLEANS

4360 Palmer, Richard F. "The Great Warship that Waited and Waited...,"
Inland Seas 40 (1984): 272-85.

4361 _____. "Sackett's Harbor and the 'New Orleans'," Yesteryears 29
(1986): 11-29.

## USS NORTH CAROLINA

4362 "Extracts from the Journal of an Officer on Board the U.S. Ship
North Carolina," Army and Navy Chronicle 5 (1837): 344-46.

4363 Merrill, James M. "Midshipman DuPont and the Cruise of the North
Carolina," American Neptune 40 (1980): 211-25.

4364 Durkin, Joseph T. "Journal of Rev. Adam Marshall, Schoolmaster,
U.S.S. North Carolina," American Catholic Historical Society of
Philadelphia Records 53 (1942): 152-68; 54 (1943): 44-65.

SEE ALSO: Samuel F. DuPont

## USS OHIO

4365 Gould, Roland F. The Life of Gould, an Ex-Man-of-War's Man, with
Incidents on Sea and Shore, Including the Three Year's Cruise of
the Line of Battleship Ohio, on the Mediterranean Station, under
the Veteran Commodore Hull. Claremont, NH: Claremont Manufacturing,
1867.

4366 Huguemin, Charles A. "The Figurehead of Hercules at Stony Brook,
L.I., " New York Folklore 9 (1955): 106-15.

4367 "Line of battleship 'Ohio'," Naval Magazine 2 (1837): 90-94.

4368 Torrey, F.P. A Journal of the Cruise of the United States Ship Ohio,
Commodore Isaac Hull, Commander, in the Mediterranean, in the Years
1839, 1840, 1841. Boston: Samuel N. Dickerson, 1841.

## USS ONTARIO

4369 Baltimore, Maryland. Floating School. A Brief History of the
Establishment of the Floating School of the City of Baltimore.
Baltimore: Bull, Tuttle, 1860.

4370 Hopkins, Fred. "From Warship to Schoolship: The History of the
U.S.S. Ontario, America's First Floating School," American Neptune
40 (1980): 38-45.

4371 Paullin, Charles O. "The Voyage of the Ontario, 1817-1819," United
States Naval Institute Proceedings 46 (1940): 213-17.

## *USS PEACOCK

4372 Poesch, Jessie. Titian Ramsey Peale, 1799-1885, and His Journal of
the Wilkes Expedition. Philadelphia: American Philosophical Society,
1961.

4373 Richardson, Charles. "Voyage via the Orient," American History
Illustrated 14 (1979): 30-35.

4374   Roberts, Edmund. An Embassy to the Eastern Courts of Cochin-China,
       Siam, and Muscat, in the U.S. Sloop of War Peacock, during the Years
       1832-34. New York: Harper, 1837.

4375   _____. "Disaster of the Flag Ship Peacock," American Foreign Service
       Journal 15 (1938): 282-84, 300-1.

## USS PENNSYLVANIA

4376   Ashmead, L.P. "The Old Pennsylvania: Launching of a Warship at
       Philadelphia in 1837," United Service 42 (1905): 528-33.

4377   "Old Line of Battleship Pennsylvania," Scientific American 80 (1899):
       346-7.

4378   Stewart, L. "The Navy: 100 Years Ago," United States Naval Institute
       Proceedings 73 (1947): 587.

## USS PHILADELPHIA

4379   Benjamin, Samuel G. "The Loss and Recapture of the Philadelphia,"
       Riverside Magazine 4 (1870): 410-12.

4380   "The Capture and Burning of the Philadelphia," Navy 7 (1913): 11-13.

4381   Companion to the Historical Paintings of the Destruction of the
       Frigate Philadelphia and the Bombardment of Tripoli. Boston: B. True,
       1807.

4382   DeSelding, Charles. Documents, Official and Unofficial, Relating to
       the case of the Capture and Destruction of the Frigate Philadelphia
       at Tripoli on 16th February, 1804. Washington, DC: J.T. Towers, 1850.

4383   Duncan, Robert B. "The Men of Mastico." In: Brave Deeds of American
       Sailors. Philadelphia: G.W. Jacobs, 1912, 58-80.

4384   Evans, Lawton B. "Decatur Burns the Philadelphia." In: With Wind and
       Tide: Sea Stories from American History. Springfield, MA: Milton,
       Bradley, 1929, 85-92.

4385   Furlong, Charles W. The Gateway to the Sahara: Observations and
       Experiences in Tripoli. New York: Charles Scribner's, 1909, 100-19.

4386   _____. "Finding the Frigate Philadelphia," Harper's 111 (1905): 50-58.

4387   Gibbs, George F. "Decatur and the Philadelphia." In: Pike and Cutlass:
       Hero Tales of Our Navy. Philadelphia: J.B. Lippincott, 1900. 46-72.

4388   _____. "The Biggest Little Fight in Naval History," Lippincott's
       Magazine 64 (1899): 632-39.

4389   Huff, Arthur B. "Preble and the Philadelphia," United States Naval
       Institute Proceedings 61 (1935): 818-22.

4390   Leeming, Joseph. "The Burning of the Philadelphia." In: The Book of
       American Fighting Ships. New York: Harper & Bros., 1939, 71-78.

4391   Lodge, Henry C. and Theodore Roosevelt. "The Burning of the Philad-
       elphia." In: Hero Tales from American History. New York: Century,
       1895, 101-13.

4392    Prudden, Theodore M. The Frigate Philadelphia. Princeton, NJ:
        Van Nostrand, 1966.

4393    Roper, William L. "With Cutlass and Sword: Decatur," Marine Corps
        Gazette 62 (1978): 51-56.

4394    "A Sailor's Letter," Military and Naval Magazine 5 (1835): 195-96.

4395    U.S. Congress. Committee on Naval Affairs. Destruction of the
        Frigate Philadelphia. 19th Cong. 2d Sess. House Report No. 74.

4396    U.S. Navy Deaprtment. Burning the Frigate Philadelphia at Tripoli.
        Washington, DC: Gales, Seaton, 1826.

4397    Webster, Hanson H. and Ella M. Powers. "Decatur Burns the Phila-
        delphia." In: Famous Seaman of America. New York: Crowell, 1928,
        51-61.

4398    Wilmer, L.A. "Loss of the Frigate Philadelphia," United States
        Military Magazine 2 (1840): 33-36.

        SEE ALSO: Stephen Decatur

                            USS PORPOISE

4399    Neeser, Robert W. "Historic Ships of the Navy," United States Naval
        Institute Proceedings 66 (1940): 647-49.

                            USS PORTSMOUTH

4400    Farenholt, Ammen. "U.S.S. Portsmouth," United States Naval
        Institute Proceedings 70 (1944): 442-43.

4401    Larmar, Howard, ed. The Cruise of the Portsmouth, 1845-1847; A
        Sailor's View of the Conquest of California. New Haven: Yale
        University Press, 1958.

4402    Montgomery, John B. "The Navy of the Pacific Coast," Journal of the
        Military Service Institute 30 (1902): 708-20.

4403    Neeser, Robert W. "Historic Ships of the Navy-Portsmouth," United
        States Naval Institute Proceedings 52 (1928): 1339-55.

4404    Selfridge, T.O. "Origin of the U.S. Ship Portsmouth," Ibid 42
        (1916): 913-14.

4405    Wood, William M. Wandering Sketches of People and Things in South
        America, Polynesia, California and other Places Visited during a
        Cruise. Philadelphia: Carey, Hart, 1849.

        SEE ALSO: John B. Montgomery

                            USS POTOMAC

4406    Foltz, Johnathan M. The Endemic Influence of Evil Government...with
        Medical Statistics of a Voyage of Circumnavigation of the Globe,
        and an Account of Other Service Ashore and Afloat. New York:
        Langley, 1843.

4407    Henshaw, Joshua S. Around the World: A Narrative of a Voyage in the
        East India Squadron. New York: C.S. Francis, 1840.

4408 Maclay, Edgar S. "An Early 'Globe-circling' Cruise," United States Naval Institute Proceedings 36 (1910): 481-500.

4409 Reynolds, Jeremiah N. Voyage of the U.S. Frigate Potomac, under the Command of Commodore John Downes, during a Circumnavigation of the Globe in the Years, 1831-1834. New York: Harper, 1835.

4410 Warriner, Francis. Cruise of the U.S. Frigate Potomac, Round the World During the Years 1831-34, Embracing the Attack on Quallah Battoo. New York: Leavitt, Lord, 1835.

4411 "Washington City," Army Navy Chronicle 3 (1836): 328-29.

4412 Woodworth, Celia. "The U.S.S. Potomac and the Pepper Pirates." In: Clayton R. Barrow, ed. America Spreads Her Sails. Annapolis: Naval Institute Press, 1973, 56-69.

SEE ALSO: John Downes

*USS PRESIDENT

4413 "Naval Reminiscence," Army and Navy Chronicle 3 (1836): 119-20.

4414 "Visit to the British Frigate President," Ibid 1 (1835): 338-39.

USS PRINCETON

4415 Adams, Scarritt. "No More Guns Tonight," Skipper 20 (1966): 26-27, 40-41.

4416 Butler, Clement M. Address by Rev. Clement M. Butler, at the President's Mansion, on the Occasion of the Funeral of Abel P. Upshur, T.W Gilmer and Others who Lost their Lives by the Explosion on Board the Princeton, February 28, 1844. Washington, DC: J. and G.S. Gideon, 1844.

4417 Ellis, George W. A Poem on the Awful Catastrophe on Board the U.S Steam Frigate Princeton, Together with a Full Description of the Terrible Calamity, the Proceedings at Washington, and the Funeral Obsequies. Boston: A.J. Wright, 1844.

4418 Handlin, Oscar. "Explosion on the Princeton: Chance or Destiny," Atlantic 195 (1955): 63-68.

4419 Miles, Alfred H. "The Princeton Explosion," United States Naval Institute Proceedings 52 (1926): 2225-45.

4420 _____. "The Princeton Explosion," Iron Worker 21 (1957): 1-11.

4421 Nash, Howard P. "The Princeton Explosion," American History Illustrated 4 (1969): 4-13.

4422 Pearson, Lee M. "The Princeton and the Peacemaker: A Study in 19th Century Naval Research and Development Procedures," Technology and Culture 7 (1986): 163-83.

4423 Pember, P.Y. "Tragedy of the United States Steamship Princeton," Independent 57 (1904): 560-63.

4424 "Report on the Explosion of the Gun on Board the Steam Frigate Princeton," Journal of the Franklin Institute 8 (1844): 206-16.

4425 Sioussat, St. George, ed. "The Accident on Board the U.S.S. Princeton, February 28, 1844: A Contemporary Newsletter," Pennsylvania History 4 (1937): 161-89.

4426 Sutherland, Robert T. "Ericsson, Stockton, and the U.S.S. Princeton," United States Naval Institute Proceedings 83 (1957): 92-94.

4427 Taylor, John M. "The Princeton Disaster," Ibid 110 (1984): 148-49.

4428 Taylor, William M. "A Sad Event in Our National History: The Explosion on the Warship Princeton," Magazine of American History 30 (1893): 63-67.

4429 Tucker, Spencer C. "U.S. Navy Steam Sloop Princeton," American Neptune 49 (1989): 96-113.

4430 U.S. Congress. Committee on Naval Affairs. Accident on Steamship Princeton. Washington, DC: Blair, Rives, 1844.

4431 Watts, Harry C. "Ericsson, Stockton and the U.S.S. Princeton," United States Naval Institute Proceedings 82 (1956): 961-67.

4432 Webster, Donald B. "The Beauty and Chivalry of the United States Assembled...," American Heritage 17 (1965): 50-53, 87-90.

   SEE ALSO: John Ericsson, Thomas W. Gilmer, Robert Stockton, Abel P. Upshur

## USS SANTEE

4433 Alden, Carroll S. "The Santee: An Appreciation," United States Naval Institute Proceedings 39 (1913): 761-79.

4434 Riley, Elihu S. "The Passing of the U.S.S. Santee," Navy 7 (1913): 100-101.

## USS SAVANNAH

4435 Braynard, Frank O. "Copper for the Savannah, 1818," American Jewish Historical Quarterly 48 (1959): 170-76.

## USS SHARK

4436 Howerton, Alfred T. "The U.S. Schooner Shark," Oregon Historical Quarterly 40 (1939): 288-91.

4437 Osborn, Burr. "Letters by Burr Osborn, Survivor of the Howison Expedition to Oregon, 1846," Ibid 14 (1913): 355-65.

## USS SOMERS

4438 Anthony, Irvin. Revolt at Sea. New York: G.P. Putnam's Sons, 1937.

4439 A.M.G. "Stern Justice," Blackwood's Magazine 279 (1956): 495-504.

4440 Arvin, Newton. "A Note on the Background of 'Billy Budd'," American Literature 20 (1948): 51-55.

4441 Baldwin, Hanson W. Admiral Death: Twelve Adventures of Men Against the Sea. New York: Simon, Schuster, 1939, 225-54.

4442 ____. Sea Fights and Shipwrecks: True Tales of the Seven Seas. New York: Hanover House, 1955, 183-206.

4443 Benton, Thomas H. Thirty Years' View; or, A History of the Working of the American Government for Thirty Years, from 1820 to 1850. 2 Vols. New York: D. Appleton, 1854–1856. Vol. 2, 522–62.

4444 "Cases of Mutiny at Sea," Southern Literary Messenger 9 (1843): 135–36.

4445 Chaille, W. Jackson. "Philip Spencer." In: H. Seger Sifer and Hiram L. Kennicott. The Chi Psi Story. Ann Arbor, MI: The Fraternity, 1951, 74–79.

4446 David, Leon T. "An Episode in Naval Justice," Los Angeles Bar Bulletin 27 (1952): 201–2, 222–26.

4447 Dutton, Arthur H. "The Death of Somers," Overland 49 (1907): 551–53.

4448 Fuller, Edmund, ed. Mutiny: Being Accounts of Insurrections, famous and infamous, on Land and Sea, from the Days of Caesar to Modern Times. New York: Crown, 1953, 118–50.

4449 Hayford, Harrison, ed. The Somers Mutiny Affair. Englewood Cliffs, NJ: Prentice Hall, 1959.

4450 Hamilton, Gail. "The Murder of Philip Spencer," Cosmopolitan 7 (1889): 133–40, 248–55, 345–54.

4451 Hill, Frederic S. "The Mutiny of the Somers." In: The Romance of the American Navy. New York: G.P. Putnam's Sons, 1910, 201–14.

4452 Hunt, Livingston. "The Attempted Mutiny on the U.S. Brig Somers," United States Naval Institute Proceedings 51 (1925): 2062–99.

4453 _____. "Commodore Ridgely's Account of the Last of Somers," Ibid 54 (1928): 486–88.

4454 Liebling, A.J. "The Navy's Only Mutiny," New Yorker 15 (1939): 35–44.

4455 Loring, Charles G. "Memoir of the Hon. William Sturgis," Massachusetts Historical Society Proceedings 7 (1864): 452–55.

4456 MacFarland, Philip. Sea Dangers: The Affair of the Somers. New York: Schocken, 1985.

4457 Morris, H.H. "The U.S.S. Somers Affair," American History Illustrated 9 (1974): 24–31.

4458 "Mutiny of the Somers," North American Review 57 (1843): 195–241.

4459 "A Naval Reminiscence," Naval Magazine 1 (1836): 172–75.

4460 Parmlee, T.N. "Recollections of an Old Stager: The Somers Tragedy," Harper's Monthly Magazine 46 (1873): 700–05.

4461 Prescott, Dana G. Rough Passage: True Stories of Ships and Men. Caldwell, ID: Caxton Printers, 1958, 94–109.

4462 Rogers, Robert C. "Some Reminiscences of Philip Spencer and the Brig Somers,' United Service 4 (1890): 23–36.

4463 Rogin, Michael. "The Somers Mutiny and Billy Budd: Melville in the Penal Colony," Criminal Justice History 1 (1980): 186–224.

4464   Sanborn, Soloman H. Exposition of Official Tyranny in the U.S. Navy. New York: N.P., 1841.

4464A  Schneiderman, David. "Mutiny! The Somers Affair," Manuscripts 40 (1988): 291-94.

4465   "A Sea Tragedy of 1840: The Execution of Midshipman Philip Spencer for Mutiny," United Service 17 (1897): 308-11.

4466   Singer, Kurt D. and Jane Sherrod. Great Adventures of the Sea. Minneapolis: T.S. Denison, 1962, 11-47.

4467   Smith, Horatio D. "The Mutiny on the Somers," American Magazine 8 (1888): 109-14.

4468   Van de Water, Frederick F. The Captain Called it Mutiny. New York: Washburn, 1954.

4469   ____. "Panic Rides the High Seas," American Heritage 12 (1961): 20-23, 97-99.

4470   Wendt, William R. "The Somers Affair," Marine Corps Gazette 39 (1955): 46-51.

4471   Whitton, F.E. "A Mutinous Midshipman," Blackwood's Magazine 233 (1933): 378-84.

       SEE ALSO: Alexander S. Mackenzie

                          *USS UNITED STATES

4472   Ames, Nathaniel. A Mariner's Sketches. Providence, RI: Cory, Marshall, Hammond, 1830.

4473   Anderson, Charles R., ed. Journal of a Cruise to the Pacific Ocean, 1842-1844, in the Frigate United States, with Notes on Herman Melville. Durham: Duke University Press, 1937.

4474   "Cruises of the Frigate United States," Army and Navy Chronicle 8 (1839): 75.

4475   Fish, Peter S. A Midshipman and an Old Lady: Journal of a Cruise Made by Peter Stuyvesant Fish in the Years 1832 and 1833. New York: Privately Printed, 1939.

4476   Franklin, Samuel R. Memories of a Rear Admiral who Has Served for More than Half a Century in the Navy of the United States. New York: Harper & Bros., 1898.

4477   Kemble, John H. "An Incident in Naval Diplomacy," United States Naval Institute Proceedings 63 (1937): 166-68.

4478   Maritime Scraps, or, Scenes in the Frigate United States During a Cruise in the Mediterranean...By a Man-of-War's Man. Boston: The Author, 1838.

4479   Schenck, James F. Journal of a Mediterranean Cruise, July 3, 1832, to December 12, 1833, by Admiral (then past Midshipman) James Schenck, United States Navy. Vallejo, CA: N.p., 1983.

4480   Willis, N. Parker. Pencillings by the Way. London: Virtue, 1842.

4481   ____. Summer Cruise in the Mediterranean on Board an American Frigate. Auburn, NY: Alden, Beardsley, 1853.

## USS VINCENNES

4482   Bolander, Louis H. "The Vincennes: World Traveller of the Old Navy,"
       United States Naval Institute Proceedings 63 (1936): 823-31.

4483   Browning, Robert L. "The Cruise of the U.S. Sloop of War Vincennes
       Circumnavigating, 1837-1838, from the Journal of Robert Lee-Wright
       Browning, Lieut., U.S.N.," United Service 13 (1885): 576-85, 717-28;
       14 (1886): 81-88, 184-210, 265-78, 400-08.

4484   Colvocoresses, George M. Four Years in the Government Exploring
       Expedition to Brazil, the Coast of Patagonia, Chile, Peru, &c.
       Commanded by Captain Charles Wilkes. New York: J.M. Fairchild, 1855.

4485   "Cruise of the Vincennes," Army and Navy Chronicle 3 (1836): 24-25.

4486   Stewart, Charles S. A Visit to the South Seas in the U.S. Ship
       Vincennes during the Years 1829 and 1830, with Scenes in Brazil,
       Peru, Manila, the Cape of Good Hope, and St. Helena. New York:
       New York: J.P. Haven, 1831.

4487   Van Natter, F.M. "First Time Around," United States Naval Institute
       Proceedings 73 (1947): 317-24.

## *USS VIXEN

4488   Middlebrook, Louis F., ed. Journal of Hezekiah Loomis, Steward of
       U.S. Brig Vixen, Captain John Smith, U.S.N., in the War with Tripoli.
       Salem, MA: Essex Institute, 1928.

## *USS WASP

4489   McCaffery, Lloyd. "U.S. Sloop of War Wasp," Nautical Research Journal
       31 (1985): 3-16.

# IV
# MILITIA, CANADA, INDIANS

*MILITIA

4490  Aldrich, Duncan M. "Frontier Militias: Militia Laws on the North American and South African Frontiers." In: William W. Savage and Steven I. Thompson, eds. The Frontier: Comparative Studies. 2 Vols. Norman: University of Oklahoma Press, 1979. Vol. 2, 153-66.

4491  Anderson, T.M. "Militia Past and Present," Journal of the Military Service Institute 19 (1916): 75-79.

4492  Asbury, Charles J. "The Right to Keep and Bear Arms in America: The Origins and Application of the Second Amendment to the Constitution." Ph. D. dissertation, University of Michigan, 1974.

4493  Ayres, George B. "Old Time Militia Training," Dauphin County Historical Society Transactions 1 (1903): 156-58.

4494  Brundage, Lyle D. "The Organization, Administration and Training of the United States Ordinary and Volunteer Militia, 1792-1861." Ph. D. dissertation, University of Michigan, 1959.

4495  Carter, William H. "The Organized Militia: Its Past and Future," United Service 41 (1903): 789-94.

4496  Cress, Lawrence D. Citizen in Arms: The Army and the Militia in American Society to the War of 1812. Chapel Hill: University of North Carolina Press, 1982.

4497  ____. "An Armed Community: The Origins and Meaning of the Right to Bear Arms," Journal of American History 71 (1984): 22-41.

4498  Cushing, John D. "A Well-Regulated Militia," New England Galaxy 5 (1963): 26-36.

4499  "The Florida War-Capt. Thistle," Army and Navy Chronicle 8 (1839): 236.

4500  Hamilton, John D. "The Elegant Elite: Volunteer Militia Companies and their Social Significance, 1790-1860," Man at Arms 2 (1980): 28-30.

4501  Knox, Henry. "A Plan for the General Arrangement of the Militia of the United States," Massachusetts Historical Society Proceedings 6 (1863): 364-403.

4502  London, Lena. "The Militia Fine, 1830–1860," Military Affairs 15
      (1951): 136–44.

4503  Mahon, John K. "A Board of Officers Considers the Condition of the
      Militia in 1826," Ibid 15 (1951): 85–94.

4504  _____. The American Militia: Decade of Decision, 1789–1800.
      Gainesville: University of Florida Press, 1960.

4505  _____. History of the Militia and the National Guard. New York:
      Macmillan, 1983.

4506  _____. "Militia in the Black Hawk War," Indiana Military History
      Journal 8 (1983): 4–11.

4507  "Militia of the United States," Military and Naval Magazine 1 (1833):
      235–43, 269–80, 352–62.

4508  "Militia of the United States," North American Review 19 (1824):
      275–96.

4509  "Militia of the United States," New York Review 7 (1840): 277–306.

4510  "Militia Reform," New England Magazine 7 (1834): 51–59.

4511  Mook, H. Telfer. "Training Days in New England," New England
      Quarterly 11 (1938): 675–97.

4512  Nihart, Bruce, ed. "A Humorous Account of a Militia Muster Circa
      1807," Military Collector and Historian 10 (1958): 11–14.

4513  Reinders, Robert. "Militia and Public Order in Nineteenth Century
      America," Journal of American Studies 11 (1977): 81–101.

4514  "Reminiscences Connected with the War of 1812," New England
      Historical and Genealogical Quarterly 19 (1865): 338–42.

4515  Riker, William H. Soldiers of the States: The Role of the National
      Guard in American Democracy. Washington, DC: Public Affairs, 1957.

4516  Shalhope, Robert E. "The Ideological Origins of the Second Amendment,"
      Journal of American History 69 (1982): 599–614.

4517  _____. "The Armed Citizen in the Early Republic," Law And Contemp-
      orary Problems 49 (1986): 125–41.

4518  Sumner, William H. An Inquiry into the Importance of the Militia to
      a Free Commonwealth. Boston: Cummings, Hilliard, 1823.

4519  Todd, Frederick P. "Our National Guard: An Introduction to its
      History," Military Affairs 5 (1941): 73–86, 152–70.

4520  Weiler, Harold J. "The Development of the National Guard,"
      Quartermaster Review 54 (1940): 25–35.

4521  Whisker, James. "The Second Amendment: The Right to Keep and Bear
      Arms." Ph. D. dissertation, University of Maryland, 1969.

4522  Wienre, Frederick B. "The Militia Clause of the Constitution,"
      Harvard Law Review 54 (1940): 181–220.

      SEE ALSO: 4653, 4887, 5618

## ALABAMA

4523  Koerper, Phillip E. and David T. Childress. "The Alabama Volunteers in the Second Seminole War, 1836," Alabama Review 37 (1984): 3-12.

## CONNECTICUT

4524  Gates, Stewart L. "Disorder and Social Organization: The Militia in Connecticut Public Life, 1660-1860." Ph. D. dissertation, University of Connecticut, 1975.

4525  Lucke, Jerome B. History of the New Haven Grays from September 13, 1776, to September 13, 1876. New Haven: Tuttle, Morehouse, 1876.

4526  Maples, Philip G. "The Dress Regulations for the Connecticut Militia, 1812: A Backyard Study," Military Collector and Historian 31 (1979): 74-77.

4527  _____. "Connecticut Militia Flank Companies, 1824," Ibid 32 (1980): 19-23.

## FLORIDA

4528  Bittle, George C. "In Defense of Florida: The Organized Florida Militia from 1821 to 1920." Ph. D. dissertation, Florida State University, 1965.

4529  _____. "The Florida Militia's Role in the Battle of Withlacoochee," Florida Historical Quarterly 44 (1966): 303-11.

4530  Cobb, Samuel E. "The Spring Grove Guards," Ibid 22 (1944): 208-16.

4531  _____. "The Florida Militia and the Affair at Withlacoochee," Ibid 19 (1940): 128-39.

4532  "Florida Volunteers," Army and Navy Chronicle 5 (1837): 352-57.

4533  Hawk, Robert. Florida's Army: Militia/State Troops/National Guard, 1565-1985. Englewood, FL: Pineapple Press, 1986.

## GEORGIA

4534  "The Militia Drill." In: Georgia Scenes: Characters, Incidents, in the First Half-Century of the Republic. New York: Harper, 1840, 145-51.

4535  "Militia Papers Relating to the Indian War, 1836," DeKalb Historical Society Collections 1 (1952): 15-25.

## ILLINOIS

4536  Wood, Walter S. "The 130th Infantry, Illinois National Guard: A Military History, 1778-1919," Illinois State Historical Society Journal 30 (1937-1938): 193-255.

SEE ALSO: Abraham Lincoln

## INDIANA

4537  Lockhart, Paul D. "The Lafayette Guard in the Black Hawk War," Indiana Military History Journal 12 (1987): 16-19.

### IOWA

4538  Gardner, Hamilton. "The Nauvoo Legion, 1840-1845: A Unique Military
      Organization," Iowa State Historical Society Journal 54 (1961):
      181-97.

4539  Richards, Charles B. "Organization and Service of the Frontier
      Guards," Annals of Iowa 11 (1913): 1-15.

4540  Upham, Cyril B. "Historical Survey of the Militia in Iowa, 1838-
      1865," Iowa Journal of History and Politics 17 (1919): 299-405.

### KENTUCKY

4541  Clift, J. Glenn. The 'Cornstalk' Militia of Kentucky, 1792-1811.
      Frankfort, KY: Kentucky Historical Society, 1911.

4542  Stone, Richard G. A Brittle Sword: The Kentucky Militia, 1776-1912.
      Lexington: University of Kentucky Press, 1977.

4543  Thacker, Joseph A. "The Kentucky Militia from 1792 to 1812."
      Master's Thesis, University of Kentucky, 1954.

### MICHIGAN

4544  "The Brady Guards," Michigan Pioneer 12 (1889): 525-46.

4545  Solvick, Stanley D. Let the Drum Beat: A History of the Detroit
      Light Guard. Detroit: Wayne State University Press, 1988.

### MAINE

4546  Southard, Frank E. "The Portland Federal Volunteers, 1798-1803,"
      Military Collector and Historian 12 (1959): 44-56.

### MASSACHUSETTS

4547  Russell, Samuel H. "A Contemporary Letter written from Fort Sewall
      in Marblehead to the Gurnet Fort near Plymouth Detailing the 'Sandy
      Bar Surprise' of September 5, 1814, with other Matters," Essex
      Institute Historical Collections 36 (1900): 214-16.

4548  Wade, Herbert T. "The Essex Regiment in Shays' Rebellion, 1787,"
      Ibid 90 (1954): 317-49.

### MISSOURI

4549  "The Army," Army and Navy Chronicle 6 (1838): 108.

4550  "Battle of Okeechobee," Ibid 6 (1838): 154-56, 250.

4551  Gentry, William R. "The Missouri Soldier One Hundred Years Ago,"
      Missouri Historical Review 12 (1917-1918): 216-23.

4552  _____. 'Full Justice': The Story of Richard Gentry and His Missouri
      Volunteers in the Seminole War. St. Louis: N.p., 1937.

4553  Missouri. National Guard. History of the Missouri National Guard.
      Jefferson City: Military Council, Missouri National Guard, 1934.

4554  Westover, John G. "The Evolution of the Missouri Militia, 1804-
      1919." Ph. D. dissertation, University of Missouri, 1949.

NEW YORK

4555   Clark, Charles S. "Centennial of A Famous Regiment," Army and Navy
       Life 8 (1906): 57-60.

4556   Clark, Emmons. History of the Second Company of the 7th Regiment,
       New York State Militia. New York: J.G. Gregory, 1864.

4557   Noble, Henry H. "General Orders of the Commander-in-Chief of the
       New York State Forces, 1812," American Historical Register 1 (1897):
       16-26.

PENNSYLVANIA

4558   Holmes, Joseph I. "Decline of the Pennsylvania Militia, 1815-1870,"
       Western Pennsylvania Historical Magazine 57 (1974): 199-217.

4559   Porland, W.A. "The Second Troop, Philadelphia City Cavalry,"
       Pennsylvania Magazine of History and Biography 47 (1923): 147-77.

RHODE ISLAND

4560   Richards, John J. Rhode Island's Early Defenders and Their
       Successors. East Greenwich, RI: R.I., 1937.

SOUTH CAROLINA

4561   Cardwell, Guy A. "William Henry Timrod, the Charleston Volunteers,
       and the Defense of St. Augustine," North Carolina Historical Review
       18 (1941): 27-37.

4562   Flynn, Jean M. "South Carolina's Compliance with the Militia Act of
       1792," South Carolina Historical Magazine 69 (1968): 26-43.

VERMONT

4563   Blackwell, Marilyn S. and James M. Holway. "Reflections on Jacksonian
       Democracy and Militia Reform: The Witsfield Militia Petition of
       1836," Vermont History 55 (1987): 5-15.

4564   Dutcher, L.L. "June Training in Vermont: A Serio-Comic History,"
       Vermont Historical Gazetteer 2 (1871): 347-55.

4565   Haraty, Peter H. Put the Vermonters Ahead: A History of the Vermont
       National Guard, 1764-1978. Burlington, VT: Queen City Printers, 1979.

4566   Marro, Anthony. "Vermont Local Militia Units, 1815-1860,"
       Vermont History 40 (1972): 28-42.

VIRGINIA

4567   Butler, Stuart L. A Guide to Virginia Militia Units in the War of
       1812. Athens, GA: Iberian Publishing Co., 1988.

4568   Courtenay, William A. "The Washington Light Infantry, 1807-1861,"
       Southern Historical Society Papers 31 (1903): 1-11.

4569   Kochan, James L. "Virginia Cavalry in the War of 1812," Military
       Collector and Historian 38 (1986): 110-13.

4570    Huntsberry, Thomas V. Western Maryland, Pennsylvania, and Virginia
        Militia in the Defense of Maryland. Baltimore: J. Mart, 1983.

4571    "Richmond Light Infantry Blues," U.S. Military Magazine 3 (1841):
        25-30.

                            UNIFORMS

4572    Curtis, John O. and William H. Guthman. New England Militia Uniforms
        and Accoutrements. Sturbridge Village, MA: Old Sturbridge Village
        Press, 1971.

4573    Gero, Anthony and Philip G. Maples. "Observations on the Infantry
        Uniforms of the New York State Militia, 1820 to 1835," Military
        Collector and Historian 36 (1984): 154-61.

                            *CANADA

4574    Anderson, Stuart. "British Threats and the Settlement of the Oregon
        Boundary Dispute," Pacific Northwest Quarterly 66 (1975): 153-60.

4575    Bemis, Samuel F. "Canada and the Peace settlement of 1782-3,"
        Canadian Historical Review 14 (1933): 265-84.

4576    Bourinot,  John G. "The United States and Canada: A Historical
        Retrospective," American Historical Review 5 (1891): 89-147.

4577    Braver, Kinley J. "The United States and British Imperial Expansion,
        1815-1860," Diplomatic History 12 (1988): 19-37.

4578    Brown, George. "The St. Lawrence in the Boundary Settlement of 1783,"
        Canadian Historical Review 9 (1928): 223-28.

4579    Campbell, Charles S. From Revolution to Rapproachment: The United
        States and Great Britain, 1783-1900. New York: Wiley, 1974.

4580    Corbett, Percy E. The Settlement of Canadian-American Disputes: A
        Critical Study of Methods and Results. New Haven: Yale University
        Press, 1937.

4581    Elkins, Wilson H. "British Policy in Relation to the Commerce and
        Navigation of the United States of America from 1794 to 1807."
        Ph. D. dissertation, Oxford University, 1936.

4582    Gash, Norman. The Life and Political Career of Robert Banks Jenkinson,
        Second Earl of Liverpool, 1770-1828. Cambridge: Harvard University
        Press, 1984.

4583    Golladay, U. Dennis. "The United States and the British North American
        Fisheries, 1815-1845," American Neptune 33 (1973): 246-57.

4584    Hodgins, Thomas. British and American Diplomacy Affecting Canada,
        1782-1899. Toronto: Publishers Syndicate, 1900.

4585    Jones, Howard. To the Webster-Ashburton Treaty: A Study in Anglo-
        American Relations, 1783-1843. Chapel Hill: University of North
        Carolina, 1977.

4586    Jones, Wilbur D. The American Problem in British Diplomacy, 1841-1861.
        Athens, GA: University of Georgia Press, 1974

4587    _____ . and J. Chal Vinson. "British Preparedness and the Oregon
        Question," Pacific Historical Review 22 (1953): 353-64.

4588   Leavitt, Ophra E. "British Policy on the Canadian Frontier, 1782-1792," Wisconsin Historical Society Proceedings (1915): 151-85.

4589   McLaughlin, A.C. "The Western Posts and the British Debts," American Historical Association Annual Report (1894): 413-44.

4590   Masterson, William H. Tories and Democrats: British Diplomats in Pre-Jacksonian America. College Station: Texas A&M University Press, 1986.

4591   Moore, Charles. "Retaining the Northwest Posts: How England Gained by It," Magazine of American History 28 (1892): 189-95.

4592   Moore, David R. Canada and the United States, 1815-1830. Chicago: Jennings, Graham, 1910.

4593   Mugridge, Ian. "The Old West in Anglo-American Relations, 1783-1803." Ph. D. dissertation, University of California, Santa Barbara, 1969.

4594   Nunis, Doyce B. "The Diplomatic Defense of the Old Northwest, 1781-1789: America's Quest for Empire." Ph. D. dissertation, University of Southern California, 1958.

4595   Osgood, Howard L. "The British Evacuation of the United States," Rochester Historical Society Publications 6 (1927): 55-63.

4596   Payne, Charles E. "The Influence of Castlereagh on Anglo-American Friendship." In: Stuart G. Brown, ed. Internationalism and Democracy: Essays Personal, Historical and Political in memory of Charles E. Payne. Syracuse: Syracuse University Press, 1949, 131-41.

4597   Ritchieson, Charles R. Aftermath of the Revolution: British Policy Towards the United States, 1783-1795. Dallas: Southern Methodist University Press, 1969.

4598   _____. "Anglo-American Relations, 1783-1794," South Atlantic Quarterly 58 (1959): 364-80.

4599   Russell, Nelson V. "The End of the British Regime in Michigan and the Northwest," Michigan Alumnus Magazine 44 (1938): 189-206.

4600   _____. The British Regime in Michigan and the Old Northwest, 1760-1796. Northfield, MN: Carleton College Press, 1939.

4601   Schafer, Joseph. "The British Attitude towards the Oregon Question, 1815-1846," American Historical Review 16 (1911): 273-99.

4602   Smith, Joe P. "A United States of North America: Shadows or Substance, 1815-1915," Canadian Historical Review 26 (1945): 109-18.

4603   Tevis, Raymond H. "American Opinions and Attitudes Toward British Retention of the Western Posts and American Attempts to Obtain the Western Posts, 1783-90." Ph. D. dissertation, St. Louis University, 1976.

4604   Thistlewaite, Frank. The Anglo-American Connection in the Early Nineteenth Century. Philadelphia: University of Pennsylvania Press, 1959.

4605   Wright, J. Leitch. Britain and the American Frontier, 1783-1815. Athens, GA: University of Georgia Press, 1975.

4606  Younge, Charles D. Life and Administration of Robert Banks, Second Earl of Liverpool. 3 Vols. London: Macmillan, 1868.

SEE ALSO: British-Indian Relations

CANADIAN DEFENSE

4607  Banks, W.J. "Old Forts along the Unfortified Border," Landmark 13 (1931): 629-32.

4608  Bourne, Kenneth. Britain and the Balance of Power in North America, 1815-1908. Berkeley: University of California Press, 1967.

4609  Corey, Albert B. "Canadian Defense Problems after 1814 and their Culmination in the 'Forties'," Canadian Historical Association Annual Report (1938): 110-20.

4610  Davis, John W. "The Unguarded Boundary," Geographic Review 12 (1922): 585-601.

4611  Hitsman, J. McKay. Safeguarding Canada, 1763-1871. Toronto: University of Toronto Press, 1968.

4612  Dykstra, David L. "The United States and Great Britain and the Balance of Power on the North American Continent, 1837-1848." Ph. D. dissertation, University of Virginia, 1973.

4613  McInnis, Edgar W. The Unguarded Frontier: A History of American-Canadian Relations. Garden City, NY: Doubleday, Doran, 1942.

4614  Preston, Richard A. The Defense of the Undefended Border. Montreal: McGill-Queen's University Press, 1977.

4615  Stacey, Charles P. "The Myth of the Unguarded Frontier, 1815-1871," American Historical Review 56 (1950): 1-18.

4616  Stuart, Reginald C. United States Expansionism and British North America, 1775-1871. Chapel Hill: University of North Carolina, 1987.

4617  _____. "United States Expansion and the British North American Provinces, 1783-1871." In: Joan R. Challinor and Robert L. Beisner, eds. Arms at Rest: Peacemaking and Peacekeeping in American History. Westport, CT: Greenwood Press, 1987, 101-32.

4618  Wager-Smith, Elizabeth. "Historic Attempts to Annex Canada to the United States," Journal of American History 5 (1911): 215-30.

SEE ALSO: John G. Simcoe

MILITARY AFFAIRS

4619  Arnell, J.C. "Trooping to the Canadas," Mariner's Mirror 53 (1967): 143-60.

4620  Bond, C.C. "The British Base at Carleton Island," Ontario History 52 (1960): 1-16.

4621  Blanco, Richard L. "The Development of British Military Medicine, 1793-1814," Military Affairs 38 (1974): 4-10.

4622 Borroughs, Peter. "Tackling Army Desertion in British North America," Canadian Historical Review 61 (1980): 28-68.

4623 Boss, William. The Stormont, Dundas, and Glengarry Highlanders, 1783-1951. Ottawa: Range Press, 1952.

4624 Bradley, Arthur G. "Military Traditions of Canada: The Importance of the United Empire Loyalists," Canadian Magazine 112 (1915): 845-56.

4625 Bull, Stuart. The Queen's York Rangers; the Story of a Famous Canadian Regiment. Erin, ON: Boston Mills Press, 1984.

4626 Cruikshank, Ernest A. The Origin and Official History of the Thirteenth Battalion of Infantry, and a Description of the Work of the Early Militia of the Niagara Peninsula in the War of 1812 and the Rebellion of 1837. Hamilton, ON: E.L. Ruddy, 1899.

4627 Graves, Donald E. and Anne E. Macleod. Nova Scotia Military History: A Resource Guide. Halifax, NS: The Army Museum, 1982.

4628 Greenwood, Frank M. "The Development of a Garrison Mentality Among the English in Lower Canada, 1793-1811." Ph. D. dissertation, University of British Columbia, 1970.

4629 Hamilton, C.F. The Canadian Militia from 1816 to the Crimean War," Canadian Defense Quarterly 5 (1928): 462-73.

4630 Johnson, W.K. "The Social Composition of the Toronto Bank Guards," Ontario History 64 (1972): 95-104.

4631 Krog, Carl E. "The British Great Lakes Forts," Inland Seas 42 (1986): 252-60.

4632 Philp, John. "The Economic and Social Effects of the British Garrisons on the Development of Western Upper Canada," Ontario History 41 (1949): 37-48.

4633 Raudzens, George K. "The British Ordnance Department in Canada, 1815-1855." Ph. D. dissertation, Yale University, 1970.

4634 _____. "The Military Impact on Canadian Canals, 1815-1825," Canadian Historical Review 54 (1973): 273-97.

4635 Schafer, Joseph, ed. "Documents in Relation to Warre and Vavasour's Military Reconnaissance in Oregon, 1845-6," Oregon Historical Quarterly 10 (1909): 1-99.

4636 _____. "The Secret Mission of Warre and Vavasour," Washington Historical Quarterly 3 (1912): 131-53.

4637 Senior, Elinor. "The British Garrison in Montreal in the 1840's," Journal of the Society for Army Historical Research 52 (1974): 111-27.

4638 _____. "The Provincial Cavalry in Lower Canada, 1837-50," Canadian Historical Review 57 (1976): 1-24.

4639 _____. "The Glengarry Highlanders and the Supression of the Rebellion in Lower Canada, 1837-1838," Journal of the Society for Army Historical Research 56 (1978): 143-59.

4640 Senior, Elinor. British Regulars in Montreal: An Imperial Garrison, 1832-1854. Montreal: McGill-Queen's University Press, 1981.

4641 Sherk, A.B. "Early Militia Matters in Upper Canada, 1808-1842," Ontario Historical Society Papers and Records 13 (1915): 67-73.

4642 Spurr, John W. "The Kingston Garrison, 1815-1870," Historic Kingston No. 20 (1972): 14-34.

4643 Stacey, Charles P. Canada and the British Army, 1846-1871: A Study in the Practice of Responsible Government. Toronto: Toronto University Press, 1963.

4644 "The Steamship Traveller and the Rebellion of 1837," Ontario History 52 (1960): 251-56.

4645 Sunder, John E. "British Army Officers on the Santa Fe Trail," Colorado Magazine 23 (1967): 147-58.

4646 Talman, James J., ed. "A Secret Military Document, 1825," American Historical Review 38 (1932-1933): 295-300.

4647 White, A.S. Bibliography of Regimental Histories of the British Army. London: Society for Army Historical Research, 1965.

4648 Whitfield, Carol. Tommy Atkins: The British Soldier, 1759-1870. Ottawa: Parks Canada, 1981.

4649 Young, Richard J. "Block Houses in Canada, 1749-1841: A Comparative Report and Catalogue," Canadian Historic Sites 23 (1980): 5-116.

## *WAR OF 1812 IN CANADA

4650 Bowler, R. Arthur. "Propaganda in Upper Canada in the War of 1812," American Review of Canadian Studies 18 (1988): 11-32.

4651 Burns, R.J. "The First Elite of Toronto." Ph. D. dissertation, University of Western Ontario, 1975.

4652 Carter-Edwards, Dennis. "Defending the Straits: The Military Base at Amherstburg." In: K. Pryke and L. Kulisek, eds. The Western District. Windsor, ON: Essex County Historical Society, 1983, 33-43.

4653 Dunnigan, Brian L. "To Make a Military Appearance: Uniforming Michigan's Militia and Fencibles," Michigan Historical Review 15 (1989): 29-47.

4654 Edwards, J.P. "Events in Canada from 1812 to 1815," Canadiana 1 (1889): 113-24.

4655 Errington, Jane. The Lion, The Eagle and Upper Canada. Montreal: McGill-Queen's University Press, 1987.

4656 _____. "Friends and Foes: The Kingston Elite and the War of 1812; A Case Study in Ambivalence," Journal of Canadian Studies 20 (1985): 58-79.

4657 Fraser, Edward and L.G. Carr-Laughton. The Royal Marine Artillery, 1804-1923. 2 Vols. London: Royal United Service Institute, 1930.

4658 Fraser, Robert L. "Politics at the Head of the Lake in the War of 1812: the Case of Abraham Markle," Wentworth Bygones No. 14 (1984): 18-27.

4659  Greusel, Joseph, ed. "Copies of Papers on File in the Dominion
Archives at Ottawa, Canada, Pertaining to the Relations of the
British Government with the United States during the Period of the
War of 1812," Michigan Pioneer 15 (1909): 1-745; 16 (1910): 1-775.

4660  Guitard, Michelle. The Militia of the Battle of Chaueauguay: A
Social History. Ottawa: Government Publishing Center, 1983.

4661  Hitsman, J. McKay. "The War of 1812 in Canada," History Today 12
(1962): 632-39.

4662  Hunter, A.T. "How Upper Canada was Saved in the War of 1812,"
Canadian Defense Quarterly 8 (1931): 400-04.

4663  Irving, Luken H. Officers of the British Forces in Canada during
the War of 1812-1815. Welland, ON: Tribune Printing, 1908.

4664  Luethy, Ivor C. "Swiss Mercenaries in the Service of the British
Crown: The War of 1812," Swiss-American Historical Society Newsletter
21 (1985): 9-20.

4665  Mecredy, Stephen D. "Some Military Aspects of Kingston's Development
during the War of 1812." Master's Thesis, Queen's University, 1984.

4666  Millman, Thomas R. "Jacob Mountain, First Lord Bishop of Quebec, 1776-
1828: A Study in Church-State Relations." Ph. D. dissertation,
McGill University, 1944.

4667  Rawlyk, George. "The Federalist-Loyalist Alliance in New Brunswick,
1784-1815," Humanities Association Review 27 (1976): 142-60.

4668  Smith, Alison. "John Strachan and Early Upper Canada, 1799-1814,"
Ontario History 52 (1960): 159-72.

4669  Stuart, Reginald C. "Special Interests and National Authority in
Foreign Policy: American-British Provincial Links during the Embargo
and the War of 1812," Diplomatic History 8 (1984): 311-28.

4670  Trenholm, Donald T. "The Military Defense of Nova Scotia during the
French and American Wars." Master's Thesis, Mt. Allison University,
1939.

4671  "War of 1812: Reports and Correspondence from the Canadian Archives
at Ottawa," Northwest Ohio Quarterly 2 (1930): 1-14.

SEE ALSO: Isaac Brock, James Fitzgibbon, Henry Procter

DISARMAMENT

4672  Batten field, Ester R. "150 Years of Peace under a Six-Month Pact,"
Inland Seas 23 (1967): 137-48.

4673  Boutell, H.S. "Is the Rush-Bagot Convention Immortal?" North American
Review 173 (1901): 331-48.

4674  Callahan, James M. "Agreement of 1817: Reduction of Naval Forces Upon
the American Lakes," American Historical Association Annual Report
for 1895 (1896): 369-92.

4675  _____. The Neutrality of the American Lakes and Anglo-American
Relations. Baltimore: Johns Hopkins University Press, 1898.

4676  Cruikshank, Ernest A. "The Negotiation of the Agreement for Dis-
      armament on the Lakes," Royal Society of Canada Transactions 30
      (1936): 151-84.

4677  Curti, Merle E. "The Armament on the Great Lakes, 1844," American
      Historical Review 40 (1934-1935): 473-78.

4678  Eayers, James. "Arms Control on the Great Lakes," Disarmament and
      Arms Control 2 (1964): 373-404.

4679  Falk, Stanley L. "Disarmament on the Great Lakes: Myth or Reality?"
      United States Naval Institute Proceedings 87 (1961): 69-73.

4680  Fay, Terrance J. "The Rush-Bagot Agreement: A Reflection of the
      Anglo-American Detente, 1815-1818." Ph. D. dissertation, Georgetown
      University, 1974.

4681  Foster, John W. Limitations of Armament on the Great Lakes, 1836-
      1917. Washington, DC: Carnegie Endoment for International Peace,
      1914.

4682  Glover, Wilbur H., ed. "Documents Relating to the Rush-Bagot
      Agreement," Niagara Frontier 14 (1967): 30-41.

4683  Knapland, Paul. "The Armaments of the Great Lakes, 1844," American
      Historical Review 40 (1935): 473-76.

4684  Levermore, Charles H. The Anglo-American Agreement of 1817 for
      Disarmament of the Great Lakes. Boston: World Peace Foundation, 1914.

4685  MacPherson, K., and E.C. Fisher, eds. "The End of the Great Lakes
      Navy," Warship International 7 (1970): 377-83.

4686  Morison, Samuel E. "Charles Bagot's Notes on Housekeeping and
      Entertaining at Washington, 1819," Colonial Society of Massachusetts
      26 (1927): 438-46.

4687  Perkins, Bradford. Castlereagh and Adams: England and the United
      States, 1812-1823. Berkeley: University of California, 1964.

4688  Powers, Mabel. "The Disarmament Pact between the United States and
      Canada," Current History 32 (1936): 273-76.

4689  Hill, Charles E. Leading American Treaties. New York: Macmillan, 1922.

4690  Scammell, J.H. "The Rush-Bagot Agreement, 1817," Ontario Historical
      Society Papers and Records 13 (1915): 58-66.

4691  Stacey, Charles P. "The Rush Bagot Agreement, 1817-1867," Niagara
      Frontier 14 (1967): 26-29.

4692  Walker, Bryon E. and Charles Fitzpatrick. Addresses Delivered Before
      the Lawyer's Club of New York. New York: N.p., 1917.

4693  Wild, Robert. "The Rush-Bagot Agreement." In: State Bar Association
      of Wisconsin Proceedings. Milwaukee: Evening Wire Print, 1915, 100-11.

4694  Winks, Robert W. "A Nineteenth Century Cold War," Dalhousie Review
      39 (1960): 464-70.

## *ROYAL NAVY

4695  Albion, Robert G. "Forests and Seapower: The Timber Problem of the
      English Navy, 1652-1862." Master's Thesis, Harvard University, 1924.

4696 Bartlett, Christopher J. Great Britain and Seapower, 1815-1853. New York: Oxford University Press, 1963.

4697 Byron, John D. "Crime and Punishment in the Royal Navy: Discipline on the Leeward Islands Station, 1784-1812." Ph. D. dissertation, Louisiana State University, 1987.

4698 Carr, H.J. "Naval History of Bermuda," Bermuda Historical Quarterly 8 (1951): 54-71.

4699 Dawson, Lionel. "Venezuelan Adventure, 1813," Royal United Service Institute Journal 106 (1961): 59-64.

4700 Goldberg, Joseph A. "The Royal Navy's Blockade of New England Waters, 1812-1815," International History Review 6 (1984): 424-39.

4701 Gough, Barry M. "H.M.S. America on the North Pacific Coast," Oregon Historical Quarterly 70 (1969): 292-311.

4702 _____. "The Royal Navy and the Oregon Crisis, 1844-1846," British Columbia Studies 9 (1971): 15-37.

4703 _____. "The Royal Navy and Canadian Dominion," Mariner's Mirror 72 (1986): 5-15.

4704 Graham, Gerald S. Seapower and British North America, 1703-1820: A Study in British Colonial Policy. New York: Greenwood Press, 1968.

4705 _____. and R.A. Humphreys, eds. The Navy and South America, 1807-1823: Correspondence of the Commander in Chief of the South American Station. New York: Oxford University Press, 1962.

4706 "James' Naval History of Great Britain," New York Review 10 (1842): 184-210.

4707 Lloyd, Christopher. "Above and Under Hatches: The Royal Navy, 1782-1814," History Today 29 (1979): 292-304.

4708 Longstaff, Frederick W. "The Royal Navy on the Northwest Coast, 1813-1850," British Columbia Historical Quarterly 9 (1945): 1-24, 113-28.

4709 McNeil, D.R. "Medical care aboard Australian-Bound Convict Ships, 1786-1840," Bulletin of the History of Medicine 26 (1952): 117-40.

4710 Strum, Harvey. "The Leander Affair," American Neptune 43 (1983): 40-50.

4711 Teignmouth, Henry N. "British Protection of American Shipping in the Mediterranean, 1784-1810," United Service Magazine 70 (1919): 169-78.

SEE ALSO: George Cockburn, Provo Wallis

## *INDIANS

4712 Abel, Annie H. "Proposals for an Indian State, 1778-1878," American Historical Association Annual Report for 1907 (1908): 87-104.

4713 Baker, James H. "Address at Fort Snelling in Celebration of the Centennial Anniversary of the Treaty of Pike with the Sioux," Minnesota Historical Society Collections 12 (1908): 291-301.

4714   Barce, Elmore. "Governor Harrison and the Treaty of Fort Wayne, 1809," Indiana Magazine of History 11 (1915): 352-58.

4715   Billet, Viola E. "Indian Diplomacy in the Northwest Territory, 1783-1795." Master's Thesis, Northwestern University, 1937.

4716   Blackorby, E.C. "The Return of Big White: The Tragic Sequel of the Lewis and Clark Expedition," North Dakota History 23 (1956): 109-18.

4717   Bowker, Edna B. "The Indian Policy of the United States, 1789-1841." Ph. D. dissertation, Boston University, 1926.

4718   Brown, Elton T. "Seminole Indian Agents, 1842-1874," Chronicles of Oklahoma 51 (1973): 59-83.

4719   Catlin, George. Letters and Notes on the Manners, Customs, and Conditions of North American Indians. New York: Wiley, Putnam, 1841.

4720   "The Centennial Celebration at Pike's Pawnee Village," Kansas Historical Society Transactions 10 (1908): 15-159.

4721   Clark, Ella E. "Waykeuse and Lewis and Clark," Western Folklore 12 (1953): 175-78.

4722   Covington, James W. "The Florida Seminoles in 1845," Tequesta 24 (1964): 49-57.

4723   Cox, Isaac J. "The Indian as a Diplomatic Factor in the History of the Old Northwest," Ohio Archaeological and Historical Society Quarterly 18 (1909): 542-65.

4724   Crane, Katherine E. "Some Basic Facts in Indian Land Cessions, with Special Reference to the Old Northwest before 1811." Ph. D. dissertation, University of Chicago, 1930.

4725   Davis, T. Frederick. "The Seminole Council, October 23-25, 1834," Florida Historical Quarterly 7 (1929): 330-50.

4726   Dillon, John B. "The National Decline of the Miami Indians," Indiana Historical Society Publications 1 (1897): 121-43.

4727   Dowd, Gregory E. "Paths of Resistance: American Indian Religion and the Quest for Unity, 1745-1815." Ph. D. dissertation, Princeton University, 1986.

4728   Edmunds, R. David. "Nothing has been Effected': The Vincennes Treaty of 1792," Indiana Magazine of History 74 (1978): 23-35.

4729   Evans, Emory. "Government Indian Policy, 1789-1809." Master's Thesis, University of Virginia, 1954.

4730   Ewers, John C. "Plains Indian Reaction to the Lewis and Clark Expedition," Montana 16 (1966): 2-12.

4731   Fiorato, Jacqueline. "The Cherokee Mediation in Florida," Journal of Cherokee Studies 3 (1978): 111-19.

4732   Fisher, Kenneth E. "Jefferson, Harrison, and Northwest Indian Policy." Master's Thesis, University of Virginia, 1979.

4733   Gallaher, Ruth A. "Indian Agents in Iowa," Iowa Journal of History and Politics 14 (1916): 348-94, 559-96.

4734  Gallaher, Ruth A. "The Indian Agent in the United States before 1850," Iowa Journal of History and Politics 14 (1916): 3-55.

4735  Hill, Edward F. The Office of Indian Affairs, 1824-1880: Historical Sketches. New York: Clearwater Publishing Co., 1974.

4736  Hoffman, Edna P. "The Problem of Seminole Indian Removal from Florida." Master's Thesis, Florida State University, 1935.

4737  Horsman, Reginald. "American Indian Policy in the Old Northwest, 1783-1812," William and Mary Quarterly 18 (1961): 35-53.

4738  ____. Expansion and American Indian Policy, 1783-1812. East Lansing: Michigan State University Press, 1967.

4739  ____. "American Indian Policy and the Origins of Manifest Destiny," University of Birmingham Historical Journal 11 (1968): 128-40.

4740  ____. Race and Manifest Destiny: The Origins of American Anglo-Saxonism. Cambridge: Harvard University Press, 1981.

4741  Humins, John H. "George Boyd: Indian Agent of the Upper Great Lakes, 1819-1842." Ph. D. dissertation, Michigan State University, 1975.

4742  Hunter, Juanita. "The Indians and the Michigan Road," Indiana Magazine of History 83 (1987): 244-66.

4743  Jackson, Donald. "Lewis and Clark among the Oto," Nebraska History 41 (1960): 237-48.

4744  Jenson, Merrill. "The Cessions of the Old Northwest," Mississippi Valley Historical Review 23 (1936): 27-48.

4745  Koester, Susan. "The Indian Threat Along the Santa Fe Trail," Pacific Historian 17 (1973): 13-28.

4746  Lang, Herbert. "Sources of Conflict on the Anglo-American Indian Frontier, 1776-1876, with Emphasis cn Racial and Cultural factors." Master's Thesis, University of Texas, 1950.

4747  Lee, Fred L. "Sha Ha Ka: Lewis and Clark's Mandan Indian Friend," Trail Guide 12 (1967): 1-23.

4748  Mahon, John K. "Two Seminole Treaties: Payne's Landing, 1832, and Fort Gibson, 1833," Florida Historical Quarterly 41 (1962): 1-21.

4749  Majors, Harry M. "Lewis and Clark among the Sayleeh Indians," Northwest Discovery 7 (1987): 124-246.

4750  Martin, George W. Historical Addresses Delivered at the Village of Pawnee Republic. Topeka: Morgan, State Printer, 1900.

4751  Mohr, Walter H. Federal-Indian Relations, 1774-1788. Philadelphia: University of Pennsylvania Press, 1933.

4752  Morehead, Warren K. "The Indian Tribes of Ohio," Ohio Archaeological and Historical Society Publications 7 (1898): 1-109.

4753  Munday, Frank J. "Pike-Pawnee Village Site: Review and Summary of the Evidence of the Case," Nebraska History 10 (1927): 168-92.

4754   "On the State of the Indians," North American Review 16 (1823): 30-45.

4755   Petersen, William J. "Indians and the Steamboats," Iowa Journal of History and Politics 30 (1932): 155-81.

4756   Porter, Kenneth W. "Seminole Flight from Fort Marion," Florida Historical Quarterly 22 (1944): 112-33.

4757   Prucha, Francis P. American Indian Policy in the Formative Years: The Indian Trade and Commerce Acts, 1790-1834. Cambridge: Harvard, 1962.

4758      . "Early Indian Peace Medals," Wisconsin Magazine of History 45 (1962): 279-89.

4759      . The Great Father: The United States Government and the American Indian. 2 Vols. Lincoln: University of Nebraska Press, 1984.

4760   Ray, Verne F. Lewis and Clark and the Nez Perce Indians. Washington: Potomac Corral of the Westerners, 1971.

4761   Rees, John E. "The Shoshoni Contribution to Lewis and Clark," Idaho Yesterdays 2 (1958): 2-13.

4762   Richards, Robert L. "Indian Removal in Florida, 1835-1842: A Study of the Causes and Conduct of the Seminole War." Master's Thesis, University of Kansas, 1951.

4763   Ronda, James P. Lewis and Clark Among the Indians. Lincoln: University of Nebraska Press, 1984.

4764   Sanborn, Theodore A. "The Story of the Pawnee Indian Village in Re-public County ," Kansas Historical Quarterly 39 (1973): 1-11.

4765   Satz, Ronald M. "Federal Indian Policy, 1829 to 1849." Ph. D. dissertation, University of Maryland, 1972.

4766   Scanlan, Peter L. "Nicholas Boilvin, Indian Agent," Wisconsin Magazine of History 27 (1943): 145-69.

4767   Schmeckebier, Laurence F. The Office of Indian Affairs: Its History Activities, and Organization. Baltimore: Johns Hopkins Press, 1927.

4768   Seymour, Flora W. Indian Agents of the Old Frontier. New York: D. Appleton-Century, 1941.

4769   Sherer, T.M. "Governor Hull and the Michigan Indians," Detroit Perspective 7 (1983): 33-45.

4770   Shetrone, Henry C. "The Indian in Ohio," Ohio Archaeological and Historical Society Quarterly 27 (1919): 274-509.

4771   Smith, Dwight L. "Indian Land Cessions in the Old Northwest." Ph. D. dissertation, Indiana University, 1949.

4772      . "The Problem of the Historic Indian in the Ohio valley: The Historian's View," Ohio Archaeological and Historical Society Quarterly 63 (1954): 172-80.

4773   Taylor, Elizabeth O. "Hostilities in Florida Arrising from the Removal of the Seminole Indians." Master's Thesis, Oklahoma A&M, 1934.

4774  Viola, Herman J. Thomas J. McKenny: Architect of America's Early Indian Policy, 1816-1830. Chicago: Swallow Press, 1974.

4775  Wehr, Paul W. "The Treaty of Fort Finney, 1786: Prelude to the Indian Wars." Master's Thesis, Miami University, 1958.

4776  Williams, Joyce G. and Jill E. Farrelly. Diplomacy on the Indian-Ohio Frontier, 1783-1791. Bloomington: Indiana University, 1976.

4777  Wolff, Elizabeth. "The Policy of the United States in Removing the Indians from the Old Northwest by Treaties." Master's Thesis, Wayne State University, 1935.

SEE ALSO: 5863, Lewis Cass, William Clark, Benjamin Hawkins, Henry Knox, Benjamin Lincoln, Timothy Pickering, Lawrence Taliaferro, William Wells

## CONTEMPORARY ACCOUNTS

4778  American State Papers: Indian Affairs. 3 Vols. Washington, DC: Gales, Seaton, 1832.

4779  Boyd, George. "Papers of Indian Agent Boyd-1832," Wisconsin Historical Society Collections 12 (1892): 266-98.

4780  Brandt, Penny S., ed. "A Letter of Dr. John Sibley, Indian Agent," Louisiana History 29 (1988): 365-87.

4781  Cherokee Nation. Peace Commission to the Seminole Indians. Seminole and Cherokee Indians: Memorial of the Cherokee Mediators. 25th Cong. 2d Session House Document 285 (1838).

4782  Colt, Katherine G., ed. The Letters of Peter Wilson: Soldier, Explorer and Indian Agent of the Mississippi River. Baltimore: Wirth Brothers, 1940.

4783  Foreman, Grant, ed. "Report of the Cherokee Deputation into Florida, February 17, 1838," Chronicles of Oklahoma 9 (1931): 423-38.

4784  _____. "The Journal of the Proceedings, at Our First Treaty with the Wild Indians," Ibid 19 (1936): 393-417.

4785  Kappler, John J., ed. Indian Affairs: Laws and Treaties. 2 Vols. Washington, DC: Government Printing Office, 1904.

4786  Kinzie, Juliette A. Wau-Bun, the 'Early Day' in the Northwest. New York: Derby, Jackson, 1856.

4787  "Letter Book of Thomas Forsyth, 1814-1818," Wisconsin Historical Society Collections 11 (1888): 316-55.

4788  McKenny, Thomas L. Memoirs, Official and Personal. 2 Vols. New York: Paine, Burges, 1846.

4789  Schoolcraft, Henry R. Personal Memoirs of a Residence of Thirty Years with the Indian Tribes. Philadelphia: Lippincott, Grambo, 1851.

## MILITARY RELATIONS

4790  Brown, Lizzie M. "The Pacification of the Indians of Illinois after the War of 1812," Illinois State Historical Society Journal 8 (1915-1916): 550-58.

4791  Caldwell, Dorothy J. "The Big Neck Affair: Tragedy and Farce on the
      Missouri Frontier," Missouri Historical Review 64 (1970): 391-412.

4792  Doyle, Cornelius J. "Indians and Indian Fighters," Illinois State
      Historical Society Journal 19 (1927): 115-41.

4793  Edmunds, R. David. "Wea Participation in the Northwest Indian Wars,
      1790-1795," Filson Club Quarterly 46 (1972): 241-53.

4794  Eid, Leroy V. "The Neglected Side of American Indian War in the
      Northeast," Military Review 61 (1981): 9-21.

4795  _____. "A Kind of Running Fight: Indian Battlefield Tactics in the
      Late Eighteenth Century," Western Pennsylvania Historical Magazine
      71 (1988): 147-72.

4796  _____. "Their Rules of War: The Validity of James Smith's Summary of
      Indian Woodland War," Register of the Kentucky Historical Society 86
      (1988): 4-23.

4797  _____. "The Cardinal Principle of Northeast Woodland Indian War." In:
      William Cowan, ed. Papers of the Thirteenth Algonquian Conference.
      Ottawa: Carleton University, 1982, 243-50.

4798  "Employment of Indians Against the Seminoles." American State Papers:
      Military Affairs 7: 518-25.

4799  "Frontier Fear of the Indians," Annals of Iowa 29 (1948): 315-22.

4800  Grimes, J.W. "Apprehended Indian Troubles," Ibid 2 (1897): 627-30.

4801  Hadlock, Wendell S. "War Among the Northeastern Woodland Indians,"
      American Anthropologist 49 (1947): 204-2, 601-57.

4802  Hughes, Willis B. "The Heatherly Incident of 1836," Missouri Historical
      Society Bulletin 13 (1957): 161-80.

4803  "Investigations as to Causes of Indian Hostilities West of the Missouri
      River, 1824," Annals of Wyoming 15 (1943): 198-220.

4804  "Irregulars in the War of 1812." 24th Cong. 2d Session House Document
      10, 1836.

4805  Koester, Susan. "The Indian Threat along the Santa Fe Trail," Pacific
      Historian 17 (1973): 13-28.

4806  Laubin, Reginald and Gladys. American Indian Archery. Norman:
      University of Oklahoma Press, 1980.

4807  Mahon, John K. "Anglo-American Methods of Indian Warfare," Mississippi
      Valley Historical Review 45 (1958): 254-75.

4808  Nichols, Roger L. "The Army and the Indians, 1800-1830: A Reappraisal;
      The Missouri valley Example," Pacific Historical Review 41 (1972): 151-68.

4809  Reese, Calvin L. "The United States Army and the Indian: Low Plains
      Area, 1815-1854." Ph. D. dissertation, University of Southern California,
      1963.

4810   Skelton, William B. "Army Officer Attitudes Towards Indians, 1830–1860," Pacific Northwest Quarterly 67 (1976): 113–24.

4811   Smith, Dwight L. "Provocation and Occurrence of Indian-White Warfare in the Early American Period of the Old Northwest," Northwest Ohio Quarterly 33 (1961): 132–47.

4812   Smith, James. A Treatise on the Mode and Manner of Indian War. Paris, KY: R. Lyle, 1812.

4813   Smith, Marian. "American Indian Warfare," Transactions of the New York Academy of Science 13 (1951): 348–65.

4814   "The Young warriors," Philadelphia Album 5 (1831): 285.

4815   Webb, George W. Chronological List of Engagements between the Regular Army of the United States, and Various Tribes of Hostile Indians which Occurred during the Years 1798 to 1898, Inclusive. St. Joseph, MO: Wing Printing Co., 1939.

4816   White, Lonnie J. "Disturbances on the Arkansas-Texas Border, 1827–1831," Arkansas Historical Quarterly 19 (1960): 95–110.

SEE ALSO: Andrew Jackson, David Moniac

## CONTEMPORARY ACCOUNTS

4817   Burnett, John G. "The Cherokee Removal Through the Eyes of a Private Soldier," Journal of Cherokee Studies 3 (1978): 180–85.

4818   "Military Orders and Correspondence of the Cherokee Removal," Ibid 3 (1978): 143–52.

4819   Morse, Jedidiah. A Report to the Secretary of War of the United States on Indian Affairs. New Haven: S. Converse, 1822.

4820   "The Muskogees and Seminoles, by an Officer of the Medical Staff, U.S. Army," Monthly Magazine of Religion and Literature 1 (1840): 137–47.

4821   Webster, L.B. "Letters from a Lonely Soldier," Journal of Cherokee Studies 3 91978): 153–57.

## *BRITISH-INDIAN RELATIONS

4822   Allen, Robert S. "Red and White: The Indian Tribes of the Ohio Valley and Anglo-American Relations, 1783-1796." Master's Thesis, Dalhousie University, 1970.

4823   _____. "His Majesty's Indian Allies: Native Peoples, the British Crown, and the War of 1812," Michigan Historical Review 14 (1988): 1–24.

4824   Berkhofer, Robert F. "Barrier to Settlement: British Indian Policy in the Old Northwest, 1783-1894." In: David M. Ellis, ed. The Frontier in American Development: Essays in Honor of Paul Wallace Gates. Ithaca, NY: Cornell University Press, 1969, 249–76.

4825   Calloway, Colin G. "The End of an Era: British-Indian Relations in the Great Lakes Region after the War of 1812," Michigan Historical Review 12 (1986): 1–28.

4826   _____. Crown and Calumet: British-Indian Relations, 1783-1815. Norman: University of Oklahoma Press, 1987.

4827  Calloway, Colin G. "Foundations of Sand: The Fur Trade and British
      Indian Relations, 1783-1815." In: Bruce G. Trigger, Toby Morantz,
      and Louise Decherre, eds. 'Le Castor Fait Tout': Selected Papers of
      the Fifth North American Fur Trade Conference, 1985. Montreal:
      Societe Historique du lac St. Louis, 1987, 144-63.

4828  Graham, Gerald S. "The Indian Menace and the Detention of the Western
      Posts," Canadian Historical Review 15 (1934): 46-48.

4829  Hamer, P.M. "The British in Canada and the Southern Indians, 1790-1794,"
      East Tennessee Historical Society Publications 2 (1930): 107-34.

4830  Horsman, Reginald. "The British Indian Department and the Abortive
      Treaty of Lower Sandusky, 1793," Ohio History 70 (1961): 189-213.

4831  _____. "The British Indian Department and the Resistance to General ·
      Anthony Wayne, 1793-1795," Mississippi Valley Historical Review 49
      (1962): 269-90.

4832  _____. Mathew Elliott: British Indian Agent. Detroit: Wayne State
      University Press, 1964.

4833  Kellogg, Louise P. The British Regime in Wisconsin and the Old
      Northwest. Madison: State Historical Society of Wisconsin, 1935.

4834  Leavitt, Orpha E. "British Policy on the Canadian Frontier, 1782-1792:
      Mediation and an Indian barrier States," Wisconsin Historical Society
      Proceedings (1915): 151-85.

4835  "Papers on File in the Dominion Archives of Ottawa relating to Indian
      Tribes and Military Posts, 1789-95," Michigan Pioneer 12 (1887): 1-190.

4836  Walsh, G. Mark. "We Have Heard the Great Guns': British Indian Policy
      and the Battle of Lake Erie," Journal of Erie Studies 17 (1988): 22-38.

      SEE ALSO: Billy Caldwell, Henry Procter, John G. Simcoe, Tecumseh

# V
# BIOGRAPHIES

## *JOHN ADAIR

4837   "Adair's Expedition, 1792," Western Review and Miscellaneous Magazine 3 (1821): 61-62.

4838   Adair, John. "Observations on Men and Affairs in the Old Southwest, 1809," Gulf Magazine 1 (1902): 13-18.

4839   Daveiss, M.T. "Gen. John Adair," American Historical Register 3 (1895-1896): 228-34.

## JOHN ADAMS

4840   Adams, Charles F., ed. The Life and Works of John Adams. 10 Vols. Boston: Little, Brown, 1850-1856.

4841   Adams, John. "John Adams on Warfare," Magazine of History 21 (1915): 131-32.

4842   _____. "Letter to Senator Joseph B. Varnum, January 5, 1813, and His Reply," United States Naval Institute Proceedings 67 (1941): 1813-15.

4843   _____. Correspondence of the Late President Adams. Boston: Everett, Munroe, 1809.

4844   Allen, R.S. "Adams and his Admirals." In: More Merry-Go-Round. New York: Liveright, 1932, 299-76.

4845   Anderson, William G. "John Adams and the Creation of the American Navy." Ph. D. dissertation, State University of New York, Stony Brook, 1975.

4846   _____. "John Adams, the Navy, and the Quasi-War with France," American Neptune 30 (1970): 117-32.

4847   Butterfield, L.H., ed. The Adams Papers: Diary and Autobiography of John Adams. 4 Vols. Cambridge, MA: Belknap Press, 1961.

4848   Brown, Ralph A. The Presidency of John Adams. Lawrence, KS: University Press of Kansas, 1975.

4849   Calkins, Carlos G. "The American Navy and the Opinions of one of its Founders, John Adams, 1735-1826," United States Naval Institute Proceedings 37 (1911): 453-82.

4850   Cappon, Lester J., ed. The Adams-Jefferson Letters. 2 Vols.
       Chapel Hill: University of North Carolina Press, 1959.

4851   Carr, James D. "John Adams and the Barbary Problem: The Myth and the
       Record," American Neptune 26 (1966): 231-57.

4852   Cooke, Jacob E. "Country above Party: John Adams and the 1799 Mission
       to France." In: Edmund P. Willis, ed. France and the Founding Fathers.
       Bethlemham, PA: Moravian College, 1967, 53-77.

4853   Hayes, Frederick H. "John Adams and American Seapower," American
       Neptune 25 (1965): 35-45.

4854   Holder, Jean S. "The John Adams Presidency" War Crisis Leadership
       in the Early Republic." Ph. D. dissertation, American University, 1983.

4855   Kelly, John D. "The Struggle for American Seaborne Independence as
       Viewed by John Adams." Ph. D. dissertation, University of Maine, 1974.

4856   Kurtz, Stephen G. The Presidency of John Adams: The Collapse of
       Federalism, 1795-1800. Philadelphia: University of Pennsylvania, 1957.

4857   Murphy, William J. "John Adams: The Politics of the Additional Army,
       1798-1800," New England Quarterly 52 (1979): 234-49.

4858   Saul, Norman E. "Johnathan Russell, President Adams, and Europe in
       1810," American Neptune 30 (1970): 279-93.

4859   Schultz, John A. and Douglas Adair, eds. The Spur of Fame: Dialogues
       of John Adams and Richard Rush, 1805-1813. San Marino, CA: Huntington
       Library, 1966.

4860   Smith, Page. John Adams, 1735-1826. 2 Vols. New York:  Doubleday, 1962.

4861   Trescot, William H. Diplomatic History of the Administration of
       Washington and Adams, 1789-1801. Boston: Little, Brown, 1857.

4862   Wood, John. History of the Administration of John Adams, Late
       President of the United States. New York: Barlas, Ward, 1802.

*JOHN QUINCY ADAMS

4863   Adams, John Q. "Letters of John Quincy Adams," Massachusetts
       Historical Society Proceedings 10 (1895 ): 374-92.

4864   Bergquist, Harold E. "John Quincy Adams and the Promulgation of the
       Monroe Doctrine, October-December, 1823," Essex Institute Historical
       Collections 3 (1975): 37-52.

4865   Cubberly, Frederick. "John Quincy Adams and Florida," Florida
       Historical Quarterly 5 (1926): 88-93.

4866   Ford, Worthington C. John Quincy Adams: His Connection with the Monroe
       Doctrine. Cambridge, MA: John Wilson, 1902.

4867   Parsons, Lynn H. "Perpetual harrow upon My Feelings: John Quincy Adams
       and the American Indian," New England Quarterly 46 (1973): 339-79.

4868   Potter, Kenneth. "The Hispanic-American Policy of John Quincy Adams,
       1817-1825." Ph. D. dissertation, University of California, Berkeley,
       1935.

4869  Radke, August C. "John Quincy Adams' Mission to Russia, 1809-1814."
      Master's Thesis, University of Washington, 1947.

4870  Weeks, William A. "The Origins of Global Empire: John Quincy Adams
      and the Transcontinental Treaty of 1819." Ph. D. dissertation,
      University of California, San Diego, 1986.

                        SAMUEL ADAMS

4871  Pencak, William. "Samuel Adams and Shays' Rebellion," New England
      Quarterly 62 (1989): 63-74.

                     *WILLIAM H. ALLEN

4872  Brown, John H. "William H. Allen." In: American Naval Heroes.
      Boston: Brown & Co., 1899, 291-302.


                     WILLAIM H. ASHLEY

4873  Bechdolt, Frederick R. Giants of the Old West. New York: Century,
      1930.

4874  Carter, Harvey L. "William H. Ashley." In: LeRoy R. Hafen, ed. The
      Mountain Men and the Fur Trade of the Far West. 5 Vols. Glendale,
      CA: Arthur H. Clark, 1969. Vol. 3, 23-34.

4875  Clokey, Richard M. William H. Ashley: Enterprise and Politics in the
      Trans-Mississippi West. Norman: University of Oklahoma Press, 1980.

4876  Dale, Harrison C., ed. The Ashley-Smith Explorations and the
      Discovery of a Central Route to the Pacific, 1822-1829. Cleveland:
      Arthur H. Clarke, 1918.

4877  Frost, Donald M. "Notes on General Ashley, the Overland Trail, and
      South Pass," American Antiquarian Society Proceedings 54 (1945):
      161-312.

4878  Glauert, Ralph E. "The Life and Activities of William Henry Ashley
      and His Associates, 1822-1826." Master's Thesis, Washington
      University, St. Louis, 1950.

4879  Hulbert, Archer B. "The First Wagon Train on the Road to Oregon,"
      Frontier 10 91930): 147-68.

4880  Morgan, Dale L. The West of William H. Ashley: The International
      Struggle for the Fur Trade of the Missouri. Denver: Old West
      Publishing Co., 1964.

4881  Switzler, William F. "General William Henry Ashley," American
      Monthly Magazine 32 (1908): 318-30.

                        HENRY ATKINSON

4882  Atkinson, Henry. "General Atkinson's Trip to Yellowstone in 1825,"
      American State Papers. Indian Affairs. 2: 603-08.

4883  _____. "The Yellowstone Expedition," Nebraska State Historical
      Society Quarterly 4 (1892): 20-23.

4884  _____. Expedition up the Missouri. Washington: Gales, Seaton, 1826.

4885  _____. "Letter from General Atkinson to Colonel Hamilton," Nebraska
      History 5 (1922): 9-11.

4886  Barron, Alice F. "In Defense of the Frontier: The Work of General
      Henry Atkinson, 1819-1842." Master's Thesis, Loyola University,
      Chicago, 1937.

4887  Hagan, William T. "General Henry Atkinson and the Militia," Military
      Affairs 22 (1959-1960): 194-97.

4888  Swart, Mrs. George. Footsteps of Our Founding Fathers. Fort Atkinson:
      Fort Atkinson Historical Society, 1968.

4889  Nichols, Roger L. "General Henry Atkinson's Report of the Yellowstone
      Expedition of 1825," Nebraska History 44 (1963): 65-82.

4890  _____. General Henry Atkinson: A Western Military Career. Norman:
      University of Oklahoma Press, 1965.

4891  _____. "The Battle of Bad Axe: General Atkinson's Report," Wisconsin
      Magazine of History 50 (1966): 54-58.

4892  _____. "General Henry Atkinson and the Building of Jefferson Barracks,"
      Missouri Historical Society Bulletin 22 (1966): 321-26.

                          JOHN C. AYLWIN

4893  Brown, John H. "John Cushing Aylwin." In: American Naval Heroes.
      Boston: Brown, 1899, 345-48.

                        *WILLIAM BAINBRIDGE

4894  Bainbridge, William. "Letter to General H.A.S. Dearborn, March 13,
      1831," Boston Public Library Bulletin 8 (1903): 71-72.

4895  Belluci, Janice M. "Bainbridge: Stalwart of the Navy," All Hands
      No. 812 (1984): 12-15.

4896  "Commodore Bainbridge to John Bullus, Navy Agent," Historical Magazine
      3 (1868): 159.

4897  "Biography," Army and Navy Chronicle 5 (1837): 113-15.

4898  Hunt, Livingston. "Bainbridge under the Turkish Flag," United States
      Naval Institute Proceedings 52 (1926): 1147-62.

4899  Long, David F. "William Bainbridge and the Barron-Decatur Duel:
      Mere Participant or Active Plotter," Pennsylvania Magazine of History
      and Biography 103 (1979): 34-52.

4900  Pearce, George F. "William Bainbridge: A Journal from Washington
      to Pensacola on U.S.S. Hornet, Return on U.S.S. John Adams, and by
      Stagecoach from Savannah, Georgia to Petersburg, Virginia, October-
      December, 1825," American Neptune 44 (1984): 245-56.

4901  Rea, John. Letter to William Bainbridge, Esq., Formerly Commander
      of U.S.S. George Washington, Relative to some Transactions on Board
      Said Ship during the Voyage to Algiers, Constantinople, etc.
      Philadelphia: The Author, 1802.

4902  Symonds, Craig. "William Bainbridge: Bad Luck of Fatal Flaw?" In:
      James C. Bradford, ed. Command Under Sail: Makers of American Naval
      Tradition, 1775-1850. Annapolis: Naval Institute Press, 1984, 97-125.

## GEORGE BANCROFT

4903   Gates, Lillian F. "A Canadian Rebel's Appeal to George Bancroft,"
       New England Quarterly 41 (1968): 96-104.

4904   Howe, Mark A. Life and Letters of George Bancroft. 2 Vols. New York:
       Charles Scribner's Sons, 1908.

4905   Nye, Russell B. George Bancroft: Brahmin Rebel. New York: Alfred A.
       Knopf, 1944.

4906   Rohrs, Richard C. "George Bancroft and American Foreign Relations."
       Ph. D. dissertation, University of Nebraska, 1976.

4907   Sloane, William M. "George Bancroft: In Society, In Politics, In
       Letters," Century Magazine 33 (1886-1887): 473-87.

## *ROBERT H. BARCLAY

4908   Buckie, Robert. "His Majesty's Flag Has Not Been Tarnished: The Role
       of Robert Heriot Barclay," Journal of Erie Studies 17 (1988): 85-102.

## *JOSHUA BARNEY

4909   Barney, Joshua. "Letter to Robert Lewis, 1789," Boston Public Library
       Bulletin 7 (1902): 500.

4910   Brown, John H. "Joshua Barney." In: American Naval Heroes. Boston:
       Brown, 1899, 141-47.

4911   Hoskins, Rebecca. "The Death and Internment of Joshua Barney,"
       Western Pennsylvania Historical Magazine 65 (1982): 75-78.

4912   Levin, Alexandra L. "How Commodore Barney Outwitted the British at
       Norfolk," Maryland Historical Magazine 73 (1976): 163-67.

4913   Mayo, Bernard. "Joshua Barney and the French Revolution," Ibid 36
       (1941): 357-62.

## *JAMES BARRON

4914   Barron, James. "James Barron to Richard Dale on the Barron-Decatur
       Duel," New York Public Library Bulletin 17 (1913): 979-80.

4915   "The Bladensburg Dueling Grounds," Harper's Monthly Magazine 16
       (1858): 471-81.

4916   Brown, John H. "James Barron." In: American Naval Heroes. Boston:
       Brown, 1899, 321-26.

4917   Clark, Allen C. "Samuel Nicholls Smallwood, Merchant and Mayor,"
       Columbia Historical Society Records 28 (1926): 23-61.

4918   _____. "Commodore James Barron, Commodore Stephen Decatur, and the
       Barron-Decatur Duel," Ibid 42-43 (1942): 189-215.

4919   Hussey, Jeanette M. The Code Duello in America. Washington:
       Smithsonian Institute, 1980.

4920   Marr, Janey H. "Commodore James Barron, U.S. Navy," American
       Historical Register 2 (1895): 755-59.

4921  Seitz, Don Carlos. _Famous American Duels_. New York: Crowell, 1929.

4922  Spaulding, Myra L. "Dueling in the District of Columbia," _Columbia Historical Society Records_ 29-30 (1928): 117-210.

4923  Stevens, William O. _An Affair of Honor: The Biography of Commodore James Barron_. Baltimore: Chesapeake Historical Society, 1969.

4924  ____. _Pistols at Ten Paces: The Story of the Code of Honor in America_. Boston: Houghton, Mifflin, 1940.

4925  Taylor, John M. "The Decatur-Barron Duel," _American History Illustrated_ 11 (1976): 4-9, 47-48.

SAMUEL BARRON

4926  Barron, James. "Commodore Samuel Barron," _Virginia Historical Record_. 3 (1850): 198-204.

JOHN BARRY

4927  Baird, George W. _The Father of the American Navy_. N.p., N.d.

4928  Benz, Francis E. _Commodore Barry, Navy Hero_. New York: Dodd, Mead, 1950.

4929  "Biographical Notice of Commodore John Barry," _Portfolio_ 2 (1813): 1-10.

4930  "The Brief Career of the First Commander of the Infant U.S.N.," _Literary Digest_ 132 (1915): 118-19.

4931  Brown, John H. "John Barry." In: _American Naval Heroes_. Boston: Brown, 1899, 117-26.

4932  Bryan, Dan. "Commodore John Barry," _Irish Sword_ 2 (1956): 249-56.

4933  Clark, William B. _Gallant John Barry, 1745-1803; The Story of a National Hero of Two Wars_. New York: Macmillan, 1938.

4934  Cooney, Thomas F. _John Barry_. New York: N.p., 1922.

4935  Connolly, James. "The Father of the American Navy," _Rosary Magazine_ 44 (1914): 450-61.

4936  Cooper, James F. "John Barry," _Graham's Magazine_ 24 (1845): 267-73.

4937  Coyle, John G. "Commodore John Barry, the Father of the American Navy," _Grafton Magazine_ 1 (1908): 35-45.

4938  Dow, J.E. "Some Passages in the Life of Commodore John Barry, the First Captain in the United States Navy under the Constitution," _American Catholic Historical Researches_ 6 (1910): 312-21.

4939  ____. "Some Passages in the Life of Commodore John Barry," _United States Military Magazine_ 2 (1840): 1-3.

4940  Everett, Barbara. "John Barry, Fighting Irishman," _American History Illustrated_ 12 (1977): 18-25.

4941  Fink, Leo G. _Barry or Jones, 'Father of the United States Navy', Historical Reconnaissance_. Philadelphia: Jefferies, Manz, 1962.

4942   Frost, John. The Pictorial Book of the Commodores. New York: Nafis, Cornish, 1845, 75–88.

4943   Griffin, Martin I. "Commodore John Barry," American Historical Association Annual Report (1895): 339–68.

4944   _____. "John Barry, Commodore and Father of the American Navy," American Catholic Historical Researches 4 (1908): 97–192.

4945   _____. The History of Commodore John Barry. Philadelphia: American Catholic Historical Researches, 1897.

4946   _____. Commodore John Barry, 'Father of the American Navy'; A record of His Services for our County. New York: P.J. Kennedy, 1933.

4947   Gurn, Joseph. Commodore John Barry, Father of the American Navy. New York: P.J. Kennedy, 1933.

4948   Jenrich, Charles H. "The Mantle of Valor," Rudder 73 (1957): 9–13.

4949   Lefferts, Walter. Noted Pennsylvanians. Philadelphia: Lippincott, 1913.

4950   Longacre, James B. and James Herring. The National Portrait Gallery of Distinguished Americans. 4 Vols. Philadelphia: Rice, Potter, 1868.

4951   Meany, William B. Commodore John Barry, the Father of the American Navy: A Survey of Extraordinary Episodes in his Naval Career. New York: Harper, 1911.

4952   "Memoir of Commodore John Barry, U.S.N.," Metropolitan Magazine 4 (1856): 394–403.

4953   Morgan, William M. "John Barry: A Most Fervent Patriot." In: James C. Bradford, ed. Command Under Sail: Makers of the American Naval Tradition, 1775–1850. Annapolis: Naval Institute Press, 1984, 46–70.

4954   Morris, Charles. Heroes of the Navy in America. Philadephia: J.B. Lippincott, 1907, 54–64.

4955   Pollard, Elizabeth. "John Barry, the Father of the American Navy," Americana 5 (1910): 395–401.

4956   Preble, George H. "Commodore John Barry, Senior Officer of the U.S. Navy from 1783 to 1803," United Service 12 (1885): 518–35.

4957   Purcell, Richard. "Captain John Barry of the American Revolution," Studies 23 (1934): 623–33.

4958   Reilly, Richard M. "Commodore John Barry," Lancaster County Historical Society Journal 10 (1906): 126–40.

4959   Ryan, Michael J. Address of Michael J. Ryan, Esq., at the Commemoration of the One Hundredth Anniversary of the Death of Commodore Barry, Father of the American Navy. Philadelphia: Bradley Bros., 1903.

4960   "Relics of Commodore John Barry in Philadelphia," Magazine of History 2 (1905): 386–88.

4961   Seton, William. "Commodore John Barry," U.S. Catholic Historical Magazine 1 (1887): 150–66.

4962  Taggart, Joseph. Biographical Sketches of Eminent American Patriots.
      Kansas, MO: Burton Co., 1907.

4963  Thomas, Sarah A. "John Barry: A Patriot of the Revolution," Cape May
      County Magazine 3 (1948): 33-48.

4964  Wibberly, Leonard P. John Barry, Father of the Navy. New York: Ariel
      Books, 1957.

                            WILLIAM BEAUMONT

4965  Bailey, John R. "Army Surgeon," Physician and Surgeon 22 (1900): 572-83.

4966  Brodman, Estelle. "Scientific and Editorial Relationships Between
      Joseph Lovell and William Beaumont," Bulletin of the History of
      Medicine 38 (1964): 127-32.

4967  Burns, Virginia. William Beaumont, Frontier Doctor. Bath, MI:
      Enterprise Press, 1978.

4968  Carmichael, E.B. "William Beaumont: Peripatetic Army Surgeon and
      American Physiologist," Alabama Journal of Medical Science 12 (1975):
      342-51.

4969  Cohen, I. Bernard, ed. The Career of William Beaumont. New York:
      Arno Press, 1980.

4970  Cushing, Harvey. "William Beaumont's Rendezvous with Fame," Yale
      Journal of Biology and Medicine 8 (1938): 113-26.

4971  "Dr. William Beaumont and the Code of Honor," Military Surgeon 74
      (1934): 248-50.

4972  Flexner, James T. Doctors on Horseback; Pioneers of American Medicine.
      New York: Viking Press, 1937.

4973  Martin, Deborah B. "Doctor William Beaumont: His Life in Mackinac
      and Wisconsin, 1820-1834," Wisconsin Magazine of History 4 (1920-
      1921): 263-80.

4974  Miller, William S. "William Beaumont, M.D., " Annals of Medical
      History 5 (1933): 28-51.

4975  Myer, Max W. "Dr. William Beaumont Comes to St. Louis," Missouri
      Historical Society Bulletin 8 (1952): 338-55.

4976  Phalen, James M. "The Life of William Beaumont," Military Surgeon 84
      (1939): 289-94.

4977  Pitcock, Cynthia. "The Career of William Beaumont, 1785-1853: Science
      and the Self-Made Man in America." Ph. D. dissertation, Memphis State
      University, 1985.

4978  Reasoner, M.A. "Dr. William Beaumont," Military Surgeon 78 (1936):
      389-91.

4979  Smith, A.H. "William Beaumont, 1785-1853," Journal of Nutrition 44
      (1951): 3-16.

4980  Vaughan, Victor C. "William Beaumont and His Work," Physician and
      Surgeon 24 (1902): 543-54.

4981  Zollinger, R.M. "The Legacies of William Beaumont, Pioneer
      Investigator," Pharos 46 (1983): 20-23.

WILLIAM G. BELKNAP

4982  The Belknap Family of Newburgh and Vicinity. Newburgh, NY: N.p., 1889.

4983  Foreman, Carolyn T. "General William Goldsmith Belknap," Chronicles
      of Oklahoma 20 (1942): 124-42.

4984  Ledbetter, Barbara N. General William Goldsmith Belknap (1794-1851),
      Founder of Fort Belknap, Young County, Texas. Archer City, TX:
      McGrain Publishing Co., 1975.

JOHN BELL

4985  Parks, Joseph H. John Bell of Tennessee. Baton Rouge: Louisiana
      State University Press, 1950.

4986  Parks, Norman L. "The Career of John Bell as Congressman from Tenn-
      essee, 1827-1841," Tennessee Historical Quarterly 1 (1942): 229-49.

4987  The Life, Speeches and Public Service of John Bell. New York: Rudd,
      Carleton, 1860.

SIMON BERNARD

4988  Borrensen, Thor. "Simon Bernard and American Coastal Forts,"
      Regional Review 2 (1939): 2-9.

4989  Carter, William G. "Bvt. Major General Simon Bernard," Professional
      Memoirs, Corps of Engineers 5 (1913): 306-14.

4990  _____. "General Simon Bernard," Magazine of History 15 (1912): 155-62.

4991  Cooper, James F. Letter to General Lafayette. New York: Columbia
      University Press, 1931.

4992  Harrison, Joseph H. "Simon Bernard, the American System, and the
      Ghost of the French Alliance." In: John B. Boles, ed. America, the
      Middle Period: Essays in Honor of Bernard Mayo. Charlottesville:
      of Virginia Press, 1973, 145-67.

4993  Planchot, Francoise. "Le General Simon Bernard, Ingenieur Militaire
      Aux Etats-Unis," Revue Francaise d'Etudes Americaines 7 (1982): 87-98.

*JAMES BIDDLE

4994  Barnes, James. "Our First Mission to Japan: The Story of Commodore
      Biddle's Visit in 1846," Harper's Weekly Magazine 57 (1913): 11-12.

4995  Brown, John H. "James Biddle." In: American Naval Heroes. Boston:
      Brown, 1899, 327-38.

4996  Dressel, Barry L. "The Early career of Commodore James Biddle."
      Master's Thesis, East Carolina University, 1972.

*BLACK HAWK

4997  Alexander, Edward P. "Black Hawk and the Vanishing American,"
      Wisconsin Journal of Education 76 (1943): 183-88.

4998  Beckhard, Arthur J. Black Hawk. New York: Messner, 1957.

4999    "Black Hawk," Hesperian 2 (1838): 167-70.

5000    "Black Hawk: Some Account of His Life, Death, and Resurrection,"
        Iowa Journal of History and Politics 12 (1921): 126-31.

5001    "Black Hawk," Army and Navy Chronicle 7 (1838): 110.

5002    "Black Hawk," Palimpsest 13 (1932): 41-92.

5003    Britt, Albert. "Black Hawk: The Sauk who Fought for His Village."
        In: Great Indian Chiefs. New York: McGraw Hill, 1938, 156-87.

5004    Coles, Cyrenus. I am A Man: The Indian Black Hawk. Iowa City: State
        Historical Society of Iowa, 1938.

5005    Cooke, David B. Fighting Indians of America. New York: Dodd, Mead,
        1954, 148-63.

5006    Drake, Benjamin. The Life and Adventures of Black Hawk: With Sketches
        of Keokuk, the Sac and Fox Indians, and the late Black Hawk War.
        Cincinnati: George Conclin, 1839.

5007    ____. The Great Indian Chief of the West; or, Life and Adventures
        of Black Hawk. Cincinnati: Gales, Wright, 1858.

5008    Drake, Samuel G. Biography and History of the Indians of North
        America. Boston: J. Drake, 1834, 637-78.

5009    Edmunds, R. David. "Black Hawk," Timeline 5 91988): 24-27.

5010    Engle, Paul. "Futile Defiance," Palimpsest 13 (1932): 55-73.

5011    Foster, Julia. "Black Hawk: Martyr or Villain?" The Iowan 1 (1953):
        40-43.

5012    Froncek, Thomas. "I was Once a Great warrior: Tragedy of Black Hawk,"
        American Heritage 24 (1972): 16-21.

5013    Goodrich, Samuel C. Lives of Celebrated American Indians. New York:
        J.M. Allen, 1843, 303-15.

5014    Hagan, William T. Black Hawk's Route through Wisconsin: Report of an
        Investigation made by Authority of the Legislature of Wisconsin.
        Madison: State Historical Society of Wisconsin, 1949.

5015    Hallwas, John E. Western Illinois Heritage. Macomb, IL: Illinois
        Heritage Press, 1983.

5016    Harsha, W.J. "In Memory of Chief Black Hawk," Southern Workman 66
        (1931): 524-28.

5017    Hauberg, J.M. "Black Hawk, On America's Greatest Patriotic Indian,"
        Illinois State Historical Society Journal 20 (1927): 265-81.

5018    ____. "Black Hawk's Home Country," Illinois State Historical Library
        Transactions (1914): 113-21.

5019    ____. "Black Hawk's Mississippi from Rock River to Bad Axe," Illinois
        State Historical Society Journal 22 (1929): 93-163.

5020 Heckman, Wallace. Lorado Taft's Indian Statute 'Black Hawk'; an Account of the Unveiling Ceremonies. Chicago: University of Chicago Press, 1912.

5021 Hodge, Frederick W. Handbook of American Indians North of Mexico. Washington, DC: Government Printing Office, 1912. Vol. 1, 150-52.

5022 Jackson, Donald. "Black Hawk: The Last Campaign," Palimpsest 43 (1962): 80-94.

5023 _____. "Black Hawk: The Man and His Times," Ibid 43 (1962): 65-79.

5024 Johnston, Charles H. Famous Indian Chiefs. Boston: L.C. Page, 1909, 353-67.

5025 Josephy, Alvin M. "The Rivalry of Black Hawk and Keokuk." In: The Patriot Chiefs. New York: Viking Press, 1961, 209-55.

5026 Letts, Albina M. "Black Hawk," Midland 8 (1897): 221-30.

5027 "Life of Black Hawk," North American Review 40 (1835): 68-87.

5028 "Life of Ma-ka-tai-me-she-kia-kiak, or Black Hawk," American Quarterly Review 35 (1834): 426-48.

5029 McBride, David. "The Capture of Black Hawk," Wisconsin Historical Society Collections 5 (1867-1869): 293-97.

5030 Monaghan, James. "Black Hawk Rides Again: A Glimpse of the Man," Wisconsin Magazine of History 29 (1945): 43-60.

5031 Newhall, John B. Sketches of Iowa, or, The Emigrant's Guide. New York: J.H. Colton, 1841.

5032 Palmer, Luke. "Judge Luke Palmer's Address on Black Hawk." In: Report of the 16th Annual Conference of the Iowa DAR. Burlington, IA: N.p., 1916, 137-42.

5033 Peck, Mrs. W.F. "Black Hawk," Annals of Iowa 2 (1895-1897): 450-64.

5034 Quaife, Milo M., ed. Life of Black Hawk, Ma-ka-tai-me-she-kia-kiak. Chicago: R.R. Donnelly, 1916.

5035 Reed, William C. "An Intimate View of Black Hawk, Personal Recollections of the Notable Indian Chief." In: DeMoines Register and Leader, March 10, 1907.

5036 "Reminiscences of Black Hawk, by People Who Knew Him." In: Burlington (Iowa) Hawk Eye, March 24, 1907.

5037 Richman, Irving B. John Brown Among the Quakers and other Sketches. Des Moines: Historical Department of Iowa, 1894.

5038 _____. "The Home of Black Hawk," New England Magazine 7 (1892): 305-20.

5039 Rishel, James D., ed. Black Hawk's Autobiography Through the Investigation of Antonine LeClaire. Rock Island: American Publishing, 1912.

5040 Roach, J.V. "The Story of Black Hawk and His Wars," Americana 5 (1910): 46-62.

5041  Shaw, John. "Black Hawk," Wisconsin Historical Society Collections 10 (1888): 216-19.

5042  Smith, Elbert H. The History of Black Hawk, with which is interwoven a Description of the Black Hawk War. Milwaukee: E.H. Smith, 1846.

5043  Snyder, J.F. "The Burial of Black Hawk," Magazine of American History 15 (1886): 494-99.

5044  _____. "The Burial and Resurrection of Black Hawk," Illinois State Historical Society Journal 4 (1911-1912): 47-56.

5045  Stark, William F. Along the Black Hawk Trail. Sheboygan, WS: Zimmerman Press, 1984.

5046  Swisher, Jacob A. "Chief of the Sauks," Palimpsest 13 (1932): 41-54.

5047  Treadway, Sandra G. "Triumph in Defeat: Black Hawk's 1837 Visit to Virginia," Virginia Cavalcade 35 (1985): 4-17.

5048  Wade, Mary H. Ten Big Indians; Stories of Famous Indian Chiefs. Boston: W.A. Wilde, 1905, 199-218.

5049  Wood, Norman B. Lives of Famous Indian Chiefs. Aurora, IL: American Indian Historical Publishing Co., 1906, 363-400.

GEORGE S. BLAKE

5050  Blake, Frank, Jr., ed. Memoir of George Smith Blake, Commodore, U.S.N. Cambridge, MA: The Author, 1871.

BLUE JACKET

5051  Bennett, John. Blue Jacket, War Chief of the Shawnees, and his Part in Ohio's History. Chillicothe, OH: Ross County Historical Society, 1944.

5052  Eckert, Allan W. Blue Jacket, War Chief of the Shawnees. Boston: Little, Brown, 1969.

5053  Gore, Sally. "Blue Jacket, the Famous Shawnee Chief," Kansas State Historical Society Transactions 10 (1908): 397-98.

5054  Harvey, Henry. History of the Shawnee Indians, 1681 to 1854. Cincinnati: E. Morgan, 1855.

BENJAMIN L. BONNEVILLE

5055  Baldensperger, Fernand. "Bonneville the Bold, Explorer of the West," Legion d'Honneur 14 (1943): 269-75.

5056  Barry, J. Neilson. "Captain Bonneville," Annals of Wyoming 8 (1932): 608-33.

5057  "The Bonneville Documents," Washington Historical Quarterly 18 (1927): 60-65.

5058  Bonneville, Benjamin L. "Captain Bonneville's Letter," Contributions to the Historical Society of Montana 1 (1876): 105-10.

5059    Brackett, William S. "Bonneville and Bridger," Contributions to the
        Historical Society of Montana 3 (1900): 175-200.

5060    Ford, Anne E. "A De Bonneville Sketch," Americana 22 (1928): 148-52.

5060A    ____. "Some Adventures of Captain Bonneville," Chronicles of Oklahoma
        6 (1928): 129-39.

5061    Foreman, Grant, ed. "An Unpublished Report by Captain Bonneville,"
        Ibid 10 (1932): 326-30.

5062    "General B.L.E. Bonneville," Washington Historical Quarterly 18
        (1927): 207-30.

5063    Irving, Washington. The Rocky Mountains, or Scenes, Incidents and
        Adventures in the Far West Digested from the Journal of Captain
        B.L.E. Bonneville. Philadelphia: Carey, Lea, Blanchard, 1837.

5064    Lockley, Fred and Marshall N. Dana. More Power to You. Portland:
        Oregon Journal, 1934.

5065    McDermott, John F. "Washington Irving and the Journal of Captain
        Bonneville," Mississippi Valley Historical Review 43 (1956): 459-67.

5066    Major, Donald M. "Benjamin Bonneville: He Played Well his Part in
        the Winning of the West," Journal of American History 21 (1927):
        127-36.

5067    Meacham, Walter E. Bonneville the Bold. Portland, OR: N.p., 1934.

5068    Todd, Edgeley W., ed. The Adventures of Benjamin L.E. Bonneville,
        U.S.A., in the Rocky Mountains and the Far West. Norman: University
        of Oklahoma Press, 1961.

5069    Warren, Gouverneur K. "Bonneville's Expedition to the Rocky Mountains,"
        Annals of Wyoming 15 (1943): 220-33.

                              NATHAN BOONE

5070    "Colonel Nathan Boone: Biography of the Adventurous Pioneer,"
        Annals of Iowa 10 (1872): 226-29.

5071    Fessler, W. Julian, ed. "Captain Nathan Boone's Journal," Chronicles
        of Oklahoma 7 (1929): 58-105.

5072    Foreman, Carolyn T. "Nathan Boone, Trapper, Manufacturer, Surveyor,
        Militiaman, Legislator, Ranger and Dragoon," Ibid 19 (1941): 322-47.

5073    Foreman, Grant, ed. "Captain Nathan Boone's Survey, Creek-Cherokee
        Boundary Line," Ibid 4 (1926): 356-65.

5074    Graham, Charles W. "Presenting the Long-Hidden History of Nathan
        Boone's Life." In: Kansas City Star, July 21 1946.
        At Kansas State Historical Society Library.

5075    Lucas, Corydon L. The Milton Lott Tragedy; a History of the First
        White Death in Boone County, and the Events which lead up to the
        Dark Tragedy. Madrid, IA: Madrid Historical Society, 1906.

5076  Skaggs, Jimmy M. "Captain Nathan Boone." In: Joseph A. Stout, ed.
      Frontier Adventurers: American Exploration in Oklahoma. Oklahoma
      City: Oklahoma Historical Society, 1976, 111-23.

5077  Upton, Lucile M. Nathan Boone, the Neglected Hero. Republic, MO:
      Western Printing Co., 1984.

5078  Walker, Wayne T. "Nathan Boone: The Forgotten Hero of the Missouri,"
      Journal of the West 18 (1979): 85-94.

BILLY BOWLEGS

5079  Eyma, Louis X. La Vie dans le nouveau, par Xavier Eyma. Paris:
      Poulet-Malassis, 1862, 212-17, 237-56.

5080  Foreman, Carolyn T. "Billy Bowlegs," Chronicles of Oklahoma 33
      (1955-1956): 512-32.

5081  Gifford, John D. Billy Bowlegs and the Seminole War. Coconut Grove,
      FL: Triangle Co., 1925.

5082  Howard, Oliver O. Famous Indians I Have Known. New York: Century,
      1908.

5083  Porter, Kenneth W. "Billy Bowlegs (Holata Micco) in the Seminole
      Wars," Florida Historical Quarterly 45 (1967): 219-42.

*HUGH BRADY

5084  Brady, Hugh. "The Battle of Lundy's Lane," Historical Magazine 10
      (1866): 272.

5085  _____. "General Hugh Brady: A Biographical Sketch," Michigan
      Pioneer 3 (1881): 84-87.

5086  Prucha, Francis P., ed. "Reports of General Brady on the Patriot
      War," Canadian Historical Review 31 (1950): 56-68.

*ISAAC BROCK

5087  Kosche, Ludwig. "Contemporary Portraits of Isaac Brock: An Analysis,"
      Archivaria 20 (1985): 22-66.

JOHN BRANCH

5088  Haywood, Marshal D. "John Branch, Secretary of the Navy," North
      Carolina Booklet 15 (1915): 49-103.

*JACOB BROWN

5089  Brown, Jacob. "Battle of Sackett's Harbor, 1813," Journal of the
      Military Service Institute 32 (1903): 408-13.

5090  "Jacob Brown," Military and Naval Magazine 6 (1836): 397-410.

5091  Jones, Roger. "General Brown's Inspection Tour up the Lakes in 1819,"
      Buffalo Historical Society Publications 24 (1920): 295-323.

5092  "The Late Major General Brown," Army and Navy Chronicle 2 (1836):
      264-65.

MOSES BROWN

5093  Jones, Augustine. Moses Brown: His Life and Services. Providence:
      Rhode Island Printing, 1892.

5094   Maclay, Edgar S. Moses Brown, Captain, U.S.N. New York: Baker, Taylor, 1904.

5095   Swett, Samuel. Sketches of a Few Distinguished Men of Newbury and Newburyport. Boston: S.N. Dickinson, 1846.

FRANKLIN BUCHANAN

5096   Brown, John H. "Franklin Buchanan." In: American Naval Heroes. Boston: Brown, 1899, 507-13.

5097   Lewis, Charles L. Admiral Franklin Buchanan: Fearless Man of Action. Baltimore: Norman, Remington, 1929.

HENRY BURBECK

5098   Gardner, Asa B. Memoir of Brevet. Brig. Gen. Henry Burbeck, Founder of the U.S. Military Academy. New York: A.S. Barnes, 1883.

5099   _____. "Henry Burbeck: Brevet Brigadier General, United States Army," Magazine of American History 9 (1883): 251-65.

5100   Murdock, Richard K. "The Case of the Spanish Deserters, 1791-1793," Georgia Historical Quarterly 44 (1960): 278-305.

*WILLIAM BURROWS

5101   Brown, John H. "William Burrows." In: American Naval Heroes. Boston: Brown, 1899, 339-44.

PIERCE M. BUTLER

5102   Foreman, Carolyn T. "Pierce Mason Butler," Chronicles of Oklahoma 30 (1952): 6-28.

BILLY CALDWELL

5103   Burley, C.A. Sauganash, 1780-1848. Chicago: Koester, Zander, 1920.

5104   Clifton, James A. "Merchant, Soldier, Broker, Chief: A Corrected Obituary of Captain Billy Caldwell," Illinois State Historical Society Journal 71 (1978): 185-210.

5105   _____. "Billy Caldwell's Exile in Early Chicago," Chicago History 6 (1977-1978): 218-28.

5106   _____. "Personal and Ethnic Identity on the Great Lakes Frontier: The Case of Billy Caldwell, Anglo-Canadian," Ethnohistory 25 (1978): 69-94.

5107   Hickling, William. "Caldwell and Shabonee." In: Addresses Delivered at the Annual Meeting of the Chicago Historical Society. Chicago: Fergus Printing Co., 1877, 29-41.

5108   Walsh, G. Mark. "Your Humble and Obedient Servant: William Caldwell." Master's Thesis, University of Windsor, 1984.

*JOHN C. CALHOUN

5109   Barsness, Richard W. "John C. Calhoun and the Military Establishment, 1817-1825," Wisconsin Magazine of History 50 (1966): 43-53.

5110  Cushman, George F. "John C. Calhoun," Magazine of American History
      8 (1882): 612-19.

5111  Derosier, Arthur H. "John C. Calhoun and the Removal of the Choctaw
      Indians," South Carolina Historical Association Proceedings (1957):
      33-45.

5112  Fisher, Vincent J. "Mr. Calhoun's Army," Military Review 37 (1957):
      52-58.

5113  Meriwether, Robert L. and W. Edwin Hemphill, eds. The Papers of John
      C. Calhoun. 13 Vols. Columbia: University of South Carolina Press,
      1959-1980.

5114  Niven, John. John C. Calhoun and the Price of Union. Baton Rouge:
      Louisiana State University Press, 1988.

5115  "Rip Rap Contract," Nile's Weekly Register 31 (1826-1827): 292-387.

5116  Smith, Carleton B. "John C. Calhoun, Secretary of War, 1817-1825:
      The Cast Iron Man as Administrator." In: John B. Boles, ed. America,
      the Middle Period: Essays in Honor of Bernard Mayo. Charlottesville:
      University of Virginia, 1973, 132-45.

5117  Spiller, Roger J. "John C. Calhoun as Secretary of War, 1817-1825."
      Ph. D. dissertation, Louisiana State University, 1977.

5118  _____. "Calhoun's Expansible Army: The History of a Military Idea,"
      South Atlantic Quarterly 79 (1980): 189-203.

5119  Weigley, Russell. The American Military; Readings in the History of
      the Military in American Society. Reading, MA: Addison-Wesley, 1969.

5120  Wiltse, Charles M. John C. Calhoun: Nationalist, 1782-1828.
      Indianapolis: Bobbs-Merrill, 1944.

5121  Young, Frances P. "John C. Calhoun as Secretary of War, 1817-1825,"
      Oregon Historical Quarterly 12 (1912): 297-337.

## RICHARD K. CALL

5122  Brevard, Caroline M. "Richard Keith Call," Florida Historical
      Quarterly 1 (1908): 3-12, 8-20.

5123  Doherty, Herbert J. Richard Keith Call: Southern Unionist.
      Gainesville: University of Florida Press, 1961.

5124  _____. "Richard Keith Call vs the Federal Government on the Seminole
      War," Florida Historical Quarterly 31 (1953): 163-80.

5125  "Gov. Call and the Seminole Campaign," Army and Navy Chronicle 3
      (1836): 330-31.

5126  Halsell, Willie D. "Early Letters from R.K. Call," Florida Historical
      Quarterly 39 (1961): 266-69.

5127  Martin, Sidney W. "Richard Keith Call; Florida Territorial Leader,"
      Ibid 21 (1943): 332-51.

5128  "Official," Army and Navy Chronicle 3 (1836): 372-76.

5129   No entry

5130   "Operations of the American Army Under R.K. Call," American State
       Papers: Military Affairs 6: 992-1002.

                          EDWARD R.S. CANBY

5131   Heyman, May L. Prudent Soldier: A Biography of General E.R.S. Canby,
       1817-1873. Glendale, CA: Arthur C. Clarke, 1959.

                          JAMES H. CARLETON

5132   Clendenen, Clarence C. "General James Henry Carleton," New Mexico
       Historical Review 30 (1955): 23-43.

5133   Gibson, Arrell M. "James H. Carleton." In: Paul A. Hutton, ed. Soldiers
       West: Biographies from the Military Frontier. Lincoln: University of
       Nebraska Press, 1987, 59-77.

5134   Hunt, Aurora. Major General James Henry Carleton, 1814-1873: Western
       Frontier Dragoon. Glendale, CA: Arthur C. Clarke, 1958.

5135   Perkins, Mary W. "James Henry Carleton," Sprague's Journal of Maine
       History 14 (1926): 14-17.

5136   "Occidental Reminiscences-Prairie Log Book; or Rough Notes of a
       Dragoon campaign to the Pawnee Villages in '44," Spirit of the Times
       14 (1844): No. 37-46, 48, 50-52; Vol. 15 (1845): Nos. 5-7.

5137   Pelzer, Louis, ed. The Prairie Logbooks: Dragoon Campaigns to the
       Pawnee Villages in 1844, and to the Rocky Mountains. Lincoln:
       University of Nebraska Press, 1983.

                          *LEWIS CASS

5138   Brown, Ralph H. "With Cass in the Northwest in 1820: Journal of
       Charles G. Trowbridge," Minnesota Historical Collections 23 (1942):
       126-48, 233-52, 328-48.

5139   Comfort, Benjamin F. Lewis Cass and the Indian Treaties: A Monograph
       on the Indian Relations of the Northwest Territory from 1813 to 1831.
       Detroit: Charles F. May, 1923.

5140   Doty, James D. "Official Journal, 1820, Expedition with Cass and
       Schoolcraft," Wisconsin Historical Society Collections 13 (1895):
       163-219.

5141   "General Cass at St. Marie in 1820," Ibid 5 (1867-1869): 410-16.

5142   General Lewis Cass. Norwood, MA: Plimpton Press, 1916.

5143   Heibron, Bertha L. "Lewis Cass, Exploring Governor," Minnesota History
       31 (1950): 93-97.

5144   Hewlett, Richard G. "Lewis Cass in National Politics, 1842-1861."
       Ph. D. dissertation, University of Chicago, 1952.

5145   Miriani, Ronald. "Lewis Cass and Indian Administration in the Old
       Northwest, 1815-1836." Ph. D. dissertation, University of Michigan,
       1974.

5146   Naegely, Henry E. "Lewis Cass and the Treaty of 1819," Michigan
       Historical Magazine 3 (1919): 610-16.

5147 Prucha, Francis P. Lewis Cass and the American Indian Policy. Detroit: Wayne State University Press, 1967.

5148 ____. and Donald F. Carmony, eds. "A Memorandum of Lewis Cass: Concerning a System for the Regulation of Indian Affairs," Wisconsin Magazine of History 52 (1968-1969): 35-50.

5149 Quaife, Milo M. "Detroit's Presidential Candidate," Burton Historical Collection Leaflet 3 (1924): 17-32.

5150 "Seminole Campaign," Army and Navy Chronicle 4 (1837): 241-46.

5151 Unger, Robert W. "Lewis Cass: Indian Superintendent of the Michigan Territory, 1813-1831: A Survey of Public Opinion as Reported by the Newspapers of the Old Northwest." Ph. D. dissertation, Ball State University, 1967.

5152 Woodford, Frank B. Lewis Cass: The Last Jeffersonian. New Brunswick, NJ: Rutgers University Press, 1950.

JOHN CASSIN

5153 "Commodore John Cassin, U.S.N.," American Catholic Historical Records 22 (1911): 103-05.

5154 Richardson, Edgar P. "The Cassin Medal," Winterthur Portfolio 4 (1968): 75-82.

JAMES L. CATHCART

5155 Baker, Liva. "Cathcart's Travels, or a Dey in the Life of an American Sailor," American Heritage 26 (1975): 52-60, 82-85.

5156 Calkin, Homer L. "James Leander Cathcart and the United States Navy," Irish Sword 3 (1958): 145-52.

5157 Cathcart, James L. The Captives: Eleven Years a Prisoner in Algiers. La Porte, IN: Herald Print, 1899.

5158 ____. Tripoli: First War with the United States; Letterbook by James Leander Cathcart, First Consul to Tripoli. La Porte, IN: Herald Print, 1901.

5159 ____. "The Diplomatic Journal and Letterbook of James Leander Cathcart, 1788-1796," American Antiquarian Society Proceedings 64 (1954): 303-436.

5160 Prichard, Walter, ed. "Southern Louisiana and Southern Alabama in 1819: The Journal of James Leander Cathcart," Louisiana Historical Quarterly 28 (1945): 735-921.

5161 Ross, Frank E. "James Leander Cathcart-'Troublesome, Litigious Trifler'," Americana 28 (1934): 478-85.

*ISAAC CHAUNCEY

5162 "Biographical Notice of Commodore Isaac Chauncey," Army and Navy Chronicle 10 (1844): 148-49.

5163 Brown, John H. "Isaac Chauncey." In: American Naval Heroes. Boston: Brown, 1899, 361-72.

### WILLIAM CHAUVENET

5164  Coffin, John H. "Memoir of William Chauvenet, 1820–1870," National Academy of Sciences Biographical Memoirs 1 (1877): 227–44.

5165  "The First Academic Staff," United States Naval Institute Proceedings 61 (1935): 1384–1403.

5166  Johnson, William W. "William Chauvenet," Ibid 43 (1917): 2283–88.

5167  Littehales, George W. "William Chauvenet and the U.S. Naval Academy," Ibid 31 (1905): 605–12.

5168  Roever, William H. "William Chauvenet," Washington University Studies 12 (1925): 97–117.

5169  Tiernay, John A. "William Chauvenet–Father of the Naval Academy," Shipmate 32 (1969): 6–11.

5170  Woodward, Calvin M. "Personal Recollections of William Chauvenet," Washington University Association Bulletin No. 3 (1905): 123–28.

### THOMAS CHILDS

5171  Childs, Thomas. "General Childs, U.S.A.: Extracts from His Correspondence with his Family," Historical Magazine 2 (1873): 299–304, 371–74; 3 (1874): 169–71, 280–84.

5172  Fredriksen, John C. "Colonel Childs and His Quadrant: Reflections on the Career of a Distinguished American Soldier," Military Collector and Historian 39 (1987): 122–25.

### SYLVESTER CHURCHILL

5173  Churchill, Frank H. Sketch of the Life of Bvt. Brig. General Sylvester Churchill, Inspector General, United States Army. New York: Willis McDonald, 1888.

### *WILLIAM CLARK

5174  Barry, Louise, ed. "William Clark's Diary, May, 1826–February, 1831," Kansas Historical Quarterly 16 (1948): 1–39, 136–74, 274–305, 384–410.

5175  "Biography," Army and Navy Chronicle 7 (1838): 196–97.

5176  Butterfield, Lyman H. "More Fruits of the Expeditions: The Field Notes of Captain William Clark, 1803–1805," Yale Review 54 (1965): 446–50.

5177  "Captain Lewis's Expedition," Literary Magazine 6 (1806): 442–45.

5178  Coues, Eliott, ed. "Letters by William Clark and Nathaniel Pryor," Annals of Iowa 1 (1893–1895): 613–20.

5179  Gregg, Kate L., ed. Westward with the Dragoons: The Journal of William Clark on his Expedition to Establish Fort Osage. Fulton, MO: Ovid Bell Press, 1937.

5180  Isern, Thomas D., ed. "Exploration and Diplomacy: George Champlin Sibley's Report to William Clark, 1811," Missouri Historical Review 72 (1978): 85–102.

5181   Lindley, Harlow. "William Clark–The Indian Agent," Mississippi Valley Historical Review 2 (1908-1909): 64-65.

5182   Loos, John. "A Biography of William Clark, 1770-1813." Ph. D. dissertation, Washington University, St. Louis, 1953.

5183   _____. "William Clark's Part in the Preparation of the Lewis and Clark Expedition," Missouri Historical Society Bulletin 10 (1954): 490-503.

5184   McGrane, Reginald C., ed. "William Clark's Journal of General Wayne's Campaign," Mississippi Valley Historical Review 1 (1914): 418-44.

5185   Osgood, Ernest S. The Field Notes of Captain William Clark, 1803-1805. New Haven: Yale University Press, 1964.

5186   Russell, Robert P. "The Public Career of William Clark." Master's Thesis, Washington University, St. Louis, 1945.

5187   Smith, Walter R. "General William Clark," Washington University Association Bulletin No. 4 (1906): 49-69.

5188   Steffen, Jerome O. "William Clark: A New Perspective of Missouri National Politics, 1813-1820," Missouri Historical Review 67 (1973): 171-97.

5189   _____. "William Clark: A Reappraisal," Montana 25 (1975): 52-61.

5190   _____. William Clark: Jeffersonian Man on the Frontier. Norman: University of Oklahoma, 1977.

5191   _____. "William Clark." In: Paul A. Hutton, ed. Soldiers West: Biographies from the Military Frontier. Lincoln: University of Nebraska Press, 1986, 11-24.

5192   Thomas, Samuel W. "William Clark's 1795 and 1797 Journals and their Significance," Missouri Historical Society Bulletin 25 (1969): 277-95.

5193   Thwaites, Reuben G. "William Clark: Soldier, Explorer, Statesman," Missouri Historical Society Collections 2 (1906): 1-24.

5194   U.S. War Department. Civilization of the Indians. Washington, DC: Gales, Seaton, 1826.

## DUNCAN L. CLINCH

5195   "General Clinch and the Indians," Army and Navy Chronicle 2 (1836): 114-16.

5196   "Military Anecdote," Ibid 4 (1837): 76.

5197   Patrick, Rembert W. Aristocrat in Uniform: General Duncan L. Clinch. Gainesville: University of Florida Press, 1961.

5198   Quigg, Joyce E. "Brevet Brigadier General Duncan Lamont Clinch and His Florida Service." Master's Thesis, University of Florida, 1963.

5199   "Seminole Campaign," Army and Navy Chronicle 3 (1836): 85-87.

5200   "Seminole Campaign," Ibid 4 (1837): 385-91.

5201 "Seminole War," Army and Navy Chronicle 5 (1837): 385-92.

COACOOCHEE

5202 Cooke, David B. Fighting Indians of America. New York: Dodd, Mead, 1954, 192-206.

5203 Francke, Arthur E. Coacoochee, Made of the Sands of Florida: An Account of a Once-Free Seminole Chief. Deleon Springs, FL: E.O. Painter, 1986.

*ALEXANDER COCHRANE

5204 Henderson, William A. "Vice Admiral Sir Alexander Cochrane and the Southern campaign to New Orleans, 1814-1815," Southern Historian 8 (1987): 24-38.

*GEORGE COCKBURN

5205 Pack, A. James. The Man Who Burned the White House: A Biography of Admiral Sir George Cockburn. Annapolis: Naval Institute Press, 1987.

5206 _____. "A Naval Sidelight in the 1812 War with America," Mariner's Mirror 73 (1987): 287-92.

*DAVID CONNER

5207 Brown, John H. "David Conner." In: American Naval Heroes. Boston: Brown, 1899, 385-92.

5208 Proceedings of the Courts-Martial in the Cases of Lieutenants Weaver and Conner. Washington, DC: Gales, Seaton, 1825.

PHILIP ST. GEORGE COOKE

5209 Burton, E.B. "Texas Raiders in New Mexico in 1843," Old Santa Fe 2 (1915): 407-29.

5210 Carroll, Horace B. "Steward A. Miller and the Snively Expedition of 1843," South Western Historical Quarterly 54 (1951): 261-86.

5211 Connelly, William E., ed. "A Journal of the Santa Fe Trail," Mississippi Valley Historical Review 12 (1925): 72-98, 227-55.

5212 Cooke, Philip St G. "Our Cavalry," United Service 1 (1879): 329-46.

5213 _____. "One Day's Work of a Captain of Dragoons," Magazine of American History 18 (1887): 35-44.

5214 _____. Scenes and Adventures in the Army, or, the Romance of Military Life. Philadelphia: Lindsay, Blakston, 1857.

5215 Foreman, Carolyn T. "General Philip St. George Cooke," Chronicles of Oklahoma 32 (1954): 195-213.

5216 Gardner, Hamilton. "Romance at Old Cantonment Leavenworth: The Marriage of 2nd Lieutenant Philip St. George Cooke in 1830," Kansas Historical Quarterly 22 (1956): 97-113.

5217 _____. "Captain Philip St. George Cooke and the March of the First Dragoons to the Rocky Mountains in 1845," Colorado Magazine 30 (1953): 246-69.

5218  Gardner, Hamilton. "A Young West Pointer Reports for Duty at Jefferson
      Barracks, 1827," Missouri Historical Society Bulletin 9 (1952): 124-38.

5219  Merritt, Wesley. "Life and Services of General Philip St. George Cooke,"
      Journal of the United States Cavalry Association 8 (1895): 79-92.

5220  Young, Otis E. The West of Philip St. George Cooke, 1809-1895.
      Glendale, CA: Arthur H. Clarke, 1955.

                              JAMES F. COOPER

5221  Bolander, Louis H. "The Naval Career of James Fenimore Cooper,"
      United States Naval Institute Proceedings 66 (1940): 541-50.

5222  Clagett, John H. "Cooper and the Sea: Naval Life and Naval History in
      the Writings of James Fenimore Cooper." Ph. D. dissertation, Yale
      University, 1954.

5223  Cooper, James F.  Correspondence of James Fenimore Cooper. 2 Vols.
      New Haven: Yale University Press, 1922.

5224  _____. "Comparative Resources of the American Navy," Naval Magazine
      1 (1836): 19-33.

5225  _____. "Hints on Managing the Navy," Ibid 1 (1836): 176-91.

5226  _____. The Cruise of the Somers: Illustrative of the Despotism of
      the Quarterdeck, and the Unmanly Conduct of Commodore Mackenzie.
      New York: J. Winchester, 1844.

5227  Egan, Hugh M. "Gentlemen Sailors: The First Person Sea Narratives of
      Dana, Cooper, and Melville." Ph. D. dissertation, University of
      Iowa, 1983.

5228  Green, Martin. "Cooper, Nationalism, and Imperialism," Journal of
      American Studies 12 (1978): 161-68.

5229  Grossman, James. James Fenimore Cooper. New York: William S.oan, 1949.

5230  Hall, Edwin M. "Cooper and the Navy." Ph. D. dissertation,
      Pennsylvania State University, 1959.

5231  Lewis, D.D. "James Fenimore Cooper: Novelist, Historian and Lawyer,"
      United States Naval Institute Proceedings 89 (1963): 171-72.

5232  Lounsbury, Thomas R. James Fenimore Cooper. Boston: Houghton, Mifflin,
      1890.

5233  Nelson, Paul D. "James Fenimore Cooper's Wartime Nationalism, 1820-
      1850," Military Affairs 41 (1977): 129-32.

5234  Palmer, Richard F. "James Fenimore Cooper and the Navy Brig Oneida,"
      Inland Seas 40 (1984): 90-99.

5235  Philbrick, Thomas. James Fenimore Cooper and the Development of
      American Sea Fiction. Cambridge: Harvard University Press, 1961.

5236  _____. "Cooper's Naval Friend in Paris," American Literature 52 (1980-
      1981): 634-38.

*LEONARD COVINGTON

5237  Adams, Charles S. "General Leonard Covington, 1768-1813," Christopher
      Gist Historical Society Papers 1 (1949-1950): 104-12.

*WILLIAM H. CRAWFORD

5238  Cutler, Everette W. William H. Crawford. Charlotte: University of
      Virginia Press, 1965.

5239  Wendel, Arthur G. "William Harris Crawford and the Jeffersonian
      Republican party, 1806-1825." Master's Thesis, Catholic University
      of America, 1962.

JOHN A. DAHLGREN

5240  Alden, Carroll S. and Ralph Earle. "John Adolphus Dahlgren." In:
      Makers of Naval Tradition. Boston: Ginn, 1925, 130-45.

5241  Allison, David K. "John A. Dahlgren: Innovator in Uniform." In: James
      C. Bradford, ed. Captains of the Old Steam Navy. Annapolis: Naval
      Institute Press, 1986, 26-45.

5242  Brown, John H. "John Adolphus Dahlgren." In: American Naval Heroes.
      Boston: Brown, 1899, 485-90.

5243  Dahlgren, Madeleine. Memoirs of John A. Dahlgren, Rear Admiral, United
      States Navy, by His Widow. Boston: J.R. Osgood, 1882.

5244  Earle, Ralph. "John Adolphus Dahlgren," United States Naval Institute
      Proceedings 51 (1925): 424-36.

5245  Holmberg, L.G. "Dahlgren: Father of Modern Naval Ordnance," All Hands
      No. 755 (1980): 12-17.

5246  Hornsby, Thomas. "Dahlgren's Boat Armament," Mariner 10 (1936): 1-10.

5247  Petersen, Clarence F. Admiral John A. Dalhgren, Father of U.S. Naval
      Ordnance. New York: Hobson Book Press, 1945.

5248  Preble, George H. "Rear Admiral John Adolphus Dalhgren, United States
      Navy," United Service 8 (1883): 67-86.

5249  Turner, D.K. "Admiral John A. Dahlgren, U.S.N., " Bucks County
      Historical Society Collections 3 (1909): 603-20.

RICHARD DALE

5250  "American Naval Affairs, 1798-1802," New York Library Bulletin 11
      (1907): 411-19.

5251  Brown, John H. "Richard Dale." In: American Naval Heroes. Boston:
      Brown, 1899, 97-116.

5252  Cooper, James F. Lives of Distinguished American Naval Officers. 2 Vols.
      Philadelphia: Carey, Hart, 1845. Vol. 2, 233-64.

5253  Frost, John. The Pictorial Book of the Commodores. New York:
      Nafis, Cornish, 1845, 33-59.

5254  Hannon, Bryan. Three American Commodores. New York: Robert's Book
      Co., 1935.

5255  Kern, Gregory B. "Descendants of Joran Kyn-Commodore Richard Dale,"
      Pennsylvania Magazine of History and Biography 4 (1880): 494-500.

5256  "Life of Commodore Dale," Portfolio 3 (1814): 499-515.

5257  Longacre, James B. and James Herring. The National Portrait Gallery
      of Distinguished Americans. 4 Vols. Philadelphia: Rice, Rutter, 1868.
      Vol. 3.

5258  Morris, Charles. Heroes of the Navy in America. Philadelphia: J.B.
      Lippincott, 1907, 45-53.

5259  Seawell, Molly F. Twelve Naval Captains. New York: Charles Scribner
      1906, 28-41.

5260  Sheburne, John H. Life and Character of the Chevalier John Paul Jones.
      Washington, DC: Vanderpool, Cole, 1825, 361-64.

5261  Simpson, Henry. The Lives of Eminent Philadelphians. Philadelphia:
      William Brotherhood, 1859, 278-81.

FRANCIS G. DALLAS

5262  Allen, Gardner W., ed. The Papers of Francis Gregory Dallas, United
      States Navy: Correspondence and Journal 1837-1859. New York: Naval
      Historical Society Publications, 1917.

CHARLES H. DAVIS

5263  Brown, John H. "Charles Henry Davis." In: American Naval Heroes.
      Boston: Brown, 1899, 491-506.

5264  Davis, Charles H. Life of Charles Henry Davis, Rear Admiral, 1807-
      1877. Boston: Houghton, Mifflin, 1899.

5265  Rear Admiral Charles Henry Davis, United States Navy. N.p., 1877.

JEFFERSON DAVIS

5266  Aldrich, Charles. "Jefferson Davis and Black hawk," Midland Monthly
      5 (1896): 406-11.

5267  Davis, Jefferson. "A Letter by Jefferson Davis," Annals of Iowa 4
      (1899): 230-32.

5268  Davis, Varina. Jefferson Davis, Ex-President of the Confederate States
      of America; a Memoir by His Wife. 2 Vols. New York: Belford Co., 1890.
      Vol. 1, 104-44.

5269  Dodd, William E. Jefferson Davis. New York: Russell, Russell, 1966.

5270  Eaton, Clement. Jefferson Davis. New York: Free Press, 1977.

5271  Evans, W.A. "Davis, his Diseases, and his Doctors," Mississippi Doctor
      20 (1941): 14-26.

5272  Fleming, Walter L. "The Early Life of Jefferson Davis," Mississippi
      Valley Historical Review 4 (1917): 151-76.

5273 Fleming, Walter L. "Jefferson Davis at West Point," <u>Mississippi Historical Society Publications</u> 10 (1909): 247-67.

5274 _____., ed. "Some Documents Relating to Jefferson Davis at West Point," <u>Mississippi Valley Historical Review</u> 7 (1920): 146-52.

5275 Langhein, Eric. <u>Jefferson Davis, Patriot</u>. New York: Vantage, 1962.

5276 Lasswell, Lynda J., ed. "Jefferson Davis Ponders his Future, 1829," <u>Journal of Southern History</u> 41 (1975): 517-22.

5277 Macbride, Dorothy. "Lieutenant Jefferson Davis," <u>Palimpsest</u> 4 (1923): 346-57.

5278 Monroe, Haskell M. and James T. McIntosh, eds. <u>The Papers of Jefferson Davis; Vol. 1: 1808-1840</u>. Baton Rouge: Louisiana University, 1977.

5279 Morgan, James F. "Jefferson Davis: The Military man and the Politician." Master's Thesis, California State University, Fullerton, 1973.

5280 Quaife, Milo M. "The Northwestern Career of Jefferson Davis," <u>Illinois State Historical Society Journal</u> 16 (1923-1924): 1-19.

5281 Riley, Harris D. "Jefferson Davis and His Health: Part 1, June 1808-December, 1860," <u>Journal of Mississippi History</u> 49 (1987): 179-203.

5282 Scanlan, Paul L. "The Military Record of Jefferson Davis in Wisconsin," <u>Wisconsin Magazine of History</u> 24 (1940-1941): 174-82.

5283 Shelton, William A. "The Young Jefferson Davis, 1808-1846." Ph. D. dissertation, University of Kentucky, 1977.

5284 Strode, Hudson. <u>Jefferson Davis; American Patriot, 1808-1861</u>. New York: Harcourt, Brace, 1955.

## *STEPHEN DECATUR

5285 Adkins, Milton S. "The Bladensburg Dueling Ground," <u>Magazine of American History</u> 25 (1891): 18-34.

5286 Bouve, Pauline C. <u>American Heroes and Heroines</u>. Boston: Lothrop, 1095, 149-57.

5287 Brady, Cyrus T. "Stephen Decatur and the 'Philadelphia'," <u>McClure's Magazine</u> 14 (1900): 62-67.

5288 Calkins, Carlos G. "Decatur and Coleridge," <u>United States Naval Institute Proceedings</u> 34 (1908): 917-55.

5289 Cochran, Hamilton. "Stephen Decatur." In: <u>Noted American Duels and Hostile Encounters</u>. Philadelphia: Chilton, 1963, 51-79.

5290 Cook, Edward M. "Stephen Decatur: The Man Who Loved Honor More," <u>DAR Magazine</u> 113 (1979): 532-35.

5291 Cooke, Mary L. amd Charles L. Lewis. "An American Naval Officer in the Mediterranean, 1802-1807," <u>United States Naval Institute Proceedings</u> 67 (1941): 1533-39.

5292   Correspondence Between the Late Commodore S. Decatur and Commodore
       J. Barron, which led to the Unfortunate Meeting of the 22nd of March.
       Washington: Gales, Seaton, 1820.

5293   Creel, George. Sons of the Eagle: Soaring Figures from America's Past.
       Indianapolis: Bobbs-Merrill, 1927.

5294   Decatur, Susan. Documents Relative to the Claim of Mrs. Decatur, with
       Her Earnest Request that the Gentlemen of Congress will Take the
       Trouble to Read Them. Georgetown, DC: J.C. Dunn, 1827.

5295   Forester, Cecil S. "Bloodshed at Dawn," American Heritage 15 (1964):
       40-45, 73-76.

5296   Gibbs, George F. "The Revenge of Decatur," Cosmopolitan 31 (1901):
       400-02.

5297   Hinteruhuff, John E. Decatur of High Barbary. New York: Holt, 1955.

5298   Holmes, Charles N. "Stephen Decatur-A Brave American," Journal of
       American History 12 (1918): 379-84.

5299   Krafft, Herman F. "A Dare-Devil Champion of our Early Navy," DAR
       Magazine 65 (1931): 3-9.

5300   Lewis, Charles. "Stephen Decatur and the Barbary Pirates." In: Famous
       American Naval Officers. Boston: L.C. Page, 1924, 39-70.

5301   _____. "Reuben James or Daniel Frazier?" Maryland Historical Magazine
       19 (1924): 30-36.

5302   "Naval Anecdotes," Army and Navy Chronicle 10 (1840): 149.

5303   "The Old Salt," Ibid 4 (1837): 116-17.

5304   Oliver, Vickie J. "Decatur-Man of Conflict," All Hands No. 786 (1982):
       38-41.

5305   Reydon, Royana B. "Com. Stephen Decatur," Historic Preservation 19
       (1967). 30 47.

5306   Read, Harlan E. "Stephen Decatur." In: Fighters for Freedom. New York:
       McBride, 1946, 231-37.

5307   Schroeder, John H. "Stephen Decatur: Heroic Ideal of the Young Navy."
       In: James C. Bradford, ed. Command under Sail: Makers of the American
       Naval Tradition, 1775-1850. Annapolis: Naval Institute Press, 1984,
       199-219.

5308   Simpson, Henry. The Lives of Eminent Philadelphians. Philadelphia:
       William Brotherhead, 1859, 299-305.

5309   Smith, Charles H. Stephen Decatur and the Supression of Piracy in
       the Mediterranean. New Haven: Order of the Founders and Patriots of
       of America, 1901.

5310   Sultana, Donald E. "Samuel Taylor Coleridge and an American Hero
       on Malta," Malta University Faculty of Arts Journal 1 (1958): 121-27.

5311   Webster, Hanson H. and Ella M. Powers. "Decatur burns the Philadelphia."
       In: Famous Seamen of America. New York: T.Y. Crowell, 1928, 51-61.

## EBENEZER DENNY

5312  Denny, Ebenezer. "Diary of Lieutenant Denny," Ohio Archaeological and Historical Society Quarterly 20 (1911): 102-08.

5313  _____. "Military Journal of Major Ebenezer Denny," Historical Society of Pennsylvania Memoirs 7 (1860): 237-409.

5314  _____. Military Journal of Major Ebenezer Denny, an Officer in the Revolutionary and Indian Wars with an Introductory Memoir. Philadelphia: J.B. Lippincott, 1859.

5315  Denny, William H. "Soldier of the Republic: The Life of Major Ebenezer Denny." Ph. D. dissertation, Miami University, 1978.

5316  Lambing, A.A. "Major Ebenezer Denny, the First Mayor of Pittsburgh," Historical Society of Western Pennsylvania Report (1899): 11-27.

## RENE E. DERUSSY

5317  Herman, Frederick W. "Rene Edward DeRussy," Professional Memoirs, Corps of Engineers 7 (1915): 758-60.

## MAHLON DICKERSON

5318  Beckwith, Robert R. "Mahlon Dickerson of New Jersey, 1770-1853." Ph. D. dissertation, Columbia University, 1964.

## *DANIEL DOBBINS

5319  Johnson, Theodore. "The Life-Saving Service of the Lakes: The Relation of Captain Dobbins there to," Magazine of Western History 5 (1886): 229-41.

5320  Meakin, Alexander C. "The Other Hero of the Battle of Lake Erie," Inland Seas 44 (1988): 274-80.

## JOHN DOWNES

5321  Hill, Henry. Recollections of an Octogenarian. Boston: Lothrop, 1884.

5322  Huntoon, David T. History of the Town of Canton, Norfolk County, Massachusetts. Cambridge: J. Wilson, 1893, 448-57.

5323  Krafft, Herman F. "Commodore John Downes, from His Official Correspondence," United States Naval Institute Proceedings 54 (1928): 36-48.

5324  "Sketch of the Life of John Downes, Esq., of the United States Navy," American Monthly Magazine 8 (1836): 71-78.

## HENRY DODGE

5325  Clark, James I. Henry Dodge, Frontiersman: First Governor of Wisconsin Territory. Madison: University of Wisconsin Press, 1957.

5326  Crook, Richard J. "Henry Dodge, Frontier Soldier and Politician," Westerner's Brand Book 33 (1977): 72-75.

5327  Dodge, Henry. "Report on the Expedition of Dragoons, Under Colonel Henry Dodge, to the Rocky Mountains, 1835. American State Papers, Military Affairs 6: 130-46.

5328 Hagan, William T. "The Dodge-Henry Controversy," Illinois State Historical Society Journal 50 (1957): 377-84.

5329 Harlan, Edgar R., ed. "Colonel Henry Dodge and his Regiment of Dragoons on the Plains in 1834," Annals of Iowa 13 (1929-1931): 173-97.

5330 Pelzer, Louis. Henry Dodge. Iowa City: State Historical Society of Iowa, 1911.

5331 _____. "A Frontier Officer's Military Order Book," Mississippi Valley Historical Review 6 (1919-1920): 260-67.

5332 Petersen, William J. "Henry Dodge," Palimpsest 19 (1938): 41-49.

5333 Salter, William. "The Letters of Henry Dodge to Gen. Goerge W. Jones," Annals of Iowa 3 (1897-1898): 220-23, 290-96, 384-99.

5334 _____. "Henry Dodge, Part IV: Colonel, U.S. Dragoons, 1833-6," Iowa Historical Record 7 (1891): 101-19; 8 (1892): 251-67.

5335 _____. "Henry Dodge in the Black Hawk War, 1832," Ibid 6 (1890): 391-427.

5336 Shambaugh, Benjamin F., ed. The Messages and Proclamations of the Governors of Iowa. Iowa City: State Historical Society of Iowa, 1903. Vol. 1, 1-70.

## SAMUEL F. DUPONT

5337 Anderson, Roger. "Samuel Francis Dupont and the Voyage of the North Carolina, 1825-1827." Bachelor's Thesis, University of Delaware, 1970.

5338 Dupont, Henry A. Rear Admiral Samuel Francis Dupont, United States Navy: A Biography. New York: National American Society, 1926.

5339 Dupont, Samuel F. "The War with Mexico: The Cruise of the U.S. Ship Cyane during the Years 1845-48," United States Naval Institute Proceedings 8 (1882): 419-37.

5340 McPherson, James M. "The First Cruise of a Delaware Midshipman: Samuel Francis Dupont and the Franklin," Delaware History 20 (1983): 256-68.

5341 Merrill, James M. Dupont, the Making of an Admiral: A Biography of Samuel Francis Dupont. New York: Dodd, Mead, 1986.

5342 Sketch of the Public Services of Rear Admiral S.F. Dupont, United States Navy. Wilmington, DE: H. Eckel, 1865.

## WILLIAM EATON

5343 Abbatt, William. "A Forgotten Hero," Magazine of History 6 (1907): 1-11.

5344 Eaton, Arthur W. A Memorial Sketch of William Eaton. New York: Privately Printed, 1893.

5345 Eaton, William. Interesting Detail of the Operations of the American Fleet in the Mediterranean. Springfield, MA: Bliss, Brewer, 1805.

5346   Eaton, William. "Letters of William Eaton," Collector 22 (1909): 120-21.

5347   Felton, Cornelius. Life of William Eaton. New York: Harper & Bros, 1854.

5348   Gerson, Noel B. Barbary General: The Life of William H. Eaton. Englewood Cliffs, NJ: Prentice Hall, 1968.

5349   Hale, William H. "General Eaton and His Improbable Legion," American Heritage 9 (1960): 26-33.

5350   "Life of the Late General William Eaton," Analectic Magazine 5 (1815): 299-320, 398-408.

5351   Macleod, Julia H. "William Eaton's Relations with Aaron Burr," Mississippi Valley Historical Review 31 (1944-1945): 523-36.

5352   Minnigerode, Meade. Lives and Times: Four Informal American Biographies. New York: G.P. Putnam's Sons, 1925.

5353   Moran, Charles. "William Eaton-Hero of Derne," United States Naval Institute Proceedings 67 (1941): 497-500.

5354   Morgan, Forrest. "General William Eaton, the First American Imperialist," Americana 6 (1911): 586-614, 697-713.

5355   "Notice of the Life of General William Eaton," General Repository and Review 4 (1813): 174-94.

5356   Powell, Edward A. Gentlemen Rovers. New York: Scribner, 1913, 45-72.

5357   Prentis, Charles. The Life of the Late General William Eaton. Brookfield: E. Merriam, 1813.

5358   Rodd, Francis J. General William Eaton: The Failure of an Idea. New York: Minton, Balch, 1939.

5359   Sedgwick, John H. "William Eaton: A Sanguine Man," New England Quarterly 1 (1928): 107-23.

5360   Shippen, Edward. "A Forgotten General: William Eaton," United Service 5 (1881): 1-21.

5361   Wright, Louis B. "William Eaton, Timothy Pickering, and Indian Policy," Huntington Library Quarterly 9 (1946): 387-400.

5362   _____. and Julia H. Macleod. The First Americans in North Africa: William Eaton's Struggle for a Vigorous Policy against the Barbary Pirates, 1799-1805. Princeton: Princeton University Press, 1945.

## HENRY ECKFORD

5363   DeKay, George C. "George DeKay Writes from Constantinople," American Neptune  6 (1946): 84-85.

5364   "The Late Henry Eckford," U.S. Nautical Magazine 7 (1858): 65-72.

5365   Wheelock, Phyllis D. "Henry Eckford (1775-1832): An American Shipbuilder," American Neptune 7 (1948): 177-95.

## *JESSE D. ELLIOTT

5366   Brown, John H. "Jesse Duncan Elliott." In: American Naval Heroes.
       Boston: Brown, 1899, 373-77.

5367   Elliott, Jesse D. Speech of Com. Jesse Duncan Elliott, U.S.N.,
       Delivered in Hagerstown, Maryland, on 12 November, 1843. Philadelphia:
       G.B. Zieber, 1844.

5368   Runyan, Timothy J. and Jan M. Copes. "The Battle of Lake Erie After
       175 Years: Commemoration and Controversy," Inland Seas 44 (1988):
       264-73.

5369   "The Testimony in the Court of Inquiry on Capt. Elliott following
       the Battle of Lake Erie," Ibid 40 (1984): 110-20.

## JOHN ERICSSON

5370   Church, William C. The Life of John Ericsson. 2 Vols. New York:
       Scribner, 1890.

5371   Creese, James. "John Ericsson, Engineer," American Scandanavian Review
       14 (1926): 286-301.

5372   Headley, Phineas C. The Miner Boy and His Monitor: The Career and
       Achievements of John Ericsson, Engineer. Boston: Lee, Shepard, 1883.

5373   Hirsch, Mark O. "John Ericsson: His Influence on My Community and
       Beyond," Swedish Pioneer Historical Quarterly 5 (1954): 3-12.

5374   Lamb, Martha J. "John Ericsson, the Builder of the 'Monitor', 1803-
       1889," Magazine of American History 25 (1891): 1-17.

5375   Robinson, George H. "Recollections of Ericsson," United Service 13
       (1895): 10-26.

5376   White, Ruth. Yankee from Sweden: The Dream and Reality in the Days
       of John Ericsson. New York: Holt, 1960.

## *DAVID G. FARRAGUT

5377   Brown, John H. "David Glasgow Farragut." In: American Naval Heroes.
       Boston: Brown, 1899, 445-58.

5378   Farragut, Loyal. The Life and Letters of Admiral Farragut, First
       Admiral of the United States Navy. New York: D. Appleton, 1879.

5379   Forney, John W. Anecdotes of Public Men. 2 Vols. New York: Harper
       & Bros., 1873-1881. Vol. 2, 200-11.

5380   Frothingham, Jesse P. Seafighters from Drake to Farragut. New York:
       New York: Charles Scribner's Sons, 1902.

5381   Goodrich, Caspar F. "Farragut," United States Naval Institute
       Proceedings 49 (1923): 1961-86.

5382   Headley, Phineas C. The Life and Naval Career of Vice-Admiral David
       Glascow Farragut. New York: H. Appleton, 1865.

5383   Lewis, Charles L. David Glasgow Farragut: Admiral in Making. 2 Vols.
       Annapolis: Naval Institute Press, 1941.

5384 Mahan, Alfred T. Admiral Farragut. New York: University Society, 1905.

5385 Morris, Charles. Heroes of the Navy in America. Philadelphia: J.B. Lippincott, 1907, 273-85.

5386 Paullin, Charles O. "The Father of Admiral Farragut," Louisiana Historical Quarterly 13 (1930): 37-45.

5387 Rawson, E.K. "Admiral Farragut," Atlantic Monthly 69 (1892): 483-89.

5388 Stevens, William O. David Glasgow Farragut: Our First Admiral. New York: Dodd, Mead, 1942.

5389 Talbot, James J. "Admiral David Glagow Farragut," United Service 3 (1880): 11-22.

5390 Thwaites, Reuben G. "Letter of David G. Farragut concerning his Father and Early Life," American Historical Review 9 (1904): 537-41.

## *JAMES FITZGIBBON

5391 McKenzie, Ruth. James Fitzgibbon, Guardian of Upper Canada. Toronto: Dundurn Press, 1983.

## CHARLES FLOYD

5392 Brooks, Mary E. "Sergeant Floyd's Grave," Midland Monthly 4 (1895): 419-24.

5393 Butler, James D., ed. "The New-found Journal of Charles Floyd, a Sergeant under Captains Lewis and Clark," American Antiquarian Society Proceedings 9 (1891): 225-52.

5394 Caldwell, Ernest W. "The Floyd Monument," Iowa Historical Record 17 (1901): 362-70.

5395 Catlin, George. "The Grave of Sergeant Floyd," Palimpsest 7 (1926): 337-41.

5396 Coues, Elliott. In Memoriam. Sergeant Charles Floyd. Sioux City, IA: Perkins Bros., 1897.

5397 Garver, Frank H. "The Story of Sergeant Charles Floyd," Mississippi Valley Historical Association Proceedings (1910): 76-92.

5398 Holman, Albert M. Pioneering in the Northwest. Sioux City, IA: Deitch, Larmar, 1924.

5399 "Newspaper Clippings Regarding Charles Floyd, his re-internment, etc." Clippings at Wisconsin Historical Society Library.

5400 Wakefield, George W. "Sergeant Charles Floyd," Annals of Iowa 2 (1896): 305-14.

## ANDREW H. FOOTE

5401 Foote, Andrew H. Africa and the American Flag. New York: D. Appleton, 1854.

5402 Hoppin, James M. The Life of Andrew Hull Foote, Rear Admiral, U.S.N. New York: Harper, 1874.

5403  Keller, Allan. Andrew Hull Foote, Gunboat Commodore. Hartford, CT:
      Connecticut Civil War Centennial Commission, 1961.

                          JOSIAH FOX

5404  Lewis, Clifford M., ed. "Career of Josiah Fox as Ship Builder for
      the U.S. Navy: His Own Story," Upper Ohio Valley Historical Review
      10 (1980): 22-31.

5405  Stanton, Elizabeth R. "Builder of the First American Navy: Attested
      Claims of Josiah Fox as Contractor of the First American War Vessels,"
      Journal of American History 2 (1908): 102-12.

5406  Westlake, Merle T. "Josiah Fox, Gentleman, Quaker, Shipbuilder,"
      Pennsylvania Magazine of History and Biography 88 (1964): 316-27.

                        JOHN C. FREMONT

5407  Bartlett, Ruhl J. "The Political and Military Career of John C.
      Fremont." Ph. D. dissertation, Ohio State University, 1927.

5408  Bashford, Herbert. A Man Unafraid: The Story of John Charles Fremont.
      San Francsico: Harr Wagner, 1927.

5409  Bigelow, John. Memoir of the Life and Public Services of John Charles
      Fremont. New York: Derby, Jackson, 1856.

5410  Bradley, G.D. "John C. Fremont," Santa Fe Employee's Magazine 5
      (1911): 25-32.

5411  Davis, William C. "John C. Fremont: A Profile of the Pathfinder,"
      American History Illustrated 5 (1970): 41-11, 44-47.

5412  Egan, Ferol. Fremont: Explorer for a Restless Nation. New York:
      Doubleday, 1977.

5413  _____. "Fremont at Bent's Fort," American West 13 (1976): 18-21.

5414  Eyre, Alice. The Famous Fremonts and their America. Santa Ana, CA:
      Fine Arts Press, 1948.

5415  Fremont, Jesse C. Memoirs of my Life; Including the Narratives of
      Five Journeys of Western Exploration during the Years 1842, 1843-4,
      1845-6-7, 1848-9, 1853-4. Chicago: Belford, Clarke, 1887.

5416  _____. "Pathfinding in Iowa," Palimpsest 9 (1928): 176-84.

5417  _____. Report of the Exploring Expedition to the Rocky Mountains in
      the Year 1841 and to Oregon and North California in the Years 1843-
      1844. 28th Cong. 2d Session. Senate Executive Document 175, 1845.

5418  _____. A Report of an Exploration of the Country Lying Between the
      Missouri River and the Rocky Mountains on the Line of the Kansas
      and Great Platte Rivers. 27th Cong. 3d Session Senate Document 243,
      Serial 416, 1843.

5419  _____. "Early Reports Concerning the Des Moines River," Iowa Journal
      of History and Politics 16 (1918): 108-20.

5420  Glazier, Willard. Heroes of Three Wars. Philadelphia: Hubbard, 1882,
      352-56.

5421  Goodwin, Cardinal L. John Charles Fremont; an Explanation of His Career. Stanford, CA: Stanford University Press, 1930.

5422  Greeley, Horace. Life of Colonel Fremont. New York: Tribune Office, 1856.

5423  Hawthorne, Hildegarde. Born to Adventure; the Story of John Charles Fremont. New York: D. Appleton, 1947.

5424  Jackson, Donald and Mary Lee Spence, eds. The Expeditions of John Charles Fremont. 2 Vols. Urbana: University of Illinois Press, 1974.

5425  Nevins, Allan. "A Record Filled with Sunlight," American Heritage 7 (1956): 12-19, 106-7.

5426  _____., ed. Narratives of Exploration and Adventure by John Charles Fremont. New York: Longmans, Green, 1956.

5427  _____. Fremont: The West's Greatest Adventurer. 2 Vols. New York: Harper, 1928.

5428  _____. Fremont: Pathmaker of the West. New York: Longmans, Green, 1939.

5429  Royce, Josiah. "Fremont," Atlantic Monthly 66 (1890): 548-57.

5430  Smucker, Samuel M. The Life of Col. John Charles Fremont, and His Narrative of Explorations and Adventures, in Kansas, Nebraska, Oregon, and California. New York: Miller, Orton, Mulligan, 1856.

5431  Stenberg, Richard R. "Polk and Fremont, 1845-1846," Pacific Historical Review 7 (1938): 211-27.

5432  Upham, Charles W. Life, Explorations and Public Services of John Charles Fremont. Boston: Ticknor, Fields, 1856.

5433  Zabriskie, George A. "The Pathfinder," New York Historical Society Quarterly 31 (1947): 5-17.

*EDMUND P. GAINES

5434  Gaines, Edmund P. Memorial of Edmund Pendleton Gaines to the Senate and House of Representatives of the United States in Congress. Memphis: Enquirer Office, 1840.

5435  _____. To the Young Men of the States of the American Union, Civil and Military. N.p., 1838.

5436  "Seminole Campaign," Army and Navy Chronicle 4 (1837): 163-68.

5437  Silver, James W. "Edmund Pendleton Gaines and Frontier Problems, 1801-1849," Journal of Southern History 1 (1935): 320-44.

5438  _____. "General Edmund P. Gaines and the Protection of the Southwest Frontiers," Louisiana Historical Quarterly 20 (1937): 183-91.

5439  _____. "Edmund Pendleton Gaines: Railroad Propagandist," East Tennessee Historical Society Publications No. 9 (1937): 3-18.

5440  _____. "A Counter-proposal to the Indian Removal Policy of Andrew Jackson," Journal of Mississippi History 4 (1942): 207-15.

5441  Silver, James W. "General Gaines Meets Governor Troup: A State-Federal
      Clash in 1825," Georgia Historical Quarterly 27 (1943): 248-70.

*ALBERT GALLATIN

5442  Balinky, Alexander S. "Albert Gallatin, Navy Foe," Pennsylvania
      Magazine of History and Biography 82 (1958): 293-304.

5443  Burrows, Edwin G. "Albert Gallatin and the Political Economy of
      Republicanism." Ph. D. dissertation, Columbia University, 1974.

5444  Ferguson,  Russell J. "Albert Gallatin, Western Pennsylvania Polit-
      ician," Western Pennsylvania Historical Magzine 16 (1933): 183-95.

5445  Gallatin, Albert. The Speech of Albert Gallatin, a Representative
      from the County of Fayette, in the House of Representatives of the
      General Assembly of Pennsylvania. Philadelphia: W. Woodward, 1795.

5446  Merk, Frederick. Albert Gallatin and the Oregon Question: A Study
      in Anglo-American Diplomacy. Cambridge: Harvard University, 1956.

5447  Shenk, Sarah L. "Albert Gallatin and the Whiskey Insurrection."
      Master's Thesis, University of Pittsburgh, 1930.

*JOHN M. GAMBLE

5448  "An Old Time Fighting Marine," Marine Corps Gazette 13 (1928): 125-30.

5449  Kirk, Neville T. "The U.S. Marines enter the South Seas," United
      States Naval Institute Proceedings 81 (1955): 360-61.

5450  McClellan, Edwin N. "John M. Gamble," 35th Annual Report of the
      Hawaiian Historical Society (1927): 32-55.

PATRICK GASS

5451  Forrest, Earle R. Patrick Gass, Lewis and Clark's Last man.
      Independence, PA: A.M. Painter, 1950.

5452  _____. "Patrick Gass: Carpenter of the Lewis and Clark Expedition,"
      Missouri Historical Society Bulletin 4 (1948): 217-22.

5453  Gass, Patrick. A Journal of the Voyages and Travels of a Corps of
      Discovery under the Command of Captains Lewis and Clark of the Army
      of the United States. Philadelphia: Mathew Carey, 1810.

5454  Jacobs, John G. The Life and Times of Patrick Gass. Wellsburg, VA:
      Jacob, Smith, 1859.

5455  McGirr, Newman F. "Patrick Gass and his Journal of the Lewis and Clark
      Expedition," West Virginia History 3 (1942): 205-12.

5456  Smith, James S. "Sedulous Sergeant: Patrick Gass: An Original Biography
      by Direct Descendants," Montana 5 (1955): 20-27.

5457  Sparks, Edwin E. "Patrick Gass, American Explorer," Dial 37 (1904):
      270-71.

JAMES M. GILLIS

5458  Gould, Benjamin A. Biographical Notice of James Melville Gillis.
      Cambridge, MA: Welch, Bigelow, 1867.

## THOMAS W. GILMER

5459   Gilmer, Thomas W. "Letters of Thomas Walker Gilmer," Tyler's Historical and Genealogical Register 6 (1924-1925): 15-22, 187-99, 240-49.

5460   Speed, John G. "Thomas Walker Gilmer." In: The Gilmers in America. New York: Privately Printed, 1897, 108-15.

## SIMON GIRTY

5461   Beers, Paul R. "A Wild Beast in Human Form," American History Illustrated 3 (1968): 20-24.

5462   Bowersox, Charles A. Standard History of Williams County, Ohio 2 Vols. Chicago: Lewis Publishing Co., 1920. Vol. 1, 39-49.

5463   Boyd, Thomas. Simon Girty, the White Savage. New York: Minton, Balach, 1928.

5464   Butterfield, Consul W. History of the Girtys; being a Concise Account of the Girty Brothers-Thomas, Simon, James and George. Cincinnati: R. Clarke, 1890.

5465   Cattermole, E.G. Famous American Frontiersmen, Pioneers and Scouts; the Vanguards of American Civilization. Chicago: M.A. Donohue, 1890, 87-99.

5466   Chauvin, Francois X. Simon Girty (1741-1818). An Address before the Descendants of Simon Girty at Lakeside Park, Kingsville, Ontario, September 5th, 1932. Windsor, ON: Sequin Brothers, N.d.

5467   "A Clash of Cultures: Simon Girty and the Struggle for the Frontier," Timeline 2 (1985): 2-17.

5468   Gallagher, William D. "Girty, the Renegade," Hesperian 1 (1838): 343-49, 423-27.

5469   Hall, William M. Reminiscences and Sketches, Historical and Biographical. Harrisburg, PA: Meyers Printing House, 1890, 173-81.

5470   McEldowney, John C. History of Wetzel County, West Virginia. N.p., 1901.

5471   Macleod, J. "A Sketch of the Life of Simon Girty," Michigan Pioneer 7 (1886): 123-29.

5472   Nye, Russell B. A Baker's Dozen: Thirteen Unusual Americans. East Lansing, MI: Michigan State University Press, 1956.

5473   Ranck, George W. "Girty, the White Indian," Magazine of American History 15 (1886): 256-77.

5474   Riddell, William R. "Simon Girty's Marriage," Canadian Magazine 58 (1921): 169-71.

5475   Rodgers, T.L. "Simon Girty and Some of His Contemporaries," Western Pennsylvania Historical Magazine 8 (1925): 148-58.

5476   Scomp, Henry A. "The Girty Legends and Romances," Magazine of History 12 (1910): 243-52; 13 (1911): 219-29.

5477  "Simon Girty," Notes and Queries 1 (1894): 66-70; 2 (1895): 366-68.

CHARLES GORDON

5478  Calderhead, William R. "A Strange Career in a Young Navy," Maryland
Historical Magazine 72 (1977): 18-41.

5479  Radoff, Morris L. "Captain Gordon of the 'Constellation'," Ibid
67 (1972): 389-418.

CHARLES GRATIOT

5480  Bale, Florence G. "When the Gratiots Came to Galena," Illinois State
Historical Society Journal 24 (1932): 671-82.

5481  Darley, John F. Personal Recollections of Many Prominent People.
St. Louis: G.I. Jones, 1880.

5482  Jenks, William L. "Fort Gratiot and its Builder, Gen. Charles Gratiot,"
Michigan Historical Magazine 4 (1920): 141-55.

5483  "Mrs. Adele P. Gratiot's Narrative," Wisconsin Historical Society
Collections 10 (1888): 261-75.

5484  Myer, May W. "Charles Gratiots's Land Claim Problems," Missouri
Historical Society Bulletin 21 (1965): 237-44.

5485  Quaife, Milo M., ed. "Journals and Reports of the Blach Hawk War,"
Mississippi Valley Historical Review 12 (1925): 392-409.

5486  Smith, Mildred L. General Charles Gratiot: Acres and Avenues Bear
His Name. Ithaca, MI: Gratiot County Historical and Genealogical
Society, 1987.

5487  Washburne, E.H. "Col. Henry Gratiot," Wisconsin Historical Society
Collections 10 (1888): 235-60.

DUNCAN N. INGRAHAM

5488  Bradlee, Francis B. A Forgotten Chapter in Our Naval History: A
Sketch of the Career of Duncan Nathaniel Ingraham, Commander, U.S.N.,
and Commodore, C.S.N. Sale, MA: Essex Institute, 1923.

JAMES HALL

5489  Hall, James. Trial and Defense of First Lieutenant James Hall of the
Ordnance Department, United States Army. Pittsburgh: Eichbaum,
Johnston, 1820.

5490  _____. "Reminiscences of the Last War," Illinois Monthly Magazine 2
(1832): 202-07.

5491  _____. "A Reminiscence," Knickbocker Magazine 6 (1835): 10-19.

5492  Randall, Randolph. James Hall: Spokesman of the New West. Columbus:
Ohio State University Press, 1964, 26-26.

HENRY W. HALLECK

5493  McGinty, Brian. "Old Brains' in the New West," American History
Illustrated 13 (1978): 10-19.

## ALEXANDER HAMILTON

5494  Bates, Charles F. "Alexander Hamilton's Military Plans," Infantry Journal 21 (1922): 409-12.

5495  Bemis, Samuel F. "Alexander Hamilton and the Limitation of Armaments," Pacific Review 3 (1922): 587-602.

5496  Cooke, Jacob E. Alexander Hamilton. New York: Charles Scribner's Sons, 1982.

5497  Duncan, Louis I. "Alexander Hamilton's Plan for a Military Establishment," Military Surgeon 70 (1932): 488-91.

5498  Hamilton, John C., ed. History of the Republic of the United States as Traced in the Writings of Alexander Hamilton. 7 Vols. New York: D. Appleton, 1857-1865.

5499  Hunt, Richard C. "Alexander Hamilton and the Regular Naval Establishment," United States Naval Institute Proceedings 83 (1957): 806-07.

5500  Johnson, Helene V. "Alexander Hamilton and the British Orientation of American Foreign Policy, 1783-1803." Ph. D. dissertation, University of Southern California, 1963.

5501  Lodge, Henry C., ed. The Works of Alexander Hamilton. 12 Vols. New York: G.P. Putnam's Sons, 1904.

5502  Mitchell, Broadus. Alexander Hamilton: The National Experience, 1788-1804. New York: Macmillan, 1962.

5503  Nelson, John R. "Hamilton and Gallatin: Political Economy and Policy Making in the New Nation, 1789-1812." Ph. D. dissertation, Northern Illinois University, 1979.

5504  Syrett, Harold C. and Jacob E. Cooke, eds. The Papers of Alexander Hamilton. 26 Vols. New York: Columbia University Press, 1977.

5505  Wills, Merlin V. "Hamilton and the Whiskey Insurrection." Master's Thesis, University of Pittsburgh, 1930.

## *WADE HAMPTON

5506  Bridwell, Ronald E. "The South's Wealthiest Planter: Wade Hampton I of South Carolina, 1754-1835." Ph. D. dissertation, University of South Carolina, 1980.

## JOHN HAMTRAMCK

5507  Bald, Clever F. "Colonel John Francis Hamtramck," Indiana Magazine of History 44 (1948): 335-54.

5508  Catlin, George B. "Col. John F. Hamtramck," Ibid 26 (1930): 237-52.

5509  "Letters of Col. John F. Hamtramck pertaining to Wayne's Campaign," Michigan Pioneer 34 (1904): 734-40.

5510  "Letter of Colonel John F. Hamtramck to General Charles Scott," Magazine of History 4 (1906): 363.

5511  O'Hair, Mary C. "The Rock and the Hospital on the Wabash," Indiana
      History Bulletin 35 (1958): 99-107.

5512  Thornbrough, Gayle, ed. Outpost on the Wabash, 1787-1791: Letters
      of Brigadier General Josiah Harmar and Major John Francis Hamtramck.
      Indiana Historical Society Publications 19 (1957): 7-305.

5513  Van Cleve, John W., ed. "Letters of Colonel Hamtramck," American
      Pioneer 2 (1843): 293-96, 388-94.

5514  Willis, Richard S. "Colonel John F. Hamtramck," Burton Historical
      Collection Leaflet 1 (1922): 17-24.

## WILLIAM J. HARDEE

5515  Hughes, Nathaniel C. General William J. Hardee, Old Reliable.
      Baton Rouge: Louisiana State University Press, 1965.

## JOHN HARDIN

5516  Blue, Herbert T. Centennial History of Hardin County, Ohio. Canton:
      Rogers-Miller Co., 1933.

5517  Bogart, William H. Daniel Boone, and the Hunters of Kentucky. New York:
      Lee, Shepard, Dillingham, 1872.

5518  Sanders, Robert S. "Colonel John Hardin and His Letters to His Wife,
      1792," Filson Club Quarterly 49 (1965): 5-12.

5519  Walworth, Mansfield T. "Colonel John Hardin," Historical Magazine 5
      (1869): 233-37.

## JOSIAH HARMAR

5520  "General Harmar's Journal," Ohio Archaeological and Historical Society
      Quarterly 20 (1911): 89-96.

5521  Harmar, Josiah. Proceedings of the Court of Inquiry held at the
      Special Request of General Josiah Harmar to Investigate His Conduct
      as Commanding Officer of the Expedition Against the Miami Indians
      in 1790. Philadelphia: John Fenno, 1791.

5522  Harmar, Josiah. "Letters of General Josiah Harmar and Others,"
      Memoirs of the Historical Society of Pennsylvania 7 (1860): 413-77.

5523  Heart, Johnathan. Journal of Captain Johnathan Heart on the March
      with His Company from Connecticut to Fort Pitt, in Pittsburgh,
      Pennsylvania, from the Seventh of September to the Twelfth of
      October, 1785, inclusive, to which is Added the Dickinson-Harmar
      Correspondence of 1784-5. Albany: J. Munsell's Sons, 1885.

5524  Khasigian, Amos. "The Military Career of Josiah Harmar." Master's
      Thesis, University of Southern California, 1958.

5525  Peckham, Howard H. "The Papers of General Josiah Harmar," Michigan
      Alumnus Quarterly Review 43 (1937): 428-32.

5526  Smith, Dwight L. "Josiah Harmar, Diplomatic Courier," Pennsylvania
      Magazine of History and Biography 87 (1963): 420-30.

5527  Thornbrough, Gayle, ed. Outpost on the Wabash, 1787-1791: Letters
      of Brigadier General Josiah Harmar and Major John Francis Hamtramck.
      Indiana Historical Society Publications 19 (1957): 7-305.

5528  Warren, Louis A. "A Harmar Sesquientennial Symposium," Ohio Archaeo-
      logical and Historical Society Quarterly 50 (1941): 47-58.

## WILLIAM S. HARNEY

5529  Adams, George R. "General William Selby Harney: Frontier Soldier,
      1800-1899." Ph. D. dissertation, University of Arizona, 1983.

5530  Clow, Richmond L. "William S. Harney." In" Paul A. Hutton, ed.
      Soldiers West: Biographies from the Military Frontier. Lincoln:
      University of Nebraska Press, 1987, 42-58.

5531  "Expedition Through the Everglades by One who was With Col. Harney."
      In: Hester M. Walker. The Pathetic and Lamentable Narrative of Miss
      Perine, on the Massacre and Destruction of Indian Key Village in
      August, 1840. Philadelphia: E.C. Gill, 1840.

5532  "Florida War-Correspondents," Army and Navy Chronicle 7 (1838): 329-30.

5533  Griswold, Oliver. "William Selby Harney: Indian Fighter," Tequesta
      9 (1949): 73-80.

5534  Johnston, Charles H. Famous Scouts, Including Trappers, Pioneers and
      Soldiers of the Frontier. Boston: L.C. Page, 1910, 211-31.

5535  Kelsey, D.M. Our Pioneer Heroes and Their Daring Deeds. Philadelphia:
      Scammell, 1890, 449-74.

5536  Reavis, Logan V. The Life and Military Services of General William
      Selby Harney. St. Louis: Bryan, Brand, 1878.

## *BENJAMIN HAWKINS

5537  Henri, Florette. The Southern Indians and Benjamin Hawkins.
      Norman: University of Oklahoma Press, 1986.

## ARCHIBALD HENDERSON

5538  Donnelly, Ralph W. "Archibald Henderson, Marine," Virginia Cavalcade
      20 (1971): 39-47.

5539  Jenkins, James C. "Brigadier General Archibald Henderson, U.S.M.C.,"
      Marine Corps Gazette 25 (1941): 18, 50-54.

5540  Metcalfe, Clyde H. "When our Commandant took the Field," Ibid 20
      (1936): 35-59.

5541  Pierce, Philip N. and Frank O. Hough. "Archibald Henderson: An Era,"
      Ibid 44 (1960): 28-33.

## ETHAN A. HITCHCOCK

5542  Cohen, I. Bernard. Ethan Allen Hitchcock, Soldier, Humanitarian,
      Scholar," American Antiquarian Society Proceedings 61 (1951): 30-136.

5543  Croffut, W.A., ed. Fifty Years in Camp and Field: The Diary of Major-
      General Ethan Allen Hitchcock, U.S.A. New York: G.P. Putnam's, 1909.

5544  Foreman, Grant, ed. A Traveler in Indian Territory: The Journal of
      Ethan Allen Hitchcock. Cedar Rapids, IA: Torch Press, 1930.

5545  Hitchcock, Ethan A. "A Crisis of Conscience." In: Peter Karsten, ed.
      The Military in America: From Colonial Era to the Present. New York:
      Free Press, 1980, 111-16.

5546  Leger, Mary C. "A Study of the Public Career of Ethan Allen Hitchcock."
      Ph. D. dissertation, City University of New York, 1971.

5547  "Letter from Captain Hitchcock," Army and Navy Chronicle 2 (1836):
      380-81.

5548  Robinson, H.E. "General Ethan Allen Hitchcock," Missouri Historical
      Review 2 (1908): 173-87.

5549  True, Marshall M., ed. "Ethan Allen Hitchcock and the Texas Rebellion:
      a Letter Home," Vermont History 45 (1977): 102-06.

5550  "War in Florida," Army and Navy Chronicle 2 (1835): 225-27.

                              DAVID HOLMES

5551  Conrad, David. "David Holmes, First Governor of Mississippi,"
      Mississippi Historical Society Publications 4 (1921): 234-57.

5552  Horton, William B. "The Life of David Holmes." Master's Thesis,
      University of Colorado, 1935.

5553  McCain, William D. "The Administration of David Holmes, Governor of
      the Mississippi Territory, 1809-1817," Journal of Mississippi History
      29 (1967): 328-47.

5554  Melton, Elizabeth M. "The Public career of David Holmes, 1809-1820."
      Master's Thesis, Emory University, 1966.

5555  Smith, Robert. "Letter to David Holmes Concerning the Proposed Attack
      on Mobile, 1810," Gulfstream Historical Magazine 1 (1903): 441-42.

                          THEOPHILUS H. HOLMES

5556  Foreman, Carolyn T. "Lieutenant General Theophilus Hunter Holmes,"
      Chronicles of Oklahoma 35 (1957): 425-34.

                              *ISAAC HULL

5557  Anderson, Leslie J. "Isaac Hull Memorabilia at the U.S.S. Constitution
      Museum," Magazine of Antiques 126 (1984): 119-23.

5558  "Arrival of the Frigate Constitution at Malta," Army and Navy
      Chronicle 2 (1836): 295-96.

5559  Brown, John H. "Isaac Hull." In: American Naval Heroes. Boston:
      Brown, 1899, 269-76.

5560  Dunn, Lucius C. "Some Unpublished History of Old Glory," United States
      Naval Institute Proceedings 61 (1935): 965-72.

5561  Eller, Ernest M. "Is Defeat Inevitable?" Ibid 60 (1934): 1201-13.

5562  Hamilton, John D. "The Isaac Hull Collection," Man at Arms 5 (1983): 31-36.

5563  Hull, Isaac. "I. Hull to Nathaniel Silsbee," Massachusetts Historical Society Proceedings 45 (1912): 29-30.

5564  _____. Minutes of Proceedings of the Court of Inquiry into the Official Conduct of Capt. Isaac Hull, as Commandant of the United States Navy Yard at Charlestown, in the State of Massachusetts. Washington, DC: Davis, Force, 1822.

5565  Lewis, Charles. "Isaac Hull and Old Ironsides." In: Famous American Naval Officers. Boston: L.C. Page, 1924, 71-99.

5566  Maloney, Linda M. "Isaac Hull: Commodore in Transition." In: James C. Bradford, ed. Command Under Sail: Makers of American Naval Tradition. Annapolis: Naval Institute Press, 1984, 251-72.

5567  _____. The Captain from Connecticut: The Life and Naval Times of Isaac Hull. Boston: Northeastern University Press, 1986.

5568  Richmond, Helen. Isaac Hull, A Forgotten American Hero. Boston: U.S.S. Constitution Museum, 1983.

5569  Russo, John P. "Hull's First Victory: One Painting, Three Famous Men," American Neptune 25 (1965): 29-34.

5570  Shelton, J.D. "Birthplace of Commodore Isaac Hull," Harper's Monthly Magazine 85 (1892): 30-36.

5571  Ward, G.C. "A Seafarer's Legacy," Americana 11 (1983): 26-32.

ANDREW A. HUMPHREYS

5572  Humphreys, Andrew H. "Historical Sketch of the Corps of Engineers." In: Historical Papers Relating to the Corps of Engineers and to Engineer Troops of the United States Army. Washington, DC: Press of the Engineer School, 1904, 1-54.

5573  Humphreys, Henry H. Andrew Atkinson Humphreys, a Biography. Philadelphia: John C. Winston, 1924.

JOSHUA HUMPHREYS

5574  Brewington, Marion V. "The Design of our First Frigates," American Neptune 8 (1948): 11-25.

5575  Chapelle, Howard I. "The Design of American Frigates of the Revolution and Joshua Humphreys," Ibid 9 (1949): 161-68.

5576  Dorsey, Ella L. "Our First Naval Constructor," DAR Magazine 62 (1928): 211-16.

5577  Faris, John T. The Romance of Forgotten Men. New York: Harper & Bros., 1928.

5578  Humphreys, Henry H. "Who Build the First United States Navy," Journal of American History 10 (1916): 49-89.

5579  Humphreys, Joshua. "Letters from Joshua Humphreys," Pennsylvania Magazine of History and Biography 30 (1906): 376-78, 503.

5580  Pinhowski, Edward. "Joshua Humphreys." In: Forgotten Fathers.
      Philadelphia: Sunshine Press, 1953, 273-87.

5581  Simpson, Henry. The Lives of Eminent Philadelphians, now Deceased.
      Philadelphia: W. Brotherhead, 1859.

DAVID HUNTER

5582  Schenck, Robert C. "Major General David Hunter," Magazine of American
      History 17 (1887): 138-52.

*ANDREW JACKSON

5583  Belohlavek, John M. Andrew Jackson and the Malaysian Pirates: A
      Question of Diplomacy and Politics," Tennessee Historical Quarterly
      36 (1977): 19-29.

5584  Chace, James and Caleb Carr. "The Odd Couple who Won Florida and Half
      the West," Smithsonian 19 (1988): 134-60.

5585  Clark, Ana. "Jackson's Administration of Florida," Florida Historical
      Quarterly 5 (1926): 44-49.

5586  "Correspondence between Major General Jackson and Brevet Major General
      Scott, on the Subject of an Order Bearing date the 22nd of April, 1817,"
      Army and Navy Life 9 (1906): 83-92.

5587  Davis, T. Frederick. "Pioneer Florida: Jackson's Premature
      Proclamation," Florida Historical Quarterly 24 (1945): 39-44.

5588  Doherty, Herbert J. "The Governorship of Andrew Jackson," Ibid 33
      (1954): 3-31.

5589  Dovell, Junius. "The Influence of Andrew Jackson on the History of
      Florida." Master's Thesis, Stetson University, 1934.

5590  Eaton, John H. Life of Major General Andrew Jackson, Containing a
      Brief History of the Seminole War, and Cession of the Government of
      Florida. Philadelphia: McCarty, Davis, 1828.

5591  Bassett, John. "Jackson in Florida." In: Life of Andrew Jackson.
      New York: Macmillan, 1931, 233-93.

5592  Bruce, H.A. "Andrew Jackson and the Acquisition of Florida," Outlook
      88 (1908): 730-42.

5593  Jackson, Andrew. Memorial of Major General Andrew Jackson. Washington:
      Gales, Seaton, 1820.

5594  _____. "General Jackson's Proclaimation to the Negroes," Massachusetts
      Historical Society Proceedings 6 (1962): 244-47.

5595  _____. "Letter to Richard K. Call," Gulf Stream Historical Magazine
      1 (1903): 438-39.

5596  James, Marquis. "The Florida Adventure." In: Andrew Jackson, the Border
      Captain. Indianapolis: Bobbs-Merrill, 1933, 285-301.

5597  McGovern, James R., ed. Andrew Jackson in Florida. Pensacola: Jackson
      Day Sesquicentennial Committee, 1971.

5598   McGuire, Phillip. "Andrew Jackson Revisited: An Analysis of Jackson's Views Toward his Slaves and Black Soldiers," Journal of Social and Behavioral Sciences 28 (1982): 39-45.

5599   McQueen, Ray A. "The Role of Andrew Jackson in the Acquisition of the Floridas." Ph. D. dissertation, University of Pittsburgh, 1942.

5600   Moser, Harold D. and Sharon MacPherson, eds. The Papers of Andrew Jackson. Vol. 2: 1804-1813. Knoxville: University of Tennessee Press, 1984.

5601   Parton, James. "Jackson in Florida." In: The Life of Andrew Jackson. 3 Vols. Boston: Houghton, Mifflin, 1888. Vol. 2, 391-531.

5602   Perkins, Samuel. General Jackson's Conduct in the Seminole War Delineated in a History of that Period, affording Conclusive Reasons Why he should not be the Next President. Brooklyn: Advertiser, 1828.

5603   Remini, Robert V. "The First Seminole War." In: Andrew Jackson and the Course of American Empire. New York: Harpers, Row, 1977, 351-77.

5604   Rogin, Michael P. Fathers and Children: Andrew Jackson and the Subjugation of the American Indian. New York: A.A. Knopf, 1975.

5605   Thomas, David Y. "Jackson's Attitude in the Seminole War," American Historical Magazine 9 (1904): 145-52.

5606   Wert, Jeffery. "Old Hickory and the Seminoles," American History Illustrated 15 (1980): 28-35.

*THOMAS JEFFERSON

5607   Adams, Henry. History of the United States of American During the Administration of Thomas Jefferson. 9 Vols. New York: Albert and Charles Boni, 1930.

5608   Adams, Mary P. "Jefferson's Reaction to the Treaty of San Ildefonso," Journal of Southern History 21 (1955): 173-88.

5609   Allen, Milford F. "Thomas Jefferson and the Louisiana-Arkansas Frontier," Arkansas Historical Quarterly 20 (1961): 39-64.

5610   Baker, Denise R. "Thomas Jefferson and the West." Master's Thesis, Western Kentucky University, 1981.

5611   Bergh, Albert E., ed. The Writings of Thomas Jefferson. Washington: Thomas Jefferson Memorial Association, 1903-1907.

5612   Borne, O.S. "Jefferson and the Dark Days of '14," National Magazine 11 (1900): 551-56.

5613   Boyd, Julian P. The Papers of Thomas Jefferson. 19 Vols. Princeton: Princeton University Press, 1950-.

5614   Chuinard, Eldon G. "Thomas Jefferson and the Corps of Discovery: Creating the Lewis and Clark Expedition," American West 12 (1975): 4-13.

5615   Chinard, Gilbert, ed. The Correspondence of Jefferson and Dupont de Nemours. Baltimore: Johns Hopkins University Press, 1931.

5616 Cutright, Paul R. "Jefferson's Instructions to Lewis and Clark," _Missouri Historical Society Bulletin_ 22 (1965): 302-20.

5617 Ford, Paul L., ed. _The Works of Thomas Jefferson._ 12 Vols. New York: Putnam, 1904-1905.

5618 Forman, Sidney. "Thomas Jefferson on Universal Military Training," _Military Affairs_ 11 (1947): 177-78.

5619 Gray, Francis C. _Thomas Jefferson in 1814; Being an Account of a Visit to Monticello, Virginia._ Boston: Club of Odd Volumes, 1924.

5620 Hamilton, J.G. "The Pacifism of Thomas Jefferson," _Virginia Quarterly Review_ 31 (1955): 607-20.

5621 Hoffman, Thomas J. "Jefferson and the West Through the Ordnance of 1784." Master's Thesis, Ohio State University, 1932.

5622 Jackson, Donald. _Thomas Jefferson and the Stony Mountains: Exploring the West from Monticello._ Urbana: University of Illinois Press, 1981.

5623 "The Jefferson Papers," _Massachusetts Historical Society Collections_ 1 (1900): 1-378.

5624 Jefferson, Thomas. _Message from the President of the United States Respecting the Application of Hamet Caramalli, Ex-Bashaw of Tripoli, January 13, 1806._ Washington, DC: A. & G. Way, 1806.

5625 ____. _Message from the President of the United States, Communicating Discoveries Made in Exploring the Missouri, Red River, and Washita._ Washington, DC: A. and G. Way, 1806.

5626 Kimball, Marie G., ed. "Unpublished Correspondence of Mmme de Sted with Thomas Jefferson," _North American Review_ 208 (1918): 63-71.

5627 Lacey, Alexander B. "Jefferson and the Congress: Congressional Methods and Politics, 1801-1809." Ph. D. dissertation, University of Virginia, 1964.

5628 Landerholm, Carl. "Jefferson's Interest in Western Exploration." Master's Thesis, University of Oregon, 1929.

5629 Leiner, Frederick C. "The Whimsical Phylosophic President and his Gunboats," _American Neptune_ 43 (1983): 245-66.

5630 Losse, Winifred J. "Thomas Jefferson and the West." Master's Thesis, University of Virginia, 1943.

5631 Lydon, James G. "Thomas Jefferson and the Mathurins," _Catholic Historical Review_ 49 (1963): 192-202.

5632 McCarthy, Richard E. "Some Philosophical Foundations of Jefferson's Foreign Policy." Ph. D. dissertation, St. John's University, 1958.

5633 Malone, Dumas. _Jefferson the President: First Term, 1801-1805._ Boston: Little, Brown, 1970.

5634 ____. _Jefferson the President: Second Term, 1805-1809._ Boston: Little, Brown, 1974.

5635   Macleod, Julia H. "Jefferson and the Navy: A Defense," Huntington
       Library Quarterly 8 (1945): 153-84.

5636   Mead, Edwin D. "Washington, Jefferson and Franklin on War," World
       Peace Foundation Pamphlet 3 (1913): 1-15.

5637   Norton, Paul F. "Jefferson's Plans for Mothballing the Frigates,"
       United States Naval Institute Proceedings 82 (1956): 737-41.

5638   O'Malley, Richard F. "The Attitude of Thomas Jefferson Toward American
       Naval Affairs, 1775-1826." Master's Thesis, University of Notre Dame,
       1959.

5639   Owen, Joanne C. "Thomas Jefferson and the Barbary Problem: A Study
       of his Use of Force Against Barbary Powers." Master's Thesis,
       Uuniversity of Georgia, 1973.

5640   Patton, John S. "Thomas Jefferson's Contributions to Natural History,"
       Natural History 19 (1919): 405-10.

5641   Rooney, William E. "Thomas Jefferson and the New Orleans Marine
       Hospital," Journal of Southern History 22 (1956): 167-82.

5642   Sears, Louis M. Jefferson and the Embargo. Durham, NC: Duke University
       Press, 1927.

5643   Skeen, Carl E. "Jefferson and the West, 1789-1808." Master's Thesis,
       Ohio State University, 1960.

5644   Stuart, Reginald C. "Thomas Jefferson and the Origins of War,"
       Peace and Change 4 (1977): 22-27.

5645   _____. "Encounter with Mars: Thomas Jefferson's View of War."
       Ph. D. dissertation, University of Florida, 1974.

### *THOMAS S. JESUP

5646   "General Jesup, the Secretary of War, and the Military Academy,"
       Army and Navy Chronicle 6 (1838): 137-40.

5647   Jesup, Thomas S. Seminole Saga: The Jesup Report. Fort Myers, FL:
       Island Press, 1973.

### ALBERT S. JOHNSTON

5648   Johnston, William P. The Life of General Albert Sidney Johnston.
       New York: D. Appleton, 1879.

5649   Moore, Avery C. Destiny's Soldier. San Francisco: Fearon Publishers,
       1958.

5650   Roland, Charles P. Albert Sidney Johnston, Soldier of Three Republics.
       Austin: University of Texas Press, 1964.

### *JACOB JONES

5651   Brown, John H. "Jacob Jones." In: American Naval Heroes. Boston:
       Brown, 1899, 277-84.

## *THOMAS Ap C. JONES

5652  "Biographical Sketch of Thomas ap Catesby Jones," Military and Naval Magazine 3 (1834): 127-34.

5653  Bradley, Harold W. "Thomas ap Catesby Jones and the Hawaiian Islands, 1826-1827," Hawaiian Historical Society Report 39 (1931): 17-30.

5654  Bradley, Udolpho T. "Thomas ap Catesby Jones: A Personality of the Days of Sail," United States Naval Institute Proceedings 69 (1933): 1154-56.

5655  Gapp, Frank W. "The Kind-eyed Chief': Forgotten Champion of Hawaii's Freedom," Hawaiian Journal of History 19 (1985): 101-21.

5656  Johnson, Robert E. "A Long Chase," United States Naval Institute Proceedings 85 (1959): 144-46.

5657  ____. "Commodore and Virginia Planter," Virginia Cavalcade 16 (1967): 4-11.

5658  Jones, Thomas Ap C. "A Visit to Los Angeles in 1843," Historical Society of Southern California Quarterly 17 (1935): 123-34; 18 (1936): 7-19.

5659  ____. "Letter of Com. Jones Relative to the Capture of Monterey," Army and Navy Chronicle and Scientific Repository 1 (1843): 480-86, 526-34.

5660  ____. "The Sandwich Islands," Military and Naval Magazine 6 (1835): 282-88.

5661  Threlkeld, Georgia M. "The Three Pacific Cruises of Thomas ap Catesby Jones." Master's Thesis, University of Southern California, 1961.

5662  Workman, Gilbert. "A Forgotten Firebrand," United States Naval Institute Proceedings 94 (1968): 79-87.

## *WILLIAM JONES

5663  Owsley, Frank L. "William Jones." In: Paolo Coletta, ed. American Secretaries of the Navy. 2 Vols. Annapolis: Naval Institute Press, 1980. Vol. 1, 101-10.

## LAWRENCE KEARNY

5664  Alden, Carroll S. Lawrence Kearny: Sailor Diplomat. Princeton: Princeton University Press, 1936.

5665  Hanks, Robert J. "Commodore Lawrence Kearny, the Diplomatic Seaman," United States Naval Institute Proceedings 96 (1970): 70-72.

5666  Dennett, Tyler. "How Old is American Policy in the Far East," Pacific Review 2 (1921): 463-74.

5667  Kearny, Thomas. "Commodore Lawrence Kearny and the Open Door and Most Favorite Nation Policy in China in 1842 to 1843," New Jersey Historical Society Proceedings 50 (1932): 162-90.

5668  Kearny, Thomas. "The Tsiang Documents," Chinese Social and Political Science Review 16 (1932): 75-104.

5669 Kendall, David W. "The Navy in the Orient in 1842," United States Naval Institute Proceedings 68 (1942): 645-50.

5670 "Lawrence Kearny," United States Magazine and Democratic Review 28 (1851): 260-69.

5671 McSweeney, Edward F. "Lawrence Kearny, 1789-1868," American Irish Historical Society Journal 22 (1923): 108-22.

PHILIP KEARNY

5672 DePeyster, John W. "A Character Sketch of Phil Kearny," Volunteer 1 (1869): 1-16.

5673 ____. Personal and Military History of Philip Kearny, Major General, United States Volunteers. New York: Rice, Gage, 1869.

5674 Flynn, David M. "Philip Kearny," American Irish Historical Society Journal 14 (1915): 127-39.

5675 "General Philip Kearny," Ibid 32 (1941): 105-10.

5676 Glazier, Willard. Heroes of Three Wars. Philadelphia: Hubbard Bros., 1884, 387-90.

5677 Kearny, Thomas. General Philip Kearny, Battle Soldier of Five Wars. New York: G.P. Putnam's Sons, 1937.

5678 Kearny, Thomas. "Philip Kearny (1815-1862): Soldier of America-Soldier of France," Legion D'Honneur 7 (1936): 115-23.

5679 Parker, Cortlandt. Philip Kearny: Soldier and Patriot. Newark, NJ: N.p., 1868.

5680 Reid, Mayne. "A Dashing Dragoon; the Murat of the American Army." In: Philip Kearny. Service with the French Troops in Africa. New York: N.p., 1844, 86-95.

STEPHEN W. KEARNY

5681 Bradley, Glenn D. Winning the Southwest; a Story of Conquest. Chicago: A.C. McClurg, 1912, 31-43.

5682 Clarke, Dwight L. Stephen Watts Kearny: Soldier of the West. Norman: University of Oklahoma Press, 1962.

5683 Crimmins, Martin L. "General Stephen Watts Kearny," Frontier Times 9 (1932): 145-50.

5684 Hughes, Willis B. "The Army and Stephen Watts Kearny in the West, 1819-1846." Ph. D. dissertation, University of Minnesota, 1955.

5685 Kearny, Stephen W. "An Expedition Across Iowa in 1820," Annals of Iowa 10 (1912): 343-71.

5686 ____. "A Group of Kearny Letters," New Mexico Historical Review 5 (1930): 17-37.

5687 ____. Report of a Summer campaign to the Rocky Mountains &c. in 1843. 29th Cong. 1st Session Senate Executive Document 1, Serial 470, 210-20.

5688 Kearny, Thomas. "General Stephen Watts Kearny," New Jersey Historical Society Proceedings 2 (1926): 90-93.

5689 Petersen, William J. "Stephen Watts Kearny," Palimpsest 12 (1931): 289-97.

5690 _____. "Kearny in Iowa," Ibid 44 (1963): 1-47.

5691 Porter, Valentine M. "Journal of Stephen Watts Kearny," Missouri Historical Society Collections 3 (1908): 8-29, 99-131.

5692 Smith, Eudora. "Stephen Watts Kearny as a Factor in the Westward Movement, 1812-1834." Master's Thesis, Washington University, St. Louis, 1925.

5693 Taylor, Mendell L. "The Western Services of Stephen Watts Kearny, 1815-1848." Ph. D. dissertation, University of Oklahoma, 1944.

5694 _____. "The Western Services of Stephen Watts Kearny, 1815-1848," New Mexico Historical Review 21 (1946): 171-84.

5695 Twitchell, Ralph E. "Major General Stephen Watts Kearny." In: Old Santa Fe: The Story of New Mexico's Ancient Capital. Santa Fe: Santa Fe New Mexican Publishing Corporation, 1925, 245-74.

KEOKUK

5696 Auman, Francis R. "The Watchful Fox," Palimpsest 9 (1928): 121-32.

5697 _____. "Indian Oratory," Ibid 9 (1928): 149-54.

5698 _____. and J.E. Briggs. "Keokuk," Ibid 39 (1958): 289-320.

5699 Briggs, John E. "The Council on the Iowa," Ibid 9 (1928): 133-48.

5700 Clemens, Orion. City of Keokuk in 1856. Keokuk, IA: O. Clemens, 1856.

5701 Cole, Cyrenus. Iowa Through the Years. Iowa City: State Historical Society of Iowa, 1940, 63-98.

5702 Finley, James B. Life Among the Indians, or, Personal Reminiscences and Historical Incidents Illustrative of Indian Life and Character. Cincinnati: Methodist Book Concern, 1857, 531-43.

5703 Fulton, A.R. The Red Man of Iowa. Des Moines, IA: Mills, 1882, 231-47.

5704 Lockwood, Myna. Indian Chief: The Story of Keokuk. New York: Oxford University Press, 1943.

5705 McKenny, Thomas L. History of the Indian Tribes of North America. Philadelphia: E.C. Biddle, 1836-1838. Vol. 3, 115-49.

5706 Metcalfe, John R. "Who Should Rule at Home? Native American Politics and Indian-White Relations," Journal of American History 61 (1974): 651-65.

5707 Richman, Irving B. John Brown Among the Quakers and Other Sketches. Des Moines, IA: Historical Department of Iowa, 1904, 79-119.

5708 "Sketch of Keokuk," Hesperian 1 (1838): 199-204.

## *FRANCIS S. KEY

5709 Meyer, Sam. "Francis Scott Key: He Gave the Nation its Anthem," CAMP Periodical 25 (1987): 35-45.

5710 Mullaly, Frank R. "A Forgotten letter of Francis Scott Key," Maryland Historical Magazine 55 (1960): 359-60.

5711 "Origin of the Star Spangled Banner," Historical Magzine 5 (1861): 282-83.

## HENRY KNOX

5712 "A Biographical Sketch of Major General Henry Knox," Portfolio 6 (1811): 99-108.

5713 Brooks, Noah. Henry Knox, A Soldier of the Revolution. New York: G.P. Putnam's Sons, 1900.

5714 Callahan, North. Henry Knox: General Washington's General. New York: New York: A.S. Barnes, 1958.

5715 Denzil, Justin F. Champion of Liberty, Henry Knox. New York: Julian Messner, 1969.

5716 Diffenderffer, F.R. "A General Knox Letter," Lancaster County Historical Society Papers 3 (1898-1899): 212-15.

5717 Drake, Francis S. Life and Correspondence of Henry Knox. Boston: Samuel Drake, 1873.

5718 _____. "Henry Knox," New England Historical and Genealogical Register 34 (1880): 347-58.

5719 Dunnack, Henry. "General Henry Knox, American Patriot," DAR Magazine 59 (1925): 354-57.

5720 Dyer, Weston A. "The Influence of Henry Knox on the Formation of American Indian Policy in the Northwest Department, 1786-1795." Ph. D. dissertation, Ball State University, 1970.

5721 Elliott, Charles W. "Bookseller in Arms," Infantry Journal 47 (1940): 580-91.

5722 Griffith, Thomas. Major General Henry Knox and the Last Heirs to Montpelier. Lewiston, ME: Twin City Printing, 1965.

5723 Grose, Ada M. "Major General Henry Knox, Master of Montpelier," Down East 3 (1957): 24-27, 57-59.

5724 Historical Records Survey. Massachusetts. A Calender of the General Henry Knox Papers, Chamberlain Collection, Boston Public Library. Boston: Historical Records Survey, 1939.

5725 Knollberg, Bernard. "John Adams, Knox and Washington," American Antiquarian Society Proceedings 56 (1946): 207-38.

5726 Otis, Harrison G. "Major General Henry Knox," New England Historical and Genealogical Register 30 (1876): 360-66.

5727 Pell, S.H. "Major General Henry Knox," Field Artillery Journal 23
     (1933): 542-49.

5728 Sandham, William R. "General Henry Knox, after whom Knox County, was
     Named," Illinois State Historical Society Journal 18 (1925): 436-39.

5729 Society of the Cincinnati. Memorials of the Society of the Cincinnati
     of Massachusetts. Boston: The Society, 1873.

5730 Spaulding, Oliver L. "General Henry Knox," Field Artillery Journal
     21 (1931): 517-23.

5731 Stevens, Benjamin F. "Henry Knox, the Great Artillerist of the American
     Revolution," United Service 5 (1904): 685-87.

5732 Williamson, Joseph. "General Henry Knox," Maine Historical Society
     Collections 1 (1890): 1-27.

                              *JAMES LAWRENCE

5733 Dudley, William S. Captain James Lawrence, U.S.N.: Fallen Hero.
     Burlington, NJ: Burlington County Cultural and Heritage Commission,
     1983.

5734 "The Life of James Lawrence," Portfolio 3 (1817): 3-21.

                              ALBERT M. LEA

5735 Gallaher, Ruth A. "Albert Miller Lea," Iowa Journal of History and
     Politics 33 (1935): 195-259.

5736 _____. "Albert Miller Lea," Palimpsest 16 (1935): 65-80.

5737 Lathrop, H.W., ed. "Early Explorations in Iowa," Iowa Historical Record
     6 (1890): 535-53.

5738 Lea, Albert M. "Albert Miller Lea," Ibid 8 (1892): 200-07.

5739 _____. Notes on the Wisconsin Territory, Particularly with Reference
     to the Iowa District, or Black Hawk Purchase. Philadelphia: H.S.
     Tanner, 1836.

5740 Merryman, Robert M. A Hero Nonetheless: Albert Miller Lea, 1808-1891.
     Lake Mills, IA: Graphic Publications Co., 1983.

5741 Powell, Clifford. "The Contribution of Albert Miller Lea to Literature
     of Iowa History," Iowa Journal of History and Politics 9 (1911): 3-32.

5742 U.S. Congress. Committee on the Territories. Northern Boundary of
     Missouri...The Report of Albert M. Lea in Reference to the Northern
     Boundary of Missouri. 27th Cong. 3d Session House Document 38.

                              *HENRY LEAVENWORTH

5743 "Brigadier General Leavenworth," Military and Naval Magazine 4 (1834):
     101-04.

5744 " A Criticism of Leavenworth by Captain Chittenden," South Dakota
     Historical Collections 1 (1902): 235-41.

5745   Delaney, Donald J. "The Catlin Portrait of General Leavenworth," Kansas Historical Quarterly 37 (1971): 345-50.

5746   Geiser, Samuel W. "Heinrich Carl Beyrich in Arkansas Territory," Field and Labratory 24 (1956): 77-96.

5747   Parker, Henry S. Henry Leavenworth, Pioneer General. N.p., N.d. At Kansas State Historical Society.

5748   Wharton, Clarence R. "General Leavenworth and his Expedition from Fort Gibson." In: Satanta, the Great Chief of the Kiowas, and His People. Dallas: Upshaw, 1935, 37-56.

ROBERT E. LEE

5749   Cuthbert, Norma B. "To Molly: Five Early Letters from Robert E. Lee to His Wife, 1832-1835," Huntington Library Quarterly 15 (1952): 257-76.

5750   Drumm, Stella, ed. Letters of Robert E. Lee to Henry Kaysen, 1838-1846," Glimpses of the Past 3 (1936): 1-43.

5751   _____. "Robert E. Lee and the Improvement of the Mississippi River," Missouri Historical Society Collections 6 (1929): 151-71.

5752   Ellis, Robert R. "The Lees at Fortress Monroe," Military Engineer 42 (1950): 1-5.

5753   Freeman, Douglas S. R.E. Lee, a Biography. 4 Vols. New York: Charles Scribner's Sons, 1945.

5754   Musser, Ruth, and John C. Krantz. "The Friendship of Robert E. Lee and Dr. William Beaumont," Johns Hopkins Institute of the History of Medicine Bulletin 6 (1938): 467-76.

5755   Preston, Walter C. Lee, West Point, and Lexington. Yellowsprings, OH: Antioch Press, 1934.

5756   Rhodes, Charles D. Robert E. Lee, the West Pointer. Richmond: Garrett, Massie, 1932.

5757   Shackelford, George G., ed. "Lieutenant Lee Reports to Captain Talcott on Fort Calhoun's Construction on the Rip Raps," Virginia Magazine of History and Biography 60 (1952): 458-87.

5758   Simpson, Ida E. "Robert E. Lee at Fort Monroe," Iron Worker 22 (1958): 24-28.

5759   Swift, Eben. "Military Education of General R.E. Lee," Virginia Magazine of History and Biography 35 (1927): 97-160.

URIAH P. LEVY

5760   Abrahams, Robert D. The Commodore. Philadelphia: Jewish Publications of America, 1954.

5761   Blandford, Benjamin W. "Levy the Lion-Hearted: The Story of Uriah P. Levy and the War of 1812," American Hebrew 117 (1925): 461-62, 472.

5762   Cameron, Joshua. "Commodore Levy: He Changed the Navy," Destination: Philadelphia 3 (1975): 11-27.

5763 Eiseman, Alberta. Rebels and Reformers: Biographies of Four Jewish Americans. Garden City, NY: Zenith Books, 1976.

5764 Fitzpatrick, Donovan and Saul Saphire. Navy Maverick: Uriah P. Levy. New York: Doubleday, 1963.

5765 Gersh, Harry. "Uriah P. Levy." In: These are My People. New York: Behrman, 1959, 263-71.

5766 Kanof, Abram. "U.P. Levy: The Story of a Pugnacious Commodore," American Jewish Historical Society Publications 39 (1949): 1-66.

5767 Marcus, Jacob R., ed. Memoirs of American Jews, 1775-1865. 3 Vols. Philadelphia: Jewish Publication Society of America, 1955. Vol. 1, 76-116.

5768 Morgan, J.M. "American Forerunner of Dreyfus," Century Magazine 58 58 (1899): 796-800.

5769 Rezneck, Samuel. The Saga of an American Jewish family Since the Revolution: A History of the Family of Jonas Phillips. Washington, DC: University Press of America, 1980.

5770 Sanderson, William A. "The Yankee Boy for Fighting: The Story of Uriah Phillips Levy." Master's Thesis, Hebrew Union College, 1951.

5771 Sobel, Samuel. Intrepid Sailor. Philadelphia: Cresset Publications, 1980.

5772 Strenlicht, Sanford V. Uriah P. Levy, the Blue Star Commodore. Norfolk, VA: Jewish Community Council, 1961.

5773 _____. "Incident at Rio," United States Naval Institute Proceedings 89 (1963): 156-57.

5774 Wolf, Simon. "Biographical Sketch of Commodore Uriah P. Levy," American Jewish Yearbook (1902-1903): 42-45.

## MERIWETHER LEWIS

5775 Abrams, Rochanne. "Meriwether Lewis: Two Years with Jefferson, the Mentor," Missouri Historical Society Bulletin 36 (1979): 3-18.

5776 _____. "Meriwether Lewis: The Logistical Imagination," Ibid 36 (1980): 228-40.

5777 _____. "The Colonial Childhood of Meriwether Lewis," Ibid 34 (1978): 218-27.

5778 Bentley, James R., ed. "Two letters of Meriwether Lewis to Major William Preston," Filson Club Quarterly 44 (1970): 170-75.

5779 Bond, Octavia Z. "Lewis's Tomb," Land of Sun 12 (1900): 358-66.

5780 Brown, Alexander D. "The Mysterious Death of a Hero," American History Illustrated 5 (1971): 18-27.

5781 Cappon, Lester J. "Men of Albemarle and the Louisiana Purchase," Magazine of Albemarle County History 13 (1953): 1-22.

5782   Carter, Clarence E., ed. The Territorial Papers of the United States: The Territory of Louisiana-Missouri, 1806-1814. Washington, DC: Government Printing Office, 1949.

5783   Cutright, Paul R. "Meriwether Lewis Prepares for a Trip," Missouri Historical Society Bulletin 23 (1966): 3-20.

5784   ____. "Lewis on the Marias, 1806," Montana 18 (1968): 30-43.

5785   Dillon, Richard. Meriwether Lewis, A Biography. New York: Coward, McCann, 1965.

5786   Fisher, Vardis. Suicide or Murder? The Strange Death of Governor Meriwether Lewis. Denver: Alan Swallow, 1962.

5787   Hays, Wilma P. The Meriwether Lewis Mystery. Philadelphia: Westminister Press, 1971.

5788   Jackson, Donald. "On the Death of Meriwether Lewis's Servant," William and Mary Quarterly 21 (1964): 445-48.

5789   Kushner, Howard I. "The Suicide of Meriwether Lewis: A Psychoanalytic Inquiry," Ibid 38 (1981): 464-81.

5790   Lewis, Andrew. "Meriwether Lewis," Oregon Historical Quarterly 6 (1905): 391-462.

5791   Lewis, Grace. "The First Home of Governor Lewis in Louisiana Territory," Missouri Historical Society Bulletin 14 (1958): 357-68.

5792   "Life of Captain Lewis," Portfolio 4 (1814): 133-47.

5793   Meriwether, Lee. "Meriwether Lewis, his Work and his Place in American History," Virginia Magazine of History and Biography 45 (1937): 329-45.

5794   Moore, John H. "The Death of Meriwether Lewis," American Historical Magazine 9 (1904): 218-30.

5795   Moulton, Gary E. "New Documents of Meriwether Lewis," We Proceed On 13 (1987): 4-7.

5796   ____. "The Missing Journals of Meriwether Lewis," Montana 35 (1985): 28-39.

5797   "Notice of Captain M. Lewis," Analectic Magazine 7 (1816): 329-33.

5798   Phelps, Dawson A. "The Tragic Death of Meriwether Lewis," William and Mary Quarterly 13 (1956): 305-18.

5799   Seymour, Flora W. Meriwether Lewis, Trail Blazer. New York: D. Appleton, 1937.

5800   "Particulars of the Death of Captain Lewis," Portfolio 7 (1812): 34-38.

5801   Wilson, Charles M. Meriwether Lewis of Lewis and Clark. New York: Thomas Y. Crowell, 1934.

5802   Wright, Marcus J. "Governor Meriwether Lewis, 1774-1809," Magazine of American History 26 (1891): 135-42.

## ABRAHAM LINCOLN

5803   Alexander, Edward P. Lincoln Comes to Wisconsin. Madison: Lincoln
       Fellowship of Wisconsin, 1944.

5804   Bigelow, J. "Mr. Bryant's Impression of Abraham Lincoln, a Captain
       in the Black Hawk War," Magazine of American History 23 (1890): 343.

5805   Brown, Marion E. "Abraham Lincoln, Captain," Manuscripts 6 (1954):
       136-41.

5806   Burford, C.C. "Abraham Lincoln and the American Indian in the Central
       West," Journal of Illinois State Anthroplogical Society 6 (1949):
       15-21.

5807   Cain, Marvin R. "Lincoln as a Soldier of the Union: A Reappraisal,"
       Lincoln Herald 83 (1981): 592-603.

5808   Davis, Charles G. "March of Captain Abraham Lincoln's Company in
       the Black Hawk War," Illinois State Historical Society Transactions
       31 (1924): 25-27.

5809   East, Ernest E., ed. "New Lincoln Black Hawk War Document," Illinois
       Libraries 34 (1952): 359-63.

5810   Harlan, E.R. "Lincoln's Iowa Lands," Annals of Iowa 15 (1927): 621-23.

5811   Jackson, Alfred A. "Abraham Lincoln in the Black Hawk War," Wisconsin
       Historical Society Collections 14 (1896): 118-36.

5812   Murphy, James P. "Abraham Lincoln, Doughboy," Infantry Journal 34
       (1929): 121-23.

5813   Pratt, Harry E. "Abraham Lincoln in the Black Hawk War." In: O. F.
       Ander, ed. The John Hauberg Historical Essays. Rock island: Augustana
       College Library, 1954, 18-28.

5814   Temple, Wayne C. "Lincoln's Arms and Dress in the Black Hawk War,"
       Lincoln Herald 71 (1969): 145-49.

5815   _____. Lincoln's Arms, Dress, and Military Duty During and After the
       Black Hawk War. Springfield: State of Illinois, Military and Naval
       Department, 1981.

5816   _____. "Lincoln's Military Service After the Black Hawk War,"
       Lincoln Herald 72 (1970): 87-88.

5817   Thwaites, Reuben G. "Criticism of Nicolay and Hay's Life of Abraham
       Lincoln," Magazine of Western History 5 (1886-1887): 435-36.

## BENJAMIN LINCOLN

5818   "Biography of Benjamin Lincoln," Military Magazine and Record of the
       Volunteers of the United States 1 (1840), No. 11.

5819   Bowen, Francis. Life of Benjamin Lincoln. Boston: Charles Little,
       James Brown, 1847.

5820   Cavanaugh, John C. "The Military Career of Major General Benjamin
       Lincoln." Ph. D. dissertation, Duke University, 1969.

5821  Kirkland, John T. "Notices of the Life of Benjamin Lincoln,"
      Massachusetts Historical Society Collections 3 (1815): 233-55.

5822  Lincoln, Benjamin. "Observations on the Indians," Ibid 5 (1798):
      6-12.

5823  ____. "Journal of a Treaty Held in 1793 with the Indian Tribes
      Northwest of the Ohio, by Commissioners of the United States,"
      Ibid 5 (1836): 109-76.

5824  Shipton, Clifford K. "Benjamin Lincoln: Old Reliable." In: George A.
      Billias, ed. George Washington's Generals. New York: William Morrow,
      1964, 193-211.

                              LITTLE TURTLE

5825  Blaine, Harry S. "Little Turtle's Watch," Northwest Ohio Quarterly
      37 (1965): 27-32.

5826  Carter, Harvey L. The Life and Times of Little Turtle: First Sagamore
      of the Wabash. Urbana: University of Illinois Press, 1987.

5827  Cooke, David B. Fighting Indians of America. New York: Dodd, Mead,
      1954, 66-96.

5828  Drake, Samuel G. Biography and History of the Indians of North
      America. Boston: J. Drake, 1834, 569-74.

5829  Dunn, Jacob B. True Indian Stories. Indianapolis: Sentinel, 1908.

5830  Finley, James B. Life Among the Indians, or Personal Reminiscences
      and Historical Incidents Illustrative of Indian Life and Character.
      Cincinnati: Methodist Book Concern, 1857, 514-17.

5831  "A Frenchman's View of Little Turtle," Old Fort News 6 (1941):
      398-433.

5832  Fort Wayne and Allen County Public Library. Chief Little Turtle.
      Fort Wayne, IN: The Library, 1952.

5833  Hoel, William B. "Little Turtle, the Miami Chieftain." Master's
      Thesis, Miami University, 1938.

5834  Johnston, Charles H. Famous Indian Chiefs. Boston: L.C. Page, 1909,
      284-308.

5835  Langtry, Rosa A. "Historical Retrospect of a Fort Wayne Resident,"
      Indiana History Bulletin 4 (1927): 112-17.

5836  Lockridge, Ross F. "Highlights in Indiana History," Ibid 3 (1926):
      29-42.

5837  Love, Nathaniel B. "Me-she-kun-nogh-quah, or Little Turtle, 1783-
      1812," Ohio Archaeological and Historical Society Publications 18
      (1909): 115-48.

5838  Mansfield, Edward D. Personal Memories; Social, Political, and
      Literary. Cincinnati: Robert Clarke, 1879, 22-26.

5839  Potterf, Rex M. "Little Turtle," Old Fort News 21 (1958), 11pp.

5840  Smith, Dwight L. The Great Indian Leaders in the Indian Wars, 1790-
      1794. Columbus: Anthony Wayne Parkway Board, 1950.

5841   Stouder, J.M. "The Grave of Little Turtle," _Indiana Magazine of
       History_ 8 (1912): 119-21.

5842   Sweet, James S. _Jacob M. Storder_. Fort Wayne, IN: Allen County-
       Fort Wayne Historical Society, 1958.

5843   Teetor, Henry D. "The Miami Indians: Little Turtle, the Last Chief,"
       _Magazine of Western History_ 12 (1890): 3-6.

5844   Thatcher, Benjamin B. _Indian Biography_. 2 Vols. New York: Harper Bros.,
       1837. Vol. 2, 243-69.

5845   Whitsett, Robert B. "Snake-Fish Town, the Eighteenth Century Metropolis
       of Little Turtle's Eel River Miami," _Indiana History Bulletin_ 15
       (1938): 72-82.

5846   Winger, Otho. _The Kenapocomoco, Eel River, the Home of Little Turtle_.
       North Manchester, IN: N.p., 1934.

5847   _____. _The Last of the Miamis_. North Manchester, IN: N.p., 1935.

5848   _____. "A Pioneer Experiement in Teaching Agriculture." In: _The News
       Journal_ (North Manchester, Ind. N.d.
       At Indiana Historical Society Library.

5849   _____. _Little Turtle: The Great Chief of Eel River_. North Manchester:
       News-Journal, 1942.

5850   Wood, Norman B. _Lives of Famous Indian Chiefs_. Aurora, IL: American
       Indian Historical Publishing Co., 1906, 283-316.

5851   Young, Calvin D. "The Birthplace of Little Turtle," _Ohio Archaeological
       and Historical Society Publications_ 23 (1914): 105-49.

5852   _____. _Little Turtle, Me-she-kin-no-quah; The Great Chief of the Miami
       Indian Nation_. Indianapolis: Sentinel, 1917.

JOHN LONG

5853   Burroughs, Charles. _A Tribute to the Memory of Commodore John Long,
       of the U.S. Navy_. Portsmouth, NH: C.W. Brewster, 1865.

STEPHEN H. LONG

5854   Dillon, Richard. "Stephen H. Long's Great American Desert," _American
       Philosophical Society Proceedings_ 111 (1967): 93-108.

5855   _____. "Stephen Long and the Great American Desert," _Montana_ 18 (1968):
       58-74.

5856   DuBose, Beverly M. "Stephen Harriman Long," _Atlanta History Bulletin_
       3 (1938): 169-78.

5857   Friis, Herman R. "Stephen Long's Unpublished Manuscript Map of the
       United States, compiled in 1820-1822 (?)," _California Geographer_ 8
       (1967): 75-87.

5858   Halley, Patrick L. "The Western Experiences of Major Stephen H. Long."
       Ph. D. dissertation, University of Oklahoma, 1951.

5859  Kane, Lucile M., June D. Holmquist and Carolyn Gilman, eds. The Northern Expeditions of Stephen H. Long: The Journals of 1817 and 1823, and Related Documents. St. Paul: Minnesota Historical Society, 1978.

5860  Lamar, Mirbeau B. "Life of James Long." In: The Papers of Mirabeau Bonaparte Lamar. 6 Vols. Auston, TX: A.C. Baldwin, 1922. Vol. 2.

5861  Livingston, John. "Colonel Stephen H. Long of the United States Army." In: Portraits of Eminent Americans Now Living. 4 Vols. New York: Cornish, Lamport, 1853-1854. Vol. 4, 477-89.

5862  Long, Stephen H. "Long's Plan for a New Fort at Peoria, Illinois," Illinois State Historical Society Journal 47 (1954): 417-21.

5863  _____. "Major Long's Account of the Republican Pawnee and the Kansas Villages," Nebraska History 10 (1927): 204-16.

5864  _____. "A Letter from Stephen H. Long to George Graham, in Washington, March 4, 1817," National Register 3 (1817): 193-98.

5865  _____. "Voyage in a Six-oared Skiff to the Falls of St. Anthony in 1817," Minnesota Historical Society Collections 2 (1889): 7-88.

5866  Martin, Lawrence. "A Pennsylvanian's Discovery of a Driftless Area," Philadelphia Geographical Society Bulletin 21 (1923): 140-47.

5867  Nichols, Roger L. and Patrick L. Halley. Stephen Long and American Frontier Exploration. Newark, DE: University of Delaware Press, 1980.

5868  _____. "Stephen Long and Scientific Exploration on the Plains," Nebraska History 52 (1971): 51-64.

5869  _____. "Stephen H. Long." In: Paul A. Hutton, ed. Soldiers West: Biographies from the Military Frontier. Lincoln: University of Nebraska Press, 1986, 25-41.

5870  Sampson, F.A. "Books of Early Travel in Missouri," Missouri Historical Review 9 (1915): 94-101.

5871  Smallwood, James. "Major Stephen Harriman Long." In: Joseph A. Stout. Frontier Adventurers: American Exploration in Oklahoma. Oklahoma City: Oklahoma Historical Society, 1976, 51-60.

5872  Smith, Alice E. "Stephen H. Long and the naming of Wisconsin," Wisconsin Magazine of History 26 (1942): 67-71.

5873  Wood, Richard G. Stephen Harriman Long, 1784-1864: Army Engineer, Explorer, Inventor. Glendale, CA: Arthur H. Clark, 1966.

5874  _____. "Stephen Harriman Long at Belle Point," Arkansas Historical Quarterly 13 (1954): 338-48.

5875  _____., ed. "Exploration by Steamboat," Journal of Transportation History 3 (1955): 121-23.

GUSTAVUS LOOMIS

5876  Foreman, Carolyn T. "Gustavus Loomis, Commandant, Fort Gibson and Towson," Chronicles of Oklahoma 18 (1940): 219-28.

## NATHANIEL LYON

5877   Phillips, Christopher W. "The Court-Martial of Lieutenant Nathaniel Lyon," Missouri Historical Review 81 (1987): 296-304.

5878   Woodward, Ashbel. Life of General Nathaniel Lyon. Hartford, CT: Case, Lockwood, 1862.

## GEORGE A. MCCALL

5879   McCall, George A. Letters from the Frontiers: Written During a Period of Thirty Years Service in the Army of the United States. Philadelphia: Lippincott, 1868.

5880   "Seminole Campaign," Army and Navy Chronicle 3 (1834): 81-84.

## THOMAS MACDONOUGH

5881   Brown, John H. "Thomas MacDonough." In: American Naval Heroes. Boston: Brown, 1899, 377-84.

5882   Eckert, Edward K. "Thomas MacDonough: Architect of a Wilderness Navy." In: James C. Bradford, ed. Command Under Sail: Makers of the American Naval Tradition, 1775-1850. Annapolis: Naval Institute Press, 1984, 147-72.

## JAMES MCHENRY

5883   Boles, John B. "Politics, Intrigue and the Presidency: James McHenry to Bishop John Carroll, May 16, 1800," Maryland Historical Magazine 69 (1974): 64-85.

5884   Brown, Frederick J. A Sketch of the Life of Dr. James McHenry. Baltimore: Maryland Historical Society, 1877.

5885   "Correspondence of James McHenry, 1796-1801," William and Mary Quarterly 13 (1904-1905): 102-07.

5886   Essary, Jesse F. Maryland in National Politics. Baltimore: John Murphy, 1915.

5887   "Letters of Jefferson, etc., Found Among the papers of James McHenry," Virginia Magazine of History and Biography 12 (1905): 257-68, 406-14.

5888   McClellan, Edwin N. "When the Same Man was Secretary of War and Navy," United States Naval Institute Proceedings 59 (1933): 534-36.

5889   "McHenry Letters, 1796-1817," Southern Historical Association 9 (1905): 99-110, 311-20, 374-88.

5890   McHenry, James. "Maryland Politics in 1798-9," Ibid 10 (1906): 31-38, 101-06, 150-57.

5891   _____. "Papers of Dr. James McHenry on the Federal Convention of 1787," American Historical Review 11 (1906): 595-624.

5892   Mattsson-Boze, M. Howard. "James McHenry, Secretary of War, 1796-1800." Ph. D. dissertation, University of Minnesota, 1965.

5893   Phalen, James M. "Doctor at Arms; James McHenry-Secretary to the Chief," Military Surgeon 99 (1946): 223-25.

5894   "Selections from the McHenry papers," Historical Magazine 2 (1867): 260-68.

5895   Smith, William L. "Letters to James McHenry, Secretary of War, 1797," Sewanee Review 14 (1906): 76-104.

5896   Steiner, Bernard C. The Life and Correspondence of James McHenry. Cleveland: Burrows Bros., 1907.

WILLIAM MCINTOSH

5897   Chapman, George. Chief William McIntosh. Atlanta: Cherokee Publishing Co., 1988.

5898   Corbini, Harriet T. A History and Genealogy of Chief William McIntosh. Long Beach, CA: N.p., 1967.

5899   Griffith, Benjamin W. McIntosh and Weatherford, Creek Indian Leaders. Tuscaloosa: University of Alabama Press, 1988.

5900   Montgomery, Horace, ed. Georgians in Profile. Athens, GA: University of Georgia Press, 1958, 114-43.

5901   White, George. Historical Collections of Georgia. New York: Pudney, Russell, 1854, 170-73.

ALEXANDER S. MACKENZIE

5902   Shufeldt, R.W. "An Interesting Historical letter: Commodore Alexander Slidell Mackenzie to Hon. Ogden Hoffman," Magazine of American History 17 (1887): 128-31.

5903   DiMona, Joseph. Great Court-Martial Cases. New York: Grosset, Dunlap, 1972, 43-71.

5904   Hayes, John D. "Alexander Slidell Mackenzie," Shipmate 25 (1962): 12.

5905   Mackenzie, Alexander S. "Thoughts on the Navy," Naval Magazine 2 (1837): 5-42.

5906   _____. Case of the Somer's Mutiny: Defense of Alexander S. Mackenzie. Commander of the U.S. Brig Somers. New York: Tribune Office, 1843.

5907   _____. "Flogging in the Navy," United States Magazine and Democratic Review 25 (1849): 97-115, 417-32.

WILLIAM L. MACKENZIE

5908   Donnelly, F.K. "The British Background of William Lyon Mackenzie," British Journal of Canadian Studies 2 (1987): 61-73.

5909   Flint, David. William Lyon Mackenzie: Rebel Against Authority. Toronto: Oxford University Press, 1971.

5910   Gates, William. After the Rebellion: The Later Years of William Lyon Mackenzie. Toronto: Dundern Press, 1987.

5911   Hathaway, E.J. "William Lyon Mackenzie in Toronto," Canadian Magazine 42 (1914): 311-15, 431-35, 527-30, 594-98.

5912  Keilty, Greg, ed. <u>1837: Revolution in the Canadas as Told by William</u>
      <u>Lyon Mackenzie</u>. Toronto: N.C. Press, 1974.

5913  Kilbourne, William M. "The Fire Brand: William Lyon Mackenzie and
      the Rebellion in Upper Canada." Ph. D. dissertation, Harvard
      University, 1957.

5914  Leacock, Stephen. <u>Mackenzie, Baldwin, Lafontaine, Hincks</u>. New York:
      Oxford University Press, 1926.

5915  Le Sueur, William D. <u>William Lyon Mackenzie: A Reinterpretation</u>.
      Toronto: Macmillan of Canada, 1979.

5916  Lindsey, Charles. <u>The Life and Times of William Lyon Mackenzie</u>.
      Toronto: C.W., P.R. Randall, 1862.

5917  Mackay, R.A. "The Political Ideals of William Lyon Mackenzie,"
      <u>Canadian Journal of Economics and Political Science</u> 3 (1937): 1-22.

5918  Mackenzie, William L. <u>Mackenzie's Own Narrative of the Late Rebellion</u>.
      Toronto: Palladium Office, 1838.

5919  Olney, M. "William Lyon Mackenzie: The Rochester Years, 1838-1842."
      Master's Thesis, University of Rochester, 1962.

5920  "Personal Narrative of the Escape of W.L. Mackenzie from Toronto to
      the United States," <u>Living Age</u> 16 (1848): 331-34.

5921  Rasporich, Anthony W. <u>William Lyon Mackenzie</u>. Toronto: Holt, Rinehart,
      Winston, 1972.

5922  Salutin, Rick. <u>1837: William Lyon Mackenzie and the Canadian</u>
      <u>Revolution</u>. Toronto: J. Lorimer, 1976.

5923  Yeigh, Frank. "Some Reminders of William Lyon Mackenzie," <u>Canadian</u>
      <u>Magazine</u> 19 (1902): 195-203.

## ALEXANDER MCLEOD

5924  Bonham, Milledge L. "Alexander McLeod: Bone of Contention," <u>New York</u>
      <u>History</u> 18 (1937): 189-217.

5925  Colquhoun, A.H. "Famous Canadian Trials: Alexander McLeod," <u>Canadian</u>
      <u>Magazine</u> 44 (1914-1915): 201-04.

5926  Corey, Albert B. "Public Opinion and the McLeod Case," <u>Canadian</u>
      <u>Historical Association Report</u> (1936): 53-64.

5927  Jennings, R.Y. "The Caroline and McLeod Cases," <u>American Journal of</u>
      <u>International Law</u> 32 (1938): 82-99.

5928  "McLeod's Case," <u>Fraser's Magazine</u> 24 (1841): 492-504.

5929  "The Supreme Court of New York and Daniel Webster on the McLeod Case,"
      <u>United States Magazine and Democratic Review</u> 10 (1842): 487-500.

5930  <u>Trial of Alexander McLeod for the Murder of Amos Durfee and as An</u>
      <u>Accomplice in the Niagara River during the Canadian Rebellion in 1837-</u>
      <u>1838</u>. New York: Sun Office, 1841.

5931   Watt, Alastair. "The Case of Alexander McLeod," Canadian Historical
       Review 12 (1931): 145-67.

*JOHN MCNEIL

5932   Webb, James W. To the Officers of the Army. New York: N.p., 1827.

*JAMES MADISON

5933   "A Colored Man's Reminiscences of Mr. Madison," Historical Magazine
       7 (1863): 17-20.

5934   Ketcham, Ralph. "James Madison." In: Henry F. Graff, ed. The Presi-
       dents: A Reference History. New York: Charles Scribner's, 1985.

5935   McCoy, Drew R. The Last of the Founding Fathers: James Madison and
       the Republican Legacy. New York: Cambridge University Press, 1985.

5936   Rutland, Robert A. James Madison: Founding Father. New York:
       Macmillan, 1987.

5937   Warfield, J.D. "President Madison's Retreat," American Historical
       Register 2 (1895): 857-61.

JOHN B. MAGRUDER

5938   Settles, Thomas M. "The Military Career of John Bankhead Magruder."
       Ph. D. dissertation, Texas Christian University, 1972.

DENIS H. MAHAN

5939   Abbot, Henry L. Memoirs of Denis H. Mahan, 1802-1871. Washington, DC:
       N.p., 1878.

5940   Cullum, George W. "Professor D.H. Mahan," Army and Navy Journal 9
       (1871): 119-20.

5941   Griess, Thomas E. "Denis Hart Mahan: West Point Professor and Advocate
       of Military Professionalism, 1830-1871." Ph. D. dissertation, Duke
       University, 1969.

5942   Mahan, F.A. "Professor Denis Hart Mahan," Professional Memoirs,
       Corps of Engineers 9 (1917): 72-76.

5943   Mahan, Denis H. A Complete Treatise on Field Fortifications, with
       the General Outlines of the Principles Regulating the Arrangement,
       the Attack, and the Defense of Permanent Works. New York: Wiley,
       Long, 1836.

5944   Niu, Sien-chong. "Two Forgotten American Strategists," Military Review
       46 (1966): 53-54.

MAIN POC

5945   Edmunds, R. David. "Main Poc: Potawatomi Wabeno," American Indian
       Quarterly 9 (1985): 259-72.

STEPHEN R. MALLORY

5946   Clubbs, Occie. "Stephen Russell Mallory, the Elder." Master's Thesis,
       University of Florida, 1936.

5947  Clubbs, Occie. "Stephen Russell Mallory," Florida Historical Quarterly 25 (1947): 221-45, 295-318.

5948  Durkin, Joseph T. Stephen R. Mallory, Confederate Navy  Chief. Chapel Hill: University of North Carolina Press, 1954.

5949  Melvin, Philip. "Stephen Russell Mallory, Southern Naval Statesman," Journal of Southern History 10 (1944): 137-60.

JARED MANSFIELD

5950  Dudley, Charlotte W. "Jared Mansfield: United States Surveyor General," Ohio History 85 (1976): 231-46.

5951  Livermore, W.R. "Jared Mansfield," Professional Memoirs, Corps of Engineers 11 (1919): 123-27.

JAMES B. MANY

5952  Foreman, Carolyn T. "Colonel James B. Many: Commandant at Fort Gibson, Fort Towson, and Fort Smith," Chronicles of Oklahoma 9 (1941): 119-28.

RANDOLPH B. MARCY

5953  Hollon, W. Eugene. Beyond the Cross Timbers: The Travels of Randolph B. Marcy, 1812-1887. Norman: University of Oklahoma Press, 1955.

5954  Marcy, Randolph B. Thirty Years of Army Life on the Border. New York: Harper & Bros., 1866.

5955  _____. Border Reminiscences. New York: Harper & Bros., 1872.

5956  Tate, Michael. "Randolph B. Marcy: First Explorer of the Wichitas," Great Plains Journal 15 (1976): 80-113.

WILLIAM L. MARCY

5957  Mackenzie, William L. Sketches of William L. Marcy, Jacob Barker, and Others. Boston: N.p., 1845.

5958  Mattina, Benjamin. "The Early Life of William Learned Marcy, 1789-1832." Ph. D. dissertation, Georgetown University, 1949.

5959  Spencer, Ivor D. The Victor and the Spoils: A Life of William L. Marcy. Providence: Brown University Press, 1959.

5960  _____. "William L. Marcy: An 'Educated' Democrat," New York History 22 (1941): 180-90.

5961  "William L. Marcy," United States Magazine and Democratic Review 40 (1857): 161-70.

RICHARD B. MASON

5962 Foreman, Carolyn T. "Gen. Richard Barnes Mason," Chronicles of Oklahoma 19 (1941): 14-36.

MONTGOMERY C. MEIGS

5963 Weigley, Russell F. Quartermaster General of the Union Army: A Biography of Montgomery C. Meigs. New York: Columbia University, 1959.

MATTHEW F. MAURY

5964  Alden, Carroll S. and Ralph Earle. "Matthew Fontaine Maury." In: Makers of Naval Tradition. Boston: Ginn, 1925, 111-29.

5965  Anderson, Anton B. "Science of the Sea," United States Naval Institute Proceedings 61 (1935): 1732-35.

5966  Blair, Maria. Matthew Fontaine Maury. Richmond: Shepperson, 1918.

5967  Brandt, George E. "Maury's Genius Shown in an Old Letter: How the First Superintendent of the Naval Observatory Saved Fifty years," United States Naval Institute Proceedings 51 (1925): 1197-1201.

5968  Caskie, Jacquelin A. Life and Letters of Matthew Fountaine Maury. Richmond: Richmond Press, 1926.

5969  Chandler, A.B. "Matthew Fontaine Maury," Southern Historical Society Papers 44 (1923): 223-28.

5970  Coleman, Elizabeth P. "The Pathfinder of the Seas," Virginia Cavalcade 2 (1952): 11-16.

5971  Corbin, Diana F. Life of Matthew Fontaine Maury, Compiled by his Daughter. London: S. Low, 1888.

5972  Cowen, Robert C. Frontiers of the Sea. Garden City, NY: Doubleday, 1960.

5973  Coxe, Lewis. "Matthew Fontaine Maury, U.S.N., " United States Naval Institute Proceedings 51 (1925): 1193-96.

5974  Cronie, William J. "The First American Oceanographer," Ibid 90 (1964): 56-59.

5975  Darter, Lewis J. "Federal Archives Relating to Matthew Fontaine Maury," American Neptune 2 (1941): 149-58.

5976  Dill, Jacob S. "The American Scientist who Charted the Oceans," Journal of American History 4 (1910): 319-37.

5977  DuVal, Miles P. Matthew Fontaine Maury: Benefactor of Mankind. Washington, DC: Naval Historical Foundation, 1971.

5978  Hawthorne, Hildegarde. Matthew Fontaine Maury, Trailmaker of the Seas. New York: Longmans, Green, 1943.

5979  Heath, Winifred. "Matthew Fontaine Maury," Catholic World 168 (1949): 349-53.

5980  Hellweg, J.F. "The Pathfinder of the Seas," United States Naval Institute Proceedings 59 (1933): 93-96.

5981  Iselin, Columbus O. Matthew Fontaine Maury, 1806-1873: Pathfinder of the Seas. New York: Newcomen Society, 1957.

5982  Klapp, Orrin E. "Matthew Fontaine Maury, Naval Scientist," United States Naval Institute Proceedings 71 (1945): 1315-25.

5983  Lewis, Charles. "Matthew Fontaine Maury," Confederate Veteran 33 (1925): 296-301.

5984    Lewis, Charles L. Matthew Fontaine Maury, the Pathfinder of the Seas. Annapolis: Naval Institute Press, 1927.

5985    _____. "Maury and the 'Messenger'," Southern Literary Messenger 1 (1939): 165-71.

5986    "A Life of Maury," Literary World 19 (1888): 280-82.

5987    Lyman, John. "The Centennial of Pressure Pattern Navigation," United States Naval Institute Proceedings 74 (1948): 212-28.

5988    McIlwaine, Richard. "Matthew Fontaine Maury." In: Addresses and Papers Bearing Chiefly on Education. Richmond: Whittet, Shepperson, 1908.

5989    "Matthew Fontaine Maury," Atlantic Monthly 63 (1889): 128-32.

5990    "Matthew Fontaine Maury, the Pathfinder of the Seas: A Profile," Civil War Times Illustrated 2 (1963): 10-16.

5991    Maury, Matthew F. "Letters to Mr. Clay," Southern Literary Messenger 7 (1841): 724-29.

5992    _____. "The Navy and its Use," Hunt's Merchant Magazine 7 (1842): 383-411.

5993    _____. "Of Reorganizing the Navy," Southern Literary Messenger 7 (1841): 3-25.

5994    _____. "Our Navy," Ibid 7 (1841): 345-79.

5995    _____. "Lake Defense and Western Interests," Ibid 11 (1845): 83-91.

5996    _____. "On the Navigation of Cape Horn," Military and Naval Magazine 5 (1835): 123-30.

5997    Pancake, Frank. "Matthew Fontaine Maury," Huguenot 16 (1954): 110-19.

5998    Rawson, Geoffrey. "Pathfinder of the Seas," United States Naval Institute Proceedings 74 (1948): 219-20.

5999    "Sketch of Matthew Fontaine Maury," Popular Science 37 (1890): 400-07.

6000    Smith, C. Alphonso. Matthew Fontaine Maury. Charlottesville: University of Virginia Press, 1924.

6001    Stanton, William. "Matthew Fontaine Maury: Navy Science for the World." In: James C. Bradford, ed. Captains of the Old Steam Navy. Annapolis: Naval Institute Press, 1986, 46-63.

6002    Stevens, William O. "Two Early Proposals for Naval Education," United States Naval Institute Proceedings 39 (1913): 127-33.

6003    Stewart, William H. The Spirit of the South. New York: Neale, 1908.

6004    Tillman, G.N. "Matthew Fontaine Maury: A Great Tennessean," Methodist Quarterly Review 64 (1915): 533-40.

6005    Towle, Edward L. "Science, Commerce, and the Navy on the Seafaring Frontier (1842-1861): The Role of Lieutenant M.F. Maury." Ph. D. dissertation, University of Rochester, 1966.

6006   Towle, Edward L. "Matthew Fontaine Maury's 1845 Defense Plan for the Great Lakes Frontier," Inland Seas 22 (1966): 267-82.

6007   Wayland, John W. The Pathfinder of the Seas: The Life of Matthew Fontaine Maury. Richmond: Garrett, Massie, 1930.

6008   Wickham, Julia P. "Matthew Fontaine Maury: Pathfinder of the Seas," Huguenot Society of South Carolina Transactions No. 36 (1931): 39-59.

6009   Williams, Frances L. Matthew Fontaine Maury, Scientist of the Seas. New Brunswick, NJ: Rutgers University Press, 1963.

6010   _____. Ocean Pathfinder: A Biography of Matthew Fontaine Maury. New York: Harcourt, Brace, World, 1966

ORMSBY M. MITCHEL

6011   Headley, Phineas C. Old Stars: The Life and Military Career of Major-General Ormsby M. Mitchel. Boston: Lee, Shepard, 1864.

6012   Mitchel, Frederick A. Ormsby Macnight Mitchel, Astronomer and General, a Biographical Narrative. Boston: Houghton, Mifflin, 1887.

DAVID MONIAC

6013   Benton, Kenneth L. "Warrior from West Point," Soldiers 29 (1974): 21-24.

6014   Foreman, Carolyn T. "The Brave Major Moniac and the Creek Volunteers," Chronicles of Oklahoma 23 (1945): 96-106.

6015   Griffith, Benjamin. "Lieut. David Moniac, Creek Indian: First Minority Graduate of West Point," Alabama Historical Quarterly 41 (1981): 99-110.

JOHN B. MONTGOMERY

6016   Ellicott, John M. "John Berrien Montgomery," United States Naval Institute Proceedings 60 (1934): 533-36.

6017   Rodenbough, Theophilus F. "John Berrien Montgomery, Rear Admiral, U.S. Navy," Magazine of American History 2 (1878): 420-34.

6018   Rogers, Fred B. Montgomery and the Portsmouth. San Francisco: J. Howell, 1958.

ALFRED MORDECAI

6019   Falk, Stanley L. "Alfred Mordecai, American Jew," American Jewish Archives 10 (1958): 125-32.

6020   _____. "Soldier-Technologist: Major Alfred Mordecai and the Beginnings of Science in the United States Army." Ph. D. dissertation, Georgetown University, 1959.

6021   Mordecai, Alfred. Report of Experiments on Gunpowder, Made at Washington Arsenal in 1843 and 1844. Washigtnon, DC: Gideon, 1845.

6022   _____. Artillery for the United States Land Service, As devised and Arranged by the Ordnance Board. Washington, DC: Gideon, 1849.

6023    Padgett, James A., ed. "The Life of Alfred Mordecai as Related by
        Himself," North Carolina Historical Review 22 (1945): 58-108.

## DANIEL MORGAN

6024    Callahan, North. Daniel Morgan: Ranger of the Revolution. New York:
        Rinehart, Winston, 1961.

6025    Higginbotham, Don. Daniel Morgan, Revolutionary Rifleman. Chapel Hill:
        University of North Carolina, 1961.

6026    Graham, James. The Life of General Daniel Morgan of the Virginia Line
        of the United States. New York: Derby, Jackson, 1856.

## *CHARLES MORRIS

6027    Brown, John H. "Charles Morris." In: American Naval Heroes. Boston:
        Brown, 1899, 285-90.

6028    Larned, Ellen D. "An Old-Time Hero-Commodore Charles Morris,"
        Connecticut Magazine 5 (1899): 478-80; 6 (1899): 411-15.

## RICHARD V. MORRIS

6029    Morris, Richard V. Defense of the Conduct of Commodore Morris during
        his Command in the Mediterranean. New York: I. Riley, 1908.

## ALEXANDER MURRAY

6030    Brown, John H. "Alexander Morris." In: American Naval Heroes. Boston:
        Brown, 1899, 157-68.

6031    Folsom, Benjamin. Compilation of Biographical Sketches of Distinguished
        Officers of the United States Navy. Newburyport, MA: H.G. Allen,
        1814, 148-61.

6032    Frost, John. The Pictorial Book of the Commodores. New York: Nafis,
        Cornish, 1845, 60-74.

6033    "The Life of Commodore Murray," Portfolio 3 (1814): 399-409.

6034    Waldo, Samuel P. Biographical Sketches of Distinguished American Naval
        Heroes. Hartford: S. Andrus, 1823.

## PRESLEY O'BANNON

6035    Averill, Rebecca G. "Brief Sketch of Services of Lieutenant P.N.
        O'Bannon, a Kentucky Soldier in the War with Tripoli," Register
        of the Kentucky Historical Society 18 (1920): 73-76.

6036    _____. "Lieutenant Presley Neville O'Bannon," Ibid 18 (1920): 21-24.

6037    Cooke, F.O. "O'Bannon in Libya," Leatherneck 25 (1942): 5-6, 70-71.

6038    Gaines, William H. "Sword of Honor: Virginia Awarded a Handsome
        Weapon to a Native Son, in recognition of His Heroism on a Foreign
        Shore," Virginia Cavalcade 15 (1965): 4-10.

6039    Lanier, William D. "The Shores of Tripoli," United States Naval
        Institute Proceedings 68 (1942): 72-78.

6040  Lewis, Charles L. "Presley Neville O'Bannon and the 'Shores of Tripoli'." In: Famous American Marines. Boston: L.C. Page, 1950, 38-54.

6041  Magruder, John H. and Brooke Nihart. "The O'Bannon Sword," Military Collector and Historian 10 (1958): 102-04.

6042  Simmons, Edwin H. "Presley O'Bannon: Archtypical Marine," Register of the Kentucky Historical Society 71 (1973): 439-44.

6043  _____. "O'Bannon's Sword?" Fortitudine 14 (1984): 3-9.

6044  Sundberg, Trudy J. "O'Bannon and Company," Marine Corps Gazette 60 (1976): 35-39.

OSCEOLA

6045  Alderman, Clifford L. Osceola and the Seminole Wars. New York: Messner, 1973.

6046  Boyd, Mark F. "Asi-Yaholo, or, Osceola," Florida Historical Quarterly 33 (1955): 249-305.

6047  "The Capture of Osceola," El Scribano 4 (1967): 4-15.

6048  "The Case of Osceola," Magazine of American History 5 (1880): 447-50.

6049  Catlin, George. Letters and Notes on the manners, Customs, and Condition of the North American Indians. New York: Wiley, Putnam, 1841. Vol. 2, 247-51.

6050  Coe, Charles H. "The Parentage and Birthplace of Osceola," Florida Historical Quarterly 17 (1939): 304-11.

6051  _____. "The Parentage of Osceola," Ibid 33 (1955): 202-05.

6052  Collins, LeRoy. Forerunners Courageous, Stories of Frontier Florida. Tallahassee: Colcade Inc., 1971.

6053  Cooke, David B. Fighting Indians of America. New York: Dodd, Mead, 1954, 164-91.

6054  Duke, Seymour R. Osceola, or, Fact and Fiction: A Tale of the Seminole War. New York: Harper & Bros., 1838.

6055  _____. A Narrative of the Early Days and Remembrances of Osceola Nikkanochee, Prince of Econchatti, a Young Seminole Indian. London: Hatchland & Son, Picadilly, 1841.

6056  Gaillard, Frye. "Two Osceolas and the White Man," New South 26 (1971): 79-86.

6057  Goggin, John M. "Osceola: Portraits, Features, and Dress," Florida Historical Quarterly 33 (1955): 161-92.

6058  Hall, Gordon L. Osceola. New York: Holt, Rinehart, Winston, 1944.

6059  Hartley, William B. and Ellen. Osceola, the Unconquered Indian. New York: Hawthorne Books, 1973.

6060    Johnston, Charles H. Famous Indian Chiefs. Boston: L.C. Page,
        1919, 368-78.

6061    Josephy, Alvin M. "The Death of Osceola." In: The Patriot Chiefs.
        New York: Viking Press, 1961, 175-208.

6062    McCarthy, Joseph E. "Portraits of Osceola and the Artists who painted
        them," Papers of the Jackosnville Historical Society 2 (1949): 23-44.

6063    McKenny, Thomas L. The Indian Tribes of North America with Biograph-
        ical Sketches and Anecdotes of the Principle Chiefs. 3 Vols.
        Philadelphia: E.C. Biddle, 1836-1844. Vol. 2, 360-92.

6064    McSpadden, Joseph W. Indian Heroes. New York: T.Y. Crowell, 1950.

6065    Neill, Wilfred T. "The Site of Osceola's Village in Marian County,
        Florida," Florida Historical Quarterly 33 (1955): 240-46.

6066    Porter, Kenneth. "The Episode of Osceola's Wife: Fact or Fiction?"
        Ibid 26 (1947): 92-98.

6067    _____. "Osceola and the Negroes," Ibid 33 (1955): 235-39.

6068    Rutlidge, Archibald. "The Duke and the Medicine Man," South Atlantic
        Quarterly 36 91937): 400-18.

6069    "The Seminole War," Army and Navy Chronicle 3 (1836): 57-58.

6070    Simms, W.C. Osceola, Fact and Fiction: A Tale of the Seminole War.
        New York: Harper & Bros., 1838.

6071    Sprague, Lynn T. "Osceola, Chief of the Seminoles," Outing Magazine
        49 (1907): 644-52.

6072    Storrow, Thomas W. "Osceola, the Seminole," Knickerbocker
        24 (1844): 427-48.

6073    Sturtevant, William C. "Notes on Modern Seminole Traditions of
        Osceola," Florida Historical Quarterly 33 (1955): 206-17.

6074    _____. "Osceola's Coats," Ibid 34 (1958): 315-20.

6075    Wade, Mary H. Ten Big Indians: Stories of Famous Indian Chiefs.
        Boston: W.A. Wildes, 1905, 175-98.

6076    Ward, May M. "The Disappearance of the Head of Osceola," Florida
        Historical Quarterly 33 (1955): 193-201.

6077    Wells, William A. "Osceola and the Second Seminole War." Master's
        Thesis, University of Oklahoma, 1936.

6078    "The White Flag," Florida Historical Quarterly 33 (1955): 218-34.

6079    Whitney, Edison L. and Frances M. Perry. Four American Indians: King
        Philip, Pontiac, Tecumseh, Osceola. New York: American Book, 1904.

6080    Wilson, Minnie M. Osceola; Florida's Seminole Chieftain. Palm Beach:
        Davies Publishing Co., 1936.

## USHER PARSONS

6081  Brazer, Marjorie C., ed. "An Afterword to the Battle of Lake Erie," Inland Seas 37 (1977): 180-83.

6082  Chase, P.P. "Doctors Afield: Usher Parsons," New England Journal of Medicine 254 (1956): 757-60.

6083  Cushman, Paul. "Usher Parsons, M.D. (1788-1868): Naval Surgeon in the Battle of Lake Erie," New York State Journal of Medicine 71 (1971): 2891-94.

6084  Goldowsky, Sebert J. "Usher Parsons: The Battle of Lake Erie," Rhode Island Medical Journal 69 (1986): 525-31.

6085  _____. Yankee Surgeon: The Life and Times of Usher Parsons, M.D., 1788-1868. Boston: Francis A. Countway Library of Medicine, 1988.

6086  Parsons, Usher. "Negroes in the Navy," Massachusetts Historical Society Proceedings 6 (1862): 239-42.

6087  "Usher Parsons," Historical Magazine 10 (1866): 169-71.

## ALDEN PARTIDGE

6088  "Alden Partridge," American Journal of Education 13 (1863): 49-64, 683-88.

6089  Baker, Dean P. "The Partridge Connection: Alden Partridge and Southern Military Education." Ph. D. dissertation, University of North Carolina, 1986.

6090  Beane, S.C. "Captain Alden Partridge," Granite Monthly 12 (1889): 92-97.

6091  Bornemann, Alfred. "Captain Alden Partridge and Political Economy," Vermont History 25 (1957): 142-47.

6092  "Captain Alden Partridge," United States Military Magazine 3 (1841): 87-88.

6093  Colvocoresses, G.P. "Captain Alden Partridge," United Service 2 (1902): 25-29.

6094  Dupuy, Richard E. "Mutiny at West Point," American Heritage 7 (1955): 22-27.

6095  Grabowski, John E. "Alden Partridge and Military Education, 1818-1834." Master's Thesis, University of Pittsburgh, 1972.

6096  Harmon, Ernest N. Norwich University, its Founder and His Ideals. New York: Newcomen Society in North America, 1951.

6097  Painter, Jacqueline S., ed. The Trial of Captain Alden Partridge, Corps of Engineers. Northfield, VT: Norwich University Press, 1988.

6098  Partridge, Alden. The Military Academy at West Point, Unmasked, or Corruption and Military Despotism  Exposed. Washington, DC: N.p., 1830.

6099  _____. Memorial of Alden Partridge and Edmund Burke, in Behalf of the State Military Convention of Vermont, Praying for the Adpotion of a Plan proposed by them For the Reorganization of the Militia of the United States. 25th Cong. 3d Session Senate Document 197.

6100  Sheldon, Nelson L. "Captain Alden Partridge, A.M.: Founder of Technical Education in America," New England Magazine 31 (1904): 228-36.

6101  Sheldon, Nelson L. "Norwich University," New England Magazine 20
      (1899): 65-86.

6102  Walker, Joseph T. "Old Pewter: A Biographical Sketch of Captain
      Alden Partridge," Vermont History 33 (1965): 313-25.

6103  Webb, Lester A. "Captain Alden Partridge, Cadet, Professor, and
      Superintendent, United States Military Academy from 1806 to 1818."
      Master's Thesis, University of North Carolina, 1957.

6104  _____. Captain Alden Partridge and the United States Military
      Academy, 1806-1833. Northport, AL: American Southern, 1965.

                        HIRAM PAULDING

6105  "Olde Ulster and the American Navy," Olde Ulster 9 (1913): 267-74.

6106  Paulding, Hiram. Journal of a Cruise of the U.S. Schooner Dolphin
      Among the Islands of the Pacific Ocean, and a Visit to the Mulgrave
      Islands in Pursuit of the Mutineers of the Whaleship Globe. New
      York: G. & G. & H. Carvill, 1831.

6107  Meade, Rebecca. Life of Hiram Paulding, Admiral, U.S.N. New York:
      Baker, Taylor, 1910.

6108  Meade, R.W. "Admiral Hiram Paulding," Harper's Monthly Magazine 58
      (1878): 358-64.

                        JAMES K. PAULDING

6109  Aderman, Ralph M., ed. The Letters of James Kirke Paulding.
      Madison: University of Wisconsin Press, 1962.

6110  Herold, Amos L. James Kirke Paulding: Versatile America. New York:
      Columbia University Press, 1926.

6111  Paulding, William I. The Literary Life of James K. Paulding.
      New York: Charles Scribner, 1867.

                        JOHN PERCIVAL

6112  Blacklington, Alton H. "Mad Jack," Yankee 25 (1961): 40-42, 74-76.

6113  Conrad, D.B. "Some Yarns Spun by an Officer of the Old Navy,"
      United Service 8 (1892): 326-29.

6114  Facts Representing the Conduct of Lieut. John Percival of the United
      States Schooner Dolphin, at the Sandwich Islands in the Year 1826.
      N.p., 1828.

6115  Hilliard, Jack E. "The First Time," United States Naval Institute
      Proceedings 95 (1969): 147-49.

6116  Long, David F. "Mad Jack' Percival in Vietnam: First American
      Hostilities, May, 1845," American Neptune 47 (1987): 169-73.

6117  McKee, Linda. "Mad Jack' and the Missionaries," American Heritage
      22 (1971): 30-37, 85-87.

6118  Safford, Mary J. "A Commander of the 'Constitution'," Army and Navy
      Life 9 (1906): 385-88.

6119  Wagner, John P. "Sandal Wood Bonanza." In: Clayton J. Barrow, ed. America Spreads Her Sails. Annapolis: Naval Institute Press, 1973, 21-40.

6120  Westcott, Allan. "Captain 'Mad Jack' Percival," United States Naval Institute Proceedings 61 (1935): 313-19.

6121  Wise, Henry A. Tales for Marines. New York: J.C. Derby, 1855.

MATTHEW C. PERRY

6122  Alden, Carroll S. and Ralph Earle. "Matthew Clabraith Perry." In: Makers of Naval Tradition. Boston: Ginn, 1925, 93-110.

6123  Barrows, Edward M. The Great Commodore: The Exploits of Matthew Calbraith Perry. Indianapolis: Bobbs-Merrill, 1935.

6124  Griffis, William E. "Commodore Matthew Calbraith Perry," Magazine of American History 13 (1885): 417-35.

6125  _____. Matthew Calbraith Perry: A Typical American Naval Officer. Boston: Cupples, Hurd, 1887.

6126  Morison, Samuel E. 'Old Bruin': Commodore Matthew C. Perry, 1794-1858. Boston: Little, Brown, 1962.

6127  Morris, Charles. Heroes of the Navy in America. Philadelphia: J.B. Lippincott, 1907, 261-72.

6128  Robinson, Robert L. "Commodore Matthew C. Perry and the Protection of American Rights in West Africa, 1843-45," Southern Quarterly 5 (1966): 47-63.

6129  Schroeder, John H. "Matthew Calbraith Perry: Antebellum Precursor of the Steam Navy." In: James C. Bradford, ed. Captains of the Old Steam Navy. Annapolis: Naval Institute Press, 1986, 3-25.

6130  Wright, Donald R. "Matthew Perry and the African Squadron." In: Clayton J. Barrow, ed. America Spreads Her Sails. Annapolis: Naval Institite Press, 1973, 80-99.

6131  Zabriskie, G.A. "Commodore Matthew Calbraith Perry," New York Historical Society Quarterly 30 (1946): 196-207.

*OLIVER H. PERRY

6132  Altoff, Gerry T. "Oliver Hazard Perry and the Battle of Lake Erie," Michigan Historical Review 14 (1988): 25-58.

6133  Baker, Henry D. Commodore Oliver Hazard Perry, U.S.N., and His Historic Connection with Trinidad. Washington, DC: American Consular Association, 1924.

6134  Baker, Maury D., ed. "The Voyage of the U.S. Schooner Nonsuch up the Orinoco: Journal of the Perry Mission of 1819 to South America," American Historical Review 30 (1950): 480-98.

6135  Brown, John H. "Oliver Hazard Perry." In: American Naval Heroes. Boston: Brown, 1899, 351-60.

6136  Cherpak, Evelyn M. "The Naval Officer as Diplomat: Oliver Hazard Perry's Mission to Angostura, Venezuela, 1819," Newport History 57 (1984): 6-15.

6137  Coletta, Paolo E. "A Selected Annotated Bibliography of Oliver Hazard Perry," Journal of Erie Studies 17 (1988): 123-29.

6138  Edwards, J. Dixon. "The Commodore Perry We do not Know," Foreign Service Journal 30 (1953): 20-23, 52-56.

6139  Mahon, John K. "Oliver Hazard Perry: Savior of the Northwest." In: James C. Bradford, ed. Command Under Sail: Makers of the American Naval Tradition, 1775-1850. Annapolis: Naval Institute, 1984, 126-46.

6140  Palmer, Michael D. "A Failure of Command, Control and Communications: Oliver Hazard Perry and the Battle of Lake Erie," Journal of Erie Studies 17 (1988): 7-26.

6141  Van Denmark, Herry. "Oliver Hazard Perry, Diplomat: Some Facts About a Little-Known Episode in the Life of One of Our Greatest Naval Heroes," Education 54 (1933): 177-81.

6142  Vivian, James F. "The Orinoco River and Angostura, Venezuela, in the Summer of 1819: The Narrative of a Maryland Naval Chaplain," The Americas 24 (1967-1968): 160-83.

6143  Ward, Annette P. Lest We Forget: Oliver Hazard Perry, the War of 1812, and the Battle of Lake Erie. Columbus: Champlain Press, 1912.

## ISAAC PHILLIPS

6144  Palmer. Michael. "The Dismission of Capt. Isaac Phillips," American Neptune 45 (1985): 94-103.

6145  Phillips, Isaac. Impartial Examination of the Case of Isaac Phillips Late of the Navy and Commander of the U.S. Sloop of War Baltimore in 1798. Baltimore: R. Edes, 1825.

## *TIMOTHY PICKERING

6146  Brown, Jefferey P. "Timothy Pickering and the Northwest Territory," Northwest Ohio Quarterly 53 (1981): 117-32.

6147  Clarfield, Gerald H. Timothy Pickering and American Diplomacy, 1795-1800. Columbia: University of Missouri Press, 1969.

6148  Phillips, Edward H. "The Public Career of Timothy Pickering, Federalist, 1745-1802." Ph. D. dissertation, Harvard University, 1950.

6149  _____. "Timothy Pickering at His Best: Indian Commissioner, 1790-1794," Essex Institute Historical Collections 102 (1966): 163-202.

6150  Wright, Louis B. "William Eaton, Timothy Pickering and Indian Policy," Huntington Library Quarterly 9 (1946): 387-400.

## BENJAMIN K. PIERCE

6151  Burbey, Louis H. Our Worthy Commander: The Life and Times of Benjamin K. Pierce, in whose Honor Fort Pierce Was Named. Fort Pierce, FL: Indian River Community College, 1976.

### * ZEUBULON M. PIKE

6152  Abel, Annie H. "The Retirement of General Pike." In: The American Indian as Participant in the Civil War. Cleveland: Arthur H. Clark, 1919, 185-201.

6153  Backes, William J. "General Zeubulon M. Pike, Somerset Born," Somerset County Historical Quarterly 8 (1919): 241-51.

6154  Baker, Nina. Pike of Pike's Peak. New York: Harcourt, Brace, 1953.

6155  Bolton, Herbert E., ed. "Papers of Zeubulon M. Pike, 1806-1807," American Historical Review 13 (1908): 798-827.

6156  Carpenter, John C. "Pike, a Typical American Soldier," Kansas Historical Collections 7 (1901-1902): 284-87.

6157  Carter, Harvey L. Zeubulon Montgomery Pike: Pathfinder and Patriot. Colorado Springs: Dentan Printing Co., 1956.

6158  Castel, Albert. "Zeubulon Pike, Explorer," American History Illustrated 7 (1972): 4-11, 45-48.

6159  "Correspondence of General Pike," Western Reserve Historical Society Tracts No. 39, 22-24.

6160  Coues, Elliot, ed. The Expeditions of Zeubulon Montgomery Pike to the Headwaters of the Mississippi River, through Louisiana Territory and in New Spain, during the Years, 1805-6-7. New York: Francis P. Harper, 1895.

6161  Crichton, Kyle S. "Zeb Pike," Scribner's Magazine 82 (1927): 462-67.

6162  Curran, Ruth A. "Biography of Zeubulon Montgomery Pike." Master's Thesis, Washington University, St. Louis, 1944.

6163  Davis, W.W. "Five Bucks County Generals," Bucks County Historical Society Collections 3 (1909): 258-73.

6164  DeWitt, Donald. Pike and Pike's Peak: A Brief Life of Zeubulon Montgomery Pike, and extracts from His Journal of Exploration. Colorado Springs: Collarado College, 1906.

6165  Hafen, LeRoy. "Zeubulon M. Pike," Colorado Magazine 8 (1931): 132-42.

6166  Hart, Stephen H. and Archer B. Hulbert, eds. Zeubulon Pike's Arkansas Journal: In Search of the Southern Louisiana Purchase Boundary Line. Denver: Denver Public Library, 1932.

6167  Harvey, Charles M. "Captain Zeubulon M. Pike, Expansionist," Putnam's Monthly 1 (1906): 138-46.

6168  Hoffman, M.M. "A Yankee Captain and a Spanish Priest," Catholic World 136 (1933): 672-79.

6169  Hollon, W. Eugene. "Zeubulon Montgomery Pike and the Wilkinson-Burr Conspiracy," American Philosophical  Society Proceedings 91 (1947): 447-56.

6170  _____ . "Zeubulon Montgomery Pike's Lost papers," Mississippi Valley Historical Review 34 (1947): 265-73.

6171  Jackson, Donald, ed. The Journals of Zeubulon Montgomery Pike with Letters and Related Documents. 2 Vols. Norman: University of Oklahoma Press, 1966.

6172  Jones, Warren H. "Pike of Pike's Peak," Army in Europe (February, 1965): 8-11.

6173  "Life and Military Services of Zeubulon M. Pike," Minnesota Historical Society Collections 12 (1906): 220-429.

6174  Lykes, Lily W. "Zeubulon Pike, National Hero," DAR Magazine 62 (1928): 597-603.

6175  McSpadden, J. Walker. Pioneer Heroes. New York: Crowell, 1929.

6176  Pike, Zeubulon M. An Account of Expeditions to the Sources of the Mississippi, and Through Western Parts of Louisiana. Philadelphia: C. & A. Conrad, 1810.

6177  _____. "An Account of Expeditions to the Source of the Mississippi," General Repository And Review 1 (1812): 374-410.

6178  Prentis, Noble L. "Pike of Pike's Peak," Kansas State Historical Society Transactions 6 (1900): 325-36.

6179  Terrell, John U. Zeubulon Pike: The Life and Times of an Adventurer. New York: Weybright, Tally, 1968.

6180  Thompson, Albert W. "Where is Zeubulon M. Pike Buried?" Colorado Magazine 13 (1936): 149-55.

6181  Warner, Robert M. "The Death of Zeubulon M. Pike," Annals of Iowa 33 (1955): 44-46.

EDGAR A. POE

6182  Allan, Carlisle. "The Military Service of Edgar Allen Poe." Master's Thesis, Columbia University, 1925.

6183  _____. "Cadet Edgar Allen Poe," American Mercury 29 (1933): 446-55.

6184  _____. Sergeant Major Perry and Cadet Poe," Infantry Journal 51 (1942): 70-78.

6185  Cameron, Kenneth W. "Young Poe and the Army-Victorian Editing," American Transcendental Quarterly No. 20 (1973): 154-82.

6186  Gibson, Thomas W. "Poe at West Point," Harper's Monthly Magazine 35 (1867): 754-56.

6187  Helfers, Melvin C. "The Military Career of Edgar Allen Poe." Master's Thesis, Duke University, 1949.

6188  Johnson, Tom. "Cadet Edgar Allen Poe," American Heritage 27 (1976): 60-63, 87-88.

6189  Oelke, Karl E. "Poe at West Point-A Re-evaluation," Poe Studies 6 (1973): 1-6.

6190  Redmond, Catherine. "Edgar Allen Poe-Soldier," Field Artillery Journal 26 (1936): 255-62.

JOEL R. POINSETT

6191 Hruneni, George A. "Palmetto Yankee: The Public Life and Times of Joels Roberts Poinsett, 1824-1851." Ph. D. dissertation, University of California, Santa Barbara, 1972.

6192 "Joel R. Poinsett," United States Magazine and Democratic Review 1 (1838): 361-68, 443-56.

6193 Putnam, Herbert E. Joel Roberts Poinsett: A Political Biography. Washington: Mimeoform Press, 1935.

6194 Rippy, J. Fred. Joel R. Poinsett: Versatile American. Durham: Duke University Press, 1935.

6195 Stille, Charles J. "The Life and Service of Joel R. Poinsett," Pennsylvania Magazine of History and Biography 12 (1888): 129-64, 257-303.

*DAVID PORTER

6196 Beach, Edward L. "The Pioneer of America's Pacific Empire: David Porter," United States Naval Institute Proceedings 34 (1908): 543-71.

6197 _____. "The Court-Martial of Commodore David Porter," Ibid 33 (1907): 1391-1402.

6198 Bidwell, Robert L. "The First Mexican Navy, 1821-1830." Ph. D. dissertation, University of Virginia, 1960.

6199 Brown, John H. "David Porter." In: American Naval Heroes. Boston: Brown, 1899, 303-20.

6200 Flaccus, Elmer W. "Commodore David Porter and the Mexican Navy," Hispanic American Historical Review 34 (1954): 365-73.

6201 Lewis, Charles. "David Porter and the Cruise of the Essex." In: Famous American Naval Officers. Boston: L.C. Page, 1924, 99-131.

6202 Long, David F. "David Porter: Pacific Ocean Gadfly." In: James C. Bradford, ed. Command Under Sail: Makers of American Naval Tradition, 1775-1850. Annapolis: Naval Institute Press, 1984, 173-98.

6203 Matthews, C.W. "Rise and Fall of Madison's Ville: From Captain Porter's Account of the Navy's First Advanced Base," Navy Civil Engineer 12 (1971): 10-13.

6204 Minutes of the Proceedings of the Court of Inquiry and Court-Martial in Relation to Captain David Porter. Washington, DC: Davis, 1825.

6205 Porter, David. "The Northwest Coast," Washington Historical Quarterly 10 (1919): 149-52.

6206 _____. An Exposition of the Facts and Circumstances which Justify the Expedition to Foxardo, and the Consequences Thereof. Washington, DC: Davis, Force, 1825.

6207 _____. Constantinople and Its Environs: In a Series of Letters Exhibiting the Actual States of the Manners, Customs, and Habits of the Turks, Armenians, Jews and Greeks. 2 Vols. New York: Harper, 1835.

## DAVID D. PORTER

6208  Bassett, F.S. "Admiral David Dixon Porter," United Service 5 (1891):
      381–84.

6209  Cagle, Malcom W. "Lieutenant David Dixon Porter and His Camels,"
      United States Naval Institute Proceedings 83 (1957): 1327–33.

6210  Colvocoresses, George P. "Admiral Porter," Ibid 34 (1908): 309–14.

6211  Gerson, Noel B. Yankee Admiral: A Biography of David Dixon Porter.
      New York: D. McKay, 1968.

6212  Melia, Tamara M. "David Dixon Porter: Fighting Sailor." In: James C.
      Bradford, ed. Captains of the Old Steam Navy: Makers of the American
      Naval Tradition, 1840–1880. Annapolis: Naval Institute Press, 1986,
      227–49.

6213  Morris, Charles. Heroes of the Navy in America. Philadelphia: J.B.
      Lippincott, 1907, 286–93.

6214  Parker, John C. "Admiral David D. Porter." In: Military Order of the
      Loyal Legion of the United States, Missouri Commandery. St. Louis:
      The Commandery, 1892. Vol. 1, 434–42.

6215  Porter, David D. Memoir of Commodore David Porter of the United States
      Navy. Albany: J. Munsell, 1875.

6216  Soley, James R. Admiral Porter. New York: D. Appleton, 1913.

6217  West, Richard S. The Second Admiral: A Life of David Dixon Porter,
      1813–1891. New York: Coward, McCann, 1937.

## EDWARD PREBLE

6218  Bainbridge-Hoff, Arthur. "Preble and the Philadelphia," United States
      Naval Institute Proceedings 61 (1935): 818–22.

6219  Brown, John H. "Edward Preble." In: American Naval Heroes. Boston:
      Brown, 1899, 183–206.

6220  Brown, Gilbert P. "Commodore Edward Preble, U.S.N., First to Carry
      the Flag Around the Cape of Good Hope," New Age 5 (1906): 267–70.

6221  "Commodore Preble and Tripoli," American Historical Record 1 (1872):
      53–60.

6222  Cooper, James F. Lives of Distinguished American Naval Officers. 2 Vols.
      Philadelphia: Carey, Hart, 1846. Vol. 1, 171–252.

6223  "Diary of Commodore Edward Preble Before Tripoli-1804," Magazine of
      American History 3 (1879): 182–93.

6224  Kirkland, John T. Life of Commodore Preble. N.p., 1810.

6225  "Life of Commodore Edward Preble," Portfolio 3 (1810): 353–65.

6226  McKee, Christopher. "Edward Preble and the 'Boys': The Officer Corps
      of 1812 Revisited." In: James C. Bradford, ed. Command Under Sail:
      Makers of the American Naval Tradition, 1775–1850. Annapolis: Naval
      Institute Press, 1984, 71–96.

6227  McKee, Christopher. *Edward Preble: A Naval Biography*. Annapolis: Naval Institute Press, 1972.

6228  Morris, Charles. *Heroes of the Navy in America*. Philadelphia: J.B. Lippincott, 1907, 104-12.

6229  Pratt, Fletcher. "Edward Preble." In: *Preble's Boys*. New York: Sloane, 1950, 13-39.

6230  _____. "Edward Preble," *United States Naval Institute Proceedings* 59 (1933): 1683-89.

6231  Preble, Edward. "Edward Preble to Robert R. Livingston, 19 February, 1804," *New York Historical Society Quarterly* 35 (1951): 410-11.

6232  _____. "Edward Preble's Report on the Frigates, 1806," *American Neptune* 18 (1958): 183.

6233  Riley, Elihu S. "Commodore Preble's Infernal," *Southern Magazine* 5 (1873): 30-35.

6234  Sabine, Lorenzo. *The Life of Edward Preble, A Commodore in the Navy of the United States*. Boston: C.C. Little, J. Brown, 1855.

6235  Seawell, Molly E. *Twelve Naval Captains*. New York: Charles Scribner, 1906, 87-101.

*HENRY PROCTER

6236  Antal, Sandor. "Myths and Facts Concerning General Procter," *Ontario History* 29 (1987): 251-62.


NATHANIEL PRYOR

6237  Coues, Elliot, ed. "Letters by William Clark and Nathaniel Pryor," *Annals of Iowa* 1 (1893-1895): 613-20.

6238  Douglas, Walter B., ed. "Captain Nathaniel Pryor," *American Historical Review* 24 (1919): 253-65.

6239  Foreman, Grant. "Nathaniel Pryor," *Chronicles of Oklahoma* 7 (1929): 152-63.

*SAMUEL C. REID

6240  Brown, John H. "Samuel Chester Reid." In: *American Naval Heroes*. Boston: Brown, 1899, 393-420.


BENNETT RILEY

6241  Foreman, Carolyn T. "General Bennett Riley, Commandant at Fort Gibson and Governor of California," *Chronicles of Oklahoma* 19 (1941): 225-44.

6242  Hutchins, James S. "Dear Hook': Letters from Bennett Riley, Alphonzo Wetmore and Reuben Holmes, 1822-1823," *Missouri Historical Society Bulletin* 36 (1980): 203-20.

6243  Murdock, Victor. "Notes on Western History," *Chronicles of Oklahoma* 20 (1942): 372-75.

6244  Riley, Bennett. "Report of Four Companies of the 6th Regiment of United States Infantry, *American State Papers: Military Affairs* 4: 277-80.

6245   Sweeney, William M. "General Bennett Riley, U.S. Army," American Irish
       Historical Society Journal 26 (1927): 266-68.

*JOHN RODGERS

6246   Bauer, K. Jack. "John Rodgers: The Stalwart Conservative." In:
       James C. Bradford, ed. Command Under Sail: Makers of the American
       Naval Tradition, 1775-1850. Annapolis: Naval Institute Press, 1984,
       220-50.

6247   Bradley, Udolpho T. "Commodore Rodgers and the Bureau System of Naval
       Administration," United States Naval Institute Proceedings 57 (1931):
       307-08.

6248   Brown, John H. "John Rodgers." In: American Naval Heroes. Boston:
       Brown, 1899, 263-68.

6249   Hall, A. "Biographical Memoir of John Rodgers," National Academy of
       Science Biographical Memoirs 6 (1909): 81-92.

6250   Paullin, Charles O. "The Services of Commodore John Rodgers in Our
       Wars with the Barbary Pirates," United States Naval Institute
       Proceedings 34 (1908): 1141-88.

6251   Rodgers, John. "Letter of Commodore Rodgers to Secretary Crowinshield
       in 1815," Massachusetts Historical Society Proceedings 4 (1887-1889):
       207-08.

JOHN RODGERS, Jr.

6252   Johnson, Robert E. Rear Admiral John Rodgers, 1812-1882. Annapolis:
       Naval Institute Press, 1967.

SACAJAWEA

6253   Anderson, Irving W, "Probing the Riddle of the Bird Woman," Montana
       23 (1973): 2-17.

6254       . Sacajawea, Sacagawea, Sakakawea," South Dakota History 8 (1978):
       303-11.

6255   Blassingame, Wyatt. Sacajawea, Indian Guide. Champaign, IL: Garrard
       Publishing Co., 1965.

6256   Bragg, William F. "Sacajawea's Role in Western History." Master's
       Thesis, University of Wyoming, 1953.

6257   Chandler, M.G. "Sidelights on Sacajawea," Masterkey 43 (1969): 58-66.

6258   Chuinard, Eldon G. "The Actual Role of the Bird Woman," Montana 26
       (1976): 18-29.

6259   Clark, Ella and Margot Edmonds. Sacajawea of the Lewis and Clark
       Expedition. Berkeley: University of California Press, 1979.

6260   Crawford, Helen. "Sakakakwea," North Dakota Historical Quarterly 1
       (1927): 5-15, 30-45.

6261   Defenbach, Byron. Red Heroine of the Northwest. Caldwell, ID:
       Caxton Printer, 1929.

6262 Farnsworth, Frances J. Winged Moccasins: The Story of Sacajawea. New York: Messner, 1954.

6263 Fletcher, F.N. "Sacajawea," Out West 23 (1905): 223-37.

6264 Frazer, Neta L. Sacajawea, the Girl Nobody Knows. New York: David Makay, 1967.

6265 Gilbert, B. Miles. "Sacajawea: A Problem in Plains Anthropology," Plains Anthropologist 17 (1972): 156-60.

6266 Hebard, Grace R. Sacajawea, A Guide and Interpreter of the Lewis and Clark Expedition. Glendale, CA: Arthur H. Clark, 1933.

6267 _____. "Pilot of the First White Men to Cross the American Continent," Journal of American History 1 (1907): 467-84.

6268 Howard, Harold P. Sacajawea. Norman: University of Oklahoma, 1972.

6269 Howard, Helen A. "The Mystery of Sacagawea's Death," Pacific Northwest Quarterly 58 (1967): 1-6.

6270 Humphrey, Grace. Women in American History. Indianapolis: Bobbs-Merrill, 1919.

6271 Karolevitz, Robert F. "Sacajawea: Heroine of the Lewis and Clark Expedition," True West 5 (1958): 4-6, 28-30.

6272 Kingston, C.S. "Sacajawea as A Guide: The Evaluation of a Legend," Pacific Northwest Quarterly 35 (1944): 2-18.

6273 Libby, Orin G. "Sakakawea, the 'Bird Woman'," Magazine of History 19 (1914): 23-24.

6274 McCoy, Timothy J. "Sacajawea, the Bird Woman," Westerner's Brand Book 5 (1953): 96-102.

6275 McCreight, Milton F. Sac-a-ja-wea; America's Greatest Heroine. Sykesville, PA: Nupp Print Co., 1948.

6276 Mumey, Nolie. "Sacajawea, the Great American Indian Heroine Who Accompanied Lewis and Clark up the Missouri River in 1804-1805; Buried in Wyoming," Westerner's Brand Book 14 (1958): 333-48.

6277 Madsen, Brigham P. The Lemhi: Sacajawea's People. Caldwell, ID: Caxton Printers, 1979.

6278 Reid, Russell. "Sakakawea," North Dakota History 30 (1963): 101-13.

6279 _____. Sakakawea, the Bird Woman. Bismark: North Dakota State Historical Society, 1950.

6280 Robinson, Doane. "Sac-a-jawe vs Sa-kaka-wea," South Dakota Historical Collections 12 (1924): 71-81.

6281 Schroer, Blanche. "Boat-Pusher' or 'Bird Woman'," Annals of Wyoming 52 (1980): 46-54.

6282 Schultz, James W. Bird Woman (Sacajawea); The Guide of Lewis and Clark. Boston: Houghton, Mifflin, 1918.

6283  Scott, Laura T. Sacajawea: The Unsung Heroine of Montana. Dillon, MT: Federation of Women's Clubs, 1915.

6284  Spencer, Lloyd. "Early Phases of the History of the State of Washington," Americana 29 (1935): 369-429.

6285  Waldo, Anna Lee. Sacajawea. New York: Avon Books, 1978.

6286  Wheeler, William F. "Sacajawea: A Historical Sketch," Contributions to the Montana Historical Society 7 (1910): 271-303.

## ARTHUR ST. CLAIR

6287  "Arthur St. Clair," Mad River Valley Pioneer 1 (1870): 5 pp.

6288  Beals, Ellis. "Arthur St. Clair in the History of Western Pennsylvania." Master's Thesis, University of Pittsburgh, 1928.

6289  ____. "Arthur St. Clair, Western Pennsylvania's Leading Citizen, 1764-1818," Western Pennsylvania Historical Magazine 12 (1929): 75-96, 175-96.

6290  Bond, Beverly W. "An American Experiment in Colonial Government," Mississippi Valley Historical Review 15 (1928): 221-35.

6291  Boucher, John N. "General Arthur St. Clair: First Governor of the Northwest Territory," Americana 12 (1918): 381-404.

6292  Brown, Jeffrey P. "Arthur St. Clair and the Northwest Territory," Northwest Ohio Quarterly 59 (1987): 75-90.

6293  Carter, James G. "First Governor of the Northwest Territory," Knight Templar 24 (1978): 9-13.

6294  Douglas, Albert. "Major General Arthur St. Clair," Ohio Archaeological and Historical Society Publications 16 (1907): 455-76.

6295  ____. "Major General Arthur St. Clair, Governor of the Northwest Territory," Firelands Pioneer 15 (1906): 1020-42.

6296  Downs, Randolph C. "Thomas Jefferson in the Removal of Governor St. Clair," Ohio Archaeological and Historical Society Quarterly 36 (1927): 62-77.

6297  Hunter, William H. "General Arthur St. Clair," Old Northwest Genealogical Quarterly 9 (1906): 33-44, 166-68.

6298  Ferguson, R.J. "General St. Clair: The Gallant Loser," Carnegie Magazine 29 (1955): 64-66.

6299  Furlong, Patrick L. "The Investigation of General Arthur St. Clair, 1792-1793," Capitol Studies 5 (1977): 65-86.

6300  Greenleaf, Kate V. "Major General Arthur St. Clair," American Historical Register 3 (1895): 364-72.

6301  Heathcothe, Charles W. "General Arthur St. Clair-A Patriotic Pennsylvanian Military Officer and Colleague of Washington," Picket Post No. 74 (1961): 4-10.

6302 Hill, M. Therese. "St. Clair, Stateman or Tyrant?" Master's Thesis, Xavier University, 1957.

6303 Historical Sketches. A Collection of Papers Prepared for the Historical Society of Montgomery County, Pennsylvania. Norristown, PA: Montgomery County Historical Society, 1895. Vol. 4, 158-64.

6304 Krull, Theresa V. "The Bicentennial of Major Arthur St. Clair," Indiana History Bulletin 11 (1934): 83-93.

6305 Longacre, James A. and James Herring. The National Portrait Gallery of Distinguished Americans. 4 Vols. Philadelphia: Rice, Rutter, 1868. Vol. 3.

6306 McCarty, Dwight G. The Territorial Governors of the Old Northwest; A Study in Territorial Administration. Iowa City: State Historical Society of Iowa, 1910, 48-74.

6307 Moore, George H. Libels on Washington, with A Critical Examination Thereof. New York: The Author, 1889.

6308 Murray, Eleanor M. "The Court-Martial of General Arthur St. Clair," Fort Ticonderoga Museum Bulletin 7 (1947): 3-20.

6309 Nash, George K. "Arthur St. Clair," Ohio Archaeological and Historical Society Centennial Anniversary (1903): 53-58.

6310 "Notes and Queries," Pennsylvania Magazine of History and Biography 6 (1882): 119-22.

6311 Okey, George B. "History of the Veto in Ohio," Ohio Magazine 1 (1906): 570-73.

6312 Poole, W.F. "General Arthur St. Clair," Dial 2 (1882): 227-29, 251-54.

6313 _____. "General Arthur St. Clair and the Ordnance of 1787," Ibid 3 (1883): 13-15.

6314 Rorison, Arda B. Major General Arthur St. Clair, A Biographical Sketch. New York: N.p., 1910.

6315 St. Clair, Arthur. A Narrative of the Manner in Which the Campaign Against the Indians, in the Year One Thousand Seven Hundred and Ninety One, was Conducted. Philadelphia: Jane Aitken, 1812.

6316 "St. Clair, Arthur. Miscellaneous Material." Clippings at the Burton Historical Collection, Detroit Public Library.

6317 Sears, Alfred B. "The Political Philosophy of Arthur St. Clair," Ohio Archaeological and Historical Society Quarterly 49 (1940): 41-57.

6318 Siebeneck, Henry K. "Hervey Allen vs Arthur St. Clair," Western Pennsylvania Historical Magazine 30 (1947): 73-94.

6319 Smith, William H. The St. Clair Papers: The Life and Public Services of Arthur St. Clair, Soldier of the Revolutionary war. 2 Vols. Cincinnati: Arthur Clark, 1882.

6320 Smith, William H. "General St. Clair and the Ordnance of 1787," Dial 2 (1882): 293-96.

6321   Thompson, Joseph J. "Penalties of Patriotism," Illinois State
       Historical Society Journal 9 (1917): 401-19.

6322   Trenary, Donald C. "Major General Arthur St. Clair, First Governor
       of the Northwest Territory." Ph. D. dissertation, University of
       Wisconsin, 1928.

6323   Tweedy, Malcom. "Arthur St. Clair, Patriot," DAR Magazine 98 (1964):
       374-76, 390.

6324   West, J. Martin. "Arthur St. Clair," Timeline 5 (1988): 51-55.

6325   Westrate, Edwin V. Those Fatal Generals. New York: Knight, 1936.

6326   Williams, William W. "Arthur St. Clair and the Ordnance of 1787,"
       Magazine of Western History 1 (1884-1885): 49-61.

6327   Wilson, Fraser E. Arthur St. Clair, Rugged Ruler of the Old
       Northwest. Richmond: Garrett, Massie, 1944.

6328   Wilson, Gordon L. "Arthur St. Clair and the Administration of the
       Old Northwest, 1788-1802." Ph. D. dissertation, University of
       Southern California, 1957.

## *CHARLES DE SALABERRY

6329   Wohler, Patrick. Charles de Salaberry: Soldier of Empire, Defender
       of Quebec. Toronto: Dundurn Press, 1984.

## BENJAMIN F. SANDS

6330   Sands, Benjamin F. From Reefer to Rear Admiral: Reminiscences of
       Nearly a Half Century of Naval Life, 1827-1874. New York: F.A.
       Stokes, 1899.

## WINTHROP SARGENT

6331   Hamilton, William B. "The Printing of the 1799 Laws of the Missi-
       ssippi Territory," Journal of Mississippi History 2 (1940): 88-99.

6332   Pershing, Benjamin H. "Winthrop Sargent: A Builder in the Old
       Northwest." Ph. D. dissertation, University of Chicago, 1927.

6333   _____. "Winthrop Sargent," Ohio Archaeological and Historical
       Society Quarterly 33 (1924): 229-82; 35 (1926): 583-602.

6334   _____. "A Surveyor on the Seven Ranges," Ibid 46 (1937): 257-70.

6335   _____. "Winthrop Sargent and the American Occupation of Detroit,"
       Northwest Ohio Quarterly 18 (1946): 114-25.

6336   _____. "Winthrop Sargent—Patriot and Pioneer," Society of Colonial
       Wars in Pennsylvania Historical Publications 6 (1944): 1-31.

6337   Rowland, Dunbar, ed. The Mississippi Territorial Archives, 1798-1818:
       Executive Journals of Governor Winthrop Sargent and Governor William
       C.C. Claiborne. Nashville: Brandon Printing Co., 1905.

6338   Sargent, Charles S., ed. "Winthrop Sargent's Diary while with General
       Arthur St. Clair's Expedition Against the Indians," Ohio Archaeological
       and Historical Society Publications 33 (1924): 228-82.

6339   Sargent, Winthrop. Papers in Relation to the Official Conduct of
       Governor Sargent. Boston: Thomas, Andrews, 1801.

6340        . Diary of Col. Winthrop Sargent, Adjutant General of the United
       States Army During the Campaign of 1791. Worsloe, GA: Privately
       Printed, 1851.

6341        . "St. Clair's Defeat, From Winthrop Sargent's Journal,"
       American Historical Record 1 (1872): 480-87.

6342        . "Journal of the General Meeting of the Cincinnati in 1784,"
       Historical Society of Pennsylvania Memoirs 6 (1858): 57-115.

6343   Toulmin, George B. "The Political Ideas of Withrop Sargent, A New
       England Federalist on the Frontier," Journal of Mississippi History
       15 (1953): 207-29.

6344   Wunder, John. "American Law and Order Comes to the Mississippi
       Territory: The Making of Sargent's Code," Ibid 38 (1976): 131-55.

## CHARLES SCOTT

6345   "Anecdote of Old General Scott," Army and Navy Chronicle 3 (1836):
       258-59.

6346   Burnley, Pattie. "Biographical Sketch of General, Afterwards Governor,
       Charles S. Scott," Register of the Kentucky Historical Society 1
       (1903): 11-18.

6347   Crittenden, Thomas L. "General Charles Scott." In: Sons of the
       Revolution, Kentucky Chapter Yearbook (1913): 124-29.

6348   Fort Wayne and Allen County Public Library. Scott's Wabash Campaign,
       1791. Fort Wayne, IN: The Library, 1953.

6349   Heathcote, Charles W. "General Charles Scott-An Able Officer on Whom
       Washington Depended," Pickett Post No. 57 (1957): 4-11.

6350   Knopf, Richard C., ed. "Two Journals of Kentucky Volunteers, 1793
       & 1794," Filson Club Quarterly 27 (1963): 247-81.

6351   Nelson, Paul D. "General Charles Scott, the Kentucky Mounted
       Volunteers, and the Northwest Indian Wars, 1784-1794," Journal
       of the Early Republic 6 (1986): 219-51.

6352   Obituary Addresses Delivered Upon the Occasion of the Re-Internment
       of Remains of Gen. Charles Scott. Frankfort, KY: A.&.G. Hodges, 1855.

6353   Smucker, Isaac. "General Charles Scott," Historical Magazine 3 (1874):
       88-90.

6354   Ward, Harry M. Charles Scott and the 'Spirit of 76'. Charlotteville:
       University of Virginia Press, 1988.

6355   Whickar, John W. "General Charles Scott on his March to Ouiatenon,"
       Indiana Magazine of History 21 (1925): 90-99.

## MARTIN SCOTT

6356   Heston, Alfred M. "A Partial View of South Jersey History,"
       Americana 18 (1924): 426-29.

6357   Marcy, Randolph B. Thirty Years of Army Life on the Border.
       New York: Harper Bros., 1866, 384-402.

6358   Marrayat, Frederick. A Diary in America with Remarks on Its Instit-
       utions. 3 Vols. London: Longman, Orme, Brown, Greene, Longman, 1839.
       Vol. 2, 78-125.

6359   Sachse, Nancy D. "Frontier Legend: Bennington's Martin Scott,"
       Vermont History 34 (1966): 157-68.

6360   Seitz, Don C. Uncommon Americans. Indianapolis: Bobbs-Merrill, 1925,
       43-59.

6361   Williams, J.F. "Memoir of Captain Martin Scott," Minnesota
       Historical Society Collections 3 (1870-1880): 180-87.

### *WINFIELD SCOTT

6362   Aldrich, Charles. "A Characteristic Order of General Scott,"
       Magazine of American History 24 (1890): 352-53.

6363   Carrington, H.B. Winfield Scott. Boston: N.p., 1910.

6364   Castel, Albert. "Winfield Scott, Part II: The Commander," American
       History Illustrated 16 (1981): 20-29.

6365   Downey, Fairfax. "Winfield Scott," National Defense 62 (1977): 236-8.

6366   Elliott, Charles W. "Winfield Scott and the Black Hawk War,"
       Infantry Journal 41 (1934): 333-37.

6367   _____. "Some Unpublished Letters of a Roving Soldier-Diplomat:
       General Winfield Scott's Reports to Secretary of State James Monroe
       on Conditions in France and England in 1815-1818," American Military
       Historical Foundation Journal 1 (1937): 165-73.

6368   Events and Incidents in the History of General Winfield Scott.
       Washington, DC: Kirkwood, McGill, 1852.

6369   "Fuss and Feathers," Virginia Historical Society Bulletin No. 11
       (1965): 2-5.

6370   Hamilton, Schuyler. "Anecdotes of General Winfield Scott," Southern
       Historical Association Publications 4 (1900): 187-98.

6371   "General Winfield Scott," American Whig Review 5 (1846): 148-57.

6372   "General Scott and the Volunteers," Army and Navy Chronicle 2 (1836):
       378-80.

6373   Johnson, Ludwell H. "Old Fuss and Feathers: William and Mary's
       Greatest Soldier," William and Mary Quarterly 54 (1985): 24-28.

6374   "Major General Winfield Scott," United States Military Magazine 2
       (1840): 81-83.

6375   "Major General Scott's Address," Army and Navy Chronicle 4 (1837):
       168-76.

6376   Memoir of General Scott, from Records Contemporaneous with Events.
       Washington, DC: C. Alexander, 1852.

6377    "Miscellany," Army and Navy Chronicle 6 (1838): 117-19.

6378    Nance, Joseph M. "Adrian Woll; Frenchman in the Mexican Military
        Service," New Mexico Historical Review 33 (1958): 177-86.

6379    Phalen, James M. "General Winfield Scott-Sanitarian," Military Surgeon
        90 (1942): 694-96.

6380    Pratt, Julius W. "General Scott's Headquarters," Niagara Frontier 18
        (1971): 31-39.

6381    "Puffing," Army and Navy Chronicle 7 (1838): 348-49.

6382    Scott, Winfield. "General Winfield Scott on Native Americanism,"
        American Catholic Historical Researches 7 (1911): 10-12.

6383    _____. Proceedings of the Military Court of Inquiry in the Case of
        Major General Scott and Major General Gaines. Washington, DC: N.p.,
        1837.

6384    _____. "Strictures on General Brown's Report on the Battle of Lundy's
        Lane," Historical Magazine 10 (1866): 253-55.

6385    "Seminole Campaign," Army and Navy Chronicle 4 (1837): 177-92.

6386    Stacey, Charles P. "A Private Report of General Winfield Scott on
        the Border Situation in 1839," Canadian Historical Review 21 (1940):
        407-14.

                            RAPHAEL SEMMES

6387    Meriwether, Colyer. Raphael Semmes. Philadelphia: Jacobs, 1913.

6388    Semmes, S. Spencer. "Admiral Raphael Semmes," Southern Historical
        Society Papers 38 (1910): 28-40.

6389    Summersell, Charles G. "The Career of Raphael Semmes prior to the
        Cruise of the 'Alabama'." Ph. D. dissertation, Vanderbilt University,
        1940.

                                SHABBONA

6390    "Dedication of Shabbona Park, LaSalle County, Illinois," Illinois
        Historical Library Publications 12 (1908): 332-41.

6391    Dowd, James. Built Like a Bear. Fairfield, WA: Ye Galleon Press, 1979.

6392    Hatch, Luther A. The Indian Chief Shabbona. DeKalb: L.A. Hatch, 1915.

6393    "The Life and Death of Shabbona," Illinois State Historical Society
        Journal 31 91938): 344-48.

6394    Marsh, Charles W. "Shabbona-His Great Services and Shameful Treatment."
        In: Recollections, 1837-1910. Chicago: Farm Implement News, 1910, 49-62.

6395    Matson, Nehemiah. Memories of Shaubena. With Incidents Relating to
        the Early Settlement of the West. Chicago: D.B. Cooke, 1878.

6396    _____. "Sketch of Shau-be-na, A Pottawatamie Chief," Wisconsin
        Historical Society Collections 7 (1876): 415-21.

6397  Miller, Anson S. "Shaubenna, the Indian Chieftain," Lakeside Monthly
      6 (1871): 53-57.

6398  Robinson, Solon. Me-Won-I-Toc: A Tale of Frontier Life and Indian
      Character. New York: New York News, 1867.

6399  Stevens, Frank E. "The Life and Death of Shabbona," Illinois State
      Historical Society Journal 31 (1938): 344-48.

6400  Temple, Wayne C. Shabbona, a Friend of the Whites. Springfield,
      Illinois State Museum, 1957.

6401  Thornton, N.W. "Shabbona, the White Man's Friend," Illinois State
      Historical Society Journal 5 (1912): 256-60.

6402  Vanderworth, W.C. "The Potowatomi Peace Chief," DAR Magazine 108
      (1974): 668-72.

6403  Walters, Alta P. "Shabonee," Illinois State Historical Society
      Journal 17 (1924-1925): 381-97.

6404  Wick, B.L. "Chief Shabbona and the Part He Played in the Pioneer
      History of the Mississippi Valley," Annals of Iowa 17 (1930): 168-72.

6405  Wood, Norman B. Lives of Famous Indian Chiefs. Aurora, IL: American
      Indian Historical Publishing Co., 1906, 401-42.

JOHN SHAW

6406  Cooper, James F. Lives of Distinguished American Naval Officers.
      2 Vols. Philadelphia: Carey, Hart, 1845. Vol. 1, 123-46.

6407  Shaw, John. Trial of Captain John Shaw, by the General Court-Martial,
      Holden on Board the U.S. Ship Independence. Washington, DC: Davis,
      Force, 1822.

DANIEL SHAYS

6408  "Domestic Miscellany," Army and Navy Chronicle 5 (1837): 90-94.

6409  Feer, Robert A. "The Devil and Daniel Shays," Cambridge Historical
      Society Publications 40 (1964-1966): 7-22.

6410  Gregg, Arthur B. "The Lost Years of Daniel Shays," Schoharie County
      Historical Review 18 (1954): 11-15.

JOHN T. SHUBRICK

6411  "Biographical Sketch of Lieutenant John Templar Shubrick," Analectic
      Magazine 8 (1816): 247-51, 401-04.

6412  Cooper, James F. Lives of Distinguished American Naval Officers.
      2 Vols. Philadelphia: Carey, Hart, 1845. Vol. 1, 147-70.

6413  "Lieutenant John T. Shubrick," Military and Naval Magazine 5 (1835):
      373-76.

6414  "Memoirs of John Templar Shubrick," Portfolio 19 (1825): 360-63.

WILLIAM B. SHUBRICK

6415  Cooper, Susan F. "Rear Admiral William Branford Shubrick," Harper's
      Monthly Magazine 53 (1876): 400-07.

JOHN G. SIMCOE

6416   Brown, Alan S. "Governor Simcoe, Michigan, and Canadian Defense," _Michigan History_ 67 (1983): 18-23.

6417   Caldwell, F.L. "John Graves Simcoe: The First Lieutenant Governor of Ontario," _Canadian Defense Quarterly_ 13 (1936): 327-45.

6418   Clark, Mattie M. _The Positive Side of John Graves Simcoe_. Toronto: Forward Publishing Co., 1943.

6419   Cruikshank, Ernest A. _The Correspondence of Lieutenant Governor John Graves Simcoe_. 2 Vols. Toronto: Ontario Historical Society, 1923-1924.

6420   _____. "Lieutenant Governor Simcoe in Canada: A Chronological Record," _Ontario Historical Society Papers and Records_ 26 (1930): 16-36.

6421   Cross, Barney E. "General John Graves Simcoe as a Disturbing Factor in the Old Northwest." Master's Thesis, Colorado State University, 1935.

6422   Danglade, James K. "John Graves Simcoe and the United States: A Study in Anglo-American Frontier Diplomacy." Ph. D. dissertation, Ball State University, 1972.

6423   Givens, W.R. "Unpublished Letters of Governor Simcoe," _Canadian Magazine_ 30 (1908): 402-04.

6424   Green, James A. "General John Graves Simcoe: The Canadian Governor who Attempted to Make Ohio a Part of Canada," _Ohio Archaeological and Historical Society Quarterly_ 43 (1934): 35-60.

6425   Letcher, H.K. "The Imperial Designs of John Graves Simcoe: First Lieutenant Governor of Upper Canada, 1792-1796." Master's Thesis, Wayne State University, 1935.

6426   Lucas, Charles P. John Graves Simcoe," _United Empire_ 3 (1912): 947-50.

6427   MacLeod, Malcom. "Fortress Ontario or Forlorn Hope? Simcoe and the Defense of Upper Canada," _Ontario History_ 53 (1972): 149-78.

6428   Parnell, F.R. "Lieutenant General John Graves Simcoe, First Governor of Upper Canada," _Niagara Historical Society Publications_ No. 36 (1924): 9-25.

6429   Read, David B. _The Life and Times of General John Graves Simcoe_. Toronto: G. Virtue, 1890.

6430   Riddell, William R. _The Life of John Graves Simcoe, First Lieutenant Governor of the Province of Upper Canada_. Toronto: McClelland, Stewart, 1926.

6431   Scott, Duncan C. _John Graves Simcoe_. Toronto: Oxford University Press, 1926.

6432   Smith, William. _Political Leaders of Upper Canada_. Toronto: T. Nelson, 1931.

6433   Van Steen, Marcus. _Governor Simcoe and His Lady_. Toronto: Hodder, Stoughton, 1968.

6434   Wise, Sidney F. "The Indian Diplomacy of John Graves Simcoe,"
       Canadian Historical Association Annual Report (1953): 36-44.

ARTHUR SINCLAIR

6435   Barnett, Lelia S. "Commodore Sinclair and the 'Nautical School',"
       DAR Magazine 54 (1920): 553-63.

JOHN D. SLOAT

6436   "Commodore John Drake Sloat," Hunt's Merchant Magazine 15 (1846):
       446-56.

6437   Sherman, Edwin A. The Life of the Late Rear Admiral John Drake Sloat
       of the United States Navy. Oakland, CA: Carruth & Carruth, 1902.

6438   Van Duzer, Mrs. George. Rear Admiral John Drake Sloat. Port Jervis,
       N.p., 1916.

ROBERT SMITH

6439   Davis, George E. "Robert Smith and the Navy," Maryland Historical
       Magazine 14 (1919): 305-22.

6440   Steiner, Bernard C., ed. "Some Papers of Robert Smith, Secretary of
       the Navy, 1801-1809, and Secretary of State, 1809-1811," Ibid 20
       (1925): 139-50.

JOSIAH SNELLING

6441   Dick, Helen D. "A Newly Discovered Diary of Colonel Josiah Snelling,"
       Minnesota History 18 (1937): 399-406.

6442   Johnston, Patricia C. "Guarding the Colonel's Place in History,"
       Twin Cities 4 (1981): 66-70, 106-10.

6443   Kunz, Virginia. "Colonel Snelling's Journal," Ramsey County History
       6 (1969): 9-11.

6444   Woodall, Allen E. "William Joseph Snelling and the Early Northwest,"
       Minnesota History 10 (1929): 367-85.

RICHARD SOMERS

6445   Brown, John H. "Richard Somers." In: American Naval Heroes. Boston:
       Brown, 1899, 253-58.

6446   Calver, William L. "A Yankee Hero: How Captain Richard Somers Gave
       His Life for His Country."
       Clippings at the Mariner's Museum Library.

6447   Cooper, James F. Lives of Distinguished American Naval Officers.
       Philadelphia: Carey, Hart, 1846. Vol. 1, 73-122.

6448   Daly, Robert W. "Richard Somers," United States Naval Institute
       Proceedings 74 (1948): 1139-45.

6449   Dutton, Arthur H. "The Death of Somers," Overland 49 (1907): 420-22.

6450   Gibbs, George F. "Somers and the Intrepid." In: Pike and Cutlass: Hero
       Tales of Our Navy. Philadelphia: J.B. Lippincott, 1900, 170-80.

6451  Hoopes, Edna M. Richard Somers, 1778-1804, Master Commandant of the United States Navy. Atlantic City, NJ: N.p., 1933.

6452  "A Naval Reminiscence," Naval Magazine 1 (1836): 172-75.

6453  Seawell, Molly. Twelve Naval Captains. New York: Charles Scribners, 1906, 130-44.

6454  Stewart, Frank H., ed. Letters and Papers of Richard Somers. Woodbury, NJ: Constitition Co., 1942.

## CHARLES STEDMAN

6455  Mason, Amos L., ed. Memoirs and Correspondence of Charles Stedman, Rear Admiral, United States Navy. Cambridge, MA: Riverside Press, 1912.

## ISAAC I. STEVENS

6456  Hazard, Joseph T. Companion of Adventure: A Biography of Isaac Ingalls Stevens, First Governor of Washington Territory. Portland, OR: Binford, Mort, 1952.

## JOHN STEVENS

6457  Gregg, Dorothy. "The Exploitation of the Steamboat: The Case of Colonel John Stevens." Ph. D. dissertation, Columbia University, 1951.

6458  Martin, T.C. "John Stevens: A Family of Engineers," Cosmopolitan 25 (1898): 23-34.

6459  Mitman, Carl W. "Stevens' 'Porcupine' Boiler, 1804: A Recent Study," Newcomen Society Transactions 19 (1940): 165-71.

6460  Thurston, Robert H. The Messrs. Stevens of Hoboken, as Engineers, Architects, and Philanthropists. Philadelphia: W.P. Kildane, 1874.

6461  Turnbull, Archibald. "John Stevens," North American Review 223 (1926): 440-55.

6462  _____. John Stevens, an American Record. New York: Century, 1928.

## ALEXANDER P. STEWART

6463  Wingfield, Marshall. "Old Straight': A Sketch of the Life and Campaigns of Lieut. Gen. Alexander P. Stuart, C.S.A.," Tennessee Historical Quarterly 3 (1944): 99-130.

6464  _____. General A.P. Stewart: His Life and Letters. Memphis: West Tennessee Historical Society, 1954.

## *CHARLES STEWART

6465  Gilder, Richard W. "Old Ironsides," Hours at Home 10 (1870): 268-76, 468-77.

6466  "Commodore Charles Stewart," Gentleman's Magazine 2 (1838): 5-27.

6467  Krafft, Herman F. "Old Ironsides and the Academy," United States Naval Institute Proceedings 55 (1929): 564-66.

6468 Stewart, Charles. "Commodore Stewart's Letter," United States Nautical
     Magazine 2 (1845): 172-85.

                           ROBERT F. STOCKTON

6469 "The Adventures of Captain Stockton, '13'," Princeton Alumni Weekly
     3 (1902-1903): 38-40.

6470 Bayard, Samuel J. A Sketch of the Life of Commodore Robert F. Stockton.
     New York: Derby, Jackson, 1856.

6471 Bradley, Glenn D. Winning the Southwest; A Story of Conquest.
     Chicago: A.C. McClurg, 1912.

6472 Brown, Madeline F. "A New Jersey Sailor Who Served His Country Well,"
     Journal of American History 22 (1928): 298-302.

6473 Duke, Marvin L. "Robert F. Stockton: Early U.S. Naval Activities in
     Africa," Naval War College Review 24 (1972): 86-94.

6474 Egbert, Donald D. and D.M. Lee. "Robert F. Stockton." In: Princeton
     Portraits. Princeton: Princeton University Press, 1947, 189-91.

6475 Forney, John W. Anecdotes of Public Men. 2 Vols. New York: Harper &
     Bros., 1873-1881. Vol. 2, 30-34.

6476 Langley, Harold D. "Robert F. Stockton: Naval Officer and Reformer."
     In: James C. Bradford, ed. Command Under Sail: Makers of the American
     Naval Tradition, 1775-1850. Annapolis: Naval Institute Press, 1984,
     273-304.

6477 Parker, Joel. Address on the Life, Character and Services of Commodore
     Stockton. Newark, NJ: N.p., 1868.

6478 Price, Glenn W. "Robert F. Stockton and the American Character in the
     Middle of the 19th Century," Pacific Historian 8 (1964): 203-10.

6479     . Origins of the War with Mexico: The Polk-Stockton Intrigue.
     Austin: University of Texas Press, 1967.

6480 Quincy, Josiah. Figures of the Past, from the Leaves of Old Journals.
     Boston: Roberts Bros., 1883, 230-41.

6481 Stenberg, Richard R. "Intrigue for Annexation," Southwestern Review
     25 (1939): 58-69.

6482 Stockton, R.T. The Stockton Family of New Jersey. Washington: Carnahan,
     1911.

6483 Watkins, John E. Biographical Sketches of John Stevens...and Robert
     F. Stockton. Washington, DC: W.F. Roberts, 1892.

                           BENJAMIN STODDERT

6484 Carrigg, John J. "Benjamin Stoddert and the Foundation of the American
     Navy." Ph. D. dissertation, Georgetown University, 1953.

6485 Jones, Robert F. "The Naval Thought and Policy of Benjamin Stoddert,
     First Secretary of the Navy, 1798-1801," American Neptune 24 (1964):
     61-69.

6486  Lippincott, Horace M. "Peters and Stoddert, First Secretaries of the Army and Navy," University of Pennsylvania Alumni Register 19 (1916): 71-77.

6487  Millis, Walter, ed. "Benjamin Stoddert Calls for Massive Naval Expansion." In: American Military Thought. Indianapolis: Bobbs-Merrill, 1966, 74-78.

6488  Rowland, Kate M. "Philadelphia a Century Ago," Lippincott's Magazine 62 (1898): 804-18.

6489  Scheina, Robert L. "Benjamin Stoddert, Politics, and the Navy," American Neptune 35 (1976): 54-68.

6490  Stoddert, Benjamin. "Letters of Benjamin Stoddert, First Secretary of the Navy, to Nicholas Johnson of Newburyport, 1798-1799," Essex Institute Historical Collections 74 (1938): 350-60.

6491  Turner, Harriot S. "Memoirs of Benjamin Stoddert, First Secretary of the United States Navy," Columbia Historical Society Records 20 (1917): 141-66.

## SILAS H. STRINGHAM

6492  Brown, John H. "Silas Horton Stringham." In: American Naval Heroes. Boston: Brown, 1899, 459-62.

## EDWIN V. SUMNER

6493  Crocchiola, Stanley F. E.V. Sumner: Major General, United States Army, 1797-1863. Borger, TX: J. Hess, 1968.

6494  Long, William W. "A Biography of Major General Edwin Vose Sumner, 1797-1863." Ph. D. dissertation, University of New Mexico, 1971.

## JOSEPH G. SWIFT

6495  Cullum, George W. Biographical Sketch of Brigadier General Joseph G. Swift, Chief Engineer of the U.S. Army, July 21, 1817 to November 12, 1818. New York: C.A. Coffin, 1877.

6496  Ellery, Harrison, ed. The Memoirs of General Joseph Gardner Swift. Worcester, MA: Privately Printed, 1890.

6497  "Journal of General Joseph Gardner Swift," James Sprunt Historical Monographs No. 4 (1903): 91-117.

6498  Patten, William. General Joseph G. Swift, First Graduate of West Point. Rhinebeck, NY: N.p., N.d.

## SILAS TALBOT

6499  Johnston, Charles H. Famous Privateersmen and Adventurers of the Sea. Boston: L.C. Page, 1911.

6500  The Life and Surprising Adventures of Captain Talbot. London: Barnard Sultzer, 1803.

6501  Schultz, Charles R. Inventory of the Silas Talbot Papers, 1767-1867. Mystic Seaport, CT: Marine Historical Association, 1965.

6502 Tuckerman, Henry T. The Life of Silas Talbot: A Commodore in the Navy of the United States. New York: J.C. Riker, 1859.

LAWRENCE TALIAFERRO

6503 Babcock, Willoughby M. "Major Lawrence Taliaferro, Indian Agent," Mississippi Valley Historical Review 11 (1924): 358-75.

6504 Taliaferro, Lawrence. "Autobiography," Minnesota Historical Society Collections 6 (1894): 189-255.

6505 Zylla, Paul. "Major Lawrence Taliaferro, Indian Agent in Minnesota, 1819-1839." Master's Thesis, Catholic University, 1948.

JOSIAH TATTNALL

6506 Chase, John. Correspondence Between Captain John Chase of the Buenos Ayrean Privateer Congress, and Lieut. Josiah Tattnall of the U.S. Ship Erie. Baltimore: N.p., 1832.

6507 Curtis, Edith R. The Tattnalls of Savannah. N.p., 1980.

6508 Farley, M. Foster. "Josiah Tattnall-Gallant American," Georgia Historical Quarterly 58 (1974): 172-80.

6509 _____. "Josiah Tattnall: American Seadog," History Today 29 (1979): 163-71.

6510 Jones, Charles C. The Life and Services of Commodore Josiah Tattnall. Savannah: Morning News Steam Printing House, 1878.

*ZACHARY TAYLOR

6511 Bauer, K. Jack. Zachary Taylor: Soldier, Planter, Statesman of the Old Southwest. Baton Rouge: Louisiana State University, 1985.

6512 Castel, Albert. "Zachary Taylor: A Profile," American History Illustrated 5 (1970): 4-11, 48.

6513 Caygill, H.W. "Zachary Taylor and His Hounds of War," National Guardsman 16 (1962): 12-13.

6514 "Gen. Taylor and the Missouri Volunteers," Army and Navy Chronicle 8 (1839): 236.

6415 Hamilton, Holman. "Zachary Taylor and the Black Hawk War," Wisconsin Magazine of History 24 (1941): 305-15.

6516 _____. "Zachary Taylor and Fort Snelling," Minnesota History 28 (1947): 15-19.

6517 _____. "Zachary Taylor and Minnesota," Ibid 30 (1949): 97-110.

6518 Hoyt, William P., ed. "Zachary Taylor on Jackson and the Military Establishment, 1835," American Historical Review 51 (1945): 480-84.

6519 Schauffer, Edward R. "Zachary Taylor in Florida," Infantry Journal 26 (1925): 280-85.

6520 "Sketch of the Life of Major Zachary Taylor," Western Review 1 (1819): 36-46.

6521 "Taylor's Report of the Battle of Okeechobee," American State Papers: Military Affairs 7: 985-92.

*TECUMSEH

6522 "Battle of the Thames," Army and Navy Chronicle 6 91838): 349-50.

6523 Cook, Darius B. "The Death of Tecumseh," Century Magazine 38 (1885): 332.

6524 Doyle, Cornelius J. "Indians and Indian Fighters," Illinois State Historical Society Journal 19 (1926-1927): 115-41.

6525 Edmunds, R. David. "The Thin Red Line: Tecumseh, the Prophet, and Shawnee Resistance," Timeline 4 (1987-1988): 2-19.

6526 Galt, William R. "Who Killed Tecumseh?" Historical Magazine 1 (1866): 318.

6527 Gilbert, Bil. God Gave Us This Land: Tecumseh and the First Civil War. New York: Athenaeum, 1989.

6528 Hill, Leonard V. John Johnston and the Indians in the Land of the Three Miamis. Piqua, OH: Stoneman Press, 1957, 147-92.

6529 Horsman, Reginald. "Tecumseh and Indian Resistance, 1805-1814," Westerner's Brand Book 25 (1968): 17-19, 22-24.

6530 Kingston, John T. "Death of Tecumseh," Wisconsin Historical Society Collections 4 (1859): 375-76.

6531 Lossing, Benson J. "Was Tecumseh Skinned?" American Historical Record 1 (1872): 285.

6532 Risjord, Norman K. "Tecumseh, Indian Statesman." In: Representative Americans: The Revolutionary Generation. Lexington, MA: D.C. Heath, 1980, 213-30.

6533 Smith, Seba. "The Western Captive, or, the Times of Tecumseh," New World 2 (1842): 1-39.

6534 Sprague, Stuart S. "The Death of Tecumseh and the Rise of Rumpsey Dumpsey: The Making of a Vice President," Filson Club Quarterly 59 (1985): 455-61.

6535 Stecker, C.C. "Philip, Pontiac and Tecumseh," New England Magazine 5 (1891): 121-31.

6536 Sugden, John. Tecumseh's Last Stand. Norman: University of Oklahoma Press, 1985.

6537 _____. "Early Pan-Indianism: Tecumseh's Tour of the Southern Indian Country, 1811-1812," American Indian Quarterly 10 (1986): 275-305.

6538 "Tecumseh and Black Hawk," Army and Navy Chronicle 7 (1838): 295-96.

6539 Van Hoose, William H. Tecumseh: An Indian Moses. Canton, OH: Darling Books, 1984

6540 Wood, Norman B. "Indian Wars and Warriors of Michigan," Michigan Historical Magazine 3 (1919): 547-63.

## HENRY K. THATCHER

6541 Preble, George H. Henry Knox Thatcher: Rear Admiral, U.S. Navy.
Boston: Williams, 1882.

6542 ____. "Henry Knox Thatcher, Commodore," New England Historical and
Genealogical Register 36 (1882): 5-19.

## SYLVANUS THAYER

6543 Adams, Cindy. The West Point Thayer Papers, 1808-1872. West Point:
Association of Graduates, 1965.

6544 Braintree, Massachusetts. Tercentennary Committee. A Brief History
of the Town of Braintree. Boston: Thomas, Todds, 1940.

6545 Cullum, George W. Biographical Sketch of Sylvanus Thayer. New York:
A.G. Sherwood, 1883.

6546 Dupuy, R. Ernest. "Mutiny at West Point," American Heritage 7 (1955):
22-28.

6547 ____. Sylvanus Thayer: Father of Technology in the United States.
West Point: Association of Graduates, 1958.

6548 Eliot, George. Sylvanus Thayer of West Point. New York: Messner, 1959.

6549 Ford, Norman R. Thayer of West Point. St. Johnsbury, VT: Thayer Book
Press, 1953.

6550 Forman, Sidney. "Sylvanus Thayer, More than the 'Father of the U.S.
Military Academy'," Assembly 17 (1958): 14-15.

6551 Frazier, Ronald F. "The General Sylvanus Thayer Birthplace,"
Antiques 123 (1983): 1027-35.

6552 George, Field E. "Tempered by Fire," Ordnance 44 (1959): 214-17.

6553 Kershner, James W. "Sylvanus Thayer: A Biography." Ph. D. dissertation,
University of West Virginia, 1976.

6554 Southworth, Stacy B. The Life and Character of General Sylvanus Thayer.
Braintree, MA: N.p., 1924.

## TIGER TAIL

6555 Ewan, J.W. "A Seminole Reminiscence," Tequesta 40 (1980): 43-46.

6556 "Old Tiger Tail Dead," Florida Historical Quarterly 4 (1926): 192-94.

6557 Porter, Kenneth W. "Tiger Tail," Ibid 24 (1946): 216-17.

6558 Williams, Isabelle M. "The Truth Regarding 'Tiger Tail'," Ibid 4 (1925):
68-75.

## JAMES TILTON

6559 Adams, T.R. "The Medical and Political Activities of Dr. James Tilton,"
John Carter Brown Library Annual  Report 7 (1972): 30-32.

6560  Montgomery, Elizabeth. Reminiscences of Wilmington, in Familiar Village Tales, Ancient and New. Philadelphia: T.K. Collins, 1851, 53-57.

6561  Saffron, M.H. "The Tilton Affair," Journal of the American Medical Association 236 (1976): 67-72.

6562  Shands, A.R. "James Tilton,  M.D., Delaware's Greatest Physician," Delaware Medical Journal 46 (1974): 24-35.

6563  Thatcher, James. American Medical Biography. Boston: Richardson, Lord, 1828, 129-40.

6564  Tilton, Francis T. History of the Tilton Family in America. Clifton: N.p., 1927.

6565  No entry

6566  Tilton, James. Economical Observations on Military Hospitals and the Preservation and Cure of Diseases Incident to an Army. Wilmington, DE: J. Wilson, 1813.

6567  Wooden, Allen C. "James Tilton: Outstanding Military Medical Administrator," Delaware Medical Journal 46 (1974): 24-35.

6568  _____. "James Tilton, M.D. (1745-1822), Military Medical Reformer." In: International Congress of the History of Medicine. Budapest: Acta, 1976, 393-96.

LOUIS DE TOUSARD

6569  Graves, Donald E. "Louis De Tousard and his 'Artillerists Companion': An Investigation of Source Material for Napoleonic Period Ordnance," Arms Collecting 21 (1983): 51-60.

6570  "Original Documents," Magazine of History 25 (1917): 40-48.

6571  Wilkinson, Norman B. "The Forgotten Founder of West Point," Military Affairs 24 (1960-1961): 177-88.

STEPHEN D. TRENCHARD

6572  Maclay, Edgar S., ed. Reminiscences of the Old Navy, From the Journals and Private Papers of Captain Edward Trenchard and Rear Admiral Stephen Decatur Trenchard. New York: Putnam, 1898.

AMASA TROWBRIDGE

6573  Biographical Sketches of Dr. Amasa Trowbridge and Amasa Trowbridge, Jr. of Watertown, N.Y. N.p., 1859.

6574  "Biography of a Surgeon of the War of 1812," American Medical Times 2 (1861): 341-43, 358-59.

6575  Trowbridge, Francis B. The Trowbridge Genealogy. New Haven, CT: Tuttle, Morehouse, Taylor, 1908.

THOMAS TRUXTON

6576  "Biographical Notice of Commodore Thomas Truxton," Portfolio 1 (1809): 30-36.

6577  Brown, John H. "Thomas Truxton." In: American Naval Heroes. Boston: Brown, 1899, 169-83.

6578    "Captain Truxtun and the Constellation," New From Home 15 (1954): 3–18.

6579    Chance, Maria S. A Chronicle of the Family of Edward F. Beale of Philadelphia. Haverford: N.p., 1943.

6580    Cook, Lewis D. "Commodore Thomas Truxtun," Pennsylvania Genealogical Magazine 17 (1949): 3–32.

6581    Daly, John J. "Truxton of the United States Navy," Washington Post October 21, 1928.

6582    Eller, Ernest M. "Truxtun–The Builder," United States Naval Institute Proceedings 63 (1937): 1445–52.

6583    Ferguson, Eugene S. "Thomas Truxtun in New Jersey: Some Unanswered Questions," New Jersey Historical Society Proceedings 77 (1959): 91–102.

6584    _____. Commodore Thomas Truxtun, 1755–1822: A Description of the Truxton–Biddle Letters. Philadelphia: Free Library, 1947.

6585    _____. Truxton and the Constellation: The Life of Commodore Thomas Truxton, U.S. Navy, 1755–1822. Baltimore: Johns Hopkins University Press, 1956.

6586    Frost, John. The Pictorial Book of the Commodores. New York: Nafis, Cornish, 1845, 173–84.

6587    Garland, Charles T. "Truxton: Number One Naval Commander," Navy 5 (1962): 22–23.

6588    Powell, Edward A. Gentlemen Rovers. New York: Scribner, 1913.

6589    Randolph, Evan. "The Spirit of Commodore Truxton," Yankee 41 (1977): 80–85, 132–37.

6590    Robison, Samuel S. "Commodore Thomas Truxton, U.S. Navy," United States Naval Institute Proceedings 58 (1932): 541–54.

6591    Seawell, Molly. Twelve Naval Captains. New York: Charles Scribner, 1906, 42–52.

6592    Stott, A.C. "Early Naval Strategy," United States Naval Institute Proceedings 62 (1936): 229–30.

6593    Truxtun–Decatur Naval Museum. Commodores Thomas Truxton and Stephen Decatur and the Navy of Their Time. Washington, DC: The Museum, 1950.

6594    Truxton, Thomas. "Account of the Engagement Between the U.S. Frigate Constellation and a French Frigate," Naval Chronicle 4 (1800): 119–23.

6595    _____. "Occurences on Board the U.S. Frigate Constellation, February 1, 1800," Naval Chronicle 3 (1800): 514–15.

6596    _____. "Letter to Daniel Smith, 13 October, 1813," Pennsylvania Magazine of History and Biography 19 (1895): 531.

6597    _____. Reply of Thomas Truxton to an Attack made on Him in the National Intelligencer in June, 1806. Philadelphia: N.p., 1906.

JOHN R. TUCKER

6598 Rochelle, James H. Life of Rear Admiral John Randolph Tucker, Commander in the Navy of the U.S. Washington, DC: Neale Publishing Co., 1903.

DANIEL TURNER

6599 "Report of the Committee on the Militia and Public Defense, upon the Resolution Relating to the Naval Services of Captain Daniel Turner," Naval Magazine 1 (1836): 287-90.

DAVID E. TWIGGS

6600 Brown, Russell K. "David Emanuel Twiggs," Richmond County History 15 (1983): 12-16.

ABEL P. UPSHUR

6601 Allin, Lawrence C. "Abel Parker Upshur and the Dignity of Discipline," Naval War College Review 12 (1970): 85-91.

6602 Hall, Claude H. "Abel P. Upshur and the Navy as an Instrument of Foreign Policy," Virginia Magazine of History and Biography 69 (1961): 290-99.

6603 _____. Abel Parker Upshur: Conservative Virginian, 1790-1844. Madison: State Historical Society of Wisconsin, 1964.

6604 _____. "Abel Parker Upshur: An Eastern Shoreman Reforms the United States Navy," Virginia Cavalcade 23 (1974): 29-37.

6605 "Judge Abel P. Upshur," Southern Literary Messenger 7 (1841): 865-72.

6606 M'Cabe, R.E. "Abel Parker Upshur," John P. Branch Historical Papers 3 (1903): 188-205.

6607 Miller, Russell E. "Abel Parker Upshur: A Study in Antebellum Social and Political Philosophy." Ph. D. dissertation, Princeton University, 1952.

6608 Mitchell, Donald W. "Abel Upshur: Forgotten Prophet of the Old Navy," United States Naval Institute Proceedings 75 (1949): 1366-75.

6609 Sturges, Mary U. "Abel Parker Upshur," Magazine of American History 1 (1877): 542-60.

*STEPHEN VAN RENSSELAER

6610 Forney, John W. Anecdotes of Public Men. New York: Harper Bros, 1873, 281-83.

6611 McClave, Elizabeth W. Stephen Van Rensselaer III: A Pictorial Reflection and Biographical Commentary. Stephentown, NY: Stephentown Historical Society, 1984.

DECIUS WADSWORTH

6612 Reed, C. Wingate. "Decius Wadsworth, First Chief of Ordnance, U.S. Army, 1812-1821," Army Ordnance 24 (1943): 113-16.

6613 Rosecrans, George A. and Bill Turner. "Decius Wadsworth-An Enigma," Ordnance 3 (1985): 2-6.

PROVO WALLIS

6614 Heine, William C. Ninety Six Years in the Royal Navy: The Astonishing Story of Halifax-Born Admiral of the Fleet Sir Provo Wallis. Halifax, NS, Lancelot Press, 1987.

*LEWIS WARRINGTON

6615 "The Late Commodore Warrington," Virginia Historical Register 5 (1852): 100-03.

GEORGE WASHINGTON

6616 Amber, Charles H. George Washington and the West. Chapel Hill: University of North Carolina Press, 1936.

6617 Anderson, Ray M. "George Washington and the Whiskey Insurrection." Master's Thesis, American University, 1970.

6618 Baker, William S. Washington After the Revolution, 1784-1799. Philadelphia: J.B. Lippincott, 1898.

6619 Bernath, Stuart L. "George Washington and the Genesis of American Military Discipline," Mid America 49 (1967): 83-100.

6620 Boller, P.F. "Washington and Civilian Supremecy," Southwestern Review 39 (1954): 9-23.

6621 Clarfield, Gerald. "Protecting the Frontiers: Defense Policy and the Tariff Question in the First Washington Administration," William and Mary Quarterly 32 (1975): 443-64.

6622 Fitzpatrick, John C., ed. The Diaries of George Washington, 1748-1799. 4 Vols. Boston: Houghton, Mifflin, 1925.

6623 _____. The Writings of George Washington. 39 Vols. Washington, DC: Government Printing Office, 1931-1944.

6624 Flexner, James T. George Washington and the New Nation, 1783-1793. Boston: Little, Brown, 1970.

6625 _____. George Washington: Anguish and Farewell. Boston: Little, Brown, 1972.

6626 Flower, Lenore E. Visit of George Washington to Carlisle, 1794. Carlisle, PA: Hamilton Library and Cumberland County Historical Society, 1932.

6627 Freeman, Douglas S. "Washington's Hardest Decision," Atlantic 190 (1952): 45-51.

6628 "George Washington and Fort Wayne," Indiana History Bulletin 1 (1924): 69-70.

6629 "George Washington and the American Indians," American Catholic Historical Researches 4 (1908): 203-11.

6630   Green, William. "Administrations of Washington and Adams,"
       Christian Review 17 (1852): 237-62.

6631   Hume, Edgar E. "George Washington and the Society of the Cincinnati,"
       Publications of the United States George Washington Bi-Centennial
       Commission 3 (1933): 567-76.

6632   _____. General Washington's Correspondence Concerning the Society of
       the Cincinnati. Baltimore: Johns Hopkins University Press, 1941.

6633   Knopf, Richard C. "Cool Cat George' and the Indian Wars in Ohio." In:
       Randall Buchman, ed. The Historic Indian in Ohio. Columbus: Ohio
       Historical Society, 1976, 20-28.

6634   "Letter of General Washington to Johnathan Williams, 1795,"
       Massachusetts Historical Society Proceedings 9 (1866-1867): 473.

6635   Lossing, Benson J. The Diary of George Washington from 1789 to 1791.
       Richmond: Virginia Historical Society, 1861.

6636   Marshal, John. The Life of George Washington. 5 Vols. Philadelphia:
       C.P. Wayne, 1807. Vol. 5.

6637   Orr, John G. 1794. General Washington in Franklin County. Chambersburg:
       Presses of the Valley Spirit, 1898.

6638   Paxton, Frederic L. "Washington and the Western Fronts, 1753-1795,"
       Illinois State Historical Society Journal 24 (1932): 589-605.

6639   Rich, Bennett M. "Washington and the Whiskey Rebellion." In: Presidents
       and Civil Disorder. Washington, DC: Brookings Institute, 1941, 2-20.

6640   _____. "Washington and the Whiskey Rebellion," Pennsylvania Magazine
       of History and Biography 65 (1941): 334-52.

6641   Skaggs, David C. "Washington's Legacies to the Modern Army," Engineer
       12 (1982): 12-15.

6642   Sparks, Jared, ed. Writings of George Washington. 12 Vols. Boston:
       Russell, Shattuck, Williams, 1863.

6643   Tachau, Mary B. "George Washington and the Reputation of Edmund
       Randolph," Journal of American History 73 (1986): 15-34.

6644   Townsend, Elizabeth J. "George Washington and the Resolution of the
       Quasi-War with France." Master's Thesis, Cornell University, 1961.

6645   Twohig, Dorothy, ed. The Papers of George Washington: The Journal of
       the Proceedings of the President, 1793-1797. Charlottesville:
       University of Virginia Press, 1981.

6646   Washington, George. Fifty-five Letters of George Washington to Benjamin
       Lincoln, 1777-1799. New York: N.p., 1907.

ANTHONY WAYNE

6647   Armstrong, John. Life of Major-General Anthony Wayne. Boston: Histard,
       Gray, 1835.

6648   _____. "Life of Wayne," North American Review 42 (1836): 116-24.

6649   Bald, F. Clever. "General Anthony Wayne Visits Detroit," Michigan History 26 (1942): 439-56.

6650   ____. "A Portrait of Anthony Wayne painted from Life by Jean Pierre Henri Elovis in 1796," Clements Library Bulletin No. 52 (1948): 7-15.

6651   Barnes, James. The Hero of Stony Point, Anthony Wayne. New York: D. Appleton, 1916.

6652   Bicknell, Thomas W. "Major General Anthony Wayne," American Irish Historical Society Journal 10 (1911): 277-300.

6653   "A Biographical Sketch of the Late Major General Anthony Wayne," Portfolio 1 (1809): 402-08.

6654   Boyd, Thomas A. Mad Anthony Wayne. New York: Scribner, 1929.

6655   Brooke, John M. "Anthony Wayne: His Campaigns Against the Indians of the Northwest," Pennsylvania Magazine of History and Biography 19 (1895): 387-96.

6656   Burton, Clarence M. "General Wayne's Orderly Book," Michigan Pioneer 34 (1904): 341-733.

6657   Chappell, Absalom H. Miscellanies of Georgia; Historical, Biographical, Descriptive, etc. Columbus, GA: T. Gilbert, 1874.

6658   DePeyster, John W. "Anthony Wayne," Magazine of American History 15 (1886): 127-43.

6659   Heathcote, Charles W. "Anthony Wayne re-appraisal," Picket Post No. 45 (1954): 4-9.

6660   Holland, Rupert S. Mad Anthony, The Story of Anthony Wayne. New York: Century Co., 1931.

6661   Galbreath, Charles B. "Ohio Honors Anthony Wayne: Beautiful Statue Unveiled at the Battlefield of Fallen Timbers," Ohio Progress 1 (1929): 9-12.

6662   Glazier, Willard. Heroes of Three Wars. Philadelphia: Hubbard Bros, 1884, 153-59.

6663   Hamm, Margherita A. Builders of the Republic. New York: J. Pott, 1902, 370-84.

6664   Knopf, Richard C. "Anthony Wayne and the Founding of the United States Army." Ph. D. dissertation, Ohio State University, 1960.

6665   ____. "Wayne's Campaign: The Wayne-Knox Correspondence, 1793-1794," Pennsylvania Magazine of History and Biograpy 78 (1954): 298-341, 424-55.

6666   ____. Anthony Wayne: A Name in Arms. Pittsburgh" University of Pittsburgh, 1960.

6667   Lefferts, Walter. American Leaders. 2 Vols. Philadelphia: Lippincott, 1919. Vol. 1, 159-74.

6668   "Letters Relating to the Death of Major General Anthony Wayne," Pennsylvania Magazine of History and Biography 19 (1895): 112-15.

6669   Life of General Warren; to Which are added Sketches of the Lives of DeKalb, Wayne, and Morgan. New York: Nafis, Cornish, 1847.

6670   Millis, Wade. "A Rugged Patriot: Major General Anthony Wayne," Michigan Historical Magazine 20 (1936): 127-51.

6671   Moore, Horatio N. Life and Services of General Anthony Wayne. Philadelphia: Leary, Getz, 1845.

6672   Nelson, Paul D. "Anthony Wayne; Soldier as Politician," Pennsylvania Magazine of History and Biography 106 (1982): 463-82.

6673   _____. Anthony Wayne: Soldier of the Republic. Bloomington, IN: University of Indiana Press, 1985.

6674   _____. "Mad' Anthony Wayne and the Kentuckians of 1790," Register of the Kentucky Historical Society 84 (1986): 1-17.

6675   Niles, J.H. "Anecdote of General Wayne," Firelands Pioneer 7 (1866): 60.

6676   Norm, Isaac. Wayne-Ohio's Wilderness Warrior. Dublin, IN: Print Press, 1982.

6677   Ohio State Archaeological and Historical Society. "Ohio's Monument to General Anthony Wayne Unveiled," Ohio Archaeological and Historical Society Quarterly 38 (1929): 575-600.

6678   Pennsylvania Wayne Monument Commission. Ceremonies at the Dedication of the Equestrian Statue of Major General Anthony Wayne, Commander-in -Chief of the U.S. Army. Harrisburg, PA: Harrisburg Publishing Co., 1909.

6679   Pennypacker, Samuel. "Anthony Wayne," Pennsylvania Magazine of History and Biography 26 (1902): 257-301.

6680   _____. Anthony Wayne. Philadelphia: J.B. Lippincott, 1908.

6681   _____. Pennsylvanians in American History. Philadelphia: William J. Campbell, 1910, 1-80.

6682   Pleasants, Henry. Anthony Wayne. West Chester, PA: H.F. Temple, 1936.

6683   Pratt, Fletcher. "Anthony Wayne, the Last of the Romans," In: Eleven Generals: Studies in American Command. New York: William Sloan, 1949, 37-58.

6684   _____. "Last of the Romans," Infantry Journal 45 (1938): 433-41.

6685   Preston, John H. A Gentleman Rebel: The Exploits of Anthony Wayne. New York: Farrar, Rinehart, 1930.

6686   Rankin, Hugh F. "Anthony Wayne: Military Romanticist." In: George A. Billias, ed. George Washington's Generals. New York: William Morrow, 1964, 260-90.

6687   Roberts, Bessie K. Anthony Wayne, His Fort, 1794. Fort Wayne, IN: Allen County-Fort Wayne Historical Society, 1944.

6688   Ruston, Jay C. "Anthony Wayne and the Indian Campaign, 1792-1794," Indiana Military History Journal 7 (1982): 21-25.

6689   Stille, Charles J. Major General Anthony Wayne and the Pennsylvania
       LIne in the Continental Army. Philadelphia: J.B. Lippincott, 1893.

6690   Stoddart, R.H. "Revolutionary Heroes-Wayne," National Magazine 12
       (1858): 213-20.

6691   Spears, John R. Anthony Wayne, Sometimes Called 'Mad Anthony'.
       New York: D. Appleton, 1903.

6692   Tucker, Glenn. Mad Anthony Wayne and the New Nation: The Story of
       Washington's Front Line General. Harrisburg, PA: Stackpole Books,
       1973.

6693   Victor, Orville J. The Life, Times and Services of Anthony Wayne.
       New York: Beadle, Adams, 1861.

6694   Wayne, Anthony. "Official Account of General Wayne's Defeat of the
       Indians," New York Magazine, or Literary Repository 5 (1794): 643-48.

6695   Wayne, Isaac. "Biographical Memoir of Major General Anthony Wayne,"
       The Casket 4 (1820): 193-203, 241-51, 297-317, 349-61, 389-411, 445-57,
       493-505, 531-40; 5 (1830): 4-14, 16-72, 109-20.

6696   Whitney, Herbert P. "The Military Career of Anthony Wayne," Northwest
       Ohio Quarterly 1 (1928-1929): 17-24.

6697   Wildes, Harry E. Anthony Wayne, Trouble Shooter of the Revolution.
       New York: Harcourt, Brace, 1941.

## *WILLIAM WELLS

6698   Grissom, Donald B. "William Wells-Indian Agent," Old Fort News 42
       (1979): 51-59.

6699   Hunt, John E. "Sketch of Col. Thomas Hunt," Maumee Valley Pioneer
       Association Transactions (1877): 28-37.

6700   Hutton, Paul A. "William Wells: Frontier Scout and Indian Agent,"
       Indiana Magazine of History 74 (1978): 183-222.

6701   Mason, Edward G. Chapters from Illinois History. New York: Duffield,
       1906.

6702   Pritts, Joseph. Incidents of Border Life. Chambersburg, PA: J. Pritts,
       1839, 367-75.

6703   Roberts, Bessie K. "William Wells: A Legend in the Council of Two
       Nations," Old Fort News 17 (1954): Nos. 3 & 4.

6704   Smith, Dwight L. "William Wells and the Indian Council of 1793,"
       Indiana Magazine of History 56 (1960): 217-26.

6705   Sutphen, Richard H. "The Scouts," Northwest Ohio Quarterly 13 (1941):
       7-11.

## GEORGE W. WHISTLER

6706   Allan, Carlisle. "George W. Whistler, Military Engineer," Military
       Engineer 29 (1937): 177-80.

6707   Parry, Albert. Whistler's Father. Indianapolis: Bobbs-Merrill, 1939.

6708   Teall, Gardner C. "Whistler's father," New England Magazine 29 (1903–1904): 235–39.

6709   Vose, George L. A Sketch of the Life and Works of George W. Whistler, Civil Engineer. Boston: Lee, Sheppard, 1887.

### WILLIAM WHISTLER

6710   Foreman, Carolyn T. "Colonel William Whistler," Chronicles of Oklahoma 18 (1940): 313–27.

### CHARLES WILKES

6711   Farrow, Elise B. "The Man who named the Antarctic and His Expedition," Social Studies 39 (1948): 359–64.

6712   Greely, Adolphus W. "Charles Wilkes, the Discoverer of the Antarctic Continent." In: Explorers and Travelers. New York: Scribner, 1893, 194–212.

6713   Henderson, Daniel. The Hidden Coasts: A Biography of Admiral Charles Wilkes. New York: William Sloane, 1953.

6714   Hill, Jim D. "Charles Wilkes–Turbulent Scholar of the Old Navy," United States Naval Institute Proceedings 57 (1931): 867–87.

6715   Jaffe, David. The Stormy Petrel and the Whale: Some Origins of Moby Dick. N.p., 1976.

6716   Krout, Mary H. "Rear Admiral Charles Wilkes and his Exploits," United States Naval Institute Proceedings 50 (1924): 405–16, 1131–33.

6717   Meany, Edward S., ed. "Diary of Wilkes in the Northwest," Washington Historical Quarterly 16 (1925): 49–61, 137–45, 206–23, 290–301; 17 (1926): 43–65, 129–44, 223–29.

6718   Morgan, William J. Autobiography of Rear Admiral Charles Wilkes, United States Navy, 1798–1877. Washington: Naval Historical Center, 1979.

6719   Riesenberg, Felix. "Wilkes: America's Captain Cook." In: The Pacific Ocean. New York: McGraw, 1940, 267–93.

6720   Schmucker, Samuel M. The Life of Elisha Kent Kane, and Other Distinguished American Explorers. Philadelphia: J.W. Bradley, 1859.

6721   Silverberg, Robert. Stormy Voyager: The Story of Charles Wilkes. Philadelphia: J.B. Lippincott, 1968.

6722   Smith, Geoffrey S. "Charles Wilkes and the Growth of American Diplomacy." In: Frank J. Merli and Theodore A. Wilsons, ed. Makers of American Diplomacy. New York: Scribner's 1974, 135–63.

6723   _____. "Charles Wilkes: The Naval Officer as Explorer and Diplomat." In: James C. Bradford, ed. Captains of the Old Steam Navy. Annapolis: Naval Institute Press, 1986, 64–86.

6724   Vorse, A.W. "American Seamen in the Antarctic," Scribner's Magazine 26 (1899): 700–04.

6725  Wilkes, Charles. "Synopsis of the Cruise of the U.S. Exploring Expedition," North American Review 50 (1843): 257-70.

6726  _____. Narrative of the United States Exploring Expedition During the Years, 1838, 1839, 1840, 1841, 1842. 5 Vols. Philadelphia: C. Sherman, 1844.

6727  _____. Voyage Round the World, Embracing the Principal Events of the United States Exploring Expedition. New York: Putnam, 1851.

6728  _____. "Report on the Territory of Oregon," Oregon Historical Society Quarterly 12 (1911): 269-99.

## *JAMES WILKINSON

6729  Abernethy, Thomas P. The Burr Conspiracy. New York: Oxford University Press, 1954.

6730  Bolton, H.E. "James Wilkinson as Advisor to the Emperor Iturbide," Hispanic American Historical Review 1 (1918): 163-80.

6731  Carter, Clarence E. "The Burr-Wilkinson Intrigue in St. Louis," Missouri Historical Society Bulletin 10 (1954): 447-64.

6732  Caldwell, Norman W. "Cantonment Wilkinsonville," Mid America 20 (1949): 3-28.

6733  Christian, P.W. "General Wilkinson and Kentucky Separatism, 1784-1798." Ph. D. dissertation, Northwestern University, 1935.

6734  Clark, Daniel. Proofs of the Corruption of General James Wilkinson. Philadelphia: William Hall, George W. Pierce, 1809.

6735  Cox, Isaac J. "The Pan-American Policy of Jefferson and Wilkinson," Mississppi Valley Historical Review 1 (1914-1915): 212-239.

6736  _____. "Wilkinson's First Break With the Spaniards," Ohio Valley Historical Association Report 8 (1915): 49-56.

6737  _____. "General Wilkinson and his Later Intrigues with the Spaniards," American Historical Review 19 (1913-1914): 794-812.

6738  Crocchiola, Stanley. "Two to a Triangle," Palacio 56 (1948): 35-48.

6739  Davis, Elvert M. "By Invitation of Mrs. Wilkinson: An Incident of Life at Fort Fayette," Western Pennsylvania Historical Magazine 13 (1930): 145-81.

6740  Drewry, Elizabeth B. "Episodes in Westward Expansion as Reflected in the Writings of General James Wilkinson." Ph. D. dissertation, Cornell University, 1933.

6741  Duty, Tony E. "James Wilkinson, 1757-1825," Texana 9 (1971): 291-355.

6742  Farley, M. Foster. "General James Wilkinson: Soldier and Intriguer," DAR Magazine 114 (1980): 44-50.

6743  Foley, William E. "James A. Wilkinson: Territorial Governor," Missouri Historical Society Bulletin 25 (1968): 3-17.

6744   Green, T. Marshall. The Spanish Conspiracy: A Review of Early Spanish Movements in the Southwest. Cincinnati: Robert Clarke, 1891.

6745   Hamilton, Raphael. "General James Wilkinson's Religious Affiliations," Mid America 12 (1929): 122-32.

6746   Hay, Thomas R., ed. "Letters of Anne Biddle Wilkinson, 1788-1789," Pennsylvania Magazine of History and Biography 56 (1932): 33-55.

6747   _____. "Some Reflections on the Career of General James Wilkinson," Mississippi Valley Historical Review 21 (1934-1935): 470-84.

6748   _____. "General James Wilkinson-The Last Phase," Louisiana Historical Quarterly 19 (1936): 407-35.

6749   Holmes, Jack D. "Show Down on the Sabine: General James Wilkinson vs Lieutenant Colonel Simon de Herra," Louisiana Studies 3 (1964): 46-76.

6750   Jefferson, Thomas. Messages from the President Communicating Documents and Information Touching Upon the Official Conduct of Brigadier General James Wilkinson. Washington: A & G Way, 1808.

6751   Jillson, Willard R. Some Kentucky Obliquities in Retrospect: Meade, Rafinesque, Wilkinson. Frankfort, KY: Roberts Printing Co., 1952.

6752   Kohn, Richard H. "General Wilkinson's Vendetta with General Wayne: Politics and Command in the American Army, 1791-1796," Filson Club Quarterly 45 (1971): 361-72.

6753   Marshall, John. "Letters of John Marshall to James Wilkinson, 1787," American Historical Review 12 (1906-1907): 346-48.

6754   McGrane, Reginald C. "Anthony Wayne and James Wilkinson: A Study in Frontier Characters," Ohio Valley Historical Association Annual Report (1913): 30-39.

6755   McKernan, Frank W. "The Intrigues of James Wilkinson in the Old Southwest, 1783-1807." Master's Thesis, University of Cincinnati, 1939.

6756   Pemberton, Gilbert. "Notes on General Wilkinson's Memorial and Miro and Navarro's Dispatch," Louisiana Historical Society Publications 1 (1917): 45-54.

6757   Quaife, Milo M., ed. "General James Wilkinson's Narrative of the Fallen Timbers Campaign," Mississippi Valley Historical Review 16 (1929): 81-90.

6758   Risjord, Norman K. "James Wilkinson, Imperial Schemer." In: Representative Americans: The Revolutionary Generation. Lexington, MA: D.C. Heath, 1980, 193-212.

6759   Shepherd, William R. "Wilkinson and the Beginnings of the Spanish Conspiracy," American Historical Review 9 (1904): 490-506.

6760   _____., ed. A Letter of General James Wilkinson, 1806," Ibid 9 (1904): 533-37.

6761   Simmons, David A. "The Military and Administrative Abilities of
       James Wilkinson in the Old Northwest, 1792-1793," Old Northwest
       3 (1977): 237-50.

6762   Taylor, John M. "An Accomplished Villain," American History
       Illustrated 13 (1979): 4-9, 47-50.

6763   United States Congress. House. Report of the Committee Appointed to
       Inquire into the Conduct of Brigadier General Wilkinson. Washington,
       DC: Roger C. Weightman, 1810.

6764   _____. Report of the Committee Appointed to inquire into the Conduct
       of General Wilkinson. Washington, DC: A. & G. Way, 1811.

6765   Weems, John E. Men without Countries: Three Adveturers of the Early
       Southwest. Boston: Houghton, Mifflin, 1969.

6766   Wensorski, John F. "A Wilkinson Conspiracy," Oklahoma State Historical
       Review 4 (1983): 35-44.

6767   Whitaker, A.P. "James Wilkinson's First Descent to New Orleans,"
       Hispanic American Historical Review 8 (1928): 82-97.

6768   Wilkinson, James. A Brief Examination of Testimony to Vindicate the
       Character of General James Wilkinson Against the Imputation of a
       Sinister Connection with the Spanish Government. Washington, DC:
       W. Cooper, 1811.

6769   _____. "Wilkinson to Brown, December 12, 1791," New England Historical
       and Genealogical Register 21 (1867): 339-40.

6770   _____. "Letter of James Wilkinson," American Historical Register 3
       (1874): 133-35.

6771   _____. "Letters of General James Wilkinson Addressed to Dr. James
       Hutchinson," Pennsylvania Magazine of History and Biography 12
       (1888): 55-64.

6772   _____. "On the Mexican Revolution, 1823," New York Public Library
       Bulletin 3 (1899): 361-64.

6773   _____. "Letters of James Wilkinson," Register of the Kentucky
       Historical Society 24 (1926): 259-67.

6774   _____. "The Battle of Olde Towne near Logan Port, " Indiana History
       Bulletin 5 (1928): 243-47.

6775   Wilkinson, James. "General James Wilkinson," Louisiana Historical
       Quarterly 1 (1917): 79-116.

6776   Wray, Francis M. "The Administration of General James Wilkinson,
       Governor of the Territory of Louisiana, 1805-1806," Master's Thesis,
       University of Virginia, 1854.

## JOHNATHAN WILLIAMS

6777   Longacre, James B. and James Herring. The National Portrait Gallery
       of Distinguished Americans. 4 Vols. Philadelphia: Rice, Rutter,
       1868, Vol. 1.

6778  Smith, Dwight L., ed. "The Ohio River in 1801: Letters of Johnathan Williams," Filson Club Quarterly 27 (1953): 199-222.

6779  Wade, Arthur P. "A Military Offspring of the American Philosophical Society," Military Affairs 38 (1974): 103-07.

6780  Zuersher, Dorothy. "Benjamin Franklin, Johnathan Williams, and the United States Military Academy." Ph. D. dissertation, University of North Carolina, 1974.

### JOHN A. WINSLOW

6781  Ellicot, J.M. Life of John Ancrum Winslow, Rear Admiral, U.S. Navy. New York: G.P. Putnam's Sons, 1902.

### LEVI WOODBURY

6782  Capowski, Vincent J. "The Making of a Jacksonian Democrat: Levi Woodbury, 1789-1831." Ph. D. dissertation, Fordham University, 1966.

6783  Woodbury, Levi. Writings of Levi Woodbury. 3 Vols. Boston: Little, Brown, 1852.

### *JOHN E. WOOL

6784  "Battle of Plattsburg," Army and Navy Chronicle 9 (1839): 103-04.

6785  "A Letter from General John E. Wool," Historical Magazine 2 (1873): 243.

### *MELANCTHON T. WOOLSEY

6786  "Death of Commodore Woolsey," Army and Navy Chronicle 6 (1838): 341-42.

# NAME INDEX

This index lists editors and compilers, as well as authors. The numbers below refer to entry numbers, not page numbers.

Coates, G.H., 264
Cobb, J.A., 4043
Cobb, Samuel E., 4530, 4531
Cochran, Hamilton, 5289
Cochrane, John, 2136
Coe, Charles H., 1255, 6050, 6051
Coe, Edwin D., 1090
Coffin, John H., 5164
Coffin, Patricia, 2347
Coffman, Edward M., 1708, 2106,
  2213, 2754, 6620
Croghan, George, 3495
Cohen, I. Bernard, 4969, 5542
Cohen, Myer M., 1353
Coker, William S., 791, 3751
Colby, Chester, 3835
Cole, Allan B., 3918, 3919
Cole, Harry E., 2891
Cole, Cyrenus, 1091, 1092, 5004,
  5701
Coleman, Elizabeth D., 5970
Coleman, Irene, 2963
Coleman, James C., 2963
Coles, Harry, 680, 1709
Coletta, Paolo E., 6137
Colgrove, Kenneth W., 2715
Collins, LeRoy, 6052
Collum, Richard S., 3723
Colquhoun, A.H., 1426, 5925
Colt, Katherine G., 4782
Colton, Walter, 4213, 4225
Colvocresses, George M., 4484
Colvocoresses, G.P., 6093, 6210
Comfort, Benjamin F., 5139
Compton, H.W., 288
Compton, Harvey W., 121
Compton-Smith, C., 1515
Cone, Stephen D., 3169, 3141
Conklin, Edwin G., 3969
Conlin, Mary Lou, 695
Connolly, James, 4935
Connelley, William E., 2607, 2667,
  5211
Conover, Cheryl, 2068
Conrad, D.B., 6113
Conrad, David, 5551
Cook, Darius B., 6523
Cook, Edward M., 5290
Cook, Kermit A., 358
Cook, Lewis D., 6580
Cooke, David B., 5005, 5202, 5827,
  6053
Cooke, David C., 1256
Cooke, F.O., 6037
Cooke, Jacob E., 397, 1830, 4852,
  5496, 5504

Cooke, Jean-Marie, 567
Cooke, John, 331
Cooke, Mary L., 5291
Cooke, Philip St. G., 5212, 5213,
  5214
Cooley, Mary E., 3970
Coolidge, Richard H., 3150
Cooling, Benjamin F., 2273, 1862
Cooney, James P., 2801
Cooney, Thomas F., 4934
Cooper, James F., 739, 837, 4261,
  4991, 4936, 5223, 5224, 5225,
  5226, 5252, 6222, 6406, 6412,
  6415, 6447
Copeland, Charles H., 907
Copeland, Peter F., 3760
Copes, Jan M., 5368
Corbett, Percy E., 4580
Corbett, William P., 2892
Corbin, Diana F., 5971
Corbin, Harriet T., 5898
Corey, Albert, 1427
Corey, Albert B., 1533, 4609,
  5926
Cornish, Dudley T., 3338
Correll, John T., 2293
Corson, O.T., 398
Coues, Elliott, 2464
Coues, Eliott, 5178, 5396, 6160,
  6237
Coughlin, Magdalen, 1623
Coulter, Ellis M., 1005
Couper, William, 2044
Courtnay, William A., 4568
Coutts, H.B., 4204, 4262
Coventry, George, 1428
Covington, James W., 1257, 1258,
  1259, 2991, 2992, 4722
Cowan, William, 4797
Cowdery, Jonathan, 665
Cowen, Robert C., 5972
Cox, Henry B, 483
Cox, Isaac J., 2422, 4723, 6735,
  6736, 6737
Cox, Lewis, 5973
Coyle, Wallace, 1764
Coyle, John G., 4937
Crackel, Theodore J., 712, 1710,
  1711, 2019
Craig, Gerald M., 1534
Craig, Harden, 4263
Craig, Neville, 198, 398, 400
Craig, Oscar, 122
Craighead, Erwin, 3410
Crampton, Emeline J., 1429
Crane, Charles J., 1758

Davis, John W., 4610
Davis, Julia, 2468
Davis, Madison, 4172
Davis, Paris M., 974
Davis, Paul T., 2208
Davis, Susan B., 3112
Davis, T. Frederick, 1261, 1893,
    4725, 5587
Davis, Varnia, 5268
Davis, W.B., 289
Davis, W.W., 6163
Davis, William C., 5411
Daugherty, James H., 2467
Dawson, Henry B., 239, 290, 568,
    1094, 1262, 3332, 4229
Dawson, John W., 216
Dawson, Lionel, 4699
Day, Grove A., 3893
Day, Hannibal, 1355
Dean, Bashford, 2368
Dearden, Seton, 569
DeBlois, C.J., 4338
DeCaindry, William A., 1853
Decatur, Stephen, 5294
Decatur, Susan, 5294
DeCelles, Alfred D., 1434, 1536
Dechere, Louise, 4827
DeChristofaro, S., 3701
Decker, Leslie E., 1692
DeConde, Alexander, 513, 514, 515,
    516
Defenbach, Byron, 6261
DeGrummond, Jane L., 792
Dekay, George C., 5363
Delafosse, F.M., 1579
Delaney, Donald J., 5745
Dellenbaugh, Frederick S., 2577
Delta, 4044
DeMeissner, Sophie K., 4046
Demeritt, Dwight B., 2295
DeMorgan, John, 570
Denison, John L., 3510
Dennett, Tyler, 3885
Denny, Ebenezer, 5312, 5313, 5314
Denny, William H., 5315
Dent, John C., 1435
Denton, Edgar, 2021
Denzil, Justin F., 5715
DePaoli, Neill, 3027
DePeyster, F. Watts, 3486, 5672,
    5673, 6658
Derbine, Stewart, 1537
De Ross, John F., 4047
Derosier, Arthur H., 5111
DeSelding, Charles, 4382
Des Montaignes, Francois, 2656

Destler, C.M., 1045
DeVoto, Bernard, 1624, 2469, 2556
Dewhurst, W.W., 1008
DeWitt, Donald, 6164
DeWitt, John L., 1805
Dexter, Franklin B., 85
Deyrup, Felicia J., 2282
De Zurko, Edward R., 3235
Dibble, Ernest F., 1046
Dick, Helen, 6441
Dickens, P.D., 3861
Diffenderffer, F.R., 5716
Dill, Jacob S., 5976
Dillon, John B., 4726
Dillon, Richard B., 5785, 5854,
    5855
DiMona, Joseph, 5903
Dinnen, Catherine M., 3456
Dix, John A., 571
Dixon, Benjamin F., 4336
Dobbs, Judy, 2266
Dodd, Dorothy, 1356
Dodd, William F., 5269
Dodge, Ernest S., 3971
Dodge, Henry, 5327
Dodge, Jacob, 126
Doherty, Herbert J., 5123, 5124,
    5588
Donahue, Bernardo, 2164
Donaldson, Gordon, 741
Donnelly, F.K., 5908
Donnelly, Ralph W., 3724, 5538
Donovan, Bernard F., 12
Don Passos, John R., 404
Dorsey, Ella L., 5576
Doty, James D., 3365, 5740
Dougall, James, 1437
Dougherty, Dolorita M., 3423
Douglas, Albert, 6294, 6295
Douglas, Marjory S., 1263
Douglas, R. Alan, 1438
Douglas, Walter B., 6238
Douglass, David B., 932
Dovell, Junius V., 5589
Dow, J.E., 4265, 4938, 4939
Dowd, Gregory E., 4727
Dowd, James, 6391
Dowdy, Clifford S., 3004
Downes, Randolph C., 127, 128, 6296
Downey, Fairfax, 129, 1959, 6365
Doyle, Cornelius J., 4792, 6524
Drake, Benjamin, 5006, 5007
Drake, Francis S., 5717, 5718
Drake, Frederick C., 742, 3817
Drake, Samuel, 1264, 5008, 5828
Drake-Wilkes, L.P., 1993

Mackenzie, William L., 5918, 5957
McKernan, Frank W., 6755
McKinley, Mike, 3520, 3684
McKnight, Charles, 150
McKusick, Marshall B., 3072, 3073,
  3134, 3257
McLarty, Vivian K., 2932
McLaughlin, A.C., 4589
McLaughlin, Patrick L., 845
McLaughlin, Philip K., 963
McLaughlin, W.M., 3135
Maclay, Edgar S., 493, 819, 1235,
  4201, 4408, 5094, 6572
McLemore, Richard A., 531, 801
Macleod, Anne E., 4627
McLeod, Donald, 1474
Macleod, J., 5471
Macleod, Julia A., 650, 5351, 5361,
  5635
Macleod, Malcom, 6427
Macleod, William C., 151
McMaster, Richard K., 2031, 3812,
  3822
McMillen, Florence C., 3098
McMurry, Donald L., 3196
McMurray, John C., 2319
McNally, William, 3685
McNeil, D.R., 4709
McNeilly, Earl E., 3823
McNutt, William S., 829
Macomb, Alexander, 727, 1866, 2245
McPheeters, Addison, 1200
McPherson, James M., 5340
MacPherson, K., 4685
MacPherson, Sharon, 5600
McQueen, Ray A., 5599
McRae, J.H., 1902
McReynolds, Edwin C., 1284
McSpadden, Joseph W., 6064
McSpadden, J. Walker, 6175
McSweeney, Edward F., 5671
Meacham, Walter E., 5067
Mead, Edwin D., 5636
Meade, Rebecca, 6107
Meade, R.W., 6108
Meader, John R., 43, 157, 427, 603,
  1480
Meakin, Alexander C., 5320
Meany, Edward S., 2822, 6717
Meany, William B., 4951
Mecredy, Stephen D., 4665
Meehan, Thomas F., 3696
Meek, Basil, 224
Meese, William A., 1124, 3066
Meigs, Cornelia, 2594
Melia, Tamara, 6212
Mellon, T.A., 1288

Melton, Elizabeth M., 5554
Meltzer, Milton, 1290
Melville, Herman, 4060
Melvin, Philip, 5949
Mercer, Charles F., 1016
Mercier, Henry J., 4284
Meriwether, Colyer, 6387
Meriwether, David, 3319
Meriwether, Lee, 5793
Meriwether, Robert L., 5113
Merk, Frederick, 1637, 1675, 5446
Merli, Frank J., 6722
Merlin, John R., 2880
Merriam, Charles E., 1780
Merrick, George B., 2933
Merrill, James M., 4363, 1698, 1923,
  3892, 5341
Merrill, Walter M., 4061
Merritt, Wesley, 5219
Merritte, Weber I., 2824
Merryman, Robert M., 5740
Metcalfe, C.H., 3745
Metcalfe, Clarence S., 4347
Metcalfe, Clyde H., 5540
Metcalfe, John R., 5706
Metcalfe, Samuel, 347
Mewha, John, 2196
Meyer, Sam, 5709
Meyers, William H., 4303
Miceli, Augusto P., 2613
Michael, William, 473, 474
Michener, James A., 3893
Middendorf, J. William, 4283
Middlebrook, Louis F., 4488
Middleton, Jesse E., 1481
Middleton, Larmar, 44, 428
Middleton, William H., 2118
Miles, Alfred H., 4419
Miles, Edwin A., 1638
Miles, Jack L., 1781
Miles, Richard D., 305
Miles, Thomas W., 2246
Miles, Wyndham P., 2614
Miller, Anson S., 6397
Miller, Arthur P., 604
Miller, Clifford A., 2269
Miller, Gerald H., 3067
Miller, H.Orlo, 1594
Miller, Linus W., 1595
Miller, Russell E., 6607
Miller, Stanley, 1125
Miller, William, 430
Miller, William C., 3171, 3172
Miller, William J., 3961
Miller, William S., 4974
Milligan, James C., 814
Millis, Wade F., 429, 3466, 6670

Murphy, Dan, 2508
Murphy, James, 1810
Murphy, James P., 5812
Murphy, John M., 4133
Murphy, Rowley, 748
Murphy, William D., 3086
Murphy, William J., 4857
Murray, Eleanor M., 6308
Murray, Robert A., 2934, 3227
Murrell, Benjamin, 3946
Murrell, William M., 4208
Musham, H.A., 4155, 4348
Musick, Michael P., 4334
Musser, Ruth, 5754
Myer, Max W., 4975, 5484
Myers, Harry C., 3340
Myers, Minor, 2151

Nadeau, Remi, 3228
Nadler, Soloman, 878
Naegely, Henry E., 5146
Nalty, Bernard C., 1236
Nance, Joseph M., 6378
Nasatir, Abraham P., 815, 1061
Nash, George K., 6309
Nash, Howard P., 495, 4420
Natress, Thomas, 1487
Neal, Annie, 2746
Needler, George H., 1488
Neeser, Robert W., 3590, 3715,
   4209, 4216, 4314, 4399, 4403
Nehrbass, Arthur F., 2320, 2321,
   2359
Neil, Edward D., 3394, 3395, 3396
Neill, Wilfred T., 6065
Nelson, Dan, 749
Nelson, Dennis D., 3671
Nelson, George A., 831
Nelson, Gladys G., 729
Nelson, Harold L., 2901
Nelson, John R., 5503
Nelson, Larry L., 2413, 3276, 3277
Nelson, Paul D., 306, 5233, 6351,
   6672, 6673, 6674
Nelson, Peter, 1489
Nelson, Ray E., 3087
Nelson, Robert, 3229
Nenninger, Timothy K., 1703
Ness, George T., 2057
Neumann, William L., 3903
Nevins, Allan, 5425, 5426, 5427,
   5428
Nevin, Robert P., 432
New, Chester W., 1490
Newell, Thomas M., 3856
Newhall, John B., 5031

Newlands, R.W., 1126
Ney, Virgil, 2257, 3088, 3089, 3090,
   3091, 3092
Nicholls, C.L., 48
Nichols, Roger L., 1062, 1963, 1127,
   1128, 1661, 2509, 2629, 2634,
   2730, 2886, 2909, 2935, 3074,
   3093, 4808, 4889, 4890, 4891,
   4892, 5867, 5868, 5869
Nichols, Roy F., 643
Nicholson, Thomas, 984
Nicolosi, Anthony S., 3616
Nihart, Brooke, 6041
Nihart, Bruce, 4512
Niles, J.H., 6675
Niu-Sien-chong, 5944
Niven, John, 5114
Noah, Mordecai M., 985
Nobles, Gregory H., 50
Nobles, Henry H., 4557
Nobles, John, 49
Nofziger, David R., 845
Nolan, J. Bennett, 435
Nolan, L.C., 3904
Nordhoff, Charles, 4065
Norm, Isaac, 6676
Norman, Charles B., 496
Norris, C.H., 3287
Norris, Caleb H., 307
Norris, Walter B., 3548
North, Ralph H., 2339
North, S.D., 2339
Norton, Herman A., 2871
Norton, Lewis A., 1596
Norton, Paul F., 5637
Norton, W.T., 3104
Nothstein, Ira O., 2270
Nunis, Doyce B., 4594
Nye, Russell B., 4905, 5472

Oberly, James M., 2227, 2228, 2229
O'Brien, William J., 2271
Observer, 3686
O'Byrne, Michael C., 1129
O'Callaghan, E.B., 249
O'Callaghan, Jerry A., 2230
O'Connell, Charles F., 1797, 2005
O'Connor, Raymond G., 1749, 3570
O'Connor, Thomas, 977
Oelke, Karl E., 6189
Ogden, Warren C., 894
Oglesby, Eliza, 3420
O'Hair, Mary C., 5511
Ohio State Archaeological and
   Historical Society, 308, 369,
   3443, 6677

# SUBJECT INDEX

Plain numbers refer to pages; those in brackets refer to entry numbers.

**About the Compiler**

JOHN C. FREDRIKSEN holds a master's degree in American history from the University of Michigan and a master's of library science from the University of Rhode Island.